INTERNATIONAL LAW

VOLUME 4

THE LAW OF PEACE

PARTS VII AND VIII

WITHDRAWN

INTERNATIONAL LAW

BEING THE COLLECTED PAPERS OF

HERSCH LAUTERPACHT

Q.C., LL.D., F.B.A.

SYSTEMATICALLY ARRANGED AND
EDITED BY

E. LAUTERPACHT, Q.C.

VOLUME 4

THE LAW OF PEACE

PARTS VII AND VIII

CAMBRIDGE UNIVERSITY PRESS

CAMBRIDGE

LONDON · NEW YORK · MELBOURNE

Published by the Syndics of the Cambridge University Press
The Pitt Building, Trumpington Street, Cambridge CB2 1RP
Bentley House, 200 Euston Road, London NW1 2DB
32 East 57th Street, New York, NY 10022, USA
296 Beaconsfield Parade, Middle Park, Melbourne 3206, Australia

First published 1978

Printed in Great Britain by
Western Printing Services Ltd.
Bristol

Library of Congress Cataloguing in Publication Data (Revised)

Lauterpacht, Sir Hersch, 1897–1960.
International law, being the collected papers of
Hersch Lauterpacht.
1. International law. I. Lauterpacht, Elihu, ed.
JX3225.L32   341   70–92250
ISBN 0 521 21524 2 (v. 4)

CONTENTS

CONTENTS OF PREVIOUS VOLUMES

1. GENERAL WORKS

2. THE LAW OF PEACE

PART I INTERNATIONAL LAW IN GENERAL

3. THE LAW OF PEACE

PART II STATES AS SUBJECTS OF INTERNATIONAL LAW

PART III STATE TERRITORY AND TERRITORIAL JURISDICTION

PREFACE

With the material on State Responsibility and Treaties the present volume concludes the presentation of Lauterpacht's writings on the Law of Peace. There remains for publication in the next volume only his significant contribution to the law governing disputes, including the jurisdiction of the International Court, and to the law of war and neutrality.

Two chapters in the present volume have never been published before: Lauterpacht's professional opinion in the *Nottebohm* case and his draft of the legal argument for the British Memorial in the *Anglo-Iranian Oil Company* case. And the chapter on 'Preparatory work in the interpretation of treaties', which is the original version of his Hague lectures of 1934, has not previously been printed in English – though much of it subsequently appeared in an article published in the *Harvard Law Review* (which, for the reasons given at p. 449 below, is not reprinted here).

As will be seen (and is more fully explained in the note at p. 95 below) Lauterpacht's important writing on the Law of Treaties has been set in a framework basically of his own making and identified from the scheme which he outlined, but did not complete, for his work as rapporteur of the International Law Commission on that subject. I have not wanted to disturb the flow of his approach to the subject by breaking up too much the reports which he prepared for the Commission; but it has seemed right to fuse the relevant parts of his two reports and, in addition, to reprint at appropriate points in that framework a few other items on the same subjects.

I express my gratitude to Dr E. Loewenfeld, LL.B. for his kindness in giving permission for the printing of chapter 1 of Part VII; to the British Petroleum Company Ltd. (formerly the Anglo-Iranian Oil Company Ltd.) for consenting to the publication of chapter 2 of Part VII; to the Editor of the *Law Quarterly Review* for permission to reprint 'Contracts to break a contract' in chapter 16 of Part VIII; to the Oxford University Press for permission to reprint part of chapter 16, as well as chapter 20, in Part VIII; and to the Hague Academy of International Law for permission to reproduce as chapter 21 of Part VIII the English text of lectures delivered at the Academy.

In preparing the volume for publication I have had invaluable aid from those who have helped me before and upon whom I have come so gratefully to rely: Professor Gillian White; Mrs C. A. Hopkins; Mr D. J. Driscoll and Mr W. M. Bush. I am also much indebted to Mrs Rainbow, my secretary in Cambridge, and to Miss P. Paton, my secretary in Canberra.

E. LAUTERPACHT

Department of Foreign Affairs
Canberra
July 1976

TABLE OF CASES

ABBREVIATIONS

OF TITLES OF BOOKS, ETC., QUOTED IN
THIS VOLUME

The books referred to in the bibliographies and notes are, as a rule, quoted with their full titles and the date of their publication. But certain books and periodicals which are often referred to in this volume are quoted in an abbreviated form, as follows:

Accioly	Accioly, *Tratado de Direito internacional público*, 3 vols. (1933–5).
A.J.	*American Journal of International Law.*
Annuaire	*Annuaire de l'Institut de Droit International.*
Annual Digest	*Annual Digest and Reports of Public International Law Cases*: 1919–22, edited by Sir John Fischer Williams and H. Lauterpacht (1932); 1923–4, edited by the same (1933); 1925–6, edited by A. D. McNair and H. Lauterpacht (1929); 1927–8, edited by the same (1931); 1929–30 (1935); 1931–2 (1938); 1933–4 (1940); 1935–7 (1941); 1938–40 (1942); 1941–2 (1945); 1919–42 (supplementary volume) (1947); 1943–5 (1949); 1946 (1951); 1947 (1951); 1948 (1953); 1949 (1955) – all edited by H. Lauterpacht.
Anzilotti	Anzilotti, *Corso di diritto internazionale*, vol. I, 3rd ed. (1928), French translation by Gidel (1929); vol. III, part I (1915).
A.S. Proceedings	*Proceedings of the American Society of International Law.*
Balladore Pallieri	Balladore Pallieri, *Diritto internazionale pubblico* (1937).
Baty	Baty, *The Canons of International Law* (1930).
Bibliotheca Visseriana	*Bibliotheca Visseriana Dissertationum Jus Internationale Illustrantium.*
Bittner	Bittner, *Die Lehre von völkerrechtlichen Urkunden* (1924).
Bluntschli	Bluntschli, *Das moderne Völkerrecht der zivilisierten Staaten als Rechtsbuch dargestellt*, 3rd ed. (1878).
Borchard	Borchard, *The Diplomatic Protection of Citizens Abroad* (1915).

Br. and For. St. Papers	British and Foreign State Papers (Hertslet), vol. 1 (1841), continued up to date.
Brierly	Brierly, The Law of Nations, 5th ed. (1955).
Bustamante	Bustamante, Derecho internacional público, 3 vols. (1933–5).
B.Y.	British Year Book of International Law.
Calvo	Calvo, Le Droit international théorique et pratique, 5th ed., 6 vols. (1896).
Cavaglieri	Cavaglieri, Lezioni di diritto internazionale (general part, 1925).
Clunet	Journal du droit international.
Cruchaga	Cruchaga-Tocornal, Nociones de Derecho internacional, 3rd ed., 2 vols. (1923–5).
Dicey	Dicey, Conflict of Laws, 4th ed. (1927).
Dickinson, Cases	Dickinson, Cases and Other Materials on International Law (1950).
Documents	Documents on International Affairs.
Fauchille	Fauchille, Traité de droit international public, 8th ed. of Bonfils' Manuel de droit international public, vol. 1, part 1 (1922), vol. 1, part 2 (1925), vol. 1, part 3 (1926), vol. 11 (1921).
Fenwick	Fenwick, International Law, 3rd ed. (1948).
Fiore	Fiore, Nouveau droit international public. French translation by Antoine from the 2nd Italian edition, 3 vols. (1885).
Fiore, Code	Fiore, International Law Codified. Translation by Borchard from the 5th Italian edition (1918).
Fischer Williams, Chapters	Fischer Williams, Chapters on Current International Law and the League of Nations (1929).
Fontes Juris Gentium	Fontes Juris Gentium, edited by V. Bruns.
Garner, Developments	Garner, Recent Developments in International Law (1925).
Gemma	Gemma, Appunti di diritto internazionale (1923).
Genet	Genet, Traité de diplomatie et de droit diplomatique, 3 vols. (1931–2).
Gidel	Gidel, Le droit international public de la mer, le temps de paix: vol. 1, Introduction – La haute mer (1932); vol. 11, Les eaux intérieures (1932); vol. 111, La mer territoriale et la zone contiguë (1934).
Grotius	Grotius, De Jure Belli ac Pacis (1625).
Grotius Annuaire	Grotius Annuaire International.
Grotius Society	Transactions of the Grotius Society.
Guggenheim	Guggenheim, Lehrbuch des Völkerrechts, Parts 1 and 2 (1947).

Guggenheim, *Traité*	Guggenheim, *Traité de Droit International Publique*, vol. I (1953); vol. II (1954).
Hackworth	Hackworth, *Digest of International Law*, 7 vols. (1940–3).
Hague Recueil	*Recueil des Cours, Académie de Droit International de La Haye.*
Hall	Hall, *A Treatise on International Law*, 8th ed. (1924), by A. Pearce Higgins.
Harvard Research	*Research in International Law.* Under the Auspices of the Harvard Law School. Draft Conventions Prepared for the Codification of International Law. Directed by M. O. Hudson: (1929) I. *Nationality* (Reporter: Flournoy); II. *Responsibility of States* (Borchard); III. *Territorial Waters* (G. G. Wilson); (1932) I. *Diplomatic Privileges and Immunities* (Reeves); II. *Legal Position and Functions of Consuls* (Quincy Wright); III. *Competence of Courts in regard to Foreign States* (Jessup); IV. *Piracy* (Bingham); V. *A Collection of Piracy Laws of Various Countries* (Morrison); (1935) I. *Extradition* (Burdick); II. *Jurisdiction with respect to Crime* (Dickinson); III. *Treaties* (Garner).
Heffter	Heffter, *Das europäische Völkerrecht der Gegenwart*, 8th ed. by Geffcken (1888).
Heilborn, *System*	Heilborn, *Das System des Völkerrechts entwickelt aus den völkerrechtlichen Begriffen* (1896).
Hertslet's *Commercial Treaties*	Hertslet, *Collection of Treaties and Conventions between Great Britain and Other Powers, so far as they relate to Commerce and Navigation*, vol. I (1820), continued to date.
Higgins and Colombos	Higgins and Colombos, *The International Law of the Sea*, 2nd ed. (1951).
H.L.R.	*Harvard Law Review.*
Holland, *Lectures*	Holland, *Lectures on International Law*, edited by T. A. and W. L. Walker (1933).
Holland, *Studies*	Holland, *Studies in International Law* (1898).
Holtzendorff	Holtzendorff, *Handbuch des Völkerrechts*, 4 vols. (1855–9).
Hudson, *Cases*	Hudson, *Cases and Other Materials on International Law*, 3rd ed. (1951).
Hudson, *Legislation*	Hudson, *International Legislation*: vols. I–XI (1931–50).
Hyde	Hyde, *International Law, chiefly as interpreted and applied by the United States*, 2nd ed., 3 vols. (1945).

I.C.J. Reports	*International Court of Justice Reports.*
I.C.L.Q.	*International and Comparative Law Quarterly.*
I.L.R.	*International Law Reports*, being the continuation of *Annual Digest*, edited by H. Lauterpacht until volume 24 and thereafter by E. Lauterpacht.
J.C.L.	*Journal of Comparative Legislation and International Law.*
Keith's Wheaton	*Wheaton's Elements of International Law*, 6th English edition by A. Berriedale Keith, vol. I (1929); vol. II (7th ed., 1944).
Klüber	Klüber, *Europäisches Völkerrecht*, 2nd ed. by Morstadt (1851).
Lapradelle-Politis	Lapradelle-Politis, *Recueil des arbitrages internationaux*, vol. I (1905), vol. II (1924), vol. III (1954).
Lauterpacht, *Analogies*	Lauterpacht, *Private Law Sources and Analogies of International Law* (1927).
Lauterpacht, *The Function of Law*	Lauterpacht, *The Function of Law in the International Community* (1933).
Lawrence	Lawrence, *The Principles of International Law*, 7th ed., revised by P. H. Winfield (1923).
Lindley	Lindley, *The Acquisition and Government of Backward Territory in International Law* (1926).
Liszt	Liszt, *Das Völkerrecht*, 12th ed. by Fleischmann (1925).
L.N.O.J.	*League of Nations, Official Journal.*
L.N.T.S.	*League of Nations Treaty Series.* Publication of Treaties and International Engagements registered with the Secretariat of the League of Nations.
Lorimer	Lorimer, *The Institutes of International Law*, 2 vols. (1883–4).
De Louter	De Louter, *Le droit international public positif*, French translation from the Dutch original, 2 vols. (1920).
L.Q.R.	*Law Quarterly Review.*
McNair	McNair, *The Law of Treaties: British Practice and Opinions* (1938).
McNair, *Opinions*	McNair, *International Law Opinions* (1956).
Maine	Maine, *International Law*, 2nd ed. (1894).
Martens	Martens, *Völkerrecht*, German translation from the Russian original, 2 vols. (1883–6).
Martens, G. F.	G. F. Martens, *Précis du droit des gens moderne de l'Europe*, new edition by Vergé, 2 vols. (1858).

Martens, R.
Martens, N. R.
Martens, N. S. } These are the abbreviated quotations of
Martens, N. R. G. } the different parts of Martens, *Recueil de*
Martens, N. R. G., 2nd ser. } *Traités*, which are in common use.
Martens, N. R. G., 3rd ser.

Martens, *Causes célèbres* Martens, *Causes célèbres du droit des gens*, 2nd ed.,
  5 vols. (1858–61).

Mérignhac Mérignhac, *Traité de droit public international*,
  vol. I (1905), vol. II (1907), vol. III (1912).

Möller Möller, *International Law in Peace and War*, English
  translation from the Danish, vol. I (1931), vol. II
  (1935).

Moore Moore, *A Digest of International Law*, 8 vols. (1906).

Moore, *International* Moore, *History and Digest of the International*
  Arbitrations *Arbitrations to which the United States has been a Party*,
  6 vols. (1898).

Nordisk T.A. *Nordisk Tidskrift for International Ret. Acta scandi-*
  navica juris gentium.

Nys Nys, *Le droit international*, 2nd ed., 3 vols. (1912).

Oppenheim, I, II Oppenheim, *International Law*, vol. I, 8th ed.
  (1955), by H. Lauterpacht; vol. II, 7th ed. (1952),
  by H. Lauterpacht.

O.Z̧.ö.R. *Österreichische Zeitschrift für öffentliches Recht.*

P.C.I.J. *Publications of the Permanent Court of International*
  Justice:
  Series A: Judgments.
    B: Advisory Opinions.
    A/B: Cumulative Collection of Judgments
      and Advisory Opinions given since 1931.
    C: Acts and Documents relating to
      Judgments and Advisory Opinions.
    D: Collection of Texts governing the
      Jurisdiction of the Court.
    E: Annual Reports.

Perels Perels, *Das internationale öffentliche Seerecht der*
  Gegenwart, 2nd ed. (1903).

Phillimore Phillimore, *Commentaries upon International Law*,
  3rd ed., 4 vols. (1879–88).

Praag Praag, *Juridiction et droit international public* (1915).
Praag, *Supplément* Supplement to the above (1935).
Pradier-Fodéré Pradier-Fodéré, *Traité de droit international public*,
  8 vols. (1885–1906).

Pufendorf Pufendorf, *De Jure Naturae et Gentium* (1672).

Ralston	Ralston, *The Law and Procedure of International Tribunals*, revised ed. (1926). Supplement (1936).
Ray, *Commentaire*	Ray, *Commentaire du Pacte* (1930).
Recueil T.A.M.	*Recueil des décisions des tribunaux arbitraux mixtes.*
Reddie, *Researches*	Reddie, *Researches, Historical and Critical, in Maritime International Law*, 2 vols. (1844).
Répertoire	Lapradelle et Niboyet, *Répertoire de droit international.* Founded by Darras in 1929.
R.G.	*Revue générale de droit international public.*
R.I.	*Revue de droit international et de législation comparée.*
R.I. (Geneva)	*Revue de droit international, de sciences diplomatiques, politiques et sociales.*
R.I. (Paris)	*Revue de droit international.*
R.I.F.	*Revue internationale française du droit des gens.*
Rivier	Rivier, *Principes du droit des gens*, 2 vols. (1896).
Rivista	*Rivista di diritto internazionale.*
Rousseau	Rousseau, *Principes généraux du droit international public*, vol. 1 (1944).
Satow	Satow, *A Guide to Diplomatic Practice*, 3rd ed. by Ritchie (1932).
Scelle	Scelle, *Précis de droit des gens*, vol. 1 (1932), vol. 11 (1934).
Schücking und Wehberg	Schücking und Wehberg, *Die Satzung des Völkerbundes*, 2nd ed. (1924).
Schwarzenberger	Schwarzenberger, *International Law as Applied by International Courts and Tribunals*, vol. 1 (1945).
Scott, *Hague Reports*	Scott, *Hague Court Reports* (1916).
Scott, *Hague Reports* (2nd)	Scott, *Hague Court Reports (Second Series)* (1932).
Sibert	Sibert, *Traité du droit international public*, 2 vols. (1951).
Sirey	*Recueil général des lois et des arrêts* (founded by Sirey).
Smith	Smith, *Great Britain and the Law of Nations, a Selection of Documents*, vol. 1 (1932), vol. 11 (1935).
Spiropoulos	Spiropoulos, *Traité théorique et pratique du droit international public* (1933).
Stowell	Stowell, *International Law. A Restatement of Principles in Conformity with Actual Practice* (1931).
Strupp, *Éléments*	Strupp, *Éléments du droit international public, universel, européen et américain*, 2nd ed., 3 vols. (1930).
Strupp, *Wört.*	*Wörterbuch des Völkerrechts und der Diplomatie*, ed. by Strupp (begun by Hatschek), 3 vols. (1924–9).

Suarez	Suarez, *Tratado de Derecho internacional público*, 2 vols. (1916).
Temperley	Temperley, *History of the Peace Conference of Paris*, 6 vols. (1920–4).
Testa	Testa, *Le droit public international maritime*, translation from the Portuguese by Boutiron (1886).
Toynbee, *Survey*	Toynbee, *Survey of International Affairs.*
Travers	Travers, *Le droit pénal international*, 5 vols. (1920–2).
Treaty Series	United Kingdom Treaty Series, vol. I (1892), and a volume every year.
Twiss	Twiss, *The Law of Nations*, etc., 2 vols., 2nd ed., vol. I (Peace, 1884), vol. II (War, 1875).
U.N.R.I.A.A.	United Nations, *Reports of International Arbitral Awards.*
U.N.T.S.	*United Nations Treaty Series.*
Vattel	Vattel, *Le droit des gens*, 4 books in 2 vols., new edition (1773).
Verdross	Verdross, *Die Verfassung der Völkerrechtsgemeinschaft* (1926).
Walker	Walker, *A Manual of Public International Law* (1895).
Walker, *History*	Walker, *A History of the Law of Nations*, vol. I (1899).
Walker, *Science*	Walker, *The Science of International Law* (1893).
Westlake	Westlake, *International Law*, 2 vols., 2nd ed. (1910–13).
Westlake, *Chapters*	Westlake, *Chapters on the Principles of International Law* (1894).
Westlake, *Papers*	*The Collected Papers of John Westlake on Public International Law*, ed. by L. Oppenheim (1914).
Wharton	Wharton, *A Digest of the International Law of the United States*, 3 vols. (1886).
Wheaton	Wheaton, *Elements of International Law*, 8th American edition by Dana (1866).
Z.I.	*Zeitschrift für internationales Recht.*
Z.ö.R.	*Zeitschrift für öffentliches Recht.*
Z.ö.V.	*Zeitschrift für ausländisches öffentliches Recht und Völkerrecht.*
Z.V.	*Zeitschrift für Völkerrecht.*

PART VII
STATE RESPONSIBILITY

I TREATMENT OF PERSONS

CHAPTER I

IN RE FRIEDRICH NOTTEBOHM

Editor's note   The *Nottebohm* case between Liechtenstein and Guatemala
(*I.C.J. Reports* 1955, p. 4) is best known as the case in which the International Court of Justice developed the concept of 'genuine connection' as
a factor affecting the obligation of one State to recognize the validity of
a naturalization granted by another. Though the reasoning of the Court's
approach was criticized at the time (e.g. by Mervyn Jones in the *I.C.L.Q.*
5 (1956)), the concept has commended itself to the international community in the context, for example, of the nationality of ships. See,
especially, the separate opinion of Judge Jessup in the *Barcelona Traction*
case: *second phase, I.C.J. Reports* 1970, pp. 186–8.

The fact remains, however, that the extension by the Court of the
notion of the genuine link to naturalization, as opposed to the determination of effective nationality in cases of dual nationality, represented an
unexpected development in the law. This is to some extent illustrated by
the present chapter, which consists of an opinion on the position of Mr
Nottebohm which Lauterpacht prepared for the Government of Liechtenstein. The opinion contains no suggestion that the concept of the genuine
link might be relevant in a case of naturalization. The thought clearly did
not occur to Lauterpacht, who carefully canvassed other possible grounds
on which the effectiveness of Mr Nottebohm's nationality might in theory
be challenged.

Lauterpacht made no public comment on the case. The last edition
which he prepared of volume 1 of Oppenheim's *International Law* was
completed before the date of the Court's judgment. And the other work of
Lauterpacht in which one might have expected to find some reference to
the decision, namely, *The Development of International Law by the International
Court*, which was published in 1958, contains in its preface the statement
that: '. . . I have considered it proper not to comment upon or refer to any
of the judgements . . . given by the Court since I became one of its
members.' Though Lauterpacht did not sit in the second phase of the
Nottebohm case, in which the judgment was rendered on 6 April 1955, he
had been elected to the Court in the preceding September and had
assumed his duties in February 1955.

The opinion is undated. In the last paragraph, however, there is a
suggestion that if the Government of Guatemala fails to give satisfaction
to the Government of Liechtenstein, proceedings should be commenced
before the International Court of Justice 'not later than 1 May 1950'. As

the opinion also refers to a Guatemalan Law of 25 May 1949, it is clear that it must have been written between those two dates – probably in the early months of 1950.

Lauterpacht prepared the Application instituting proceedings in the case, which was dated 20 December 1951. Thereafter, he did not participate in the case, as he retired from the Bar early in 1952.

Permission to print the opinion has kindly been given on behalf of the Principality of Liechtenstein by Dr E. H. Loewenfeld, who acted as solicitor and agent for the Principality in the *Nottebohm* case.

I

1 I have been asked for an opinion on the legal issues arising from the detention and internment in Guatemala of Mr Friedrich Nottebohm, a national of Liechtenstein, and from the attempted confiscation of his property by the Guatemalan Government. I am also requested to advise on the remedies open to the Government of Liechtenstein.

2. There has been no previous correspondence on this subject between the Governments of Liechtenstein and Guatemala and the present opinion is accordingly based on the statement of facts as suggested to me on behalf of Mr Friedrich Nottebohm.

II THE FACTS

3 Mr Friedrich Nottebohm is a national of Liechtenstein at present resident in Vaduz, in the Principality of Liechtenstein. He became a national of Liechtenstein on 13 October 1939 in accordance with the Liechtenstein Law of 10 January 1934 concerning acquisition of nationality. Although he was associated with Liechtenstein in various ways and although he appears to have, prior to his naturalization, paid frequent visits to Liechtenstein, he was at the time of his naturalization domiciled in Guatemala where he had resided since 1906. He was a German national by birth. In the special circumstances of the case the Liechtenstein Government, in granting his naturalization, applied section 6(d) of the Law of 1934 which, while providing that a person seeking naturalization must have resided at least three years in Liechtenstein, permitted of exceptions to be made from that requirement of residence in special cases.

4 It appears from Article 25 of the German Nationality Law of 22 July 1913 that as the result of the acquisition of Liechtenstein nationality Mr Friedrich Nottebohm lost his German nationality. It

6

appears also from the documents submitted to me that after the acquisition of Liechtenstein nationality he was constantly treated both by Liechtenstein and by Switzerland, through which he repeatedly passed, as a Liechtenstein national. On 5 February 1940 he was duly registered by the Guatemalan authorities as a national of Liechtenstein. He continued to reside in Guatemala until 20 November 1943 when, after having been arrested on the previous day, he was taken on board an American vessel to the United States and interned there. Guatemala entered the war at the end of 1941.

5 Some time after the beginning of his internment – apparently at the beginning of 1944 – the property, moveable and immoveable, of Mr Friedrich Nottebohm was sequestrated. In so far as the Guatemalan authorities supplied an explanation of the measures taken against Mr Friedrich Nottebohm, they referred to the fact that he had been put on the British and American black list. It may be noted in this connection that on 7 March 1944 the following document was issued by the civil attaché to the British legations in Central America:

As civil attaché to His Britannic Majesty's legations in Central America, I conducted a thorough investigation into the firm of Nottebohm Hermanos and its directors. The business transactions of the firm since August 1939 up to September 1943 were scrutinized by myself and by a chartered accountant, and we were unable to find any instance of the firm having aided the enemy. As the result of the investigation I was satisfied that the charges made against Nottebohm Hermanos, which resulted in its being placed on the Statutory List in 1939, were based on erroneous evidence or on confused statements given in good faith. – At the same time I conducted an investigation into the life of the partners, Frederico Nottebohm and Karl Heinz Nottebohm, and came to the conclusion that neither had aided the Nazis in a business or private capacity. From the investigations and from personal knowledge of the partners I am of opinion that they should not be considered Nazi sympathizers.

Signed Arthur Neale.

About the same time, on 7 March 1944, a document to similar effect was issued by the Swiss consul in Guatemala.

6 On 26 January 1946 the legal representatives of Mr Friedrich Nottebohm were informed that his registration as Liechtenstein national was cancelled by the Foreign Ministry of Guatemala apparently in pursuance of a provision of a Guatemalan law which provides that registered aliens whose absence from the country

exceeds two years must re-register. While this aspect of the factual situation – in particular the relevant dates – is not quite clear, it appears that as the result of the cancellation of his registration as a national of Liechtenstein Mr Friedrich Nottebohm was subsequently refused permission to re-enter Guatemala.

7 During all this period he was deprived of his property. A list of these assets, as submitted to me, shows that their total value is estimated at $1,509,566 (or Swiss Francs 6,491,133). It is also estimated that the normal annual income from these assets is in the neighbourhood of $70,000.

8 Some time in 1948 the Guatemalan Government published a draft of a law providing, in effect, for the confiscation of the property of aliens who on 7 October 1938 were nationals of a State which subsequently was engaged in war against the Allies or who were placed on the American black list. That draft, which in its original form was apparently vetoed by the President of Guatemala, became subsequently law on 25 May 1949 (Ley de Liquidacion Asuntos de Guerra). The law apparently provides for the possibility of re-course to judicial and other organs with the view to proving that a person *prima facie* affected by its operation falls within some of the complicated exceptions exempting his property from confiscation. It is understood that the legal representatives of Mr Friedrich Nottebohm in Guatemala have been pursuing, so far without success, the remedies nominally open to them under the Confiscation Law of 1949.

9 It is not clear whether the continued sequestration of the property of Mr Friedrich Nottebohm is now taking place by virtue of the provisions of the Confiscation Law of 1949 or of previous war-time legislation affecting alien enemies.

10 The above exposition of facts is based on statements supplied to me on behalf of Mr Friedrich Nottebohm. No authoritative state-ment on behalf of the Guatemalan Government has been laid before me and I am therefore unable to judge to what extent the position as recounted by Mr Friedrich Nottebohm and by his representative corresponds to fact. The present opinion is based on the assumption that the statements supplied to me are substantially correct. They involve, on the face of it, the question of the treatment by Guatemala of a national of Liechtenstein, an independent sovereign State.

8

III. THE LAW

(a) *The question of nationality*

11 It is not clear from the documents as submitted whether the measures taken by the Government of Guatemala against Mr Friedrich Nottebohm were taken and are being taken against him notwithstanding his Liechtenstein nationality or whether the Government denies that he now possesses or ever validly acquired the nationality of Liechtenstein. Whatever may be the attitude of the Guatemalan Government in the matter, it is of importance to ascertain whether, as a matter of international law, Guatemala is under an obligation to consider and to treat Mr Friedrich Nottebohm as a national of Liechtenstein.

12 I am of the opinion that, on the facts as submitted to me, Mr Friedrich Nottebohm must be considered as being a national of Liechtenstein and as not being a national of any other State. He seems to have validly acquired the nationality of Liechtenstein. As the result of the acquisition of the nationality of Liechtenstein he seems to have effectively lost his German nationality by virtue of German law. There is no evidence to show that, having once become a national of Liechtenstein, he has done anything to divest himself of it or to retain German nationality.

13 The question must now be considered whether Guatemala is under an obligation to recognize the change, which took place in October 1939, in the nationality of Mr Friedrich Nottebohm and, in particular, whether Guatemala is bound to recognize and treat Mr Friedrich Nottebohm as a national of Liechtenstein. In general, there ought to be little doubt that Guatemala is under an obligation of that nature. It is an accepted rule of international law that the conferment of nationality is a matter within the exclusive competence of the State concerned subject to such limitations as may follow from customary international law, from treaties, and from general principles of law. Unless Guatemala is in the position to show that the conferment of Liechtenstein nationality upon Mr Friedrich Nottebohm was at variance with the restrictions thus imposed by international law, she is bound to treat him as a Liechtenstein national. The fact that by registering him as a Liechtenstein national she did in fact recognize him as such is directly relevant to the matter. I am not expressing an opinion on the question whether by thus recognizing Mr Friedrich Nottebohm as a Liechtenstein

9

national Guatemala is irrevocably estopped from challenging his Liechtenstein nationality or whether she may be permitted to do so on the ground of evidence, subsequently discovered, that the conferment of Liechtenstein nationality upon Mr Friedrich Nottebohm was contrary to customary international law or to any treaties existing between the two countries or to general principles of law. It does not appear that, so far, Guatemala has relied on any such evidence.

14 In this connection reference may be made to the question whether Guatemala is entitled to refuse to recognize the Liechtenstein nationality of Mr Friedrich Nottebohm on the ground that it was acquired at a time when Germany, of which he had been a national, was at war. There is clearly no rule of international law which prohibits the renunciation of nationality at a time when the State of origin of the person concerned is at war. Undoubtedly the law of some States – such as Great Britain – prohibits the subject of the State to assume, during the war, the nationality of the enemy. (Although it will be noted that even in such cases English courts have refused to recognize the change of nationality thus effected only so far as English law is concerned. They have acted on the view that for other purposes – in particular in connection with international treaties – the change thus effected must be treated as valid.) Also, a State which is a belligerent, does not act contrary to international law if it refuses to recognize the right of alien enemies to change their nationality during the war either by their own action or as the result of the action of their State. None of these circumstances existed in connection with the assumption of Liechtenstein nationality by Mr Friedrich Nottebohm. Guatemala was not a belligerent at the time of the naturalization of Mr Friedrich Nottebohm. She did not become so for another two years.

15 Undoubtedly, although, with the possible exception of its own nationals, a State is bound to recognize the nationality conferred by another State – this does not mean that it is not entitled to deny that the person in question is in fact and law the national of that State. It is, for instance, not sufficient for Liechtenstein to say that Mr Friedrich Nottebohm is a Liechtenstein national and that Mr Friedrich Nottebohm has validly acquired Liechtenstein nationality. It is open to Guatemala to maintain that according to Liechtenstein law Mr Friedrich Nottebohm never acquired Liechtenstein nationality or that, after having acquired it, he lost it as the result of Liechtenstein law. If the assertion of a State that a person is its national and

that therefore it is entitled to protect him diplomatically and before international tribunals were conclusive, the rule of nationality of claims – which is still a rule of international law – would be of very limited importance. It would be sufficient for a State to assert that a person is its national and thus to acquire absolutely the right to protect him regardless of the rule of nationality of claims. International arbitral practice provides sufficient authority in support of the view that a State is entitled to challenge the acquired foreign nationality of a person on the ground that such nationality was not in fact acquired in accordance with the law of the naturalizing State or that it was lost subsequently to it. It does not appear that, so far, Guatemala has put forward or substantiated any contention to that effect. So long as she has not done so, she is under a legal duty to treat Mr Friedrich Nottebohm as a national of Liechtenstein.

16 For these reasons – as already stated – I am not decisively impressed by the possible argument that as the Guatemalan Government recognized Mr Friedrich Nottebohm as a Liechtenstein national by entering him in the list of foreigners in his capacity as a Liechtenstein national it was at any subsequent date estopped from denying his Liechtenstein nationality. In my opinion if the Guatemalan Government had rightly come to the conclusion that Mr Friedrich Nottebohm never in fact acquired Liechtenstein nationality according to Liechtenstein law or that he subsequently lost it according to Liechtenstein law then it would not have been bound to continue to regard him as such. The legal position is, in this respect, the same as with regard to any evidence, subsequently discovered, that the conferment of Liechtenstein nationality upon Mr Friedrich Nottebohm was contrary to international law. However, the burden of proof of substantiating any such assertion would rest upon the Guatemalan Government.

17 Occasionally – though not frequently – the courts of some States have refused to recognize a change of nationality if it was effected *in fraudem legis* as, for instance, in order to circumvent the law of the State in the matter of divorce. There are also indications that some mixed arbitral tribunals after the First World War were inclined to disregard a change of nationality effected with the view to escape the operation of the clauses of the Peace Treaties. None of these circumstances appears in the present case.

18 I am not of the opinion that an international tribunal would regard a change of nationality on the part of Mr Friedrich Nottebohm as being *in fraudem legis* on the ground that he apprehended the

possibility – which did not materialize till 1941 – of Guatemala becoming a belligerent on the side of the United States (which latter country was in 1939 emphatic in its declarations of the resolve to continue a policy of neutrality). It is possible – although there is no proof of that – that Mr Friedrich Nottebohm apprehended that possibility and that by acquiring Liechtenstein nationality in accordance with Liechtenstein law he intended to avoid the disabilities resulting from his German nationality. This would have constituted the legitimate exercise of foresight on the part of a businessman and no international tribunal could properly regard it as a naturalization *in fraudem legis*. It will be noted, on the other hand, that that renunciation of German nationality in October 1939 could have implied an act of deliberate dissociation from the National-Socialist régime. In any case no such charge of naturalization *in fraudem legis* occurred to the Guatemalan Government when she recognized in 1939 the change of nationality on the part of Mr Friedrich Nottebohm.

19 The preceding observations lead me to the conclusion that since October 1939 Mr Friedrich Nottebohm was a Liechtenstein national according to the law both of Liechtenstein and Guatemala as well as according to international law, and that when in 1941 Guatemala entered the war he became the national of a neutral State, and that he was entitled to be treated as such. There is no evidence to show that facts occurred which gave the Government of Guatemala the right to discontinue to regard him as a national of Liechtenstein and of a neutral State.

20 It must now be considered whether the conduct of the Guatemalan Government towards Mr Friedrich Nottebohm as an alien and neutral subject has been in accordance with international law. This question may be considered under four heads: (i) the treatment of Mr Friedrich Nottebohm and his internment during the time of Guatemalan belligerency; (ii) the refusal of the Government of Guatemala to allow him to return to Guatemala subsequent to his internment in the United States; (iii) the sequestration; and (iv) the attempted confiscation of his property. These questions will now be treated in turn.

(b) Liability for the internment of a neutral subject

21 On the facts as submitted to me I am of the opinion that the conduct of the Guatemalan Government in interning a neutral national, in deporting him to a foreign country and in permitting his

continued detention without an adequate inquiry as to his guilt or innocence was contrary to international law and entails the duty of compensation. Undoubtedly, in time of war a neutral subject resident in the territory of a belligerent submits himself and his property to many of the obligations, risks and inconveniences which weigh upon the nationals of the belligerent. His property may be requisitioned, subject to compensation. He may be asked to leave certain zones or localities and to reside in districts assigned to him. He may be requested to participate in certain branches of national service as distinguished from military service proper. There is also authority for the view that a belligerent, either in his own territory or in the territory occupied by him, may, in the presence of strong suspicion calling for immediate action in the interest of his own safety, intern a neutral subject pending inquiries, or expel him regardless of any restrictions which international law imposes upon States in the matter of expulsion of aliens. It does not appear that there existed in the present case any such ground for strong suspicion other than the fact that Mr Nottebohm's enterprises were included on the black list of Great Britain and the United States. It is well known that the inclusion in the black list of persons of former enemy origin or association is often a precautionary measure and does not imply any charge of active assistance to or sympathy for the enemy. Moreover the inclusion in the black list, forming as it does part of the general policy of preventing trading and intercourse with the enemy, does not – even if justified – imply a degree of guilt and active assistance to the enemy warranting the drastic measure of arrest and internment. Neither is it without significance that the British consul in Guatemala was subsequently able to testify officially to the irreproachable conduct and character of Mr Friedrich Nottebohm. It cannot be claimed that the interests of immediate safety of Guatemala called for the summary and hard measures of internment taken by the Guatemalan Government against Mr Friedrich Not-tebohm. Guatemala was not in the neighbourhood of military operations; she was not a region of war; she was not in danger of invasion. Her position was not analogous to that in which, for instance, Great Britain found herself in June 1940 and when provisional measures of internment against a highly suspected neutral national might have been justified.

22 However, even granted that when interning Mr Friedrich Nottebohm the Guatemalan Government acted in the interests of what it believed to be the threatened safety of the country, it was the

duty of that Government – especially in relation to an alien who had been residing in the country for thirty-three years – to take steps to verify any suspicion against Mr Friedrich Nottebohm. No such steps were taken. Accordingly even if the initial act of interning Mr Friedrich Nottebohm was justified – and there is no evidence to prove that – his continued detention, unaccompanied by any positive proof of hostile disposition or action or by any attempt to produce such proof, must be regarded as involving clearly the responsibility of the Guatemalan Government.

23 In view of this, the Government of Liechtenstein would, in my opinion, be justified in holding the Guatemalan Government responsible both for the internment and the continued detention of Mr Friedrich Nottebohm and claiming compensation for the direct and indirect damages resulting to Mr Friedrich Nottebohm from the conduct of the Government of Guatemala in this matter. There is abundant international arbitral authority for the assessment of damages in cases of this nature.

(c) Liability for the refusal to re-admit an unlawfully deported alien

24 I have now to consider the legality of the decision of the Guatemalan Government not to re-admit Mr Friedrich Nottebohm to Guatemala and thus to cause his enforced absence which that Government has treated, in turn, as one of the relevant factors in removing Mr Friedrich Nottebohm from the list of aliens and in purporting to deprive Mr Friedrich Nottebohm of his property by way of confiscation. It is now a fairly well established principle of international law that a State is not entitled to resort arbitrarily to the expulsion of an alien who has been long resident in the country, who has established a business there and who has not been guilty of any serious violation of the law of the State. On the facts presented to me there was in this case no justifiable cause of expulsion. In my opinion, the refusal to re-admit Mr Friedrich Nottebohm subsequent to his forcible removal from the country – a removal for which there was no ground other than the German origin of Mr Friedrich Nottebohm – was tantamount to expulsion. The fact that, by virtue of the provisions of certain Aliens Orders and the Confiscation Law, Mr Friedrich Nottebohm's enforced absence from the country has been treated as a relevant factor in depriving him of his status as a lawfully admitted alien and of his property, adds emphasis to this aspect of the international liability of the Government of Guatemala. It is unlikely that an international tribunal would refrain from dis-

approving the conduct of a Government which relies on its own wrong of unlawful internment and, in effect, of expulsion as a ground for invoking the enforced absence of the alien as a further reason for depriving him of his status and property. It will also be noted that no reasons of national safety militated against the re-admission of Mr Friedrich Nottebohm subsequent to the general cessation of hostilities.

(d) Liability for sequestration and withholding of property

25 It is not apparent from the documents submitted to me on what date subsequent to the forcible detention and deportation of Mr Friedrich Nottebohm the Government of Guatemala took over his property. Neither is it clear whether the Government of Guatemala now holds the property of Mr Friedrich Nottebohm as the administrator of it in connection with the said detention and the subsequent enforced inability of Mr Friedrich Nottebohm to return to Guatemala, or in pursuance of the provisions of the Confiscation Law of 1949. In so far as Mr Friedrich Nottebohm has been deprived of the use of his property in connection with or as the result of his detention, continued internment, or enforced absence from the country – of which at least the last two seem to be contrary to international law – the Government of Guatemala is responsible for any damage resulting from such deprivation of property. That responsibility is additional to the principal obligation to restore without delay the property in question to Mr Friedrich Nottebohm or his legal representatives.

(e) Liability for the confiscation of property

26 Regardless of the question of the legality of what has been in effect the expulsion of Mr Friedrich Nottebohm, he has remained an alien and his property has remained that of an alien. It is from this point of view that there must be judged the legality and any resulting responsibility of the Government of Guatemala in connection with the attempted confiscation of the property of Mr Friedrich Nottebohm in pursuance of the Confiscation Law of 1949. The confiscation, without compensation, of the property of an alien for a reason other than punishment, consistent with justice, for an offence against the law of the State is illegal under international law. The fact that the alien in question was for a time a national of a State with which Guatemala is formally at war is altogether irrelevant for the purpose of judging the legality of the confiscation. The position might be

different if Mr Friedrich Nottebohm had changed his nationality at a time when Guatemala was already at war with Germany and if Guatemala had therefore declined to recognize the change of nationality. Neither of these exculpating circumstances exist in the present case. Mr Friedrich Nottebohm became a Liechtenstein national long before Guatemala entered the war. Moreover, he had been recognized as such by Guatemala. The proceeding adopted by Guatemala in purporting to confiscate the property of an alien for the reason that he was the national of Germany at a date, arbitrarily chosen, at which not only Guatemala was not at war with Germany, but at which Germany was not at war with any other country, creates the impression of being unprecedented. It is certainly contrary to international law. This may be said without advancing the contention that the Confiscation Law although framed in general terms is in fact aimed specifically at Mr Friedrich Nottebohm. Any such assertion would be disrespectful to Guatemala and, in my opinion, ought not be advanced. At the same time, there seems to be little doubt, on the facts as submitted to me, that the action of Guatemala is patently inconsistent with the generally recognized principles of international law in the matter of the treatment of property of aliens and that an international tribunal would hold it to be so.

27 The purely confiscatory nature of the proposed measure appears also from the fact that, even if Mr Friedrich Nottebohm were a German national, there would probably be no justification for Guatemala to confiscate the property of German nationals by way of reparation for damage suffered by Guatemala as the result of the war. It is unlikely that Guatemala suffered direct damage as the result of military, naval, or air operations. She was not in the region of war. It will be noted that in the Peace Treaties of 1947 the victorious belligerents, other than Soviet Russia, renounced all claims to reparations. In so far as the Peace Treaties provided for the retention of private property of subjects of the former enemies, it was laid down that enemy assets in excess of claims – other than requisitions – must be returned. However, these considerations are here adduced only as pointing to the general impropriety – as distinguished from illegality – of the action of Guatemala. They do not enter as a factor in the legal claim to be advanced by Liechtenstein. For Mr Friedrich Nottebohm is a Liechtenstein – and not a German – national.

IV. THE REMEDIES AVAILABLE

28 It would thus appear that the claim of the Liechtenstein Government against Guatemala falls under five heads: (i) the internment of Mr Friedrich Nottebohm; (ii) his continued detention unaccompanied by an inquiry as to his guilt or innocence; (iii) the unjustified refusal, amounting to expulsion, to allow him to return to Guatemala; (iv) the seizure and continued sequestration of the property of Mr Friedrich Nottebohm; (v) the attempted confiscation of his property. The proper procedure for the Liechtenstein Government would be to address a formal communication to the Guatemalan Government bringing to its notice the facts recounted in the present opinion and the views of the Government of Liechtenstein on the question of the legality of the conduct pursued by the Government of Guatemala. That communication ought to be accompanied by a request for compensation with regard to the first four of these heads; with a request for the authorization for Mr Friedrich Nottebohm to re-enter Guatemala; with a claim for restitution in respect of the seizure of property; and with a request to desist from the announced intention to confiscate his property.

29 These steps can properly be undertaken concurrently with any attempts which are being made by the legal representatives of Mr Friedrich Nottebohm in Guatemala to obtain redress. I am not of the opinion that the rules of international law relating to the necessity of the exhaustion of local remedies as a condition of putting forward an international claim preclude the Government of Liechtenstein from taking immediate steps with the Government of Guatemala or, in case such steps should not be successful, from bringing the matter before the International Court of Justice by virtue of the Optional Clause of Article 36 of its Statute. That Clause is now effectively in operation between the two countries – Guatemala having signed it on 27 January 1947 for a period of five years and Liechtenstein on 29 March 1950 without a time limit. While recognizing the general justification of the requirement of exhaustion of legal remedies, international courts and tribunals have declined to permit it to defeat the ends of justice. It is an established principle that it is not necessary to exhaust local remedies where, to all appearance, there are no local remedies to be exhausted, where the acts complained of emanate from governmental or legislative acts against which the law provides, in effect, no remedy, or when the processes for securing justice within the State concerned operate with a slowness which may

make the prospects of an ultimate remedy purely illusory. It will be noted that nearly seven years have now elapsed since Mr Friedrich Nottebohm was interned and since he was first deprived of his property. Throughout that period continuous efforts have been made on behalf of the legal representatives of Mr Friedrich Nottebohm to obtain redress. Similarly unceasing efforts have been made since the enactment of the Confiscation Laws to obtain an exemption of the property of Mr Friedrich Nottebohm from the operation of that law.

30 There is a further feature in the situation which is relevant to the question of the exhaustion of legal remedies. As stated, the Guatemalan Government subscribed, in 1947, for a period of five years, to the obligations of the Optional Clause of the Statute of the International Court of Justice. Unless renewed, that signature will expire in February 1952. There is no reason to believe that Guatemala which for a long time has been a strong adherent of the cause of international justice would not renew its signature. On the other hand that is a possibility which the Government of Liechtenstein is entitled to take into consideration and which it is not entitled to disregard consistently with its obligations to its nationals. This is a factor which the International Court of Justice is not likely to disregard in assessing whether the local remedies have been exhausted.

31 It must also be noted that this is not a question of a complaint being brought against Guatemala by virtue of a law which may prove merely theoretical in relation to the alien concerned. Whatever may be the chances of Mr Friedrich Nottebohm bringing himself within the orbit of the exceptions exempting his property from confiscation, it is probable that action – however provisional – has already been taken and is being taken in pursuance of the Confiscation Law. Mr Friedrich Nottebohm is now deprived of the use of his property not only in consequence of the previous measures of sequestration taken in connection with his internment but, probably, also by virtue of the Confiscation Law. He is already suffering damage thereunder. The Government of Liechtenstein is entitled to complain not only of any actual and accomplished confiscation, but also of the fact – and this is not a mere attempt – that the Confiscation Law disregards the Liechtenstein nationality of Mr Friedrich Nottebohm and purports to throw upon him the burden of proof that he is exempted from the operation of that law. This is in itself a violation of the international rights of the alien.

32 While the representatives of Mr Friedrich Nottebohm in pursuing the legal remedies available under the Confiscation Law of 1949 must necessarily invoke the provisions of that law and proceed on the basis of that law, it is of importance that the Government of Liechtenstein should make it clear at this juncture that it in no way recognizes the right of the Government of Guatemala to proceed against a national of Liechtenstein on the basis of that law which arbitrarily transforms a national of Liechtenstein into a national of an enemy of Guatemala.

33 It is for the Government of Liechtenstein to consider, as a matter of policy, whether, with the view to a speedy and amicable termination of the controversy which has arisen, it ought not to limit its claim against the Government of Guatemala to the full restitution of the property of Mr Friedrich Nottebohm, to a formal and final abandonment of any attempts at confiscation by virtue of the Law of 1949, to compensation for any direct damage caused to him as the result of the administration by the Guatemalan authorities, to compensation for unjustified detention and to an accounting for the profits which the Guatemalan Government has derived from the properties administered by it. This would mean the abandonment of what, on the facts before me, I believe to be a good legal claim in respect of the internment, the unjustified refusal – amounting to expulsion – to re-admit Mr Friedrich Nottebohm, and the indirect damage resulting from the seizure of the property of Mr Friedrich Nottebohm.

34 Should the Government of Guatemala fail to give immediate satisfaction to that part of the communication of the Government of Liechtenstein which refers to the attempted confiscation of property, it may be advisable for the Government of Liechtenstein to consider an application to the International Court of Justice for an indication of interim measures of protection, under Article 41 of the Statute and Article 61 of the Rules of the Court, with the view to preventing the Government of Guatemala from proceeding with the implementation of the Confiscation Law of 1949. Such application ought to be made, in my opinion, not later than six weeks from the receipt of the request of Liechtenstein by the Government of Guatemala, provided that no satisfactory answer has been received from the Government of Guatemala.

35 In case the Government of Guatemala should fail to give satisfaction to the Government of Liechtenstein with respect to all or some aspects of the case, it is in my opinion advisable that the

Government of Liechtenstein should institute proceedings before the International Court of Justice by unilateral submission not later than 1 May 1950 in accordance with Articles 36 and 40 of the Statute of the Court and Article 32 of its Rules.

II TREATMENT OF PROPERTY

CHAPTER 2

THE *ANGLO-IRANIAN OIL COMPANY* CASE – DRAFT OF LEGAL SUBMISSIONS

Editor's Note From the moment of the nationalization of the Anglo-Iranian Oil Company's concession in Iran on 1 May 1951 until early in 1952 when Lauterpacht retired from the Bar, he was closely involved in the various legal moves made by the company to assert its legal rights. On the international plane, the first of these was the commencement of proceedings before the International Court of Justice asserting the international illegality of the nationalization. This was soon followed by an application for the indication of interim measures of protection – in which Lauterpacht appeared as one of the British counsel. This application led to the Court's Order of 5 July 1951 (*I.C.J. Reports* 1951, p. 89). Lauterpacht was then engaged by the company to prepare on its behalf the first draft of the legal argument in the Memorial on the merits of the case. This draft was conveyed to the Foreign Office and, after amendment, formed the central part of the Memorial filed by the British Government on 10 October 1951 (see *I.C.J. Pleadings, Anglo-Iranian Oil Company Case*, p. 64).

The draft was prepared by Lauterpacht under extraordinary pressure. My personal recollection is that he was asked to complete it in about ten days – and did so. I have thought it right to include it here because it is the only extended work on the treatment of alien property rights which Lauterpacht wrote. It is, moreover, an outstanding elaboration of the traditional view of the sanctity of foreign property rights in international law as it stood before the period of challenge heralded by the post-Second World War nationalizations in Europe, encouraged by this very episode of nationalization and furthered by the first General Assembly resolution on 'Permanent Sovereignty over Natural Resources'.

Whether Lauterpacht, in his academic capacity, fully shared the views which he here developed in his professional capacity is open to some doubt. Some of the statements in this chapter may be compared with his brief observations in the next chapter (see below, p. 90). Also, in his eighth edition of volume 1 of Oppenheim's *International Law* he qualified the statement of the rule that alien property is entitled to respect by the following observation (at p. 352): '[A] modification must be recognized in cases in which fundamental changes in the political system and economic structure of the State or far-reaching social reforms entail interference, on a large scale, with private property. In such cases neither the principle of absolute respect for alien private property nor rigid equality with the dispossessed nationals offers a satisfactory solution of the difficulty. It is probable that, consistently with legal principle, such solution must be sought in the granting of partial compensation.'

The same requirements of forensic presentation which explain the fact that some statements in the draft Memorial go some way beyond Lauterpacht's own academic views also explain the divergencies between Lauterpacht's draft and the final text as eventually presented to the Court by the British Government. The Government were clearly and properly entitled to amend Lauterpacht's draft so as to present to the Court as cogent an argument as possible. For this reason it would be unwise and might well be misleading to attach any particular significance to differences between the two texts. Only the Memorial, as finally submitted to the Court, can be read as an authoritative statement of the views of the British Government at that time.

The text printed here differs slightly from the original in a few minor respects, involving principally the omission of notes and queries introduced by Lauterpacht indicating passages which might require further expansion or discussion before the text of the Memorial was settled.

CONTENTS

THE LAW

25

THE LAW

1. Applicable principles of law   It is convenient to preface the exposition
of the contentions of the Government of the United Kingdom by the
following summary of legal submissions:

(i) While a State possesses the right to nationalize and, generally,
to expropriate the property of aliens, it is entitled to do so only
subject to conditions laid down by international law. Such property
includes concessions granted by a State to foreign nationals. Their
treatment, like that of other property rights, is governed by the
general principle of international law obliging the State to respect
the property and other vested rights of aliens.

(ii) The termination or cancellation for the purpose of nationalization – or, generally, of expropriation – of a concession granted
to a foreign national is unlawful if the State granting the concession has expressly undertaken either in a treaty or in the
particular concessionary contract not to terminate it unilaterally.

(iii) The nationalization of the property of aliens – including
concessions granted to them – is unlawful unless accompanied
by compensation which is adequate, prompt and effective. In
addition the amount and manner of such compensation – including,
in proper cases, restitution in kind – depend, apart from other
factors, on the question whether the nationalization is lawful or
unlawful, for instance, whether it is in conformity with obligations
expressly undertaken by the State or with the principle prohibiting
discrimination against aliens. The Government of the United
Kingdom will rely in this connection on the rule which is an
established principle of international jurisprudence and which
was formulated by the Permanent Court of International Justice
in the *Chorzów Factory (Claim for Indemnity)*, case.

(iv) A measure of expropriation and nationalization even if
otherwise lawful, becomes unlawful under international law if in
effect it is exclusively or primarily directed against aliens as such.
The latter factor enhances the unlawfulness of an act of nationalization which may be unlawful for other reasons.

(v) A measure of confiscation or of nationalization which is contrary to international law on account of being confiscatory in nature or for other reasons engages directly the international responsibility of the State if it is the result of legislation admitting of no recourse to or remedy by local courts or tribunals provided for by the concessions agreement.

2. *Submissions of the United Kingdom*   The Government of the United Kingdom will submit that in the light of the principles set out above the Iranian Oil Nationalization Law of 1 May 1951 constitutes an unlawful act which engages the international responsibility of Iran for the reasons:

(a) that it is in violation of an express undertaking not to terminate the concession unilaterally by legislative or governmental action;

(b) that, notwithstanding an apparent promise to compensate the Anglo-Iranian Oil Company, it is in fact confiscatory in nature;

(c) that, notwithstanding its apparent general character, it is in fact directed primarily, if not exclusively, against a foreign national – the Anglo-Iranian Oil Company; and

(d) that as it does not – and, by virtue of its terms cannot – provide for any municipal remedy open to the Anglo-Iranian Oil Company in Iran or before an appropriate tribunal in accordance with the terms of the Convention of 1933, it engages directly the responsibility of the Iranian State.

3. *Submissions of the United Kingdom as to the judgment of the Court*   The Government of the United Kingdom will submit accordingly that it is entitled to a declaration and judgment of the Court that the Government of Iran is bound:

(a) to restore the Anglo-Iranian Oil Company to the position as it existed prior to the Oil Nationalization Law;

(b) in the alternative, to abide by the obligation of Article 22 of the Convention of 1933 providing for the arbitration of all differences between the parties;

(c) in the alternative, to grant the company full compensation in accordance with the principles accepted in international jurisprudence and formulated by the Permanent Court of International Justice in the *Chorzów Factory* case – such compensation including both an indemnity which is due in case of a lawful expropriation of the property of an alien national and an indemnity which international law prescribes in cases in which expropriation has been effected in violation of the international obligation of the State.

II. CONCESSIONS AND NATIONALIZATION OF PROPERTY AND ALIENS

4. A concession is a vested right protected by international law   The Government of the United Kingdom does not consider it necessary to elaborate the proposition that rights acquired by alien nationals by virtue of concessionary contracts are property rights and that as such they are entitled to the same protection which international law grants to property of aliens. This proposition is generally recognized and, to the knowledge of the Government of the United Kingdom, has not been seriously challenged. 'Concessions', says a modern authority, 'are acquired rights' (Professor Verdross in *Hague Recueil*, 37 (1931), 364). See also to the same effect Gidel, *Des effets de l'annexation sur les concessions* (1904); Kaeckenbeeck in *B.Y.* 17 (1936), 10; Scelle, II, 120, who points out that respect for property implies respect for contractor and debts; Dr Mosler, the author of the most recent work on concessions in relation to State succession, says: 'The protection of concessionary rights has its roots in the protection of acquired rights of private persons' (*Wirtschaftskonzessionen bei Änderung der Staatshoheit* (1948), 92). In the *compromis* and in the award of the *Delagoa Bay* arbitration of 1891 – an arbitration concerned with the cancellation of a concession – the concession was treated as an acquired right. The *compromis* instructed the Tribunal to fix 'le montant de la compensation due par le gouvernement portugais aux ayants droit'. As stated in a frequently quoted passage from the judgment of Chief Justice Marshall in *Soulard* v. *United States* (4 Peters. 511): 'The term "property" as applied to lands, comprehends every species of title, inchoate or complete. It is supposed to embrace those rights which lie in contract; those which are executory, as well as those which are executed.' Reference may also be made to the various communications of the Department of State addressed after the First World War to the Government of the United Kingdom in the matter of American concessions in the territories formerly belonging to the Ottoman Empire and referring throughout to these concessions as 'vested rights' (*U.S. For. Rel.* (1920), II, 650; (1922), II, 273; (1923), II, 1033). Finally, to refer to a modern example, in the Agreement of 2 November 1949 between the

Netherlands and Indonesia the latter undertook to 'adhere to the basic principle of recognizing concessions'. This obligation was undertaken in connection with the provision of Article 3 of the agreement which laid down that 'expropriation, nationalization, compulsory cession and transfer of property rights' can take place only if they are for the public benefit, and then only 'against previously enjoyed or guaranteed indemnity to be fixed by judicial decision at the real value of the object involved' (*Staatsblad*, 21 December 1949). In the *Oscar Chinn* case the Permanent Court of International Justice seemed to have no doubt that a concession created a vested right. The main question, to which it gave a negative answer, was whether the particular privileges claimed on behalf of Mr Chinn were 'anything in the nature of a genuine vested right' (Series A/B, no. 63, p. 88).

5. Concessions and State succession   The extent of recognition of concessionary rights as 'vested' or 'acquired' rights is illustrated by the fact that, with slight exceptions, international practice in the matter of State succession has treated them as coming within the rule that acquired private rights must be respected by the successor State.

6. Legality of nationalization of concessions   The Government of the United Kingdom do not dissent from the proposition that a State is entitled to nationalize and, generally, to expropriate concessions granted to aliens in the same way as it is entitled to do with regard to other property owned by aliens. The exercise of that right, with regard to concessions and other property rights, is, however, subject to limitations clearly established by international practice and resting on well-recognized principles of international law. These limitations include, in particular, the principle that a State is not entitled to nationalize a concession if by a treaty or contract it has expressly divested itself of the right to do so; the rule that the nationalization must not be discriminatory against aliens or exclusively or primarily directed against them; and the requirement that nationalization must be accompanied by compensation in accordance with international law. It is not necessary for the Government of the United Kingdom, for the purpose of the present case, to express an opinion on the question – which is controversial – whether the absence of discrimination against aliens, in the matter of compensation or otherwise, relieves the State of international responsibility. For the reasons stated below, the Government of the United Kingdom will submit that the Iranian Oil Nationalization Act of 1 May is, in fact and in law, directed against a foreign national – to wit, the Anglo-Iranian Oil Company – and that it is therefore discriminatory.

7. International responsibility for violation of concessions. Arbitral practice
The principle that a State which enacts legislation in violation of contracts concluded with or concessions granted to aliens incurs international responsibility is very generally recognized by the international practice of States, by judicial and arbitral decisions, and by writers. It is not considered necessary at this stage to give an exhaustive survey of these decisions. Reference may, however, usefully be made to some of them in so far as they bear on the principles set out in this section of the Memorial.

In a long series of arbitral awards the principle of the responsibility of the State for the unilateral and arbitrary cancellation of concessions granted to and contracts made with aliens has been expressly recognized. In the *Rudloff* case between the United States and Venezuela the Umpire said:

The taking away or destruction of rights acquired, transmitted, and defined by a contract is as much a wrong, entitling the sufferer to redress, as the taking away or destruction of tangible property; and such an act committed by a Government against an alien resident gives, by established rules of international law, the Government to which the alien owns allegiance and which in turn owes him protection, the right to demand and to receive just compensation. (Ralston, *Venezuelan Arbitrations* (1903), pp. 188–9.)

Identical principles were expressed in substance in the cases of *Kunhard (United States)* v. *Venezuela* (Ralston's *Report*, p. 63); *Selwyn* v. *Venezuela* (*ibid.* p. 322); *North and South American Construction Co.* v. *Clark* (Moore, *International Arbitrations*, p. 2318); and *Milligan* v. *Peru* (*ibid.* p. 1643). All these cases are referred to in support of the proposition here contended for, in the comment to Article 8 of the Harvard Research Draft on Responsibility of States for Damage Done in their Territory to the Person or Property of Foreigners and in Borchard, pp. 293–6.

The well-known and frequently cited cases of the *Delagoa Bay Railroad Company* (Moore, *International Arbitrations*, pp. 1865–99, and Moore, vi, 648) and of the *El Triunfo* claim (Moore, vi, 649; *U.S. For. Rel.* (1902), pp. 838–52) provide authority for the same proposition.

In the *Mariposa* claim (*United States* v. *Panama*, Hunt's *Report* (1934), pp. 556 *et seq.*) the Tribunal held as follows:

The Commission does not assert that legislation might not be passed of such a character that its mere enactment would destroy the marketability of private property, render it valueless and give rise forthwith to an international claim, but it is the opinion of the Commission that ordinarily, and in this case, a claim for the expropriation of property must be held to have arisen when the possession of the owner is interfered with and not when the legislation is passed which makes the later deprivation of possession possible.

In the *De Sabla* case, decided between the United States and Panama, the Tribunal said:

It is axiomatic that acts of a Government in depriving an alien of his property without compensation impose international responsibility. Panama has attempted to justify the result reached by asserting that the claimant failed to comply with the duties and take advantage of the remedies created by Panaman law. This justification the Commission, for the reasons stated, finds to be unsustained. In so finding, no imputation of bad faith or discrimination is made against the Government of Panama or its land authorities. As the public statements of its high officials show, it was endeavouring throughout this period to bring order out of a chaotic system of public land administration. In such a period of development and readjustment, it is perhaps inevitable that unfortunate situations like the present one should arise. It is no extreme measure to hold, as this Commission does, that if the process of working out the system results in the loss of the private property of aliens, such loss should be compensated. (Hunt's *Report* (1934), pp. 432, 447.)

In the *Walter Fletcher Smith* case, decided in 1930 between the United States and Cuba, the Arbitrator used language even more emphatic:

From a careful examination of the testimony and of the records, the Arbitrator is impressed that the attempted expropriation of the claimant's property was not in compliance with the constitution, nor with the laws of the Republic; that the expropriation proceedings were not, in good faith, for the purpose of public utility . . .

While the proceedings were municipal in form, the properties seized were turned over immediately to the defendant company, ostensibly for public purposes, but, in fact, to be used by the defendant for purposes of amusement and private profit, without any reference to public utility. The Arbitrator is of the opinion, then, that all the acts of expropriation shown in testimony, and the proceedings based upon them, were not of

34

such a character as to give an indefeasible title to the defendant company. (*A.J.* 24 (1930), 384–8; *Annual Digest* (1929–30), case no. 163.)

In the *Shufeldt* case, decided in 1931 between the United States and Guatemala, the Arbitrator said:

It is perfectly competent for the Government of Guatemala to enact any decree they like and for any reasons they see fit, and such reasons are no concern of this Tribunal. But this Tribunal is only concerned where such a decree, passed even on the best of grounds, works an injustice to an alien subject, in which case the Government ought to make compensation for the injury inflicted and can not invoke any municipal law to justify their refusal to do so. (*A.J.* 24 (1930), pp. 799–822; *Annual Digest* (1929–30), case no. 110.)

In the case of the *International Fisheries Company*, decided in 1931 by the United States–Mexican Special Claims Commission, the same principle was again affirmed although in the circumstances the Commission found that the 'case was not one of unilateral nullification without reasons' (*Annual Digest* (1931–2), case no. 142). Some of the decisions of the mixed arbitral tribunals follow directly or indirectly the same principle. Thus in *Rosenstein* v. *German State* the Germano–Roumanian Mixed Arbitral Tribunal did so indirectly by finding that Germany was not, in the circumstances, responsible for the unilateral cancellation on the ground that:

A State had the right to take away, on the ground of the general interest, concessions relating to public works from a contractor who had become in consequence of a declaration of war a national of an enemy Power, and as such not only suspect but also liable to be interned at any time. The rescission of the contract was in such cases based upon the loss of an essential quality in the person of the contractor. (*Annual Digest* (1929–30), case no. 283.)

The case of *Kemeny* v. *État Serbe-Croat-Slovène*, decided in 1928 by the Hungarian–Yugoslav Mixed Arbitral Tribunal and referred to below in paragraph 40 is on the same lines. The same applies to the *Suez Canal* case, decided in 1864, and the *Markin* case, decided in 1930 between Italy and Venezuela. The principle of the responsibility of the State – the successor State – for cancellation of concessionary contracts was also affirmed with clarity in the arbitration decided by Dr Unden in 1933 between Greece and Bulgaria (*Annual Digest* (1933–4), case no. 39). Last – but not least – there is the fundamental and exhaustive pronouncement of the Permanent Court of International Justice in the *Chorzów Factory* case, detailed reference to which is made elsewhere in this Memorial.

As mentioned, not all these decisions have resulted in an award against the defendant State. Some of them, while affirming the principle of responsibility, declined to find that the defendant State was responsible. In some of them the vested right which was interfered with was not a concession, but some category of contract. But the uniformity of these awards is impressive.

8. The same. Practice of Governments The practice of Governments in urging the illegality of unilateral cancellation of contracts and concessions and the resulting international responsibility of the offending State has been particularly prominent in connection with the cases referred to above. Thus, for instance, in a note addressed to the Portuguese Government in 1887 in connection with the Delagoa Bay–Lourenço Marques Railway the British Government said:

Her Majesty's Government are of the opinion that the Portuguese Government had no right to cancel the concessions nor to forfeit the lines already constructed.

They hold the action of the Portuguese Government to have been wrongful, and to have violated the clear rights, and injured the interests, of the British company which was powerless to prevent it, and which, as the Portuguese company is practically defunct, has no remedy except through the intervention of its own Government. In their judgment the British investors have suffered a grievous wrong in consequence of the forcible confiscation by the Portuguese Government of the line and materials belonging to the British Company, and of the security on which the debentures of the British Company had been advanced; and for that wrong Her Majesty's Government are bound to ask for compensation. (*Br. and For. St. Papers*, 81, 691.)

The statements by the British, American and Dutch Governments in connection with the expropriations in Mexico are quoted below. The earlier statements of Mr Cass, the American Secretary of State, have often been quoted in this connection, and they are suitably reproduced here. He said, in 1860:

It is quite true, for example, that under ordinary circumstances when citizens of the United States go to a foreign country they go with an implied understanding that they are to obey its laws, and submit themselves, in good faith, to its established tribunals. When they do business with its citizens, or make private contracts there, it is not to be expected that either their own or the foreign Government is to be made a party to this business or these contracts, or will undertake to determine any disputes to which they may give rise. The case, however, is very much changed when no impartial tribunals can be said to exist in a foreign country, or when they have been arbitrarily controlled by the Government to the injury of our citizens. So, also, the case is widely different when the foreign Government becomes itself a party to important contracts, and then not only fails to fulfil them, but capriciously annuls them, to the great loss of those who have invested their time and labour and capital from a reliance upon its own good faith and justice. (Moore, VI, 287.)

In a previous communication to Mr Lamar, Minister to Central America, Mr Cass stated:

What the United States demand is that in all cases where their citizens have entered into contracts with the proper Nicaraguan authorities, and questions have arisen or shall arise respecting the fidelity of their execution, no declaration of forfeiture, either past or to come, shall possess any binding force unless pronounced in conformity with the provisions of the contract, if there are any; or if there is no provision for that purpose, then unless there has been a fair and impartial investigation in such a manner as to satisfy the United States that the proceeding has been just and that the decision ought to be submitted to. (*Ibid.* p. 725.)

Professor Borchard summarizes the practice of the Government of the United States in the following words:

Perhaps the most zealous interposition on the part of the United States has been in cases where the confiscatory act of the foreign Government consisted in the arbitrary annulment of the entire contract or of some of its essential provisions without a resort to the courts. (Borchard, p. 293.)

9. The same. The Hague Codification Conference In view of this impressive volume of arbitral decisions and the practice of States it is not surprising that in their *Bases of Discussion* submitted to the Hague Codification Conference the Preparatory Committee gave, in general, an affirmative answer to the question:

Does the State become responsible in the following circumstances:
    Enactment of legislation incompatible with the terms of concessions or contracts granted to or concluded with foreigners or of a nature to obstruct their execution?

Its answer was:

A State is responsible for damage suffered by a foreigner as the result of the enactment of legislation which directly infringes rights derived by the foreigner from a concession granted or a contract made by the State.

It depends upon the circumstances whether a State incurs responsibility where it has enacted legislation general in character which is incompatible with the operation of a concession which it has granted or the performance of a contract made by it. (League of Nations, Conference for the Codification of International Law, *Bases of Discussion*, vol. III: Responsibility of States for Damage caused in their Territory to the Person or Property of Foreigners, p. 33.)

The following passage – which is directly relevant to the Oil Nationalization Law – from the Observations of the Committee on the subject may suitably be quoted:

It seems, on the other hand, that certain difficulties will be met if a distinction is made between legislation which directly infringes rights conferred by the State upon a foreigner in a concession or a contract and legislation of a general character which is incompatible with such concession or contract; as regards the latter, the responsibility of the State would seem to depend to some extent on the circumstances of the case. (*Ibid.*)

The answer of the British Government to the question put by the committee is relevant. It said:

Where the contract or concession with which the legislation is irreconcilable has been concluded or granted by the State itself, the State is responsible and must make reparation if its legislative organ thereafter enacts legislation which is incompatible with such contract or concession or prevents its fulfilment. (*Ibid.* p. 31.)

The view that it is unlawful to infringe the right of an alien resting on a contract with the State or on a concession is generally supported by writers. Verdross expresses the view that

La responsabilité de l'État se trouve engagée lorsqu'une disposition législative porte directement atteinte aux droits d'un étranger découlant d'une concession accordée par l'État où d'un contrat passé par lui. (*Hague Recueil* (1931) (iii), p. 373.)

Similarly, Kaeckenbeeck writes:

While a foreigner's right rests on a contract with the State or on a concession, its infringement through legislative action is often held to render the State internationally liable, but this would seem to be certain only when the concession has been granted or the contract has been entered into by the State as such, that is as sovereign, and not simply as Fisc. (In *B.Y.* 17 (1936), 15.)

10. The same. Views of writers The views of writers and unofficial bodies give expression to the rule which follows so clearly from general principle and precedent. Article 8 (*a*) of the Harvard Research Draft on State Responsibility lays down that 'A State is responsible if an injury to an alien results from its non-performance of a contractual obligation which it owes to the alien, if local remedies have been exhausted without adequate redress.' It is clear from the comment on that Article that it covers both contracts in general and concessions in particular and that it refers both to administrative and to legislative action of the organs of the State.

Writers who have devoted special attention to the question of State Responsibility express the same view. Thus Professor Eagleton says:

Similarly, the State may be held responsible for confiscatory breaches of contracts. The United States has often intervened on this account; and such intervention has been justified as against a tortious, rather than against a contractual, injury. It has been said that the United States today requires 'that a breach of contract must constitute also a tort in order to be regarded as internationally illegal conduct'; and the diplomatic correspondence includes various statements in which this term of private law is introduced into the realm of international law. In those cases, the basis for the claim is to be found in the fact that the circumstances accompanying the breach of the contract constitute in themselves internationally illegal conduct. (*The Responsibility of States in International Law* (1928), p. 165.)

It will be noted from sections III, IV and V of this Memorial that it is exactly the tortious aspect of the conduct of Iranian authorities which is the subject matter of the complaint of the Government of the United Kingdom in the present case.

Dr Freeman's view is to the same effect.

Professor Borchard (*Borchard*, p. 292) says:

Cases have frequently occurred in which the contracts of citizens of the United States with foreign Governments were arbitrarily annulled by the contracting Government without recourse to a judicial determination of the contract or of the legitimacy of its act. An act of this kind has generally been held by the Department of State to be a confiscatory breach of the contract and to warrant diplomatic interposition as in cases of tort.

Finally, reference may be made to the following passage in Dr Feller's book on *The Mexican Claims Commissions, 1923–1934* (1935), pp. 173–4:

What is the basis of international responsibility for breach by a Government of a contract which it has concluded with an alien? One possible basis is that the breach of contract is in and of itself a confiscation of property. It is thus violative of international law and the responsibility of the Government arises immediately. This is the view taken by American Commissioner Nielsen in the General Claims Commission and by one or two international tribunals. The overwhelming weight of opinion, both of writers and tribunals, has been, however, to the effect that international responsibility for a breach of contract does not arise until there has been a 'denial of justice', i.e., until the alien has applied to the local authorities and courts and adequate redress has been denied him. The one apparent exception has been with respect to 'confiscatory' breaches of contract, where, it is said, international responsibility arises immediately. On examination these 'confiscatory' breaches resolve themselves into cases where no means of local redress exist and the denial of justice is therefore established without the necessity of going through the futile forms of seeking redress, or where there has been an arbitrary annulment of the contract by the executive without resort to judicial procedure.

11. Conclusions The conclusions of this section of the Memorial are that a concession granted to an alien is a 'vested', 'acquired', right protected by international law; that while international law does not prohibit the nationalization or expropriation of the vested rights in question the lawfulness of measures, in the international sphere, is conditioned by their compliance with the limitations imposed by international law; that the disregard of such limitations engages the international responsibility of the State; and that the principles thus formulated are supported by international judicial and arbitral practice, by the practice of Governments, and by opinions of writers. The limitations which international law imposes upon the right of the State to nationalize concessions granted to foreign nationals will now be considered.

III. CANCELLATION OF THE CONCESSION IN VIOLATION OF AN EXPRESS RENUNCIATION OF THE RIGHT OF UNILATERAL TERMINATION

12. Article 21 of the Convention of 1933 It is contended by the Government of the United Kingdom, in the first instance, that, whatever may be the legal position – in other respects – with regard to the right of a State to nationalize a concession granted by it, in the present case the unilateral cancellation of the Convention of 1933 amounts to a breach of international law inasmuch as it deprives the Anglo-Iranian Oil Company of a vested right in violation of an explicit undertaking of the Imperial Iranian Government. Article 21 of the convention lays down that the 'Concession shall not be annulled by the Government and the terms therein contained shall not be altered either by general or special legislation in the future, or by administrative measures or any other acts whatever of the executive authorities'. That Article of the convention was inserted with the specific object of making it legally impossible for the Government of Iran to put an end to the concession by some such measure of nationalization. Contrasted with the previous concession, which it replaced, it was a new provision calculated to remove, once and for all, the danger of contingencies such as gave rise to the situation which brought about an international crisis in 1932 and which caused the dispute between the United Kingdom and Persia to be brought before the League of Nations.

13. The consequences of the renunciation of the right of unilateral termination
There is, in the submission of the Government of the United Kingdom, a fundamental difference between an ordinary concession, even if granted for a term of years, and a concession in which the State has expressly divested itself of the right to exercise the power of terminating it by unilateral action whether its purpose be for other reasons or, generally, the exercise of the power of nationalization, expropriation, eminent domain. It is arguable that normally a foreign national who obtains a concession from a Government must realize that the vested right thus acquired is subject to the contingency of its being terminated, on payment of compensation as prescribed by international law and, in accordance with other rules of international law, by the law of the State. He must, on that view, be assumed to have willingly taken the risk to which the nationals of the State in question are exposed. However, the position is quite different, as a matter of law and good faith, if the foreign company or national expressly stipulates in the contract – with the full, formal, and express concurrence of the other contracting party – that the concession shall be immune from termination by legislative or governmental action. It is only on the strength of such express and formal assurance that they are willing to undertake the risks and burdens of such a prodigious investment. They do so for the reason, among others, that, in their view, no ordinary compensation such as normally accompanies nationalization can meet their case. As is

pointed out in another part of this Memorial, this is exactly the position with regard to the investments and the interests of the Anglo-Iranian Oil Company in Persia. For a Government to attempt, in relation to a concession of that nature, to proceed to nationalization is to become guilty not only of a, possibly controversial, breach of contract, but of a breach of contract in relation to a matter which the parties by an explicit provision removed from the orbit of any possible controversy and against which they provided what they considered to be an absolute safeguard. The question whether a cancellation, for the purposes of nationalization, of a concession granted involves a breach of international law has been a matter of dispute. But there is, in the contention of the Government of the United Kingdom, no room for controversy in relation to a case in which the State in question has expressly renounced such power of legislative action.

14. Unilateral denunciation and breach of contract It may be asserted that the distinction which the Government of the United Kingdom is seeking to establish between the two instances of unilateral cancellation of a concession is only a matter of degree. For in both cases there appears to have taken place a breach of contract. It may be maintained that, after all, there is no substantial difference between a breach of contract *tout court* and a breach of contract where one of the parties expressly bound itself not to break it. Such an undertaking, it may be argued, is essentially redundant and without effect, seeing that, in the last resort, in every contract there is an implied undertaking against breaking it. However, in the submission of the Government of the United Kingdom the difference – even if it be a matter of degree – is of a most substantial and decisive character. This is so in particular if we consider that in one case, according to a view which is widely accepted and which the Government of the United Kingdom does not challenge in the present proceedings, the cancellation of a concession for the purpose of nationalization effected in accordance with international law – although *prima facie* constituting a breach of the contract – is not necessarily unlawful. In the other case the illegality – being in violation of a most explicit undertaking not to exercise the legislative power in question – is patent and incontestable.

15. Limitation of legislative freedom by treaty or contract There is no warrant, in the submission of the Government of the United Kingdom, for the view that a specific undertaking given by a State not to exercise its legislative power for the purpose of the unilateral termination of a contract is a meaningless formula for the alleged reason that a State cannot fetter its future legislative action. States certainly assume some such obligation in the treaties which they conclude. Most treaties concluded by the State – whether relating to the treatment of aliens or otherwise – restrict *pro tanto* the legislative freedom of the contracting parties. The position is not substantially dissimilar with regard to contracts made with foreign nationals. Courts may be under a duty to give effect to legislation violative of the provisions of contracts made with an alien, but that circumstance in no way affects the rule that such legislation is internationally unlawful and that it engages the international responsibility of the State. The right of expropriation for the purpose of nationalization or otherwise is admittedly an important right of sovereignty and a matter which is in principle exclusively within the domestic jurisdiction of the State. Yet it does not follow that a State cannot part with the exercise of that right in respect of any specific property or category of property or in relation to any class of persons. Thus there is no doubt that State A may in a treaty concluded with State B bind itself not to nationalize in any circumstances the property of the nationals of State B; or it may do so with regard to any particular property, right or concession belonging to the nationals of State B. To give another example, the right to regulate immigration or the right to impose tariffs are an important prerogative of sovereignty. But a State may validly and with binding effect agree to a limitation or renunciation of that right. The Government of the United Kingdom contend that, with regard to nationalization or any other legislative measure affecting the property of aliens, it is irrelevant that the limitation of the legislative freedom of the State – such as is most clearly expressed in Article 22 of the Concession with the Anglo-Iranian Oil Company – is provided not in a treaty proper but in a contract with a foreign national. For although the contract in question may in the first instance be governed by the law of that country – it need not necessarily be so – its fulfilment is placed in the last resort, through the right of diplomatic protection on the part of the home State, under the protection of international law.

Undoubtedly, as in the matter of treaties so also with regard to a concessionary contract absolutely overriding reasons of State, a vital change of circumstances, or non-fulfilment of an essential clause of the contract by the other party may justify, subject to a

finding by an impartial international agency, the denunciation of
the contract notwithstanding an express provision against unilateral
denunciation. The Government of Iran has not brought – and has
not attempted to bring – its action within the purview of some such
justification.

16. The Convention of 1933 as an engagement of an international character
The considerations adduced in the preceding paragraph acquire
particular significance if it is borne in mind that the Convention of
1933 cannot be regarded as an ordinary contract, governed exclusively by municipal law, between Iran and a foreign company.
The Concession of 1933 lies, in a substantial sense, half-way between
a contract with a private party and a treaty. The concession agreement is described throughout, in French, as 'une convention'.
Disputes as to its interpretation and application are submitted to the
jurisdiction not of the Persian courts but of arbitrators agreed upon
by the parties and, in the absence of agreement, of an arbitrator to be
appointed by the President of the International Court. Moreover,
the sources of law to be applied in the arbitration are those contained in Article 38 of the Statute of the Court. Article 27 of the
convention provided for ratification by the Majlis. As recounted
above (paragraph 12), the origin of the convention, concluded as
part of an international arrangement following upon the settlement
of the dispute between the United Kingdom and Persia under the
auspices of the League of Nations, was distinctly international in
character. When in 1933 an inquiry was made of the Court whether
its President would accept the exercise of the function conferred
upon him by Article 22 of the convention the inquiry was addressed
to the Court through official communications of the Governments of
the United Kingdom and Iran. In view of this approximation, in
various respects, of the Convention of 1933 to an engagement of an
international character any assertion that the Persian legislature could
not validly undertake not to terminate the convention unilaterally
amounts to some extent to an assertion that the Government of Iran
could not undertake international obligations effectively binding the
future action of its legislature.

17. English law and limitation of legislative action   In submitting that a
State can validly bind itself by treaty or by a contract of an inter-
national character not to interfere with concessionary rights the
Government of the United Kingdom is not unmindful of the circum-

stance that the courts of some States – including English courts – have made occasional pronouncements to the effect that the State cannot by contract fetter the freedom of its executive and legislative action. Thus in an English case decided in 1921 – *Rederiaktiebolaget Amphitrite* v. *The King* [1921] 3 K.B. 500 – the Court, by reference to the rule as stated above, held unenforceable an undertaking by the Government promising freedom from detention to a Swedish ship trading with Great Britain during the First World War. However, while in the circumstances it is deemed proper to refer to that decision for the sake of the completeness of this section of the Memorial, it seems doubtful whether that decision was intended to have an effect as wide as its wording seemed to some to imply. Thus in a recent case – *Robertson* v. *Minister of Pensions* [1948] 2 A.E.R. 767 – the Court said:

That doctrine was propounded by Rowlatt J., in *Rederiaktiebolaget Amphitrite* v. *R.*, but it was unnecessary for the decision because the statement there was not a promise which was intended to be binding but only an expression of intention. Rowlatt J. seems to be influenced by the cases on the right of the Crown to dismiss its servants at pleasure, but those cases must now all be read in the light of the judgment of Lord Atkin in *Reilly* v. *R.* [1934] A.C. 179. That judgment shows that, in regard to contracts of service, the Crown is bound by its express promises as much as any subject. The cases where it has been held entitled to dismiss at pleasure are based on an implied term which cannot, of course, exist where there is an express term dealing with the matter. In my opinion, the defence of executive necessity is of limited scope. It only avails the Crown where there is an implied term to that effect, or that is the true meaning of the contract.

It will thus be seen that English law can hardly be regarded as providing clear authority for the view that the State cannot validly bind itself in a contract. Neither can support be found for any such proposition in those cases in which courts have held that it is *ultra vires* for statutory authorities to deprive themselves by contract of powers conferred upon them by the legislature.

18. The law of the United States of America, France and Germany The same applies to the cases decided by some courts of the United States in which it was held that the legislature cannot deprive itself by contract of powers indispensable to the public welfare. Any such limitation of the powers of the legislature has been held to apply only to matters relating to the 'police power' in its narrow sense, i.e. as affecting public health and morals. With regard to France, the legal position has been described by Duguit, one of the greatest constitutional lawyers, in the following words:

aucun organe de l'État, pas même le legislateur, n'est compétent pour faire un acte individuel et unilateral supprimant ou modifiant la situation subjective née d'un contrat auquel il est partie. L'acte serait sans valeur et les tribunaux administratifs ou judiciaires devraient statuer comme s'il n'éxistait pas. Il faut incontestablement donner cette solution, même si l'acte public qui porte atteinte au contrat est une loi formelle . . . Sans doute, [les tribunaux] doivent réspecter les décisions des chambres; mais ils doivent aussi respecter et sanctionner les contrats qui obligent l'État. Au cas de contradiction, ce sont ces derniers qui s'imposent à eux. (*Traité de droit constitutionnel*, III, 3rd ed. (1930), 437.)

In thus formulating the legal position Duguit relies on two decisions of the Conseil d'État, of 1899 and 1904 respectively, ordering the French State to honour a contract to pay an annuity to certain ecclesiastical establishments although the two Houses of Parliament had refused to vote credits for that purpose. He also relied on a judgment of the same Court in the case of *Orcibal*, decided in 1902 (Sirey(1905), III, 93), where the Minister for War ceased to execute a contract relating to the payment of compensation for damage caused by manoeuvres on certain land, and where it was held that 'les conventions légalement formées tiennent lieu de loi à ceux qui les ont faites et ne peuvent être revoquées que de leur consentement mutuel'. As to the position in Germany before the advent of the National-Socialist régime, Jellinek, a recognized authority on the subject, says in his *Verwaltungsrecht* (2nd ed., 1929), p. 270:

The subjective public right created by the administrative act sets a limit to its free revocability. Admittedly the argument may be tautologous if one says that an administrative act cannot be revoked because it has created subjective rights, for the subjective right often refers to the maintenance of the legal position created by the administrative act, i.e. it consists in the very thing which still requires to be proved, namely, that the administrative act cannot be revoked. However, the reference to subjective law is not quite meaningless. The administrative act may expressly confer a 'right' on an individual, or it may bring into being legal relations, not only between the State and the individual, but between the latter and a third party, as in the case of mining concessions.

19. Maintenance of the arbitration clause of the convention   Having regard to considerations of principle as set out above and to the authorities and precedents on the subject, the Government of the United Kingdom submit that the Government of Iran was not entitled to terminate by legislative action a convention which it expressly undertook not to terminate by legislative action; that, in particular, it was not entitled to do that with regard to a convention which, having regard to the circumstances of its conclusion and to its provisions, partakes in many ways of an engagement of an international character; and that the unilateral termination of the convention constituted therefore a violation of the rights, protected by international law, of the Anglo-Iranian Oil Company. However, assuming – though the Government of the United Kingdom deny the validity of any such assumption – that the Government of Iran was entitled, notwithstanding the express provision of the convention to the contrary, to terminate it unilaterally, it is submitted that such right of unilateral termination did not – or did not necessarily – extend to Article 22 of the convention. That Article provides for the arbitration of all disputes relating to the interpretation of the convention. It is arguable – and the argument is not devoid of apparent logic – that if the convention is denounced such denunciation must include the whole of it and cannot stop short of any particular Article. The Government of the United Kingdom submit that this is not necessarily so, in particular in relation to the present case:

(a) It may be possible for the Government of Iran to assert that the unilateral denunciation of the convention for the purpose of nationalization was dictated by the highest interests of the State and by the political impossibility or undesirability of its continued existence. Even if that were so, it does not follow that the imperative interests of the State demanded that the termination of the concession be combined with the cancellation of the clause which is the proper instrument for providing a remedy – in the form of adequate compensation determined in accordance with law as applied by the arbitrators – for what is undeniably a breach of the contract. Even assuming that unilateral termination was admissible, it would still have been possible – and proper – for the Iranian Government to approach the Anglo-Iranian Oil Company and say: 'We find ourselves under a necessity, for inescapable reasons of State, to put an end to the concession. We cannot, therefore, admit that under Article 22 of the convention the arbitrators or the sole arbitrator have the right to pass upon the legality of the measure taken and, in particular, to decree the restitution of the concession. However, as a matter of law and, in the words of Article 21 of the convention, "on principles of mutual good will and good faith" as well as on a "reasonable interpretation" of this agreement, we are prepared to abide by an award of arbitrators as to the compensation due to the company for the breach of the convention.' Instead, the Iranian Government have refused to submit the dispute, even within the limited compass as suggested, to arbitration. And they have pushed logic to the extreme of crudity by declaring that the Anglo-Iranian Oil Company – an entity which does not owe its existence to Iranian law – has ceased to exist as the result of the unlawful and unilateral act of the Iranian Government.

(b) It will be noted, in so far as the unilateral termination of the convention is based on allegations that the company has been guilty of a breach of the convention, that Article 26 provides that 'in any other cases of breach of the present agreement by one party or the other, the Arbitration Court shall establish the responsibilities and determine their consequences'. The *Martini* case, decided in 1930 between Italy and Venezuela, provides an instructive example of judicial determination of the existence of reasons adduced as a justification for the cancellation of a concession (*Annual Digest* (1929–30), case no. 93).

(c) There is high authority for the view that even if a contract comes to an end – for instance, as the result of frustration – the clauses of the contract relating to arbitration may nevertheless continue to operate. Reference may be made here to the decision of the English House of Lords in *Heyman* v. *Darwins* [1942] A.C. 356, where Viscount Simon, then Lord Chancellor, in reliance upon ample precedent, formulated the legal position as follows:

If the dispute is whether the contract which contains the clause has ever been entered into at all, that issue cannot go to arbitration under the clause, for the party who denies that he has ever entered into the contract is thereby denying that he has ever joined in the submission. Similarly, if one party to the alleged contract is contending that it is void *ab initio* (because, for example, the making of such a contract is illegal), the arbitration clause cannot operate, for on this view the clause itself also is void. But, in a situation where the parties are at one in asserting that they entered into a binding contract, but a difference has arisen between them whether there has been a breach by one side or the other, or whether circumstances have arisen which have discharged one or both parties from further performance, such differences shall be regarded as differences which have arisen 'in respect of', or 'with regard to', or 'under' the contract, and an arbitration clause which uses these, or similar expressions should be construed accordingly. By the law of England (though not, as I understand, by the law of Scotland), such an arbitration clause would also confer authority to assess damages for breach, even though it does not confer on the arbitral body express power to do so . . . If, therefore, when parties have entered into a contract, circumstances arise before the performance of the contract is completed which, in the view of one party, bring the contract to an end by frustration, and, therefore, discharge both parties from further performance, but the other party does not agree, this is a difference about the applicability of the implied term and is just as much within the arbitration clause as if it were a difference about an express term of the contract.

If this is the position in relation to the termination of a contract as the result of frustration independent of the will of the parties, there would appear to be particularly cogent reasons for the effective maintenance of the arbitration clause where the purported termination of the concession is due to a discretionary – if not arbitrary – act of one party.

(d) Reference may be made in this connection to various arbitral decisions which stress the importance of the jurisdiction of arbitral tribunals in matters relating to the cancellation of a concession. Thus in the *Turnbull* case the Umpire said:

the nonfulfillment of the pledged obligations by one party does not annul the contract *ipso facto*, but forms a reason for annulment, which annulment must be asked of the tribunals, and the proper tribunal alone has the power to annul such a contract – this rule of the law of almost all civilized nations being in absolute concordance with the law of equity – that nobody can be judge in his own case. (Ralston, p. 83.)

In the *El Triunfo* case against Salvador it was said:

In any case, by the rule of natural justice obtaining universally throughout the world wherever a legal system exists, the obligation of parties to a contract to appeal for judicial relief is reciprocal. If the republic of Salvador, a party to the contract which involved the franchise to El Triunfo Company, had just grounds for complaint that under its organic law the grantees had, by misuser or nonuser of the franchise granted, brought upon themselves the penalty of forfeiture of their rights under it, then the course of that Government should have been to have itself appealed to the courts against the company and there, by the due process of judicial proceedings, involving notice, full opportunity to be heard, consideration, and solemn judgment, have invoked and secured the remedy sought. (*Ibid.*)

In the *Milligan* case before the Mixed Commission of Lima it was contended by the American Commissioner that the Government of Peru, in declaring the contract null and void, deprived itself automatically of the right to insist that the company should submit the dispute to the local courts. The observation, on that argument, of the learned commentator in Lapradelle-Politis, II, 595, is relevant:

L'argumentation du commissaire américain ne semble pas admissible, car la question de savoir si le Pérou avait eu le droit de révoquer son contrat était precisement une question d'interprétation de ce contrat, qui devait, d'après ses propres termes, être soumise aux tribunaux du Pérou.

La clause, en droit international, était nulle, comme fermant tout recours à l'arbitrage.

20. *The importance of the arbitration clause* It is this refusal of the Iranian Government to abide at least by the clause of the convention providing for arbitration which enhances the unlawfulness of the unilateral termination of the convention and which adds to it the element of an international delinquency consisting in denial of justice. For some such procedure of arbitration is essential if the principle of the nationalization of the oil industry is conceded. The Oil Nationalization Law itself provides for some semblance of compensation, but such compensation is illusory and nominal if the Iranian Government is to remain judge of the justification of the claims of the company. There is no principle of law more fundamental than that a party cannot be judge in its own case. The Permanent Court of International Justice applied that principle in a radical manner in the Twelfth Advisory Opinion relating to the interpretation of the Treaty of Lausanne when it held it to be superior to the apparently paramount principle of unanimity of the Council of the League of Nations. It was possible for the Government of Iran while insisting on its right to terminate the Convention of 1933 on account of the law nationalizing the oil industry to leave the arbitration clause of Article 22 intact subject to the maintenance of the Oil Nationalization Law. International practice provides frequent instances of the parties limiting in advance the scope of the arbitration in order to safeguard rights which one or both parties consider to be absolutely essential. The *compromis* concluded between Great Britain and Venezuela in 1897 prior to the *British Guiana* arbitration and making absolute the title by presumption of fifty years is an instructive example of an arrangement of this nature. With regard to the practice of national courts and municipal legislation in granting specific performance in relation to arbitration clauses in private agreements,

the following extract from the Oral Statement of the representative of the United States before the International Court of Justice in connection with the advisory opinion relating to the *Interpretation of Peace Treaties* with Bulgaria, Hungary and Roumania may be quoted:

Although some countries including the United States have found difficulty in the absence of legislation to give full effect to, or adequate redress for, the breach of an agreement to arbitrate, judicial decisions of national courts as well as national legislation reveal a definite trend not only towards more complete legal recognition of an agreement to arbitrate but towards more effective legal redress for the breach of such agreement. In *Red Cross Line* v. *Atlantic Fruit Co.* ((1923), 264 U.S. 109, at p. 123), Justice Brandeis, speaking for the United States Supreme Court, declared that 'the substantive right created by an agreement to submit disputes to arbitration is recognized as a perfect obligation'. (See *Berkovitz* v. *Arbib and Houlberg* (1921), 230 N.Y. 261, 130 N.E. 288, opinion by Cardozo recognizing that a Statute which provided for specific enforcement of arbitration may be applied to an arbitration agreement concluded prior to the Statute . . . *I.C.J. Pleadings, Oral Arguments, Documents* (1950), p. 294.)

21. Conclusions The following are the conclusions of this section of the Memorial: The first reason why the application of the Iranian Oil Nationalization Law of 1 May 1951 would constitute a violation of international law is that it is in breach of an express undertaking, in the Convention of 1933, not to terminate the concession by unilateral action. That express undertaking was, for the Anglo-Iranian Oil Company, a most material consideration in concluding the concession agreement. The violation of that undertaking constitutes, in addition to a breach of the contract, a tortious act on the part of the Iranian Government. There is no warrant either in international law or in municipal law for the proposition that a State cannot fetter by treaty or contract the future action of its legislative organs. The converse proposition, with regard to contracts, applies in particular to engagements which – like the Convention of 1933 – are, in some material aspects, of an international character. Finally, even if the Iranian Government were entitled to cancel unilaterally the Convention of 1933, such cancellation need not, necessarily or automatically, extend to the arbitration clause of the convention. Reasons of legal principle, supported by precedent, and considerations of good faith require that that clause should be given effect in any case.

The refusal of the Government of Iran to give effect to the arbitration clause of the convention and its determination to remain the sole judge in matters arising out of the unilateral cancellation of the convention in themselves amount to a tortious action which engages the international responsibility of Iran.

IV. CONFISCATORY NATURE OF
THE OIL NATIONALIZATION LAW

22. Article 2 of the Nationalization Law The Government of the United Kingdom contend that even if the Oil Nationalization Law of 1 May were otherwise in accordance with international law, it is unlawful for the reason that it is essentially confiscatory in nature having regard to the terms of compensation as offered by the Oil Nationalization Law. Article 2 of that law requires the Iranian Government 'to dispossess at once the former Anglo-Iranian Oil Company'. It then proceeds to lay down that 'if the company refuses to hand over at once ... the Government can, by mutual agreement, deposit in the Bank Melli Iran or in any other bank up to 25 per cent of current revenue from the oil after deduction of exploitation expenses in order to meet the probable claims of the company'.

23. Compensation in case of nationalization. The practice of States Before examining the provisions of Article 2 it is desirable to recall the rule of international law governing compensation in case of expropriation. That rule was stated repeatedly and emphatically in 1940 by the Government of the United States – as well as by other Governments – in connection with the expropriation of American-owned and other oil companies in Mexico. In the first instance, the Government of the United States while readily recognizing the right of a sovereign State to expropriate property for public purposes 'stated with equal emphasis that the right to expropriate property is coupled with and conditioned on the obligation to make adequate, effective and prompt compensation' (note of Secretary Hull of 3 April 1940 to the Mexican Ambassador in Washington, reproduced in Hackworth, 3, 662, and commented upon, with approval, by Hyde, 1, § 217 C). Moreover, the Government of the United States gave expression, on that occasion, to the second, well-recognized, rule of international law that 'the legality of an expropriation is in fact dependent upon the observance of this requirement [i.e. of compensation which is adequate, effective and prompt]'. On a previous occasion, in connection with the expropriation of agrarian properties in Mexico, the Secretary of State formulated on 21 July 1938 the same principle in clear language. He said:

The taking of property without compensation is not expropriation. It is confiscation. It is no less confiscation because there may be an expressed intent to pay at some time in the future.

If it were permissible for a Government to take the private property of the citizens of other countries and pay for it as and when, in the judgment of that Government, its economic circumstances and its local legislation may perhaps permit, the safeguards which the constitutions of most countries and established international law have sought to provide would be illusory. Governments would be free to take property far beyond their ability or willingness to pay, and the owners thereof would be without recourse. We cannot question the right of a foreign Government to treat its own nationals in this fashion if it so desires. This is a matter of domestic concern. But we cannot admit that a foreign Government may take the property of American nationals in disregard of the rule of compensation under international law. Nor can we admit that any Government unilaterally and through its municipal legislation can, as in this instant case, nullify this universally accepted principle of international law, based as it is on reason, equity and justice. (Hackworth, 3, 656.)

In another communication, of 22 August 1938, addressed to Mexico the Government of the United States said:

The fundamental issues raised by this communication from the Mexican Government are therefore, first, whether or not universally recognized principles of the law of nations require, in the exercise of the admitted right of all sovereign nations to expropriate private property, that such expropriation be accompanied by provision on the part of such Government for adequate, effective and prompt payment for the properties seized; second, whether any Government may nullify principles of international law through contradictory municipal legislation of its own; or, third, whether such Government is relieved of its obligations under universally recognized principles of international law merely because its financial or economic situation makes compliance therewith difficult.

The Government of the United States merely adverts to a self-evident fact when it notes that the applicable precedents and recognized authorities on international law support its declaration that, under every rule of law and equity, no Government is entitled to expropriate private property, for whatever purpose, without provision for prompt, adequate, and effective payment therefore. In addition, clauses appearing in the constitutions of almost all nations today, and in particular in the constitutions of the American republics, embody the principle of just compensation. These, in themselves, are declaratory of the like principle in the law of nations.

The universal acceptance of this rule of the law of nations, which, in truth, is merely a statement of common justice and fair-dealing, does not in the view of this Government admit of any divergence of opinion. (*Ibid.* pp. 658–9.)

The attitude of the Government of Holland was the same. In a note to the Mexican Government of 27 October 1938, the Government of the Netherlands stated as follows:

The Government of the Netherlands maintains that even in cases where circumstances oblige a Government to expropriate private property, it is a condition *sine qua non* that the properties expropriated must be exactly defined, and that if the authority takes immediate possession of such goods a just and prompt indemnity shall be immediately and effectively guaranteed. . . In the attitude of the Mexican Government after the decree of expropriation, the Netherlands Government regrets that it can only see a refusal to acknowledge these fundamental rules. Six months have passed since the day of expropriation, and the properties expropriated have not yet even been defined. Therefore, the Netherlands Government feels obliged to express new hope for a satisfactory arrangement of this controversy, an arrangement that cannot consist in less than adequate, prompt, and effective compensation or in return of the properties expropriated to the companies affected. (*Documents* (1938), I, 472.)

The British Government, while denying the right of Mexico to expropriate the properties in the circumstances of the case and while claiming restitution, at the same time emphatically subscribed to the view that 'an essential condition of the validity of [expropriation] would be the payment of full and adequate compensation' (note to the Mexican Government of 11 May 1938, in *ibid.* p. 471).

The Mexican Government itself, in a note to the British Government of 12 April 1938, stated that they wished 'to place on record that there is a universally accepted principle of international law which attributes to all sovereign and independent countries the right to expropriate in the public interest with the payment of adequate compensation' (*ibid.* p. 462). In a note to the United States Government of 1 May 1940, the Government of Mexico affirmed that it had declared its support to the principle of the 'right to an equitable and prompt compensation for the expropriated properties' (Hackworth, III, 664). Earlier, in 1922, in relation to expropriation of the property of citizens of the United States in China the following instruction was issued by the State Department:

Concerning the question of whether the Chinese authorities may exercise the right of eminent domain over property owned by American citizens in

China, the Department may state that since the right is so essential to the existence of any sovereign State, the Department would not be inclined to question the exercise of the right by China in an appropriate case, that is, for a public purpose, but would of course be under the necessity of insisting that just compensation be made for any property taken or damaged and that there shall be no discrimination in this respect against American citizens. (*Ibid.* p. 654.)

More recently, at the International Conference of American States at Bogotá, the United States successfully opposed the proposal of the Mexican Delegation that there ought to be prompt, adequate and effective compensation for expropriation 'except when the constitution of any country provided otherwise' (*Report of Ninth International Conference of American States*, United States Department of State Publication 3263, pp. 66–7).

This insistence on the duty, in case of expropriation for public purposes, to pay adequate compensation was not a new feature of international practice. The earlier practice of States has shown a number of examples of recognition of the duty of compensation for expropriation. In 1853 the Greek Government expropriated the land of the Rev. Jonas King, an American citizen, for a public purpose. The United States demanded, and the Greek Government readily agreed to, the payment of compensation. Similarly, the Greek Government paid the value of expropriated land which had been the property of George Finlay, a British subject, and which had been seized, allegedly for public purposes, in 1836 (*Br. and For. St. Papers, 1849–1850,* 39, 467).

24. The same. The practice of international tribunals The practice of international tribunals is uniform on the subject, and it is not considered necessary to substantiate that proposition by an exhaustive examination of international practice. By way of example, in addition to the clear pronouncement of the Permanent Court of International Justice in the *Chorzów Factory* case, referred to below, reference – which is far from being exhaustive – may be made to a number of arbitral decisions directly bearing on the subject. In the case of *David Goldenberg* v. *German State* (*R.I. (Paris),* 3 (1929), 552), a claim for compensation for the requisition, by Germany, of the property of a Roumanian national during the First World War was submitted to a specially appointed arbitrator. Some compensation, amounting to approximately one-sixth of the value of the property, had been paid some six months after the requisition. The Arbitrator condemned

Germany to pay the amount requisite to make the compensation equivalent to the value of the property. In an award given in 1928 he said:

Le respect de la propriété privée et des droits acquis des étrangers fait sans conteste partie des principes généraux admis par le droit des gens. . .

'La réquisition militaire est une forme *sui generis* de l'expropriation pour cause d'utilité publique. Cette dernière est une dérogation admise au principe du respect de la propriété privée des étrangers. Il en est de même de la réquisition . . .

Toutefois, si le droit des gens autorise un État, pour des motifs d'utilité publique, à déroger au principe du respect de la propriété privée des étrangers, c'est à la condition *sine qua non* que les biens expropriés ou réquisitionnés seront équitablement payés le plus rapidement possible.

L'application des ces règles aboutit au résultat suivant: la réquisition operée par l'autorité militaire allemande ne constituait pas *initialement* un 'acte contraire au droit des gens'. Pour qu'il continuat à en être ainsi, il fallait, cependant, que dans un délai raisonnable les demandeurs obtinssent une indemnité équitable. Or tel n'a pas été le cas, l'indemnité atteignant à peine le sixième de la valeur des biens expropriés.

Il est dès lors constant que Mm. Goldenberg et fils ont été privés des 5/6 de leurs biens, sans compensation. Il y a là un 'acte contraire au droit des gens', que l'on applique le principe général qui s'oppose à l'expropriation de la propriété privée des étrangers sans juste indemnité.

Similarly, the Arbitral Tribunal established in pursuance of the Anglo-American Arbitration Agreement of 1910, in the case of *Eastern Extension, Australasia and China Telegraph Co., Ltd.*, found the rule to be established, although inapplicable to the case before them. In the course of the award, which was given in 1923, they said:

It is contended that the cutting [of cables], however legitimate, may create an obligation to compensate the neutral owner of the cable, and various instances are given of legitimate acts which, it is said, do create such an obligation. We do not think that the instances given furnish a just analogy. In those instances the right is not absolute but limited, and is in reality only itself acquired in consideration of payment of compensation, and has no existence as a right apart from the obligation to make compensation. Such is the case in respect of requisition, either for the purposes of ownership or user; of expropriation; or, to take a case from maritime law, of the exercise of the right of angary. (Nielsen's *Report*, p. 76.)

After the secularization of religious properties in Portugal in 1910 claims by foreign nationals in respect of property so taken were submitted to arbitration. In awards rendered on 2 September 1920, a tribunal constituted from the panel of the Permanent Court of Arbitration awarded full compensation to British and French claimants, stressing that it was not the intention of the Government of the Portuguese Republic to seek in the seizure a source of pecuniary gain (Scott, *Hague Reports* (2nd), p. 7).

In the *Savage* claim, which referred to the seizure by the Salvadorean Government, in pursuance of general legislation, of the stock-in-trade of a United States citizen, an arbitral commission in 1852 awarded full compensation (Lapradelle-Politis, II, xii). In *Marks'* case, the Umpire appointed in a dispute between the United States and Mexico concerning the seizure in a public emergency of property belonging to an American citizen held that, while the seizure was justified, the claimant was clearly entitled to full compensation for the property (Moore, *International Arbitrations*, p. 3722).

In the award rendered by the Permanent Court of Arbitration on 13 October 1922, in the dispute between the United States and Norway relating to the requisitioning of Norwegian contracts for the building of ships by the United States Government for public purposes during a period of emergency, the Tribunal held: 'Whether the action of the United States was lawful or not, just compensation is due to the claimants under the municipal law of the United States, as well as under the international law, based upon the respect for private property.' The Court rejected the contention of the United States Government that there could be no compensation when the contract had been destroyed or rendered void, or delayed, in consequence of 'restraint of princes'. It held that 'no State can exercise towards the citizens of another civilized State the "power of eminent domain" without respecting the property of such foreign citizens or without paying just compensation as determined by an impartial tribunal, if necessary' (*A.J.* 17 (1923), 392). The Tribunal held that it was common ground that compensation for property which has been lawfully expropriated is measured by the fair actual value of the property at the time and place it was taken.

In the *Spanish Zone of Morocco* claims, brought by Great Britain against Spain in 1924, where expropriation was not actually in question, the rapporteur held, in general terms, that under international law an alien cannot be deprived of his property without just compensation (*Annual Digest* (1923–4), case no. 85).

In the *De Sabla* claim, which came before the United States–Panama General Claims Commission in 1933, the Panamanian Government had granted land belonging to the claimant to third parties, in pursuance of a general land law. The Commission considered it 'axiomatic that acts of a Government in depriving an alien of his property without compensation impose international responsibility' (*Annual Digest* (1933–4), case no. 92).

Other arbitral decisions are referred to below in connection with the question of compensation in cases of unlawful deprivation of property and with reference to the question of restitution in kind.

As stated, the arbitral decisions referred to above are not intended to give a complete picture of the judicial and arbitral practice on the subject. Should the principle of international law which that practice has uniformly applied be challenged, the Government of the United Kingdom will be in a position to submit to the Court a more complete statement on the subject.

25. The same. Views of writers   Writers have registered, with impressive uniformity, the existing practice on the subject. Miss Whiteman, in the most comprehensive and authoritative work on the subject – *Damages in International Law* (1937) – states, at p. 1386: 'If land belonging to an alien (other than an alien enemy) is expropriated, requisitioned or confiscated by a government "just compensation" must be paid for it. The international duty to make compensation exists apart from the provisions of municipal law.' The same conclusion is reached by Professor Hyde (Hyde, 1, at pp. 710–17). Freeman, in *The International Responsibility of States for Denial of Justice* (1938), states, at p. 518, that 'the preponderance of legal authority accepts the view that no foreigner may be deprived of his property without adequate compensation' and that 'it would seem difficult to maintain that the right to compensation does not exist just as fully in the case of general legislation under which an alien is expropriated as it does in individual cases of confiscation'. Nielsen, in *International Law Applied to Reclamations* (1933), at p. 39, summarizes his experience of international claims in the matter as follows:

Land and other property may of course properly be taken by public authority in the exercise of the right of expropriation. It is possible that laws relating to this subject might be of such an odd character that their application to property of aliens might be found objectionable. A Government cannot justifiably insist that 'public purpose' within the meaning of its own laws must be given precisely the same definition in the terms of another nation's laws. But it may properly insist that a taking without compensation, or with inadequate compensation, is a form of confiscation violative of international law.

Similarly, Fachiri (in *B.Y.* 6 (1925), 170–1) concludes that:

> if a claim were referred to judicial settlement by an international court in respect of the expropriation of a foreigner's land . . . the plaintiff state would have a reasonable prospect of success if one of two conditions were fulfilled and proved:
>
> (2) that no compensation was given in respect of the expropriation, or if there was compensation, that it was so inadequate as to involve a substantial degree of confiscation.

Professor Scelle, in Scelle, II, writes, at p. 113:

> La reconnaissance du droit de propriété se concrétise dans la règle généralement adoptée que les étrangers, comme les nationaux, ne peuvent être privés de leurs propriétés que moyennant une *juste et préalable indemnité*, et *pour cause d'utilité publique régulièrement constatée*. Il y a là un principe si généralement établi qu'un certain nombre de traités se contentent d'y renvoyer comme à un principe de droit universel, et que la doctrine le consacre à peu près unanimement.

Professor Erich Kaufmann (in *Hague Recueil* 54 (1935), at 429) expresses the view that 'La propriété des étrangers ne peut être expropriée que pour cause d'utilité publique dans une procédure qui remplit toutes exigences de la justice procédurale et contre une juste compensation.' Professor Gidel, citing with approval Anzilotti, writes as follows:

> Le vice de cette comparaison [between expropriation and liquidation] est qu'il néglige le trait capital qui distingue l'expropriation pour cause d'utilité publique de toutes les dépossessions de propriété exorbitantes du droit commun. Dans sa célèbre consultation, M. Anzilotti l'a rappelé en ces termes: 'Sans doute l'expropriation pour utilité publique s'impose aux étrangers autant qu'aux nationaux, mais à la condition qu'elle soit accompagnée des garanties dont toutes les législations modernes l'entourent dans le but de la rendre compatible avec le droit de propriété. L'expropriation n'est compatible avec le droit de propriété que si elle est justifiée par l'utilité générale qui prime l'utilité individuelle et accompagnée d'une équitable indemnité qui couvre le dommage subi.' (*R.I.* (*Paris*), 1 (1927), 117.)

More recently, Professor A. de La Pradelle says, in the 'Projet provisoire de Résolutions' attached to his Report on International Effects of Nationalizations presented to the Institute of International Law at Bath in 1950:

> La nationalisation, acte unilatéral de souveraineté, doit respecter les engagements valablement conclus, soit par traité, soit par contrat.

Faute de ce respect, il y aurait déni de justice donnant naissance, non pas à une simple indemnité, valeur pour valeur, mais à des dommages-intérêts, à caractère pénalisateur. (*Annuaire* (1950) (i), 68.)

Witenberg says, in *Clunet*, 55 (1928), at 576:

Toujours l'indemnisation doit accompagner l'expropriation. Cette indemnisation doit représenter la valeur exacte de la propriété dont l'étranger est dépossédé.

Fauchille and Sibert say, in *R.G.* (1925), p. 22:

L'indemnité devra présenter les traits suivants:
1. Il va de soi qu'elle doit être générale, c'est à dire exister dans tous les cas et s'appliquer sans distinction à tous les biens frappés d'expropriation;
2. l'indemnité doit être intégrale, c'est à dire tenir compte au propriétaire de la valeur de ce qu'il transmet et de la dépréciation subie par ce qui lui est laissé;
3. elle doit etre préalable, ou tout au moins coincider avec la prise de la propriété . . .

26. Relevance of the plea of non-discrimination   The Government of the United Kingdom appreciate that there has been a divergence of opinion among Governments and international lawyers on the question whether, in case of a general measure of expropriation for the purpose of nationalization or in pursuance of measures of social reform, the expropriating State may not lawfully limit the indemnity paid to aliens to the amount and kind of compensation received by the nationals of the expropriating State. The Government of the United Kingdom adhere in this matter to the view which it has expressed on various occasions and which is shared by the majority of Governments, namely, that the plea of non-discrimination does not, in general, provide adequate justification for State action which falls short of the minimum standard of treatment of aliens with regard both to their persons and property. However, it is submitted that this aspect of State responsibility is not relevant to the present case. There is no question here of a general measure affecting Iranian nationals and aliens alike. As is pointed out below in the present Memorial, notwithstanding the generality of the language of the Oil Nationalization Law, this is a discriminatory measure in fact directed exclusively against a single foreign company – a circumstance which in itself is a substantial factor adding to the illegality of the action taken by the Iranian Government.

27. Relevance of postponement of payment of compensation Neither is the complaint of the Government of the United Kingdom in the present case based on the contention that the action of the Iranian Government is illegal for the reason that the compensation offered by it is not prompt inasmuch as there has been no offer of immediate compensation in cash. There have been in fact pronouncements by Governments and arbitral tribunals that prompt compensation means immediate payment in cash. Thus in the arbitration between the United States and Norway relating to the requisitioning of contracts for the building of ships in the United States it was held: 'The Tribunal is of opinion that full compensation should have been paid . . . at the latest on the day of the effective taking' (Scott, *Hague Reports* (2nd), at p. 77).

Similarly, the Government of the United States stated, during the negotiations with Mexico arising out of the Constitution of 1917 and subsequent laws in 1923, that 'under the rules of international law there can be no taking of lands, water rights or other property of American citizens . . . without indemnification in cash at the time of the taking for the just value thereof' (*Proceedings* of the United States–Mexican Commission Convened at Mexico City, 14 May 1923, p. 29). The Government of the United Kingdom is prepared to admit that deferred payment accompanied by suitable and adequate guarantees may be interpreted as satisfying the requirement of payment in accordance with international law. As Professor Hyde puts it:

The matter of time of payment is among the factors that must always be considered because, if payment is to be deferred, the total amount will fail to be fully compensatory if it does not make provision, among other things, for interest on the investment or for loss of benefits to the owner after the property was taken and prior to payment. Thus the adequacy of compensation is to be tested in cases where deferred payments are contemplated, by the respect which the arrangement pays for the consequences of postponement. It should be clear that a deferred payment, or series of deferred payments, is not truly compensatory if the loss sustained by the owner in consequence of postponement be unrequited. In his correspondence with the Mexican Government, Secretary Hull did not intimate that arrangements for deferred payments which would make requisite provision for the period of delay would be inadequate. There is hardly room to impute to him the thought that the fiscal equivalent of prompt payment, if duly arranged for at the outset, would violate any requirement of international law. (Hyde, I, 718–19.)

28. Analysis of the compensation envisaged in the Oil Nationalization Law
While the Government of the United Kingdom are thus willing to admit that the requirement of 'adequate, prompt and effective' compensation ought to be interpreted in a liberal manner by reference to the circumstances of each particular case, it maintains that the compensation envisaged contained in Article 2 of the Oil Nationalization Law in no sense fulfils these requirements; that the offer of compensation contained therein is arbitrary and largely nominal; that, to that extent, the Oil Nationalization Law amounts to confiscation, and is for that reason alone unlawful. Such offer of compensation as is contained in Article 2 of the Oil Nationalization Law is not an offer of compensation for the value of the property of which the company is dispossessed. It is an offer of a deposit of 'up to 25 per cent of current revenue from the oil after deduction of exploitation expenses in order to meet the probable claims of the company'. It is clear that the compensation offered under that formula is arbitrary, uncertain, and largely nominal.

(a) It is fundamental that compensation payable in the event of expropriation and nationalization should be an ascertained sum of money. This requirement is illustrated by the terms of compensation paid to the various British industries nationalized during recent years and by the terms ultimately agreed between the Mexican Government and the expropriated oil companies. This has been the method followed uniformly in the various agreements concluded after the Second World War and arising out of nationalization of the property of foreign nationals.[1] It is a requirement of obvious cogency and reasonableness. Persons deprived of their property cannot be expected to rely for their compensation on the uncertain profits of an undertaking managed by the new owners in circumstances and other conditions which cannot be foreseen – an aspect of the situation which is developed below. As stated, there is in proper cases no objection to the amount of compensation being liquidated over a period. In such cases it is usual that interest, at some agreed rate, becomes payable

---

[1] Thus the Swiss–Yugoslav Agreement, of 27 September 1948, provides for the payment of 75 million Swiss Francs within not more than ten years; the Swiss–Polish Agreement, of 25 June 1949, provides for the payment of 53 million Swiss Francs beginning in June 1951; the Swiss–Czechoslovak Agreement, of 22 December 1949, provides, in addition to an initial payment of 28 million Swiss Francs, for twenty half-yearly payments of the balance; the Agreements between the United Kingdom and Yugoslavia, of 23 December 1948 and 26 December 1949, provide, in addition to an initial payment of £450,000, for the payment of the balance in fifteen half-yearly instalments; the Agreement between the United Kingdom and Czechoslovakia provides for the payment of £8 million within seventeen years.

periodically in respect of that part of the compensation which remains outstanding. This was the practice followed in the case of the expropriation of the Mexican oil companies.

(b) Even assuming – an assumption which, as stated below does not necessarily follow from the terms of Article 2 of the Oil Nationalization Law – that the Government of Iran is willing to set aside 25 per cent of current revenue for the purpose of satisfying the claims of the company, the compensation thus offered is wholly dependent on the future success or failure of the Iranian Government in conducting the Iranian oil operations. It will be noted that the Iranian oil industry has hitherto been sustained not only by an extensive overseas marketing organization fed by a considerable tanker fleet but also by an extensive overseas buying and supply organization which provides the oilfields and refinery areas with essential materials, spare parts, equipment and stores of all kinds, including cargoes of food to supplement local supplies. It is very probable that without this organization Iranian production of oil for export shipment would decline, with a consequential reduction in profits. Moreover, the maintenance of crude oil production levels is of little value if refinery facilities in Iran and elsewhere are not available for its treatment. The possibility – if not the probability – must also be taken into account that the fact of the unilateral repudiation of the Convention of 1933 by the Iranian Government may have the effect in some countries of diminishing confidence in contracts made with the Iranian Government. The result might be that some markets might be closed to Iranian oil. It is stated in the issue of the *Economist* of 21 July 1951, that 'during the period immediately after expropriation Mexico was unable to find markets for its oil despite its proximity to the United States. World stocks at the time were high and fed competitively by American, Venezuelan, Persian and Roumanian oils. Moreover, Mexico had great difficulty in its attempts to charter oil tankers.' In 1939, the year following Mexican expropriation, the director of the Mexican exchequer admitted that the national oil industry lost £5 million because of unfavourable sales in the United States and the closure of European markets. However, the decisive factor with regard to this aspect of the question is the absence of any assurance that, apart from the purely commercial considerations, the efficiency of the industry managed by the Iranian Government will be such as to make 25 per cent of the profit approximate to what constituted till May 1951 that proportion of the profits of the company.

(c) Even assuming that under Iranian control the Iranian oil industry is capable of continuing as a profitable economic unit, there is no assurance that the profits to which the 25 per cent are to be applied may not be artificially whittled down as the result of (i) local industries being subsidized by the provision of oil, materials and services free of charge; (ii) excessive customs duties, local taxes, etc., being imposed on the oil industry; (iii) a large and expensive 'administrative' organization being foisted on the oil industry; (iv) unorthodox accounting practices being adopted, such as capital expenditure which should be charged against profits over a period being charged against profits of one year, extravagant provisions being made for contingencies, and incomplete records being kept.

(d) The anticipation of these possibilities seems less pessimistic than may appear at first sight if it is considered that the proportion of 25 per cent is the maximum provided for in Article 2 and that no provision is made for an impartial tribunal to be responsible for the assessment of compensation. The Iranian Government has repudiated both the Convention of 1933 and the arbitration provisions of that convention. As the result, the Oil Nationalization Law leaves it open to the Government to be the judge in its own case. It is most probable that, particularly in view of what is said under (e) below, no compensation would be agreed upon except as a result of negotiations between the Government and the company in which the scales would be heavily weighted in favour of the Government. No provision is made in Article 2 of the Oil Nationalization Law for any right of appeal against the Government's assessment of compensation following upon negotiations.

(e) There is a distinct possibility that the Iranian Government may, in assessing the amount due to the company up to the maximum of 25 per cent, raise claims which it has in the past put forward against the company. These claims run into millions of pounds. Their nature may be gauged from the examples adduced in an annex to this paragraph. However fanciful these claims may be, there is no assurance that the Iranian Government would not bring them up again at the time of the compensation negotiations and seek to set off the total amount of these claims against the amount of compensation claimed by the Company. Some such claims have in fact already been made by the Iranian Government upon the company in the course of previous negotiations. Actually the annex showing the nature of these claims merely reproduces copies of two documents which were handed by the Iranian Government to the company during the negotiations for the supplemental agreement. The Iranian Government has also in the past made other claims, including one for duties on war-time supplies to the Russian Government.

(f) Finally, it will be noted that no attempt is made in the Oil Nationalization Law to secure an impartial evaluation of the assets owned by the company or to estimate – assuming that such an estimate is possible – the real value of '25 per cent of current revenue from the oil after deduction of exploitation expenses'. Neither is it stated for how long the Iranian Government are to be bound to 'deposit in the Bank Milli Iran or in any other bank up to 25 per cent' of the revenues.

It is submitted that the above analysis fully bears out the contention advanced at the beginning of this paragraph that the compensation offered under the formula adopted by the Oil Nationalization Law is 'arbitrary, uncertain, and largely nominal'. The Government of the United Kingdom attach the utmost importance to disclosing the legal implications of the fact, which is not apparent from a cursory reading of the terms of the Iranian Oil Nationalization Law, that the latter far from providing for compensation as required by international law actually conceals a denial thereof behind a nebulous and misleading form of words.

29. The question of the solvency of the debtor Government   Such offer of compensation as is contained in Article 2 of the Oil Nationalization Law does not contain an offer of the global amount liquidated over a period of years and accompanied by periodic payment of interest in respect of the outstanding part of the compensation. It contains an offer contingent upon the undetermined future revenues of the oil industry. If compensation were offered commensurate with the magnitude of the interests involved the question would arise as to the value of such an offer on the part of the Government which by its own act has most substantially impaired the prospects and potentialities of its main economic asset. Reference may be made in this connection to some relevant observations of Professor Hyde. He says:

The arrangement suggests the inquiry whether a like plan would be feasible were a State to expropriate immovable property of very great value, and for which it had no visible means of compensating the owners even through a series of deferred payments extended over a protracted period of time. It raises the question whether a State may rightfully expropriate alien owned immovable property under circumstances when it can not give reasonable assurance of ultimate and complete reimbursement to the titleholders. (Hyde, 1, 719.)

30. Conclusions It is submitted, in conclusion of this section of the present Memorial, that the action of the Government of Iran with regard to the Oil Nationalization Law is unlawful for the reason that the expropriation of the Anglo-Iranian Oil Company is not accompanied by compensation as provided by international law and that it is in effect to a large extent of a confiscatory character. Such compensation, according to uniform governmental pronouncements, judicial practice and writers of authority, must be adequate, prompt, and effective. Even if the Oil Nationalization Law were otherwise from the point of view of international law lawful – which, for the reasons stated in sections III and V of this Memorial, the Government of the United Kingdom denies – the absence of requisite compensation is sufficient to render it unlawful. The position in this respect is the same as that arising in connection with requisitions in time of war. As tribunals have repeatedly held, a requisition otherwise in conformity with the requirements of Hague Convention no. IV ceases to be lawful if it is not accompanied by payment of compensation. Reasons have been given why the purported compensation terms offered in the Oil Nationalization Law can be regarded as neither adequate, prompt, nor effective, and why the Oil Nationalization Law must therefore be considered as contrary to international law. It may be added that even if the compensation offered were such as is otherwise adequate with regard to lawful expropriation, it could not be regarded as adequate in the present case. For in the view of the Government of the United Kingdom the Oil Nationalization Law is also unlawful for the reason that it constitutes a unilateral termination of the Convention of 1933 in violation of a specific undertaking to the contrary. It is also unlawful for the reason that, as will be submitted in the section which follows, it is in fact directed exclusively against a foreign national.

Annex to paragraph 28 (e): Estimate of the possible claims of the Iranian Government against the Anglo-Iranian Oil Company on the basis of the note handed to the company on 24 April 1949

1. On account of gold premium in
   1947 total tonnage royalty and
   taxation   £4,198,955

Gold premium at the rate of 172
shillings and three pence   1,828,294
Gold premium at the rate of 255
shillings   4,723,824

Due to the Government on account
of gold premium   £2,895,530

2. On account of 20 per cent of taxes
paid to the British Government:
Total taxes paid to British
Government from the year 1933
to 1947   £72,268,487

20 per cent of above: £14,453,697

3. 20 per cent of the difference be-   (Computation not possible
tween sums allocated to de-   due to unavailability of
preciation and amortization and   necessary data.)
what should normally have been
allocated to depreciation and
amortization of properties

4. Payment of the difference in the
Government's share of dividends
without taking into account the
rules concerning dividend restriction. $10\frac{1}{2}$ million pounds has
been carried into the General
Reserve on account of Dividend
Restriction

20 per cent of above: £2,100,000

5. 20 per cent of the difference be-   (Computation not possible
tween sale prices of oil products   due to unavailability of
to the British Navy and Air Force   necessary data.)
and normal international rates

6. Royalty on oil products consumed
in the company's operations
from the year 1933 to the year
1947   £3,650,000

V. UNLAWFULNESS OF THE OIL NATIONALIZATION LAW AS DIRECTED EXCLUSIVELY AGAINST A FOREIGN NATIONAL

31. The Oil Nationalization Law in fact directed exclusively against the Anglo-Iranian Oil Company The Government of the United Kingdom have contended so far that the Government of Iran has incurred international responsibility on the grounds: (i) that the Iranian Oil Nationalization Law is in violation of an express undertaking not to terminate the concession unilaterally by legislative action; and (ii) that that law provides for no such compensation as is required by international law. The Government of the United Kingdom now submit, thirdly, that expropriation of the Anglo-Iranian Oil Company is unlawful for the reason that it is a measure which, although purporting to be of a general character, is in fact directed exclusively against a particular foreign company. That the Oil Nationalization Law is, for all practical purposes, directed exclusively against the Anglo-Iranian Oil Company is a fact which appears directly from the text of the law and which therefore requires no further elaboration. Apart from the concession of the Anglo-Iranian Oil Company there is only one other concession, operated by the Kavir-i-Khuriar Company and owned jointly by Russia and an Iranian group. The concession is of negligible size and it is understood that it has not been working for some time.

32. Illegality of expropriation in fact directed exclusively against aliens The principle that it is unlawful to expropriate the property of aliens by an act which is either openly or by implication directed exclusively against them is generally recognized. A clear and authoritative statement of the rule that legislation, even if general in its terms, which expropriates the property of aliens and is directed exclusively against aliens is unlawful is contained in the Report to the Council of the League of Nations on the question of the 'Hungarian Optants in Roumania'. That report was drawn up after consultation with international lawyers of distinction. While the report was concerned with the interpretation of certain Articles of the Treaty of Trianon, the statement on the subject here under discussion is of general applicability seeing that the treaty prohibited only seizures of property which were unlawful under general international law. The relevant passage reads as follows:

1. *The provisions of the peace settlement effected after the war 1914–1918 do not exclude the application to Hungarian nationals (including those who have opted for Hungarian nationality) of a general scheme of agrarian reform.*

Article 250 forbids the application of Article 232 to the property of Hungarian nationals in the transferred territory. Under the terms of Article 250, the prohibition to retain and liquidate cannot restrict Roumania's freedom of action beyond what it would have been if Articles 232 and 250 had not existed. Even if none of these provisions appeared in the treaty, Roumania would none the less be entitled to enact any agrarian law she might consider suitable for the requirements of her people, subject to the obligations resulting from the rules of international law. There is, however, no rule of international law exempting Hungarian nationals from a general scheme of agrarian reform.

The question of compensation, whatever its importance from other points of view, does not here come under consideration.

2. *There must be no inequality between Roumanians and Hungarians, either in the terms of the Agrarian Law or in the way in which it is enforced.*

Any provision in a general scheme of agrarian reform which either expressly or by necessary implication singled out Hungarians for more onerous treatment than that accorded to Roumanians or to the nationals of other States generally, would create a presumption that it was intended to disguise a retention or liquidation of the property of Hungarian nationals *as such* in violation of Article 250 and would entitle the Mixed Arbitral Tribunal to give relief. The same would apply in the case of a discriminatory application of the Agrarian Law. (*L.N.O.J.* Special Supplement no. 64 (Plenary Meetings), p. 230.)

33. The same. Opinions of writers   There is general support among writers for the view that expropriation is unlawful if it is directed exclusively against aliens, whether such intention is plain or disguised. Professor Brierly writes:

Les biens des étrangers ne peuvent être confisqués pour la raison que leurs propriétaires sont étrangers; nous avons là un cas où la discrimination entre nationaux et étrangers, que celle-ci soit ouverte ou dissimulée, constituerait avec certitude un facteur décisif de la responsabilité de l'État. (*Hague Recueil*, 58 (1936) (iv), at 171.)

Professor Gidel writes, in *R.I.* (*Paris*), 1 (1927), at 117:

Si l'expropriation pour cause d'utilité publique qui permet, sous certaines conditions, la dépossession d'un individu, en dehors de son consentement, est admise par le droit international commun, cela implique précisément que la mesure est indépendante de la nationalité de l'individu.

Similarly, Freeman (*The International Responsibility of States for Denial of Justice* (1938)) states (at p. 517) that 'Any measures expropriating private property without compensation and directed against the property of aliens as such would violate international law.' This is also the view of Fachiri (in *B.Y.* 6 (1925), 171). Herz (in *A.J.* 35 (1941), at 249) expresses a similar view:

An important distinction is that between measures directed against foreigners only and those which concern aliens and nationals alike. It will be shown in more detail later that there is much doubt as to the legal consequences of measures of expropriation which refer indiscriminately to citizens and foreigners, especially in case of measures of general reform enacted in general legislation. No such doubt exists, however, when the act is one of discrimination against foreigners. Here the usual legal consequences (in particular, the obligation to pay compensation) arise even should the expropriation, directed only against foreigners, be effected as part of a general legislative programme. In this sense the principle of 'national treatment' of foreigners is admitted by all those who have dealt with the problem, irrespective of whether they consider this principle as the minimum or the maximum of what a foreigner may rely on. 'Non-discrimination' has formed the basis of all those claims where measures had been directed against single foreigners. It does not matter whether the discrimination is open or veiled, if only there is evidence that in its effects the measure affects practically aliens alone.

Professor A. de La Pradelle, in the 'Projet provisoire de Résolutions' submitted to the Institute of International Law at Bath in 1950, says that 'Elle [la nationalisation] peut porter sur les nationaux sans porter sur les étrangers; elle ne peut atteindre les étrangers sans atteindre les nationaux' (*Annuaire* (1950) (i), 68).

34. Equality in fact and equality in law   It is well recognized that the generality of the language used in an enactment is not decisive for the question whether it is in fact discriminatory against aliens. The Permanent Court of International Justice on several occasions made it clear that discriminatory legislation which is couched in general terms is nevertheless unlawful. In the case of the *German Settlers in Poland* (Series B, no. 6), where the Court was concerned with legislation passed by Poland and expropriating all lands title to which was derived from the German State, the Court found that the legislation, although general in its terms, was directed at persons of German origin, and was thus contrary to the Minorities Treaty which, in this case, protected a certain category of Polish nationals against discrimination. The Court said, on this point:

Article 8 of the treaty guarantees to racial minorities the same treatment and security 'in law and in fact' as to other Polish nationals. The facts that no racial discrimination appears in the text of the Law of 14 July 1920, and that in a few instances the law applies to non-German Polish nationals who took as purchaser from original holders of German race, make no substantial difference. Article 8 is designed to meet precisely such complaints as are made in the present case. There must be equality in fact as well as ostensible legal equality in the sense of the absence of discrimination in the words of the law.

That principle was applied in favour of Polish nationals in the case of the *Treatment of Polish Nationals in Danzig*. There the Court said:

The prohibition against discrimination, in order to be effective, must ensure the absence of discrimination in fact as well as in law. A measure which in terms is of general application, but in fact is directed against Polish nationals and other persons of Polish origin or speech, constitutes a violation of the prohibition. (Series A/B, no. 44, p. 28.)

The same principle was reaffirmed in the case of the *Minority Schools in Albania* (Series A/B, no. 64, at p. 19).

A series of cases decided by mixed arbitral tribunals illustrates, indirectly, the same principle. In the case of *Schmidt* v. *Yugoslav State*, which came before the Hungaro-Yugoslav Mixed Arbitral Tribunal in 1929, the question at issue was whether the expropriation of the landed property of Hungarian nationals in pursuance of Czech laws of agrarian reform was a confiscation or liquidation in the meaning of Article 250 of the Treaty of Trianon, which prohibited such measures. It was recognized that the prohibition did not apply to expropriation in pursuance of general legislation for a public purpose and in return for adequate compensation. However, it was contended by the Hungarian Government that the legislation in this case, while general in tenor, was in effect aimed mainly at Hungarian nationals. The Tribunal reserved the question on the merits for a later decision. It found that there was a sufficient *prima facie* case under Article 250 of the Treaty of Trianon to give it jurisdiction over the case (Lapradelle, *Causes célèbres: la réforme agraire yugoslave* (1930)). In the case of *Kulin, Emeric* v. *Roumanian State*, decided by the Hungaro-Roumanian Mixed Arbitral Tribunal in 1927 (*Recueil T.A.M.* 7 (1928), 138) the facts and the decision were similar. The same applies to the *Pallavicini* case, which came before the Hungaro-Czechoslavak Mixed Arbitral Tribunal in 1929 (Lapradelle, *Causes célèbres: la réforme tchécoslovaque devant la justice internationale* (1930)).

35. Evidence that the Oil Nationalization Law is directed exclusively against the Anglo-Iranian Oil Company The Government of the United Kingdom does not deny that cases may arise in which a measure of expropriation solely affecting foreign nationals is dictated by such overwhelming considerations of public utility and general welfare that they must be regarded, in the circumstances of the case, as an exculpating or mitigating factor. In such cases the fact that the expropriation affects aliens only is, in a distinct sense, accidental. The State, when acting in good faith, cannot be expected to refrain from a measure which it considers to be of vital importance for the sole reason that the persons affected are aliens. However, the situation is altogether different when the circumstances of the case point cogently to the conclusion that the action taken was embarked upon not in pursuance of a general purpose but with the object of nullifying a transaction which is deemed to be inconvenient or less lucrative than was expected at the time when it was entered into. The situation is altogether different when there is clear evidence pointing to the conclusion that the measure taken was dictated by sentiments of resentment, animosity and vindictiveness against the foreign national in question and that the official reference to a general measure of nationalization in fact attaches itself spuriously and unconvincingly to a thinly disguised predatory design of confiscation. The conspicuous feature of the statements of the Government of Iran preceding, accompanying and following the passing of the Oil Nationalization Law has been a succession of accusations and vituperation against the Anglo-Iranian Oil Company. The malevolence of the charges levelled against the company as justifying a breach of the concession in itself points to the true object of the Oil Nationalization Law. The company has been accused of malpractice, dishonesty, and corruption; it has been saddled with responsibility for the miseries of the people of Iran; and the virtual confiscation of its rights and assets has been represented as the first and indispensable condition of any attempt to secure the economic prosperity of Iran. The treatment to which the officials of the company have been exposed since the passing of the Oil Nationalization Law throws light on the true motives which underlay the passing of that enactment. It substantiates the contention of the Government of the United Kingdom that this is not a case of genuine nationalization which happens to affect an alien, but that it is a case of a deliberate attempt at confiscation under the guise of a general act of nationalization.

36. Nationalization as disguise for confiscation Neither has an attempt been made on the part of the Iranian Government to show that, on any long-range view, the Oil Nationalization Law was dictated by imperative requirements of the Iranian economy. In the submission of the Government of the United Kingdom the contrary is the case. Economic conditions in Iran: its financial stability; the industrial efficiency and commercial prosperity of the oil industry; and considerations of the peace of the world and of respect for law upon which the economic well-being of Iran, like that of other countries ultimately depends – all these demanded that such measures of nationalization as were considered to be dictated by paramount interests of the Iranian economy and sovereignty should have been accomplished by negotiation and agreement, as repeatedly urged by the Government of the United Kingdom and the company, in accordance with the solemn pledges enshrined in the explicit Articles of the convention. Instead, the Government of Iran has resorted to action, closely approximating to confiscation, against a foreign company in pursuit of a short-term advantage and in high-handed disregard of the prosperity of its own country and the economic needs of the world. It would appear that in a case such as the present one where the operation of an enactment couched in general language actually and exclusively affects a particular foreign national, the Iranian Government should have taken all requisite precautions to dispel the charge that the Oil Nationalization Law was in fact no more than a cloak for confiscation. It could have done so, *inter alia,* by providing both for adequate compensation in principle and for proper machinery, either through agreement or through the determination of an impartial agency, for fixing its amount. But this is the very thing which the Government of Iran, with deliberate and transparent evasion, has failed to do.

37. Nationalization and exhaustion of local remedies In this connection, without embarking upon an elaborate legal argument in relation to a question which constitutes essentially a provisional question relating to the jurisdiction of the Court, the Government of the United Kingdom attach importance to stating that the Oil Nationalization Act of 1 May 1951 engages immediately and directly the international responsibility of Iran. There cannot be any question of the jurisdicton of the Court being dependent upon any previous exhaustion of available local remedies. It is an established principle of international judicial and arbitral practice that the requirement of exhaustion of local remedies does not apply in cases where there are no local remedies to exhaust. There are no legal remedies under the law of Iran against a law passed by the Iranian legislature. Moreover, the legal remedies for a breach of the Convention of 1933 are the remedies provided for in Article 22 of the convention, namely, recourse to arbitration. That legal remedy the Government of Iran has repudiated expressly and repeatedly – a repudiation which in itself constitutes the international delinquency of denial of justice.

38. Conclusions The conclusions of this section are as follows: The Oil Nationalization Law of 1 May 1951, although general in phraseology, is in fact directed only against the Anglo-Iranian Oil Company. It is a generally recognized principle of international law that it is unlawful to expropriate the property of aliens by an act which is openly or by implication directed exclusively against them. That principle has the support of judicial and arbitral decisions and of writers. It was adopted by the Council of the League of Nations. There is direct and circumstantial evidence to the effect that the Oil Nationalization Law is actually directed against the Anglo-Iranian Oil Company. That evidence is corroborated by the confiscatory character of the law and by the repudiation by the Iranian Government of its obligation to submit the interpretation of the convention to impartial determination. In view of the latter fact and having regard to the legislative character of the measures taken, the international responsibility of Iran has become directly and immediately engaged.

VI. THE LEGAL REMEDIES FOR UNLAWFUL EXPROPRIATION

A. *Full compensation for unlawful expropriation*

39. Compensation for lawful and unlawful expropriation The Government of the United Kingdom contend that should the Court find that the action of the Government of Iran is unlawful for all or any of the reasons adduced in the preceding sections of this Memorial, then any such finding of the Court will be directly relevant to the question of the remedy to which the Government of the United Kingdom is entitled. That relevance lies in the distinction, well recognized in international law, between the consequences of expropriation which is lawful and that which is in violation of the international obligations of the State. That distinction was formulated by the Permanent Court of International Justice, with all requisite clarity and emphasis in the *Chorzów Factory (Claim for Indemnity)* case. In view of the importance of the ruling of the Court in that case it is considered necessary to quote the relevant passage in full. The Court said:

The action of Poland which the Court has judged to be contrary to the Geneva Convention is not an expropriation – to render which lawful only the payment of fair compensation would have been wanting; it is a seizure of property, rights and interests which could not be expropriated even against compensation, save under the exceptional conditions fixed by Article 7 of the said convention. As the Court has expressly declared in Judgment no. 8, reparation is in this case the consequence not of the application of Articles 6 to 22 of the Geneva Convention, but of acts contrary to those articles.

It follows that the compensation due to the German Government is not necessarily limited to the value of the undertaking at the moment of dispossession, plus interest to the day of payment. This limitation would only be admissible if the Polish Government had had the right to expropriate, and if its wrongful act consisted merely in not having paid to the two companies the just price of what was expropriated; in the present case, such a limitation might result in placing Germany and the interests protected by the Geneva Convention, on behalf of which interests the German Government is acting, in a situation more unfavourable than that in which Germany and these interests would have been if Poland had respected the said convention. Such a consequence would not only be unjust, but also and above all incompatible with the aim of Article 6 and following Articles of the convention – that is to say, the prohibition, in principle, of the liquidation of the property, rights and interests of German nationals and of companies controlled by German nationals in Upper Silesia – since it would be tantamount to rendering lawful liquidation and unlawful dispossession indistinguishable in so far as their financial results are concerned.

The essential principle contained in the actual notion of an illegal act – a principle which seems to be established by international practice and in particular by the decisions of arbitral tribunals – is that reparation must, as far as possible, wipe out all the consequences of the illegal act and re-establish the situation which would, in all probability, have existed if that act had not been committed. Restitution in kind, or, if this is not possible, payment of a sum corresponding to the value which a restitution in kind would bear; the award, if need be, of damages for loss sustained which would not be covered by restitution in kind or payment in place of it – such are the principles which should serve to determine the amount of compensation due for an act contrary to international law.

This conclusion particularly applies as regards the Geneva Convention, the object of which is to provide for the maintenance of economic life in

Upper Silesia on the basis of respect for the *status quo*. The dispossession of an industrial undertaking – the expropriation of which is prohibited by the Geneva Convention – then involves the obligation to restore the undertaking and, if this be not possible, to pay its value at the time of the indemnification, which value is designed to take the place of restitution which has become impossible. To this obligation, in virtue of the general principles of international law, must be added that of compensating loss sustained as the result of the seizure. The impossibility, on which the parties are agreed, of restoring the Chorzów factory could therefore have no other effect but that of substituting payment of the value of the undertaking or restitution; it would not be in conformity either with the principles of law or with the wish of the parties to infer from that agreement that the question of compensation must henceforth be dealt with as though an expropriation properly so called was involved. (*P.C.I.J.* Series A, no. 17, pp. 46–8).

If the above judgment of the Court expresses – as in the opinion of the Government of the United Kingdom it does – a sound and equitable rule of international law, then it is submitted by the Government of the United Kingdom that even if the compensation offered by the Government of Iran in the Oil Nationalization Law were such as international law provides for cases of lawful expropriation, it would not provide the remedy to which the Government of the United Kingdom is entitled in the circumstances of this case. For the expropriation, in this case, is unlawful. Accordingly, the remedy to which the Government of the United Kingdom is entitled is that laid down by the Permanent Court of International Justice in the *Chorzów Factory* case and based on the distinction between lawful and unlawful expropriation. As has been shown, the compensation which is envisaged in – or which may be deduced from – the Oil Nationalization Law is not even such as international law requires in case of lawful expropriation.

40. Arbitral practice as to compensation for unlawful expropriation Before attempting to apply to the present case the principle laid down by the Court in the *Chorzów Factory* case reference may be made to some arbitral precedents and to writers as fully substantiating the rule laid down by the Court in the *Chorzów Factory* case as to the completeness of the remedy in circumstances amounting to unlawful expropriation of – and, generally, unlawful interference with – the property of aliens.

The decision of the Permanent Court of International Justice in the *Chorzów Factory* case was cited and applied in the *Martini* case, an arbitration between Italy and Venezuela, the award in which was given in 1930. In that case a mining concession had been rescinded as the result of a judicial decision on the ground of the non-performance of certain obligations by the concessionaire. Severe damages were also imposed on the latter by reason of other alleged defaults. The Arbitrators, while holding that the rescission of the concession was itself lawful, found that the damages had been unlawfully imposed. The Tribunal thereupon expressly annulled the obligation of payment, and said:

Bien que ce paiement n'ait jamais été effectué – ainsi qu'il ressort de déclarations faites par les Agents des deux Parties au cours des débats oraux – les obligations existent en droit. Ces obligations doivent être annullées, à titre de réparation. En prononçant leur annulation, le Tribunal Arbitral souligne qu'un acte illicite a été commis et applique le principe que les conséquences de l'acte illicite doivent être effacées. (*U.N.R.I.A.A.* II (1949), 975, at 1002; *A.J.* 25 (1931), 584.)

A decision analogous to that in the *Chorzów Factory* case was given in an award rendered in the same year in the dispute between Portugal and Germany. The claim arose out of the requisition of Portuguese property in German-occupied territory. The Arbitrators laid down the following rules relating to the calculation of the indemnity:

Il faut, dès lors, distinguer entre les actes que ce droit autorise dans certaines limites, comme la réquisition, et ceux qu'il réprime d'une manière absolue, comme le pillage. Dans le premier cas, il ne peut être question d'appliquer, même par analogie, les règles du droit privé sur la résponsabilité découlant des actes illicites. Les arbitres ne peuvent fixer des indemnités excédant le paiement qui, effectué au comptant ou intervenue aussitôt que possible, eut exclu tout acte contraire au droit des gens. L'État allemand s'étant reconnu obligé de rembourser la valeur des objets réquisitionnés à l'époque de la réquisition, il n'est pas nécéssaire d'examiner théoriquement si l'État doit, au sens de l'Article 52 du règlement de la Haye, payer la valeur *intégrale* de ce qu'il a requisitionné, ou s'il ne satisferait pas aux exigences minimes du droit des gens en allouant, aux propriétaires neutres, ce qu'il eut accordé à ses propres ressortissants en vertu de sa législation interne.

Dans le second cas, l'indemnité devrait, *a fortiori*, s'élever au minimum à la valeur des objets disparus au cours du pillage. (*U.N.R.I.A.A.* II (1949), 1037, at 1040.)

In the *Shufeldt* claim, a dispute between the United States and

Guatemala, the Arbitrator also emphasized that *restitutio in integrum* must be given to a person injured by an unlawful act. In that case a concession held by a United States citizen was abrogated by the legislature of Guatemala. In an award given on 24 July 1930, the Arbitrator assessed damages on the following principle:

I will now consider the question of damages and will, to begin with, quote the words of the Arbitrator in the claim of *R. H. May* v. *Guatemala* and *Guatemala* v. *May*, reported in *U.S. For. Rel.* ((1900), p. 673): 'I cannot pretend to lay down the law concerning damages in clearer words than those of the advocate of the Guatemalan Government who uses the following language in the counter-claim: "The law of Guatemala says Don Jorge Munoz (to which the claimant is subject in this case) establishes, like those of all civilized nations of the earth, that contracts produce reciprocal rights and obligations between the contracting parties; that whoever concludes a contract is bound not only to fulfil it but also to recoup or compensate (the other party) for damages and prejudice which result directly or indirectly from the nonfulfilment or infringement by default or fraud of the party concerned and that such compensation includes both damage suffered and profits lost: *damnum emergens et lucrum cessans*." '

The *damnum emergens* is always recoverable, but the *lucrum cessans* must be the direct fruit of the contract and not too remote or speculative.

I will deal with the profits lost first and it seems to me that this is essentially a case where such profits are the direct fruit of the contract and may reasonably be supposed to have been in the contemplation of both parties as the probable result of a breach of it. (*U.N.R.I.A.A.* II (1949), 1083, at 1099.)

In the award in the arbitration between the United States and Norway relating to the requisition of Norwegian ships by the United States Government during the First World War, rendered by the Permanent Court of Arbitration on 13 October 1922, the 'just compensation' for the taking of the ships was increased by 'damages for the unlawful retaining of the title and use of the ships after all emergency ceased' (*A.J.* 17 (1923), at 394). The Court held that 'just compensation implies a complete restitution of the *status quo ante* based . . . upon the loss of profits of the Norwegian owners as compared with other owners of similar property' (*ibid.* p. 392).

In the case of *Walter Fletcher Smith*, which was submitted to arbitration by the United States and Cuba, the property of the claimant was expropriated, ostensibly in pursuance of a general law for the urbanization of the district but in fact, as the Arbitrator found, by a measure specifically directed against him. In an award given in 1929 the Arbitrator, after holding that, according to law, the property should be restored to the claimant, assessed compensation to cover both the value of the land, buildings and personal effects, and the deprivation of the use of the property. The following passage of the award may properly be cited:

From a careful examination of the testimony and of the records, the Arbitrator is impressed that the attempted expropriation of the claimant's property was not in compliance with the constitution, nor with the laws of the Republic; that the expropriation proceedings were not, in good faith, for the purpose of public utility. They do not present the features of an orderly attempt by officers of the law to carry out a formal order of condemnation. The destruction of the claimant's property was wanton, riotous, oppressive. It was effected by about 150 men whose action appears to have been of a most violent character. There is some evidence tending to show that, before the expropriation proceedings, certain persons, being unable to purchase the property from the claimant, threatened to destroy it.

While the proceedings were municipal in form, the properties seized were turned over immediately to the defendant company, ostensibly for public purposes, but, in fact, to be used by the defendant for purposes of amusement and private profit, without any reference to public utility. The Arbitrator is of the opinion, then, that all the acts of expropriation shown in testimony, and the proceedings based upon them, were not of such a character as to give an indefeasible title to the defendant company. (*U.N.R.I.A.A.* II (1949), at 917–18; *A.J.* 24 (1930), 384)

In *Kemeny* v. *État Serbe-Croat-Slovene*, decided on 13 September 1928, by the Hungaro-Yugoslav Mixed Arbitral Tribunal, the plaintiff had been deprived, in 1920, of a mining concession which would have expired in 1921 and which, apparently, was not yet being worked at a profit. The Tribunal laid down the following principles with regard to the payment of damages:

Attendu qu'il est de jurisprudence du Tribunal de ceans que dans pareil cas, l'État dont les fonctionnaires auraient pris une mesure pareille est tenu de rétablir les choses dans l'état où elles se trouvaient avant l'application de la mesure; . . . Attendu qu'il est d'évidence qu'il ne peut être question de rétablir effectivement les choses dans l'état antérieur; . . . Attendu que le Tribunal estime que la seule solution possible et équitable consiste en une indemnité en argent à payer par l'État S.C.S. au requérant; cette indemnité devra s'élever jusqu'à concurrence de la valeur commerciale qu'avaient le 16 août 1920, les droits exclusifs de fouille et de récherche, en tant que ces droits se rapportaient aux terrains mentionnés dans la décision prise, à cette dernière date, par la Direction des Mines de Zagreb; qu'en vue de déterminer cette valeur, il devra être tenu compte de toutes les conditions de la vie commerciale et économique prévalant à la date indiquée au lieu auquel les droits susmentionnés se rapportaient. (*Recueil T.A.M.* 8 (1928), at 596–7.)

In the *Delagoa Bay Railway* case, the award in which was given in 1900, the Portuguese Government had rescinded the concession of the Lourenço Marques Railroad, which was financed by English and American capital, and had taken possession of the line already constructed. A Tribunal, nominated by the Swiss Federal Council, found that the decree of rescission and the taking possession of the railway had not been carried out in conformity with the contract of concession. It then held that there was but one principle of law applicable to the fixing of the compensation – that of *dommages et intérêts*, comprising, in accordance with the rules of law universally admitted, *damnum emergens* and *lucrum cessans* (*Archives Diplomatiques*, LXXIV, 214). The Tribunal added that, had the company been the victim of arbitrary treatment which was wholly unmerited, penal damages might have been awarded.

In the *Suez Canal* case the Emperor Napoleon III, who had been appointed Arbitrator in a claim of the Suez Canal Company against the Egyptian Government for the breach of the concession for the building of the canal, laid down the following basic principle as applicable to the question submitted to him:

Lorsque des conventions ont été librement formées par le consentement de parties capables et éclairées, elles doivent être fidèlement exécutées. Celle des parties contractantes qui refuse ou néglige d'accomplir ses engagements est tenue de réparer le dommage qui résulte de son infraction à la loi qu'elle s'est volontairement imposée. En général, sauf à tenir compte des circonstances et des motifs de l'infraction, la réparation consiste dans une indemnité représentant la perte qu'éprouve l'autre partie et le bénéfice dont elle est privée. (Lapradelle-Politis, II, 364.)

In the *Antioquia Railway* case, a case of breach of a contract made with British nationals by the Colombian Government, the Arbitral Tribunal laid down as the guiding principle for cases of that nature that the damage caused to one party by the wrongful breaking of the contract includes, on the one hand, all the expenses and losses which it has incurred in fulfilling its contractual obligations (*damnum emergens*) and, on the other hand, the profits which were likely to arise from its regular execution (*lucrum cessans*) (La Fontaine, *Pasicrisie Internationale*, p. 552).

In the case of *Marion Cheek*, a dispute between the United States and Siam, in which the property of the claimant had been unlawfully seized, the amount of indemnity was determined by the Arbitrator, in an award given in 1878, on the basis 'that the estate should as far as possible be placed in the same position as it would have been in had not the Siamese Government seized the property...' (Moore, *International Arbitrations*, p. 5069).

In the arbitration between France and Venezuela in the *Fabiani* case, in which Venezuela was found to have been responsible for a denial of justice to a French national, the award given on 30 December 1896 stated the following principles to be the basis of the assessment of damages:

Les dénégations de justice qu'a eprouvées Fabiani sont pour le moins des delits civils ou des quasi-delits. En droit moderne, l'auteur d'une faute aquilienne est, en principe, tenu de réparer *tout* le prejudice qui peut raisonnablement en être envisage comme la consequence directe ou indirecte (*damnum emergens* et *lucrum cessans*). (Moore, *International Arbitrations*, at p. 5908.)

In the case of the *Cape Horn Pigeon*, a dispute between the United States and Russia relating to the unlawful detention of a vessel and its crew by the Russian Government, the Arbitrator emphasized that restitution for an unlawful act, in order to be complete, must cover both *damnum emergens* and *lucrum cessans*. He said:

Considérant que le principe général du droit civil, d'après lequel les dommages-intérêts doivent contenir une indemnité non seulement pour le dommage qu'on a souffert, mais aussi pour le gain dont on a été privé, est également applicable aux litiges internationaux et que, pour pouvoir l'appliquer, il n'est pas nécéssaire que le montant du gain dont on se voit privé puisse être fixe avec certitude, mais qu'il suffit de démontrer que dans l'ordre naturel des choses on aurait pu faire un gain dont on se voit privé par le fait qui donne lieu à la réclamation.

Considérant qu'il n'est pas question en ce cas d'un dommage indirect, mais d'un dommage *direct*, dont le montant doit faire l'objet d'une évaluation. (*R.I.*(*Paris*), 2nd ser., 5 (1903), 78.)

41. The same. Opinions of writers Writers on the question of state responsibility have given full support to the view that in case of illegality the measure of damages is determined by the principle of *restitutio in integrum*. Thus Freeman (*The International Responsibility of States for Denial of Justice* (1938), p. 573) writes:

Speaking generally the reparation of an international wrong may take two possible forms; that of *restitutio in integrum* or of compensation by way of damages (*dommages-intérêts*) for the injuries suffered. The first is simply the re-establishment of the state of facts which would exist if the unlawful act had not been committed, the second an economic satisfaction given either in lieu of restitution where that, for some reason, has become impossible, or as a complement thereof when it itself is inadequate to repair the wrong.

Professor Eagleton adopts the same principle as the basis for establishing detailed rules of the measure of damages:

The start must be made from the universally accepted rule that full compensation must be made; that the situation must be restored as it was before the injurious act took place; that the injured party must be made whole. If this rule be accepted it would appear that compensation should be made for all damages which were caused by the illegal act and are traceable exclusively to it. (*Yale Law Journal*, 39 (1929–30), 73–4.)

Similarly, Yntema states (in *Columbia Law Review*, 24 (1924), 137):

According to the doctrine which is now accepted generally by the Continental writers on international law, a State which is responsible for an occurrence giving rise to an international injury is under an international obligation to make complete compensation. This implies a duty to make satisfacton in kind, where possible and desirable, and furthermore, in cases where a specific remedy is impossible, unjust or insufficient, to make payment of a money compensation. The basis upon which the latter is to be estimated is the restoration of the injured party substantially to the condition which would have been enjoyed had not the occurrence causing injury taken place.

B. *Restitution in kind*

42. Arbitral practice and restitution in kind   It will have been noted from the survey of authorities referred to above that the principle of *restitutio in integrum* may assume two forms. In the first instance, it may take the form of complete restitution, *in specie*, of the *status quo ante*. There is nothing in international law which is opposed to full restitution thus conceived. As the Permanent Court of International Justice said in the above-quoted judgment in the *Chorzów Factory* case, 'restitution in kind' is in the first instance the natural expression of the duty of *restitutio in integrum*. It is only 'if this is not possible' that consideration must be given to the 'payment of a sum corresponding to the value which a restitution in kind would bear'. There is, so far as the Government of the United Kingdom are aware, no case on record in which an international arbitral tribunal has held that, for reasons connected with the sovereignty of the State, no restitution in kind is admissible in international law. In many cases, while admitting it in principle, they give detailed reasons why in the case before them such restitution was not practicable. The following passage from the Award of Undén, Arbitrator, given in 1933 in the arbitration between Greece and Bulgaria, illustrates that aspect of the matter:

The Arbitrator is of the opinion that the obligation of restoring the forests to the claimants cannot be imposed upon the defendant. There are several reasons which may be given in favour of this opinion. The claimants in whose behalf a claim put forward by the Greek Government has been held admissible, are partners in a commercial organization composed of other partners as well. It would therefore be inadmissible to compel Bulgaria to restore integrally the disputed forests. Moreover, it is hardly likely that the forests are in the same condition that they were in 1918. Assuming that most of the rights in the forests are rights of cutting a fixed quantity of wood, to be removed during a certain period, a decision holding for restitution would be dependent upon an examination of the question whether the quantity contracted for could be actually obtained. Such a decision would also require examining and determining the rights which may have arisen meanwhile in favour of other persons, and which may or may not be consistent with the rights of the claimants.

The only practicable solution of the dispute, therefore, is to impose upon the defendant the obligation to pay an indemnity. (*Annual Digest* (1933–4), case no. 39, at pp. 99–100.)

Practical considerations, coupled with the recognition in principle of restitution in kind underlay the award, referred to above, in the *Walter Fletcher Smith* case. In some of the awards rendered in 1920 in the arbitration arising out of the expropriation of religious properties in Portugal, the Arbitrators decreed restitution of the properties taken (*U.N.R.I.A.A.* 1 (1948), 11 *et seq.*).[1] A writer who has devoted a

---

[1] The case of *Salvador* v. *Nicaragua*, decided in 1917 by the Central American Court of Justice, provides an extreme example of a decision decreeing *restitutio in integrum*. In the Bryan–Chamorro Treaty between the United States and Nicaragua, concluded in 1914, the United States had obtained from Nicaragua the lease of a naval base in the Gulf of Fonseca. Salvador complained that this endangered her security. The Court, after having found that this was so, said: 'Whereas: as a logical consequence of the violation of rights claimed by the Government of El Salvador and recognized by this tribunal, the Government of Nicaragua is impressed with the obligation to take all possible means sanctioned by international law to re-establish and maintain the legal status that existed between the two countries prior to the conclusion of the Bryan–Chamorro Treaty.

'It is clear that under the principles of international law and the previous stipulations agreed to in the Treaty of Washington, the high party defendant was without power to enter into a new treaty that undermined in any degree the moral and legal structure of

monograph to the study of the question of reparation for illicit acts in international law summarizes the position as follows: 'Depuis plus d'un siècle, les commissions et tribunaux internationaux appliquent la règle qui prescrit une *restitution en nature* au profit du lèse et seulement en cas d'impossibilité une indemnité pecuniaire' (Reitzer, *La réparation comme conséquence de l'acte illicite en droit international* (1938), p. 171). Reference may be made in this connection to Article IX of the Convention of 8 September 1923 between the United States and Mexico providing for the setting up of a General Claims Commission. That Article laid down as follows:

In any case the Commission may decide that international law, justice and equity require that a property right be restored to the claimant in addition to the amount awarded in such case for all loss or damage sustained prior to the restitution. In any case where the Commission so decides the restitution of the property or right shall be made by the Government affected after such decision has been made, as hereinbelow provided. The Commission, however, shall at the same time determine the value of the property or right decreed to be restored and the Government affected may elect to pay the amount so fixed after the decision is made rather than to restore the property or right to the claimant.

In the event the Government affected should elect to pay the amount fixed as the value of the property or right decreed to be restored, it is agreed that notice will be filed with the Commission within thirty days after the decision and the amount fixed as the value of the property or right shall be paid immediately. Upon failure so to pay the amount the property or right shall be restored immediately.

Feller (*The Mexican Claims Commissions, 1923–1924* (1935), p. 291) comments on this Article: 'This interesting provision for *restitutio in integrum* was undoubtedly inserted in order to provide for possible claims for the restoration of oil or agrarian lands by Americans in Mexico.'

43. The same. The Hague Codification Conference In connection with the attempted codification of international law on the subject of state responsibility most States which dealt in their answer with the substance of the matter gave an affirmative answer to the question whether reparation for the damage caused should include the

those principles and stipulations. Hence, the obligation imposed on the Government of Nicaragua to re-establish and maintain, by all means possible, the legal status respecting the matters here in controversy that existed with El Salvador prior to 5 August 1914, on which date that memorable treaty was concluded' (*A.J.* 11 (1917), 728).

performance of the obligation. Some of the replies may suitably be quoted:

Germany

In principle, reparation should as far as possible consist of restitution in kind. If it is impossible wholly or partly to re-establish the *status quo*, a pecuniary indemnity should be granted in lieu of or in addition to reversion to that *status quo*. It is not possible to reply absolutely in the affirmative to the question whether restitution in kind is excluded by the fact that the object to be restored has legally passed into the possession of others under the national law. It is quite easy to conceive of cases in which the State responsible ought to be required to incur considerable expenditure with a view to restoring the object in question. Such cases arise mainly when true compensation for damage can only be obtained by the restitution of the object. (*Bases of Discussion*, III (1929), at p. 146.)

Holland

Yes, where performance of the obligation is still possible and where it still possesses any value for the claimant. (*Ibid.* at p. 149.)

Poland

(*a*) If it is possible simply to re-establish the *status quo* violated by the State, or to fulfil the obligation which the State was endeavouring to evade, the State in question (if this is in the interests of the injured party) may be required in principle to re-establish the *status quo* or to comply with its obligation.

In other cases, pecuniary reparation will be required. (*Ibid.* at p. 150.)

Switzerland

As regards damages, doctrine takes its stand on the principle that, as far as circumstance allow, we should endeavour to obtain *restitutio in integrum*, i.e. reversion to the situation in which the injured individual would be if the wrongful act had not been committed. Only where no *restitutio in integrum* is possible can the injured State claim for its nationals compensation for the material, and perhaps moral, wrong caused. (*Ibid.* at pp. 150–1.)

44. Opinions of writers The opinions of writers are uniformly and emphatically in favour of the admissibility, in principle, of restitution in kind. Decencière-Ferrandière, *La responsabilité internationale des États* (1927), says, at p. 246:

Il n'existe aucun principe de droit qui oblige l'État demandeur à se contenter d'une indemnité, s'il préfère voir les choses remises dans leur situation primitive, s'il préfère, par exemple, recouvrir en nature un bien confisqué à l'un de ses nationaux.

Lais, *Rechtsfolgen Völkerrechtlicher Delikte* (1932), says, at p. 29:

Die Naturalrestitution ist das vollendeste Mittel zum Schadenersatz; der Geschädigte wird hier so gestellt, als ob nichts geschehen wäre, denn es wird ja der alte Zustand wieder herbeigeführt, und der Geschädigte hat nichtnötig, sich eine Ersatzleistung aushändigen zu lassen. Wie in jeder anderen Rechtsordnung muss auch im Völkerrecht die Naturalrestitution gelten, weil sie der einzige Weg ist, den Schaden in der volkommensten Weise wieder gutzumachen. Es liegt kein Grund vor, weshalb ein Staat nach Völkerrecht sich mit einer anderen Form der Entschädigung, die doch immer nur einen Ersatz bietet, zufrieden stellen soll, wenn eine Wiederherstellung des früheren Zustandes möglich ist.

Strupp, *Das völkerrechtliche Delikt* (1920), says, at pp. 209 *et seq.*:

(a) *Die Naturalrestitution.* An erster Stelle ist, und zwar ohne Rücksicht darauf, ob das völkerrechtliche Delikt durch das Medium eines Individuums ausgelöst worden ist oder nicht an Naturalrestitution zu denken. Sie bedeutet die Verpflichtung des Taterstaates zur Wiederherstellung des Zustandes, der vorliegen würde, wenn das rechtswidrige Tun oder Unterlassen nicht stattgefunden hätte . . .

Salvioli (in *Hague Recueil*, 28 (1929) (iii), 239) expresses a similar view:

Dans le cas où la restitution en nature n'est pas possible l'arbitre doit déterminer *la valeur de remplacement* en tenant compte de deux éléments:
  1. quelle serait la valeur de la chose, exprimée en monnaie – actuelle – d'indemnité à la date de la décision;
  2. quel serait le développement normal que la chose aurait raisonnablement prise, si elle était restée entre les mains de son proprietaire.

This is also the view of Sibert (in *R.G.* 44 (1937), 539–42) and Spiropoulos (in *Z.I.* 35 (1925–6), 116). He says:

Grundsätzlich ist nach geltendem Völkerrecht der aus einem völkerrechtlichen Delikte entstandene Schaden in Falle einer Haftungsbergründung auf Grund des allgemeinen Schadenersatzbegriffes in seinem GESAMTEM Umfange zu ersetzen (*Damnun emergens* und *lucrum cessans*).

45. Restitution in kind and solvency of the defendant State The authorities adduced above show that there is nothing in the principles of international law and in international practice which prevents the Court from decreeing restitution in kind. There is, in this connection, a further material factor to which the Government of the United

Kingdom attach importance: While it may be admitted that in certain circumstances restitution in kind may not be either possible or necessary for safeguarding the true interests of the parties, there may be cases in which such restitution provides the only practicable and just solution. Such cases include those in which the offending State is unlikely to be in a position to grant adequate pecuniary compensation and in which the situation, wrongfully created by it, is calculated, if allowed to subsist, to affect adversely its solvency. Reference is made here to the considerations adduced above in paragraph 28.

c. *Full compensation*

46. '*Fair market value*' Should the Court decide that in the circumstances of the present case compensation, as distinguished from the restitution of the *status quo ante*, is the proper remedy, then it is contended by the Government of the United Kingdom that the second alternative envisaged in the judgment in the *Chorzów Factory* case must apply, namely, 'payment of a sum corresponding to the value which a restitution in kind would bear'. That sum, according to well-established international arbitral practice – some instances of which are enumerated as an appendix to this paragraph – includes both the value of the actual investment and loss of profits. In fact, the prospective profits – the *lucrum cessans* – are, in case of unlawful deprivation of property – an integral part of the 'fair market value' – used as a basis of compensation in the award of the Permanent Court of Arbitration in the *Norwegian Shipowners* case. Or, to use the language of the Arbitrator in the above-quoted case between Greece and Bulgaria:

According to the general principles of international law, interest-damages must be determined on the basis of the value of the forests, respectively of the exploitation contracts, at the date of the actual dispossession, that is, on 20 September 1918, in addition to an equitable rate of interest estimated on that value from the date of dispossession. [The Arbitrator took as a basis of his valuation the value of the forest enterprise as declared by the members of the partnership in a memorandum drafted in 1918, several months before the expropriation, with a view to selling the business.] (*Annual Digest* 1933–4), case no. 39, at p. 101.)

Appendix to paragraph 46: Some instances of awards of prospective profits as part of the 'fair market value'

In the *Aboilard* case the claimant had been granted a concession by the Haitian Government, approval of which was subsequently refused by the legislature of Haiti. France and Haiti submitted to arbitration the questions whether the contract of concession had been valid, and, if so, whether the Haitian Government was liable to pay compensation. In an award given on 26 July 1905, the Arbitrators held that the contract was valid and that the duty to pay compensation followed logically therefrom:

> Si les contrats étaient pleinement valables, la conséquence suivrait d'elle-même logiquement, le gouvernement haitien devant naturellement procurer au concessionaire tous les avantages qui seraient resultés pour lui de l'exécution complète des concessions . . .

They assessed the compensation by reference both to *damnum emergens* and *lucrum cessans*:

> Aboilard a éprouvé certains dommages direct dont l'existence n'est pas douteuse, bien que la Commission regrette que des justifications précises et detaillées ne lui aient pas fourni . . .
>
> S'il y a lieu de constater qu'il n'y avait encore qu'un Société d'étude et non pas le Société d'exploitation prévue par les concessions, des sérieuses bénéfices pouvaient être légitimement espérés par Aboilard. . .
> (*R.G.* 12 (1905), Documents, 13.)

The principle that compensation must be given for loss of profits as well as for direct damage has been applied in a number of cases arising out of the unlawful detention of vessels. In the *Favourite*, a claim decided in 1921 by the American–British Claims Tribunal set up under the Treaty of 1910, damages for the detention of the vessel were calculated, in part with reference to the trouble occasioned, but mainly on the basis of the prospective profits of the vessel (Nielsen's *Report* (1926), p. 515). The same view was taken by the same Tribunal in the *Wanderer* (*ibid.* p. 459); the *Kate* (*ibid.* p. 472); and, with reference to the unlawful denial of the right to execute repairs, in the *Horace B. Parker* (*ibid.* p. 570). Other examples of the application of this principle are the decisions of the United States–Chilean Claims Commission of 1862 in the case of the *Hop On* (Moore, *International Arbitrations*, p. 326); the award in the dispute between Great Britain and the Netherlands relating to the *Costa Rica Packet* (*ibid.* p. 4948); the award in the dispute between the United States and Spain concerning the *Colonel Lloyd Aspinwall* (*ibid.* p. 1007); and the award of the United States–Peruvian Claims Commission in the case of the *William Lee* (Lapradelle-Politis, II, 282–3). In the case of the *Masonic*, an American vessel which had been unlawfully seized and sold by Spanish authorities in the Phillipines, the Arbitrator, in a detailed award rendered in 1885, calculated the compensation payable under two main heads: the value of the vessel at the time of seizure and the value of the prospective earnings of the vessel (Moore, *International Arbitrations*, p. 1055). In the case of *Yuille, Shortridge and Co.* the Senate of Hamburg, which had been empowered to settle this dispute between Great Britain and Portugal arising out of the failure to execute a judgment in favour of British subjects in Portugal, granted *restitutio in integrum* by assessing damages to cover the payment of the cost of the Portuguese judgment, the immediate loss caused by the failure to execute it, and the loss of prospective business profits occasioned by the uncertainty resulting from that failure. (Lapradelle-Politis, II, 101.) In the case of *Joseph Smith*, a United States–Mexican Commission in 1842 awarded the value of goods wrongfully seized and a reasonable mercantile profit as damages. (Moore, *International Arbitrations*, p. 3374.)

D. *Provisional character of the statement of the United Kingdom in the matter of restitution and compensation*

47. General nature of submissions of the present Memorial on the question of damages   The above observations on the question of damages must, at the present stage of the proceedings, of necessity be of a general character. The same applies to the statement, attached to this Memorial, of the damage suffered by the company and the resulting claims for compensation. The summary submissions on the question of damages have been adduced here on account of their connection with the submission of the Government of the United Kingdom relating to the illegality of the Oil Nationalization Law. Any more specific legal submissions of the Government of the United Kingdom on the question of compensation will be presented if and when the Court has found that this is the proper legal remedy to which the Government of the United Kingdom is entitled and provided that the Government of Iran has not in the meantime complied with any judgment of the Court to the effect that that Government is bound to submit to arbitration, in accordance with Article 22 of the convention, either the dispute as a whole or the question of compensation.

CHAPTER 3

OBSERVATIONS ON THE REPORT OF PROFESSOR DE LA PRADELLE

Editor's Note. This chapter consists of Lauterpacht's observations on the Report on the 'International Effects of Nationalization' prepared by Professor A. de La Pradelle for the Institut de Droit International. The report appears in *Annuaire*, 43 (1950) (i), 42; and the Observations *ibid.* p. 92.

I have read with great interest the admirable and, in my view, very important, report of Professor de La Pradelle. The report raises, in a highly original manner, new and far-reaching problems in one of the most controversial spheres of national and international life. However, because of the controversial and political nature of the issues involved, I confess to considerable doubt as to whether the Resolutions of the Institute on the subject ought to cover a very wide field – such as proposed by the distinguished rapporteur – of rules *de lege ferenda*. This applies not only to such Articles as Article 21 (relating to the prohibition, in the Charter of the United Nations, of economic war and of 'cold' war) or Article 22 (referring to nationalization on the international plane). It applies also to other Articles which, in my view, have a somewhat political complexion. I feel that if the Institute is to make a useful contribution to this intricate subject the number of the Articles of the Resolutions ought to be substantially reduced and that we must avoid anything which – as, for instance, is probably the case with respect to Articles 6 and 7 – is in the nature of censure or of mere advice to Governments.

I am in general agreement with what I consider the principal proposition of the rapporteur, namely, that contained in the last paragraph of Article 11 and relating to the basis of compensation to be paid in case of nationalization. But I find some difficulty in following the rapporteur's distinction, on which a great deal of the Report is based, between nationalization and expropriation. He does not define these terms. Undoubtedly there are cases in which the distinction between them is obvious. But it is not clear to me what difference there is, from the point of view of the duty of compensation, between the taking away of property for the purpose of nationalization and between the expropriation of certain defined categories of property for the purpose, for instance, of land reform as in the well-known case of agrarian reform in Roumania before the Second World War. The taking away of the property of the oil companies in Mexico in 1937 and 1938 was generally referred to as expropriation, but it is probable that the rapporteur would prefer to describe it as 'nationalization'. It is possible that what the rapporteur had primarily in mind when referring to 'expropriation' is isolated deprivation of or interference with property for limited specific purposes such as building a railway or destruction of buildings for sanitary purposes. But if that is so then I am not sure that the categorical terms of full compensation, as suggested by the rapporteur, constitute an existing or desirable rule of international law.

Apart from that major difficulty, there are points of detail as to which I am not sure that I can follow the learned rapporteur.

Thus, with regard to Article 4, I doubt whether it is proper to connect the question of recognition *de jure* with the question of nationalization. I am aware of the fact that on some occasions in the past States have made recognition – either *de facto* or *de jure* – dependent upon the ability or the willingness of a foreign State or Government to fulfil its international obligations and that they considered the inability or unwillingness to pay proper compensation in cases of nationalization or expropriation as a sign of the lacking ability or will to fulfil international obligations. However, I doubt whether that occasional practice constitutes an established or desirable rule of international law.

Secondly, with regard to Article 5, I do not see any decisive reason for giving preferential treatment to property rights grounded in a contract or treaty as distinguished from ordinary rights of property.

Thirdly, with regard to Article 10, I am not sure that it is consistent with international practice to say that aliens may not renounce their right to 'international treatment'. It is true that as laid down in a number of arbitral decisions the Calvo Clause cannot be used for anticipatory acquiescence in treatment clearly contrary to international law. It does not necessarily follow that, in the matter of compensation for deprivation of or interference with property, aliens cannot in advance agree to be treated on the same footing as nationals. However, I do not feel strongly as to this particular point.

Fourthly, with regard to the same Article, I doubt whether, in any case, companies registered within the territory of a State have the right to 'international' treatment for the mere reason that they are in fact controlled by foreign interests. There are cases in which States may protect the rights of their nationals who have an interest in a foreign company, but to say that, because of that, the controlling foreign interest is invariably decisive for the determination of the rights and of the status of a company under its domestic law is, in my view, to go too far.

Fifthly, for reasons stated above, I am not sure that there is room for the differentiation in the matter of international remedies between expropriation and nationalization as proposed by the rapporteur in Article 12.

There are some points of detail in the text of the Report which perhaps the rapporteur might like to modify:

On pages 3 and 4 his account of the controversy between the United States and Mexico concerning the oil expropriations leaves an impression of a lack of accommodation and comprehension on the part of the United States which, as I read it, is not quite borne out by the diplomatic correspondence on the subject.

On page 6 the relevant passage creates the impression that Soviet Russia adhered to the Universal Declaration of Human Rights adopted in 1948. In fact Soviet Russia abstained from voting.

On pages 10–11 the relevant passage creates the impression that the sole reason of the delay of recognition of Soviet Russia by some of the Allied and Associated Powers was the question of compensation in connection with nationalization. Probably this was not so.

On page 15 the rapporteur may perhaps wish to modify the statement that nationalization the true object of which is to eliminate the element of alien control is unlawful.

PART VIII
TREATIES

I GENERAL INTRODUCTION TO THIS PART

The presentation here in systematic form of Lauterpacht's considerable contribution to the law of treaties unavoidably deprives the
reader of contact with the chronological evolution of the author's
thoughts. However, in keeping with the basic principle on which
these volumes rest – namely, the presentation of Lauterpacht's
individual writings within his concept of the general framework of
the whole subject – the materials which appear in this Part have been
placed under headings he contemplated for the series of reports on the
Law of Treaties which he began to prepare for the International Law
Commission in 1953. In fact, because of his election to the International Court of Justice, his work as rapporteur did not proceed
beyond the third of these headings, on 'Conditions of Validity of
Treaties'. However, other material is available to supplement these
reports.

Throughout his career, Lauterpacht was greatly interested in the
problem of the interpretation of treaties. In 1934 he delivered a
course of lectures at the Hague Academy on International Law on
'Preparatory Work in the Interpretation of Treaties'; and in 1950
he prepared a substantial report for the Institute of International Law
on the interpretation of treaties generally, followed by a brief supplementary report in 1951. Both these exercises led to the publication of
parts of his thought in the *Harvard Law Review* and the *B.Y.* respectively.

The last item in this Part is drawn from Lauterpacht's work as a
judge of the International Court of Justice: his separate opinion in
the *Guardianship* case in 1958. Though this is by no means the only
opinion in which Lauterpacht dealt with aspects of treaty law, it is
the only one in which his consideration of treaty problems was not
subordinated to his examination of other subjects requiring separate
classification and treatment.

The fact that the reports on the Law of the Treaties prepared for
the International Law Commission cover a number of important
topics also examined in other of Lauterpacht's writings compelled a
choice between presenting the reports as unbroken items and dividing

them up under the titles of their main parts so as to allow the introduction at appropriate places of other material bearing on the same questions. Guided again by the basis principle of 'systematic' presentation, I was led to adopt the latter alternative. Clearly this is not a choice which could be applied to every item of Lauterpacht's writings which covers more than one subject, such as his judgment in the *Norwegian Loans* case, which deals with both the jurisdiction of the Court and the exhaustion of local remedies. But the decision in the present instance appears justified because the reports on Treaties are themselves presented on an Article-by-Article basis and the text as a whole is therefore exposed to no strain when its various parts are separated from one another by other writings related to the subject matter of a particular Article. Factors such as the importance of maintaining the integrity of the text so as to preserve the sweep of the author's treatment of the subject do not here play a predominant role.

It is appropriate to provide at this point some background to the two reports on the Law of Treaties which Lauterpacht prepared during the period of his membership of the International Law Commission. The Law of Treaties was one of the topics which, at the beginning of its work, the International Law Commission selected as ripe for codification. Professor J. L. Brierly, the first British member of the Commission, was appointed rapporteur in 1949. He produced three reports relating exclusively to the conclusion of treaties. When Lauterpacht was elected to the Commission upon Brierly's resignation in 1952, he was also nominated by the Commission to succeed Brierly as rapporteur. Lauterpacht made a fresh start and on 24 March 1953 produced his first report (hereinafter called 'the 1953 Report'). This appeared as a document of the International Law Commission under the symbol A/CN.4/63 and was subsequently printed in *Yearbook of the International Law Commission* (1953), II, 90–162. Lauterpacht produced a second report on 8 July 1954 consisting of some changes in the text and commentaries of the 1953 Report. The second report (hereinafter called 'the 1954 Report') first appeared as U.N. document A/CN.4/87 and was reprinted in *Yearbook of the International Law Commission* (1954), II, 123–33. Neither report was specifically debated by the Commission either during Lauterpacht's membership (he resigned after the 1954 session upon his election to the International Court of Justice) or subsequently.

In 1955 Sir Gerald Fitzmaurice, whom the Commission elected to fill the rest of Lauterpacht's term, was appointed rapporteur and he too chose to begin again. In his turn, he produced five reports which covered the topics of framing and conclusion of treaties, validity and effect. When Sir Humphrey Waldock replaced Sir Gerald Fitz-maurice in 1961 he also made a fresh start and was able to conclude his treatment of the whole subject with a series of reports which led eventually to the adoption by the Commission in 1966 of a complete set of draft Articles on the Law of Treaties. These formed the basis of discussion at the Vienna Conference on the Law of Treaties which in 1969 produced a convention on that subject. The evolution of this convention, through the International Law Commission and the Conference, is traced in detail by Dr S. Rosenne in *The Law of Treaties* (1970).

The 1953 Report is introduced by the following Preface:

1. This section of the Report on the Law of Treaties is composed of the following three parts: Part I (Definition and Nature of Treaties); Part II (Conclusion of Treaties); and Part III (Conditions of Validity of Treaties). It is intended that the subsequent sections of the report should cover the following other topics of the Law of Treaties: Part IV (Operation and Enforcement of Treaties); Part V (Interpretation of Treaties); Part VI (Termination of Treaties); Part VII (Rules and Principles Applicable to Particular Types of Treaties).

2. The draft Articles formulated by the rapporteur are accompanied throughout by comments and notes. While the former is intended to constitute part of the work of the Commission to be submitted to the General Assembly, the notes are merely in the nature of explanations for the convenience of the Commission. However, the border-line between the comment and the notes is not contemplated as being rigid and it is probable that eventually substantial sections of the notes may be included in the comment.

3. The present report is intended primarily as a formulation of existing law. It is largely for this reason that the rapporteur has thought it necessary in a number of cases – as, for instance, in the case of Article 9 relating to Reservations – to append alternative formulations *de lege ferenda*. In some cases it has been thought necessary to include, for the consideration of the Commission, alternative formulations of *lex lata*. However, in general the rapporteur has attached importance to the preservation of the distinction between the two main tasks which, in relation to this and other topics, confront the Commission, namely, those of codification and development of international law.

In order to identify more precisely the material which appears under each of the sections below, I introduce each with a brief note which, for purposes of comparison, includes the text of the relevant Article of the Vienna Convention of 1969.

II DEFINITION AND NATURE OF TREATIES

CHAPTER I

ESSENTIAL REQUIREMENTS
OF A TREATY

Editor's note   The material on this subject consists of Article 1 of the 1953 Report followed by a revised text and commentary contained in the 1954 Report.

The Vienna Convention, which of course differs somewhat in approach, deals with the matters covered here in the following provisions.

ARTICLE 1

Scope of the present convention

The present convention applies to treaties between States.

ARTICLE 2

Use of terms

1. For the purposes of the present convention:

(*a*) 'treaty' means an international agreement concluded between States in written form and governed by international law, whether embodied in a single instrument or in two or more related instruments and whatever its particular designation. . .

ARTICLE 3

International agreements not within the scope of the present convention

The fact that the present convention does not apply to international agreements concluded between States and other subjects of international law or between such other subjects of international law, or to international agreements not in written form, shall not affect:

(*a*) the legal force of such agreements:

(*b*) the application to them of any of the rules set forth in the present convention to which they would be subject under international law independently of the convention;

(*c*) the application of the convention to the relations of States as between themselves under international agreements to which other subjects of international law are also parties.

1953 REPORT

ARTICLE I

ESSENTIAL REQUIREMENTS OF A TREATY

Treaties are agreements between States, including organizations of States, intended to create legal rights and obligations of the parties.

Comment

The object of this Article is not so much a definition of a treaty as a statement of its essential requirements and characteristics.

1. 'Treaties are *agreements* . . .' The consensual – the contractual – nature of treaties constitutes their principal characteristic which underlies the rules of customary international law in the matter of the conclusion, the binding force, the validity, the interpretation and the termination of treaties. The view is occasionally put forward that in the case of certain multilateral treaties of a general character approaching in some respects the process of international legislation or intended to provide a settlement of a general nature there is room for the application of rules somewhat different from those governing treaties at large. This view will be examined in Part VII of this draft which will be devoted to a consideration of special types of treaties and of the question of the extent to which they call for the application of rules differing from those applied to treaties generally. At least one significant pronouncement of the International Court of Justice shows that that view cannot be dismissed without detailed examination. Thus in the advisory opinion on *Reparation for Injuries Suffered in the Service of the United Nations* the Court considered the question whether the Charter of the United Nations could legally endow the United Nations with an international legal personality with an effect extending not only to its members but also to States outside the United Nations. The Court answered that question in the affirmative. It said: 'On this point, the Court's opinion is that fifty States, representing the vast majority of the members of the international community, had the power, in conformity with international law, to bring into being an entity possessing objective international personality, and not merely personality recognized by them alone, together with the capacity to bring international claims' (*I.C.J. Reports* 1949, p. 185). In a different sphere an authoritative Committee of Jurists appointed in 1920 by the Council of the League of

Nations to report on the question of the fortification of the Aaland Islands expressed the opinion that the Convention of 1856 between Great Britain, France and Russia embodying the principle of demilitarization of these islands was in the nature of 'a settlement regulating European interests' and that, as such, it 'constituted a special international status for the Aaland Islands' with the result that every interested State had the right to insist upon compliance with it (*L.N.O.J.* Special Supplement (1920), no. 3, pp. 17–19). In the advisory opinion on the *International Status of South-West Africa* the International Court of Justice held that the international rules regulating the Mandate constituted an international status for the territory (*I.C.J. Reports* 1950, p. 132). In his separate opinion in this case Judge McNair cited the Report of the Committee of Jurists in the *Aaland Islands* case in support of his view that Article 22 of the Covenant of the League of Nations relating to Mandates established a régime which 'has more than a purely contractual basis' with the result that 'the territories subjected to it are impressed with a special legal status' (at p. 154).

However, these and similar pronouncements which lend support to the view that some treaties may, in a sense, partake of the character of international legislation reaching out beyond the parties thereto are not inconsistent with the basic proposition that as between the parties such treaties are instruments of a contractual character. The practice in the matter of reservations, which was adhered to by the great majority of States in the past, was entirely based on the conception of treaties as contracts, namely, that a State appending a reservation to a treaty in law rejects an agreement reached by the signatories and makes a new offer. It is possible that in this particular case (see below, comment to Article 9) – as, indeed, with regard to other specific cases – it may be desirable, having regard to special problems of a multilateral treaty, to modify the automatic application of a rule otherwise generally applicable. However, this fact emphasizes rather than detracts from the consensual nature of all treaties. The principle that treaties are agreements of a contractual character is believed to be not only consistent with but also dictated by the preponderant practice in the matter of their validity, interpretation and termination. The persistency with which international tribunals resort to preparatory work for the elucidation of the intentions of the authors of multilateral treaties of a constitutional character – at least in cases in which that intention cannot be ascertained by other means – provides an instructive example of that attitude.

2. 'Treaties are agreements *between States, including organizations of States* . . .'

(i) This part of the definition of treaties, in so far as it excludes individuals and bodies other than organizations of States from being parties to treaties, follows from the fact that States only – acting either individually or in association – are the normal subjects of international intercourse and of international law. This means that agreements between States and individuals or juridical entities which are not States or organizations of States are not treaties even if the law governing such agreements is not the law of any particular State but general principles of law independent of any particular municipal system – as was, for instance, the case in the *Lena Goldfields* arbitration decided in 1930 between the Lena Goldfields Company and Soviet Russia (*Annual Digest*, 5 (1929–30), case no. 1). In the arbitration between the Sheikh of Abu Dhabi and the Petroleum Development Company, decided in 1951, the Umpire, Lord Asquith, held that no municipal law of any particular country was applicable to the interpretation of the concession agreement and that the terms of the agreement 'invite, indeed prescribe, the application of principles rooted in the good sense and common practice of the generality of civilized nations – a sort of "modern law of nature" ' (*I.C.L.Q.* 1 (1952), 251). The Concession Agreement between Persia and the Anglo-Iranian Oil Company of 1933 was described as a 'convention' and the arbitration clause of the agreement provided for the application of the law laid down in Article 38 of the Statute of the Permanent Court of International Justice. But the International Court of Justice declined to admit that the agreement partook of the nature of a treaty. It held that it was 'nothing more than a concessionary contract between a Government and a foreign corporation' (*I.C.J. Reports* 1952, p. 112). Occasionally it may be difficult to decide whether one of the contracting parties is a State or a subordinate agency thereof assimilated to a private corporation. This applies, for instance, to the Loan Agreement between the Government of the United Kingdom and the Export–Import Bank of Washington, described in the agreement as 'an agency of the United States of America' (Treaty Series, no. 78 (1950), Cmd. 8126). It is not feasible to provide in a general code of the law of treaties for border-line cases of this description.

(ii) The reference to 'States' in the above definition contains an element of ambiguity which it may be difficult to resolve in the definition itself. Normally 'States' would mean 'States which are independent members of the international community' or 'States which are normal subjects of international law'. The result of some such interpretation of the term would be, for instance, that agreements made between the protected and the protecting State, either at the time of the establishment of the protectorate or subsequently, could not be regarded as treaties. However, they have been so treated judicially – by both international and municipal tribunals. Rules and principles of international law applicable to treaties have been applied to them. Opinion is divided whether States which are protectorates are subjects of international law. Yet in the case between France and the United States concerning *Rights of Nationals of the United States of America in Morocco*, decided on 27 August 1952, the International Court of Justice seemed to associate itself with the view, not disputed by either party, that 'Morocco, even under the protectorate, has retained its personality as a State in international law' (*I.C.J. Reports* 1952, p. 185). It has been often – and correctly – stated that the question whether the protected State can conclude certain international treaties must be decided according to the terms of the particular treaty of protectorate. Agreements between the protecting and the protected State are frequent and there has often been no disposition, even on the part of the protecting State, to question their international character. Thus, for instance, in the proceedings before the Permanent Court of International Justice in connection with its advisory opinion on the *Jurisdiction of the Courts of Danzig* Poland did not seem to question the international character of the agreement concluded between her and Danzig – a protected State (*P.C.I.J.*, Series B, no. 15, p. 17). On 5 April 1947, the United Kingdom and the Sultanate of Muscat and Oman (which is a British protectorate) signed a Civil Air Agreement which was registered with the United Nations (*U.N.T.S.* 27, 287). In 1951 a comprehensive treaty of friendship, commerce and navigation was signed between the United Kingdom and the Sultan of Muscat and Oman and Dependencies (Muscat no. 1 (1952), Cmd. 8462). If the protecting and the protected State while disagreeing as to the interpretation of a particular provision in the agreement establishing the protectorate or of any treaty subsequently concluded between themselves were to agree to submit their dispute to an international tribunal, would the latter be entitled to consider the agreement to be a treaty and interpret it by reference to rules applicable to the interpretation of treaties? It may be difficult to give a negative answer to this question. Thus, to mention once more the judgment of the International Court of Justice in the case concerning *Rights of Nationals of the United States of America in Morocco*, the Court referred to and interpreted the treaties concerned with the establishment of the protectorate, in particular the Treaty of Fez of 1912 between the Sultan of Morocco and France. 'Under this treaty,' the Court said, 'Morocco remained a sovereign State but it made an arrangement of a contractual character whereby France undertook to exercise certain sovereign powers in the name and on behalf of Morocco, and, in principle, all of the international relations of Morocco' (*I.C.J. Reports* 1952, at p. 188).

Neither is it necessary – or, perhaps, permissible – to deny to an instrument the character of a treaty for the mere reason that a party to it is a State member of a federal State – a subject discussed in greater detail in Article 10. Thus according to the constitutions of many federal States members of the federation are authorized to enter into agreement either with one another or, to a much more limited degree, with foreign States. There has been no disposition, on the part of municipal courts, to deny to such agreements the character of treaties. In general, the relations between members of federations have been considered by the supreme tribunals of the countries in question as governed by international law. Of this tendency an instructive example is provided by the manner in which the German *Staatsgerichtshof* (in *Bremen* v. *Prussia, Annual Digest*, 3 (1925–6), case no. 266) and the Swiss Federal Court in *Canton of Thurgau* v. *Canton of St Gallen* (*ibid.* 4 (1927–8), case no. 289) applied the doctrine *rebus sic stantibus* to member States of a federal State. An international arbitral tribunal is unlikely to be confronted with the interpretation or application of treaties of this description, though it is conceivable that it may be called upon to do so either incidentally or by way of agreed submission by two parties. The International Court of Justice would probably be unable to do so, having regard to the terms of Article 34 of its

Statute – although the matter might not be free of difficulty in the case of treaties of member States of federal States such as the Ukraine or Byelorussia which have acquired a degree of formal international personality by nature of the constitution of the federation of which they are members and of their position in international organization (see below, comment to Article 10).

For these reasons, while the term 'States' in this Article must be deemed primarily to refer to contractual agreements concluded by fully independent States, its effect is not such as to preclude international judicial or other agencies from considering as treaties instruments to which the parties are communities which have been customarily described as States and which as a matter of internal and constitutional law can be considered States by virtue of their political cohesion, their internal autonomy and their historical status. On the other hand, whenever such dependent or subordinate States purport to conclude a treaty in disregard of international obligations and arrangements which limit their contractual capacity the instrument may be void because of incapacity. The matter – as well as the international position of federal States generally – is examined in Part III of the present draft (Conditions of Validity of Treaties, Article 10). The difficulty surrounding the subject is that it may be as inaccurate to say that the treaty-making power belongs only to fully independent States as it may be incorrect to assume that it belongs to every political unit described by the name of 'State'. It is equally unsatisfactory to attempt what is no more than a nominal solution by laying down, as is occasionally done, that the power to conclude treaties rests with States which are members of the international community. The latter expression is not self-explanatory – unless it signifies States endowed with the plenitude of international rights, including the right to conclude treaties in which case the statement merely begs the question. For this reason the formulation adopted in Article 1 is necessarily of a general character – leaving it to the application of Article 10 which is concerned with the capacity of the parties to resolve in a pragmatic manner the particular situations which may arise.[1]

---

[1] Up to the passing of the Act of 3 March 1871 which denied to Indian tribes the status of independent nations 'with whom the United States may contract by treaty' numerous treaties had been concluded between the United States and Indian tribes and ratified by

3. 'Treaties are agreements between States, *including organizations of States . . .*' States can exercise their capacity to conclude treaties either individually or when acting collectively as organizations created by a treaty. It follows that agreements concluded by international organizations with States or other international organizations must be regarded as treaties provided that they otherwise qualify as treaties under the terms of this Article. These include treaties concluded by the United Nations[1] with Members of the United Nations (such as the Agreement between the United Nations and the United States of America regarding the Headquarters of the United Nations: *U.N.T.S.* 11, 11), and with States which are not members of the United Nations (such as those with Switzerland on the Privileges and Immunities of the United Nations: *ibid.* 1, 163; concerning the Ariana Site: *ibid.* p. 153; and concerning postage stamps for the Geneva Office of the United Nations: *ibid.* 43, 327); and a number of agreements with specialized agencies and other international organizations. They also include agreements concluded between or by international organizations other than the United Nations such as those concluded by the specialized agencies between themselves (such as the Agreement of 1948 between the Food and Agriculture Organization and the World Health Organization providing for close co-operation and consultation in matters of common concern: *ibid.* 76, 172), or with States (for instance, the Agreement and accompanying instruments between the International Labour Organization and Switzerland of 27 May 1948: *ibid.* 15, 377). These agreements to which the United Nations or a specialized agency are parties have been properly registered under the provision of Article 102 of the Charter which requires the registration of treaties and international agreements. It has been suggested that the circumstance which makes them registrable is not that the United Nations or a specialized agency is a party but that at least one party is a member of the United Nations. However, a considerable number of agreements have been properly registered to which only the United Nations and specialized agencies

the President with the consent and approval of the Senate according to a procedure identical with that followed with regard to ordinary treaties. For details see Reiff in *A.J.* 30 (1936), 67–9. See also Octavio in *Hague Recueil* (1930)(i), p. 252. If the United States had agreed, prior to 1871, to submit to an international tribunal a dispute with an Indian tribe concerning the interpretation of a treaty concluded with it and duly ratified by the President as a treaty, would that tribunal have been prevented from considering it as such and from applying to it rules of international law?

[1] See generally Parry, 'Treaty Making Power of the United Nations', *B.Y.* 26 (1949), 108–49.

are parties.[1] Neither has the use of the instrumentality of registered agreements been limited, among organizations of States, to specialized agencies as may be seen from the Agreement of 25 January 1951 between the United Nations International Children's Emergency Fund and the Government of Paraguay concerning the activities of the former in Paraguay (*ibid.* 79, 10). On occasions a number of international organizations appear as a contracting party on the one side and a State on the other.[2] International practice shows examples, even prior to the establishment of the United Nations, of agreements concluded between States and international organizations or international organs. Thus on 28 June 1932 an agreement, registered with the League of Nations, was concluded between Yugoslavia, Roumania and the International Commission of the Danube concerning the setting up of special services at the Iron Gates (*L.N.T.S.* 140, 191; Hudson, *Legislation*, VI, 47). On 4 August 1924, the Reparations Commission concluded a comprehensive agreement with Germany (*L.N.T.S.* 41, 432; Hudson, *Legislation*, II, 1301). There are other examples of such treaties.

There appears to be no decisive reason why, subject to any modification as examined in Part VII of this draft of a code of the law of treaties, the rules otherwise applicable to treaties should not apply to those concluded by or between international organizations created by and composed of States. On the contrary, it would seem desirable to direct political and juristic effort to making available, in the interest of the progressive integration of international society on a functional basis, the experience of the law of treaties to the collective activities of States in their manifold manifestations.[3] This is so also for the additional reason that the part of multilateral treaties is likely to grow in a world of growing inter-dependence – not only because of the emergence of new interests calling for international regulation of general character, but also because in many cases the essential uniformity or identity of the subject matter of questions regulated in

[1] The reasons which, it may be assumed, have prompted the Secretary-General to register these and other international agreements to which specialized agencies are parties are cogently stated in an article contributed to the *B.Y.* 25 (1948), by Mr O. Schachter, a member of the Secretariat of the United Nations (pp. 130–2).

[2] For instance, in the Basic Agreement of 15 December 1950 between the United Nations, the Food and Agriculture Organization, the International Civil Aviation Organization, the International Labour Organization, the United Nations Educational, Scientific and Cultural Organization and the World Health Organization, and the United Kingdom being the Administrative Power of Cyrenaica and Tripolitania, for the provision of technical assistance: *U.N.T.S.* 76, 122.

[3] Article 748 of Fiore's *Code* lays down that the capacity to conclude treaties may be 'possessed by associations to which international personality has been attributed'.

the past by bilateral agreements may increasingly call for the adoption of the machinery of multilateral treaties as being best suited to give effect to such uniformity or identity. The achievement of that object will not be facilitated by questioning the fundamental quality of treaties in relation to the instruments in question.

4. 'Treaties are agreements between States, including organizations of States, *intended to create legal rights and obligations . . .*' There exist formal international instruments solemnly declared or signed by representatives of States or unilaterally proclaimed by them which, however, are in the nature of statements of policy rather than instruments intended to lay down legal rights and obligations. Examples of such instruments are the so-called Atlantic Charter of August 1941 in which the President of the United States and the British Prime Minister representing His Majesty's Government in the United Kingdom agreed 'on certain common principles in the national policies of their respective Governments on which they base their high hopes of a better future for the world' (*A.J.* 35 (1941), Special Supplement, 191); the Agreed Declaration by the President of the United States of America, the Prime Minister of the United Kingdom of Great Britain and Northern Ireland, and the Prime Minister of Canada relating to Atomic Energy, signed at Washington on 15 November 1945 (*U.N.T.S.* 3, 131); the Moscow Instrument of 1 November 1943 made by the Heads of the United States, British and Soviet Governments containing the solemn declaration relating to the punishment of war criminals (Cmd. 6668); and the Universal Declaration of Human Rights adopted by the General Assembly of the United Nations in 1948. In some cases the absence of a true contractual nexus in the instruments in question is somewhat obscured by the form, expressed in the traditional form of agreement, given to the instrument. Thus the communiqué on the Moscow Conference, signed on 27 December 1945, and the Report of the Ministers of Foreign Affairs of Soviet Russia, the United States of America and the United Kingdom, dated 26 December 1945, was registered with the United Nations (*U.N.T.S.* 20, 272) as 'together constituting an agreement relating to the preparation of Peace Treaties and to certain other problems'. The registered text of the instrument states that it 'came into force on 27 December 1945, by signature'. Yet the communiqué which forms part of the instrument merely stated that 'discussions took place on an informal and exploratory basis and agreement was reached on the following questions'. The legal nature of assurances given in an instrument may

be problematical notwithstanding the fact that it is couched in the form usually given to binding agreements such as an exchange of notes.[1] The same applies to cases in which the formal character of an otherwise general undertaking is emphasized by the fact that, like an ordinary treaty, it contains provisions for adhesion by other States. This was the case, for instance, with regard to the 'Declaration by the United Nations' of 1 January 1942 subscribing to the common programme of principles and purposes embodied in the Atlantic Charter, pledging the full employment of the resources of each Government in the common struggle, and undertaking not to make a separate armistice and peace with the enemy (*A.J.* 36 (1942), Supplement, 191).

The fact that the obligation provided for in the instrument can be fulfilled by a somewhat nominal act of the parties does not necessarily detract from its character as a treaty. To this category belong treaties embodying the obligation of consultation such as the Nine-Power Treaty of 6 February 1922 concerning China. Similarly an undertaking to negotiate implies a legal obligation to do so although it necessarily leaves a wider margin of discretion to the State bound by it.[2] A legal duty must also be deemed to exist in those marginal cases in which, by virtue of the instrument in question, a State reserves for itself the right to determine both the existence and the extent of the obligation undertaken by it, as, for instance, in the case of some declarations of acceptance of the optional clause of Article 36 of the Statute of the International Court of Justice in which the declaring States have reserved for themselves the right to determine whether a matter falls within their domestic jurisdiction. For such determination must take place in accordance with the implied obligation to act in good faith. The fact that the interested

---

[1] On 4 June 1940 the Prime Minister of the United Kingdom issued a statement to the effect that should the British Isles become untenable for British ships of war, the British Fleet would in no event be surrendered or sunk but would be sent overseas for the defence of other parts of the Empire. On 29 August 1940 the following inquiry was received by the British ambassador to the United States: 'The Government of the United States would respectfully inquire whether the foregoing statement represents the settled policy of the British Government.' An affirmative answer was given. The inquiry and the answer were published in the form of an exchange of notes: *Department of State Bulletin* (7 September 1940), 3, 63, 191; *A.J.* 35 (1941), Supplement, 37.

[2] Also, although the Declaration of Denmark, Finland, Iceland, Norway and Sweden of 27 October 1938 for the purpose of establishing similar rules of neutrality did not probably amount to a reciprocal treaty obligation, with regard to the substance of the matters regulated therein, the Declaration (which was registered with the League of Nations: *L.N.T.S.* 188, 293; Hudson, *Legislation*, VIII, 56) included an element of obligation by virtue of the agreement not to modify such rules 'without first giving, if possible, sufficient notice to the other four Governments to permit an exchange of views on the matter'.

State is the sole judge of the existence of the obligation is, while otherwise of considerable importance, irrelevant for the determination of the legal character of the instrument.[1] This is also the position with regard to treaties, such as the North Atlantic Treaty of 4 April 1949, in which each party agrees to assist others by 'such action as it deems necessary' in case of attack directed against them. In other cases, as with regard to the reservation of action in self-defence proclaimed by some States in connection with their signature of the General Treaty for the Renunciation of War of 27 August 1928 and coupled with an assertion of the right of these States to determine

---

[1] The position may be different when the effective fulfilment of the obligation does not depend upon the will of the contracting State. Thus it has been held, in effect, by the International Court of Justice in the advisory opinion concerning the *Status of South-West Africa* that an obligation to conclude an agreement is a contradiction in terms and cannot legally exist. The Court said: 'An "agreement" implies consent of the parties concerned, including the Mandatory Power in case of territories held under Mandate ... The parties must be free to accept or reject the terms of the contemplated agreement. No party can impose its terms on the other party' (*I.C.J. Reports* 1950, p. 139). There is, however, room for the view that, like any other obligation, an agreement to conclude an agreement must be interpreted in good faith and in a reasonable manner and that, accordingly, the State undertaking to conclude an agreement is legally bound to fulfil that undertaking in so far as it lies in its power. There is an obligation to accept an agreement offered by the other party if its terms are such that an impartial tribunal would consider them as taking into account the legitimate interests of both parties. The awards in the *Tacna–Arica* arbitration of 1925 between Chile and Peru (*Annual Digest*, 4 (1925–6), case no. 269) and in the *Spanish Zone of Morocco* case between Great Britain and Spain (*Annual Digest*, 2 (1923–4), case no. 8) seem to affirm the legal nature of *pactum de contrahendo*. In its advisory opinion of 18 October 1931 concerning the *Railway Traffic between Poland and Lithuania*, the Permanent Court of International Justice stated that 'The Court is indeed justified in considering that the engagement incumbent on the two Governments in conformity with the Council Resolution is not only to enter into negotiations, but also to pursue them as far as possible, with a view to concluding agreements ... But an obligation to negotiate does not imply an obligation to reach agreement, nor in particular does it imply that Lithuania, by undertaking to negotiate, has assumed an engagement, and is in consequence obliged to conclude the administrative and technical agreements indispensable for the establishment of traffic on the Landwarow-Kaisiadorys railway sector' (*P.C.I.J.* Series A/B, no. 42, p. 116). The relevant part of the Resolution of the Council was a recommendation to 'the two Governments to enter into direct negotiations as soon as possible in order to establish such relations between the two neighbouring States as will ensure "the good understanding between nations upon which peace depends" '. However, where the terms of the *pactum de contrahendo* are precise and mandatory and, in particular, where they are coupled with the conferment, upon an international tribunal, of jurisdiction in disputes arising out of the interpretation or application of the treaty, the legally binding character of the obligation seems to admit of little doubt. Thus Article 9 of the Treaty of Peace with Japan of 8 September 1951 provided that 'Japan will enter promptly into negotiations with the Allied Powers so desiring for the conclusion of bilateral and multilateral agreements providing for the regulation or limitation of fishery and development of fisheries on the high seas'. Identical provisions are contained in Article 12 (in the matter of trading, maritime and other commercial relations) and Article 13 (in the matter of civil air transport). Article 22 of the treaty confers upon the International Court of Justice jurisdiction in disputes, not otherwise settled, concerning the interpretation or execution of the treaty. There is a definite obligation and no mere *pactum de contrahendo* in cases such as Articles 284 and 354 of the Treaty of Versailles in which a party agrees to accept a treaty or arrangement to be placed before it.

when the contingency of recourse to self-defence has arisen, the freedom of action thus claimed refers only to the decision called for by the exigencies of the situation and permitting of no delay. As in other cases of self-defence, it does not exclude a final impartial determination of the legitimacy of the action thus taken. There is in instruments of this description no ground for questioning their legal character as treaties.

On the other hand the absence of a true treaty relationship, notwithstanding the formality and the solemnity of the instrument, may be apparent from the terms, the designation and the history of the instrument in question. This was probably the position with regard to the Agreement – often referred to as the Lansing–Ishii Gentlemen's Agreement of 2 November 1917 – between the United States and Japan on the subject of immigration. On occasion, as was the case with regard to the Universal Declaration of Human Rights approved by the General Assembly in 1948, the absence of a legal obligation is not open to doubt when the parties expressly disclaim the intention to assume an obligation of this nature. In all such cases the form given to an instrument is not decisive for the determination of its legal character as a treaty. In the event of a dispute on the subject it must properly be a question for judicial determination whether the instrument, whatever its description, is in fact intended to create legal rights and obligations between the parties and as such comes within the category of treaties. The circumstance that it has been registered with the United Nations, by one or more of the parties, as an international treaty or engagement is not decisive for determining this question – although the fact of its registration as the result of joint action by the parties raises a strong presumption in that direction.

5. 'Treaties are agreements between States, including organizations of States, intended to create legal rights and obligations *of the parties*.' As a rule, treaties create legal rights and obligations between the parties only – a subject which will be examined in detail in Part IV of this draft relating to the operation of treaties. However, the principle that treaties are instruments intended to create legal rights and obligations between *the parties thereto* does not necessarily mean that their legal effect is necessarily restricted to the parties. Attention has been drawn above (paragraph 1) to the pronouncement of the International Court of Justice in that sense. The report, already referred to, of the Commission of Jurists appointed in 1920 by the Council of the League of Nations in connection with the

Aaland Islands shows in a different sphere – in the creation of a so-called public law of Europe in relation to a general international settlement – the possibility of the same overreaching effect of treaties. Some instruments of a general, quasi-legislative character appear to claim to regulate the conduct of States not parties thereto. To this category belongs Article 2 (6) of the Charter of the United Nations which lays down that 'the Organization shall ensure that States which are not Members of the United Nations act in accordance with these Principles [of Article 2] so far as may be necessary for the maintenance of international peace and security'. The Article in question imposes no legal obligation upon non-member States. It claims for the United Nations the right to regulate, in the interest of the maintenance of international peace and security, the conduct of non-member States. It is possible that, with the growing integration of international society, collective treaties may, by general consent, be held to produce not only actual compliance but also legal rights and obligations in relation to States which are not parties thereto. To that extent, without losing their character as treaties as between the parties, they may also become instruments of international legislation properly so called.

Notes

1. Treaties as agreements. This element of the definition of a treaty is open to the objection that it fails to distinguish between the purely contractual type of treaty and the so-called legislative type, the *traités-lois*. The special rapporteur ventures to hope that, in the present context, that objection will not be advanced. For whatever may be the legal consequences of that distinction – a controversial matter examined in Part VII of this draft – it does not alter the fact that at present international instruments creating legal rights and obligations have their source in the agreement either of the parties who accept them in the first instance or of those who adhere to them. It may be noted, however, in this connection that the general trend of legal opinion is to deny any essential difference – for the purpose of the elaboration of rules governing their creation, operation and termination – between the two types of treaties.[1] The essence of both is that they lay down rules governing the conduct of the parties.

2. Treaties as agreements to which organizations of States are parties. The expression 'organizations of States' is here intended as

---

[1] See, for example, *Harvard Research*, vol. III, *A.J.* 29 (1935), Supplement (general comment to Article 1, pp. 688, 689); Rousseau, p. 136; Pallieri, *Hague Recueil*, 74 (1949) (i), 513.

synonymous with the expression 'international organizations' conceived as entities which are created by treaty between States, whose membership is composed primarily of States, which have permanent organs of their own, and whose international personality is recognized either by the terms of their constituent instrument or in virtue of express recognition by a treaty concluded by them with a State.

The question, already referred to in the comment, whether the Code on the Law of Treaties to be drafted by the Commission should concern itself with treaties concluded by international organizations was discussed by the Commission during its sessions in 1950 and 1951. The view which it provisionally adopted was that agreements by or between organizations of States do not fall within the province of the law of treaties to be formulated by the Commission. That view, it is submitted, needs revision. The fact of the existence of the very great number of agreements concluded by and between the various international organizations would render incomplete and deficient any codification of the law of treaties which would leave such agreements out of account. Numerous agreements of this type have been entered into by the United Nations as such. A substantial number of them have been concluded by the Economic and Social Council in pursuance of Article 63 of the Charter which provides that the Economic and Social Council may enter into agreements with specialized agencies defining the terms on which the agency concerned should be brought into relationship with the United Nations.[1] A large number of agreements have been concluded between the various specialized agencies such as the International Labour Organization, the Food and Agriculture Organization, the United Nations Educational, Scientific and Cultural Organization and the World Health Organization. These agreements are what has been described as 'essentially treaties of amity and goodwill'[2] inasmuch as they provide for close co-operation and consultation in matters of common concern. That feature does not deprive them of the character of treaties. The same applies, more conspicuously, to the great number

[1] Such agreements are now in force between the United Nations and ten specialized agencies, namely, the International Labour Organization, United Nations Educational, Scientific and Cultural Organization, Food and Agriculture Organization, International Civil Aviation Organization, the Fund, the Bank, World Health Organization, the Universal Postal Union, International Telecommunication Union and World Meteorological Organization. A detailed study of the history of these agreements and an analysis of their provisions is contained in the *Report of Action taken in pursuance of the Agreements between the United Nations and the Specialized Agencies (Official Records of the Economic and Social Council*, Ninth Session, E/1317). See also Sharp, *International Organization*, I (1947), 460–74 and II (1948), 247–67.

[2] Jenks, *B.Y.* 28 (1951), 68.

of agreements concluded between the specialized agencies with various States concerning the legal status and the immunities of these organizations, as well as in other matters, within the territories of the States concerned. These include agreements between the United Nations and the United States of America, the United Nations and Switzerland, the United Nations Educational, Scientific and Cultural Organization and France, the International Labour Organization and Switzerland, the World Health Organization and Switzerland, the Food and Agriculture Organization and Italy, the International Civil Aviation Organization and Canada, the International Refugee Organization and Switzerland, the International Telecommunication Union and Switzerland, and the Universal Postal Union and Switzerland. An analysis of any of these treaties will show how closely they approach the traditional type of treaty. Thus the final clauses of the Agreement concluded between the Swiss Federal Council and the World Health Organization on 12 January 1949 and regulating the legal status of the World Health Organization in Switzerland read like the final clauses of most other treaties with regard to settlement of disputes as to the interpretation and application of the agreement, entry into force, approval by the competent constitutional authorities, modification and denunciation of the agreement, and the like (*U.N.T.S.* 26, 333). The degree to which agreements concluded by international organizations exhibit and have been judicially treated as exhibiting the common characteristics of treaties may be gauged from the manner in which Judge Read in his opinion in the case concerning the *International Status of South-West Africa* considered the question whether as the result of a series of acts and declarations of the Government of South Africa an agreement had been brought about between the United Nations and South Africa. He said: 'It is unnecessary to discuss the juridical nature of an international agreement. It is sufficient, for the present purposes, to state that an "arrangement agreed between" the United Nations and the Union [of South Africa] necessarily included two elements: a meeting of minds; and an intention to constitute a legal obligation' (*I.C.J. Reports* 1950, p. 170).

Agreements by and between international organizations have now become a prominent feature of international relations. The international personality of international organizations – i.e. of organizations of States – is becoming generally recognized. The capacity to conclude treaties is both a corollary of international personality and a condition of the effective fulfilment of their functions on the part of the international organizations. It is, for instance, with the help, *inter alia*, of some such chain of reasoning that the International Court of Justice in the advisory opinion on *Reparation for Injuries Suffered in the Service of the United Nations* affirmed the international personality of the United Nations. After referring to the Convention on the Privileges and Immunities of the United Nations of 1946 which 'creates rights and duties between each of the signatories and the Organization', it said: 'It must be acknowledged that the Members [of the United Nations], by entrusting certain functions to it, with the attendant duties and responsibilities, have clothed it with the competence required to enable those functions to be effectively discharged' (*I.C.J. Reports* 1949, p. 179). The treaty-making power of international organizations is one of the significant instruments for their proper functioning and it seems desirable that that instrument should receive adequate recognition and elaboration. In fact, there would appear to be no reason why, in the sphere of the treaty-making power, States acting collectively should not be in the position to do what they can do individually. Quite apart from the function of the International Law Commission to develop international law, the treaty-making power of international organizations has become so much part of international practice that the inclusion, within the category of treaties, of the agreements made by and between them will come in fact within the function of the Commission concerned with the codification of existing law. It would be unsatisfactory, it is submitted, to adopt the position that although agreements made by international organizations are treaties they ought, for one reason or another, somehow to be left out of the orbit of the law of treaties as codified by the International Law Commission. Any such limitation of the codification of the law of treaties is probably as open to objection as the exclusion, from its purview, of exchanges of notes – a subject discussed, from this point of view, in the comment to Article 2. Reasoning of that character might lead to the exclusion of what some consider to be legislative treaties – which, in their opinion, differ radically from the traditional type of contractual treaties. The result might be to reduce to inconspicuous dimensions the entire task of codification of the law of treaties. The work of the Commission on the subject ought to be complete both as a matter of principle and as a matter of assisting in the development of what is becoming a growing and beneficent aspect of relations of States. For these reasons although at its session of 1951 the Commission seems to have decided not to include in the codification of the law of treaties agreements made by and between international organizations, it is submitted that that decision ought not to be adhered to. In so far as, in particular matters, specific types of treaties require regulation differing from that applying to treaties generally, the consideration and formulation of such modifications falls properly within the purview of codification.

3. The wording 'agreements between States including organizations of States' has not been adopted without a previous consideration of alternative formulations. The purpose of the wording as formulated is to lay down, in the first instance, that only States or organizations of States can be parties to treaties. The present formulation is also intended to exclude the inference that it is sufficient if an instrument is concluded, *on the one part*, by a State or an organization of States and that the other party need not be a State or an organization of States. The wording 'agreements between States and (or) organizations of States' might equally lend itself to a wrong interpretation. In fact there are three kinds of agreements, from the point of view of the parties thereto, contemplated in the present article: (1) agreements between States; (2) agreements between States and organizations of States; (3) agreements between organizations of States. It is believed that the present wording includes all three categories.

4. No reference is made in this article to the requirement adopted in Article 1 (*a*) of the Harvard Draft Convention and, for a time, in the tentative Articles approved by the Commission that an instrument, in order to be a treaty, must establish a relationship under international law. The apparent intention of that formula was that, in order to constitute a treaty, the instrument must, according to the intention of the parties or otherwise, be governed by rules of international law. The reason underlying the view thus adopted was, it would seem, the existence of agreements which regulate matters usually falling within the sphere of private law such as loans of money, purchase of foods, regulation of prices, leases or purchase of immovable property, and the like. With the growth of economic activity under the management of the State the scope of agreements of this kind has tended to increase. This applies, in particular, to the wide range of so-called commodity agreements. Yet, it is doubtful whether such agreements can be put in a special category so far as the law applicable is concerned. They are all governed, in the last resort, by international law. It is not the subjection of an agreement to international law which makes of it a treaty. It is its quality as a

treaty which causes it to be regulated by international law. This is so even if – which is an exceptional occurrence – the parties stipulate that it shall be governed by the municipal law of one of them. For in that case the specific law thus agreed upon is the consequence of the will of the parties. As the result of some such provision the law applicable is transformed into conventional international law expressing, in the terminology of Article 38 of the Statute of the International Court of Justice, 'rules expressly recognized by the contesting parties'. Usually, however, such transactions are governed by general principles of law applicable to them and the rules relating to the interpretation of treaties. For this reason, provided that the instrument otherwise fulfils the requirements of a treaty, it establishes *ipso facto* a relationship under international law between the States or organizations of States in question. This applies even to the case, exceptional in modern conditions, of treaties containing marriage arrangements between members of reigning houses.[1] The definition of a treaty as formulated in Article 1 is wide enough to include treaties of this description.

1954 REPORT

ARTICLE I

ESSENTIAL REQUIREMENTS OF A TREATY

1. This article of the special rapporteur's first report[2] runs as follows:

> Treaties are agreements between States, including organizations of States, intended to create legal rights and obligations of the parties.

2. In the light of further study the special rapporteur submits for consideration of the Commission the question whether it may not be desirable to add either in the article itself or in the accompanying comment some such statement of the law as follows:

In the absence of evidence to the contrary, an instrument finally accepted by

---

[1] Such as the Treaty of 27 October 1923 between Great Britain and Sweden concerning the marriage of Lady Louise Mountbatten to the Crown Prince of Sweden. The treaty, signed by the plenipotentiaries of the two sovereigns, was subject to ratification and was registered with the League of Nations (*L.N.T.S.* 22, 387). For other examples of such treaties see Rousseau, p. 145.

[2] A/CN.4/63, in *Yearbook of the International Law Commission*, 1953, vol. II.

both parties in the customary form of an international undertaking and registered with the United Nations in accordance with Article 102 of the Charter shall be deemed to be an instrument creating legal rights and obligations.

3. This aspect of the definition of a treaty is covered by paragraph 4 of the relevant comment to Article 1 of the first report. At the end of this part of the comment the special rapporteur stated as follows: 'The circumstance that it [the instrument] has been registered with the United Nations, by one or more of the parties, as an international treaty or engagement is not decisive for determining this question [i.e. whether the instrument is intended to create legal rights and obligations] – although the fact of its registration as the result of joint action by the parties raises a strong presumption in that direction.' The special rapporteur now believes that this passage requires reconsideration in the light of the amendment as formulated above. This is so for the reason that unless some such rule is adopted, the legal nature – and the binding character – of a large number of instruments may remain uncertain.

4. In the first instance, as already stated in the first report, the fact that the extent of the application of the instrument is left in some respects to the appreciation of the parties and that, as the result, the scope of the obligation is indefinite and elastic, is not a decisive factor for denying that there is in existence a legal duty to be fulfilled in good faith. This is so even if, in what must be regarded as the typical case in treaties of this nature, the instrument contains no provisions, or purely nominal provisions, for the settlement of disputes arising out of the application or the interpretation of the treaty. A number of instruments will illustrate this aspect of the problem:

5. Thus Article 6 of the Agreement of 27 April 1951 between the United States of America and Denmark covering the defence of Greenland (*U.N.T.S.* 94 (1951), 45) provides that 'the Government of the United States of America agrees to co-operate to the fullest degree with the Government of the Kingdom of Denmark and its authorities in Greenland in carrying out operations under this agreement', and that 'every effort will be made to avoid any contact between United States personnel and the local population which the Danish authorities do not consider desirable for the conduct of operations under this agreement'. The reference to 'every effort' being made by the American authorities in circumstances which the Danish authorities 'consider desirable' is indefinite and elastic. It is

not believed, however, that they derogate from the legal nature of the obligations thus undertaken.[1]

6. The same applies to instruments such as the Preliminary Agreement between the United States of America and Czechoslovakia of 11 July 1942 relating to the principles applying to mutual aid in the prosecution of the war against aggression (*U.N.T.S.* 90 (1951), 258). On the face of it, the agreement is non-committal. In Article 1 the Government of the United States of America binds itself to continue to supply the Provisional Government of Czechoslovakia with such defence articles, defence services and defence information *as the President of the United States of America shall authorize* to be transferred or provided – a, *prima facie*, nominal obligation. In Article 11 the Provisional Government of Czechoslovakia undertakes to continue to contribute to the defence of the United States of America and the strengthening thereof and to provide such articles, services, facilities and information *as it may be in the position to supply*. While other parts of the Agreement incorporate clear legal obligations in the matter of the transfer, payment and return of the goods supplied by the United States, Article 7 seems to formulate what is no more than a principle of policy. It lays down that the final determination of the benefits to be provided to the United States of America by the Provisional Government of Czechoslovakia, in return for the aid furnished under the Act of Congress of 11 March 1941, shall be such as not to burden commerce between the two countries, but to promote mutually advantageous economic relations between them and the betterment of the world. Notwithstanding the vague and indefinite formulation

---

[1] This is also probably the position with respect to various types of agreement of an economic nature such as the Agreement concerning the exchange of commodities between Denmark and Poland of 7 December 1949 (*U.N.T.S.* 81 (1951), 22). While some provisions of that agreement admit of elasticity of interpretation, such as the provision that the parties shall grant to each other as *favourable treatment as possible* in the issue of import and export authorization so as to facilitate the development of reciprocal exchanges, other clauses are of a definite nature, such as the obligation of the two Governments to authorize the export of goods specified in the schedule to the agreement. Similar considerations apply to such instruments as the Exchange of Notes constituting an agreement between the Netherlands and Luxembourg regarding the placement of Netherlands agricultural workers in Luxembourg of 17 and 25 August 1950 (*U.N.T.S.* 81 (1951), 14). While the notes contain a number of provisions of a somewhat vague character such as that 'in principle, the entire territory of the Grand Duchy shall be available for permanent or temporary settlement by Netherlands agricultural workers', or that the Luxembourg authorities shall provide Netherlands agricultural workers with all information that might be useful to them, other provisions are couched in terms of clear legal obligations such as that the Netherlands agricultural workers and their families shall receive in Luxembourg for equal work and performance remuneration equal to that customary in Luxembourg for workers of the same category in the same district, or that Netherlands agricultural workers shall be entitled to make transfers each month of their surplus wages and savings.

of those provisions, they are not such as to render impossible their interpretation, by reference to the overriding principle of good faith, by an arbitral or judicial body proceeding on the basis of law. The widest possible latitude of appreciation was implied in the advisory opinion of the Permanent Court of International Justice given in 1931 in deciding whether the customs union between Germany and Austria endangered or alienated Austrian independence (Series A/B, no. 41). This fact did not deprive the relevant provisions of the Treaty of St Germain and of the Geneva Protocol of 1922 of their character as binding treaty obligations.

7. The recent series of mutual defence assistance agreements between the United States of America and some other countries provides, to a more conspicuous degree, another example of instruments of that character. Thus Article 1 of the Mutual Defence Assistance Agreement between the United States of America and France of 27 January 1950 (*U.N.T.S.* 80 (1951), 172) provides 'that each Government, consistently with the principle that economic recovery is essential to international peace and security and must be given clear priority, will make or continue to make available to the other, and to such other Governments as the parties hereto may in each case agree upon, such equipment, materials, services or other military assistance as the Government furnishing such assistance may authorize and in accordance with such terms and conditions as may be agreed'. The agreement also provides, in Article 2, for the obligation of the French Government to facilitate the production and the transfer to the Government of the United States of raw and semi-processed materials required by the United States as a result of deficiencies or potential deficiencies of its own resources; and it provides, in Article 3, for such security measures 'as may be agreed in each case between the two Governments in order to prevent the disclosure or compromise of classified military articles, services or information'.[1] In a sense these provisions, which leave for future agreement the determination of the extent of the substantive

---

[1] Similar provisions are contained in the Mutual Defence Assistance Agreement with Luxembourg of 27 January 1950 (*U.N.T.S.* 80 (1951), 188); with the Netherlands of 27 January 1950 (*ibid.* p. 220); with Norway of 27 January 1950 (*ibid.* p. 242); and with the United Kingdom of 27 January 1950 (*ibid.* p. 262). The same applies to the Exchange of Notes constituting an agreement between the United States of America and Italy relating to mutual defence assistance of 27 January 1950 (*U.N.T.S.* 80 (1951), 146). In that agreement the two Governments undertook to take appropriate measures, consistent with security, to keep the public informed of operations under the agreement. They also agreed to take security measures, to be agreed upon in the future, in order to prevent disclosure or compromise of classified military articles, services or information. An annex to the agreement makes provision for privileges and immunities to the missions of the two States.

obligations of the parties, are no more than *pacta de contrahendo*. They are further weakened by qualifications such as that the amount of assistance shall be such as the Government in question shall authorize. Nevertheless, it would not be accurate to maintain that an instrument of that character is no more than a pious statement of intention as distinguished from an assumption of binding legal obligations.

8. Neither is the legal nature of the instrument affected by its designation as a declaration of policy, especially if it is described as an agreement and if in other respects it imposes ascertainable obligations upon the parties. This applies, for instance, to the Declaration by the French Republic constituting an agreement on commercial policy and related matters of 28 May 1946 (*U.N.T.S.* 84 (1951), 152). While the Declaration opens with the statement that 'the Government of the United States of America and the Provisional Government of the French Republic, having concluded comprehensive discussion on commercial policy and related matters, find themselves in full agreement on the general principles which they desire to see established to achieve the liberation and expansion of international trade, which they deem to be essential to the realization of world-wide prosperity and lasting peace', and continues that 'the two Governments have agreed that important benefits would accrue to both countries from a substantial expansion of French exports to the United States', it contains definite clauses on such matters as the obligation of the French Government to accord to American nationals who have suffered damage to their properties in France, through causes originating in the war, compensation equal to that payable to French nationals having the same types and extent of losses.

9. The same considerations apply to purely administrative agreements which, having regard to their nature and subject matter, leave a considerable measure of discretion to the authorities in question. Thus Article 19 of the Agreement of 12 July and 28 August 1948 between the Post Office of the United Kingdom of Great Britain and Northern Ireland and the Shereefian Post and Telegraph Administration for the exchange of money orders (*U.N.T.S.* 90 (1951), 84) provides as follows (*ibid.* p. 94): 'Each of the two administrations may, in extraordinary circumstances which would be of a nature to justify the measure, suspend temporarily or definitely the money order service on condition of giving immediate notice thereof (if necessary by telegraph) to the other administration. The administration of the United Kingdom may also in case of abuse by

the transmission of large sums of money as money orders raise the rate of commission charged.' There is no warrant for the suggestion that instruments of that nature do not, on account of either the large measure of discretion inherent in their application or of their purely administrative character, exhibit the essential characteristics of an international treaty.

10. As will be seen presently (see paragraph 14), there are types of treaties which raise the same problem, namely, whether an instrument cast in the usual forms of an international undertaking – i.e. an instrument signed and formally accepted by the parties or a unilateral declaration having the same effect – constitutes a treaty conferring legal rights and imposing legal obligations. The same problem arises occasionally in the sphere of the private law of contract when courts are called upon to determine whether an instrument creates legal rights and duties. It was stated in the following terms by Lord Justice Atkin in *Rose & Frank Co.* v. *J. R. Crompton Bros. Ltd.*:[1] 'To create a contract there must be a common intention of the parties to enter into legal obligations . . . Such an intention ordinarily will be inferred when parties enter into an agreement which in other respects conforms to the rules of law as to the formation of contracts. It may be negatived impliedly by the nature of the agreed promise or promises.'

11. The difficulties inherent in the problem are shown in the statement that 'the intention of the parties to enter into legal obligations . . . may be negatived impliedly by the nature of the agreed promise or promises.' The special rapporteur does not consider that that formulation can be of assistance in determining whether what on the face of it appears to be a treaty is in fact a treaty, namely, whether it creates legal rights and obligations. While in the sphere of private law the informality and variety of private arrangements may permit an inquiry into the question whether the nature of the promise is such as to create legal rights and obligations, it is believed that with regard to formal international compacts such intention must be implied from the fact of the formality of the instrument unless there is cogent and conclusive evidence to the contrary. Undoubtedly, the legal rights and obligations do not extend further than is warranted by the terms of the treaty. The fact that the instrument is a treaty does

---

[1] [1923] 2 K.B. 261, at p. 293. In *Balfour* v. *Balfour* ([1919] 2 K.B. 571) he said: '[such agreements] are not sued upon, not because the parties are reluctant to enforce their legal rights when the agreement is broken, but because the parties, in the inception of the arrangement, never intended that they should be sued upon'.

not imply an intention of the parties to endow it with the fullest possible measure of effectiveness. They may intend its effectiveness to be drastically limited. But, subject to that consideration which must be evidenced by the terms of the treaty and any other available evidence, the guiding assumption is that the instrument creates legal rights and obligations. Any measure of discretion and freedom of appreciation, however wide, which it leaves to the parties must be exercised in accordance with the legal principle of good faith. Although the parties may have intended a treaty to mean little, no assumption is permissible that they intended it to mean nothing and that the instrument concluded in the form of a treaty – with the concomitant solemnity, formality, publicity and constitutional and other safeguards – is not a treaty.

12. In particular, there is probably no warrant for the suggestion[1] that an instrument is not a treaty unless it contains provisions for the compulsory judicial or arbitral settlement of disputes as to its interpretation or application. While most multilateral treaties of a general character and many other treaties contain clauses of this nature, this is not the case in many treaties which clearly create legal rights and obligations. The legal nature of rules of customary international law does not depend upon the existence of a compulsory machinery for their arbitral or judicial ascertainment. There is no reason for more stringent requirements in this respect in the matter of treaties.

13. While in his first report the special rapporteur did not regard the question of registration with the United Nations as decisive, he now considers that that view requires modification – but no more – in accordance with the text as proposed above in paragraph 1. He continues to believe that the mere fact of registration is not *decisive*. In particular, it cannot be admitted that the Secretary-General can be entrusted with the function of giving, by complying with the request for registration, the complexion of a legal instrument to something which otherwise would not possess that character. However, although the fact of registration is not decisive – what is decisive is the formality of a written instrument couched in the traditional terms of a treaty obligation – registration constitutes an addition to those essential requirements of form which make of an instrument a treaty. It may be a matter for consideration whether weight ought to be attached in this connection to the protest of one of the parties against registration, on the ground that the instrument

[1] For an elaboration of which see the article by Fawcett in *B.Y.* 30 (1953), 381 *et seq.*

does not constitute a treaty or an international agreement creating legal rights and obligations.

14. The special rapporteur has devoted further study to – and has to some extent modified his view on – this question for the reason that, in his opinion, the codification of the law of treaties ought to provide an opportunity not for devitalizing such legal element as is contained in international instruments but for salvaging from them any existing element of legal obligation. There are, in addition to the types of instrument referred to above, other categories of treaties whose legal importance and beneficence may be jeopardized unless that principle is adopted. Thus the numerous agreements between the United Nations and the specialized agencies, as well as the agreements of the specialized agencies *inter se*, have been regarded by some as purely administrative arrangements of co-ordination[1] devoid of legal character. It is not believed that that view is substantiated either by their content or form. The same applies to the numerous inter-State treaties for cultural co-operation;[2] for technical assis-

---

[1] It will be noted that in some cases the obligations in question although described as co-operation go substantially beyond mere co-operation. This applies, for instance, to Article 6 of the Agreement between the United Nations and the International Labour Organization which provides that 'the International Labour Organization agrees to co-operate with the Economic and Social Council in furnishing such information and rendering such assistance to the Security Council as that Council may request including assistance in carrying out decisions of the Security Council for the maintenance or restoration of international peace and security' (*U.N.T.S.* 1 (1946–7), 192). In some cases the obligation is of a declaratory nature as in the case of Article 6 of the Agreement between the United Nations and the International Monetary Fund which provides as follows: 'The Fund takes note of the obligation assumed, under paragraph 2 of Article 48 of the United Nations Charter, by such of its members as are also Members of the United Nations, to carry out the decisions of the Security Council through their action in the appropriate specialized agencies of which they are members, and will, in the conduct of its activities, have due regard for decisions of the Security Council under Articles 41 and 42 of the United Nations Charter' (*U.N.T.S.* 16 (1948), 332).

[2] Such as the Cultural Convention between the Government of the United Kingdom of Great Britain and Northern Ireland and the Netherlands Government of 7 July 1948 (*U.N.T.S.* 82 (1951), 260). Of these conventions, which often provide for ratification, there is a great number. To the same category belong instruments such as the Agreement between the United States of America and France relating to the financing of certain educational exchange programmes of 22 October 1948 (*U.N.T.S.* 84 (1951), 174). The legal character of the provisions of such agreements is illustrated by Article 1 of the above agreement. It provides as follows: 'There shall be established a Commission to be known as the United States Educational Commission for France (hereinafter designated 'The Commission'), which shall be recognized by the Government of the United States of America and the Government of the French Republic as an organization created and established to facilitate the administration of an educational programme financed by funds made available in accordance with the Memorandum of Understanding dated 28 May 1946 and the Supplement thereto. Except as hereinafter provided, the Commission shall be exempt from the domestic and local laws of the United States of America as they relate to the use and expenditure of currencies and credits for currencies for the purposes set forth in the present Agreement. The funds shall enjoy on the part of the Government of the French Republic the exemption and immunities accorded to the property of a foreign

tance;[1] for co-operation between Governments and public international organizations of a humanitarian character, such as the Agreement of 19 July 1950 between the United Nations International Children's Emergency Fund and the Government of the Republic of China concerning the activities of the former in China;[2] and agreements relating to military co-operation by way of establishment of military missions and otherwise.[3]

Government.' The Agreement between Thailand and the United States of America of July 1950 (*U.N.T.S.* 81 (1951), 62), providing for the establishment of a foundation, to be known as the United States Educational Foundation in Thailand, contains specific obligations such as that the funds of the Foundation shall be regarded in Thailand as the property of a foreign Government. The Exchange of Notes constituting an agreement of 21 June 1949 between the United States of America and Mexico relating to anthropological research and investigation (*U.N.T.S.* 89 (1951), 4) provides for detailed obligations concerning the supply of services of officials and scholars, payment of salaries, publication of results of research, communication of data, customs facilities and the like. The same applies to a similar agreement between the United States of America and Peru of 17 and 25 March 1949 (*ibid.* p. 16).

[1] Such as the Basic Agreement between the United Nations, the Food and Agriculture Organization of the United Nations, the International Civil Aviation Organization, the International Labour Organization, the United Nations Educational, Scientific and Cultural Organization, the World Health Organization and France for the provision of technical assistance of 20 March 1951 (*U.N.T.S.* 82 (1951), 174); the Basic Agreement between the United Nations, the Food and Agriculture Organization of the United Nations, the International Civil Aviation Organization, the International Labour Organization, the United Nations Educational, Scientific and Cultural Organization, the World Health Organization and Colombia for the provision of technical assistance of 24 November 1950 (*U.N.T.S.* 81 (1951), 190); the Basic Agreement between the United Nations and the Government of Thailand for the provision of technical assistance of 11 June 1951 (*U.N.T.S.* 90 (1951), 46).

[2] *U.N.T.S.* 94 (1951), 22. The agreement lays down obligations governing the distribution of supplies, maintenance by the Government of accounting and statistical records, access to records, immunities of various kinds, and settlement of disputes by reference 'for appropriate action' to the Programme Committee of the Executive Board of the International Children's Emergency Fund. The legal nature of the Agreement is not impaired by some unorthodox provisions such as that relating to the duration of the Agreement. Thus Article 9 lays down that 'it shall remain in force at least until any supplies furnished by the Fund are finally consumed or used, plus a reasonable period for the completion of an orderly liquidation of all Fund activites in the Republic of China'.

[3] Thus the Agreement between the United States of America and Haiti of 14 April 1949 relating to a naval mission to Haiti (*U.N.T.S.* 80 (1951), 38), in addition to the detailed provisions concerning the personnel, duties, rank, pay and allowances of the mission to be provided by Haiti, contains other obligations of Haiti such as the undertaking not to engage the services of a mission of any other foreign Government for duties connected with the coastguard of Haiti except by the mutual agreement of the two Governments. To similar effect are such instruments as the Agreement between the United States of America and Ecuador relating to a military mission to Ecuador of 29 June 1944 (*ibid.* p. 284); the Agreement of 6 March 1950 between the United States of America and Honduras for the establishment of a United States Air Force mission to Honduras (*ibid.* p. 52); the Agreement between the United States of America and Honduras of 6 March 1950 for the establishment of a United States Army mission to Honduras (*ibid.* p. 72); the Agreement between the United States of America and Argentina of 6 October 1948 concerning a military advisory mission to Argentina (*ibid.* p. 92); the Agreement between the United States of America and Brazil relating to a military advisory mission to Brazil of 29 July 1948 (*ibid.* p. 112).

CHAPTER 2

FORM AND DESIGNATION OF A TREATY

Editor's note This section is taken from the 1953 Report, Article 2. For the relevant provision of the Vienna Convention, namely, Article 2(1) (*a*), see p. 101 above.

ARTICLE 2

FORM AND DESIGNATION OF A TREATY

Agreements, as defined in Article 1, constitute treaties regardless of their form and designation.

Alternative version of Article 2

[Agreements, as defined in Article 1, constitute treaties regardless of their form and designation and regardless of whether they are expressed in one or more instruments. A treaty obligation may be created by a unilateral instrument accepting an offer or followed by acceptance.]

Comment

1. The principle laid down in this Article is generally recognized. While the terms 'treaty', 'convention', 'agreement' and 'exchange of notes' are the most common and while they account for the great majority – probably four-fifths – of instruments of a contractual character to which States or organizations of States are parties, a great variety of other terms are occasionally also used. They include such terms as 'protocol', 'declaration', 'statute', 'final act', 'general act', 'pact', '*modus vivendi*', 'arrangement', 'covenant', 'exchange of notes constituting an agreement', '*compromis d'arbitrage*', 'additional articles', 'agreed minutes', 'instrument', and others.[1] The terms used are of no legal consequence, so long as the instrument in question can properly be interpreted as creating legal rights and obligations. As the Permanent Court of International Justice said in its advisory opinion concerning the *Customs Régime between Germany and Austria*, 'from the standpoint of the obligatory character of international

[1] See below, paragraph 5 of the note to the present Article.

agreements, it is well known that such engagements may be taken in the form of treaties, conventions, declarations, agreements, protocols or exchanges of notes'.[1] In its judgment on the *Interpretation of the Statute of the Memel Territory* the Permanent Court of International Justice declined to attach importance to the fact that the Statute was in the form of a Lithuanian municipal enactment and gave its decision on the basis that the Statute was 'a conventional arrangement binding upon Lithuania and that it must be interpreted as such' (*P.C.I.J.* Series A/B, no. 49, p. 300).

2. Neither is it of importance that the assumption of obligations (and, in some cases, of corresponding rights) takes place in the form of a unilateral declaration relating to a pre-existing instrument such as the various declarations recognizing as compulsory the jurisdiction of the International Court of Justice in conformity with Article 36, paragraphs 2 and 3, of its Statute; or the Declaration of Switzerland of 6 July 1948 (*U.N.T.S.* 17, 111) accepting the conditions determined by the General Assembly of the United Nations for Switzerland to become a party to the Statute of the International Court of Justice; or the various 'instruments of adherence' to the United Nations, such as those of Iceland, Sweden, Siam and others (*ibid.* 1, 41, 43, 47). Such unilateral declarations are in some cases in the nature of adherence or accession to a pre-existing treaty (see below, Article 7). This is so even if, as in the case of the declarations under the so-called optional clause of Article 36 of the Statute of the International Court of Justice, the terminology used does not expressly refer to adhesion in its technical sense. For it is clear that the totality of the declarations under Article 36 of the Statute of the Court constitutes a treaty as between the parties making the declaration. They have been so interpreted by the International Court of Justice, namely, by reference to the paramount consideration of the intention of the parties. This is so notwithstanding the fact that as the text of the declaration is not 'a treaty text resulting from negotiations between two or more States', but 'is the result of unilateral drafting' by one party, particular rules of interpretation of treaties may not be applicable (judgment of the International Court of Justice of 22 July 1952 in the *Anglo-Iranian Oil Co.* case (Preliminary Objection): *I.C.J. Reports* 1952, p. 105). The same applies to such instruments as the declarations made by various States and addressed to the Council

[1] *P.C.I.J.*, Series A/B, no. 41. Hudson has pointed out that 'this list was not intended to be exhaustive and that the names chosen for an instrument, frequently due to political or casual considerations, is seldom of juridical significance' (*Permanent Court of International Justice, 1920–1942* (1943) p. 632).

of the League of Nations in the matter of protection of minorities. In its advisory opinion of 6 April 1935 concerning the *Minority Schools in Albania* the Permanent Court of International Justice interpreted the Albanian Declaration on the subject as if it were one of the Minorities Treaties (*P.C.I.J.* Series A/B, no. 62). In fact, the declaration substantially reproduced the text of these treaties. It provided for the compulsory jurisdiction of the Permanent Court of International Justice in the matter of disputes as to questions of law or fact arising out of its provisions. As in the case of many other treaties, its ratification was deposited with the Secretary-General of the League. It may be added that these and similar declarations demonstrate also that a specifically expressed, exact reciprocity or correspondence of rights and obligations is not an essential prerequisite of a treaty. The benefits which accrue to a State from the assumption of an obligation need not appear directly either in the instrument in question or in any other instrument. Thus the declaration made by the Kingdom of Iraq on 30 May 1932 concerning the minorities in Iraq was made in pursuance of a resolution adopted by the Council of the League of Nations requesting such a declaration as a condition precedent to the termination of the Mandate (*L.N.O.J.* (1932), p. 474). The Council then approved the text of the declaration – which, in Article 16, stated that its provisions constituted 'obligations of international concern'. In circumstances such as these – i.e. of the existence of a resolution of the Government, of a declaration adopted in pursuance of the resolution, and of a further resolution approving the declaration — the 'obligations of international concern' must be regarded as partaking of the character of a treaty.[1]

An apparently unilateral assumption of obligations which accepts the provisions of an already existing instrument or which is followed by acceptance of the party to which it is addressed constitutes a treaty obligation. This is also one of the reasons why, apart from cogent evidence of the practice of States, exchanges of notes must be regarded as constituting a treaty (see below, Note, paragraph 4). The following passage from the report of the rapporteur of the San Francisco Committee IV/2, which is concerned with the registration of treaties under Article 102 of the Charter, may be noted in this connection: 'The word "agreement" must be understood as including unilateral engagements of an international character which have

---

[1] For a different view as to the nature of these and similar unilateral declarations see the comment to Article 4 of the Harvard Draft Convention. *Harvard Research* (1935), vol. III in *A.J.* 29 (1935), Supplement.

been accepted by the State in whose favour such an engagement has been entered into.'[1] Thus viewed, the object of Article 2 is, it is believed, adequately expressed by the statement that 'agreements, as defined in Article 1, constitute treaties regardless of their form and designation'. The alternative version, which is enclosed in brackets, merely elaborates the principle inherent in it. The alternative version of the article is attached in case it should be considered that such elaboration is necessary.

3. The designation of an instrument is irrelevant not only in so far as its character as a treaty is concerned but also in respect of the rules governing its conclusion, the conditions of its validity, its operation and interpretation, and its termination. Thus, as already stated, it does not follow from the mere fact that an instrument is described as an exchange of notes that it does not require ratification. The normal absence of the requirement of ratification in instruments of this description follows from the circumstance that as a rule they expressly dispense with ratification by providing that they shall enter into force on a specified date or on the completion of the exchange of notes, i.e. on the acceptance and confirmation by one contracting party of the document submitted and drafted – usually as the result of a joint effort – by the other party.

4. The same applies to those differences in the form of treaties which spring from the fact that some of the parties to them are Heads of States while in other cases the parties are designated as the respective States or Governments, or Heads of Governments or delegations of Governments, or governmental departments, or heads of departments. Thus, for instance, there is no rule of international law which lays down that the answer to the question as to the requirement of ratification depends on who is designated as a party to the treaty – although according to the practice of some States treaties concluded by the Head of the State in person or between departments are not as a rule considered to require ratification. It is impossible to say that according to international practice any particular type of treaty requires a particular description of parties, although as a rule, but not invariably, political treaties of importance – such as treaties of alliance – are concluded between Heads of States. Occasionally, for reasons of internal constitutional law, some States prefer to adhere to a particular description. Thus, for a time, members of the British Commonwealth of Nations attached importance to treaties being concluded in the form of agreements between

[1] *United Nations Conference on International Organization*, 13, 705 (Doc. 933, IV/2/42 (2)).

Heads of States and States as such.[1] Other States, such as the United States of America, have preferred, without insisting on such preference in the face of contrary wishes of the other contracting parties, to describe the United States of America as such as party to the treaty. In the case of the General Treaty for the Renunciation of War of 27 August 1928, which was concluded between Heads of States, Japan was reported to have raised objections to Article 1 of the Treaty in which the parties declared, 'in the names of their respective peoples', that they condemned war as an instrument of national policy. The objection was raised on the ground that under the Japanese constitution the Emperor signs treaties in his own name and not on behalf of his people. The Preamble to the Charter of the United Nations, which is a document accepted by the 'respective Governments', commences with the words 'We the peoples of the United Nations'. In the Constitution of the Food and Agriculture Organization of the United Nations of 16 October 1945 the parties seem to be the 'Nations accepting this constitution'. However, interesting as these innovations may be from other points of view, they are, like other variations of terminology on the subject, without legal significance in the field of the law of treaties.

Note

1. The main principle embodied in this article is generally admitted. That principle is that the designation of the instrument or combination of instruments is, as a rule, irrelevant for the purpose of its (or their) being regarded as a treaty so long as the intention to assume an obligation is reasonably clear. Thus a unilateral declaration constitutes a treaty if the party to whom it is directed accepts it or acts upon it. Similarly, an apparently unilateral declaration – such as that of the optional clause of Article 36 of the Statute of the International Court of Justice – may in itself constitute an acceptance of an already established instrument and as such constitute a treaty. Alternatively, a declaration may be regarded as an act of accession to an already established text. Similarly, the governing consideration seems to be that it is irrelevant in what way the text expressing the common intention of the parties has been established – whether it is composed of one instrument or a number of instruments (as in the case of exchanges of notes or accession) and whether the text of the instrument is established by the parties or by some other body and

---

[1] For the statement on the subject made to the Council of the League of Nations by the British Secretary of State for Foreign Affairs in 1927, see *L.N.O.J.* (1927), p. 377.

subsequently accepted by the parties. It is probably by reference to some such considerations that the Permanent Court of International Justice held in the *Jaworzina* case that a joint declaration of Czecho-slovakia and Poland accepting a decision of the Conference of Ambassadors was in the nature of 'two agreements' and that 'the two agreements give to the decision arrived at . . . the force of a contractual obligation entered into by the parties' (Series B, no. 8, p. 30). This is so although it may not be easy to state which document constituted, in the opinion of the Court, the treaty binding the parties – the joint declaration accepting the decision or the decision itself. Probably the treaty was constituted by both documents. There would be no difficulty in assuming, following the language of the Court, that the decision constituted the treaty and the joint declaration was in the nature of an acceptance of the treaty thus established.

2. There may indeed arise border-line cases in which the character of a unilateral act conceived as a treaty is less apparent and therefore controversial. Thus in the *Free Zones* case the Permanent Court of International Justice held that a manifesto of the Royal Chamber of Accounts of Sardinia of 1829 embodying the assent of the King of Sardinia to a claim made by the Canton of Valais terminated an international dispute relating to the interpretation of the Treaty of Turin, that it thus represented *un accord des volontés*, and that in consequence it possessed 'the character of a treaty stipulation' (Series A/B, no. 46, p. 145). It is not clear from the judgment who were the parties to the treaty relationship thus constituted. In the same case the Permanent Court of International Justice held that a declaration made by the Swiss Agent in the course of the proceedings before the Court was binding upon Switzerland notwithstanding the statement of the French Agent to the effect that he had no power to accept the offer contained in the declaration (Series A/B, no. 46, p. 170). It may be difficult to treat an offer not accepted by the other party as constituting a treaty obligation – although, as held by the Court, the declaration was binding. Otherwise the principle must be accepted that whenever there exist in fact the elements of an offer and an acceptance thereof – a recorded instrument or succession or combination of recorded instruments – there may fairly be held to exist a treaty. The object of Article 2 is to give expression to that principle.

3. Similar considerations apply to the question, which Article 2 is intended to answer with a clear affirmative, as to whether an exchange of notes constitutes a treaty. The Commission, in the course of the discussion on the subject in 1952, decided, by a majority of six

to five, not to omit exchanges of notes from the purview of its codification of the law of treaties.[1] That provisional decision was not reached without considerable hesitation. In the Harvard Draft Convention reasons are given, in the comment to Article 4, for excluding exchanges of notes from the Draft. For reasons which are set out below in some detail it is believed that there is no foundation for the exclusion, from the sphere of the law of treaties, of a class of agreements which accounts for a large proportion of the international agreements actually concluded by Governments.

4. It appears that the principal consideration which animated some members of the Commission on this question was the view that as exchanges of notes do not require ratification, and that as any procedure which dispenses with ratification is contrary to the requirements of democratic constitutional processes, no encouragement ought to be given, by way of elevating them to the dignity of a treaty, to international agreements which as a rule dispense with ratification. These assumptions – and the conclusions drawn from them – are in need of reconsideration. In general, in examining the question of exchanges of notes the following considerations ought to be borne in mind:

(a) In the last three decades exchanges of notes have constituted more than one-fourth – probably one-third – of the total number of international agreements. That proportion has been increasing.[2] The reason for that tendency is that that procedure of concluding international agreements provides a simplified form of reaching and recording agreements, in particular when concluded between Government departments and agencies. It supplies the appropriate method for agreements of a technical character and of limited scope as well as for those which, notwithstanding the importance of their subject matter, require expeditious action for their initiation and execution. The character of exchanges of notes as being in the nature of agreements is emphasized in numerous instruments by the fact that they are expressly described as 'exchanges of notes constituting agree-

---

[1] See *Yearbook of the International Law Commission, 1950*, vol. 1, 51st meeting, para. 38.

[2] Thus it has been estimated that in the years 1921 to 1930, out of 338 instruments published in the Treaty Series, 93 were exchanges of notes. Out of 453 instruments published in that Series between 1941 and 1950 no less than 195 have been exchanges of notes. In the years 1951 and 1952 about one-half of the instruments in that Series were exchanges of notes. Out of the first thousand instruments registered with the Secretariat of the League of Nations 212 were exchanges of notes. Out of the total 4,831 instruments published with the League of Nations between 1920 and 1946 nearly 25 per cent were exchanges of notes. Out of the 1,000 instruments first registered with the United Nations 280 were exchanges of notes. See Weinstein in *B.T.* vol. 29 (1952).

ments'.[1] In fact, it seems almost as if, in order to remove what are essentially unfounded doubts, that terminology is assuming a complexion of regularity.[2]

(b) The fact that numerous exchanges of notes cover technical subjects of limited scope does not mean that exchanges of notes in general are confined to questions of minor importance.[3] Exchanges of notes have regulated such matters as limitation of armaments (as between Great Britain and the United States in 1813 covering the number and size of warships on the Great Lakes, or between Great Britain and Germany on 18 June 1935 limiting the future strength of the German navy in relation to the aggregate naval strength of the members of the British Commonwealth (Treaty Series, no. 22 (1935), Cmd. 4953)), renunciation of extraterritorial rights, grant of perpetual leases, establishment of diplomatic relations, agreements on diplomatic and consular representation, commerce and navigation (as between the United States and Nepal (*U.N.T.S.* 16, 97) and Yemen (*ibid.* 4, 165)), maintenance of armed forces on foreign soil, cessions of territory, settlement of boundary disputes (e.g. between the United Kingdom and Brazil (*ibid.* 5, 71) or between the United Kingdom and China (*ibid.* 10, 227)), aviation, shipping and, generally communications, settlement of war claims, and the like. Nearly one-fourth of the commercial agreements concluded by the United Kingdom have been in the form of exchanges of notes.

(c) In so far as the objection to considering exchanges of notes as treaties arises from the notion that they are not subject to ratification, it must be remembered:

(i) That in some cases exchanges of notes *are* subject to ratification

[1] See, for instance, the series of 'exchanges of notes constituting an agreement' relating to passport visas between the United States and a number of countries: *U.N.T.S.* 88, 3, 11, 19, 33, 43, 255, 265, 275, 283.

[2] See, for example, exchanges of notes constituting an agreement between Denmark and the Union of South Africa providing for reciprocal exemption from Government and local government taxation of income derived from the exercise of shipping activities and operation of aircraft services (30 November 1950: *U.N.T.S.* 84, 51); between Belgium and Chile concerning the reciprocal protection of industrial and commercial trade marks (10 February 1947: *ibid.* 76, 113); between the United States and China concerning claims resulting from activities of the United States military forces in China (13 October 1947: *ibid.* p. 157); between the United States and Denmark concerning exchange of official publications (27 July 1949: *ibid.* 79, 147); between the United Kingdom and Italy concerning British military fixed assets in Italy (30 December 1947: *ibid.* 77, 33); between the United Kingdom and the Netherlands concerning the settlement of wartime debts (11 March 1948: *ibid.* p. 69); between Greece and Italy concerning cultural institutions (21 September 1948: *ibid.* p. 259).

[3] '. . . it is the fact that at the present time it can scarcely any longer be said that an exchange of notes habitually deals with matters of smaller importance than do treaties or conventions' (Fitzmaurice in *B.Y.* 15 (1934), 120).

(see, for example the exchange of notes between Germany and Spain (*L.N.T.S.* 26, 455) providing for ratification by both parties; between the United Kingdom and Denmark (*U.N.T.S.* 45, 324) providing for approval by the Parliament of one party; between the United States and Denmark (*ibid.* 27 (1949), 35); between South Africa and Germany (Treaty Series, no. 25 (1935), Cmd. 4961); and between the United States and Poland (*L.N.T.S.* 37, 141)).

(ii) That the omission of the requirement of ratification is not limited to exchanges of notes. The practice of many countries follows the rule that, unless otherwise provided, inter-governmental and inter-departmental agreements do not require ratification – not to mention agreements concluded directly between Heads of States. Moreover, as shown below (Article 6), a considerable and increasing number of treaties are being concluded which expressly dispense with ratification.

(d) Numerous decisions of municipal courts exhibit no hesitation in regarding exchanges of notes as treaties – although there is some divergence of practice on the question whether exchanges of notes are in the nature of inter-governmental agreements which do not require ratification or whether they must be considered as formal treaties in the sense of the constitutional law of the State concerned with the result that they cannot be enforced unless ratified. In such cases they are held to be inoperative not because they are not treaties but because, being treaties, they have not been incorporated into the law of the land.[1]

[1] This has been so particularly in France: see, for example *In re Talbot* (where the Court held that an exchange of notes cannot, without ratification and publication, have the force of law in the meaning of Article 26 of the French Constitution: *Gazette du Palais* (1947), Part II, p. 17; *Annual Digest* (1947), case no. 68). *In re Vermote* (Sirey, I (1950), Part II, p. 154) and *Benzoni* v. *Davidovici* (*ibid.* (1951), Part II, p. 79) are to the same effect. On the other hand see *In re Colman* (*Annual Digest* (1947), case no. 67) and *Zumkeller* v. *Florence* (Sirey (1946), Part I, p. 257). See also *Vicens* v. *Bonfillon* (*Annual Digest*(1933–4), case no. 180); *Huckendubler* v. *Hoeffler* (*ibid.* (1931–2), case no. 213); and *In re Société Ruegger* (*ibid.* (1933–4), case no. 179). The decision of the Italian Court of Cassation in *Russian Trade Delegation in Italy* v. *Querci* (*Foro Italiano*, 67 (1942), Part I, 11 : *Annual Digest* (1941–2), case no. 129) is to the same effect. For an analysis of these and other cases bearing on the subject see Weinstein in *B.Y.* vol. 29 (1952). See also Brandon in *A.J.* 47 (1953), 58–62, on exchanges of notes in relation to the question of registration under Article 102 of the Charter of the United Nations. In all the cases referred to above the courts were confronted with exchanges of notes interpreting previous agreements. In *Minister of Finance* v. *United States Line Co.* the French Court of Cassation applied to an independent exchange of notes what it described as *un accord diplomatique* (*Clunet*, 65 (1938), 532). In two important American cases – *United States* v. *Belmont* (1937), 301 U.S. 324, and *United States* v. *Pink* (1942), 314 U.S. 203 – the Supreme Court treated exchanges of notes accompanying the recognition of the Government of Soviet Russia as an international compact involving far-reaching – indeed startling – consequences in the sphere of municipal law. See also

(e) For the reasons stated there would appear to be strong objection to eliminating exchanges of notes from the purview of the law of treaties. As already mentioned in connection with the question of unilateral declarations, it may be unsatisfactory to leave outside the framework of codification of a particular topic a subject which, although exhibiting certain peculiarities, intrinsically falls within its purview. There is, apart from the method of establishing the text, no difference of substance between exchanges of notes and other international agreements in the matter of their validity, operation, interpretation and termination. In the municipal sphere the method of concluding a contract by way of parallel complementary instruments is generally recognized. To deny to exchanges of notes the full character of treaties may mean depriving a broad segment of international contractual relations of the authority and effectiveness which the status of a treaty imparts to an instrument. Any such course, if acted upon, would signify neglect of a method which experience has shown to be particularly suited to the growing needs of expanding international intercourse unencumbered by elaborate procedure and solemnity.[1]

The modern tendency, frequently commented upon by writers, has been in the direction of making the procedure of conclusion of treaties less formal than in the past, when difficulties of communication between Governments and their agents were a conspicuous feature of the situation and when the variety and urgency of the interests to be represented did not equal those of the modern expanding intercourse of States. Some drafts, including those previously before the Commission, have referred to a treaty as 'a solemn instrument'. The fact is that a treaty need not be a solemn instrument; nor need it consist of a single instrument. It may or may not be desirable to require ratification as an invariable prerequisite of the validity

---

United States v. *Guy W. Capps Inc.* (1951), F. Supp. 30, where it was held that an exchange of notes between the United States and Canada concerning the import and export of potatoes, although not a treaty in the meaning of the Constitution, had the force of law. And see the *Paris Agreement* case decided by the German Reichsgericht (*Annual Digest* (1919–22), case no. 225).

[1] This is so, in particular, seeing that exchanges of notes may, in effect, be used for bringing about agreements of more than two States. See, for instance, the parallel exchanges of notes between Italy and the United Kingdom and Italy and the United States of America (Treaty Series, no. 52 (1951), Cmd. 8294). These parallel notes constitute an agreement between Italy of the one part and the United Kingdom and United States of the other. The procedure of exchange of notes has also been resorted to when one of the parties has not been a State: see, for example, the Exchange of Notes between the International Court of Justice (represented by the President) and the Netherlands concerning precedence: *U.N.T.S.* 8 (1947), 61.

of a treaty. Practice has certainly not considered it as such.[1] If ratification is considered as a procedure congenial to the climate of constitutionality and democracy, that result must be achieved by the express adoption in treaties of provisions to that effect. It cannot be accomplished by eliminating from the sphere of treaties contractual agreements which properly belong there. On the contrary, such a course may be of doubtful value even when viewed as a means of discouraging the conclusion of international agreements not followed by ratification. For the reform thus achieved would be merely one of terminology. It would not prevent Governments from undertaking commitments, expressly described as not requiring ratification, by way of instruments other than exchange of notes.

(f) For these reasons the wording of Article 2 as proposed – 'Agreements, as defined in Article 1, constitute treaties regardless of their form and designation' – is intended to include exchanges of notes within the purview of treaties. In order to remove doubts from what has become a subject of some controversy and uncertainty, it may be considered whether it would not be desirable to elaborate that statement by the addition of the words 'and regardless of whether they are expressed in one or more instruments'. The alternative version of the Article is intended to serve that purpose.

5. The great variety of the designations used for describing international agreements raises the question of the justification for that diversity and of the possibility – or desirability – of keeping it within reasonable bounds. In most cases there is no apparent reason for the variation in the terms used. They often create the impression that they were dependent upon a factor no more decisive than the mood of the draftsman. Thus, to give an example provided by one volume of the *U.N.T.S.* – vol. 84 – in 1946 and 1948 the United States concluded with France a series of agreements described variously as *memorandum of understandings constituting an agreement* (relating to lend-lease, reciprocal aid, and the like: p. 59); *agreement and an accompanying supplementary understanding* (transfer of surplus United States Army and Navy property: p. 79); *agreed combined statement* (disposition of claims: p. 93); *memorandum constituting agreement* (shipping: p. 113); *declaration constituting an agreement* (commercial policy: p. 151); *understanding constituting an agreement* (exhibition of motion pictures: p. 161); *declaration* (economic and financial problems: p. 167);

---

[1] For this reason there seems to be little persuasive power in the argument, occasionally adduced, that if exchanges of notes are assimilated to treaties they would be automatically subject to the procedure of ratification.

agreement (financing of educational exchange programmes: p. 173); *joint declaration constituting an agreement* (motion pictures: p. 185). There is little method in, and no obvious explanation for, the diversity of terminology in this and many other cases. Yet it is doubtful whether there is room for a deliberate effort, by way of codification or otherwise, to introduce uniformity of terminology in this field of the law. So long as no conclusions of legal relevance are drawn from this diversity of expression the mischief, if any, resulting from it is insignificant. The same applies to the discrepancies of practice in the description of the parties.

CHAPTER 3

THE LAW GOVERNING TREATIES

Editor's note. This is taken from the 1953 Report, Article 3. There is no corresponding provision in the Vienna Convention.

ARTICLE 3

THE LAW GOVERNING TREATIES

In the absence of any contrary provisions laid down by the parties and not inconsistent with overriding principles of international law, the conditions of the validity of treaties, their execution, interpretation and termination are governed by international custom and, in appropriate cases, by general principles of law recognized by civilized nations.

Comment

To a large extent the above Article reproduces, in relation to treaties, the substance of Article 38 of the Statute of the International Court of Justice, which enumerates the sources of law to be applied by the Court. To that extent Article 3 seems to be redundant inasmuch as the sources of international law enumerated in Article 38 of the Statute of the Court govern also other parts of international law. However, as in Article 38 treaties themselves figure as the first source of international law enumerated, it is essential to state in an introductory article of a code of the law of treaties that that law is based on and owes its validity to customary international law and to the general principles of law recognized by civilized nations. Although, with few exceptions, all the pronouncements of the International Court of Justice and of its predecessor have been concerned with the interpretation of treaties, such interpretation has taken place against a background of general rules of customary international law. This subordination to international law in its entirety expresses itself in particular in relation to the fundamental aspects of the law of treaties, namely, their binding force and the principle – which is the basis of the law relating to the interpretation of treaties – that they must be interpreted in accordance with the canons of good faith. Thus the binding force of treaties is independent of the will of the States which conclude them in the exercise of their sovereignty. Their binding force and other basic conditions of their operation are grounded in customary international law. While, therefore, States are free to shape their treaty relations and the conditions of their performance in accordance with their will, they can do so only subject to the overriding principles of international law, the general principles of law and principles of good faith. The question of the degree of the overriding effect of these principles is examined in Article 15 in Part III of this draft. Accordingly, while most of the provisions of the present Code of the Law of Treaties are framed so as to give wide latitude to the autonomy and discretion of the parties and so as to be operative only if the parties have made no provision to the contrary, others are binding upon the parties in all circumstances and must be interpreted accordingly. This is so for the reason that in the matter of treaties the will of States is only one source – and in some cases only a subordinate source – of international law.

Note

On the face of it the subject matter of Article 3 seems purely doctrinal and to that extent redundant. However, it is believed that some such Article is essential in order to put in its proper perspective what may be provisionally called the Code of the Law of Treaties. As in many other spheres of international law, the parties may by treaty change or modify existing rules of international law. The Code is intended to a large extent to regulate matters which are not expressly provided for by treaty. But, as was perceived in the discussions of the Commission in connection with the Code of Arbitral Procedure, there are certain rules and principles which are above and outside the scope of the *jus dispositivum* of the parties. An express statement to that effect is particularly necessary with regard to treaties for the reason that they themselves constitute a source of international law. The Code of the Law of Treaties safeguards in many cases the freedom of action enjoyed by the parties. Its Articles will be frequently prefaced by the statement 'unless otherwise provided by the parties'. Even in the absence of some such express provision, the parties will often be entitled to adopt rules and procedures to meet their particular requirements. On the other hand, it is clear that they cannot contract out of such rules as those which lay down that treaties must not violate binding rules of international law (although it may on occasions be doubtful which rules of international law are so compelling and mandatory that they have the result of nullifying a treaty which is inconsistent with them: see Article 15 below); or that a treaty must not, lest it be void, involve the violation of a previous treaty to which the contracting States are parties; or that a treaty imposed by unlawful exercise of force is not binding. In fact, the principle underlying Article 3 as drafted provides the basis of the law relating to the validity of treaties as formulated in Part III of this draft. As such it is properly – and necessarily – included in the present general and introductory Part I.

III CONCLUSION OF TREATIES

Editor's note   Chapters 4–9 below correspond with the Articles bearing the same numbers in the 1953 Report. In addition, chapters 6 and 7 include additional passages from the 1954 Report.

The comparable provisions of the Vienna Convention are as follows:

ARTICLE 9

Adoption of the text

1.   The adoption of the text of a treaty takes place by the consent of all the States participating in its drawing up except as provided in paragraph 2.

2.   The adoption of the text of a treaty at an international conference takes place by the vote of two-thirds of the States present and voting, unless by the same majority they shall decide to apply a different rule.

ARTICLE 10

Authentication of the text

The text of a treaty is established as authentic and definitive:

  (*a*) by such procedure as may be provided for in the text or agreed upon by the States participating in its drawing up; or

  (*b*) failing such procedure, by the signature, signature *ad referendum* or initialling by the representatives of those States of the text of the treaty or of the Final Act of a conference incorporating the text.

ARTICLE 11

Means of expressing consent to be bound by a treaty

The consent of a State to be bound by a treaty may be expressed by signature, exchange of instruments constituting a treaty, ratification, acceptance, approval or accession, or by any other means if so agreed.

ARTICLE 12

Consent to be bound by a treaty expressed by signature

1. The consent of a State to be bound by a treaty is expressed by the signature of its representative when:
    (*a*) the treaty provides that signature shall have that effect;
    (*b*) it is otherwise established that the negotiating States were agreed that signature should have that effect; or
    (*c*) the intention of the State to give that effect to the signature appears from the full powers of its representative or was expressed during the negotiation.
2. For the purposes of paragraph 1:
    (*a*) the initialling of a text constitutes a signature of the treaty when it is established that the negotiating States so agreed;
    (*b*) the signature *ad referendum* of a treaty by a representative, if confirmed by his State, constitutes a full signature of the treaty.

ARTICLE 13

Consent to be bound by a treaty expressed by an exchange of instruments constituting a treaty

The consent of States to be bound by a treaty constituted by instruments exchanged between them is expressed by that exchange when:
    (*a*) the instruments provide that their exchange shall have that effect; or
    (*b*) it is otherwise established that those States were agreed that the exchange of instruments should have that effect.

ARTICLE 14

Consent to be bound by a treaty expressed by ratification, acceptance or approval

1. The consent of a State to be bound by a treaty is expressed by ratification when:
    (*a*) the treaty provides for such consent to be expressed by means of ratification;
    (*b*) it is otherwise established that the negotiating States were agreed that ratification should be required;
    (*c*) the representative of the State has signed the treaty subject to ratification; or
    (*d*) the intention of the State to sign the treaty subject to ratification appears from the full powers of its representative or was expressed during negotiation.

144

2. The consent of a State to be bound by a treaty is expressed by acceptance or approval under conditions similar to those which apply to ratification.

ARTICLE 15

Consent to be bound by a treaty expressed by accession

The consent of a State to be bound by a treaty is expressed by accession when:

(*a*) the treaty provides that such consent may be expressed by that State by means of accession;

(*b*) it is otherwise established that the negotiating States were agreed that such consent may be expressed by that State by means of accession; or

(*c*) all the parties have subsequently agreed that such consent may be expressed by that State by means of accession.

ARTICLE 16

Exchange or deposit of instruments of ratification, acceptance, approval or accession

Unless the treaty otherwise provides, instruments of ratification, acceptance, approval or accession establish the consent of a State to be bound by a treaty upon:

(*a*) their exchange between the contracting States;

(*b*) their deposit with the depositary; or

(*c*) their notification to the contracting States or to the depositary, if so agreed.

ARTICLE 18

Obligation not to defeat the object and purpose of a treaty prior to its entry into force

A State is obliged to refrain from acts which would defeat the purpose of a treaty when:

(*a*) it has signed the treaty or has exchanged instruments constituting the treaty subject to ratification, acceptance or approval, until it shall have made its intention clear not to become a party to the treaty; or

(*b*) it has expressed its consent to be bound by the treaty, pending the entry into force of the treaty and provided that such entry into force is not unduly delayed.

CHAPTER 4

ASSUMPTION OF TREATY OBLIGATIONS

1953 REPORT

ARTICLE 4

ASSUMPTION OF TREATY OBLIGATIONS

A treaty becomes binding by signature which is not subject to confirmation, ratification, accession, acceptance, or any other means of expressing the will of the parties, through a competent organ, in accordance with the provisions and practice in their constitution.

Comment

1. The object of this Article, which is of a formal character, is to state the principle that parties to treaties enjoy a wide freedom of choice in the matter of the means by which they assume treaty obligations. This includes, in addition to the traditional methods of signature, ratification and accession, not only the more recent method of so-called 'acceptance' (Article 8 below), but also such methods as concurrent action by way of exchanging notes (see comment to Article 2 above), a unilateral declaration accepted by the other party or parties (*ibid.*) and, generally, any other procedure which the parties may find it necessary to employ.

2. Although signature is enumerated in the present article as one of the means by which a party may assume a treaty obligation, it is also one of the methods for establishing – authenticating – the text of a treaty. It is difficult – and perhaps unnecessary – to decide which is its primary function. The answer to that question will depend largely upon the view eventually taken as to the nature and the necessity of ratification (see Article 6 below). It will also depend to some extent on the realization of the fact that at present over one-third of bilateral contractual instruments become binding without ratification. The purpose of these observations is merely to remove a source of misunderstanding resulting from the fact that signature is often regarded and is referred to in paragraph 4 of this comment – as one of the means of establishing the text whereas in the present Article it

appears as one of the methods of assuming a treaty obligation. Moreover, as explained in the comment to Article 5, signature is seldom, if ever, merely a means of establishing the text of the treaty, i.e. of authentication. Even if subject to ratification, it creates, within a limited sphere, certain obligations which are by no means of a merely procedural character (see Article 5 below).

3. The concluding passage of this Article, which provides that the various means of concluding a treaty must be expressed by a competent organ in accordance with the provisions of the constitution – which means both constitutional law and constitutional practice – of the parties refers to one of the conditions of the validity of a treaty and is the subject matter of Article 11 in Part III of the present draft (Validity of Treaties).

4. The present Article is not concerned with the procedural question of the methods by which the text of a treaty is established. This takes place by the signature on behalf of the parties which have taken part in the negotiation of the treaty or of the conference at which the treaty was negotiated; by incorporation in the final act of the conference; by incorporation in a resolution of an organ of an international organization in accordance with its constitutional practice; in a note or letter which provides the first link in an exchange of letters; by a unilateral declaration subsequently accepted by the party or parties to whom it is addressed; or by any other means agreed upon by the negotiating States. These other methods may include what is in effect a provisional signature, namely, initialling or signature *ne varietur*, which occasionally takes place in cases in which there is an interval between the conclusion of the negotiations and the signature of a treaty. The signature or initialling *ne varietur* is thus a guarantee of the authenticity of the text. It was resorted to in the Locarno Treaty of Mutual Guarantee of 16 October 1925. The treaty was initialled on that day *ne varietur* and it bore that date. It was signed on 1 December 1925. The establishment of the text of a treaty by a resolution of an organ of an international organization is a comparatively recent method. It has been followed in conventions adopted by resolutions of such bodies as the International Labour Organization, the Food and Agriculture Organization of the United Nations, the United Nations Educational, Scientific and Cultural Organization, and by the United Nations itself, as, for example, in the case of the Convention on Privileges and Immunities of the United Nations of 1946 or the Genocide Convention of 1948. A case in which 'other formal means' were adopted is that of the General

Act for the Pacific Settlement of International Disputes of 1928. It was signed by the President of the Assembly of the League of Nations and by the Secretary-General. There was no provision either for signatures or ratification; Article 43 of the Act merely provided for accession.

5. Signature, ratification and accession as methods of assuming treaty obligations each form the subject of a separate Article in the present section. The same applies to 'acceptance' – a procedure which, although used occasionally before the Second World War (as in the case of the United States joining the International Labour Organization), is of recent origin. It has been adopted largely owing to the desire of some States to avoid the usual reference to 'ratification', and so render unnecessary the literal observance of the constitutional procedure appropriate for ratification. Subject to minor variations it enables a party to become bound by either signature without reservation as to acceptance; or signature with reservation as to acceptance; followed by acceptance; or acceptance pure and simple. In Article 8 and in the comment thereon the question is raised whether the notion of acceptance thus conceived in fact constitutes a distinct means of assuming treaty obligations.

Note

1. As pointed out in the comment, Article 4 – which otherwise lays down no substantive rule of law – has been included largely as an occasion for stating the principle of the freedom of choice of methods for establishing the text of a treaty. Apart from that, the special rapporteur considers that the elaboration of procedural rules falls outside the scope of the Commission's work on treaties. An authoritative manual of procedure for international conferences and conclusion of treaties may be of great usefulness, and the Commission may ask at some future date whether it ought not to embark on some such study as that which was foreshadowed by the League of Nations Committee of Experts for the Progressive Codification of International Law, namely, 'whether it is possible to formulate rules to be recommended for the procedure of international conferences and the conclusion and drafting of treaties, and what such rules should be'. However, although it is not believed that that subject falls within the purview of the law of treaties now before the Commission, it is not a matter which can be altogether disregarded in this connection. A great deal of the difficulties and of the discussion surrounding the law of treaties has been due to the imperfections of the machinery

for formulating and concluding them. Thus – as will be suggested in the comment to Article 7 – the controversy, largely unreal in character, whether treaties which contain no specific provision on the question of the requirement of ratification must be ratified in order to be binding is due in most cases to an omission which could have been avoided by careful drafting. The same applies to discrepancies of practice in the matter of accession. Some treaties state that accession shall be admissible at any time; others lay down a date after which accession can be effected; still others provide that accession shall be admissible only after the treaty has entered into force. There seems to be no reason for these differences in procedure. It would not be difficult to multiply such examples. They all raise the question whether some machinery could not be devised which would obviate obscurities and the confusing absence of uniformity in matters with regard to which no apparent interest of the parties and no considerations of convenience seem to require conflicting or ambiguous regulation.

2. In this connection the Commission may wish to consider whether a measure of support should not be given to a proposal made in 1945 by an authority of recognized experience for the establishment of an international legislative drafting bureau[1] to advise Governments and conferences engaged in drafting treaties. While the exact nature of the machinery which might thus be set up must be a matter for careful examination, it is very probable that some such machinery would be useful. In many States parliamentary draftsmen attached to the legislative body have become an essential part of the legislative process. Their intimate knowledge of the entire field of the statutory law has been recognized as an invaluable means of preventing embarrassing inconsistencies in legislation and of ensuring the requisite degree of uniformity of technique. In the international sphere the need for some such assistance is even more imperative having regard to the differences of language, and above all, the baffling diversity of the municipal and, in particular, the constitutional law of States. Thus, for instance, the embarrassing problem of the relevance of constitutional limitations would be alleviated if parties to treaties could rely in this respect upon the advice given by international draftsmen whose function would embrace, *inter alia*, the provision of information on the subject. Similarly, with regard to reservations it may not be easy for a Government to assess the effect, in all its ramifications, of reservations attached by a State to a

---

[1] The proposal was put forward by Jenks in *A.J.* 39 (1945), 163–79.

particular convention. Here, again, expert information might be of assistance. Finally, although uniformity of nomenclature or structure is not an essential prerequisite of the satisfactory operation of treaties, it is possible that the elimination or the diminution of the present – and often confusing – diversity of practice would be beneficial to the authority and development of this branch of international law. Undoubtedly Governments are well served by their own legal advisers, who are fully conversant with international law. However, in the nature of things they cannot be expected to possess the detailed and specialized knowledge springing from intimate experience of the totality of treaty law and of the relevant municipal law of States. In view of this it must be a matter for consideration whether, apart from any substantive formulation of the law of treaties, the Commission should not recommend the creation of a bureau, under the responsibility and as part of the activities of the United Nations, from which Governments could enlist the assistance of experts for drafting treaties and whose presence would become a regular feature of international conferences assembled for the purpose of formulating conventions. It will be recalled that at the sixth and seventh sessions of the General Assembly proposals were made and discussed for placing under some expert guidance legal acts and instruments emanating from the General Assembly itself, including conventions concluded under the auspices of the General Assembly.[1]

---

[1] For the proposal to that effect made by the representative of the United Kingdom see *Official Records of the General Assembly, Sixth Session, Sixth Committee, Annexes*, agenda item 63. And see for a review of the relevant discussions of the General Assembly the note by Liang and Liu in *A.J.* 47 (1953), 70–83.

CHAPTER 5

SIGNATURE

1953 REPORT

ARTICLE 5

SIGNATURE

1. The signature of a treaty constitutes an assumption of a binding obligation in all cases in which the parties expressly so agree or where, in accordance with Article 6, no confirmation of the signature is necessary.

2. In all other cases the signature, or any other means of assuming an obligation subject to subsequent confirmation, has no binding effect except that it implies the obligation, to be fulfilled in good faith:

(a) To submit the instrument to the proper constitutional authorities for examination with the view to ratification or rejection;

(b) To refrain, prior to ratification, from any act intended substantially to impair the value of the undertaking as signed.

Comment

1. The subject matter of this Article is closely connected and overlaps with that of Article 6 relating to ratification. However, signature as an independent means of assuming a treaty obligation is so widely and so increasingly followed in practice that it is proper to put on record in a separate article its position as such. At the same time, signature as a means of assuming an obligation must still be regarded as a departure from what is the normal rule, namely, the requirement of ratification. For that reason it will be convenient, in connection with the Article on ratification, to comment in more detail on this part – i.e. paragraph 1 – of Article 5.

2. The statement that 'signature, or any other means of assuming an obligation subject to subsequent confirmation . . . implies the obligation, to be fulfilled in good faith, to submit the instrument to the proper constitutional authorities for examination with the view to ratification or rejection', is controversial, as expressing a rule of

international law, even in the present – conspicuously qualified – formulation. The view most frequently expressed is that there is no obligation to ratify a treaty previously signed by a State. That view accurately expresses the existing rule of international law on the subject. At the same time it must be borne in mind that, on the part of a substantial number of writers, that view has been accepted only subject to the qualification that the right to refuse ratification is not unqualified; that it must not be exercised capriciously or arbitrarily; and that misuse of that right is fraught with injury not only to the reputation of the State in question but also to the authority of international law and the needs of international intercourse. The opinion has also occasionally been voiced that there is a legal obligation to ratify in cases in which the full powers issued to the plenipotentiaries include the authority not only to negotiate but also to conclude the treaty. While these and similar views are not, it is believed, borne out to any substantial degree by the existing practice, they constitute a reminder of the inconvenience and disadvantages of the rule which recognizes an unqualified right to treat the signature as being no more than a method of authentication. Considerations of that nature underlay the resolution of the Assembly of the League of Nations of 1930 which authorized the Secretary-General of the League to address annual requests to signatories of treaties concluded under the auspices of the League as to their intentions with regard to ratification of a convention signed by them. These considerations do not affect the existing principle affirming the right to refuse to ratify a signature freely appended. However, that principle can in the long run operate in a satisfactory way only if some qualifications, however limited in compass, are adopted for modifying its rigidity. It may not be sufficient to rely on the probability that a State which habitually and without good reasons fails to ratify its signature will impair its own contractual capacity for the reason that other States will decline to conclude treaties with it. Such a probability has not prevented Governments from failing indefinitely to take action on signatures freely given – with the resulting impairment of the treaty-making process as a whole.

3. The remedy cannot lie in imposing upon the Government a duty to confirm signatures appended on the express understanding that they will be free to decide whether to confirm them or not. No such duty, unless accepted expressly or by compelling implication, is imposed by international law. However, that does not mean that the codification of the law of treaties must limit itself to the mere

statement that there is no duty to confirm the signature of a treaty. It must be regarded as a requirement of good faith, which is in itself part of the law and not merely of political prudence, that signature implies the obligation to cause the treaty thus signed to be examined by the competent constitutional authorities with the view to determining whether the signature ought to be confirmed. Of necessity it is an imperfect obligation, which must be fulfilled by the Government concerned having regard to all the circumstances. It may be occasionally, in effect, a nominal obligation in cases in which the views of the competent constitutional authorities are not likely to differ from those of the executive determined not to proceed with the treaty. It is nevertheless a legal obligation, though not an unduly onerous one. Under the Constitution of the International Labour Organization Governments are bound to submit to the national authorities, for approval or rejection, conventions against which the representatives of those Governments have voted at the Conference which adopted them. Governments have full freedom of action in confirming or rejecting a treaty which they have signed subject to the condition of subsequent confirmation – such condition being the normal rule in the absence of express or implied provisions to the contrary (see Article 6 below). What, as a matter of good faith, they cannot do is to sign a treaty and subsequently conduct themselves as if they had no concern with it or as if their signature thereto were merely a clerical act of authentication. There is no warrant in international law for reducing to that level the meaning of the signature. Signature of an instrument – even when made subject to subsequent confirmation or ratification – is more than a method of authenticating a text. In many cases the text exists already, as is the case when an established text is approved by a conference and opened for signature,[1] subject to ratification, within a prescribed period, or when accession to or acceptance of an already established text takes

---

[1] The following example shows that even from the formal point of view the function of the signature, although not amounting to a binding acceptance of obligations, may be different from that of merely establishing the text. The texts of the four Geneva Conventions of 1949 were stated in the Final Act to have been established by the conference. The Final Act was signed by all sixty-one participating States on 12 August 1949. This was not tantamount to signature of the conventions. For only sixteen of the delegations signed all four conventions; the United States of America signed only Conventions No. 1, 2 and 3. The remainder of the delegations signed the four conventions at a special meeting convened on 8 December 1949, when the United States also signed Convention No. 4. Each convention bore the date of 12 August 1949. Each was open for signature until 12 February 1950 in the name of the States represented at the Conference and by States parties to the previous relevant Geneva Convention. After that date the Conventions were open to accession (International Committee of the Red Cross, *Geneva Conventions of August 12, 1949*, Geneva).

place through signature subject to ratification. The correct principle of law with regard to the legal consequences of signature is accurately stated, it is submitted, in the following passage from the Comment to Article 9 of the Harvard Draft Convention:

It is believed that when a duly authorized plenipotentiary signs a treaty on behalf of his State, the signature is not a simple formality devoid of juridical effect and involving no obligation whatever, moral or legal, on the part of the State whose signature the treaty bears. It would seem that not only the treaty-making organ itself but also the other organs of the State which are competent to act for it, once a treaty has been signed on its behalf, are not, if they observe good faith, entirely free to act as if the treaty had never been signed. It would seem also that one signatory State has the right to assume that the other will regard the signature as having been seriously given, that ordinarily it will proceed to ratification, and that in the meantime it will not adopt a policy which would render ratification useless or which would place obstacles in the way of the execution of the provisions of the treaty, once ratification has been given.

In disregarding the question of the obligation to take appropriate measures in the matter of confirmation or otherwise of the signature the authors of the Harvard Draft failed to draw the necessary conclusions from the principle thus stated. The present draft draws these conclusions. There are compelling reasons why a signatory should not be permitted to treat his signature as a meaningless formality. In signing a treaty it exercises an important influence on some of the procedural clauses of the treaty. (These are usually referred to as the 'Final Clauses', although in some conventions they appear in the opening chapters.) Its signature is instrumental in determining such matters as the right of accession, the admissibility of reservations, the conditions of entry into force, and many others. In fact this consideration applies not only to the formal and procedural clauses of the treaty but to its substantive provisions as well. For these provisions may have been substantially – or decisively – influenced by the signatory State or States in question. The treaty is in many respects the result of a painfully achieved compromise to which some States agree, often with reluctance, in order to secure the participation of others. Often a State signs – or ratifies – a convention because the signature of another State or States is regarded by it, in case of doubt, as a sufficient inducement for its own signature. But if these other States are subsequently at liberty to treat their signature as implying no manner of obligation whatsoever, the concessions made by other signatories will have been made in vain seeing that the consideration which they could legitimately expect will not be forth-coming. Moreover, the mere fact of signature confers upon the signatory certain rights – some of them admittedly controversial – and it is proper that there should exist some obligation in consider-ation of those rights. Thus, according to the widely held view, a signatory State has a voice in determining the admissibility of reservations and, in some cases, of accessions. According to a view, which in the present Article is represented as the correct view, signature has the effect of obliging the signatories to abstain, prior to ratification, from a course of action inconsistent with the purpose of the treaty. But if signature is a mere formality which implies no obligations whatsoever on the part of others, there would appear to be no justification for such self-denying restraint. All these consider-ations prompt the conclusion that signature, although not implying an obligation of ratification, implies the duty to take some action showing a deliberate acknowledgement of the principle that eventual ratification is the natural outcome and purpose of the signature.

4. On the other hand, the authors of the Harvard Draft Convention correctly applied the principle, as stated in the passage cited above, to the question of the obligation resting upon a signatory State between signature and ratification. With regard to that question the present Article adopts, as expressing the existing law on the subject, the principle that the signature implies the obligation 'to refrain, prior to ratification, from any act intended substantially to impair the value of the undertaking as signed'. It will be noted that: (i) that obligation constitutes a legal, and not merely a moral, duty; (ii) that it refers only to such acts as are intended, and not merely calculated, to impair the value of the obligation as signed. For the purpose of that rule is to prohibit action in bad faith deliberately aiming at depriving the other party of the benefits which it legitimately hoped to achieve from the treaty and for which it gave adequate consider-ation. Thus, for instance, a State would be acting in bad faith and in violation of a legal duty if, to mention a concrete case which pre-sented itself to the Permanent Court of International Justice in the case referred to below, after having undertaken to cede to another a portion of its territory it were to proceed to alienate, in the interval between signature and ratification, all the public property of the State which would otherwise pass to the other contracting party under the rules of State succession. On the other hand, apart from deliberate action intended to deprive the other party of some of the benefits

of the treaty, a contracting party cannot be divested during a period, which may be long and occasionally indefinite, of its freedom of action with regard to normal activities of State administration. Subject to that qualification, the signature imposes upon a State the duty as formulated in the present Article. The Permanent Court of International Justice in effect affirmed that rule in the case concerning *Certain German Interests in Polish Upper Silesia.* While upholding the right of a State to dispose of State property after the signature of the treaty, it qualified that right by laying down that abuse of it would endow an act of alienation with the character of a breach of an international obligation; that such abuse cannot be presumed; and that the burden of proof rests upon the party alleging it (Series A, no. 7, p. 30). The Court then examined the facts of the case and found that the German acts of alienation did not overstep the limits of the normal administration of public property and that they were not intended to deprive Poland of a right to which she was entitled. There are decisions of other international tribunals and of municipal courts to the same effect.[1] Practically all writers who have examined the question support the rule as formulated. There exist a number of treaties which state expressly the obligation of the parties to act on that rule, for instance, Article 38 of the Final Act of Berlin of 26 February 1885, which laid down that 'en attendant la ratification, les Puissances signatoires de cet Acte général s'obligent à n'adopter aucune mesure qui serait contraire aux dispositions du dit Acte'. In so far as this and similar provisions refer to action aimed at by the present Article 5 they are no more than declaratory of an existing principle. In so far as they prohibit all action contrary to the treaty they probably go beyond that Article, which forbids only such action as is deliberately intended to deprive the other contracting party of the benefits of the treaty.

5. With regard to paragraphs 3–5 of the present comment, the reference to the legal effect of signature in some cases is amplified by the statement that this covers also 'any other means of assuming an obligation subject to subsequent confirmation'. This refers to cases in which, for instance, an accession (see Article 7 below) or an

[1] See, for example *Megalidis* v. *Turkey,* decided in 1923 by the Turkish–Greek Mixed Arbitral Tribunal (*Recueil T.A.M.* 8 (1928), 390); *Schrager* v. *Workmen's Accident Insurance Institute,* decided in 1927 by the Supreme Court of Poland (*Annual Digest* (1927–8), case no. 274); *Rentenguts-vertrag* (*Danzig*) case, decided in 1928 by the Obergericht of Danzig (*ibid.* case no. 276). In the case of *Kemeny* v. *Yugoslav State* the Hungarian–Yugoslav Mixed Arbitral Tribunal held that the conferment of mining rights on 20 March 1920, i.e. *before* the date of the signing of the Treaty of Trianon (although after the date of the armistice), was not inconsistent with the obligations of the treaty (*ibid.* case no. 374).

acceptance or a unilateral declaration (see Article 2 above) is made subject to subsequent confirmation.

Note

1. Article 5 as here formulated differs substantially from the relevant Articles tentatively adopted by the Commission, and the observations which follow may therefore be appropriate. Among these Articles there was no separate Article on signature although signature figured in the enumeration of the means of assuming a treaty obligation. This was so probably for the reason that the Commission, while recognizing that the parties may treat the signature as binding, was inclined to treat the signature primarily as a means of authentication and viewed with some disfavour, as contrary to precepts of constitutionalism, its use as a means of assuming an immediate obligation. Yet the fact is that the practice of Governments recognizes it as such to an increasing degree. Moreover, even when signature does not go to the length of the assumption of an immediate obligation, it has a legal significance going beyond mere authentication. It is a declaration of intention, whether it is subject to ratification or not, to become a party to the treaty. It is of interest to note the frequency with which multilateral conventions brought about by the signature of the States or organizations of States participating in the conferences which adopted them provide for additional possible signatures up to a fixed date and for accession subsequent to that date. Moreover, the place of signature as preliminary to accession (Article 7) or acceptance (Article 8) is conspicuous in numerous recent conventions concluded under the auspices of the United Nations and dispensing with ratification.[1]

2. The special rapporteur does not consider that the mere negative statement that there is no obligation to ratify a signature does justice to the problem from the point of view either of codification or of development of international law. That negative statement, when properly supplemented, is correct. When standing in isolation it is incomplete and to that extent inaccurate. A party which has signed a treaty is not bound to ratify it. But it cannot, consistently with legal principle and good faith, act – or refrain from acting – as if it had never signed the treaty at all. It must examine the treaty in order to come to a decision, with regard to which it enjoys full freedom of

[1] See, for example, the International Sanitary Convention for Aerial Navigation of 15 September 1944, which provides, in Article XVIII, that it shall come into force as soon as it has been signed or acceded to on behalf of ten or more Governments (*U.N.T.S.* 16, 247).

action, whether to approve the treaty or not. It is not of decisive importance that Governments have not expressly accepted that principle or that the report on the subject produced by a committee appointed by the Assembly of the League of Nations and pointing to an obligation to submit the treaty to the proper authorities for approval or rejection did not secure formal acceptance. In codifying international law the Commission is not limited to registering uniform practice. If that were its purpose its work would be partly nominal and partly redundant. While in some matters the Commission will adequately discharge its function by the mere fact of drafting rules expressive of uniform practice, in other fields – where uniform practice is lacking – it is its function to formulate rules based on what it considers *the correct legal principle*, the requirements of good faith, and such practice as it considers most conducive to the effectiveness and development of international law.

3. The same considerations apply to the second legal consequence of the signature, namely, abstention – in the period between signature and ratification – from action intended to deprive the treaty wholly or in part of its effectiveness and thus to deceive the other contracting party. This, again, is a legal obligation. The Commission refrained from laying down that principle on the ground that, as stated in its comment to tentative Article 7, the material available is 'of too fragmentary and inconclusive a nature to form the basis of codification'. However, as shown in the comment to the present Article, judicial practice, including that of the highest international tribunal, is as complete as can be desired in the circumstances. Even if there existed a regularly functioning international judiciary endowed with compulsory jurisdiction it could hardly be expected that it would produce a rich crop of cases bearing on what is in the nature of things an unusual occurrence. Here, again, what is decisive for the purpose of codification is the drawing, in the light of existing practice, of the necessary conclusions dictated by the principles of good faith (which form part of the law), of the function of signature (which goes beyond that of mere authentication), and of the requirement of honest international intercourse. Practically all writers who have examined this question have come to the conclusion formulated in the present Article – although some, including Anzilotti, base that conclusion not on the effect of the treaty as such but on the principle prohibiting abuse of rights. Thus Anzilotti says:

Il faut encore observer que, en excluant tout effet obligatoire du traité antérieurement à la ratification, on ne veut pas dire que l'État puisse ne tenir aucun compte du texte intervenu et faire comme si rien ne s'était produit. Il y a lieu, par contre, d'admettre que, lorsque la procédure de ratification d'un traité régulièrement signé est pendante, l'État doit s'abstenir d'accomplir des actes de nature à rendre impossible ou plus difficile l'exécution régulière du traité une fois ratifié. Mais il est clair qu'il ne s'agit pas alors d'un effet du traité comme tel, mais bien d'une application du principe qui défend d'abuser du droit. (Anzilotti, p. 372.)

4. The special rapporteur has not found it necessary to refer in the comment to the conventional exceptions to the principle that a party is entitled to refuse to proceed with ratification. This exception is created by Article 19 of the Constitution of the International Labour Organization which provides that, when the consent of the competent authority has been obtained, a member of the Organization is bound to communicate its ratification of the convention for which consent has been given. In the case of International Labour Conventions there is no question of ratification of a signature previously given. Such ratifications are more in the nature of accession than ratification in the accepted sense. With regard to other treaties the matter is not free from difficulty. It is frequently asserted that a contracting party is under no obligation to proceed to ratify a treaty which it has signed and which has received the legislative approval necessary for ratification. (See, for example, as to French decisions and practice in the matter Preuss in *A.J.* 44 (1950), 649.) However, refusal to ratify in such circumstances strains to breaking point the principle that a contracting party is free to decline to ratify a treaty which it has signed. For it is largely the necessity for legislative approval which is the *raison d'être* of ratification. There may be reasons justifying refusal to ratify in such circumstances – the reasons being largely identical with those which justify unilateral termination of a treaty – but they must be regarded as exceptional. The question deserves consideration by the Commission. It is particularly acute in cases in which the wording of the Article requiring ratification is such as to make legislative approval appear to be the sole reason for the requirement of ratification.

CHAPTER 6

RATIFICATION

1953 REPORT

ARTICLE 6

RATIFICATION

1. Ratification is an act by which a competent organ of a State formally approves as binding the treaty or the signature thereof.

2. In the absence of ratification a treaty is not binding upon a contracting party unless:

(*a*) The treaty in effect provides otherwise by laying down, without reference to ratification, that it shall enter into force upon signature or upon any other date or upon a specified event other than ratification;

(*b*) The treaty, while providing that it shall be ratified, provides also that it shall come into force prior to ratification;

(*c*) The treaty is in the form of an exchange of notes or an agreement between Government departments;

(*d*) The attendant circumstances or the practice of the contracting parties concerned indicate the intention to assume a binding obligation without the necessity of ratification.

Alternative version of paragraph 2

[2. Confirmation of the treaty by way of ratification is required only when the treaty so provides.]

Comment

1. *Ratification is an act of confirmation by a competent organ.* The question as to who is the competent organ to ratify a treaty is one which international law leaves to the constitution and, generally, to the law of the parties whether they be States or organizations of States. With regard to States, although as a general rule the power to ratify treaties is formally vested in the Head of the State, most constitutions qualify this rule by laying down that ratification shall not be given, or shall not be binding, unless the prior approval of the legislature or part thereof has been obtained. In some States this limitation applies to

all treaties; in others only to certain categories of treaties. The rule prevailing in some countries, such as the British Commonwealth of Nations, that the Head of the State has the unfettered power to ratify treaties is a practice modified by the convention that important treaties or certain categories of treaties are submitted for parliamentary approval prior to ratification. Also, in these countries the theoretically unrestricted power of the Head of the State to ratify treaties is limited by the principle that provisions of treaties affecting the private rights of the subject must be incorporated, by an act of legislation, into the law of the land before they can be applied by the courts. The law of only very few States – such as Ethiopia, Jordan, Morocco, Saudi Arabia and the Vatican City – reserves an unlimited power of ratification to the Head of the State. Occasionally the written constitution or constitutional practice empowers organs other than the Head of the State to ratify international agreements.[1] Such provisions, however, are infrequent for the reason that, according to the practice of many States, interdepartmental agreements are not subject to ratification (see below, paragraph 5 (c)). In any case, whatever may be the provisions, if any, of the national law on the subject, compliance with them, in so far as they are known and ascertainable (see Article 11 below), is an essential condition of the coming into force of the treaty.[2]

2. The expression 'formally approves as binding the treaty or the signature thereof' is intended to convey that, as a rule, the act of ratification may be an approval either of an instrument which the State has not previously signed or, which is the normal rule, of a signature previously appended by the representatives of the State

[1] A United States Act of 1934 provides that the Postmaster General may, with the advice and consent of the President, negotiate and conclude postal treaties or conventions. These treaties and conventions are ratified by the Postmaster General. The seal of the Post Office Department of the United States is affixed to the ratification.

[2] It must be noted in this connection that the term ratification as here used refers to *international* ratification. The law and constitutions of some countries occasionally use the term 'ratification' for what is essentially approval given by the legislature to subsequent international ratification by the Head of the State. The following message from the Peruvian Congress to the President of the Republic illustrates that terminology: 'Resolución Legislativa No. 11828, Lima, 3 de abril de 1952. Señor: El Congreso, en ejercicio de la atribución que le confiere el inciso 21 del artículo 123 de la Constitución política del Estado, ha resuelto ratificar el Convenio Comercial suscrito con la República Federal de Alemania, en Bonn, el 20 de julio de 1951' (*Revista Peruana de Derecho Internacional* (1952), pp. 130–1). On the other hand, Article 27 of the French Constitution of 1946 uses what is declared to be more precise language in this connection: 'Article 27. Treaties relative to the international organization, peace treaties, commercial treaties, treaties involving national forces, treaties relative to the personal status and property rights of French citizens abroad, and those that modify French internal legislation, as well as those involving cession, exchange or addition of territories shall not become final until they have been ratified *by virtue of a legislative act* (*en vertu d'une loi*).'

duly authorized to sign the treaty. The view is occasionally expressed (as, for instance, in the comment to Article 6 of the Harvard Draft Convention) that ratification is a confirmation not of the signature (or its equivalent) but of the treaty. It is believed that that view (adopted in the comment to the Harvard Draft Convention and in Article 5 of the tentative draft of the Commission) does violence to the language customarily used in instruments of ratification, that it is contrary to the preponderant authority, and that it fails to do justice to the independent status of the signature, which is productive of legal effects of its own. It is irrelevant for this purpose whether the signatures are those of the personal representatives of the Head of the State or of the representatives of the State as such.[1] The motive underlying this conception of signature – which is not here admitted as accurate – is, by diminishing its legal importance, to emphasize the absence of any legal obligation to confirm the signature. No such interpretation of the value of the signature is necessary in support of what is an unchallenged rule. This, as has been suggested in the comment to Article 5 and as will be suggested presently, does not mean that signature is of no legal value or effect.

The wording used in the present paragraph has been adopted in order to accommodate the eventual occurrence – as is the case with the conventions of the International Labour Organization or of some treaties constituting international organizations where the treaties are adopted by the conference and submitted for subsequent acceptance by States – of ratification of treaties which are not subject to signature (although even in these cases the signature is implied in most cases by the participation of the representative of the State in the drafting and adoption of the treaty by a conference or an organ of an international organization).

3. The second paragraph of Article 6 is concerned with the question

---

[1] The legal position in the matter has been put correctly, it is believed, by Judge Basdevant in his dissenting opinion in the *Ambatielos* case between Greece and the United Kingdom (Preliminary objection). He said: 'The drafting and the signature of an international agreement are the acts by means of which the will of the contracting States is expressed: ratification is the act by which the will so expressed is confirmed by the competent authority, for the purpose of giving it binding force' (*I.C.J. Reports* 1952, p. 69). Similarly, any tendency to distinguish between ratification as understood in the language of general jurisprudence and a conception of ratification peculiar to international law (or between the notion of ratification in earlier and in modern international law) was, in effect, discouraged by the learned judge in the following terms: 'When they signed the instruments of ratification – an act by which they confirmed the agreement reached by their respective plenipotentiaries and by which they gave the declaration a definitive character of the will of the contracting States – the President of the Greek Republic and the British Monarch were merely confirming what had already been declared by their plenipotentiaries.'

which is often discussed but whose practical importance is distinctly limited, namely, whether treaties, in the absence of an express or implied provision to the contrary, require ratification. For the reasons stated below two – seemingly contradictory – versions of the relevant paragraph may properly be considered. In the first version that question is answered in the affirmative. This version of the second paragraph by obvious implication rejects the view that treaties do not require ratification unless they provide expressly or implicitly that they are subject to ratification. The reasons under-lying that view may be stated as follows: The importance of the subject matter of treaties is such that unless the parties have waived the requirement of ratification the latter must be considered essential to the international validity of the treaty. There is little persuasive force in the argument that as numerous treaties expressly provide for ratification it must be considered that in all other cases the parties must be deemed to have waived it. For the inclusion of an express provision in the matter of ratification may mean no more than that the parties intended to emphasize the solemnity and the importance of the treaty and that they desired to leave no room for uncertainty in the matter. It has also been pointed out that by parity of reasoning it might be argued that as numerous treaties lay down expressly that they shall enter into force upon signature (i.e. that they do not require ratification), the absence of any reference to the matter would mean that ratification is indicated. The controversy surrounding the subject is to a large extent theoretical. The more formal type of instruments designated as treaties and conventions between Heads of States or States include, practically without exception, express provisions on the subject. They are to be found on occasions, ad-mittedly rare, also in exchanges of notes and inter-departmental agreements. Whatever may be their description, treaties either pro-vide that the instrument shall be ratified or, by laying down that it shall enter into force on signature or on a specified date or event, dispense with ratification. This is the regular practice. Silence on the subject is exceptional. In view of this the elaboration, in the second paragraph of Article 6, of the situations in which, in the absence of any provision on the subject, ratification is not required may seem otiose. However, it is one of the purposes of codification to provide for cases – even if rare – in which the subject is not expressly regulated by the parties.

4. As stated, the practical importance of Article 6 as formulated is somewhat reduced by the fact that an increasing number of treaties

provide, without reference to ratification, that they shall enter into force on signature or on a specified date or event thereafter. Nearly one-third of the bilateral instruments between States or organizations of States contain provisions to that effect. That circumstance may well act as a reminder of the element of exaggeration inherent in the occasional statements to the effect that modern practice has tended to reduce the importance of the signature – a statement which must be received with no less caution than the view that recent practice shows a tendency to dispense with ratification in favour either of signature or of new methods such as acceptance. The fact is that both signature and ratification are – apart from accession – the typical means of assuming treaty obligations. It might be conducive to clarity and simplicity if they were to remain so. It may now be convenient to comment on the first version of paragraph 2.

5 (a). 'In the absence of ratification a treaty is not binding upon a contracting party unless: (a) The treaty in effect provides otherwise by laying down, without reference to ratification, that it shall enter into force upon signature or upon any other date or upon a specified event other than ratification of that particular treaty.' As mentioned, the various methods of dispensing with ratification – in particular, the precise determination of the date of entry into force – have become a frequent feature of international practice in relation to bilateral agreements.[1] The 'other date', referred to in this paragraph,

[1] Thus, to give examples taken from one volume, chosen at random, of the *U.N.T.S.* – vol. 76 (1950) – more than one-third of the instruments reported there provide that they shall enter into force upon signature. In the second category – entering into force upon any other date – the Trade Agreement of 15 December 1948 between Turkey and Denmark provides that it shall enter into force on 1 January 1949 (*ibid.* p. 21). The Exchange of Notes constituting an agreement, of 28 February 1945, between the United States of America and the Provisional Government of the French Republic relating to the Principles Applying to the Provision of Aid to the Armed Forces of the United States laid down that it should enter into force on the date of signature with retroactive effect as from 6 June 1944 (*ibid.* p. 214). In the third class – entering into force upon a specified event – the Payment Agreement of 15 December 1948 between Denmark and Turkey provided that it shall enter into force on the same day as the Trade Agreement signed by the parties (*ibid.* p. 7). A similar provision was included in the Exchange of Notes between the Netherlands and New Zealand of 18 October 1947 constituting a supplementary agreement to the General Agreement on Tariffs and Trade (*ibid.* p. 42). It is of interest to note that in the above-mentioned volume of the *U.N.T.S.* only two treaties provide for ratification, and only one for 'approval' (the Agreement between the Food and Agriculture Organization and the World Health Organization). In respect of one agreement only, published in the volume in question, the position as to ratification remained partly undetermined, namely, the Agreement of the Netherlands with the International Refugee Organization of 20 June 1950 relating to the care to be given to forty refugees resident in the Netherlands (*ibid.* p. 56) – 'partly undetermined', for this agreement, in view of the urgency of its execution, probably falls within the category of agreements not requiring ratification having regard to 'attendant circumstances' (see below, paragraph 5 (c)). The footnote of the Secretariat of the United Nations states that the agreement came into force

is occasionally left to future determination by agreement of the parties. Occasionally it is stated to be the 'appointed date' or a date prior to signature.

The nature of the 'event' upon which the treaty is to enter into force is described in terms of great diversity. Thus the series of agreements concluded in 1947 between the United Kingdom and Ceylon on matters of defence, external affairs and trade provided that they 'will take effect when the constitutional measures necessary for conferring on Ceylon fully responsible status within the British Commonwealth of Nations shall come into force' (*U.N.T.S.* 86, 28). The Agreement of 5 June 1946 between the Government of the United Kingdom and the Government of Canada for the Avoidance of

on the date of signature. The only other agreement in that volume which contains no provision on the subject is the Exchange of Notes of 8 November 1945 between France and the United States of America supplementing a previous agreement, which entered into force on the date of signature, relating to the Principles Applying to Mutual Aid in the Prosecution of the War (*ibid.* p. 153). The agreement is one which probably falls within the category of declarations of policy rather than of legal instruments (see Article 1 above). A footnote appended by the Secretariat of the United Nations states that the notes came into force on the day on which they were exchanged. The above volume of the *U.N.T.S.*, which is believed to be typical with respect to bilateral treaties, in addition to providing examples of contractual instruments entering into force without ratification is instructive as providing further evidence that, in view of the normal regulation of that question in the instruments themselves, the question whether treaties require ratification is, while of considerable theoretical interest, of limited practical importance.

In a matter of this description, in which doctrinal controversy has to a considerable degree obscured the realities of the problem which confronts the task of codification, it is useful to scrutinize closely the practice of agreements, and the special rapporteur has therefore thought it useful to verify the results of the analysis of volume 76 of the *U.N.T.S.* by an examination of volumes 66, 56 and 46 of the *U.N.T.S.* Volume 56 is entirely devoted to a mimeographed reproduction of schedules of tariff concessions in connection with the General Agreement on Tariffs and Trade, and may therefore be left out of account. Volume 66 records the following position: twelve instruments, being exchanges of notes, entered into force on the date of the first or the second note; nine instruments, not being exchanges of notes, entered into force on the date of signature; six instruments entered into force on a date fixed by the treaty. It thus appears not only that in not one out of twenty-six instruments was the question of ratification left open, but that all these agreements entered into force without any ratification at all (except in one case in which the approval of the national Parliament of one party – but not ratification – was stipulated). In volume 46 ten instruments, being exchanges of notes, entered into force immediately; four other agreements entered into force upon signature; and four others upon the date of exchange of ratification. In one case – that of the Franco-Belgian Convention of 29 December 1947 (p. 112) – the convention came into force provisionally upon signature and finally upon exchange of ratification. Of the three remaining instruments the Protocol of the Circulation and Traffic in Obscene Publications (p. 170) provided that States may become parties by (a) signature without reservation as to approval; (b) acceptance to be effected by the deposit of a formal instrument with the Secretary-General of the United Nations. The Parcel Post Agreement of 15 July 1949 between the Philippines and Australia (p. 216) laid down that the agreement shall come into force upon ratification or approval by the proper authorities but that, pending ratification or approval, it may be put into force administratively on a date to be mutually settled between the postal administrations of the two countries. Again, in no case was the question of the necessity for ratification left in abeyance.

Double Taxation provides, in Article 10, that it shall come into force 'on the date on which the last of all such things have been done in the United Kingdom and Canada as are necessary to give the agreement the force of law in the United Kingdom and Canada respectively' (*ibid.* p. 5).

5 (b). 'In the absence of ratification a treaty is not binding upon a contracting party unless: (*b*) The treaty, while providing that it shall be ratified, provides also that it shall come into force prior to ratification.' There are frequent examples of this type of treaty. For instance, the Trade and Payments Agreement between Denmark and Argentina of 14 December 1948, after providing, in Article 41, that it 'shall be approved[1] in conformity with the constitutional procedure of each of the High Contracting Parties', lays down that 'without prejudice to its final approval, this agreement shall enter into force provisionally fifteen days from the date of signature and shall remain in force for five years' subject to a right of denunciation after the first year. The Franco-Belgian Convention for the Avoidance of Double Taxation signed on 29 December 1947 provided, in Article 10, that it shall be ratified and the instruments of ratification exchanged as soon as possible, but that it shall enter into force provisionally on the date of its signature (*U.N.T.S.* 46, 117).

5 (c). 'In the absence of ratification a treaty is not binding upon a contracting party unless: (*c*) The treaty is in the form of an exchange of notes or an agreement between Government departments.' Normally the form or designation of the treaty cannot be regarded as relevant to the question of necessity for ratification. For, as already mentioned, exchanges of notes have occasionally been made subject to ratification. However, as a rule – and this applies also to agreements concluded between Government departments – they specify the date on which they shall enter into force and thus, by obvious implication, dispense with ratification. That date may be – and usually is – the date of the exchange of the notes. In some cases it is laid down that the agreement established by the exchange of notes or by the inter-departmental arrangement[2] shall enter into force on

---

[1] The English text has the term 'approved', while the French text lays down that the 'accord sera ratifié'. The Spanish text provides: 'El presente Convenio sera aprobado'. It is probable that the intention was to refer to international ratification, as distinct from internal constitutional approval.

[2] Thus, for instance, the Parcel Post Agreement between the United States and Korea (signed by Korea on 17 February 1949 and by the United States on 13 April 1949) concluded between the Post Office Department of the United States of America and the Department of Communications of Korea laid down that it should take effect on a date to be mutually settled between the administrations of the two countries.

a date to be settled by the parties. To that extent the matter is governed by paragraph 2 (*a*) which lays down, in effect, that the treaty is binding without ratification if the parties, without referring to ratification, determine the date or accept a date on which the treaty shall enter into force.

In general, exchanges of notes, apart from exceptional cases, leave no doubt as to the intention of the parties to dispense with ratification. With regard to such exceptional cases, reasons of convenience, the uniformity of existing practice, and considerations of expedition which characterize exchanges of notes – and agreements between Government departments – urge acceptance of the presumptive rule that they do not require ratification.

5 (d). 'In the absence of ratification a treaty is not binding upon a contracting party unless: (*d*) The attendant circumstances or the practice of the contracting parties concerned indicate the intention to assume a binding obligation without the necessity of ratification.' The nature of the attendant circumstances which make ratification unnecessary cannot be circumscribed in advance. They will as a rule cover agreements of limited scope concluded by Governments and requiring speedy action. The Agreement, referred to above (p. 165, n. 1), between the Netherlands and the International Refugee Organization for the care of forty refugees in Holland may be mentioned as an example. Also, if it can be shown that the practice of a contracting party has been such as not to require the ratification of a particular type of agreement that party will be bound by the instrument in question unless the requirement of ratification has been expressly made part of the agreement. To that extent the subject of this paragraph 2 (*d*) is identical with that of paragraph 2 (*c*). Thus Sir Arnold McNair has pointed out that, in view of the consistent custom of inserting a provision for ratification in all cases in which the parties desire that procedure to be followed, the Government of the United Kingdom does not deem it necessary to ratify a treaty which contains no such clause. In particular, he states, ratification is unnecessary, from the point of view of the United Kingdom, with regard to inter-governmental agreements even if they are concerned with matters of importance, for instance, arbitration agreements or boundary agreements; protocols or declarations[1] or additional Articles modifying or adding to the principal agreement which does

---

[1] In the *Ambatielos* case Judge McNair was prepared to hold, if necessary, that a declaration which, in his view, did not form part of a ratified treaty was binding without ratification having regard to the practice of the United Kingdom (*I.C.J. Reports* 1952, p. 60).

or did not require ratification; and 'many exchanges of notes, agreements establishing *modi vivendi* or other provisional arrangements, and agreements prolonging the duration of commercial treaties and extradition treaties' (McNair, pp. 85–7).

6. The general manner of formulation of this part of paragraph 2 of Article 6 is deliberate. No attempt has been made to define in detail the nature of the attendant circumstances which raise the presumption that no ratification was intended and that none is required. However, in some cases the practice of States has assumed the complexion of a well-established – though not necessarily rigidly defined – custom. It is that custom which makes it permissible to state that, in general and subject to any express provisions to the contrary, inter-departmental agreements and arrangements which are obviously concerned with matters of limited importance do not require ratification. The same applies to other instruments – whatever their designation – which, within a limited sphere, are supplementary to agreements previously concluded. As already stated, in all these cases it is the content of the instrument and the attendant circumstances rather than the designation of the instrument which are decisive. Although there is occasionally some correlation between the designation of the instrument and its content, this is not always so. 'Conventions' or 'treaties' is the term often used to cover agreements on matters of a general character and of obvious political importance – just as in such cases it is frequently the Head of the State or the State as such who are described as the contracting parties. However, these designations of the instrument and of the parties thereto are occasionally used in connection with instruments of limited importance or of a purely technical character. The decisive consideration is that there are factors which make ratification appropriate and natural in some cases, but not in others. Thus, for instance, a treaty, bilateral or multilateral, requiring extensive changes in municipal law and detailed inter-departmental consultation in this connection, may require ratification notwithstanding its designation – though it is natural to assume and to expect that in such cases the designation of the treaty will not be that of an exchange of notes or of an agreement between administrative agencies. As a rule the previous practice, in the matter of ratification, of the State concerned may legitimately be relied upon. It is not possible, in commenting upon this part of Article 6, to go beyond this necessarily general statement. In practice, as previously suggested, the question arises only in rare cases. As a rule treaties, of whatever description,

leave no doubt as to the intention of the parties in the matter of ratification. But a rule there must be both in order to meet the rare cases and as an inducement to Governments, in case they desire the ratification of an instrument which is here stated as normally not requiring it, to give clear expression to their intentions. In general, with regard to multilateral treaties – because of their importance and, frequently, their resulting implications in the municipal sphere – more stringent proof will be required to show that, in the language of paragraph 2 (*d*), the 'attendant circumstances or the practice of the parties' are such as to justify the conclusion that no ratification is required.

7. However – and this consideration leads to the alternative version of the second paragraph of Article 2 – if there must be a rule, if the cases in which the parties in effect fail to regulate the matter are conspicuous for their rarity, and if the rule as stated above provides for so many exceptions as almost to be transformed into a principle opposed to that which seemingly underlies it, is it not preferable to lay down, as expressing either the existing or the desirable law, that no ratification is required unless the parties provide for it expressly? Constant practice of Governments shows that, with minor exceptions, in all cases of multilateral treaties of importance express provision is made for ratification. It would seem reasonable to assume that with regard to such treaties the absence of provision for ratification shows that the parties did not wish ratification to be a condition of entry into force. For it could hardly be assumed that the matter escaped their attention. Undoubtedly, it would be better if they had said *something*, e.g. that the treaty shall enter into force upon signature or upon some specified date or event. They do so occasionally.[1] However, having regard to the constant practice of expressly providing for ratification where the parties wish the treaty to be ratified, the implication of necessity for ratification seems an inconclusive inference from their mere silence. In fact in those rare cases in which a treaty has been silent on the matter, there has been a tendency to

---

[1] The Agreement of 31 December 1934 concerning postal exchanges between Denmark, Finland, Iceland, Norway and Sweden was concluded between the Post Office authorities of those countries. It laid down that it shall enter into force on 1 January 1935. The Agreement of 3 April 1939 between Belgium, France and the Netherlands concerning navigation on the Rhine provided that it shall enter into force on the date of signature (Hudson, *Legislation*, VIII, 283). The Nyon Arrangement of 14 September 1937 and the Supplementary Arrangement of 17 November 1937 concerning attacks upon merchantmen in the Mediterranean provided expressly that they shall enter into force immediately (*ibid.* VII, 831, 841).

assume that no requirement of ratification was intended.[1] For these reasons it has been deemed convenient to present here an alternative version of the second paragraph of Article 6 – a version according to which ratification is not required if it is not expressly provided for in the treaty. As will be submitted – in notes 1 and 2 to this comment – the actual practical difference between these two versions is not substantial. The present alternative version, in addition to the considerations outlined above, takes into account the changes which have taken place in international intercourse in the matter of conclusion of treaties. These changes, especially in relation to bilateral treaties, are the result of factors which are not of a merely transient character. In the first instance, as the result of developments in the sphere of telecommunications and facilities for travel generally, ratification is no longer a confirmation of a treaty negotiated by plenipotentiaries out of touch with the central authorities of their State and unable to receive day-by-day instructions with regard both to the details of the negotiations and to the signature itself. Secondly, whatever may be the political divisions of the world, the growing interdependence of States, and the manifold variety of their contracts have added very substantially to the range of treaties and to the necessity for expedition in bringing them into force. The increasing and already largely consummated tendency towards simplification of the procedure in the treaty-making process is an inevitable consequence of these changes.

Note

1. With regard to the main question connected with the present Article, namely, whether in the absence of relevant provisions in the treaty ratification is required in order to make the treaty binding, the solution, or solutions, outlined by the special rapporteur differ, in effect, but little from that tentatively adopted by the Commission. In the first version of paragraph 2 they differ from it in so far as they envisage a wider range of cases in which the parties must be presumed to have intended to dispense with ratification. However, even in the Article tentatively adopted by the Commission the range of exceptions was so wide as to leave but little scope for the operation of

---

[1] The Final Act of the Conference of Wheat Exporting and Importing Countries of 25 August 1933 was stated to have entered into force on that day (*L.N.T.S.* 141, 71; Hudson, *Legislation*, VI, 437). The Act contained no reference to the subject. This was also the case with regard to the Agreement of 20 December 1935 between the United Kingdom, Canada, Australia, New Zealand and South Africa, on the one hand, and Germany on the other, concerning war graves (*ibid.* VII, 213).

the principal rule laying down that in the absence of relevant provisions a treaty must be ratified in order to be binding. In view of this there is only a slight practical difference between that formulation and the seemingly contrary rule, formulated in the alternative version of paragraph 2, that in the absence of express provisions requiring ratification no ratification is necessary for the validity of the treaty. This conclusion is, on the face of it, startling. But it is startling only if we forget that a wholly unqualified rule requiring ratification is contrary to practice and that qualifying exceptions, if numerous, tend to bridge the gap between the opposing formulations.

2. As there is no substantial difference between the two seemingly opposed solutions as expressed in the two alternative versions of paragraph 2, it would appear that it does not matter very much which solution is accepted – although purely practical considerations counsel the adoption of a rule which is precise and clear. As a matter of doctrine the difference between the two methods of approach is substantial. One will recommend itself to those who, for reasons of constitutionality, of the importance of the interests affected, and of the historic function of ratification as a natural concomitant of signature, consider ratification to be essential unless expressly dispensed with. The second solution will be favoured by those who, having regard to the requirements of international intercourse in modern conditions and to cogent deductions from actual practice, see in the signature an act of a significance greater than mere authentication and establishment of the text. As stated, the practical difference in the effect of either solution is small. The importance of the subject is further reduced by the circumstance that the question hardly arises in practice. For with minor exceptions treaties either provide that they shall be ratified or, in various ways, indicate conclusively the intention of the parties to bring them into effect without ratification. While, as shown in the comment to Article 11, there are examples of States attempting to avoid a treaty on the ground that it was not ratified in accordance with the requirement of their constitution, there are probably no instances of their attempting to do so on the ground that the treaty required ratification as a condition of its international validity and that it was not in fact ratified. That circumstance does not absolve the Commission from the task of formulating a rule for the very small residuum of cases in which the parties have left the question open. For it is only the existence of a clear presumptive rule which will induce the parties to adopt an

explicit provision in case they desire a procedure differing from that as expressed within the framework of general codification.

3. In formulating the present Article the special rapporteur has avoided undue elaboration of matters of detail – some of them obvious – connected with ratification. These matters include the principle, which ought not to give rise to controversy, that wherever in an international instrument there is a reference to a 'treaty', such reference means a valid treaty, i.e. a treaty which has been ratified, and that where reference is made to 'parties to a treaty' such reference means parties who have ratified a treaty. This – and no other – is in fact the import of the relevant pronouncement in the Judgment of the Permanent Court of International Justice given in 1929 in the case concerning the *Territorial Jurisdiction of the International Commission of the River Oder* (*P.C.I.J.*, Series A, no. 23, pp. 17–22), where reference in Article 338 of the Treaty of Versailles to a convention to be drawn up by the Allied and Associated Powers was held to mean, in relation to Poland, a convention ratified by Poland. This was so, in particular, seeing that the convention in question – the Barcelona Convention – provided expressly that it was subject to ratification. In view of this the Court held that the Barcelona Convention, not having been ratified by Poland, could not be invoked against her.[1] In *Phillipson and Others* v. *Imperial Airways Ltd.* [1939] A.C. 337, the British House of Lords held that the term 'high contracting party', used in a contract of carriage and referring to the Warsaw Convention of 1929 on Air Transport, included Belgium, who had signed but not ratified the convention. The decision can probably be explained by reference to the special circumstances of a commercial contract. In a subsequent communication addressed to the United States, the Government of the United Kingdom seems to have dissociated itself from that decision. It said: 'H.M. Government are of the opinion that the ordinary meaning of high contracting party in a convention is to designate a party who is bound by the provisions of a convention and therefore does not cover a signatory who does not ratify it.' The United States Department of State agreed with that view (Hackworth, IV, 373).

4. In general, it is not the ratification, but the exchange or deposit of ratifications, which brings the treaty finally into force. That rule comes more conveniently within the purview of Part IV, which is

---

[1] This judgment of the Court is occasionally referred to as an authority for the proposition that treaties require ratification. However, this is hardly the true import of the judgment.

concerned with the operation and enforcement of treaties, and it is proposed to examine it there.

5. The special rapporteur did not consider it necessary to elaborate the principle, expressed in paragraph 1, that ratification is a formal document – which means, in any case, that it is a written document. Writers have occasionally discussed the question whether ratification may be in the form of an oral declaration. It is believed that there are no instances of such ratification and that, in any case, the considerations which require the written form for the conclusion of a treaty (see Article 17 below) apply, *a fortiori*, to its ratification. It is of the essence of ratification that it should be a deliberate and formal act directed exclusively to that purpose. For similar reasons it is difficult to admit the legal possibility of implied ratification, i.e. ratification by conduct. When a party or the parties have in fact acted upon a treaty which provided for ratification, the correct legal construction is not that they have ratified it by conduct but that their conduct amounts to a waiver of the requirement of ratification.

1954 REPORT

ARTICLE 6

RATIFICATION

1. Ratification is an act by which a competent organ of a State formally approves as binding the treaty or the signature thereof.

2. In the absence of ratification a treaty is not binding upon a contracting party unless:

(*a*) The treaty in effect provides otherwise by laying down, without reference to ratification, that it shall enter into force upon signature or upon any other date or upon a specified event other than ratification;

(*b*) The treaty, while providing that it shall be ratified, provides also that it shall come into force prior to ratification;

(*c*) The treaty is in the form of an exchange of notes or an agreement between Government departments;

(*d*) The attendant circumstances or the practice of the contracting parties concerned indicate the intention to assume a binding obligation without the necessity of ratification.

Alternative version of paragraph 2

[2. Confirmation of the treaty by way of ratification is required only when the treaty so provides. *However, in the absence of express provisions to the contrary, ratification is in any case necessary with regard to treaties which, having regard to their subject matter, require parliamentary approval or authorization of ratification in accordance with the constitutional law or practice of the countries concerned.*]

The passage italicized constitutes an addition to the previous report.[1]

1. The special rapporteur attaches importance to stating that the submission of two alternative drafts on the question is intended, to some extent, to express his view that the practical difference between the adoption of the one or the other solution is not considerable. According to one solution, which has the merit of simplicity, confirmation – through ratification – of a signed treaty is not required as a condition of its validity unless there is a clause expressly providing for ratification. According to the other solution ratification is an essential condition of the assumption of a valid treaty obligation unless the treaty either expressly provides to the contrary or unless such provision is to be implied from the previous practice of the parties, from the fact that it is concluded in the form of an exchange of notes or an agreement between Government departments, or from other 'attendant circumstances' – a potentially wide range of exceptions. These exceptions are so wide – in particular in view of the large number of treaties concluded by way of exchanges of notes and interdepartmental agreements – that their effect is to bring about a close approximation of the two alternative solutions. Moreover, the practical importance of the question is rigidly limited by the fact that treaties either expressly provide for ratification or expressly or by implication dispense with it. Reasons have been given in the first report why a codification of the subject – one way or the other – is nevertheless of importance.

2. While the special rapporteur is still of the view that there is a slight preponderance of considerations in favour of the requirement of ratification unless dispensed with expressly or by implication, he feels it necessary to draw repeated attention to the fact – already emphasized in the first report – that the most recent practice shows an increasing number of treaties which come into force without ratification. My attention has been drawn to statistical data, more detailed than those given in the first report, which reveal that tendency in a conspicuous manner. Thus it appears[2] that while about

---

[1] A/CN.4/63 in *Yearbook of the International Law Commission, 1953*, vol. II.
[2] See article by Blix in *B.Y.* 30 (1953), 352 *et seq.*

one-half of the instruments registered in the League of Nations Treaty Series came into force by ratification, this has been the case only with regard to one-fourth of the instruments registered in the United Nations Treaty Series. With this there is connected the fact that while about 40 per cent of the instruments registered with the League of Nations were described as 'treaties' or 'conventions', this has been the case only with regard to 15 per cent of the instruments registered with the United Nations. This latter development may be of significance inasmuch as it is only in the case of 'treaties' and 'conventions' that ratification constitutes the normal method of bringing them into force.[1] On the other hand, while in the case of the League of Nations about 30 per cent of the registered instruments were in the form of agreements, the percentage in the case of the United Nations is about 45 per cent – again a significant change seeing that ratification in case of agreements is not as normal a course of bringing into force as in the case of 'treaties' or 'conventions'.[2] Moreover, it appears that a large number of instruments are now being brought into force not by ordinary ratification, but by exchanges of 'notes of approval' – a method not referred to in the first report.

3. It may be asked whether, in view of this tendency as revealed by these figures, it is not desirable to formulate what may be described as the residuary rule in the matter – i.e. the rule for the small residuum of cases in which the treaty is in effect silent on the subject – by reference to the fact that ratification now takes place only in a relatively small minority of cases. It would appear legitimate to draw some such inference from what seems to be a clear trend. On the other hand, it is submitted that this is not an inescapable inference from that practice. For the only cogent deduction from that practice is that in an increasing number of cases Governments attach importance to treaties – however designated – entering into force without ratification. It does not follow that they consider the irrelevance of ratification to be the presumptive rule to which, in the absence of provisions to the contrary, they must be deemed to have submitted themselves. There is still room for the view that the general importance of the interests of States regulated by treaty requires that the presumptive – the residuary – rule must be based on the normal requirement of ratification.

[1] Thus of the 'treaties' in the League of Nations Treaty Series only one was not ratified. All 'treaties' in the United Nations Treaty Series were ratified.

[2] In the League of Nations Treaty Series 40 per cent of 'agreements' were ratified. In the United Nations Treaty Series 15 per cent of 'agreements' were ratified.

4. For this reason the Commission may consider whether, even if it arrives at the conclusion that the presumption of non-ratification is the residuary rule, it should not qualify it in turn by laying down that that rule does not apply in relation to treaties which, having regard to their subject matter, require parliamentary approval or authorization of ratification in accordance with the constitutional law or practice of the countries concerned – such as instruments involving cession or exchange of territory, changes in the internal law of the parties, financial obligation of an extensive character, and obligations of assistance in case of war. In such cases the necessity of ratification may properly be regarded as part of the residuary rule. It is, of course, open to the parties to displace that residuary rule by an express provision by virtue of which the treaty enters into force upon signature and without ratification. The special rapporteur has considered it necessary to add this qualification to the alternative residuary rule in case that rule should recommend itself to the Commission.

5. That qualification clearly complicates the residuary rule. However, this may be a case in which simplicity of the rule cannot constitute the decisive factor. A balance must be struck between the tendency to informality and expeditiousness in the conclusion of treaties and the residuary requirement of ratification which may be regarded as dictated by imperative considerations of constitutionality and democratic principles. Some countries continue to attach importance to these considerations as may be seen from the categorical language of Article 5 of the Pan-American Convention on Treaties of 20 February 1928, which provides that 'treaties are obligatory only after ratification by the contracting States, even though this condition is not stipulated in the full powers of the negotiators or does not appear in the treaty itself'.[1] Although that treaty was ratified, by 1 January 1951, only by seven Governments, it must be regarded as evidence of regional practice. On the other hand, the practice of some States, as given recent expression, seems to favour the view that unless the treaty expressly provides for ratification its signature binds the parties. Thus the French Government, in a memorandum submitted on 10 January 1953 to the Secretariat of the United Nations stated as follows: 'Certains traités ne prévoient pas qu'une ratification devra suivre la signature. Dans ce cas la signature, si elle est donnée sans condition (une signature *ad referendum* est une signature sous

---

[1] Printed in Hudson, *Legislation*, iv, 2378 *et seq.* at 2380.

condition), engage définitivement l'État.'[1] It must be assumed that this statement is to be read subject to Article 27 of the Constitution of 1946 which provides that treaties relating to international organization, commerce, financial obligations, the position of French subjects abroad, treaties providing for cession, exchange or acquisition of territory 'ne sont définitifs qu'après avoir été ratifiés en vertu d'une loi'.[2] This provision of the constitution is given effect by means of legislation authorizing the executive to proceed to ratification by virtue of which the treaty becomes internationally binding. This means apparently that, notwithstanding the statement in the French memorandum referred to above, treaties which do not provide for ratification must nevertheless be ratified, in order to become binding, if they fall within one of the categories of treaties enumerated in Article 27. Moreover, it would appear that it would be *ultra vires* of the French Government to conclude a treaty of that description as entering into force upon signature. Similarly, Article 60 of the amended Constitution of the Netherlands provides as follows: 'Agreements with other Powers and with organizations based on international law shall be concluded by or by authority of the King. *If required by such agreements* they shall be ratified by the King.'[3] There are authoritative statements to the effect that this is also the view of the United Kingdom. Thus the Secretary of State for Commonwealth Relations stated on 11 March 1953 in the House of Lords (*House of Lords Debates*, vol. 180, col. 1284) that 'there is never any necessity for ratification unless an agreement so provides'. Here again, in so far as by virtue of constitutional convention certain treaties require the previous approval of Parliament (see paragraph 9 of the comment to Article 2 of the special rapporteur's first report on the law of treaties) it would appear that with regard to such treaties ratification is required if the treaty is silent on the subject. Occasionally, in this respect, the position may not be free of doubt. Thus the Exchange of Notes constituting an agreement of 15 and 22 February 1949 between the United Kingdom and the Union of South Africa confirms 'the arrangement that His Majesty's Government in the United Kingdom should transfer to His Majesty's Government in the Union of South Africa the rights, title and interests which they formerly possessed in Marion Island and Prince Edward Island'.

[1] Printed in 'Laws and Practices Concerning the Conclusion of Treaties', *United Nations Legislative Series* (1953), p. 48.
[2] See, for example, Preuss in *A.J.* 44 (1950), 641 *et seq.*
[3] See van Panhuys in *A.J.* 47 (1953), 537, at 538 (italics added).

Note is taken of the fact that the national flag of the Union of South Africa was raised on these islands on specified dates and that consequently His Majesty's Government 'regard the transfer as complete as from those dates' (*U.N.T.S.* 93 (1951), 76). A similar exchange of notes, providing for the transfer to Australia of the Heard and MacDonald Islands was signed on 19 December 1950 (*ibid.* p. 82). There is no provision for ratification in these instruments. In view of the constitutional rule requiring parliamentary consent for cession of British territory, it may be difficult to imply from the terms of these instruments a dispensation from the requirement of ratification.

6. In this connection there must constantly be borne in mind the close relation between the question of the residuary rule in the matter of ratification and the problem of constitutional limitations upon the treaty-making power. A substantial strain is already imposed by the rule that notwithstanding the disregard of constitutional limitations a treaty which the contracting party in question expressly accepts as binding without ratification is either binding or, as suggested in the first report (Article 11), may in certain circumstances impose obligations upon the State. To say that such result may follow – in disregard of constitutional limitations – as the result of mere silence, is to strain to the breaking point a rule which is controversial in itself. This is the reason why the qualifications now added to the alternative residuary rule include the exception covering constitutional limitations.

7. The additional complication now introduced by the special rapporteur into the alternative residuary rule B adds emphasis to his preference for rule A. At the same time he submits, once more, that the practical importance of the subject is severely limited seeing that by far the greater number of treaties contain express provisions on the subject; that the practical difference between the two rules, as qualified in this report, is small; that no vital interest of States is involved in the adoption of either rule; and that the removal of doubts on the subject, through the adoption of a definite residuary rule, is feasible and desirable. The necessity for a codified rule cannot properly be judged either by the relative importance – political or other – of the rule in question or by the probable frequency of its application.

8. In connection with the subject matter of this Article it would be useful if, in its report on the subject, the Commission could draw attention to the necessity of clarifying one aspect of the practice of

the Secretariat of the United Nations with regard to registration of treaties, especially of exchanges of notes. It has been customary for the Secretariat to append in a footnote on the opening page of the registered instrument a statement to the effect that it entered into force on a specified date. While in some cases such a statement is clearly substantiated by a reference to the relevant Article or Articles of the instrument, in others it is not clear what is the source of the information given. Thus, for instance, in the case of exchanges of notes the footnote merely states that the instruments entered into force on the date (or dates) of the signature of the notes in question. It would be useful to know what is the source of the statement in question. It may perhaps be assumed that the Secretariat, in making the statement, is relying on a source of information other than the implication that exchanges of notes belong to a type of instrument which, by its nature, does not require ratification and that it therefore enters into force as a result of signature. However, the question when the absence of the requirement of ratification may be implied from the terms or the nature of the instrument is difficult to answer and it is arguable that the burden of a decision on the subject cannot properly be put on the organs of the United Nations. Admittedly in some cases such implication is obvious. Thus it is clear that a treaty requires ratification if it contains a clause permitting denunciation 'from year to year as from the date of exchange of ratifications', or, as is the case in various declarations of the acceptance of the optional clause of Article 36 of the Statute of the International Court of Justice, when it confers jurisdiction upon the Court in disputes 'which may arise after the ratification of the declaration concerning any situation or fact arising after such ratification'. On the other hand, it is not certain that dispensation from ratification can be implied from a clause which lays down that a treaty shall be operative as from a stated date or that its provisions shall continue for a stated period of years as from the date of the signing of the agreement. Article 10 of the Agreement between the Governments of the United Kingdom and South Africa concerning the avoidance of double taxation of 14 October 1946 provides that 'the present agreement shall come into force on the date on which the last of all such things shall have been done in the United Kingdom and the Union as are necessary to give the agreement the form of law in the United Kingdom and the Union respectively' (*U.N.T.S.* 86 (1951), 64). A footnote appended on p. 52 states that the treaty 'came into force on 13 February 1947 in accordance with the provisions of Article x'. It is not clear to what extent the provision as quoted implies that the treaty can be regarded as having entered into force without ratification. It seems proper that the report of the Commission should draw attention to the desirability of a clarification of this aspect of the matter.

CHAPTER 7

ACCESSION

1953 REPORT

ARTICLE 7

ACCESSION

1. A State or organization of States may accede to a treaty, which it has not signed or ratified, by formally declaring in a written instrument that the treaty is binding upon it.

2. Accession is admissible only subject to the provisions of the treaty.

3. Unless otherwise provided, accession may be effected at any time after the establishment of the text of the treaty.

Comment

1. In the present Article the expression 'accession' is used as synonymous with 'adhesion'. Attempts have occasionally been made to give different meanings to these terms. It is not believed that such attempts find support in international practice, except that as a rule 'accession' is used in the English and *adhésion* in the French language.

2. 'A State or organization of States may accede to a treaty, which it has not signed *or ratified* . . .' The explanation of the words 'or ratified' is that occasionally – though not frequently – a treaty makes it possible for the parties who participated in a conference to adhere to a treaty which they signed but for some reason failed to ratify within the period described by the treaty. In such cases there would appear to be room for a modification of the usual – and logical – practice of limiting the right of accession to non-signatory States. Thus, for instance, the Protocol of 19 September 1949 on Road Signs and Signals, which lays down that ratifications thereof could take place only up to 1 January 1950 (Article 56 (3)), provides that 'from 1 January 1950, this protocol shall be open to accession by States signatories to the Convention on Road Traffic and by States acceding or having acceded to it'. This seems also to be the case with regard to the Convention approved by the General Assembly on 9 December 1948 on the Prevention and Punishment of the Crime of

Genocide, which sets the date of 1 January 1950 as the date after which States invited to sign it may accede to the convention. This, again, may refer to States which, availing themselves of the invitation, have signed it but have failed to ratify it by 1 January 1950. Where no time limit is set for ratification by the signatories, it is difficult to see why such signatories should not at any time proceed to ratification instead of accession.[1] Most multilateral conventions expressly limit the right of accession to non-signatory States. Thus the International Telecommunications Convention of 2 October 1947 provides, in Article 17, that 'the Government of any country, not a signatory to this convention, may accede thereto at any time . . .' The Telecommunications Convention of 9 December 1932 contained, in Article 4, an identical provision (Hudson, *Legislation*, VI, 113). The Geneva Prisoners of War Convention of 12 August 1949 provides, in Article 139, that 'from the date of its coming into force, it shall be open to any Power in whose name the present convention has not been signed, to accede to this convention'. Similar provisions have been adopted in the Protocol of 23 April 1946 to prolong the International Sanitary Convention for Aerial Navigation of 1944 (*U.N.T.S.* 16, 179); in the various Peace Treaties signed in Paris on 10 February 1947; in the Convention of 2 December 1949 for the Suppression of the Traffic in Persons and the Exploitation and Prostitution of Others; in the Sanitary Convention for Air Navigation of 2 April 1933; and in many others. On the other hand, the General Agreement on Tariffs and Trade of 30 October 1947 (*U.N.T.S.* 55, 194), the Protocol of 19 September 1949 on Road Traffic and some other instruments are open to the construction that States which have signed but not ratified them may accede to them (although no time limit is provided for ratification). In view of the great – and to some extent confusing – variety of treaty provisions on the subject it seems advisable to adopt a fairly wide formulation of the relevant provision of Article 7. It must be a matter for consideration whether the codification of this subject ought not to be accompanied by an attempt to introduce in this respect a measure of uniformity into a practice which may otherwise become a source of confusion.[2]

[1] As is the case with regard to the General Treaty of Peace and Amity of 7 February 1923 between the Central American Republics which, while setting no time limit for ratification, provided that 'any of the Republics of Central America which should fail to ratify this treaty shall have the right to adhere to it while it is in force'.

[2] Thus, for instance, the Agreement of 22 November 1950 on the Importation of Educational, Scientific and Cultural Materials provides in Article IX (1) that it shall remain open for signature by all Member States of the United Nations Educational, Scientific and Cultural Organization, all Member States of the United Nations and any

3. The Article as formulated provides for the possibility of accession by international organizations. This is in accordance with the scheme of the present draft which recognizes the treaty-making power both of States and of organizations of States. Obviously the practical possibility of international organizations becoming parties to multi-lateral treaties is limited. The World Meteorological Organization cannot, consistently with its purpose, aspire to participate in the convention concerning, say, the regulation of whaling. However, any limitation of the right of international organizations to become parties, by accession, to multilateral conventions must take place, by reference to the above considerations, in accordance with paragraph 2 of the Article, in which the right of accession is dependent upon the parties to the treaty.

4. Paragraph 2 of the Article lays down the self-evident principle that parties to a treaty must agree to the participation, by way of accession, of any new parties. The principle that there is no right of accession apart from the provisions of the treaty was clearly laid down by the Permanent Court of International Justice in the case concerning *Certain German Interests in Polish Upper Silesia* (Judgment no. 7, pp. 28, 29.) A State cannot be allowed to foist itself against their will upon the parties to an existing treaty. Such consent is as a rule given in the accession clause of the treaty. It may also be given subsequent to its conclusion, as, for instance, in the North Atlantic Treaty of 4 April 1949 which provides, in Article 10, that the parties may, by unanimous agreement, invite any other European State possessing the necessary qualification to accede to the treaty (*U.N.T.S.* 34, 243). Similarly, the Treaty of 3 November 1934 establishing the Balkan Entente laid down, in Article 7, that it was open to accession by other States, 'such accession to take place only if all the high contracting parties consent thereto' (Hudson, *Legislation*, VI, 939). The treaty may limit the right of accession on the part of certain categories of States, as, for instance, in the International Civil Aviation Convention of 7 December 1944 which laid down, in Article 92, that the convention 'shall be open for adherence by Members of the United Nations and States associated with them, and States which remain neutral during the present world conflict'

non-member State if subsequently invited. The same Article provides that the agreement shall be ratified. Article x provides that States referred to in paragraph 2 of Article ix (1) may *accept* this agreement from 22 November 1950. It is difficult to follow the meaning of Article x unless its intention is to make it possible for States referred to in Article ix (1) to become parties without resorting to ratification. Article ix seems to constitute an accession clause of indefinite duration and irrespective of the question whether the agreement has entered into force.

(*ibid.* 9, 1950). A treaty may also provide that, in addition to the States referred to in the treaty, a designated body may declare any other State or any category of States eligible for accession. Thus the Convention on Road Traffic of 19 September 1949 provides, in Article 27, that, in addition to States therein designated, any other State may accede 'which the Economic and Social Council may by resolution declare eligible'. Similar provisions are contained in the Convention of 6 April 1950 on the Declaration of Death of Missing Persons (Article 13). In case of such delegation of the exercise of the right of assent to accession it must be presumed that the body thus designated determines the matter by a vote in conformity with its accepted procedure.

5. While, as a rule, definite provision for accession is made in the treaty itself, occasionally the treaty leaves to some subsequent action or condition the determination of the question of accession. Thus the General Agreement of 30 October 1947 on Tariffs and Trade lays down, in Article 23, that accession may take place, *inter alia*, by 'a Government not party to this agreement . . . on terms to be agreed between such Government and the contracting parties' (*U.N.T.S.* 55, 194). This does not necessarily mean 'all the contracting parties'. These in any case may include States which were not parties to the original agreement but which acceded at a subsequent date. When, as in the Monetary Convention of 5 November 1878, a treaty expressly provides that unanimous agreement of the contracting parties is necessary for the accession of a new party – 'contracting parties' including presumably parties which subsequently acceded to the treaty – the position leaves no room for doubt. Occasionally, as in the Geneva Convention of 6 July 1906, it is provided that non-signatory States shall have the right to accede provided that within a prescribed period no contracting party has raised objection to the adhesion. However, the treaty may provide that unanimity is not required. Thus the Convention of 13 October 1919 on the Regulation of Aerial Navigation provided, in Article 42, that after 1 January 1923 accession 'may be admitted if it is agreed to by at least three fourths of the signatory and adhering States' voting in a manner prescribed by the convention. In general, in multilateral conventions establishing international organizations the organs of the organization have been given power to permit accession by a decision falling short of unanimity.

6. In so far as the original instrument makes accession dependent upon some subsequent action or condition, there is room, so far as

the future development of the law is concerned, for relaxing in cases of doubt the requirement of unanimous consent. In theory there is force in the view that every contracting party must possess the right to agree to – or reject – the participation of a new party in the contractual relation. However, multilateral treaties regulating matters in the sphere of the general interest of the international community cannot properly be viewed as mere contractual bargains. There is in them an inherent tendency to universality which deserves encouragement. Thus, for instance, there is probably little justification, other than that of legal theory,[1] for making accession to a convention such as that for the Pacific Settlement of International Disputes dependent upon agreement between the contracting parties. This was what The Hague Conventions of 1899 and 1907 on the subject in fact provided. But it does not appear that when, after the First World War, some newly created States – such as Poland, Czechoslovakia and Finland – acceded to these conventions any serious attempt was made to act upon the provision requiring the consent of all the contracting parties. Except where the treaty contains rigid provisions to the contrary, the result ought to be avoided which would permit a single contracting party to prevent the accession of a State to a humanitarian and non-political convention intrinsically aiming at general application.

7. Such restrictive interpretation of the rule of unanimity is especially indicated when the original treaty makes accession dependent upon the fulfilment of certain conditions of status or otherwise and the question arises whether the party seeking to accede fulfils these conditions. This may include the question whether that party is a State.[2] In many cases the answer to that question can properly be given by any tribunal upon which the parties have conferred jurisdiction in the matter of interpretation of the clauses of the treaty. In the absence of such compulsory jurisdiction of an international tribunal or of voluntary submission of the ensuing dispute to judicial determination there is no occasion for adhering rigidly to the principle of unanimous consent of all the contracting parties. At the time of the original establishment of the text of the treaty the vote of one State cannot in fact prevent the insertion of the

[1] Or, possibly, for the reason – not unconnected with doctrines of legitimacy – that the contracting parties may wish to reserve for themselves freedom of action with regard to any States which may arise subsequently to the conclusion of the treaty.

[2] Thus in connection with the establishment of the so-called State of Manchukuo the question arose, in connection with possible attempts by Manchukuo to accede to multilateral conventions, whether the essential condition of accession, namely, the quality of statehood as required by international law, was present in that case.

accession clause. There is no reason why such faculty should be enjoyed by it at a subsequent stage. In view of this, the proposed second paragraph of Article 7 abstains from laying down the rule, which is to be found in some other drafts, that a State can adhere to the treaty only subject to the unanimous consent of the other contracting parties.

8. 'Unless otherwise provided, accession may be effected at any time after the establishment of the text of the treaty.' The present Article adopts, in this respect, a solution different from some previous drafts, including that of the Harvard Draft Convention (Article 9 (*b*)), which laid down that a State can accede to a treaty only after that treaty has come into force. This latter solution has occasionally been stated to be the only one which is consistent with logic seeing that unless a treaty has entered into force there is nothing to which a State can accede. The compelling character of that logical argument is open to doubt. There seems to be no convincing reason why the object of accession should not be an instrument which will enter into force and which is identical with an already established text as distinguished from an instrument which has already entered into force. Moreover, the view which underlies the present Article is believed to be supported, on the whole, by practice. Undoubtedly some, though not many, treaties provide expressly that accession can be effected only after they have entered into force. Thus the General Treaty of 27 August 1928 for the Renunciation of War provided, in Article 3, 'that it shall, when it has come into effect . . . remain open as long as may be necessary for adherence by all the Powers of the world'. The four Geneva Conventions of 12 August 1949 provide uniformly that 'from the date of its coming into force, it shall be open to any Power in whose name the present convention has not been signed, to accede to this convention'. The Convention on Aviation Salvage at Sea of 29 September 1938 was to the same effect (Hudson, *Legislation*, VIII, 145). The Convention of 22 November 1928 concerning International Exhibitions provided for accession 'at any time *after the coming into force* of the present convention' (*ibid.* IV, 2571). So did the Convention of 31 May 1928 concerning Safety of Life at Sea (Article 64: *ibid.* 2768). The same principle was followed in the Convention of 20 July 1936 concerning the Régime of the Straits (*ibid.* VII, 399) and in the Convention of 8 June 1937 concerning Regulation of Whaling (*ibid.* p. 761). The Treaty of 25 March 1936 of Limitation of Naval Armament provided expressly that accessions if made prior to the date of the coming

into force of the treaty shall take effect on that date (*ibid*. p. 283). At the second Hague Conference of 1907 it seems to have been assumed as evident that an 'adhesion may have no effect except, at the earliest, from the time the convention goes into effect'.

However, the preponderant practice of Governments has been in the opposite direction. Treaties constantly provide for accession irrespective of the date of entry into force. The Convention of 11 October 1933 for Facilitating International Circulation of Films of an Educational Character entered into force on 15 January 1935 (*ibid*. VI, 457). Article 16 of the convention provided that it may be acceded to on or after 12 April 1934. The Convention of 11 October 1933 for the Suppression of Traffic in Women and Children entered into force on 24 August 1934 (*ibid*. p. 469). Article 7 of the convention provided for accession as from 1 April 1934. The Convention of 28 October 1933 concerning the International Status of Refugees entered into force on 13 June 1935. It provided, in Article 19, for accession on or after 16 April 1934. The Convention of 8 November 1933 for the Preservation of Fauna and Flora entered into force on 14 January 1936. It provided, in Article 17, for accession as from 31 March 1934 (*ibid*. p. 519). The Convention of 14 December 1928 concerning Economic Statistics entered into force on 14 December 1930. It provided for accession as from 1 October 1929 (*ibid*. IV, 2586). The Convention of 20 April 1929 concerning Counterfeiting Currency entered into force on 22 February 1931. Provision for accession was made as from 1 January 1930 (*ibid*. p. 2702). The same system was followed in the Convention of 20 February 1935 for the Campaign against Contagious Diseases of Animals (*ibid*. VII, 9) and in the Convention of 20 February 1935 concerning Export and Import of Animal Products (*ibid*. p. 35). The Convention of 25 July 1934 concerning Protection against Dengue Fever laid down, without referring to any limitation as to the time limit, that it is open to accession of any country which has not signed it (*ibid*. VI, 934). The Universal Postal Convention of 20 March 1934 provided for accession 'at any time' (Article 2: *ibid*. p. 649). So did the European Broadcasting Convention of 15 April 1939 (*ibid*. VIII, 2961). The Arrangement of 18 August 1938 concerning the Powers of the European Commission of the Danube (Treaty Series, no. 38 (1939), Cmd. 6069) provided, in addition to ratification, for the right of accession of any State represented on the European Commission. It made provision for a procès-verbal of the deposit of instruments of ratification or accession and laid down that 'the arrangement will enter into force three months after the closing of the procès-verbal'. The Convention of 10 February 1938 concerning the Status of Refugees coming from Germany entered into force on 26 October 1938. But Article 21 of the convention provided that 'on and after 10 August 1938 any Member of the League of Nations or any other State referred to in the convention may accede to it' (Hudson, *Legislation*, VIII, 29). The Convention of 1 March 1939 on Tax Exemption in Air Traffic (Treaty Series, Misc. no. 7 (1939)) laid down, in Article 5, that after 1 June 1939 it shall be open to accession on behalf of any country on whose behalf it had not been signed. By 1946 the convention had not yet entered into force. The Convention of 7 June 1930 concerning Stamp Law and Bills of Exchange provided, in Article 5, that it shall not come into force until it has been ratified or acceded to on behalf of the seven States specified therein (*ibid.* no. 14 (1934)).

The practice as outlined above assumes an even more conspicuous complexion in cases in which accession is the only means for the entry of the treaty into force – as is the case with regard to the Convention on the Privileges and Immunities of the United Nations approved by the General Assembly on 13 February 1946 (*U.N.T.S.* 1, 15), or the Convention on the Privileges and Immunities of the Specialized Agencies, approved by the General Assembly on 21 November 1947 (*ibid.* 33, 261). The General Act of 1928 for the Pacific Settlement of International Disputes was to the same effect. So was the Revised General Act approved by the General Assembly on 28 April 1949. The International Sanitary Convention for Aerial Navigation, which was opened for signature on 15 December 1944, provided in Article 18 that it shall come into force as soon as it has been signed or acceded to on behalf of ten or more Governments (*ibid.* 16, 247). A substantially identical provision on the subject was included in the International Convention of 20 April 1929 for the Suppression of Counterfeiting Currency (*L.N.T.S.* 112, 371). The Genocide Convention approved by the General Assembly on 9 December 1948 provided, *inter alia*, for accession as from 1 January 1950. But by that date only five States had ratified the convention – which provided in Article 13 that twenty instruments of ratification or accession were required for its entry into force. There are many other examples of similar provisions.[1]

[1] See, for example, the Convention of 19 September 1949 on Road Traffic (Article 27) and the International Sanitary Convention for Aerial Navigation opened for signature on 15 December 1944 (*U.N.T.S.* 16, 247).

9. In view of the preponderance of practice, as shown here, there is no justification for regarding accession as not operative prior to the entrance of the treaty into force. Important considerations connected with the effectiveness of the procedure of conclusion of treaties seem to call for a contrary rule. Many treaties might never enter into force but for accession. Where the entire tendency in the field of conclusion of treaties is in the direction of elasticity and elimination of restrictive rules it seems undesirable to burden the subject of accession with a presumption which practice has shown to be in the nature of an exception rather than the rule.

10. For similar reasons there is no cause for limiting the freedom of a State to accede to a treaty subject to subsequent confirmation. A State may attach importance to signifying its intention to consider accession to a treaty without limiting the power of its constitutional organs to consider the question of the ratification of accession in the same way as they are free to consider treaties signed by their representatives. In view of this the matter may well be allowed to rest where it was left by a resolution of the Assembly of the League of Nations in 1927, which was to the effect that:

The procedure of accession to international agreements given subject to ratification is an admissible one which the League should neither discourage nor encourage. Nevertheless if a State gives its accession, it shall know that, if it does not expressly mention that this accession is subject to ratification, it shall be deemed to have undertaken a formal obligation. If it desires to prevent this consequence, it must expressly declare at the time of accession that the accession is given subject to ratification. (League of Nations, *Assembly Records*, Plenary Meetings, September 1927.)

Note

1. As in other Articles of the present draft, the special rapporteur has refrained from giving a definition of the procedure involved (i.e. in this case, a definition of accession). The necessary element of definition is contained in the substantive rules embodied in the Article.

2. The special rapporteur has felt compelled to depart, for reasons given in the comment above, from the Article as tentatively adopted by the Commission and to formulate conclusions which are, in some ways, in the opposite sense. This applies to the question of the requirement of consent of all the contracting parties subsequent to the entry of the treaty into force, and in particular, to the question whether accession can become operative before the treaty has fully entered into force.

3. The question has been discussed by some writers[1] whether the acceding State becomes a party to the treaty on a footing of full equality with the original contracting parties. The answer to that question really admits of no doubt. It is occasionally obscured by the argument that the effect of the accession clause if accepted is to result in a new treaty – albeit identical with the old one between the original contracting parties and the acceding State. Even if that argument were correct, it is difficult to see what difference it makes to the legal situation. However, in either case the circumstance that the acceding State becomes a party, in effect and in law, to the original treaty on a footing of equality has the further result, which will be commented upon in the Part on interpretation of treaties, that the acceding State must be deemed to possess full knowledge of the facts and records, if published, relating to the history of the negotiations preceding the conclusion of the treaty and the establishment of its text.

4. The special rapporteur does not consider it necessary to comment in detail upon the first paragraph of the Article, which lays down that accession to a treaty must be formally declared in a written instrument. That rule is no more than an application of the principle, examined below in Article 17, that the conclusion of a treaty must take place through a formal written instrument. It follows that a tacit accession is not possible. In the case concerning *Certain German Interests in Polish Upper Silesia* (Judgment no. 7, p. 28) the Permanent Court of International Justice held that 'there has been no subsequent tacit adherence or accession on the part of Poland to the Armistice Convention or Protocol of Spa'. It seems hardly permissible to deduce from this phraseology that the Court admitted by implication the admissibility of implied accession. In any case, practically all the relevant treaties provide either that accessions must be notified to the depositary of the convention or that they must be effected by the deposit of a formal instrument. The Commission may attach importance to inserting an express provision to that effect in the present Article.

---

[1] See, for example, comment to Article 9 (*e*) of the Harvard Draft Convention.

1954 REPORT

ARTICLE 7

ACCESSION

1. A State or organization of States may accede to a treaty, which it has not signed or ratified, by formally declaring in a written instrument that the treaty is binding upon it.

2. Accession is admissible only subject to the provisions of the treaty. *In case a decision is required, in pursuance of this paragraph, as to the accession, or conditions thereof, of any State, such decision shall, unless otherwise expressly provided by the treaty, be effected by a majority of two-thirds of the States which are parties to the treaty at the time at which the request for accession is made.*

1. The additional, italicized, part of paragraph 2 as proposed and the observations which follow are in accordance with the original Article 7 of the first report[1] and of the comment thereon (paragraphs 4–7 of the comment). However, the addition as formulated is intended to render the views there expressed more specific. It is also now considered appropriate, in view of the importance of the question involved, to give them the form of an express clause in Article 7. While in the comment to Article 7 doubts were expressed as to the application of the rule of unanimity to any decision required under that Article, these doubts found no expression in the body of the Article. The rule of unanimous consent of the existing parties to accession, or its conditions, by another State has the appearance of a rule of juridical logic and any derogation from it, if such derogation is considered desirable, ought probably to be given the form of a clear exception from the rule of unanimity. In some cases, unless the matter is deemed to be governed by the implied rule of unanimity, treaties normally contain no provisions on the subject. Thus, to refer to a recent instrument, Article 10 of the International Convention for the permanent control of outbreak areas of the red locust of 22 February 1949 between Belgium, the United Kingdom, South Africa and Southern Rhodesia, provides as follows: 'Any Government which is not a signatory to the present convention may be invited by the Council to accede thereto, subject to such conditions as the contracting Governments may determine' (*U.N.T.S.* 93 (1951), 138). Similarly, Article 31 of the Agreement between the United

---

[1] A/CN.4/63 in *Yearbook of the International Law Commission, 1953*, vol. II.

Kingdom, Belgium, France, Luxembourg, the Netherlands and the United States of America for the establishment of an International Authority for the Ruhr of 28 April 1949 (*U.N.T.S.* 83 (1951), 106) provides that as soon as a German Government has been established it may accede to the agreement by executing an instrument containing such undertakings with respect to the assumption of the responsibilities of the German Government under the agreement and such other provisions as may be agreed by the signatory Governments. The General Agreement on Tariffs and Trade of 30 October 1947 provides, in Article 33, for accession on terms to be agreed between the acceding Government and the contracting parties (*U.N.T.S.* 55 (1950), 284). It is arguable that, as these conventions do not refer to *unanimous* consent, a decision which falls short of unanimity is sufficient. The special rapporteur does not regard that argument to be of a cogent character. Moreover, that interpretation fails to make provision for the kind of majority, if any, required.

2. For these reasons, assuming that the Commission shares the special rapporteur's view as to the essential shortcomings of the rule of unanimity in this connection, it seems desirable to complete paragraph 2 of Article 7 by the adoption of the rule as formulated. Admittedly that rule is open to the objection that it is somewhat mechanical inasmuch as it takes no account of the relevant importance of the contracting parties. However, that defect is inherent in the existing machinery of the conclusion of multilateral treaties. It can be remedied either by express provisions of the treaty or by some such solution as is outlined below (Article 16, paragraph 16 of the comment) in connection with the revision of multilateral treaties. In any case, it is believed that, as a general rule, doubts ought to be resolved in the direction of the widest possible application of the treaty – provided that a substantial number of signatories so desire.

3. The rule as here formulated seems to be in accordance with the recent practice of multilateral conventions as to admission of new members of international organizations. Thus the Convention on International Civil Aviation of 7 December 1944 provides, in Article 93, that States other than those referred to in the convention shall be admitted to participation by means of a four-fifth vote of the Assembly and on such conditions (apparently by the same or a less exacting majority) as the Assembly may prescribe (*U.N.T.S.* 15 (1948), 358). The Constitution of the Food and Agriculture Organization of 16 October 1945 lays down, in Article 2, that additional members may be admitted by a vote concurred in by a two-thirds

majority of all the members of the Conference (*A.J.* 40 (1946), Supplement, p. 76). The Constitution of the United Nations Educational, Scientific and Cultural Organization of 16 November 1945 lays down, in Article 2, that States not members of the United Nations may be admitted, upon the recommendation of the Executive Board, by a two-thirds majority vote of the General Conference (*U.N.T.S.* 4 (1947), 280). To the same effect are the Constitution of the International Labour Organization of 7 November 1945 (*U.N.T.S.* 2 (1947), 18); of the Universal Postal Union of 5 July 1947 (Treaty Series, no. 57 (1949)); of the World Meteorological Organization of 11 October 1947; of the International Telecommunications Union of 2 October 1947; and of the Inter-governmental Maritime Consultative Organization (*United Nations Maritime Conference, 19 February–6 March 1948, Final Act and Related Documents* (1948), VIII. 2, 29). The Constitution of the World Health Organization of 26 July 1946 (*U.N.T.S.* 14 (1948), 186) requires a simple majority. The same principle underlies the constitutions of international organizations which provide for admission by a decision of one of their organs whose decisions do not, according to the constitutions, require unanimity. This is the position, for instance, with regard to the Articles of Agreement of the International Bank for Reconstruction and Development of 27 December 1945 (*U.N.T.S.* 2 (1947), 134).

4. It will be noted that the rule as formulated refers to the consent not of the original signatories of the treaty but of the States which are the contracting parties at the time when the request for accession is made. This means that the contracting parties which are entitled to take a decision on the subject include those – and those only – which have validly acceded to the treaty in accordance with its provisions.[1]

---

[1] This principle would apparently apply to such provisions as that of Article 5 of the Convention between the United States of America and Costa Rica for the establishment of an Inter-American Tropical Tuna Commission of 31 May 1949 (*U.N.T.S.* 80 (1951), 12). That Article lays down that any Government, whose nationals participate in the fisheries covered by the convention, desiring to adhere, shall address a communication to that effect to each of the high contracting parties and that, upon receiving the unanimous consent of the parties to adherence, such Government shall deposit with the Government of the United States of America an instrument of adherence. It must be assumed that the high contracting parties referred to above include those who have adhered in the meantime.

CHAPTER 8

ACCEPTANCE

1953 REPORT

ARTICLE 8

ACCEPTANCE

[Wherever provision is made for the assumption of the obligations of the treaty by acceptance a State may become a party to the treaty by a procedure which consists either: (*a*) In signature, ratification, or accession; or, (*b*) In an instrument formally described as acceptance; or (*c*) In a combination of the two preceding methods.]

Comment

1. This Article is enclosed in brackets for the reason that the necessity of including it within the codification of the law of treaties may be open to doubt. The reason which prompted the deliberate adoption, during and after the end of the Second World War, of 'acceptance' as a means of assuming treaty obligations was to provide an instrument of a less formal character than some of the traditional methods, in particular ratification, and thus to make available appropriate machinery in cases in which the municipal law of a particular State renders the assumption of treaty obligations by the traditional method of ratification more complicated than is the case if other methods are followed. Thus the Constitution of the United Nations Educational, Scientific and Cultural Organization of 16 November 1945 provided in Article 15: '1. This constitution shall be subject to acceptance ... 2. Signature may take place either before or after the deposit of the instrument of acceptance' (*U.N.T.S.* 4, 275). The relevant Articles of the Constitution of the International Monetary Fund (*ibid.* 2, 39) and of the International Bank for Reconstruction and Development included similar provisions:

Each Government on whose behalf this agreement is signed shall deposit with the Government of the United States of America an instrument setting forth that it has accepted this agreement in accordance with its law and has taken all steps necessary to enable it to carry out all of its obligations under this agreement.

This formula was followed, in a somewhat altered form, in a number of other agreements. The General Agreement on Tariffs and Trade of 30 October 1947 provided that it 'shall be open to acceptance by any Government signatory to the Final Act'. This was also the case in the Havana Charter of 24 March 1948 for an International Trade Organization. In a number of agreements[1] the parties have adopted a uniform formula providing for the assumption of the treaty obligations by: (*a*) signature without reservation as to acceptance; or (*b*) signature subject to acceptance followed by acceptance; or (*c*) acceptance. It must be noted that the contracting of international obligations by that method was not altogether novel. Thus in 1934 when accepting membership in the International Labour Organization, the United States did so not by way of ratifying any international instrument but by way of accepting an invitation extended to it – that step, in turn, following a Joint Resolution of Congress authorizing the President 'to accept membership for the Government of the United States of America in the International Labour Organization'.[2]

2. In 1948 the Sixth Committee of the General Assembly, after detailed discussion, adopted a resolution in connection with the draft Convention for the Suppression of the Traffic in Persons and of the Exploitation of the Prostitution of Others, expressing by a substantial majority (of 30 votes to none, with 4 abstentions) preference for the traditional method (of signature followed by ratification) as compared with the uniform formula of acceptance as described above.[3] Although since then it appears that only two agreements have

---

[1] E.g. Protocol approved by the General Assembly on 3 December 1948 amending the Agreement for the Suppression of Circulation of Obscene Publications (*U.N.T.S.* 30, 3); Convention of 6 March 1948 on the Inter-governmental Maritime Consultative Organization; Convention of 10 May 1948 of the International Institute of the Hylean Amazon. For a survey of the use of the term 'acceptance' in the practice of the United Nations in the matter of conclusion of treaties see Liang in *A.J.* 44 (1950), 342–9.

[2] The United States had previously assumed membership in some international organizations in accordance with that procedure, as in the case of the International Hydrographic Bureau in 1921 and the International Statistical Institute in 1924. The proclamation of acceptance of membership of the International Labour Organization was made by the President in a form not dissimilar to the proclamation of treaties in general. In the proclamation the President did 'proclaim and make public the Constitution of the International Labour Organization, a certified copy of which is hereto annexed, to the end that the same and every Article and clause thereof may be observed with good faith by the United States of America and the citizens thereof'.

[3] *Official Records of the General Assembly, Third Session, Part I, Sixth Committee,* 88th and following meetings.

provided for acceptance – in addition to signature followed by ratification[1] – there is no decisive reason for assuming that that expression of opinion was intended to cover all international instruments.

3. The term 'acceptance' does not exclude the assumption of treaty obligations by ratification or accession. Nor does it exclude signature; it is often combined with it. Its effect is to leave to Governments the option of assuming the treaty obligation either by the traditional methods of signature, ratification or accession or by using the – apparently less formal – machinery of 'acceptance'. Various objections may be raised against the conferment of a formal status of a distinct method of concluding a treaty upon 'acceptance' thus conceived. Thus it may be said that no formula used in a treaty can absolve a Government from complying with the constitutional limitations upon the final conclusion of a particular treaty. A Government ratifying a treaty may or may not be under an obligation, according to its municipal law, to obtain the necessary approval or authorization. The formula of 'acceptance' used in a treaty will not release it from that obligation. The possibility of accession, which, as has been shown, is open to States which have signed the treaty but have not ratified it and which does not depend upon the treaty having already come into force, provides an informal method of assuming a treaty obligation. For in most, if not all, States – to use the language of Sir Arnold McNair – 'an accession does not require ratification and is regarded as constitutionally equivalent to ratification'.[2] On the other hand – and that circumstance is probably decisive – if a Government finds that the use of a certain procedure may facilitate, without setting aside a legitimate and requisite expression of national will, the assumption of international obligations, there would seem to be reason for not discouraging such simplified methods by making obligatory, in effect, the use of more complicated machinery. From this point of view it would be regrettable if a treaty were to provide for ratification as the only means of finalizing the acceptance of its obligations.

4. In view of this it would appear that 'acceptance' fulfils a function different from that of merely generalizing the various methods –

[1] Agreement of 22 November 1950 on the Importation of Educational, Scientific and Cultural Materials and the Universal Copyright Convention of 6 September 1952 drawn up under the auspices of the United Nations Educational, Scientific and Cultural Organization.

[2] McNair, p. 99. He adds: 'It is not the usual practice to pass an instrument of accession under the Great Seal. A notification signed by the Secretary of State for Foreign Affairs or some other duly authorized person is considered adequate.'

more or less formal – of assuming a treaty obligation or confirming or approving an obligation provisionally undertaken by signature (or, in some cases, by accession). A number of recent agreements refer to 'approval' instead of 'acceptance'[1] while some authorize both procedures with the underlying – though by no means obvious – assumption that there is a difference between the two. Thus according to the Constitution of the World Health Organization of 22 July 1946 (*U.N.T.S.* 14, 185) States may become parties to the constitution by (1) signature without reservation as to approval; (2) signature subject to approval followed by acceptance; or (3) acceptance.

5. While the Commission believes that the law of treaties ought to encourage elasticity and flexibility in the matter of the machinery used for assuming treaty obligations, it is bound to acknowledge the force of the view that it may not be necessary to give the rigid complexion of an Article to terminology which has no specific content. The law of treaties need not ignore the tendencies implied in the terminology of 'acceptance'. But it may be sufficient to consider it as adequately accommodated within the wide orbit of Article 4, which refers to 'any other means' accepted by the parties. These means include a procedure which, while leaving room for confirmation of the signature by a subsequent act of approval, does not make such approval dependent upon formal ratification. This, of course, was the practice also prior to the explicit emergence of 'acceptance' as a means of assuming treaty obligations. On the other hand, nothing in the nature – or in the practice – of 'acceptance' prevents a party from finalizing its undertaking by way of formal ratification.

Note

The special rapporteur has included the present Article largely out of deference to Article 10 as tentatively adopted by the Commission and as a basis for discussion. He is not certain that a separate Article on the subject ought to be retained. As already mentioned in the comment, a decision to refrain from adopting a separate Article on 'acceptance' would not have the result of disregarding a practice which has found some following and which is not altogether devoid of usefulness. The case would be met by the existing reference in Article 4 to 'other means of accepting or approving' a treaty. These

[1] See, for example, the Protocol concerning the Office International d'Hygiène Publique (*U.N.T.S.* 9, 66) or the Protocol amending the Agreements, Conventions and Protocols on Narcotic Drugs (*ibid.* 12, 179).

means must necessarily be formal means. In fact, most of the various agreements providing for acceptance require the formal deposit of an instrument of acceptance. For these reasons it may be held to be conducive to clarity and the avoidance of confusion if 'acceptance', 'approval', and similar procedures are included within the whole formula of Article 4 without being created into a category of their own. Only so, it might be said, can we hope to avoid the ambiguities and contradictions which threaten to surround the subject. Thus the Article 10 tentatively adopted by the Commission defines acceptance of a treaty as 'an act by which a State, in lieu of signature or ratification or accession or all of these procedures, declares itself bound by the treaty'. Yet it is clear both from practice and from the comment which followed that Article that 'acceptance' does not necessarily take place in lieu of signature or ratification or accession. It is often effected by or combined with any of these three procedures. On the other hand, although there may be but little in the procedure of 'acceptance' – assuming that it constitutes a procedure of its own – which cannot, internationally, be achieved by the traditional methods of signature, ratification, or accession or by a combination of them, this need not necessarily be the decisive consideration. If, in some cases, Governments and the cause of international co-operation can be assisted by the use of terminology which leaves room for the desired freedom of procedure, such terminology may deserve encouragement even at the risk of some inelegancy or redundancy.

CHAPTER 9

RESERVATIONS

Editor's note The material under this head is taken from the 1953 and 1954 Reports. On 4 February 1953 (at a time when he was immersed in the preparation of the 1953 Report) Lauterpacht read a paper to the Grotius Society on 'Some possible solutions of the problem of reservations to treaties' (*Grotius Society*, 39 (1954), 97–118). As he stated in a footnote to the published version of the paper, its substance 'is embodied to a large extent' in the 1953 Report. The form of the two contributions to the subject is manifestly different, but comparison of the two texts shows that most of the Grotius Society paper appears almost verbatim in various places in the 1953 Report. I have therefore decided not to reprint the paper here.

The relevant provisions of the Vienna Convention are contained in Articles 19–23:

Section 2. Reservations

ARTICLE 19

Formulation of reservations

A State may, when signing, ratifying, accepting, approving or acceding to a treaty, formulate a reservation unless:
- (*a*) the reservation is prohibited by the treaty;
- (*b*) the treaty provides that only specified reservations, which do not include the reservation in question, may be made; or
- (*c*) in cases not falling under sub-paragraphs (*a*) and (*b*), the reservation is incompatible with the object and purpose of the treaty.

ARTICLE 20

Acceptance of and objection to reservations

1. A reservation expressly authorized by a treaty does not require any subsequent acceptance by the other contracting States unless the treaty so provides.

2. When it appears from the limited number of the negotiating States and the object and purpose of a treaty that the application of the treaty in its entirety between all the parties is an essential condition of the consent of each one to be bound by the treaty, a reservation requires acceptance by all the parties.

3. When a treaty is a constituent instrument of an international organization and unless it otherwise provides, a reservation requires the acceptance of the competent organ of that organization.

4. In cases not falling under the preceding paragraphs and unless the treaty otherwise provides:

(a) acceptance by another contracting State of a reservation constitutes the reserving State a party to the treaty in relation to that other State if or when the treaty is in force for those States;

(b) an objection by another contracting State to a reservation does not preclude the entry into force of the treaty as between the objecting and reserving States unless a contrary intention is definitely expressed by the objecting State;

(c) an act expressing a State's consent to be bound by the treaty and containing a reservation is effective as soon as at least one other contracting State has accepted the reservation.

5. For the purposes of paragraphs 2 and 4 and unless the treaty otherwise provides, a reservation is considered to have been accepted by a State if it shall have raised no objection to the reservation by the end of a period of twelve months after it was notified of the reservation or by the date on which it expressed its consent to be bound by the treaty, whichever is later.

ARTICLE 21

Legal effects of reservations and of objections to reservations

1. A reservation established with regard to another party in accordance with Articles 19, 20 and 23:

(a) modifies for the reserving State in its relations with that other party the provisions of the treaty to which the reservation relates to the extent of the reservation; and

(b) modifies those provisions to the same extent for that other party in its relations with the reserving State.

2. The reservation does not modify the provisions of the treaty for the other parties to the treaty *inter se*.

3. When a State objecting to a reservation has not opposed the entry into force of the treaty between itself and the reserving State, the provisions to which the reservation relates do not apply as between the two States to the extent of the reservation.

ARTICLE 22

Withdrawal of reservations and of objections to reservations

1. Unless the treaty otherwise provides, a reservation may be with-

drawn at any time and the consent of a State which has accepted the reservation is not required for its withdrawal.

2.   Unless the treaty otherwise provides, an objection to a reservation may be withdrawn at any time.

3.   Unless the treaty otherwise provides, or it is otherwise agreed:

(*a*) the withdrawal of a reservation becomes operative in relation to another contracting State only when notice of it has been received by that State;

(*b*) the withdrawal of an objection to a reservation becomes operative only when notice of it has been received by the State which formulated the reservation.

ARTICLE 23

Procedure regarding reservations

1.   A reservation, an express acceptance of a reservation and an objection to a reservation must be formulated in writing and communicated to the contracting States and other States entitled to become parties to the treaty.

2.   If formulated when signing the treaty subject to ratification, acceptance or approval, a reservation must be formally confirmed by the reserving State when expressing its consent to be bound by the treaty. In such a case the reservation shall be considered as having been made on the date of its confirmation.

3.   An express acceptance of, or an objection to, a reservation made previously to confirmation of the reservation does not itself require confirmation.

4.   The withdrawal of a reservation or of an objection to a reservation must be formulated in writing.

1953 REPORT

ARTICLE 9

RESERVATIONS

I

A signature, ratification, accession, or any other method of accepting a multilateral treaty is void if accompanied by a reservation or reservations not agreed to by all other parties to the treaty.

Comment

1. In the view of the Commission, Article 9 as here drafted must be regarded as probably still representing the existing law. Prior to the

advisory opinion of the International Court of Justice in the matter
of the Genocide Convention (*I.C.J. Reports* 1951, p. 15) and apart
from the so-called 'American system' initiated in 1938 as the result
of a resolution adopted at the Eighth International Conference of
American States held at Lima, the principle as stated in Article 9
was generally, if not universally, recognized as expressive of a rule of
international law. This was so notwithstanding the doubts occasionally and increasingly raised in respect of its operation. The
practice of the depositary authority of the Hague Conventions and of
the League of Nations was based on that principle. So was the report,
approved in 1927 by the Council of the League of Nations, prepared
by the Committee for the Progressive Codification of International
Law.[1] This was also the practice of the Secretary-General of the
United Nations, which, until the controversy occasioned by the
reservations to the Genocide Convention, was not seriously challenged. The report which the International Law Commission submitted in 1951 to the General Assembly was based on that principle.[2]
In the view of the Commission, in the absence of any deliberate
change in this respect effected by general agreement or constant
practice acknowledged as law, this must be regarded as still constituting the existing rule of international law.

However, although nothing decisive has occurred to dislodge the
principle of unanimous consent as a rule of existing international law,
the Commission, for reasons stated in the comment which follows,
is not now of the view that it constitutes a satisfactory rule and that it
can – or ought to – be maintained. Accordingly, the statement of law
in the present draft of Article 9 is accompanied by a number of alternative drafts which accept a different principle as the basis of
the future law on the subject. These drafts are commented upon in
considerable detail. The subject of reservations to multilateral treaties
is one of unusual – in fact baffling – complexity and it would serve
no useful purpose to simplify artificially an inherently complex
problem. This applies in particular to situations in which the task
of the Commission is one of developing international law after the
existing principle has been found to be unsatisfactory and not
acceptable to a large number of States.

In view of the fact that the Commission does not consider the
principle of unanimous consent as expressed in Article 9 as drafted to
offer a satisfactory basis for the future operation of this aspect of the

[1] League of Nations publication, *V. Legal, 1927. V.16* (Doc. C.357, M.130 (1927), v).
[2] *Yearbook of the International Law Commission, 1951*, II (Doc. A/1858, ch. II), 125–31.

law of treaties, no detailed comment on Article 9 is believed to be necessary – although a number of considerations relevant to the subject will be found in the comment to the alternative drafts, in particular in the comment to the alternative draft A.

ALTERNATIVE DRAFT A

If, in any case where a multilateral treaty does not expressly prohibit or restrict the faculty of making reservations, a State signs, ratifies, accedes to or otherwise accepts the treaty subject to a reservation or reservations limiting or otherwise varying the obligations of any Article or Articles of the treaty, the following procedure shall apply in the absence of any other provisions in the treaty:

1. Whenever a treaty provides that it shall enter into force on a specified number of States finally becoming parties thereto, the fact that a State has appended a reservation or reservations to any Article of the treaty is not taken into account for the purpose of ascertaining the existence of the requisite number of parties to the treaty.

2. If within three years of the treaty having entered into force less than two-thirds of the States accepting the treaty, whether they have accepted it with or without reservations, agree to the reservation or reservations appended by a State, that State, if it maintains the reservation, ceases to be a party thereto. If, at the end of that period and as the result of the operation of the rule as stated, the number of parties is reduced below the requisite number stipulated for the entrance of the treaty into force, the treaty is dissolved.

3. If, at the end of or subsequent to the period referred to above, a reservation is agreed to expressly or tacitly by two-thirds or more of the total number of the States accepting the obligations of the treaty, then the State making the reservation is deemed to be a party to the treaty in respect of all parties thereto subject to the right of the other parties not to consider themselves bound by the particular clause of the treaty in relation to the State making the reservation.

4. A State is deemed to have agreed to a reservation made by another State if, within three months of the receipt of notification of the reservation in question, it has not forwarded to the depositary authority a statement containing a formal rejection of the reservation.

Comment

A. General observations 1. Before proceeding to an explanation of the legal effect of draft A of Article 9 it is convenient to recall once more that with regard to the subject matter of the Article the Commission was not, more conspicuously than with regard to other Articles of the draft of the law of treaties, in a position to limit itself to a codification of the existing law. This is so to some extent for the reason that there is at present no general agreement as to the law on the subject. In the view of some States[1] this was the position even prior to the advisory opinion of the International Court of Justice in the matter of the reservations to the Genocide Convention. While what is subsequently referred to as the 'unanimity view' was followed by the generality of States and while that view found expression in the, on the whole,[2] consistent practice of the Secretary-General of the League of Nations and the Secretary-General of the United Nations, the American States have since 1938 followed a different practice. On occasions the principle of the requirement of unanimous consent was operative only by virtue of implied consent – as was probably the case with regard to some of the reservations appended to certain of the Hague Conventions relating to the law of war.[3] The advisory opinion of the International Court of Justice in the matter of the Genocide Convention has further impaired the authority of the principle of unanimous consent as expressing a generally recognized principle of international law. This is so although that opinion was, by its terms of reference and by its own language, limited to the particular issue before it. For the reasoning both of the Court and of the important dissenting opinion of four of the judges is, in many ways, of a general

---

[1] Including the United States – as shown in the written statement of the Government of the United States of America before the International Court of Justice in connection with the advisory opinion on *Reservations to the Convention on the Prevention and Punishment of the Crime of Genocide* (see I.C.J. *Pleadings, Oral Arguments, Documents*, pp. 23–47).

[2] In its advisory opinion on *Reservations to the Convention on the Prevention and Punishment of the Crime of Genocide* the International Court of Justice quoted in full (*I.C.J. Reports* 1951, p. 25) the following passage from the Report of the Secretary-General of the United Nations of 21 September 1950: 'While it is universally recognized that the consent of the other Governments concerned must be sought before they can be bound by the terms of the reservation, there has not been unanimity either as to the procedure to be followed by a depositary in obtaining the necessary consent or as to the legal effect of a State's objecting to a reservation.'

[3] See, however, the statement of the Government of the Netherlands submitted on 19 January 1951 to the International Court of Justice concerning the steps taken by that Government, as depositary of the Hague Convention of 29 July 1889 concerning the adaptation to maritime war of the principles of the Geneva Convention of 1864, to obtain the unanimous consent of the signatories of the Convention to reservations appended by some States with regard to Article x of that convention (*I.C.J. Reports* 1951 p. 288).

character applicable to reservations to any international treaty. Finally, it is impossible to disregard the fact that, subsequently to that advisory opinion, a substantial majority of States represented at the sixth session of the General Assembly declined to accept, as expressive of existing international law, the principle of unanimous consent which underlay the report of the International Law Commission presented to it in 1951. Moreover, it appears that some of the Governments, including that of the United Kingdom, who in the past have conspicuously advocated that principle, may be ready to admit that it is too rigid and that it may have to be replaced by a system based on some kind of majority[1] vote.

2. In view of the fact that the principle of unanimous consent has ceased to be regarded as supplying a satisfactory solution of the problems which have arisen and are likely to arise in this connection, the Commission no longer feels justified in limiting itself to the formulation, by way of codification, of a legal rule on the subject based on that principle. Nor does it consider itself justified in making the principle of unanimous consent the basis of the future law on the subject. At the same time the Commission has felt unable to accept, either as expressive of existing law or as a basis of future legal regulation, the so-called 'sovereignty principle' according to which a State possesses an unlimited right to append reservations coupled with the right to become a party to the convention regardless of the objections of the other parties. Finally, although the alternative drafts of Article 9 follow in some limited measure the flexibility of the so-called American system, they differ from it in substantial respects. In fact, these drafts attempt a solution independent of any of the three main principles (the 'unanimity' rule, the 'sovereignty' principle and the 'American' system) which have been advocated or which have found more or less wide acceptance in the past.

3. It may now be convenient to outline here the principal considerations underlying the alternative drafts, in particular draft A.

(a) It is desirable to recognize the right of States to append reservations to a treaty and become at the same time parties to it provided these reservations are not of such a nature to meet with disapproval on the part of a substantial number of the States which finally accept the obligations of the treaty;

(b) It is not feasible or consistent with principle to recognize an

[1] See the observations of Sir Gerald Fitzmaurice, representative of the United Kingdom, at the 267th meeting of the Sixth Committee of the General Assembly on 10 December 1951 (*Official Records of the General Assembly, Sixth Session, Sixth Committee*, pp. 86, 87). Also Sir Gerald Fitzmaurice's article in *I.C.L.Q.* 2 (1953), 1–26.

unlimited right of any State to become a party to a treaty while appending reservations however sweeping, arbitrary, or destructive of the reasonably conceived purpose of the treaty and of the legitimate interests and expectations of the other parties;

(c) The requirement of unanimous consent of all parties to the treaty as a condition of participation in the treaty of a State appending reservations is contrary to the necessities and flexibility of international intercourse.

These three principal considerations may now be reviewed.

4. *Justification of reservations.* While the right of a State to become a party to a treaty subject to reservations is not at issue, the cognate question as to the extent of its right to do so regardless of the consent of the other parties is controversial. It is a question closely, though indirectly, connected with that of the intrinsic justification of reservations, and a brief consideration of that question appears therefore to be indicated. Although the argument concerning the justification of reservations in general is inconclusive, there has been a growing tendency to acknowledge that there is nothing inherently improper in the practice of appending reservations. If the view is adopted that, in principle, it is proper and desirable to admit the right to attach reservations, then, apart from the disputed logical emanations of the doctrine of the unity of the contractual nexus between the parties to the same conventions – a subject referred to in the course of this comment – the requirement of unanimous consent to a reservation falls to the ground. Undoubtedly, the objections, in principle, to attaching reservations cannot be lightly dismissed. There is room for the view that a State must choose between, on the one hand, any particular provision of its law and constitution or any particular interest of its own and, on the other hand, participation in international treaties, and that it cannot reasonably claim both. If the interest to be safeguarded by the reservation is real and far-reaching then, it may be said, the reservation renders participation in the treaty somewhat nominal. If the interest involved is of limited significance then, it may be contended, it ought to yield to the paramount necessity of uniformity of international regulation. States cannot claim to be parties to treaties without sacrificing *some* interest; a treaty has little meaning and approaches a purely nominal declaration of principle unless the parties undertake, within a given sphere, to abandon their freedom of action, to sacrifice a particular interest and to change their legislation. If the existing law of the State is regarded as sacrosanct and if the State can agree to a

treaty only if the latter is not incompatible with its law, then the conclusion of a treaty is no more than a gesture. Naturally, the various executive departments of a State view with apprehension the inconvenience and complications resulting from the necessity of changing the law of the State and are therefore prone to encourage reservations which obviate the necessity of any such changes. This phenomenon of departmental conservatism need not be decisive. Moreover, experience has shown that very often the subject matter of the reservations, although giving expression to the views strongly held by the reserving State on a given matter, is not of great importance in comparison with the significance of the treaty as a whole and that the reservation could have been omitted without sacrificing any true interest of the State in question.

5. On the other hand, there is force in the contention that, in practice, a particular reservation, however much it detracts from the symmetry and uniformity of the treaty and although it touches upon an important point of principle, does not unduly impair the value of the treaty. That circumstance, which explains the relative rarity of objections to reservations appended in good faith, must temper the notion that the practice of attaching reservations is in itself blameworthy – especially having regard to the fact that, in a sense, it provides a safeguard for the rights of the minority of States who have agreed to become parties to a treaty drafted by the majority in disregard of the views and attitude, however well founded, of the dissenting minority. In cases of accession that minority may have had no opportunity at all to voice its objections. In such cases it may be difficult, at times, to dissent from the view that the rights of the minority must be admitted by the effective recognition of their faculty to make reservations. However, if the propriety of making reservations is admitted, then recognition of that right has a meaning only if it is coupled with the admission of the right to append reservations within the limits of propriety and good faith, even if these are not unanimously agreed to by all the other parties. On the other hand, it is important to put in proper perspective the arguments based on the rights of minorities. For, in contrast with the case of legislation within the State, no minority is compelled to become a party to a multilateral treaty. Nor is a minority entitled to impose its own view, which in practice may amount to altering drastically the character of the treaty, upon the majority.

6. *The requirement of unanimous consent.* For the reasons stated – as well as for others – the present alternative draft of Article 9 and the

other alternative drafts do not follow what is the most widely, though not uniformly, adopted opinion and practice in the matter, namely, the so-called 'unanimity' view which asserts the right of a single State – whether an actual or a potential party to the treaty – to prevent, in disregard of the attitude adopted by the other parties, the participation in the treaty of one or more reserving States. According to the present draft of Article 9 there must be one-third of the total number of States, who themselves have expressed in a binding form the wish to become parties, to prevent the participation of a State making a reservation. If two-thirds or more of the parties feel that the State making the reservation acts in good faith and in a manner which is not so unreasonable as to interfere decisively with the purpose of the treaty, then, according to draft A of Article 9 as proposed, that State ought not to be precluded from becoming a party to the treaty. It is true that many States who are prepared to take a lenient or liberal view of the reservations made by others may do so because they themselves have appended reservations. However, so long as the number of such States is substantial – two-thirds of the total number represents a substantial proportion – that consideration ought not to be decisive. A treaty cannot aspire to an excellence transcending the attitude of the parties to it. The strict requirement of unanimous consent is, on the face of it, unreasonable and out of keeping with the necessities and the flexibility of international intercourse. The requirement of unanimous consent to reservations is open to objections of an order similar to that to which the rule of absolute unanimity is open in other spheres. In the matter of reservations there may be a semblance of justification for that rule inasmuch as reliance is placed on precedent, namely, on what has admittedly been the general practice or on a somewhat technical reasoning – which, as will be suggested, is of doubtful validity. Otherwise there seems to be little justification for a rule which makes it possible for one State to prevent, however arbitrarily, the participation of another State in a convention on account of a single reservation, even if reasonable and proper. The requirement of unanimity of consent is, upon analysis, motivated alternately by the suspicion that all reservations are captious and dishonest and therefore to be discouraged or by the assumption that assent to reservations will not be arbitrarily withheld. There may often be no justification for either of these assumptions. In particular, the confidence that assent to reservations will not be capriciously or vexatiously withheld ignores the fact that the harmony and courtesies of international intercourse are more conspicuously in evidence in some periods than in other periods.

7. The requirement of unanimous consent can be upheld only by reference to considerations, which have been frequently and authoritatively stated,[1] of legal logic drawn essentially from the notion of the consensual nexus in bilateral contracts and treaties, based on strict reciprocity of obligations and on the equivalence of consideration – the *quid pro quo* – which every party is entitled to expect in return for its own unconditional acceptance of the obligations of the treaty. A party which, the argument runs, ratifies a treaty subject to reservations not previously agreed by the other parties in fact rejects the original instrument and makes a new offer; that offer, if it is to produce legal results, must be accepted by all the other parties. This is so, it is argued, quite apart from the obvious reasons of convenience and propriety which discourage the idea that a State may by unilateral action write new terms into an instrument which has evolved painfully, as the result of prolonged negotiations, amidst a process of mutual compromise and accommodation. These arguments cannot be regarded as decisive. Thus there is only limited force in the view that in accepting a multilateral treaty a State justifiably regards it as an essential part of the consideration received that all other parties accept the treaty without qualifications. This may apply to some treaties, for instance, to those of an economic character and treaties such as the conventions concluded under the auspices of the International Labour Organization where the departure by one party from the standards laid down in the treaty makes it difficult for others to adhere to it. But this is not invariably the case in humanitarian and similar conventions of a general character – in what has been described as conventions of a normative type. The conspicuous aspect of many, perhaps most, of these treaties is not the establishment of a nicely balanced system of rights and obligations – of give and take – of the parties *inter se*, but rather the assumption of an absolute obligation towards a transcending and imperative international interest subscribed to out of a sense of moral obligation and international solidarity. It is probable that in obligations of that nature the number of the parties and the conditions under which they accept the treaty are not always regarded as of decisive importance by the other parties accepting the treaty. Undoubtedly, it is inconvenient and it provides a legitimate cause of grievance if the

---

[1] See McNair, p. 105; Malkin in *B.Y.* 7 (1926), 142; Harvard Draft Convention, *A.J.* 29 (1935), Supplement, 870.

symmetry of the edifice of the treaty, so laboriously constructed, is disturbed by qualifications and limitations added, without any effort at co-ordination, by subsequent reservations. However, in relation to the general purpose and character of the treaty, this may be no more than an inconvenience. The rigid dichotomy of choice – the choice whether the reserving State or the other States ought to be excluded from the treaty – does not in fact arise.[1]

8. Moreover, while a multilateral treaty is basically a treaty and as such a contract to which it is proper to apply the fundamental notions of the general principles of the law of contract, that analogy must stop short of a reasoning which in effect transforms the requirement of consensual agreement into a negation thereof. That point is reached when the will of one party frustrates the will of all the others by rendering ineffective their consent to reservations appended by a State. It is difficult to apply to multilateral treaties the rigid requirements of the unity of the contractual relation. There is, for instance – to mention what is in effect one of the most important multilateral instruments – only a general unity and symmetry of contract in what is essentially a collective treaty of international judicial settlement resulting from the declarations of acceptance of the optional clause of Article 36 of the Statute of the International Court of Justice. We find there a multiplicity of relations brought about by the interplay of reciprocity in connection with reservations nowhere expressly authorized in the original instrument and never expressly accepted by the States parties to the optional clause. In the field of the law of war the undesirable effects of the so-called general participation clause, which is based on the notion of an exacting symmetry of treaty obligations equally applicable to all, have caused it to be abandoned in more recent conventions such as the Gas Protocol of 1925 and, in particular, the Geneva Conventions of 1949. International practice shows, in a different sphere, numerous examples of States and Governments not recognized by other parties to the same treaty and yet participating fully, in relation to other parties, in the treaty in question. There are obvious limits to the mechanical application to multilateral treaties of the logical reasoning appropriate to bilateral treaties. In the chain of relationships brought about by reservations to a multilateral treaty the element of consent – which is inescapable in any treaty, whether bilateral or multilateral – can

---

[1] The reasons underlying, from this point of view, the doctrine of unanimous consent are lucidly stated in the general comment of the Harvard Draft Convention to Articles 14, 15 and 16 (*A.J.* 29, 870, 871).

be secured only by way of giving an opportunity to withdraw from the treaty to the State or the small minority of States who find it necessary to oppose the general desire of other contracting parties to acquiesce in reservations made by other parties. The element of true consent can thus be secured by means other than that of permitting one State or a small number of States to disregard – and frustrate – the accommodating attitude of others. But it would have to be only one State or a small number of States. Otherwise the somewhat paradoxical result is reached that those very countries which are prepared to accept the treaty in its entirety, without making any reservations, are compelled to withdraw from the treaty and to leave the field to those who are willing to accept only some of its obligations.

9. *The unlimited right to make reservations.* It is also by reference to the same fundamental requirement of general – as distinguished from mere individual – consent that this alternative draft of Article 9 denies the so-called sovereignty doctrine in the matter of reservations, namely, the unlimited right of a State to append reservations, however arbitrary and however destructive of the essential purpose of the treaty, and to claim at the same time the right to participate in the treaty in disregard of the objection of a substantial number of the parties. If the reservation is of such a nature as to call seriously in question the good faith and sincerity of the State making the reservation then, it may be assumed, there will be found the requisite one-third of States who have finally accepted the treaty whether with reservations or not, who will object to the participation of that State in the treaty. In face of opposition on such grounds and in such numbers, a claim, by reference to the rights of sovereignty, to participate in the treaty amounts to a denial of the sovereignty of the other parties to the treaty. That right of effective objection, as laid down in the present draft, asserted by a substantial number of States acting, as their number shows, in the general interest, provides the necessary safeguard against an abuse of the treaty-making power which might otherwise enable a State to claim advantages, including the intangible but important advantage of participating in the treaty, without assuming substantive obligations thereunder. As experience has shown, Governments will not lightly avail themselves of that safeguard, which consists in the exclusion of the reserving State. But a safeguard there must be, in the interest of the authority of treaties and of maintaining an adequate standard of international intercourse and, in a distinct sense, of international morality.

Certainly the codification of the law of treaties should give no countenance to practices by which Governments can use the faculty of making treaties for the purpose not of undertaking international obligations but of merely creating the impression that they have undertaken them.

10. There is force in the view that one of the principal objects of the codification of the law of treaties may be to provide a safeguard of that nature. The object is not so much to secure the integrity of treaties in the sense that they must be homogeneous and of uniform application to all, but that they should exhibit a minimum degree of reality of the obligations undertaken. In the absence of such minimum of effectiveness the measure of universality, achieved at the expense of the reality of the undertaking, represents no more than a nominal advantage. It is in the light of such considerations that a compromise must be sought between the claims of universality and the integrity of the convention. These considerations provide the answer to the contention that half a loaf, secured by the universality of treaties, is preferable to no loaf at all or to its integrity achieved at the expense of drastically reducing the number of the parties to the treaty. Half a loaf[1] may be better than no bread. But there ought to be at least some approximation to half a loaf. Thus, for instance, if a Government in accepting a treaty were to add a reservation to the effect that it is under no obligation to apply the provisions of the treaty in cases in which they are in conflict with its law or if it were to reserve the right to determine in each disputed case the extent of its obligation, it might be held that the right to conclude a treaty is being diverted from its true purpose and that the reservation is of such a nature as to exclude the State in question from participation in the treaty. This is a conclusion which ought not to be made lightly. The danger of abuse or arbitrariness in reaching a conclusion of so serious a nature is effectively met by the provision of the present draft requiring the concurrence, for that purpose, of not less than one-third of the States accepting the obligations of the treaty concerned. On the other hand, there is danger of conduct inimical alike to the authority of treaties and of international law in general in the concession, for the sake of the universality of the treaty, of an absolute right to become a party to a multilateral treaty regardless of the nature of the reservations appended, or in the grant of the right to

---

[1] The deceptiveness of some manifestations of the 'half a loaf' doctrine is lucidly illustrated by Sir Gerald Fitzmaurice in a valuable article on 'Reservations to multilateral conventions', *I.C.L.Q.* 2 (1953), 1–26.

become a party so long as there is one State which does not object to a reservation. If, to use the language of the written statement of the Government of the United States of America before the International Court of Justice in connection with the Genocide Convention, a reservation is fraudulent, unreasonable, and making a mockery of ratification, then it is in the nature of an anti-climax to say that notwithstanding a reservation of that kind the reserving State may become a party if it finds one State which does not object to it. The more rational solution is that if a substantial number of parties finds that the reservation is, for the reasons stated, of a highly objectionable character, then the reserving State cannot become a party to the treaty. That number is given in the present draft as at least one-third of the parties.[1]

11. In so far as the 'American' or any other system postulates that only the refusal of all the parties to the treaty to accept a reservation should prevent the reserving State from becoming a party to the treaty, this draft adopts a solution opposed to those systems. It represents an attempt to strike a balance between the seemingly opposing considerations of universality and integrity – in either of the two meanings of the latter term – of the treaty. Universality may be an achievement which is deceptive and inimical to the dignity of international intercourse if it is obtained through acquiescence in a transparent device of participation in treaties not accompanied by acceptance of tangible and binding obligations. At the same time the so-called integrity of treaties, if attempted to be achieved through the operation of a rigid rule of unanimity in disregard of the legitimate views and interests of individual States, may become an obstructive factor in the conventional regulation of matters of common international interest. Universality, if insisted upon at all costs, can be achieved only at the expense of the reality and genuineness of treaties. 'Integrity', if an attempt is made to bring it about through the requirement of unanimous consent to reservations and the resulting possible disregard of a legitimate claim to diversity, may unnecessarily restrict the field of international co-operation.

[1] Inasmuch as the present draft is intended to strike a balance between the rival principles of unanimity of consent and of the right of the reserving State to become a party to the treaty provided that at least one State accepts the reserving State as a party, the details of the compromise implied in the proposed solution are subject to modifications, in the light of any discussion before the Commission, without affecting the essential character of that solution. Thus, for instance, the draft requires acceptance, express or implied, of the reservation by at least two-thirds of the parties. There is room for discussion whether such acceptance should not be required by a larger or smaller proportion of the total number of parties.

12. In the light of these general considerations, which to a large extent apply to all the alternative drafts here submitted, it is now convenient to distinguish between two problems which are of a different nature and which ought to be kept apart in the examination of draft A. The first problem is that connected with the entry of the treaty into force. Treaties provide, as a rule, that they shall enter into force on the occurrence of a certain event amounting to the assumption of a treaty obligation – that event being either signature, or ratification, or exchange or deposit of ratifications, or accession including ratification thereof, or deposit of an instrument of acceptance or approval – on the part of a specified number of States. When such States assume a treaty obligation subject to reservations the question arises whether – in case of objection to the reservation or until all the contracting parties have expressed approval or failed to express disapproval – the State or States making the reservation may be counted among the required number of States and whether, accordingly, the treaty has entered into force. The second, and main, question is the right of a State making a reservation to become a party to the treaty regardless of the objections of the other parties. These two questions can and, it is believed, ought to be treated separately.

B. Entry into force   13. The attempt at a solution of the first question, that of the entry into force of treaties whose signature, ratification, accession or other means of acceptance is accompanied by reservations not expressly agreed to by the other parties, constitutes the main feature of draft A of Article 9. The principal aspect of the proposed solution is that in all cases in which a treaty provides that it shall enter into force when a named number of States have definitely accepted obligations thereunder, the fact that a State has attached a reservation or reservations to any of its Articles ought to be disregarded for the purpose of ascertaining whether the requisite number of States have ratified the treaty or otherwise finally accepted its obligations. This solution, if accepted as the basis of the future law, might obviate the difficulties connected with the controversial question whether consent to reservations is required on the part of those States only which have ratified or otherwise finally assumed obligations under the treaty, or whether it extends also to States which have signed the treaty but which have not proceeded to ratify it and which may never ratify it, or, even, whether it extends to States, often indeterminate in number, which have not signed the treaty but have the right to accede to it. Reasons have occasionally been advanced why a State which has signed a treaty but has not yet ratified it shall be entitled to prevent, by its objection, the participation of a State ratifying (or otherwise finally accepting the treaty obligation) subject to reservations. These reasons, although not without some force, may not be decisive.[1] The International Court of Justice declined, in its advisory opinion on the *Genocide Convention*, to admit such a right[2] – though apparently such right was asserted, without any indication of reasons, with regard both to signatories and to States merely entitled to accede, by four judges of the Court. In its report (*Yearbook of the International Law Commission, 1951*, vol. II (Doc. A/1858, ch. II)) presented to the General Assembly at its sixth session in 1951 the Commission, while acknowledging the right of a mere signatory to prevent the participation of a reserving State, qualified the exercise of that right by the proviso that an objection by such a State should cease to have the effect of excluding the reserving State from becoming a party if within twelve months from the time of the making of its objection the objecting State has not ratified or otherwise accepted the treaty. It is probable, in the light of discussions which have since taken place, that the proposals, even if modified, acknowledging the right of actual or potential mere signatories to prevent the participation of a reserving State, are not acceptable to many States, that in some respects they are not practicable, that in other respects they

---

[1] In its report on the work of its third session (1951) the Commission expressed the view that, notwithstanding the contrary practice of the Secretary-General, 'the concern of a mere signatory State should also be taken into account'. For, as the Commission then put it, 'at the time the reservation is tendered, a signatory State may be actively engaged in the study of the convention, or it may be in the process of completing the procedure necessary for ratification, or, for some reason such as the assembling of its Parliament, it may have been compelled to delay its ratification' (section 29). These considerations probably do not outweigh the disadvantages of a rule according to which a State which is not – and may never become – a party to the treaty is entitled to prevent the participation in it of a State which declares, albeit with reservations, that it assumes binding obligations under it. These doubts apply also to conferring a right of this nature upon States which have not signed the treaty but who have been given the right to adhere to it. In view of this the Commission does not consider it necessary to express an opinion on the question whether there exists in this matter a difference in status, with a consequent difference in the right to object to reservations, between the two categories of States, namely, the signatory States and those entitled to accede. That question was answered in the affirmative, though only for a very limited and almost nominal purpose, by the majority of the Court in its advisory opinion on the *Genocide Convention (I.C.J. Reports* 1951, p. 28). The four dissenting judges, without giving reasons, answered it in the negative (*ibid.* p. 48). They recognized the right of objection, with the effect of preventing the reserving State from becoming a party to the treaty, on the part both of the signatories and of States merely entitled to accede.

[2] Although it attributed to an objection by a mere signatory the effect of a notice of objection, which acquires legal force by ratification of the treaty by the objecting State (*I.C.J. Reports* 1951, p. 30).

are open to grave objections, and that they can no longer be upheld.[1]

14. It may be convenient to draw attention to some of the possible objections to the proposals contained in the report of the Commission of 1951 which include mere signatories and States entitled to adhere among those entitled to prevent the participation of a reserving State.

(a) The system proposed may have the effect of delaying the entry into force of multilateral conventions at least for a period of twelve months and, in view of the time limits provided elsewhere for raising objections to reservations, for a considerably longer period as the result of an objection by a State which objects to the reservation and subsequently fails to ratify the treaty. Moreover, in many cases the period of twelve months allowed to an objecting State for proceeding with ratification may not be sufficient having regard to the complexity of many multilateral treaties which, in view of the necessary consequential changes in municipal law, may require prolonged inter-departmental consultation. The ratification of multilateral conventions within a period of such short duration is an exception rather than the rule.

(b) The proposals formulated by the Commission in 1951 confer the right to object only upon States which have signed or ratified the convention. They leave out of account the position of States entitled to accede. Assuming that a right of objection properly belongs to signatory States, it is difficult to see why it should be denied to States which are entitled to accede to the convention at any time on the same basis as signatory States. All the reasons adduced by the Commission for conferring that right upon signatories apply also to States entitled to adhere.

(c) The proposals disregard the complicated question as to the position arising from the fact that the States upon whose consent the participation of the reserving State depends may themselves have ratified (or otherwise finally acceded to) the treaty subject to

[1] Such scant practice as exists on the matter suggests that only those States which have finally adhered to the treaty are entitled to offer objections to reservations. Article 22 of the Convention of 20 April 1929 concerning Counterfeiting Currency provided that ratifying or acceding States desiring to be allowed to make reservations shall inform the Secretary-General to this effect and that the latter shall thereupon communicate such reservations to the high contracting parties on whose behalf ratifications or accessions have been deposited and inquire whether they have any objections thereto. 'If within six months of the date of the communication of the Secretary-General no objections have been received, the participation in the convention of the country making the reservation shall be deemed to have been accepted by the other high contracting parties subject to the said reservation' (Hudson, *Legislation*, IV, 2703).

reservations. Shall these States, whose very participation in the treaty may be in doubt on account of their own reservations, have the right effectively to object to the reserving States being counted among those whose participation is necessary for the entrance of the treaty into force?

(d) If the principle of unanimous consent is regarded as paramount, it is difficult – with respect to conventions entering into force as on the deposit of a specified number of ratifications – to regard as satisfactory a solution according to which a State which makes a reservation at the time of ratification can become a party to the convention if there is no objection on the part of any State which has previously ratified (or otherwise finally acceded to) the treaty. Apart from the difficulty which may arise from the fact that these latter States may themselves have ratified the convention subject to a reservation, the resulting situation may be that a very small number of States whose ratification or accession is required for the entrance of the treaty into force will be in a position to determine finally the participation of the reserving State with respect to a convention subsequently ratified or acceded to by thirty or forty States.

(e) As admitted in the Commission's report (paragraph 31), the proposed solution leaves out of account, as raising special problems, the question of treaties open to accession and not open to signature, such as the Convention on the Privileges and Immunities of the United Nations of 13 February 1946. The report states, in explanation, that such treaties raise special problems and are exceptional. However, in fact such conventions are quite frequent.[1] This is so in particular if it is borne in mind that the position is substantially identical with regard to treaties to which States can become parties by acceptance or approval only or to which they become parties either by signature or by acceptance (or approval). The number of such treaties has been increasing. Far from being exceptional, they may become typical. In view of this any purported solution which leaves such instruments on one side cannot be regarded as complete or satisfactory.

15. Having regard to the difficulties as outlined above, the solution which may be practicable and which is adopted in paragraph 1 of draft A of Article 9 as proposed is that the entry into force of a

---

[1] See, for example, the Convention on the Privileges and Immunities of the Specialized Agencies, approved by the General Assembly on 21 November 1947; the Revised General Act, approved by the General Assembly on 28 April 1949, for the Pacific Settlement of International Disputes; the Convention of 6 April 1950 on the Declaration of Death of Missing Persons.

treaty, at a time specified in it, should be entirely independent of the fact that the State or States upon whose final acceptance the entry into force depends have entered a reservation to any of the provisions of the treaty. Such States shall, for that purpose, be regarded as having fully accepted the obligations of the treaty and the latter shall therefore enter into force forthwith. No decision in the matter would be incumbent upon – or, in fact, admissible on the part of – the depositary authority. The latter will have to communicate the reservations to the other States which have signed the treaty, or have become parties to it, or which are entitled to accede to it. But such communication and any replies thereto, although, as is explained later on, relevant for other purposes, must be regarded as irrelevant for the purpose of the treaty entering into force. It will enter into force forthwith. As subsequently pointed out, there remains a possibility – albeit slight – that the treaty which has thus entered into force may have to be regarded as dissolved on account of the fact that, as the result of objections raised to the participation of reserving States, the number of parties to the treaty has fallen below the required minimum. However, the probability of such a contingency materializing is so small that it cannot be regarded as outweighing the advantages of the solution here proposed. Subject to these safeguards the procedure suggested in draft A of Article 9 would appear to be free from complications. The treaty which has entered into force continues to be operative in relation to any reserving State unless, after a period of adequate duration – which it is suggested should be three years – at least one-third of the number of States which have finally accepted the obligations of the convention declare a reservation to be so objectionable as to prevent the reserving State from continuing to be a party to the treaty. It must be irrelevant for that purpose whether any of the one-third (or more) States thus objecting have themselves made a reservation. The same principle would apply to a State adhering to a treaty after the expiration of the period of three years. Admittedly, in theory the solution here proposed may give opportunities for abuse and for nullifying in effect the purpose of the treaty. This might happen, for instance, if all or most of the States were to attach reservations which render the acceptance of the treaty purely nominal. However, it may be pessimistic to assume the likelihood of a large number of Governments resorting to such devices, which, in any case, may be ineffectual. In the first instance, in view of the governing principle of reciprocity such States would be unable to obtain any advantages under the treaty in the sphere covered by their own reservations. Secondly, any practical advantage accruing from recourse having been had to a device of that nature would in any case be limited to the relatively short period of three years, as explained below, at the expiry of which a majority of the parties may, by objecting to a reservation, cause the reserving State to cease to be a party to the treaty. Thirdly, even within that period, if some parties were to feel that the entry of the treaty into force was obtained by purely nominal acceptances which in effect nullify the treaty, they would be in a position to avail themselves of any right of withdrawal provided for in the treaty.

16. There are other objections to the scheme as proposed which are more cogent and which require consideration.

(a) In the first instance, Governments may be unwilling to accept a position in which they have been parties to a convention for three years subject to reservations and are subsequently excluded from participation in the treaty. A possible answer to that objection is that such Governments, if they have accepted the procedure as proposed, will have no legitimate cause for grievance seeing that they knew in advance that this might be the result of their reservations. For the provisional character, in the first three years, of the participation of a State which has made a reservation is of the essence of the solution here proposed.

(b) In view of the serious and invidious situation which is bound to arise if a State which has been a party, if only provisionally, for three years, were to cease to be a party, it is doubtful whether other States would be inclined to exercise the right of objecting to reservations unless these were obviously frivolous or made in bad faith. Reluctant as Governments are to offer a positive objection to a reservation, even if they disapprove of it, that reluctance is bound to be much greater if the convention has in fact entered into force with the reserving State as a party to it and if that reservation has in fact been in existence for some time. The result might be that reservations would be upheld which are destructive of or inconsistent with the purpose of the treaty. There cannot in the nature of things be a conclusive answer to that argument except that action resulting in termination of the membership of a reserving State would not be the result of any individual action of one party, but the cumulative result of the objection of at least one-third of the parties. Moreover, as rejection of a reservation must take place within a short period after its notification, in the event of a number of States objecting to the reservation within that period the reserving State would really not be for long in doubt as to the fate of its reservation.

(c) Finally, it may be said that there is an obvious disadvantage in a solution which makes possible the dissolution of a treaty as a result of the fact that, on account of the objection of one-third or more States, the total number of parties may fall below that required by the treaty. It is difficult to deny the inconvenience which would result from the dissolution of the treaty and the necessity of dealing with the legal effects of acts performed during its operation. However, the resulting difficulty is not insurmountable. The probability of its occurrence is small seeing that it presupposes a large number of States making reservations and a large number of States objecting to them.

C. Acceptance and rejection of reservations 17. While paragraph 2 of draft A of Article 9 is concerned with the entrance of the treaty into force, paragraph 3 is devoted to what is the principal aspect of the subject matter of that Article, namely, the question as to the conditions under which a State making reservations can definitely become a party to the treaty. (Paragraph 2, it will be noted, is intended to supply merely a provisional solution of the more limited question of the treaty entering into force.) It is convenient to preface the analysis of the solution here proposed by a statement of the technical difficulties involved, some of which have already been referred to in general terms in connection with the question of the entrance of the treaty into force.

18. When a State objects to the reservation made by another State the legal consequences of such objection are by no means automatic or uniform. Four possibilities must be envisaged: in the first instance – and this appears to be the conclusion drawn from what is described as the 'unanimity' doctrine – the State making the reservation does not, in the absence of unanimous acceptance of the reservation, become a party to the treaty in any way whatsoever. Secondly, the effect of the objection may be that the State making the reservation becomes a party to the treaty in relation to all those States which do not object to the reservation – though it does not become so in relation to the State which has objected. Thirdly, the result of the objection may be merely that there is no contractual relation, between the State making the reservation and the objecting State with regard to the particular clause covered by the reservation. Fourthly, the objecting State may be satisfied with moral or political

disapproval of the reservation without expressly attaching any legal consequences to the objection. This seems to have been the attitude, for instance, of the Government of El Salvador which expressed 'its complete disagreement' with the reservations made to the Genocide Convention by certain States and insisted that, by failing to object to them when depositing its own ratification of the convention, it did not thereby tacitly accept them. At the same time the Government of El Salvador emphasized that in ratifying the convention it did not intend to refer in any way to the reservations made, in an act of full sovereignty, by certain specified countries.[1] It is obvious that in the absence of legal regulation, by way of codification, of this aspect of the matter the position must remain confused. This is bound to be so particularly if, with regard to the State making a reservation, different parties adopt different solutions from amongst the four possible alternatives outlined above.

19. A further difficulty arises in connection with the question as to who can raise an objection resulting in any of the consequences outlined above. Is it only the States who, by a definite act of signature, of accession not requiring ratification, or of ratification, have definitely become parties to the treaty? Or does that right belong also to States who have signed or acceded subject to ratification, or who merely have the right, as yet not exercised, to do so? The considerations militating against giving the inarticulate mass of States – often comprising all the Members of the United Nations or even a potentially larger number of States – who are not bound by the treaty the right to prevent reserving States from becoming parties to it, have already been referred to. Similarly, as previously pointed out, if the number of States whose final participation is required for the purpose of the treaty entering into force is small – in the case of the Geneva Conventions of 1949, which were signed by sixty-one States, that number was laid down as two – the result may be that, whether the principle

---

[1] Annex 123 to the written statement of the United States of America before the International Court of Justice in connection with the advisory opinion on the *Genocide Convention* (I.C.J. *Reservations to the Convention on the Prevention and Punishment of the Crime of Genocide, Pleadings, Oral Arguments, Documents*, p. 185). This was also the attitude of the Government of Guatemala (*ibid.* p. 166). The attitude finally adopted by Ecuador left room for some uncertainty. On 21 March 1950 the Assistant Secretary-General addressed a letter to the Government of Ecuador drawing attention to a previous communication of that Government in which it stated that Ecuador had no objection to make concerning the submission of reservations by the Union of Soviet Socialist Republics and some other States but that 'at the same time, it expresses disagreement with the content of these reservations'. In answer to a request from the Assistant Secretary-General for clarification of that statement the Government of Ecuador replied that it 'is not in agreement with these reservations and that therefore they do not apply to Ecuador' (*ibid.* pp. 153, 154).

of unanimity of consent or some kind of majority decision to reservations is adopted or accepted, these States may acquire a power of decision of transcending consequences for the treaty as a whole.

20. Finally, if the principle is adopted that only States who have definitely become parties to the treaty may effectively object to reservations, there arises the further question whether those States must have finally accepted the treaty *without any reservations* in order to be entitled to exclude States who wish to become parties subject to reservations. For it may be argued that it is only the State whose participation is not in question who is entitled to question – and to nullify – the participation of others. Such an argument may not be altogether without force.

21. Paragraphs 2–4 of this draft of Article 9 attempt to provide an answer to these difficulties by way of the following solution:

(a) Within a period of three years subsequent to the treaty having entered into force all the parties which have finally accepted the obligations of the treaty – with or without reservations of their own – are given an opportunity to declare whether they object to the reservations appended by other States and, if they do, what effect they wish their objection to produce. They may expressly or tacitly, i.e. by failing to object, agree to the reservations; or they may adopt the position that the reservations are in their view so objectionable and contrary to the purpose and spirit of the treaty that the reserving States cannot, unless they abandon their reservations, become parties to the treaty; or they may declare – although this would in any case be the result – that while not opposing the participation of a reserving State in the treaty, they will not consider themselves bound by the treaty, in relation to that State, with regard to the operation of the particular clause in respect of which a reservation has been made. If less than one-third of the number of States which at the end of that period have finally undertaken the treaty obligation in question, with or without reservations, object to the reserving State becoming a party to the treaty, then that State will be considered a party – subject to the right of the other parties not to regard the treaty as operative as between themselves and the reserving State with respect to the clause covered by the reservation. Thus, at the end of the three years' period it will be possible to ascertain whether the treaty has definitely entered into force by having secured the final adherence of the required number of States. After the end of that period, in case a further number of States assume the obligations of the treaty subject to reservations, the question whether they can be regarded as contracting parties will be determined in the same manner – the parties up to date having an effective right of decision.

(b) It will be noted that, according to the solution here advanced, unless at least one-third of the number of the parties object to the reserving State becoming a party to the treaty, that State would become a party to the treaty not only in general but also in relation to all other parties. This would mean that no party would be in a position to declare that it does not consider itself bound by the treaty in relation to the reserving State – although it would still be in the position to insist that it will not apply the particular clause in relation to the reserving State. That solution would eliminate what some consider to be a serious defect in the 'American' system, namely, that a State which is a party to the treaty in general may not be a party to it in relation to some of the other parties (which may in extreme cases mean that a State is a party to the treaty in general although it is in effect a party to it only in relation to one State) – a situation which many regard as illogical or, in any case, undesirable. It is possible that that criticism is not absolutely decisive. However, it is a criticism which is of sufficient weight to justify the solution here proposed.

ALTERNATIVE DRAFT B

If, in any case where a multilateral treaty does not expressly prohibit or limit the faculty of making reservations, a State signs, ratifies, accedes to or otherwise accepts the treaty subject to a reservation or reservations limiting or otherwise varying the obligations of any Article or Articles of the treaty, the following procedure shall apply in the absence of any other provisions in the treaty:

1. The text of the reservations received shall be communicated by the depositary authority to all the interested States. If, on the expiry of a period of three months following the receipt of such communication, an interested State does not notify the depositary authority that it disagrees with the reservation, it shall be deemed to have accepted it.

2. Unless, after an interval prescribed by the convention, two-thirds of the States qualified to offer objections have accepted the reservation, the reserving State, if it maintains its reservation, will not be considered a party to the treaty.

3. If two-thirds or more of the States referred to in paragraph 2

agree to the reservation, the reserving State will be considered a party to the treaty subject to the right of any party not to apply to the reserving State the provision of the treaty in respect of which a reservation has been made.

Comment

1. This alternative draft follows the preceding draft with regard to its principal aspect, namely, inasmuch as it does not accept the principle of unanimous consent to reservations and considers the consent of at least two-thirds of the total number of interested States to be sufficient for the purpose. To that extent the general observations of the comment appended to the previous draft apply also to draft B.

2. On the other hand, the present draft B attempts to avoid the complications, admittedly serious, involved in the previous scheme which is based on the notion of the treaty entering into force provisionally regardless of any reservations made to it by the parties. It also leaves it, to some extent, to the treaty to determine who are the 'interested States', i.e. the States qualified to offer objections to the reservations – provided that a period is set within which objections may be raised. The practical effect would be that in most cases the treaty would enter into force on the date or event specified for the reason that the required number of States would ratify or otherwise finally accept the treaty without reservations. In cases in which that did not happen the entry into force would be delayed until the number of ratifications (or its equivalent), unaccompanied by reservations – or accompanied by reservations subsequently agreed to by the qualified States – reaches the number required by the treaty. This might mean a considerable delay in its entry into force. A further complication might arise if one of the 'qualified States', i.e. the States qualified to make objections to reservations, itself made reservations subsequently objected to by others. In that case the objection of that State would be immaterial if its own reservations were objected to by one-third or more States and if, as a result, it did not become a party to the convention.

3. The central idea underlying this scheme would be substantially clarified if the treaty were to provide expressly that the 'qualified States' are those only which themselves ratify or otherwise finally accept the treaty within the period prescribed by the treaty. Alternatively, following the recommendation made by the Commission in 1951, it could be provided that the objection of a mere signatory (or

a State entitled to accede) ceases to be valid if that State does not ratify the treaty within a prescribed period.

ALTERNATIVE DRAFT C

If, in any case where a multilateral treaty does not expressly prohibit or limit the faculty of making reservations, a State signs, ratifies, accedes to or otherwise accepts the treaty subject to a reservation or reservations limiting or otherwise varying the obligations of any Article or Articles of the treaty the following procedure shall apply in the absence of any other provisions in the treaty:

1. The parties or the organ of an international organization responsible for establishing the text of the treaty shall designate a committee, appointed in a manner to be agreed by them, competent to decide on the admissibility of reservations made by any Government subsequent to the establishment of the text of the treaty.

2. The text of the reservations received shall be communicated by the depositary authority to all the interested States. If, on the expiry of a period of three months following the receipt of such communication, an interested State does not notify the depositary authority that it disagrees with the reservation, it shall be deemed to have accepted it.

3. If a reservation is objected to by a State qualified to object, then it shall be competent for the committee, at the request of the State making the reservation, to decide whether the reservation is admissible. If the reservation is declared inadmissible then the State in question cannot become a party to the treaty if it maintains the reservation.

Comment

1. The main provision of this alternative draft is self-explanatory. It confers upon a standing committee designated by the States or the international organ which have established the text of the treaty the power to decide upon the admissibility of a particular reservation. Proposals of this character have been made in the past.[1] If adopted,

---

[1] A suggestion on these lines was made in 1932 by Sir Arnold McNair with regard to reservations to International Labour Conventions concerning points 'of minor discrepancy' between the convention and national laws. The International Labour Office did not accede to the suggestion. It may be convenient to reproduce the proposal in full:

'7. To put my suggestion into concrete form, it is this – that every convention, and,

it would eliminate the difficulties connected both with the entry of the treaty into force and with the complications arising out of the necessity for an individual decision by States.

2. The procedure as here proposed contains no answer to the question who are the States qualified to object to a reservation. That answer would be simplified – in fact, the necessity for it would be removed altogether – if it were provided that the committee should decide on the question of the admissibility of the reservation regardless of whether an objection has been raised against it.

3. It is not considered necessary to elaborate the details or possible variations of the solution here outlined, for instance, whether the committee should be the regular body to decide on the admissibility of reservations or whether it should act only if objection is raised by a State (a variation which would immediately raise the question as to what categories of States are entitled to object); whether the decisions of the committee should be by a majority, and what kind of majority; whether it should be composed of the States designated or of independent persons appointed by them; and many others. Should a solution on these lines recommend itself to Governments, further consideration might be given to an elaboration of the requisite procedure.

4. The advantages of simplicity and expedition which characterize

upon its periodical revision, every revised convention, shall contain a clause running somewhat as follows:

' "In order to obviate difficulties in the way of ratification arising from points of minor discrepancy between the text of this convention and the text of national laws or decrees in existence or to be passed to give effect to this convention each member may submit to the reservations committee of the conference the text of any reservation which it may desire to make. The reservations committee shall take such proposed reservations into consideration, and if, acting by a majority of not less than two-thirds, they are of opinion that the reservation is reasonable having regard to the legal system and other circumstances prevailing in the country of the member proposing it, and can be permitted without endangering the uniformity of the application of this convention, they shall notify their assent to the member. Thereupon a ratification to which such reservation is attached shall become effective unless and until it shall be disallowed by the general conference of the organization at the session next ensuing."

'8. Further, it would be necessary for the conference to constitute a reservations committee on some such basis as the following:

' "The reservations committee shall be a standing committee of the conference, consisting of six members, of whom four shall be permanent members (two being Government delegates, one other being a delegate representing employers, and one other being a delegate representing workers) and two shall be non-permanent and appointed *ad hoc* by the governing body and having special technical knowledge with reference to each convention" ' (I.C.J. *Reservations to the Convention on the Prevention and Punishment of the Crime of Genocide, Pleadings, Oral Arguments, Documents*, p. 259).

The Protocol to the Convention for the Simplification of Customs Formalities of 3 November 1923 empowered the Council of the League of Nations to decide upon the admissibility of certain reservations after consulting a body of experts to be appointed by it.

this particular solution may be considered by some to be so obvious as to outweigh any disadvantages or doubts inherent in it. Of these the most important is the possible – and perhaps natural – reluctance of Governments to confer upon a body over which they would have no control the essentially discretionary power to decide on modifications in the contents of the treaty in matters which may refer to fundamental aspects of its provisions and which do not admit of an answer by reference to ascertainable legal standards. This latter consideration may be held to apply, for instance, to the test laid down by the International Court of Justice in its advisory opinion on the reservations to the Genocide Convention, namely, the test of compatibility with the purpose and object of the convention. It is clear that any reservation to a particular clause is incompatible with the purpose and object of that clause. The question to be answered, therefore, is whether that particular clause constitutes an essential object and purpose of the treaty. Thus an Article conferring upon the International Court of Justice jurisdiction in disputes relating to the interpretation or application of the treaty may be regarded by some as of a purely procedural character separable from the main purpose of the treaty. Others may regard that jurisdictional clause as being of the very essence and the principal *raison d'être* of the treaty – particularly if its substantive provisions are in fact no more than declaratory of the general legal and moral sentiment of the contracting parties. It is difficult to visualize any legal answer, which is not purely subjective in nature, to questions of this character. However, this very circumstance may militate in favour of entrusting the power of decision on this question to an organ which is partly expert and partly political in its composition.

ALTERNATIVE DRAFT D

If, in any case where a multilateral treaty does not expressly prohibit or limit the faculty of making reservations, a State signs, ratifies, accedes to or otherwise accepts the treaty subject to a reservation or reservations limiting or otherwise varying the obligations of any Article or Articles of the treaty the following procedure shall apply in the absence of any other provisions in the treaty:

1. The parties or the organ of an international organization responsible for establishing the text of the treaty shall request the International Court of Justice to designate under its rules a

chamber of summary procedure to decide on the admissibility of reservations made by a Government subsequent to the establishment of the text of the treaty.

2. The text of the reservations received shall be communicated by the depositary authority to all the interested States. If, on the expiry of a period of three months following the receipt of such communication, an interested State does not notify the depositary authority that it disagrees with the reservation, it shall be deemed to have accepted it.

3. If a reservation is objected to by a State qualified to object, then it shall be competent for the chamber of summary procedure, at the request of the State making the reservation, to decide whether the reservation is admissible. If the reservation is declared inadmissible then the State in question cannot become a party to the treaty if it maintains the reservation.

Comment

As in the case of draft C, the main provision of the present alternative draft D is self-explanatory. Its object is to confer upon a chamber of summary procedure, to be constituted by the International Court of Justice under its rules, the power to decide upon the admissibility of a reservation either in the first instance or by way of appeal against the rejection of the reservation by any of the parties (or potential parties) to the treaty. A solution on these lines has a number of features in common with that proposed in draft C. It is in some respects open to the same doubts. But there is attraction in the idea that disputes of this nature – to some extent there are present the elements of a dispute in a situation in which a State puts forward a contested claim to be entitled to append a reservation – should be decided by a body of permanent composition and of acknowledged independence, and which is capable, by virtue of the continuity of its practice, of developing standards of general application. This is so although, essentially, the question of the admissibility of a particular reservation is probably not of a legal character but calls for a decision of a legislative nature. However, there would seem to be no reason why a permanent and authoritative body should not make a weighty contribution, in addition to solving concrete difficulties, to developing legislative standards of value. In so far as a particular reservation involves the issue of its compatibility with the general object and spirit of the treaty it raises the question whether the right to append reservations has been exercised in good faith. As such it is a question of fact which is not outside the proper province of the judicial function. As in the case of a standing committee designated by the signatory States, as outlined above in draft C, recourse to the summary procedure of the Court might – to an even larger extent – provide a solution conspicuous for its simplicity and expedition. Inasmuch as it could be adopted within the framework of a general codification of the law of treaties it would render unnecessary the creation of a special body for every treaty. Nor would it throw an undue burden upon the Court as a whole. The acceptance of such a function by the Court would be in keeping with its readiness in the past to assist in the settlement of disputes in cases not calling for the exercise of the judicial function proper.

Note

1. The length of the comment to this Article exceeds considerably that to other Articles of the present draft. This is not so only on account of the complexity of the subject but also because the various solutions formulated in the Article *de lege ferenda* differ from those adopted in the past by Governments and official bodies, as well as by the Commission itself. For this reason the special rapporteur considered a fuller elaboration of the comment to be appropriate.

2. The nature of the subject explains also why the special rapporteur has adopted the method of presenting a number of alternative solutions, without expressing an obvious preference for any of them. The special rapporteur is of the opinion that the formulation of principles to be adopted on the subject comes within the purview of the task of the Commission connected with the codification of the law of treaties after it has laid down what is still the existing law. Various Governments represented at successive sessions of the General Assembly have voiced the view that the Commission should devote, in connection with its work on treaties, further consideration to the matter. In presenting in 1951 its report, which was based on the predominant doctrine of the requirement of unanimous consent, the Commission probably envisaged its task in the matter as being limited substantially to codification of the existing law. The conclusions of the report, thus conceived, did not prove acceptable to a large majority of States represented at the sixth session of the General Assembly in 1951. In the view of the special rapporteur, even prior to the controversy brought about by the reservations to the Genocide Convention, it was felt increasingly that the doctrine of unanimous consent was not free from difficulties. Sir William Malkin, writing

on the subject in 1926, while still adhering to the view that every reservation must be the subject of definite acceptance by other signatories,[1] welcomed developments tending to mitigate the rigidity of the then existing system and to ensure 'the acceptance of reservations which are consistent with the intentions of the original signatories but no others'.[2] Having regard, apart from the inherent shortcomings of the traditional view, to the growing flexibility of the procedure of concluding treaties and the present unwillingness of many – perhaps a majority of – Governments to accept the unanimity principle in the matter, the subject of reservations lends itself to a combination of two methods, of codification and development, open to the Commission by virtue of its Statute. The various alternative drafts of Article 9 are drafted on that assumption. The argument that the principle of unanimous consent has operated satisfactorily in the past is, perhaps necessarily, inconclusive. It is not easy to assess to what extent the frequent absence of ratification of numerous conventions on the part of a large number of States – occasionally to the point of causing the convention not to enter into force – was due to the operation of the rule of unanimous consent and to the resulting difficulty of making reservations. The Hague Convention of 1930 relating to Conflicts of Nationality Laws did not secure wide acceptance although it provided that the parties may, when signing, ratifying, or acceding, attach reservations to all substantive provisions of the convention.[3] On the other hand, it may not be easy to accept the view that the principle of unanimous consent did not give rise to difficulties. The existence of these difficulties explains the discussions, before the League of Nations and elsewhere, of this question in the period preceding the establishment of the United Nations.

3. For reasons which appear in the comment, none of the schemes here outlined follows that aspect of the so-called 'American system', as adopted in 1938, which recognizes the possibility of a State being a

---

[1] In *B.Y.* 7 (1926), 160. Similarly, Jenks, writing in 1945, pointed to the 'marked tendency, in the case of instruments negotiated under the auspices of the League of Nations, to endeavour to expedite their acceptance by the inclusion of provisions designed to facilitate the acceptance of reservations by relaxing the ordinary rule of international law that an instrument cannot validly be accepted subject to a reservation unless the reservation is accepted by all the parties to the instrument' (*A.J.* 39 (1945), 167).

[2] *B.Y.* 7, 162.

[3] There are other instances of treaties allowing in advance reservations of wide and almost unlimited scope. Thus the Convention of 14 September 1939 on the Status of Refugees Coming from Germany provides that 'the high contracting parties may make reservations concerning Articles contained in chapters to which their obligations extend' (Hudson, *Legislation*, VIII, 32).

party to a treaty in relation to some but not to other States. As already pointed out, that feature of the American system is not without precedent. However, it is probable that decisive weight must be attached to the view that a system of that nature detracts from the unity of the treaty; that it transforms it, in many respects, into a loose combination of bilateral agreements; and, above all, that it has hardly any application to treaties which, in fact, do not create rights and obligations as between the parties but which are intended to establish an absolute obligation of all parties.[1]

4. Any procedural regulation of the subject of reservations within a general codification of the law of treaties must be purely optional in character. It must remain open to the parties, in conformity with the recommendation made in the report of the Commission in 1951[2] and approved by the resolution of the General Assembly of that year, to adopt any other provisions governing the matter. They may provide that no reservations shall be admissible, or that reservations shall not be admissible with regard to specified Articles. The relevant Article of a code would merely lay down what, in the absence of regulation by treaty, shall be the procedure governing the subject. Of necessity, that Article must be of a general character. It cannot

---

[1] As with regard to the system of unanimous consent so also with regard to the 'American system' divergent views have been expressed as to the success of its operation. The Department of International Law and Organization in the Pan-American Union has stated that that practice is well adapted 'within the limited inter-American system' and that it has successfully operated within that sphere. 'The Pan-American Union procedure is believed to be best adapted, within the limited inter-American regional system, to increasing the number of ratifications and widening the use of treaties both for purposes of a contractual character and for the development of general principles of international law. Thus far it has not had the effect, to which it might logically have given rise, of creating confusion in respect to the obligations of the various treaties which have been entered into. Whether the procedure is as well adapted to the larger organization of the United Nations, in which law-making treaties may be expected to play a larger part than in the inter-American regional system, is a question apart from the scope of the present memorandum' (I.C.J. *Reservations to the Convention on the Prevention and Punishment of the Crime of Genocide, Pleadings, Oral Arguments, Documents*, p. 20). In his article on 'Reservations to multilateral conventions' Fitzmaurice has adduced impressive evidence of the dissatisfaction, among some American countries, with the operation of the system (*I.C.L.Q.* 2, 20–2). The following quotation, included in that article, from a report of an (apparently different) organ of the Pan-American Union is of interest: 'The absence of a definite criterion as to the effect of reservations made at the time of signature . . . has given rise to various interpretations so different from one another in some cases – as in that of the Economic Agreement of Bogotà – that they have made the instrument impracticable because no State considers it wise to ratify a multilateral agreement whose application varies with each country as a result of numerous reservations' (*ibid.* pp. 20–1).

[2] The Commission suggested that 'the organs of the United Nations, specialized agencies and States should, in the course of preparing multilateral conventions, consider the insertion therein of provisions relating to the admissibility or non-admissibility of reservations and to the effect to be attributed to them' (A/1958, para. 33 in *Yearbook of the International Law Commission, 1951*, II, 130).

take fully into account the fact of the wide diversity of treaties. Thus there may be a clear difference, for the purpose of reservations, between a humanitarian treaty, such as the Genocide Convention, and a treaty of a political or economic nature in which reciprocity and uniformity of obligations may be an essential feature of the arrangement. In such cases it may be particularly desirable that the treaty should contain detailed provisions as to the admissibility and the effect of reservations. An Article of a code of the law of treaties is not the most suitable medium for impressing upon Governments the desirability of incorporating such detailed regulation. That purpose may be partly achieved by reiterating, in connection with the codification of the law of treaties, the resolution of the General Assembly on the subject.

5. Whatever scheme is eventually adopted, it is probable that the function of the depositary authority will have to be of a purely administrative nature. It will have to be relieved of any responsibility for deciding on the question whether, having regard to the reservations appended, the treaty has entered into force. Its function would be limited to that of receiving the declarations, varying in form, of acceptance of treaty obligations; communicating them, and any reservations attached to them, to the Governments concerned; and, if necessary, obtaining a clarification of any statements or declarations made by Governments in this connection. This would apply also to the question whether any particular statement or declaration does or does not constitute a reservation.[1]

---

[1] It may be noted in this connection that there is no compelling reason to regard as reservations such declarations as merely limit the effect of a provision of the treaty. As Professor C. Hyde has put it: 'The practice of States seemingly rejects the conclusion that a reservation must be confined to a proposal or condition that lessens the scope of burdens set forth in a text in relation to the reserving State. There are instances where a reservation has served to modify by enlargement obligations to be borne by other parties or prospective parties in relation to the reserving State' (Hyde, II, 1435). The question whether a declaration amounts to a reservation is independent of the designation given to it by the declaring State. The United States of America signed in 1938 a number of International Labour Conventions subject to 'understandings' which were made a part of the ratification. It was stated on that occasion by the United States that 'these understandings are deemed not to be reservations which would require the acceptance of the other Governments, but to be merely clarifications of definitions to show that the definitions accepted by the United States of America are in fact those that were intended by the Conference.' The formal notification was made 'subject to the understandings hereinafter recited and made part of this ratification' (*Official Bulletin of the International Labour Office*, 23 (1938), no. 4, 128–36). Hackworth, V, 144–53, contains an interesting section on 'Understandings short of reservations'.

1954 REPORT

ARTICLE 9

RESERVATIONS

I

Unless otherwise provided by the treaty, a signature, ratification, accession, or any other method of accepting a multilateral treaty is void if accompanied by reservations not agreed to by all parties to the treaty.

II

Alternative Proposals de lege ferenda (as in the first report)[1]

1. The italicized passage, which has been added, is not intended as any substantial modification of the original draft. It expresses a qualification which, whether explicitly stated or not, underlies most of the other Articles of the first report, namely, that the parties may, subject to any overriding principles of general international law (see Article 15 of the first report), adopt conventional rules appropriate to the nature and the circumstances of any particular treaty. In fact, the main purpose of the qualifying passage is to draw attention to the alternative proposals *de lege ferenda* as formulated in the first report. This is so mainly having regard to the fact that the unanimity rule which the Article as formulated adopts, with some hesitation though in conformity with the view previously expressed by the Commission as to the *lex lata*,[2] is unsatisfactory in many respects.

2. It is believed that, however unsatisfactory and however far short of universal acceptance a rule of international law may be, it is the function of the Commission to state that rule – even if only as a preliminary to a formulation of a more satisfactory solution *de lege ferenda*. In his first report, the special rapporteur has given reasons why the unanimity rule which the Commission – rightly, it is believed – found to be the existing rule, cannot be regarded as satisfactory. However, although open to objections of various kinds,

---

[1] A/CN.4/63 in *Yearbook of the International Law Commission, 1953*, vol. II.

[2] In his interesting memorandum on the subject, submitted in August 1953, Mr Yepes considers that the view of the Commission as to the *lex lata* cannot be sustained (*ibid.* A/CN.4/L.46). However, what is believed to be relevant is that the special rapporteur, though after some hesitation, did in fact associate himself with the view of the Commission as to the *lex lata*.

that rule nevertheless represents the existing law. The fact that it is not unanimously accepted does not mean that it is not generally accepted and that, as such, it cannot be described as the rule of international law on the subject. If unanimity of acceptance, as distinguished from generality, were to be regarded as an essential hall-mark of rules of international law, the scope of the law would be reduced to the barest minimum.

3. Nevertheless, although the Commission can, in the view of the special rapporteur, properly adhere to its statement of the existing law on the subject as formulated in its report on reservations in 1951,[1] it cannot stop there. It is a matter for reflection that while the International Court of Justice, whose function it is to *apply* existing law, in its advisory opinion on the question of Reservations to the Convention on Genocide,[2] devoted itself mainly to the *development* of the law in this sphere by laying down the novel principle of compatibility of reservations with the purpose of the treaty, the International Law Commission whose task is both to codify and develop international law, limited itself substantially to a statement of existing law. This was so notwithstanding the fact that the General Assembly requested the Commission to examine the subject from the point of view of both codification and development. In view of this the special rapporteur submits that the satisfactory fulfilment of the task of the Commission in this respect requires that it should devote attention to the elaboration of other solutions. These solutions can be conceived either as replacing the existing rule or as solutions alternative, at the option of the parties, to the existing rule which may continue to be the residuary binding principle in case the parties fail to adopt any alternative rule such as those formulated in this report.

4. Thus it will be necessary for the Commission to decide which course it will finally adopt in its codification of the law of treaties, namely, whether to formulate one of the alternative solutions as a replacement of the existing law as formulated by it in its report in 1951, or whether to reaffirm that rule as the main residuary rule and to recommend any of the alternative solutions to be adopted by the parties according to the circumstances of any particular treaty. If the Commission adopts that latter course, its task will be considerably simplified. The special rapporteur expresses no preference for either solution seeing that the practical difference between them is

[1] See chapter II of the Commission's report on its third session, *Yearbook of the International Law Commission, 1951*, II, 125.
[2] *I.C.J. Reports* 1951, p. 15.

distinctly limited. For even if the traditional rule of unanimity – admittedly unsatisfactory – is maintained, it is a rule which the parties can discard at will by selecting any of the alternative solutions. They would be bound by the unanimity rule only if they were to fail to provide for other alternatives. What the codification of the subject can usefully do is, by annexing to the main residuary rule a number of model alternative solutions, to remove the danger of the parties being bound by the residuary rule as the result of mere inadvertence. There will be no excuse for such inadvertence if the alternative solutions are clearly set out in a code of the law of treaties and if, as the result, they can be presumed to be present to the minds of the parties when engaged in drafting the final clauses of the treaty.

5. From this point of view it may be useful to bring to the attention of the Commission the discussions which took place in 1954 within the Commission on Human Rights in the matter of reservations to the proposed Covenant of Human Rights. While Chile and Uruguay proposed that 'no State Party to this covenant may make reservations in respect of its provisions' (Commission on Human Rights, tenth session, Doc. E/CN.4/L. 354, 25 March 1954), the U.S.S.R. advanced a proposal in the opposite direction – a proposal giving any State the right to formulate reservations irrespective of the attitude of the other parties. The proposal (*ibid*. Doc. E/CN.4/L.349, 22 March 1954) ran as follows:

Any State may, either at the time of signature of the present covenant followed by acceptance, i.e. ratification, or at the time of acceptance, make reservations with regard to any of the provisions contained therein. If reservations are made the covenant shall, in relations between the States which have made the reservations and all other States Parties to the covenant, be deemed to be in force in respect of all its provisions except those with regard to which the reservations have been made.

The proposal put forward by China, Egypt, Lebanon and the Philippines (*ibid*. Doc. E/CN.4/L.351, 24 March 1954) combined, in a novel fashion, the so-called Pan-American system with the principle of compatibility as enunciated by the Court. It reads as follows:

1. Any State, at the time of its signature subsequently confirmed by ratification, or at the time of its ratification or acceptance, may make any reservation compatible with the object and purpose of the covenant.

2. Any State party may object to any reservation on the ground that it is incompatible with the object and purpose of the covenant.

3. Should there be a dispute as to whether or not a particular reservation is compatible with the object and purpose of the covenant, and it

cannot be settled by special agreement between the States concerned, the dispute may be referred to the International Court of Justice by the reserving State or by any State party objecting to the reservation.

4. Unless a settlement is reached in accordance with paragraph 3, any State party objecting to the reservation may consider that the reserving State is not a party to the covenant, while any State party which accepts the reservation may consider that the reserving State is a party to the covenant.

5. Any State making a reservation in accordance with paragraph 1, or objecting to a reservation in accordance with paragraph 2, may at any time withdraw the reservation or objection by a communication to that effect addressed to the Secretary-General of the United Nations.

The detailed proposals put forward by the United Kingdom are of special interest inasmuch as they emanate from a Government which before the International Court of Justice, in the case of *Reservations to the Convention on Genocide*,[1] relied conspicuously on the unanimity rule. These proposals are in accordance with the alternative drafts A and B as formulated in the first report submitted by the special rapporteur in 1953. They follow the lines of the solution foreshadowed by the Government of the United Kingdom at the General Assembly in 1952 and elaborated in greater detail by Sir Gerald Fitzmaurice in *I.C.L.Q.* 2, 1–26. They read as follows (Doc. E/CN.4/L.345, 18 March 1954):

1. Any State may, on depositing its instrument of acceptance to this covenant, make a reservation to the extent that any law in force in its territory is in conflict with, or to the extent that its law does not give effect to a particular provision of, Part III of this covenant. Any reservation made shall be accompanied by a statement of the law or laws to which it relates.

2. As soon as the period of two years mentioned in Article 70 (3) has elapsed, the Secretary-General of the United Nations shall, subject to paragraph 5 of this Article, circulate a copy of all reservations received by him to all States which have by the date of circulation deposited an instrument of acceptance with or without reservation.

3. Copies of reservations received after the expiry of the period mentioned in Article 70 (3) shall, subject to paragraph 5 of this Article, forthwith be circulated by the Secretary-General to all States which, by the date of circulation, have deposited an instrument of acceptance with or without reservation or, if on that date the covenant has entered into force, to all States parties thereto.

---

[1] *I.C.J. Reports* 1951, p. 15.

4.   A reservation shall be deemed to be accepted if not less than two-thirds of the States to whom copies have been circulated in accordance with this Article accept or do not object to it within a period of three months following the date of circulation.

5.   If an instrument of acceptance accompanied by a reservation to any part of this covenant not mentioned in paragraph 1 of this Article is deposited by any State, the Secretary-General shall invite such State to withdraw the reservation. Unless and until the reservation is withdrawn, the instrument of acceptance shall be without effect and the procedure provided in this Article shall not be followed with respect to such instrument or the reservation or reservations accompanying it.

6.   Any State making a reservation in accordance with this Article may withdraw that reservation either by a notice addressed to the Secretary-General; such notice shall take effect on the date of its receipt; and in whole or in part at any time after its acceptance, a copy of such notice shall be circulated by the Secretary-General to all States parties hereto.

Subsequently the following paragraph was added to the foregoing text (*ibid.* Doc. E/CN.4/L.345/Add. 1, 24 March 1954):

7.   It is understood that, in order to achieve the application to the fullest extent of the provisions of this covenant, any State making a reservation in accordance with this Article should take, as soon as may be practicable, such steps as will enable it to withdraw the reservation either in whole or in part.

8. The Commission on Human Rights, without declaring itself in favour of any solution, decided to submit the various proposals to the General Assembly for a final decision. While the General Assembly may find it necessary, with regard to the particular instrument before it, to take a decision in favour of one particular system in the matter of reservations, no such determination is incumbent upon the International Law Commission. As already suggested, it may properly consider that after formulating the main residuary rule binding upon the parties in case (and only in case) they have failed to provide for a different solution, its task will be fulfilled if it formulates the various alternative solutions as outlined in this report, or, if the Commission so desires, any other methods. For the fact, which the Commission is not at liberty to disregard, is that, according to the circumstances of the various treaties, the recent practice of Governments has variously followed the different methods outlined in the report. Thus the Agreement of 25 February 1953 on German

External Debts (Cmd. 8781 (1953)) follows closely the principle of unanimity. It lays down in Article 38 as follows:

Any Government which deposits an instrument of ratification or a notification of approval or an instrument of accession to the present agreement other than in accordance with the terms of its invitation or subject to any other reservation or qualification shall not be deemed to be a party to the agreement until such reservation or qualification has been withdrawn or has been accepted by all the parties thereto.

On the other hand, the Convention of 1951 on the Legal Status of Stateless Persons allows reservations, regardless of the subsequent consent of the other contracting parties, but excludes them altogether with regard to some specified subjects, such as absence of non-discrimination (Article 3), freedom of religion (Article 4), free access to court (Article 16, para. 1), prohibition of expulsion to countries of persecution (Article 33), and the final clauses of the convention. The Convention on Declaration of Death of Missing Persons, concluded about the same time (6 April 1951), follows the so-called Pan-American system. It provides, in Article 19, that if a contracting party does not accept a reservation made by another State, it may, within ninety days of the receipt of notification thereof, notify the Secretary-General that it considers the accession of the State making the reservation as not having entered into force between that State and itself; for in that case the convention is to be considered as not having entered into force between the two States in question. These examples, which show the continuing variety of practice on the subject, suggest that it is neither necessary nor desirable to aim at a uniform solution of the problem. What is both necessary and desirable is that the codification of the law of treaties shall contain a clear rule for the cases in which the parties have made no provision on the subject.

9. It will be noted that neither the first report nor the present additional report refers to the so-called 'federal clause' or the 'colonial clause' – a subject which has given rise to considerable discussion. Essentially, the federal and colonial clauses constitute reservations; to that extent they are governed by the rules and principles bearing on that matter. However, their importance is such that they warrant separate treatment. This belongs, more conveniently, to that part of the report which will cover the operation and implementation of treaties.

IV CONDITIONS OF VALIDITY OF TREATIES

SECTION I

CAPACITY OF THE PARTIES AND OF THEIR AGENTS

Editor's note The material under this head is taken from the 1953 Report. The Vienna Convention covers the question of capacity more fully in two separate sections on conclusion and invalidity.

PART II

CONCLUSION AND ENTRY INTO FORCE OF TREATIES

Section 1. Conclusion of Treaties

ARTICLE 6

Capacity of States to conclude treaties

Every State possesses capacity to conclude treaties.

ARTICLE 7

Full powers

1. A person is considered as representing a State for the purpose of adopting or authenticating the text of a treaty or for the purpose of expressing the consent of the State to be bound by a treaty if:
   (a) he produces appropriate full powers; or
   (b) it appears from the practice of the States concerned or from other circumstances that their intention was to consider that person as representing the State for such purposes and to dispense with full powers.
2. In virtue of their functions and without having to produce full powers, the following are considered as representing their State:
   (a) Heads of State, Heads of Government and ministers for foreign affairs, for the purpose of performing all acts relating to the conclusion of a treaty;
   (b) heads of diplomatic missions, for the purpose of adopting the text of a treaty between the accrediting State and the State to which they are accredited;

(c) representatives accredited by States to an international conference
or to an international organization or one of its organs, for the
purpose of adopting the text of a treaty in that conference,
organization or organ.

ARTICLE 8

Subsequent confirmation of an act performed without authorization

An act relating to the conclusion of a treaty performed by a person who
cannot be considered under Article 7 as authorized to represent a State
for that purpose is without legal effect unless afterwards confirmed by
that State.

PART V

INVALIDITY, TERMINATION AND SUSPENSION
OF THE OPERATION OF TREATIES

Section 2. Invalidity of Treaties

ARTICLE 46

Provisions of internal law regarding competence to conclude treaties

1. A State may not invoke the fact that its consent to be bound by a
treaty has been expressed in violation of a provision of its internal law
regarding competence to conclude treaties as invalidating its consent
unless that violation was manifest and concerned a rule of its internal
law of fundamental importance.

2. A violation is manifest if it would be objectively evident to any
State conducting itself in the matter in accordance with normal practice
and in good faith.

ARTICLE 47

Specific restrictions on authority to express the consent of a State

If the authority of a representative to express the consent of a State to
be bound by a particular treaty has been made subject to a specific
restriction, his omission to observe that restriction may not be invoked
as invalidating the consent expressed by him unless the restriction was
notified to the other negotiating States prior to his expressing such
consent.

CHAPTER 10

CAPACITY OF THE PARTIES

ARTICLE 10

CAPACITY OF THE PARTIES

An instrument is void as a treaty if concluded in disregard of the international limitations upon the capacity of the parties to conclude treaties.

Comment

1. This Article overlaps to some extent with Article 1 (which contains the definition of a treaty) and Article 16 (which lays down that a treaty is void if its performance involves a breach of a treaty obligation previously undertaken by one or more contracting parties). It is thus probable that the present Article may be of a somewhat residuary character and, to that extent, of limited practical importance. Moreover, one of the many difficulties which surround this subject is the fact that while in municipal law the contractual capacity of persons is defined by overriding rules of law, in the international sphere the requisite status may be conferred by the very fact that an instrument claimed to be a treaty is concluded by an indisputably sovereign State with an entity whose legal status has hitherto been doubtful. A further difficulty is due to the circumstance that the question covered by the present Article does not seem to have received either judicial consideration or any frequent or uniform treatment, justifying the drawing of confident conclusions, on the part of Governments.

2. The following entities whose capacity to conclude a treaty may be controversial come within the purview of the present article:

(a) Dependent States, in particular protectorates;

(b) Subordinate States such as member States of federal States;

(c) Sovereign States whose contractual capacity is limited as the result of the conferment of a certain status, as in the case of neutralized States;

(d) Sovereign States whose freedom to contract has been limited as the result of the assumption of international obligations in specified spheres;

(e) International organizations inasmuch as their contractual capacity is limited by the scope of the powers assumed by them in their constitutions.

These five categories may now be considered in turn.

3. *Dependent States, in particular protectorates.* Protectorates to which reference is made here are States – and they are States probably also in contemplation of international law – which, although normally represented in the field of international relations by the protecting States, have a separate administrative existence and distinct degree of autonomy.[1] There is an occasional tendency to assume that such States, 'not being members of the international community', possess no power to conclude treaties. That statement, which is probably inaccurate, seems to beg the question. The status of a political entity as a member of the international community depends upon various factors, including the capacity to conclude treaties. This does not necessarily mean that the capacity to conclude treaties depends on the status as a member of the international community. It is probably more accurate to say that, unless the contrary is expressly provided in the treaty establishing the protectorate, the protected State does possess capacity to conclude treaties – at least with the consent of the protecting State. Thus, for instance, while France signed the International Sanitary Convention of 21 June 1926 (Hudson, *International Legislation*, III (1925–7), 1903) on her own behalf and on behalf of a number of her possessions and Mandated territories, Tunisia and Morocco were separate parties to that convention. Similarly, the Convention of 5 June 1935 concerning Unification of Methods of Analysis of Wines in International Commerce included among the parties thereto the Sultan of Morocco and the Bey of Tunis signing in their own name (*ibid.* VII, 89). This was also the case with regard to the International Convention for the Protection of Industrial Property of 2 June 1932 (*ibid.* VI, 870). Other numerous examples of the exercise of the treaty-making power of protectorates can be quoted.[2] In addition, treaties are often concluded, subsequent to the

[1] This rules out political communities such as the British colonial protectorates – although the border-line between the latter and ordinary protectorates is somewhat elastic. Thus in the case of the *Duff Development Company Ltd.* v. *Government of Kelantan* [1924] A.C. 797 the British Foreign Office informed the Court that Kelantan was an independent State notwithstanding the fact that by virtue of an agreement regulating the relations between the United Kingdom and the State of Kelantan the latter undertook to have no political relations with any foreign Power except through the medium of the Government of the United Kingdom and to follow, in all matters of administration, the advice of an adviser appointed by the Government of the United Kingdom. In the same agreement the United Kingdom undertook not to interfere with the internal administration of Kelantan save in certain exceptional contingencies.

[2] For some of them see Hackworth, V, 154.

establishment of the protectorate, between the protecting and the protected States. Thus the Treaty of 8 June 1883 between France and Tunisia confirmed the Treaty of 12 May 1881 establishing the protectorate and provided for internal reforms and French financial assistance to Tunisia. Various treaties and agreements – which subsequently gave rise to the advisory opinion of the Permanent Court of International Justice in the matter of the *Jurisdiction of Danzig Courts (P.C.I.J.* Series B, no. 15) – were concluded between Poland and Danzig.[1]

While therefore the general capacity of a protected State to conclude treaties is not at issue, the question which arises under the present Article is that connected with any express limitation or exclusion, by the treaty establishing the protectorate or any subsequent treaty with the protecting State, of the right of the protected State to conclude treaties. Thus in the Treaty of 3 August 1881 with the Transvaal Great Britain reserved for herself the 'control of the external relations of Transvaal including the conclusion of treaties'. Similarly, Article 104 (b) of the Treaty of Versailles and the Convention of Paris of 9 November 1920 between Poland and Danzig provided that the former shall undertake the conduct of the foreign relations of Danzig – a provision which the Permanent Court of International Justice described as constituting an organic limitation and essential feature of the political structure of Danzig (*P.C.I.J.* Series B, no. 18, p. 11). In some cases, as in the Treaties of France with Morocco (30 March 1912), Tunisia (12 May 1881) and Monaco (17 July 1918), the conduct of international relations of the protected states was subject to an 'entente préalable' with France. It is with regard to treaties concluded by the protected State in disregard of such limitations that the question arises as to the validity of the treaty thus concluded. There is some authority in support of the view that such treaties are void. Hall says: 'All contracts therefore are void which are entered into by such [protected] States in excess of the powers retained by, or conceded to, them under their existing relations with associated or superior States' (Hall, p. 380). In an opinion of the British Law Officers of the Crown of 27 April 1896 (reported in McNair, p. 139) the view was expressed that a treaty concluded by the South African Republic in disregard of the Treaty of 1881, referred to above, with Transvaal was invalid. They admitted that the offending treaty – a treaty of extradition – was not 'in itself of great importance', but held that 'the principle involved is obviously

[1] And see for other instances the comment to Article 1 above.

of the utmost gravity' (p. 140). In 1908 the acting Secretary of State of the United States stated in his instructions to the American ambassador to Turkey as follows:

A State proposing to enter into treaty relations with another State which is not fully *sui juris*, a State whose personality is in any way incomplete or abnormal, by reason, for instance, of its dependence in any form upon another State or its membership of a larger unit such as a federal State, is deemed to have notice of its deviation from normal and complete capacity and must satisfy itself that the proposed treaty falls within the limited capacity of the other contracting State. Treaties made by such States in excess of their capacity are void. (Hackworth, v, 153.)

On the other hand it has been suggested that treaties concluded by a dependent State in disregard of its contractual capacity are merely voidable – apparently at the option of the protecting State. Thus Sir Arnold McNair while stating that the British Government had had no opportunity to pronounce itself on the question and that the question does not admit of a general answer, suggests that where 'the dependent State is allowed to conclude treaties subject to the communication of them to the dominant State and to the latter's veto within a certain period, it would seem probable that the former's treaties are only voidable, being made subject to a resolutive condition, and are valid until timously vetoed' (McNair, p. 138). Professor C. Hyde, in a somewhat inconclusive treatment of the subject, seems to have suggested that treaties here under discussion are not necessarily 'without any legal value' and that they are voidable rather than void (Hyde, II, 492).[1] It is submitted that, in this case, the distinction is probably without a practical difference. In general, the matter must be regarded as governed by the overriding principle – elaborated below in Article 16 – that treaties concluded in violation of previous treaties are void. Any mitigation of that principle must be based on the fact of the implied consent, manifested through absence of protest, on the part of the protecting State. When such protest occurs it is sufficient to render the treaty void and as such unenforceable. As the question is one of status imposed not as

---

[1] The circumstance – to which Professor Hyde attached importance – that the protests of the superior State have often remained without effect is probably only of limited legal relevance. In some cases, these protests were not, it appears, well founded in law. Thus with regard to Bulgaria – with regard to which occasional protests were made by her Turkish suzerain against the exercise by her of the treaty-making power – British Law Officers held in 1894 that the limitations imposed upon Bulgaria in the Treaty of Berlin did not make it improper for the British Government to conclude a treaty with her (McNair, pp. 141–4).

the result of any general operation of a rule of law but in consequence of a – usually bilateral – treaty, it is probably unnecessary in this case to follow what is apparently the correct logical conclusion and to hold that a treaty concluded in disregard of the contractual capacity of the dependent State is unalterably and irremediably void. It is preferable to regard the absence of protest on the part of the superior State as equivalent to acquiescence amounting to a renunciation of the limiting provisions of the original treaty. If that is so, the question of its violation, with the resulting invalidity of the subsequent treaty, no longer arises. In the absence of such acquiescence the treaty must be regarded as void. The question whether the treaty concluded in disregard of the dependent status of a party is voidable at the option of the other party to the subsequent treaty, who – for excusable reasons – had no knowledge of the limitation, is too theoretical to require detailed treatment.

4. *Subordinate, in particular member States of federal States.* It might be maintained that no question of validity of treaties concluded by members of federal States can in fact arise on the international plane for the reason that such subordinate States, not being States in the sense of international law, cannot conclude international treaties. As pointed out above in the comment to Article 1, such argument cannot be regarded as helpful. According to the constitutions of a number of countries State members of federal States are authorized to conclude treaties. Thus an amendment of 1 February 1944 to the Constitution of the Union of Soviet Socialist Republics confers on each Republic of the Union 'the right to enter into direct relations with States, to conclude agreements with them, and to exchange diplomatic representatives with them' (Law on the Granting of Authority to the Union Republics in the Sphere of Foreign Relations). In pursuance of that law the Ukrainian S.S.R. and the Byelorussian S.S.R. became separately Members of the United Nations. They have become, in their own name, parties to numerous multilateral conventions. Article 32 of the Constitution of Western Germany of 1949 provides that in so far as the member States (Länder) are competent to legislate they may, with approval of the Federal Government, conclude treaties with foreign States.[1] Article 78 of the Weimar Constitution of 1919 was to the same effect. Article 9 of the Swiss Constitution of 1848 conferred upon the

[1] Kraus, 'Die Zuständigkeit der Länder der Bundesrepublik Deutschland zum Abschluss von Kulturabkommen mit auswärtigen Staaten nach dem Bonner Grundgesetz' in *Archiv des Völkerrechts*, III (1951–1952), 414–27.

cantons the power to conclude treaties with foreign States on the subject of public economy, relations with neighbouring States and police matters along the border provided that they are not incompatible with the interests of the confederation or the rights of other cantons. It appears that treaties of this description have been concluded between Swiss cantons and German States.[1] It is believed that treaties thus concluded by State members of federal States are treaties in the meaning of international law. They are treaties in the contemplation of the present Article 10 of this draft. They are concluded in conformity with the contractual capacity, as required by international law, of the member States in question. International law authorizes States to determine the treaty-making capacity of their political subdivisions. The conferment, by the constitutional law of the federal States in question, of the treaty-making capacity upon their member States amounts, upon analysis, to a delegation of that power on the part of the federal State. This fact is emphasized by the occasional requirement of express authorization by the federal authority and of conformity with the interest of the other members of the federation.

On the other hand, in the absence of such authority conferred by federal law, member States of a federation cannot be regarded as endowed with the power to conclude treaties. For according to international law it is the federation which, in the absence of provisions of constitutional law to the contrary, is the subject of international law and international intercourse. It follows that a treaty concluded by a member State in disregard of the constitution of the federation must also be considered as having been concluded

---

[1] In 1874 Baden and Basle concluded an agreement providing for the establishment of a ferry. In 1907 Basle-Land and Aargau concluded an agreement with Baden for the establishment of a hydro-electric plant. In 1935 Bern and Neuchâtel concluded agreements with France. See generally on the subject His in *R.I.* (1929), 454–79.

The Joint Resolution of Congress of the United States approved on 4 August 1947 in the matter of the Headquarters Agreement Act provides in section 4 as follows: 'Any States, or, to the extent not inconsistent with State law any political subdivisions thereof, affected by the establishment of the headquarters of the United Nations in the United States are authorized to enter into agreements with the United Nations or with each other consistent with the agreement and for the purpose of facilitating compliance with the same: *Provided*, that, except in cases of emergency and agreements of a routine contractual character, a representative of the United States, to be appointed by the Secretary of State, may, at the discretion of the Secretary of State, participate in the negotiations, and that any such agreement entered into by such State or States or political subdivisions thereof shall be subject to approval by the Secretary of State.' While this provision cannot be interpreted as conferring upon States any treaty-making power proper, it is of interest in this connection as covering agreements which are not of 'a routine contractual character' and as requiring the consent of the Secretary of State to what presumably must be arrangements of a public law character.

in disregard of the limitations imposed by international law upon its treaty-making power. As such it is not a treaty in the contemplation of international law. As a treaty, it is void. Moreover, as unlike in the case of protected States a State member of a federation is not *prima facie* a subject of international law, it would seem that there is in this case no question of the treaty being merely voidable at the option of the federal State.

5. *Limitation of contractual capacity of sovereign States as the result of the creation of a certain status as in the case of neutralized States.* While the limitation, by virtue of their status, of the contractual capacity of dependent and subordinate States covers, as a rule, the entirety of the treaty-making power, the latter may be limited in a particular sphere in consequence of conventional regulation amounting, within that sphere, to the creation of a status. This applies, in particular, to a neutralized State. The status of neutrality consists, on the one hand, in the guarantee of independence and integrity given to the neutralized State, and – on the other hand – in the undertaking of the latter to refrain, *inter alia*, from concluding treaties calculated to jeopardize its neutrality and to involve it in war. Switzerland being the only neutralized State in existence,[1] there is little practical importance attaching to the subject. In principle, however, in so far as arrangements of that nature amount to what has been described as an international settlement[2] of an objective character – and they do so to a large extent – they would seem to constitute a limitation of contractual capacity in a way which renders void treaties concluded in disregard of the limitation thus accepted. This is so quite apart from the fact that a treaty concluded by the neutralized State in disregard of its voluntarily accepted obligations as a neutralized State probably falls under the principle, formulated below in

---

[1] Article 24 of the Lateran Treaty of 11 February 1929 between Italy and the Holy See provided that the Vatican City shall in all circumstances be considered as neutral and inviolable territory. It is doubtful whether that Article, incorporating a declaration to that effect issuing from the Holy See, can be regarded as having the effect of constituting the Vatican City a neutralized State. There are clearly absent from the Article the typical elements of neutralization. With regard to Belgium and Luxembourg it must be assumed that their neutralized status has disappeared as the result of obligations undertaken by their acceptance of the Charter of the United Nations.

[2] See the advisory opinion of the International Court of Justice on the *International Status of South-West Africa* of 11 July 1950 where the Court held that 'the international rules regulating the Mandate constituted an international status for the territory recognized by all Members of the League of Nations' (*I.C.J. Reports* 1950, p. 132). See also for a similar explanation of the provisions of the Treaty of Paris relating to the demilitarization of the Aaland Islands the Report of the Committee of Jurists appointed in 1920 by the Council of the League of Nations (*L.N.O.J.* (1920), Special Supplement, no. 3).

Article 16, avoiding treaties inconsistent with previous treaties.[1] It may be noted that the Treaty of 31 May 1867 which effected the neutralization of Luxembourg and to which Belgium was a signatory, provided expressly that Belgium would not be one of the guaranteeing Powers on the ground that she herself was '*un État neutre*'. Her neutralized status was thus regarded as a reason for her legal incapacity to undertake the obligation of a guarantee.

6. *Sovereign States whose freedom to contract has been limited as the result of the assumption of international obligations in specified spheres.* It is probable that this category does not constitute a limitation of contractual capacity. In a sense, every obligation by which a State is bound by virtue either of customary or conventional international law constitutes a limitation of its contractual capacity inasmuch as henceforth it is not lawful for it to conclude a treaty inconsistent with its obligations. However, there seems to be no warrant for stretching to that point the notion of contractual capacity. Two examples may illustrate the situation. The Treaty of 22 May 1903 between the United States of America and Cuba provided that 'the Government of Cuba shall never enter into any treaty or other compact with any foreign Power or Powers which will impair the independence of Cuba, nor in any manner authorize or permit any foreign Power or Powers to obtain by colonization, or for military or naval purposes, or otherwise, lodgment in or control over any portion of the said island'. It might be said that the restrictions imposed upon Cuba in that Article were of such wide compass as to affect her status in the sphere of her contractual capacity. On the other hand, many may prefer the view that although in the Treaty of 1903 Cuba agreed not to enter into treaties impairing her status as an independent State, the treaty itself did not formally affect her status – including her contractual capacity – as a State. Probably it is of no considerable legal consequence which view is adopted, namely, whether a treaty concluded in violation of the restriction imposed is void on the ground of absence of contractual capacity (either in general or within

---

[1] Sir Arnold McNair in McNair, pp. 135–7 quotes a number of authorities in the form of opinions of British Law Officers of the Crown, which, however, seem to be inconclusive and partly contradictory. In an opinion given on 22 July 1872 the Law Officers considered that the only consequence of a permanently neutralized State entering into a treaty inconsistent with its status would be the release of the guaranteeing Powers from their obligations. *Sed quaere*, seeing that, in addition to the guarantee, the status of neutrality is also based on the obligation of the State whose independence is guaranteed. On the other hand, in an opinion given on 4 May 1871 the Law Officers held that the accession of Luxembourg to the Germanic Confederation 'would be a violation of the Treaty of 1867' on the part of Luxembourg.

a limited sphere) or whether it is void by virtue of the principle formulated below in Article 16, which nullifies treaties inconsistent with former treaty obligations. The same applies to the declaration, subscribed by Austria in a protocol signed on 4 October 1922 by which she undertook not to alienate her independence and to abstain from any economic or financial engagement calculated directly or indirectly to compromise her independence. In its advisory opinion given on 19 March 1931 (*P.C.I.J.* Series A/B, no. 41) the Permanent Court of International Justice held that a customs union established between Germany and Austria would not be compatible with the obligations of the Protocol of 1922. It must remain largely a question of terminology whether the obligations of Cuba and Austria, respectively, under the treaties referred to above were such as to impair their contractual capacity (and, as the result, render void treaties concluded in disregard of such limitations) or whether they merely imposed upon them the duty to refrain from undertaking a specified kind of obligations (with the result that such obligations, if entered into, could produce no legal results). The same problem arises in connection with Article 102 of the Charter of the United Nations relating to the registration of treaties. It may be said that the contractual capacity of every Member of the United Nations is limited, in relation to Members and non-members alike, to the extent that it cannot conclude a treaty enforceable by any organ of the United Nations, unless that treaty is registered. Or it may be said that the effect of Article 102 is merely to create an obligation to register treaties, without affecting the contractual capacity of Members of the United Nations and that the result of non-compliance with that provision is merely that the non-registered treaty cannot be invoked, with the view to its enforcement, before an organ of the United Nations. The same applies, in a different sphere, to Article 103 of the Charter inasmuch as its consequence is to qualify the contractual capacity of Members of the United Nations in the sense that they cannot effectively conclude treaties which may prove inconsistent with their obligations under the Charter – for such treaties must yield, when the case arises, to the provisions of the Charter. Yet it may be difficult to regard any treaty concluded by a Member of the United Nations as void – on account of incapacity to contract – on the mere ground that it does not include a reference to the overriding provision of Article 103. For these reasons the Commission is of the opinion that obligations, however wide, accepted by a State in a treaty do not constitute a limitation of its capacity to conclude treaties unless they amount to the creation of a status as in the case of neutralization.

7. *Limitations upon the contractual capacity of international organizations.* The present draft embodies, in Article 1, the principle that international organizations possess, in general, the capacity to conclude treaties. However, it must remain a matter for consideration whether such capacity is inherent in international organizations without any limit or whether its extent is determined by their purpose and constitution. In the municipal sphere it is recognized that the contractual capacity at least of some corporations is restricted. Thus in England a corporation created by or in pursuance of an Act of Parliament is limited in its contractual capacity by the language of the Act; a company incorporated under the Companies Act is bound by the terms of its constitution not to conclude contracts which are inconsistent with or foreign to its objects as formulated in the constitution. A contract made in disregard of that limitation is *ultra vires* and, to that extent, void. In the international sphere it is doubtful whether the capacity of international organizations to conclude treaties is unlimited. Undoubtedly, such capacity is the consequence of their international personality. But that personality is not co-terminous, in kind and extent, with that of States. As the International Court of Justice said in its advisory opinion on *Reparation for Injuries Suffered in the Service of the United Nations*: 'Whereas a State possesses the totality of international rights and duties recognized by international law, the rights and duties of an entity such as the organization [the United Nations] must depend upon its purposes and functions as specified or implied in its constituent documents and developed in practice' (*I.C.J. Reports* 1949, p. 180). For that reason the Court, while holding that the United Nations is an international person and that it has the capacity to conclude agreements, added the following qualifying statement: 'That is not the same thing as saying that it is a State, which it certainly is not, or that its legal personality and rights and duties are the same as those of a State' (*ibid.* p. 179).

This applies, *a fortiori*, to international organizations whose functions and purposes are less comprehensive than those of the United Nations. In some cases the constitutions of international organizations expressly indicate the fact of the limitation of their international capacity. Thus the constitution of the Food and Agriculture Organization provides that 'the organization shall have the capacity of a legal person to perform any legal act appropriate to its purpose which is not beyond the powers granted to it by this constitution'

(Article 15 (1)). An identical wording is adopted in the constitution of the World Health Organization (Article 66). Similarly, the constitution of the International Refugee Organization, approved by the General Assembly at its first session in December 1946, laid down that 'the organization shall enjoy in the territory of its members such legal capacity as may be necessary for the exercise of its functions and the fulfilment of its obligations' (Article 13). Numerous other international organizations and organs contain similar provisions. On the other hand, the constitutions of some other international organizations recognize, without any limitation 'the international personality and legal capacity' of the organization.[1] However, probably no decisive importance need be attached to the fact that some constitutions expressly limit their international personality and capacity so as to conform with their objects and purpose while others contain no provisions of that character. The general language, cited above, used by the International Court of Justice in the *Reparation for Injuries Suffered in the Service of the United Nations* case suggests that some such general limitation of capacity must be implied in all international organizations. So far no cases seem to have arisen which throw direct light on the subject so as to permit the formulation of clear and specific rules. The Commission has deemed it sufficient to accommodate the principle involved within the framework of the comprehensive language of Article 10 as proposed.

Note

The special rapporteur has found it difficult to determine to what extent the subject matter of this Article is of practical importance. With regard to such problems as the contractual capacity of protectorates and neutralized States the practical significance of the question involved tends to diminish. With regard to the possible limitation of contractual capacity as the result of the assumption of the obligation not to conclude treaties of specified character the comment suggests that this is not a case of restriction of the capacity to conclude treaties in a way amounting to the creation of a status but, rather, a case falling within the purview of Article 16 relating to the validity of treaties inconsistent with previous treaty obligations. The problem of the capacity of member States of federal States to conclude treaties raises matters of some complexity and the special rapporteur has found it necessary to examine that question at some

---

[1] See, for example Article 8 (13) of the Agreement of 1946 establishing the European Central Inland Transport Organization.

length. With regard to the limitations of the contractual capacity of international organizations any detailed regulations must be left to the activity of judicial and other bodies within the framework of the general principle laid down in Article 10. Some such general principle – giving expression to the legal consequences of any disregard of limitations of status in the matter of contractual capacity – there must be. The statement, adopted in some previous drafts, that every State has the capacity to conclude treaties, but that the capacity of some States to conclude treaties may be limited, contains information of uncontroversial character.

CHAPTER II

CAPACITY OF AGENTS —
CONSTITUTIONAL LIMITATION UPON
THE TREATY-MAKING POWER

ARTICLE II

CAPACITY OF AGENTS

Constitutional limitation upon the treaty-making power

1. A treaty is voidable, at the option of the party concerned, if it has been entered in disregard of the limitations of its constitutional law and practice.

2. A contracting party may be deemed, according to the circumstances of the case, to have waived its right to assert the invalidity of a treaty concluded in disregard of constitutional limitations if for a prolonged period it has failed to invoke the invalidity of the treaty or if it has acted upon or obtained an advantage from it.

3. In cases in which a treaty is held to be invalid on account of disregard of the constitutional limitations imposed by the law or practice of a contracting party that party is responsible for any resulting damage to the other contracting party which cannot properly be held to have been affected with knowledge of the constitutional limitation in question.

4. A party cannot invoke the invalidity of a treaty on the ground that it has been entered into in disregard of the constitutional limitations of the other contracting party.

5. A party asserting the invalidity of a treaty on account of any failure to comply with constitutional limitations is bound, in case of disagreement, to submit the substance of the dispute or the question of damage to the International Court of Justice or to any other international tribunal agreed upon by the parties.

Comment

1. This Article is intended to formulate the law on a subject of the law of treaties on which legal opinion has been divided and with regard to which the judicial and governmental practice provides no

clear answer. Only a small minority of writers now holds, without qualifications, the view that the limitations of the constitutional law or practice upon the treaty-making power are irrelevant and that a State which has finally assumed a treaty obligation is bound by it regardless of whether the constitutional limitations have been observed. The reasons for that view have been repeatedly stated. They are grounded in some cases in the deductions drawn from the so-called dualistic and monistic conceptions of the relation of international to municipal law. These deductions are inconclusive for it appears that authors starting from opposite points of view in the matter arrive at practically identical conclusions. Thus Anzilotti, adopting the typically dualistic approach held that municipal limitations of the treaty-making power are irrelevant for the reason that international law imputes to the State the will to contract through the Head of the State (or a person delegated by him in accordance with the constitutional law of the State the details of which are of no concern to international law).[1] On the other hand, Professor Scelle, starting from the monistic notion of the primacy of international law, considers the constitutional limitations irrelevant for the reason that to hold otherwise would mean to subordinate international law to the requirements of municipal law (Scelle, II, 455). This seems also to be the view of Kelsen.[2]

2. The two main reasons for the view which holds constitutional limitations to be irrelevant have been:

(a) The requirement of security of international transactions which, it has been said, would be jeopardized if parties to treaties were to be unable to rely on the ostensible authority of the organs accepting binding obligations on behalf of their State and if they were compelled to probe into the often uncertain and obscure provisions of constitutional law of the other contracting party or parties on the subject;

[1] That view is stated in the following frequently quoted passage: 'La conclusion à laquelle nous arrivons est donc que le droit international impute à l'État la déclaration de la volonté de stipuler faite en due forme par le chef de l'État, sans prendre égard aux dispositions constitutionnelles qui, d'une façon quelconque, limitent sa compétence ou lui imposent des devoirs. Nous disons "par le chef d'État", nous référant ainsi au cas le plus important et le plus grave: ajoutons immédiatement toutefois que lorsque, en conformité avec une pratique désormais bien établie, des accords internationaux sont conclus sans l'intervention des chefs des États contractants, notre conclusion vaut pour les déclarations de volonté des organes dûment autorisés à conduire les négociations et à conclure l'accord. La question, qui est le droit constitutionnel, de savoir si, dans ces cas, la compétence des organes doit se ramener à une délégation de compétence du chef d'État et si cette délégation est valable, est dénuée de pertinence au regard du droit international' (Anzilotti, I, 366–7).

[2] *Hague Recueil* 14 (1926), 270; Kelsen, *Principles of International Law* (1952), p. 324.

(b) The serious inconvenience to and the resulting invidious position of a contracting party compelled to assume the function of an arbiter of controversial questions of constitutional law of the other contracting party and occasionally to question the authority of the organ representing it.[1]

These considerations, which are of a weighty character, must be taken into account in formulating the principles governing the subject. For reasons which will be stated presently they cannot be regarded as decisive.

3. On the other hand, a substantial number – though, once more, not the majority – of writers[2] have adopted the view that a treaty concluded by the agents of the State, whether it be the Head of the State or its Government or other persons delegated for the purpose, in disregard of constitutional limitations is invalid. The reason underlying that point of view is that international law leaves it to the municipal law of States to determine the scope of representative authority conferred upon its agents; that to the extent to which an agent acts outside the scope of his authority he acts without any authority at all; that, in accordance with the maxim *qui cum alio contrahit non est vel non debet esse ignorus conditionis ejus*, a contracting party must be deemed to possess knowledge of the fact and of the nature of the constitutional limitations upon the treaty-making power of the agents of the other contracting party; and that the notion that a State may become bound by acts of persons acting outside the scope of their authority is unacceptable as being totally out of harmony with modern conceptions of representative government and principles of democracy.

4. The approach to the subject which underlies the view adopted in the present Article and which is believed to be supported by the bulk of practice is that the correct solution, both as a matter of good faith and security of international transactions, must constitute a compromise between the opposing doctrines outlined above. The

---

[1] These reasons were cogently stated by Sir Gerald Fitzmaurice in an article contributed to *B.Y.* 15 (1934), 129–37. The learned author formulates the principle that 'no State which has purported to become bound by an international engagement, through the performance of all that is necessary from the international point of view to achieve that object, ought to be permitted to deny the validity of its own action by pleading a failure to observe its own constitutional requirements' (p. 133). However, the question is: (i) whether it is really the *State* (and not its unauthorized agents) who has purported to be bound; and (ii) whether ratification by an unauthorized agent is all that is necessary from the international point of view.

[2] These include Schoen in *Z.V.* 5 (1911), 400; de Visscher in *Bibliotheca Visseriana*, 2 (1924), 98; Schücking in *Annuaire de l'Institut International de Droit Public* (1930), p. 225; Chailley, *La nature juridique des traités internationaux* (1923), pp. 175, 215.

259

compromise consists in the recognition of the fact that while constitutional limitations are, as a rule, decisive and while they must constitute the starting point of any solution of the problem, importance must be attached to such factors as the notoriety and clarity of the constitutional limitations in question, the subsequent conduct of the party attempting to avoid the treaty, and the duty to compensate any injury suffered by the innocent party. It is a solution based on some such considerations which must be considered as having secured the support of the majority of writers, including those who have examined the subject in recent years.[1] Undoubtedly, the

[1] Thus the late Professor C. Hyde after stating that 'it is reasonable and necessary for the domestic courts of a country such as the United States to regard an unconstitutional treaty as void', elaborated that proposition as follows: 'It may be said that where a contracting State holds out to another assurance that the terms of a proposed agreement are not violative of the fundamental laws of the former, and does so through an agent who is supposedly conversant with the requirements thereof by reason of the character of his connection with the particular department of his Government to which is confided the management of foreign affairs, and when no written constitution is involved, and no published and authoritative instrument notoriously proclaims an opposing view, there is ground for the conclusion that the contracting State holding out such assurance is not in a position to deny the validity of an agreement which has been concluded in pursuance thereof' (Hyde, II, 1385). Sir Arnold McNair formulates as follows a rule governing a different aspect of the question: 'It seems safe to say that, in the view of the United Kingdom Government, when an international engagement has been partly performed or otherwise treated by both parties as internationally binding, it cannot validly be repudiated by either of them on the ground that its conclusion failed to comply with some internal requirement of its constitutional or other law' (McNair, p. 44). Elsewhere Sir Arnold McNair qualifies the general conclusion as to the invalidity of the treaty in question by the following statement: 'It seems more reasonable to take the latter view and to say that in concluding a treaty if one party produces an instrument "complete and regular on the face of it" (to borrow an expression from another department of law) though in fact constitutionally defective, the other party, if it is ignorant and reasonably ignorant of the defect, is entitled to assume that the instrument is in order and to hold the former to the obligations of the treaty. If that view is correct then the repudiation of such a treaty constitutes an international wrong' (Introduction to Arnold, *Treaty-Making Procedure*, p. 6). In the Harvard Draft Convention the relevant Article 21 embodies the elements of the main qualifying considerations underlying the present Article 10: 'A State is not bound by a treaty made on its behalf by an organ or authority not competent under its law to conclude the treaty; however, a State may be responsible for an injury resulting to another State from reasonable reliance by the latter upon a representation that such organ or authority was competent to conclude the treaty' (*A.J.* 29 (1935), Supplement, Part III, 992). This, on the whole, seems also to correspond with the conclusions reached, in a careful study, by de Visscher, *De la conclusion des traités internationaux* (1943), p. 275. Similarly, Professor Verdross writes in the second edition of his treatise as follows: 'Ein ratifizierter Staatsvertrag ist aber dann anfechtbar, wenn die effektive Beschränkung der "treaty-making power" dem anderen Vertragspartner bekannt war oder bei Anwendung der nötigen Sorgfalt hätte bekannt sein mussen. Er kann sich daher in einem solchen Falle nicht beklagen, wenn der Vertrag mangels der parlamentarischen Genehmigung nicht erfüllt werden kann. Hat hingegen ein Staat bonafide einen Vertrag abgeschlossen, ohne die Beschränkung der Zuständigkeit der "treaty-making power" des Partners zu kennen, dann ist dieser Staat schadenersatzpflichtig, wenn er die Verbindlichkeit des Vertrages nicht nachträglich anerkennt' (*Völkerrecht*, 2nd ed. (1950), p. 218). This is also essentially the position adopted by Professor Guggenheim in a meticulously qualified statement of the rule laying down the invalidity of a treaty adopted in disregard of constitutional limitations.

fundamental rule of nullity of acts done in excess of authority as well as compelling claims of the democratic principle forbid the acceptance of the view that a State may become bound, by matters affecting its vital interests and in others, by acts for which there is no warrant or authority in its own law. But these considerations must not be allowed to enable Governments to conduct themselves in a manner prejudicial to the sanctity of treaties and violative of dictates of good faith; to derive benefits from a treaty and then, in reliance upon a controversial or obscure constitutional doctrine, to repudiate their obligations; and to assert the right to do so without compensating the other contracting party which relied, in good faith and without any fault of its own, on the ostensible authority of the regular constitutional organs of the State in question. There are indications in international practice, amply endorsed by writers, that these factors cannot be left out of account.

5. It is also probably for some such reasons that the practice of Governments shows relatively few instances of attempts to avoid a treaty by reference to alleged disregard of constitutional limitations. In addition to isolated cases submitted to judicial or arbitral determination and referred to below, the following list approximates, apart from some minor historical instances,[1] to completeness: the repudiation by France, in 1832, of a convention concluded in the previous year with the United States of America for the payment of compensation in respect of the spoliation of the property of American citizens during the revolutionary war – a repudiation justified on the ground of absence of legislative approval; the protest, in 1835, by the United States against a commercial agreement concluded between Peru and Chile; the controversies, in 1861, between Ecuador and Peru and in 1888 between Costa Rica and Ecuador;[2] the attempted repudiation by the Transvaal Republic of an arbitral award, rendered in 1871 in the *Western Griqualand Diamond Deposit* case, on the ground that the arbitration agreement had been concluded in

He says: 'Si l'autorité exécutive conclut un traité de commerce, contrairement à une disposition claire et non ambiguë de son droit interne et présumée connue de la partie adverse, l'organe législatif compétent a le droit de l'annuler. Toutefois, l'État dont l'organe incompétent a conclu la convention reste responsable des actes illicites'consécutifs commis dans le cadre de l'exécution du traité, malgré l'invocation de sa nullité' (*Hague Recueil*, 74 (1949), 236). Mervyn Jones' conclusions are to the same effect: *Full Powers and Ratification* (1946), p. 155.

[1] Professor Balladore Pallieri refers – in *Hague Recueil* 74 (1949), 472 – to King François I contesting the validity of a treaty concluded by him on the ground that it had not secured the approval of the Parliament of Paris.

[2] The details as to the three last mentioned disputes are recounted by Jones in *Full Powers and Ratification*, pp. 137–41.

disregard of the requirements of the constitution; the apparent reliance by China, in denying the validity of her treaties concluded with Japan in 1915, on the fact that the President had acted in excess of his constitutional authority; the attitude adopted in 1920 by the Roumanian Government, with respect to a commercial treaty concluded with Austria – which treaty, it was alleged, had not secured parliamentary approval; the doubts raised by Argentina between 1920 and 1933 with respect to the validity of her adherence to the League of Nations; the question of the validity of adherence of Luxembourg to the League of Nations;[1] the repudiation, in 1932, by the Irish Free State of agreements concluded with Great Britain with respect to the payment of certain land annuities on the ground that they had not been approved by the Dail as required by the constitution;[2] and the request made by Switzerland in 1929 to withdraw her adherence to a resolution of the Washington Conference on the Limitation of Armaments obliging the parties to furnish to each other lists of treaties and agreements made with or concerning China. The request, which did not amount to an attempt at unilateral repudiation, was made on the ground of subsequent discovery that the Swiss adherence was illegal and erroneous for the reason of the failure to comply with the requirements of the Swiss Constitution.[3] It is significant that when in 1926 Switzerland answered the questionnaire formulated on the subject by the Committee of Experts for the Progressive Codification of International Law she adopted the view that, having regard to security of international intercourse, treaties ratified by the executive organs of a State are binding upon it.

6. The practice of international tribunals on the subject is even more conspicuous for its scarcity. The arbitral award of President Cleveland, given in 1888 in a dispute between Costa Rica and Nicaragua, adopted with important qualifications as to the burden of proof and as to subsequent acquiescence by conduct, the principle that the disregard of constitutional limitations entails the invalidity of the treaty (Moore, *International Arbitrations*, II, 1946). On the other

[1] An incident discussed in detail by de Visscher, *De la conclusion des traités internationaux*, pp. 165–70.

[2] For details of these incidents see McNair's Introduction to Arnold, *Treaty-Making Procedure*, pp. 3–13, and the comment to Article 22 of the Harvard Draft Convention, pp. 1002–5. The attempted repudiation, on constitutional grounds, by the Persian Government, in 1932 and 1952, of the oil concessions agreement with the Anglo-Iranian Oil Company was directed to an agreement which that Government considered to be a private contract as distinguished from a treaty.

[3] For details see Hackworth, V, 83. Actually Switzerland complied with the resolution which, however, she then declared to have remained a 'dead letter' for the reason that the other parties had supplied no such information to Switzerland.

hand, in the Franco-Swiss arbitration of 1912 an arbitral tribunal declined to attach importance to the fact that the tariff regulations to be fixed in accordance with the commercial agreement with Switzerland had not been confirmed by the French legislature. In the view of the tribunal, that circumstance was 'a matter pertaining to internal law'.[1] In the award given in 1923 in the arbitration between Great Britain and Spain, Judge Huber declined to enter into questions of Moroccan constitutional law which, it was maintained, required a Sheriffian decree confirming an exchange of letters relied upon by Great Britain. However, he attached importance to the fact that subsequently both parties relied on the exchange of letters in question.[2] The judgment of the Permanent Court of International Justice in the case of *Eastern Greenland (P.C.I.J.* Series A/B, no. 53, p. 71) has been occasionally interpreted as having been based on the same principle. Actually the Court held that the declaration made by the Foreign Minister, which the Court – in the circumstances of the case – considered binding upon Norway, had been given by him 'in regard to a question falling within his province'. A statement made by the Permanent Court of International Justice in the case of the *Free Zones of Upper Savoy and the District of Gex (ibid.* no. 46, p. 170) as to the binding force of a declaration made by the Swiss agent in the course of the oral proceedings before the Court – a declaration which was questioned by France on the ground that it was made in disregard of the requirements of Swiss constitutional law – is probably not germane to the issue here discussed.[3]

7. The paucity and the inconclusiveness of the judicial and arbitral pronouncements on the subject make it difficult to deduce from them any rule of international law which is calculated to provide a practical solution of the problem involved. The present Article attempts a solution of that nature. Although the importance of the question may be more limited than the abundance of doctrinal discussion suggests, its detailed regulation, through codification, is desirable. Such regulation cannot be limited to the statement, such as formulated in paragraph 1 of Article 11, to the effect that

---

[1] McNair, p. 8, points out that France did not in this case maintain that the treaty was invalid on account of the absence of constitutional approval. She merely insisted that the latter circumstance pointed to an interpretation of the treaty different from that by Switzerland.

[2] *Annual Digest* (1923–4), case no. 20.

[3] No reference is here made to the award given in 1923 by President Taft in the arbitration between Great Britain and Costa Rica concerning the validity of concessions granted to a private company in disregard of the provisions of the Constitution of Costa Rica (*A.J.* 18 (1924), 147–74).

constitutional limitations are decisive and that a State can undertake binding obligations only through competent agents acting in accordance with its constitutional law and practice. Paragraphs 2 and 3 of Article 11 are intended to provide the qualifications necessary to render the major rule just and reasonable. They take into account, in paragraph 2, the possibility that the State invoking the nullity of the treaty on account of the disregard of constitutional limitations may have tacitly accepted it by acting upon it or by deriving benefits from it. A State cannot be allowed to avail itself of the advantages of the treaty when it suits it to do so and repudiate it when its performance becomes onerous. It is of little consequence whether that rule is based on what in English law is known as the principle of estoppel or the more generally conceived requirement of good faith. The former is probably no more than one of the aspects of the latter. For the same reason paragraph 2 admits of a variety of qualifications which it is not necessary to specify in detail but which are required by a reasonable application to the principal rule. Thus, for instance, the fact that a State has for a long time adopted and acted upon a treaty concluded in disregard of constitutional limitations is not of decisive importance, if owing to the continuance in power of an unconstitutional Government which concluded the treaty, there has been no way in which the constitutional will of the nation could have expressed itself and repudiated the treaty. The repudiation is improper only if the treaty has been acted upon during the régime of the repudiating Government or of the régime identical with it. Similarly, there is no more than an application of the principle of good faith in the provision of paragraph 3 which makes the right to compensation, on account of the avoidance of a treaty concluded in violation of constitutional limitations, dependent on the fact of knowledge of these limitations on the part of the State, which has taken a reasonable degree of care to ascertain these limitations, claiming compensation. On the other hand, obvious considerations of juridical logic require that such knowledge is relevant only to the question of damages, but not that of the validity of the treaty. The fact of the absence of constitutional authority cannot be remedied by excusable ignorance of the limitations in question.[1]

8. It may be noted that the above Article 11 applies to the con-

[1] It might appear that the same reasoning applies to paragraph 2. Actually that paragraph is based on the principle that the element of true consent is supplied by subsequent conduct ex ressive of the will of the State and thus remedying the original absence of constitutional authority.

stitutional limitations of the treaty-making power proper. It does not apply to situations in which a State has finally accepted a treaty by ratification or otherwise in conformity with its constitutional law and practice but in which, owing to its constitution, it finds itself unable to give effect to the treaty without further municipal legislation. The Government of a federal State may have validly ratified a treaty in accordance with its constitution and yet it may find that owing to the reserved powers of the member States it cannot implement the treaty by its own federal legislation. Thus in the case of *Attorney-General for Canada* v. *Attorney-General for Ontario* decided in 1937 by the Judicial Committee of the Privy Council for the British Empire on appeal from the Supreme Court of Canada it was held that the Parliament of Canada had no power to enact legislation to give effect to various international labour conventions validly concluded by Canada (United Kingdom, *Appeal Cases* [1937] 326; *Annual Digest* (1935–7), case no. 17). In such cases a State cannot plead any international invalidity of the treaty. If the latter was concluded in good faith and in the belief, not unreasonably held, of the power of the contracting party in question to give effect to the treaty, then probably the only proper course resulting from inability to implement it would be a request, to be addressed to the other contracting parties and which ought not to be refused, to be allowed to withdraw from the treaty regardless of any time limits laid down therein – although in cases where the State in question has derived benefits from the treaty at the expense of the other contracting party or parties there must be assumed to exist an equitable duty of compensation. In matters of this description and of obvious constitutional complexity the State ratifying the treaty may fairly be deemed to have acted in good faith even if ultimately its highest tribunals find that the constitution prevents it from implementing the treaty by legislation. Thus about the same time when the British Judicial Committee of the Privy Council, in the case referred to above, found that no legislative effect could be given to the treaty by way of federal legislation, a different conclusion – on a similar subject – was reached by the High Court of Australia in respect of federal legislation to implement the Air Navigation Convention of 1919 ((1936) 55 *Commonwealth Law Reports*, 608). In the well-known case of *Missouri* v. *Holland* the Supreme Court of the United States decided that the United States was competent by way of federal legislation to give effect to the Migratory Birds Treaty concluded with Canada in a matter normally falling within the province of the States ((1920)

252 U.S. 416). But it is equally well known that that decision, which has given rise to controversy, could not have been predicted in advance with any certainty.

9. On the other hand it is clear that the mere fact that a Government has failed to take the necessary steps to enact legislation necessary to implement a treaty – or because of reasons other than the provisions of its constitution has been unable to secure such legislation – is not a sufficient ground for absolving it from the obligations of the treaty. (That principle was explicitly affirmed by the Permanent Court of International Justice in its advisory opinion concerning the *Jurisdiction of the Courts of Danzig* (*P.C.I.J.* Series B, no. 15, p. 262) where the Court held that the failure to enact the requisite legislation in itself amounted to a non-fulfilment of an international obligation and that it could not therefore be relied upon by Poland.[1]) For this reason it seems desirable that a State should not finally become a party to a treaty unless it has assured itself that it will be in the position to take the necessary legislative measures. Thus, for instance, in the United Kingdom, while the conclusion and ratification of treaties is, as a rule, within the unfettered province of the executive, courts will not enforce treaties affecting private rights unless the relevant provisions of the treaty have been made part of the law of the land through an enabling act of Parliament. Cases have occurred in which, as the result of the operation of that rule, courts have declined to give effect to treaties validly concluded by the executive and fully operative in the international sphere.[2] In such cases there is no question of the State being entitled to avoid a treaty as the result of non-compliance with constitutional limitations. On the contrary, in situations of this nature the State is internationally responsible for the non-fulfilment of its treaty obligation. The resulting unsatisfactory position can be avoided by the adoption of a rule – whose acceptance would amount to a change in the constitutional practice – requiring the passage of the necessary enabling legislation as a condition of the ratification of the treaty. There are indications of the gradual evolution of some

[1] In the advisory opinion concerning the *Treatment of Polish Nationals in Danzig Territory* the Court held that a State cannot adduce as against another State the provisions of its own constitution in order to evade obligations incumbent upon it under international law or treaties in force (*P.C.I.J.* Series A/B, no. 44, p. 24). However, this does not apply to the provisions of the constitution relating to the treaty-making power and enacted prior to the ratification of the treaty in question.
[2] See, for example, *Administrator of German Property* v. *Knoop* [1933] Ch. 439; *Republic of Italy* v. *Hambros Bank* [1950] 1 All E.R. 430. As to Canada see to the same effect: Re *Arrow River Tributaries Slide and Boom Co.*; *Annual Digest* (1931–2), case no. 2.

such practice.[1] When that practice is established, it will amount to a constitutionally sanctioned procedure which must be presumed to be within the knowledge of the other contracting parties and whose disregard will be internationally relevant in the same way as the corresponding provisions of written constitutions. Thus it is clear that there is a definite constitutional limitation of the treaty-making power in Article 27 of the French Constitution of 1946 requiring legislative approval of enumerated categories of treaties as a condition of the final ratification by the executive. The same result may be achieved by the insertion of a clause, such as in the Agreement of 5 June 1946 between the United Kingdom and Canada concerning double taxation, which provides that it shall enter into force 'on the date on which the last of all such things has been done in the United Kingdom and Canada as are necessary to give the Agreement the force of law in the United Kingdom and Canada respectively' (*U.N.T.S.* 86, 14).

10. The question of nullity or voidability of treaties concluded in disregard of constitutional limitations has been discussed in the past from the point of view of bilateral treaties. It is only on that assumption that it is possible to subscribe to a rule, as formulated in the present Article 11, that 'a treaty is voidable, at the option of the party concerned, if it has been entered in disregard of the limitations of its constitutional law and practice'. However, it is clear that that

---

[1] In introducing in 1952 the Visiting Forces Bill intended to provide for changes in English law rendered necessary by the agreement entered into between the North Atlantic Treaty Powers relating to the status of their forces in the territory of another North Atlantic Treaty Power the Home Secretary stated as follows: 'Until our law is modified in these respects this country cannot ratify the agreement' (*Weekly Hansard*, no. 231 (1952), col. 565). However, on 11 March 1953, in answer to a question in Parliament, the British Government stated that 'strictly speaking Her Majesty's Government never have to obtain Parliamentary consent before making or ratifying a treaty' but that in practice ratification is expressly provided for in the treaty and Parliamentary approval sought in advance of ratification in two types of cases: (i) 'The first is where we should not, in fact, be able to implement the treaty without legislation. It is then necessary to ask Parliament for the legislation, and since Her Majesty's Government cannot be certain that Parliament will grant it, it is necessary that the treaty should be subject to ratification, and that we should get the legislation passed between the time when we signed the treaty and the time when we propose to ratify it.' (ii) 'The other case is that in which the political importance of a treaty is so great that Her Majesty's Government feel obliged, as a political necessity, but not as a legal necessity, to consult Parliament about it before becoming committed. Here again, it would be customary to make the coming into force of the treaty dependent upon ratification and to stage a debate about it in Parliament at some point after signature, so that, if Parliament clearly disapproved, it would still be open to Her Majesty's Government not to ratify the Agreement' (180 House of Lords Deb., col. 1284). This phenomenon of a growing constitutional practice which has not crystallized into a binding convention of the constitution in itself provides an illustration of the complexity of the problem of constitutional limitations.

phraseology cannot apply to multilateral treaties. A multilateral treaty as such is not voidable – or void – because one or more parties thereto have accepted its obligations in violation of their constitutional law or practice. The treaty remains in force as between the other contracting parties (unless – a somewhat far-fetched possibility – so many parties to the treaty have concluded it in violation of their constitutions that the number of the remaining parties has fallen below that required by the treaty for its entry into force).[1] In view of this it must be a matter for consideration whether the language of the Article as at present formulated ought not to be changed in order to cover the case of multilateral treaties. That object could be achieved by the use of some such language as '*the acceptance* of a treaty is voidable' (instead of 'a treaty is voidable') or 'a treaty is voidable, at the option of and *in relation to* the party concerned'. Similar changes would have to be introduced in other paragraphs of this Article. (The same question arises in relation to the other Articles of Part III of the present draft in which, for one reason or other, the treaty is deemed to be void or voidable.)

11. However, in relation to multilateral treaties the question is more than of phraseology. When two States negotiate and conclude a treaty it is reasonable to assume, in the first instance, that the parties must be presumed to possess knowledge of the constitutional law and practice of each other. This is not the position in the case of a multilateral treaty where the number of signatories is considerable and where, moreover, parties may sign or accede subsequent to the establishment of the text of the treaty. In the latter case the parties are hardly in the position to raise the question of any constitutional limitations upon the action of the State acceding to the treaty. While the problems arising in this connection cannot properly form the subject matter of a legal provision in a code of the law of treaties it may be proper to consider to what extent the difficulty can be met by the establishment of some permanent advisory international machinery, available to international conferences and to Governments generally, for assisting them – and, in appropriate cases, the depositary authority – in resolving what must often be a complex problem requiring an intimate knowledge of the constitutional law and practice of many States. The consideration of some such machinery has been suggested above in connection with Article 4 (note 2).

---

[1] Or – which is, once more, a somewhat strained possibility – that as the result of the failure of participation of some States other contracting parties are justifiably of the opinion that the treaty has failed in its object and is no longer binding upon the others.

Note

1. The length of the preceding comment is partly explained by the fact that the statement of the law in Article 11 departs from the view adopted by the Commission in Article 4 as tentatively formulated by it. Apparently the Commission regarded treaties concluded in disregard of constitutional limitations as being invalid *tout court*. The comment of the Commission on that article states that the view adopted therein is held by the majority of writers. This, in the opinion of the rapporteur, is not the case.[1] The Article as provisionally adopted by the Commission has the apparent merit of clarity and precision. It would be, to some extent, acceptable if constitutional limitations of the treaty-making power in various countries were precise, well known, and easily ascertainable. However, the contrary is the case. In view of this any solution which treats, without any qualifications, non-observance of constitutional limitations as the decisive and the only factor may result in introducing into the field of the law of treaties an element of arbitrariness and abuse. This might also be the result of a rule which would make it possible for Governments to avoid their treaties, on the ground of unconstitutionality, regardless of their conduct prior and subsequent to their conclusion. There may be a measure of deceptiveness in the mere simplicity of a rule designed to regulate a problem of intrinsic complexity.[2] The merits of an otherwise sound principle may be impaired by the failure to consider situations in which its unqualified application is manifestly unreasonable or productive of injustice.

2. The following consideration of a general character ought, it is believed, to be borne in mind in any attempt to codify this aspect of the law of treaties. On the whole, the appeal, on the part of Governments, to the alleged invalidity of treaties on account of non-compliance with constitutional limitations has not constituted a frequent feature of international practice. It is possible that an

---

[1] On the other hand, that comment assumes that the judgment of the Permanent Court of International Justice in the case of *Eastern Greenland* lends 'a measure of support' to the opposite view. As pointed out, in the comment to Article 11 above, this interpretation of the judgment of the Court is open to doubt.

[2] An example of that complexity is provided by the otherwise illuminating treatment by Balladore Pallieri. He states that 'les constitutions internes sont devenues toujours plus compliquées, la détermination de l'organe compétent donne naissance à des questions toujours plus subtiles; à un certain moment, il n'y a presque plus de traité dont la validité ne soit douteuse à cause de l'incompétence de l'organe' (*Hague Recueil*, 74 (1949), 475). On the following pages he says in a manner not easily reconcilable with the statement as quoted: 'Il se peut qu'un État ne se donne pas la peine de se renseigner sur l'organisation constitutionelle d'autrui, mais il le fait à ses risques et périls. Les constitutions sont des actes assez notoires, et sur lesquels il n'est pas difficile de se renseigner.'

explicit and authoritative recognition in an international code of a right to avoid a treaty on that ground may encourage allegations of invalidity of treaties in a manner inconsistent with good faith, with the stability of international relations and the observance of treaty obligations. The danger of that possibility materializing will be substantially reduced, if not removed altogether, by the provision – in addition to the safeguards provided in the preceding paragraphs – of paragraph 5 which makes the legal effectiveness of any such allegation dependent, in case of disagreement, upon the finding of a judicial or arbitral tribunal. Provision for and recognition of the compulsory jurisdiction of an international tribunal must in this case – as indeed in other cases of allegation of the nullity of a treaty – constitute an integral part of any rule of international law on the subject.

SECTION 2

REALITY OF CONSENT

CHAPTER 12

ABSENCE OF COMPULSION

Editor's note   This material is taken from the 1953 Report. The following are the corresponding provisions of the Vienna Convention:

ARTICLE 51

Coercion of a representative of a State

The expression of a State's consent to be bound by a treaty which has been procured by the coercion of its representative through acts or threats directed against him shall be without any legal effect.

ARTICLE 52

Coercion of a State by the threat or use of force

A treaty is void if its conclusion has been procured by the threat or use of force in violation of the principles of international law embodied in the Charter of the United Nations.

ARTICLE 12

ABSENCE OF COMPULSION

Treaties imposed by or as the result of the use of force or threats of force against a State in violation of the principles of the Charter of the United Nations are invalid if so declared by the International Court of Justice at the request of any State.

Comment

A. In general   1. The object of this Article is to declare the validity, in the sphere of international law, of a general principle of law which found no place in the society of States prior to the renunciation and prohibition of the use of force in general international agreements, such as the General Treaty for the Renunciation of War, the Covenant of the League of Nations and the Charter of the United Nations. The reason why traditional international law disregarded the use of force or of threats of force as a factor vitiating the validity of treaties has been repeatedly stated. In the past, international law permitted recourse to war not only as a means of enforcing rights recognized by international law, but also for the purpose of challenging and destroying the existing legal rights of States. If war was permitted as an institution, it followed that the law was bound to recognize the results of successful use of force thus used. To this explanation, unimpeachable in logic, of the legal position there was added the cogent consideration that the adoption of a different rule would have removed the legal basis of all treaties imposed by the victor upon the defeated State and thus perpetuated indefinitely a state of war. While the persuasive power of these considerations could not be denied, it was clear that the disregard of the vitiating force of duress in the conclusion of treaties tended to constitute, in a real sense, a denial of the legal nature of treaties conceived as agreements based on the free will of the contracting parties. Consensual transactions in which the true consensus of the parties, emanating from their free will, is irrelevant are an anomaly. Any rule which sanctions that anomaly is, like the admissibility of war as such, expressive of a fundamental defect in the structure of international law.

2. The cumulative result of the developments since the First World War has been to remove the foundations of the traditional rule of international law which recognized the validity of treaties imposed by force. These developments consist in the limitation and, subsequently, in the renunciation and prohibition of war, and, more generally, of force or of threats of force. Although the Covenant of the League of Nations did not abolish the right of war, it prohibited recourse to it prior to the exhaustion of means of pacific settlement prescribed by it. To that extent it rendered unlawful any recourse to war in violation of the obligations of the Covenant and authorized and prescribed sanctions against the offending State. It was generally assumed that as the result of these provisions of the Covenant the status of war in international law had undergone a fundamental change. In the General Treaty for the Renunciation of War of 27 August 1928 (Pact of Paris) the parties renounced recourse to war as an instrument of national policy in their relations with one another. The legal effect of that treaty was that war could no longer be resorted to either as a legal remedy or as an instrument for changing the law. It has been stated that 'being permanent in its nature and purpose and representing a fundamental change in the legal structure of international society, the Pact of Paris must be regarded as continuing in being and as one of the cornerstones of the international legal system' and that 'this is so although it has not been

expressly incorporated in the Charter of the United Nations' (Oppenheim, II, 197). The Charter of the United Nations provides, in paragraph 4 of Article 2, that 'all Members shall refrain in their international relations from the threat or use of force against the territorial integrity or political independence of any State, or in any other manner inconsistent with the purposes of the United Nations'. The same Article lays down, in paragraph 6, that the United Nations shall ensure that States which are not members of the United Nations act in accordance with the Principles of the Charter in so far as may be necessary for the maintenance of international peace and security. The Inter-American Treaty of Reciprocal Assistance signed at Rio de Janeiro on 2 September 1947 combined the provisions of the Pact of Paris and of the Charter of the United Nations. Article 1 of that treaty laid down that the 'high contracting parties formally condemn war and undertake in their international relations not to resort to the threat or the use of force in any manner inconsistent with the provisions of the Charter of the United Nations or of this treaty'. The cumulative result of these international enactments of a general character – of the Covenant of the League, the General Treaty for the Renunciation of War, and the Charter of the United Nations – has been to effect a change in the law, in the matter of the legal position of war, not only between the parties thereto, but in the international community as such. The prohibition of war, and of force generally, to the extent laid down by these instruments, must now be regarded as independent of these instruments and as having acquired the complexion of a general rule of international law binding upon States in the same way as rules of customary international law. That general rule prohibits aggressive war, i.e. a war undertaken as an instrument of national policy in violation or in disregard of the principles of the basic instruments referred to above. In the judgment of the International Military Tribunal of Nürnburg, whose principles have been affirmed by the General Assembly of the United Nations, aggressive war was declared to constitute an act both illegal and criminal.

3. It follows that a treaty imposed by or as the result of force or threats of force resorted to in violation of the principles of these instruments of a fundamental character is invalid by virtue of the operation of the general principle of law which postulates freedom of consent as an essential condition of the validity of consensual undertakings. The reasons which in the past rendered that principle inoperative in the international sphere have now disappeared.

Moreover, in so far as war or force or threats of force constitute an internationally illegal act, the results of that illegality – namely, a treaty imposed in connection with or in consequence thereof – are governed by the principle that an illegal act cannot produce legal rights for the benefit of the law-breaker. That principle – *ex injuria jus non oritur* – recognized by the doctrine of international law and by international tribunals, including the highest international tribunal,[1] is in itself a general principle of law.

4. The consequences of that principle have, in turn, found expression in the various declarations of policy or in declarations of the assumption of the obligation not to recognize treaties, or situations, or acquisitions of territory resulting from unlawful use of force in violation of former undertakings. Thus, in the well-known pronouncement of Mr Stimson, the United States Secretary of State, it was declared on 7 January 1932 that the United States

cannot admit the legality of any situation *de facto* nor does it intend to recognize any treaty or agreement entered into between those Governments, or agents thereof, which may impair the treaty rights of the United States or its citizens in China . . . ; and that it does not intend to recognize any situation, treaty, or agreement which may be brought about by means contrary to the covenants and obligations of the Pact of Paris of 27 August 1928, to which treaty both China and Japan, as well as the United States, are parties. (U.S. For. Rel. *Japan*, 1931–1941, I, 76.)

While the above declaration was in the nature of a declaration of a voluntarily assumed policy – of intention – of non-recognition, the resolution adopted by the Assembly of the League of Nations on 11 March 1932 gave expression to the principle of non-recognition as implying a legal obligation. It stated that 'it is incumbent upon the Members of the League of Nations not to recognize any situation, treaty, or agreement which may be brought about by means contrary to the Covenant of the League of Nations or to the Pact of Paris'. Formal pronouncements of American States have given frequent expression to the obligation of non-recognition as distinguished from a policy of non-recognition. Thus the Lima Declaration of 22

---

[1] See, for example the advisory opinion in the matter of the *Jurisdiction of the Courts of Danzig (P.C.I.J.* Series B, no. 15, pp. 26, 27); the judgment in the case concerning the *Factory at Chorzów (ibid.* Series A, no. 9, p. 31); the judgment in the case of *Eastern Greenland (ibid.* Series A/B, no. 48, p. 285 and no. 53, p. 75 – where the Court held that the Norwegian declaration of occupation and other measures taken by Norway in that connection constituted a violation of the existing legal situation and were accordingly '*illégales et non valables*' (unlawful and invalid)); the order in the case of the *Free Zones (ibid.* Series A, no. 24 – where the Court stated that France could not invoke against Switzerland any changes resulting from the illegal transfer of the French customs line).

December 1938 on Non-Recognition of the Acquisition of Territory by Force reiterated 'as a fundamental principle of the Public Law of America' that such acquisitions shall not be valid or have legal effect 'and that the pledge of non-recognition of situations arising from the foregoing conditions is an obligation which cannot be avoided either unilaterally or collectively'. In the draft Declaration of Rights and Duties of States prepared by the International Law Commission in 1949 it was laid down, in Article 11, that 'every State has the duty to refrain from recognizing any territorial acquisition by another State acting in violation' of the obligation to refrain from resorting to war as an instrument of national policy and to refrain from the threat or use force.[1] Upon analysis, non-recognition of treaties, including treaties providing for transfer of territory, imposed by unlawful exercise of force means that in the view of the States refusing recognition the treaty is invalid. While express recognition, in the field of treaties and elsewhere, is not essential as a condition of the valid creation of rights, express refusal to recognize them amounts to and is intended as a denial of their validity. It follows that, apart from the general considerations based on the principle which denies legal effect, for the benefit of the law-breaker, to unlawful acts, the nullity of treaties imposed by unlawful exercise of force must now be deemed to result, in addition to other factors, from the practice, in many cases acknowledged as an obligation, of non-recognition.

5. These factors, pointing to the invalidity of treaties imposed in connection with or as a result of unlawful exercise of force, may now be summarized. They are (i) the general principle of law avoiding consensual transactions brought about by duress; (ii) the obsolescence of the rule of international law permitting resort to or threats of war or force as a means of redress or of altering rights recognized by international law; (iii) the general principle of law denying any law-creating effect, in favour of the law-breaker, to acts which the law stigmatizes as illegal; (iv) the practice and the principle of non-recognition. Having regard to the operation of these factors, the express formulation by the Commission of the rule as laid down in Article 12 must be deemed to represent a codification, in this respect, of the existing law. That existing law is no longer what it was prior to the First World War.

6. It is arguable – and there is some apparent cogency in the argument – that the practical importance of formally sanctioning the

[1] See *Yearbook of the International Law Commission, 1949*, p. 288.

invalidity of treaties imposed by force may be inconsiderable. For, it may be said, if international society organized in the United Nations is unable to prevent unlawful recourse to force, it may not be in the position to assert, against the victorious aggressor, the principle sanctioning the invalidity of treaties imposed by force. Moreover, it is arguable that as soon as changed conditions of power permit to challenge the efficacy of treaties imposed by force such change can be effected by a political decision supported by public opinion of the world rather than by reliance on a principle of law. However, the force of these and similar arguments is more apparent than real. A general international organization such as the United Nations may not, on account of the operation of the rule of unanimity or for other reasons, be in a position to prevent aggression, or threats of aggression, and treaties imposed in consequence thereof. However, that circumstance need not necessarily signify the total breakdown either of the international organization or of the rule of law. On the contrary, the prospect that the advantages gained by an imposed treaty may prove illusory, in addition to other reasons, because of the invalidity of the settlement thus imposed – an invalidity to be formally affirmed by international tribunals, by third States and, when conditions permit, by the victim of violence himself – may in itself act as a brake upon designs of unlawful use of force. However that may be, it seems imperative that a codification of the law of treaties under the auspices of the United Nations should elevate to the dignity of a clear rule of international law a general principle of law recognized by all civilized States, namely, that freedom of consent – i.e. absence of constraint exercised otherwise than by law – is an essential condition of the validity of treaties conceived as contractual agreements. In fact, there is room for the view that if the codification of the law of treaties were to achieve no other result than to declare formally the elimination from the body of international law the traditional rule which disregarded the vitiating effect of duress, a rule which is offensive to accepted notions of law and morality and which is therefore a serious reflection upon the authority of international law – such codification would be desirable for the sake of some such Article. At the same time it is of importance to ensure that the principle thus formally incorporated should not be invoked – and abused in a manner inconsistent with the authority and the effectiveness of treaties. As intimated in the comment which follows, the present Article 12 has been formulated with this object in view.

B. *7. Treaties imposed as the result of the use of force or threats of force.*
(a) The formulation here adopted follows the language of the Charter of the United Nations. It refers to treaties imposed not as the result of war but as the result of the use of force and threats of force. The latter clearly include war. The merit of the formulation adopted in the Charter is that it obviates the doubts, which gave rise to some uncertainty under the Covenant and the Pact of Paris, as to whether in a particular case the use of force amounts to war in the technical sense of the term. Under the Charter and the Article as here formulated that distinction is devoid of relevance. (b) The expression 'by or as the result of the use of force or threats of force' is intended to express the principle that coercion, however indirect, if resulting from unlawful recourse to force or threats of force invalidates a treaty. This means that a treaty is invalid if a State, as the result of unlawful use of force, has been reduced to such a degree of impotence as to be unable to resist the pressure to become a party to a treaty although at the time of signature no obvious attempt is made to impose upon it by force the treaty in question. The formulation here adopted covers also the situation in which the victor has established within the defeated State a subservient Government which signs the treaty without a show of protest. (c) The Article refers to physical force or threats of physical force as distinguished from coercion not amounting to physical force. However, in the case of a State the border-line between these two kinds of coercion is not rigid. In fact it would appear that direct physical force can be applied only to persons, but not to the collective entity of the State. On the other hand, in cases such as attempts or threats to starve a State into submission by cutting off its imports or its access to the sea, although no physical force is used directly against persons it may be difficult to deny that the treaty must be deemed to have been concluded as the result of the use of force or threats of force. Neither would it appear to be essential that compulsion thus directly applied against a State should be the result of a war or of other use of direct physical force. The inevitably indefinite character of this cause of invalidity of treaties renders it particularly necessary to make its operation dependent upon impartial determination as provided in this Article.

8. *Upon States.* The present Article is concerned only with the coercion of States in their collective capacity. It is not concerned with physical force or threats thereof against the organs of the State in connection with the conclusion of a treaty. Force or threats of force of that character, of which text-books adduce a number of

examples,[1] eliminate altogether the element of freedom of consent which is essential for the validity of a contractual undertaking. There has been general agreement, even under traditional international law, that a treaty concluded or an undertaking given in such circumstances was without legal effect.

9. *In violation of the principles of the Charter of the United Nations.* Force ceases to have the character of mere coercion if it is exercised in execution of the law – as a legal sanction – or in accordance with the law. Although in such cases the element of consent on the part of the State concerned is lacking, the impersonal authority of the law on behalf of which – and in accordance with which – force is employed is properly deemed to supply, or to remedy, the absent element of consent. For this reason a treaty or any other undertaking imposed by the United Nations, in the course of its enforcement action, upon a State held to be guilty, in the language of Article 39 of the Charter, of a 'breach of the peace or act of aggression' does not invalidate the treaty or the undertaking. It must be assumed that force exercised by the collective action of the United Nations is exercised in accordance with its principles. This is so even in cases in which it is applied against a State not guilty of an act or of a threat of aggression. For the enforcement action of the United Nations, under chapter VII of the Charter, is not limited to action against States engaged in or threatening aggression. It is possible for such action to take in a situation amounting to a 'threat of war', i.e. in situations in which the United Nations consider that force must be exercised, if necessary, against a State whose attitude, while otherwise not unlawful, endangers peace.[2]

In this connection the question arises whether the rule as formulated in the present Article affords protection, by virtue of the principle which vitiates a treaty on account of duress, to a State which has first resorted to force in violation of its obligations. That question is here answered in the affirmative. For unless force is exercised, even against the aggressor, in accordance with, on behalf of and within the limits of the law, the fact of aggression is irrelevant – except to the extent that provision against future aggression and just reparation for damage resulting from aggression may legitimately form an element of the treaty.

[1] See Rousseau, I, 352–4.

[2] It is probably by reference to some such considerations, that an explanation may be found of the view expressed by Professor Scelle that 'le droit-loi imposé par la violence ou la pression est ou non valide selon sa conformité ou sa non-conformité avec le droit objectif' (Scelle, II, 344).

For the same reason, as in the existing state of international organization collective enforcement of peace and effective collective resistance to aggression may not always be possible, the character of legal sanction may occasionally be attributed to the action of one or more States acting for the enforcement of peace or repulsion of aggression. When acting in that capacity individual States or groups of States must, in proper cases, be deemed to act as agents of the law.[1] Whether they are so acting and whether in thus acting they remain within the orbit of the principles of the Charter of the United Nations, so that they may properly be regarded as the agents of the law, must be a matter for impartial determination by agencies other than the parties directly concerned.

10. It is necessary in this connection to explain the reference in this Article to the principles of the Charter of the United Nations as expressive of international law in general. The present Article – as indeed the present draft of the Code of the Law of Treaties – is based on the assumption that the codification of international law as a whole or any part thereof must take place within the framework of the fundamental principles of the Charter. For some purposes the law of the Charter must be regarded as the law of the international community in the sense envisaged by the International Court of Justice in its advisory opinion on the *Reparation for Injuries Suffered in the Service of the United Nations* (see above, Article 1 (1)). The prohibition of force and threats of force must be considered as falling within the orbit of these principles. These, and some other, basic principles of the Charter must be regarded as permanent and, in case of the substitution of the United Nations by any other general organization of States, as necessarily forming part of the constitution of that organization. For that reason it has been considered proper in this draft to treat the Charter of the United Nations as expressive, for some purposes, of general international law of enduring validity. Should the political condition of the world result, at any future time, in the total disappearance of any general organization of States, it is probable that any code of a law of treaties would become obsolete.

11. .... *If so declared by the International Court of Justice at the request of*

---

[1] The notion that compulsion is not a vitiating element in relation to validity of treaties in cases in which what is exacted from the coerced State does not go beyond the limits of international law is clearly expressed by Hall: 'Consent ... is conceived to be freely given in international contracts, notwithstanding that it may have been obtained by force, so long as nothing more is exacted than it may be supposed that a State would consent to give, if it were willing to afford compensation for past wrongs and security against the future commission of wrongful acts ... When this point, however is passed, constraint vitiates the agreement' (Hall, *International Law*, 3rd ed. (1890), p. 235).

any State. While other provisions of this Article are believed to express existing law, it must, *de lege ferenda,* be regarded as fundamental that any allegation of the invalidity of a treaty on account either of compulsion or of any other reason of invalidity as laid down in Articles 12–16 of this chapter may properly be made with legal effect only: (i) if accompanied by the willingness of the State making such allegation to obtain a finding of an international tribunal on the matter, and (ii) if followed by an actual finding of the tribunal to that effect. It is only if these conditions are fulfilled that reliance on the vitiating effect of duress – as well as of other reasons of invalidity – instead of constituting a disintegrating force in the treaty relations of States may become a factor in maintaining the authority of international engagements. If a State has been unlawfully coerced into entering a treaty, the proper course for it is – when conditions permit – to ask an international tribunal to make, in contentious proceedings, a declaration to that effect. The acceptance of the present Article would amount to a conferment of obligatory jurisdiction upon international tribunals in a matter of this description. In view of the gravity of the issues involved the International Court of Justice would seem to be the proper tribunal competent to declare the invalidity of the treaty.

As the continued validity of a treaty imposed by force is a matter of concern for the entire international community, the present Article gives to every Member of the United Nations – whether it has become a party to the Code of the Law of Treaties or not – the right to ask the Court to declare, in contentious proceedings, the invalidity of a treaty imposed by force. The State directly affected may not always be in the position to do so.

Note

1. As already submitted in the general observations to the comment to this Article, the Commission is confronted with an important question of principle in relation both to the present Article and most of the other Articles in this part bearing on the validity of treaties. For although there exists a certain amount of inconclusive practice in the form of allegations of duress[1] bearing on this aspect of the law

---

[1] At the Washington Conference of 1921 China raised, though in somewhat circuitous fashion, the question of the validity of her acceptance in 1915 of the so-called twenty-one demands presented to her by Japan (Willoughby, *China at the Conference* (1922), pp. 253, 255). In the course of the *Tacna-Arica* arbitration of 1925 and 1926 Peru relied frequently on the allegation that she had been compelled to sign the Treaty of 1884. When in 1920 Bolivia and Peru addressed to the Assembly of the League of Nations a request for the

of treaties that practice is not considerable either in extent or in importance. At the same time, the various causes of invalidity of treaties have loomed large in the writings of publicists and in various codes and drafts of the law of treaties. This has been so for the reason – which must be regarded as decisive – that the systematic exposition of an important branch of law cannot properly be determined by the actual or probable frequency of occurrences giving rise to the application of the rules of law in question. This is not merely a matter of *elegantia juris*. It is a question of the authority and the completeness of the law. There is no warrant for assuming that by giving to the various aspects of invalidity a place in the Code of the Law of Treaties, encouragement may be given to arbitrary appeal to them. If the safeguards of a judicial nature formulated in the present Article are adopted, they will rule out, as a matter of law, any abusive or unilateral reliance on the fact or assertion of coercion. It will not be the interested State but the International Court of Justice which will declare the treaty to be invalid. Undoubtedly, experience shows that the nullification of treaties imposed by force takes place not in pursuance of a judicial verdict but of a political action taken in conformity with changed conditions of power. But this is not an adequate or desirable reason for removing from the province of judicial determination what is essentially a question of law. The decisive feature of the Article as here formulated is that the historic foundation of the traditional rule which disregarded the vitiating effects of duress has disappeared. That historic foundation was the legal admissibility of war as an instrument both of enforcing and creating rights. The International Law Commission is now called upon to find – *constater* – that change as a matter of fact. In thus drawing the consequence of an accomplished change of the law the Commission will be codifying, not developing, the Law of Nations in one of its most essential aspects. At the same time it will be formally incorporating into the law of treaties a general principle of law of incontestable authority.

2. According to the Article as drafted treaties imposed by force or threat of force are void. They are a nullity.[1] They are not merely

revision of their treaties with Chile one of the grounds of the request was that those treaties had been imposed by force.

[1] The Harvard Research Draft Convention of 1939 on Rights and Duties of States in case of Aggression lays down, in Article 4 (3), that 'a treaty brought about by an aggressor's use of armed force is voidable'. The difference between 'absolute nullity' and mere voidability is discussed lucidly by Professor Guggenheim in his course of lectures entitled 'La validité et la nullité des actes juridiques internationaux' in *Hague Recueil*, 74 (1949), 194–236. Valuable contributions to the subject have also been made by Professor Verzijl ('La

voidable – with the effect that the coerced party may take advantage of it or of part of it, if it so chooses, or that it may become legally bound by it if it fails to exercise its right of avoidance within a reasonable time or if it has benefited from it. The attitude of acquiescence on the part of the coerced party is irrelevant. Any State may ask for a declaration of nullity. The defect of the treaty concluded in such circumstance is fundamental and nothing short of the conclusion of a freely negotiated treaty can cure it. For this reason it is difficult to accede to the reasoning adopted in Article 4 (3), and the comment thereto, of the Harvard Draft Convention of Rights and Duties of States in case of Aggression to the effect that the imposed treaty 'may offer an intrinsically fair and equitable adjustment of the controversy which led to the armed conflict'.[1] For the case is not merely one of an armed conflict; it is a case of unlawful recourse to force. In relation to a treaty concluded in these circumstances it is impracticable and contrary to principle to confer upon an international tribunal the power of scrutinizing whether it is 'intrinsically reasonable'. The governing consideration is that a treaty concluded under duress – following upon unlawful recourse to force – is not only vitiated by the absence of consent but also that its conclusion and continuation are contrary to international public policy. For the same reason, unlike in the case of error or even fraud, it is difficult to apply to such treaties the principle of severability (see below, Part IV of the draft) and try to discover which provisions of the treaty were not in fact imposed by force (and may therefore be treated as valid) and which must remain void; or, to apply another test, which provisions are intrinsically reasonable and equitable and which are not.

3. It has been noted that under the present Article no party to a treaty is entitled to declare it invalid on the ground that it has been concluded under duress. What it, or any other State, may do is to request the International Court of Justice, by a unilateral application, to declare, in contentious proceedings, that the treaty is invalid. The consent of the other party to, or its participation in, the proceedings are not required – although it is to be expected that if it has a good case it will elect to defend it before the Court. (In the absence of such participation the Court, acting in accordance with Article 53 (2) of its Statute, would still be bound to investigate the

validité et la nullité des actes juridiques internationaux' in *R.I.* (Paris), 15, 284–339) and Dr W. G. Hertz ('Essai sur le problème de la nullité' in *R.I.* third series, 20 (1939), 450–500).

[1] *A.J.* 33 (1939), Supplement, 828.

merits of the allegation that the treaty has been concluded under duress.) The essence of the relevant provision of the present Article is that there is no other way of legally pronouncing the illegality of an enforced treaty except through a judgment of the Court. There is no room for any unilateral action of the interested State save that of initiation of judicial proceedings. For that reason the present Article does not follow the suggestion embodied in Article 32 (*c*) and (*d*) of the Harvard Draft Convention on Treaties which gives to the State seeking from the Court a declaration of nullity the right to suspend provisionally the performance of its obligations under the treaty. The necessity of any such measures may be met through the exercise by the Court of the power, under Article 41 of its Statute, to indicate provisional measures to preserve the respective rights of either party. This may include, in proper cases, the right of a party to be freed, provisionally, from the performance of an invalid treaty. It may be a matter for consideration whether this Article should not give the Court the power to decree, as distinguished from mere intimation, any applicable provisional measures. In any case, it must be for the Court – and not for the States concerned – to suspend provisionally the operation of a treaty.

CHAPTER 13

ABSENCE OF FRAUD

Editor's note The material is taken from the 1953 Report. The Vienna Convention covers this matter in two Articles dealing with fraud and with the corruption of the representative of a State:

ARTICLE 49

Fraud

If a State has been induced to conclude a treaty by the fraudulent conduct of another negotiating State, the State may invoke the fraud as invalidating its consent to be bound by the treaty.

ARTICLE 50

Corruption of a representative of a State

If the expression of a State's consent to be bound by a treaty has been procured through the corruption of its representative directly or indirectly by another negotiating State, the State may invoke such corruption as invalidating its consent to be bound by the treaty.

ARTICLE 13

ABSENCE OF FRAUD

1. A treaty procured by fraud is voidable, at the instance of the International Court of Justice or, if the parties so agree, of any other international tribunal at the option and at the request of the injured party.

2. The injured party may affirm the treaty thus procured and ask for damages for the injury caused to it by the fraud of the other party.

Comment

1. The subject matter of this Article is largely theoretical. There have been no instances of judicial determination – by national or international tribunals – of disputes arising out of attempts to avoid a treaty on account of fraud. Neither does it appear that international

practice shows examples of Governments raising the issue at all – although writers have occasionally discussed the propriety of the action of Mr Webster, the United States Secretary of State, in not bringing to the attention of the British negotiators a map privately discovered and showing the boundary line in a manner favourable to the British contention. They have also discussed at some length whether treaties induced by fraud are void or voidable. For reasons substantially identical with those adduced in the general comment to Article 12 relating to coercion it is desirable that the Code of the Law to Treaties should contain, subject to suitable variations, an Article such as here proposed.

2. The reasons – including those of international public policy – which prompt the adoption of the principle that treaties concluded under duress are void, do not obtain in the case of fraud. It is sufficient to lay down the principle that such treaties are voidable at the option of the injured party and to the extent to which their provisions have been affected by fraud.

3. As in the case of coercion so also in relation to the present Article a State is not entitled unilaterally to throw off the obligations of a treaty by a unilateral assertion that it has been procured by fraud. This seems to be in accordance with existing legal principle. Only an international tribunal is entitled to make a declaration and pronounce judgment to that effect. *De lege ferenda*, in default of agreement by the parties to confer jurisdiction in the matter upon another international tribunal, the International Court of Justice must be accorded compulsory jurisdiction to adjudicate upon the allegation of fraud. The occasional disinclination of writers to recognize fraud – as well as other factors affecting the reality of consent – as a reason of nullity or voidability of treaties has been the apprehension that, in view of the deficiencies of international judicial machinery, any such elaboration of the requirements of validity of treaties may affect adversely the binding force of international engagements. The principle embodied in the present Article leaves no room for any such apprehension. It may be noted that whereas in the case of duress the seriousness of the alleged ground of nullity and the probable absence of equality in the position of the parties require the exclusive jurisdiction of the International Court of Justice, these considerations do not apply in the case of other defects of consent.

4. For the same reasons – unlike in the case of duress – the right to challenge the validity of the treaty on account of fraud must be deemed to belong to the injured party only.

5. As the treaty induced by fraud is not automatically void, the party adversely affected must possess the option: (i) of relying on the principle of severability of provisions of treaties and, in proper cases, of asking for the rescission of some of its provisions only, and (ii) of affirming the treaty as a whole and of asking for compensation of the damage resulting from the fraud perpetrated by the other contracting party. In both cases the compulsory or agreed jurisdiction of an international tribunal must be regarded as essential.

CHAPTER 14

ABSENCE OF ERROR

Editor's note This material is taken from the 1953 Report. The Vienna Convention deals with the question in Article 48:

ARTICLE 48

Error

1. A State may invoke an error in a treaty as invalidating its consent to be bound by the treaty if the error relates to a fact or situation which was assumed by that State to exist at the time when the treaty was concluded and formed an essential basis of its consent to be bound by the treaty.

2. Paragraph 1 shall not apply if the State in question contributed by its own conduct to the error or if the circumstances were such as to put that State on notice of a possible error.

3. An error relating only to the wording of the text of a treaty does not affect its validity; Article 79 then applies.

ARTICLE 14

ABSENCE OF ERROR

A treaty entered into under the mistaken belief, not due to fraud of a contracting party, as to the existence of a fact substantially affecting the treaty as a whole is voidable, at the instance of the International Court of Justice or, if the parties so agree, of any other international tribunal, at the option and at the request of the party adversely affected by the mistake.

Comment

1. The reasons, adduced in Article 12 above as to the propriety and desirability of including in the draft Code of Treaties Articles bearing on the reality of consent as a condition of validity of treaties, apply also to the present Article. Moreover, instances in international practice, both judicial and otherwise, of mistakes as affecting treaties are more frequent than those of fraud – though in some cases, occasionally discussed under the heading of mistake, the subject

matter of the difficulty more accurately falls within the category of interpretation and rectification. This applies, for instance to the case of Article 15 (1) of the Warsaw Convention of 12 October 1929 for the Codification of Certain Rules relating to International Aerial Transport. In that Article, by a mistake of translation, the word 'transporteur' was used instead of 'exporteur'. The mistake was subsequently rectified by agreement of the parties and the action of the Secretary-General of the League of Nations (for details see comment to Article 29 of the Harvard Draft Convention).[1] It is possible that interpretation, and not reality of consent, is the proper *sedes materiae* with regard to what is believed to be the most frequent example of mistake in international practice, namely, a discrepancy between maps or geographical facts and the apparent intention of the parties as expressed in the treaty. Apart from this, the problem of mistake as an element vitiating the validity of treaties, far from constituting a prominent feature of international practice, has been merely conspicuous in textbooks. The care and deliberation which precede the making of treaties in modern times and the ease of access to sources of information render it unlikely that its regulation in a code of the law of treaties will prove of direct practical assistance. However, for the reasons stated, it is not feasible or proper to disregard it in any codification of the law of treaties.

2. The mistake which in the contemplation of the present Article invalidates a treaty, is one which is not induced by misrepresentation. For in the latter case, the treaty is invalidated by fraud. The mistake must be such as to go to the root of the matter and affect an essential aspect of the treaty. The fact that it could have been discovered prior to the conclusion of the treaty, is probably irrelevant – though the circumstance that a contracting party has been guilty of negligence in failing to discover a mistake which could have been discovered by the exercise of ordinary foresight may entitle the innocent party to compensation for the loss caused by the invalidation of the treaty.

3. The considerations and principles bearing upon the voidability (as distinguished from nullity) of a treaty affected by essential mistake; the necessity of a judicial or arbitral determination of the fact and the consequence of mistake; provisional suspension of the

---

[1] *A.J.* 29 (1935), Supplement. A recent example of a rectification, by subsequent agreement, of an error made in the original treaty may be noted. In the Agreement of 1 August 1950 between Canada and France concerning air services the following error occurred: Article 5 of the agreement instead of stating 'from being used for the carriage of any international air traffic *offered*', used the word 'ordered'. By an Exchange of Notes of 28 September 1950 the parties rectified the error (*U.N.T.S.* 77, 369).

operation of the treaty; and the severability of its provisions are the same, *mutatis mutandis*, as in the case of fraud (Article 13 above). In view of the actual and probable scarcity of international practice on the subject it is unnecessary to elaborate in the present Article the details of these contingencies. These must be left to the appreciation of international tribunals in the light of general principles of law and good faith.

4. The principle of compulsory jurisdiction of international tribunals to determine the existence of error as a cause of invalidity of a treaty must, upon analysis, be regarded as a principle *de lege lata*. This is so for the reason that any acknowledgment of the right of a party to terminate unilaterally a treaty on the ground of error – or, generally, of any other allegation of absence of reality of consent – would be tantamount to a denial of the binding force of the treaty.

Note

1. As stated in the comment the main – if not the only – instances in which error has been invoked by a contracting party in relation to a treaty and in which there has been judicial or arbitral pronouncement on the subject have been instances of error in connection with maps or other geographical descriptions. Parties have found on occasions that a particular locality as described in the treaty did not exist at all or that the crucial line of delimitation was at a very considerable distance from that which they assumed.[1] Nevertheless the parties have not claimed in such cases that the treaty was void. They have asked for an interpretation or a rectification of the treaty. Writers have treated the matter largely as one of interpretation or evidence. With regard to maps, municipal jurisprudence has treated discrepancies between the description of the parcels in the contract

[1] In this class must be included the controversy which arose between Great Britain and the United States in connection with the Treaty of 1783 which referred to a range of highlands south of the St Croix River as the dividing line between two systems of rivers. No such range of highlands existed; nor was it shown on the map used by the negotiators (Moore, *International Arbitrations*, pp. 65 *et seq.*). A dispute also arose as to the identity of the St Croix River. The dispute was settled by arbitration in 1798 (Moore, *International Adjudications, Ancient and Modern* (1929–30), II, 373). The decision of the Supreme Court of the United States, in *United States* v. *Texas* (1896) 162 U.S. 1, 37–42, is another example of a rectification of a geographical description used in a treaty (of 1819 between the United States and Spain). So is also, to a conspicuous degree, the *Island of Timor* case between Portugal and the Netherlands decided in 1914 (Scott, *Hague Reports* pp. 355 *et seq.*), where the Tribunal interpreted the apparently erroneous description of the boundary by carefully elucidating the intentions of the parties at the successive stages of the negotiations. The incident between Russia and France on the one hand and Great Britain and Austria on the other, in connection with the interpretation of the Paris Treaty of 1856, recounted by McNair, p. 131, is of interest. And see generally Sandifer, *Evidence before International Tribunals* (1939), pp. 156–64, with regard to maps.

and the map attached to it as one of construction. However, even if cases of this nature fall more properly within the field of interpretation, they illustrate at the same time the principle that not every error involves the voidability of the treaty. Such effect attaches only to an essential error which goes to the roots of the treaty.

2. It will be noted that the error referred to in the above Article must be one of fact – not of law. The principle that a person – or a State – cannot plead ignorance of the law, civil or criminal, as a reason for escaping the consequences of his conduct is an indispensable legal principle. It applies with special force to Governments who are in the position to rely on the services of experts. The matter was touched upon by Judge Anzilotti in his dissenting opinion in the case of *Eastern Greenland* where he discussed the question whether the validity of a declaration made by the Norwegian Foreign Minister could have been vitiated by a mistake – the judge found that 'there was no mistake at all' – as to the consequences of the extension of Danish sovereignty: 'one can scarcely believe that a Government could be ignorant of the legitimate consequences following upon an extension of sovereignty' (*P.C.I.J.*, Series A/B, no. 53, p. 92). On a minor scale, in the matter of a contract made by a ruler of a protected State, the following observation of the Arbitrator, Lord Asquith, may be noted in relation to the allegation that as the ruler was not cognizant of the rule that territorial waters form part of the territory of the State, a concession given by him over his entire territory did not, nevertheless, cover the territorial waters. The Arbitrator said:

I am not impressed by the argument that there was in 1939 no word for 'territorial waters' in the language of Abu Dhabi, or that the Sheikh was quite unfamiliar with that conception. . . Every State is owner and sovereign in respect of its territorial waters, their bed and subsoil, whether the ruler has read the works of Bynkershoek or not. The extent of the ruler's dominion cannot depend on his accomplishment as an international jurist. (*I.C.L.Q.* 4th series, 1, Part II (1952), 253.)

SECTION 3

LEGALITY AND OBJECT OF THE TREATY

CHAPTER 15

CONSISTENCY
WITH INTERNATIONAL LAW

Editor's note   This material is taken from the 1953 Report. This question is dealt with more elaborately and in three different places in the Vienna Convention:

ARTICLE 53

Treaties conflicting with a peremptory norm of general international law
(jus cogens)

A treaty is void if, at the time of its conclusion, it conflicts with a peremptory norm of general international law. For the purposes of the present Convention, a peremptory norm of general international law is a norm accepted and recognized by the international community of States as a whole as a norm from which no derogation is permitted and which can be modified only by a subsequent norm of general international law having the same character.

ARTICLE 64

Emergence of a new peremptory norm of general international law
(jus cogens)

If a new peremptory norm of general international law emerges, any existing treaty which is in conflict with that norm becomes void and terminates.

ARTICLE 71

*Consequences of the invalidity of a treaty which conflicts with a
peremptory norm of general international law*

1.   In the case of a treaty which is void under Article 53 the parties shall:
   (*a*) eliminate as far as possible the consequences of any act performed in reliance on any provision which conflicts with the peremptory norm of general international law; and
   (*b*) bring their mutual relations into conformity with the peremptory norm of general international law.

2.   In the case of a treaty which becomes void and terminates under Article 64, the termination of the treaty:

(*a*) releases the parties from any obligation further to perform the treaty;

(*b*) does not affect any right, obligation or legal situation of the parties created through the execution of the treaty prior to its termination; provided that those rights, obligations or situations may thereafter be maintained only to the extent that their maintenance is not in itself in conflict with the new peremptory norm of general international law.

ARTICLE 15

CONSISTENCY WITH INTERNATIONAL LAW

A treaty, or any of its provisions, is void if its performance involves an act which is illegal under international law and if it is declared so to be by the International Court of Justice.

Comment

1. The principle formulated in this Article is generally – if not universally – admitted by writers who have examined this aspect of validity of treaties. Yet, mainly for two reasons, the question is not free of difficulty. In the first instance, not every treaty is void which departs from customary international law. For it is generally recognized that, in principle, States are free to modify by treaty, as between themselves, the rules of customary international law. *Modus et conventio vincunt legem.* Thus, so long as the treaty does not affect the rights of third States, there would seem to be no reason why two States shall not agree that, *as between themselves*, the width of territorial waters should be fifty miles; that their warships should be allowed to stop and otherwise exercise jurisdiction over the merchant vessels of the other contracting party on the high seas; that their diplomatic representatives should not enjoy the jurisdictional immunities otherwise prescribed by international law; that their public ships and other governmental agencies should have no immunity from suit; that their nationals should be liable to military service in the territory of the other contracting party; or that they shall have the right to nationalize without compensation the property of the nationals of the other contracting party. Numerous other examples of this nature could be adduced. In so far as any such treaty modifying or abolishing a rule of customary international law were to purport to interfere with the rights of third States they would in any case be without effect in as much as a treaty cannot lawfully affect the rights of

States which are not parties to it and in as much as, for that reason, an international tribunal would declare it to be unenforceable so far as the rights of third States are concerned.

2. Accordingly, a treaty is not void on account of illegality on the mere ground that it purports to affect, without its consent, the right of a third State. If it purports to do that it will be, to that extent, unenforceable by international tribunals by virtue of the rule *pacta tertiis nec prosunt nec nocent*. It is arguable that for that very reason, namely, because they purport to affect the rights of third States, such treaties are not only unenforceable against such States, but are also in themselves void on account of the fact that their object is illegal – such illegality consisting in the attempt to interfere with the rights of a third State in disregard of rules of international law. Thus to quote from Judge McNair's work on treaties: 'It is believed that a treaty between two States the execution of which contemplates the infliction upon a third State of what customary international law regards as a wrong is illegal and invalid *ab initio*' (McNair, p. 113). The true reason of such treaties being void is that they have for their object an act which is illegal according to customary international law.

3. The object of a treaty may be illegal – and the treaty correspondingly void – even if it does not directly affect third States. Thus it has been suggested that in so far as instruments such as the Declaration of Paris of 1856 which abolished privateering or the Slavery Convention of 1926 obliging the parties to prevent and suppress trade in slaves have become expressive of a principle of customary international law, a treaty obliging the parties to violate these principles would be void on account of the illegality of its object. The above mentioned instruments constitute also examples of inconsistency of a subsequent treaty with rules of international law which, although originating from a treaty concluded between a limited number of States, subsequently acquire the complexion of generally accepted – and, to that extent, customary – rules of international law.

4. It would thus appear that the test whether the object of the treaty is illegal and whether the treaty is void for that reason is not inconsistency with customary international law pure and simple, but inconsistency with such overriding principles of international law which may be regarded as constituting principles of international public policy (*ordre international public*). These principles need not necessarily have crystallized in a clearly accepted rule of law such

as prohibition of piracy or of aggressive war. They may be expressive of rules of international morality so cogent that an international tribunal would consider them as forming part of those principles of law generally recognized by civilized nations which the International Court of Justice is bound to apply by virtue of Article 38 (i) (c) of its Statute. Although it is not possible to cite any judicial decision in support of that view there are occasional interesting observations of individual judges to that effect. Thus in his individual opinion in the *Oscar Chinn* case Judge Schücking asserted that 'the Court would never . . . apply a convention the terms of which were contrary to public morality' (*P.C.I.J.* Series A/B, no. 63, p. 150).

5. The voidance of contractual agreements whose object is illegal is a general principle of law. As such it must find a place in a codification of the law of treaties. This is so although there are no instances, in international judicial and arbitral practice, of a treaty being declared void on account of the illegality of its object.

6. The following observations are relevant to the test of the proposed Article: (i) In referring to 'a treaty or any of its provisions' the intention is to apply the principle of severability, namely, that any single provision involving an illegality does not entail the nullity of the treaty if the latter, taken as a whole, can be upheld. This will not be possible if the provision in question constitutes an essential part of the treaty. (ii) As the offending treaty – or the offending provision – is contrary to overriding principles of international law it cannot be enforced by an international tribunal even if the State which stands to benefit from the judicial nullification of the treaty fails to raise the issue. No action will lie on a treaty of that description. On the other hand, the defendant State, although it has taken part in bringing about the illegal treaty, can plead the illegality as a defence. *In pari delicto potior est conditio defendentis.* This to a large extent answers the question whether and to what extent a State can be relieved of the the performance of an illegal treaty. It can suspend performance and leave it to the other contracting party to resort to the International Court of Justice for the vindication of the validity of the treaty. The jurisdiction of the Court in such cases is obligatory. It is the Court, and not the interested party, which is finally entitled to declare the treaty, or part thereof, to be void on account of illegality.

7. As in other Articles of this part of the present draft, so also in the matter of nullity of treaties on the ground of their inconsistency with binding rules of international law, the operation of the principle involved must be dependent upon the willingness of the party

invoking it to abide by the decision of an international tribunal upholding the allegation of invalidity or making, *proprio motu*, a finding to that effect. The reasons, which are of a general character, for that principle have been stated above in paragraph 4 of the comment on Article 14. It is a principle *de lege lata*.

Note

1. As explained in the comment the incorporation of this Article must be regarded as essential in any codification of the law of treaties. This is so notwithstanding the substantial practical and doctrinal difficulties inherent in the solution here adopted. Thus in the sphere of municipal law the legislature is often called upon to enact statutes which derogate from what has hitherto been regarded as the over-riding law of the land and imperative considerations of public policy. Courts must give effect to the statutes thus enacted. In the inter-national sphere the function of such legislation is frequently fulfilled by treaties, both bilateral and multilateral. But if, as stated in the present Article, international courts are to be judges of the validity of treaties in the light of overriding principles of international custom and international public policy as hitherto recognized, a situation may be created in which international society may be deprived of the neces-sary means of development through processes of international legislation. Probably the exceptional character of such contingencies reduces to limited proportions the practical difficulty involved. But there ought to be no doubt as to the existence of the problem and the possible necessity of an attempt at solving it, *de lege ferenda*, within the framework of the present Article. (The same problem arises, in Article 16, with regard to treaties of a general legislative character inconsistent with previous treaties.) Thus, for instance, if Article 2 (6) of the Charter were to authorize, in terms more categorical than it does at present, intervention in the affairs of non-member States, the question might arise of the validity of some provision on the face of it incompatible with the prohibition of intervention and the independence of States. *De lege ferenda* there may be room for the consideration of a principle affirming that a multilateral treaty concluded in the general international interest is valid even if departing from or contrary to what has been considered in the past to be an overriding rule of customary international law.

2. At the same time this and similar difficulties counsel caution in the matter of extending the limits of voidability of treaties. For this reason the present draft does not refer in a separate Article to

consistency with international morality as a condition of validity of treaties. To do so may result in conferring upon international tribunals a measure of discretion, in a matter admitting of highly subjective appreciation, which Governments may not be willing to confer upon them and which they could exercise only with difficulty. In so far as considerations of morality – such as conduct in accordance with canons of good faith – form a constituent part of general principles of law and of the requirements of international public policy they are provided for in the present article.

CHAPTER 16

CONSISTENCY WITH PRIOR TREATY OBLIGATIONS

Editor's note　The material is taken from the 1953 Report and the 1954 Report. The following are the relevant provisions of the Vienna Convention which appear in a section on the 'Application of treaties'.

ARTICLE 30

Application of successive treaties relating to the same subject matter

1.　Subject to Article 103 of the Charter of the United Nations, the rights and obligations of States parties to successive treaties relating to the same subject matter shall be determined in accordance with the following paragraphs.

2.　When a treaty specifies that it is subject to, or that it is not to be considered as incompatible with, an earlier or later treaty, the provisions of that other treaty prevail.

3.　When all the parties to the earlier treaty are parties also to the later treaty but the earlier treaty is not terminated or suspended in operation under Article 59, the earlier treaty applies only to the extent that its provisions are compatible with those of the later treaty.

4.　When the parties to the later treaty do not include all the parties to the earlier one:
   (*a*)　as between States parties to both treaties the same rule applies as in paragraph 3;
   (*b*)　as between a State party to both treaties and a State party to only one of the treaties, the treaty to which both States are parties governs their mutual rights and obligations.

5.　Paragraph 4 is without prejudice to Article 41, or to any question of the termination or suspension of the operation of a treaty under Article 60 or to any question of responsibility which may arise for a State from the conclusion or application of a treaty the provisions of which are incompatible with its obligations towards another State under another treaty.

1953 REPORT

ARTICLE 16

CONSISTENCY WITH PRIOR TREATY OBLIGATIONS

1. A treaty is void if its performance involves a breach of a treaty obligation previously undertaken by one or more of the contracting parties.

2. A party to a treaty which has been declared void by an international tribunal on account of its inconsistency with a previous treaty may be entitled to damages for the resulting loss if it was unaware of the existence of that treaty.

3. The above provisions apply only if the departure from the terms of the prior treaty is such as to interfere seriously with the interests of the other parties to that treaty or seriously impair the original purpose of the treaty.

4. The rule formulated under paragraphs 1 and 2 does not apply to subsequent multilateral treaties, such as the Charter of the United Nations, partaking of a degree of generality which imparts to them the character of legislative enactments properly affecting all members of the international community or which must be deemed to have been concluded in the international interest.

Comment

1. The subject matter of the present Article is of considerable importance and also of some complexity inasmuch as it raises the problem of the adaptation of a cogent legal principle to the requirements of peaceful development of international law and organization. This is so although the matter has given rise to only a relatively small number of judicial or arbitral pronouncements and although even these provide no direct authority for the principle here formulated. Thus in the *Oscar Chinn* case (*P.C.I.J.* Series A/B, no. 63), while the dissenting opinions of two judges were based in substance on the principle formulated in the present Article, the Court as a whole did not pronounce directly on the subject. The question in that case was whether the Convention of St Germain of 1919 relating to the Congo, which altered the provisions of the General Act of Berlin of 1885, was valid. The judgment of the Court relied in this respect on the fact that the parties to the dispute, the United Kingdom and Belgium, did not challenge the validity of the Convention of St Germain. In 1917 Costa Rica and Salvador brought an action

before the Central American Court of Justice on account of the violation by Nicaragua, by a treaty concluded with the United States, of her treaties with these States. The Court, for jurisdictional reasons, declared itself unable to act on the request that it should declare the treaty with the United States to be null and void (*A.J.* II (1917), 228). It declined to do so for the reason that one of the parties thereto, namely, the United States, was not a party to the dispute. But the Court found that Nicaragua 'is under the obligation – availing itself of all possible means provided by international law – to re-establish and to maintain the legal status that existed prior to the Bryan–Chamorro Treaty' (*ibid.*). The decision of the same Court in an action brought *in pari materia* by Salvador against Nicaragua was to the same effect (*ibid.* p. 729). In what is perhaps the most important incident bearing on the subject – the incident arising out of the allegation of inconsistency of the Hay–Varilla Treaty of 1903 between the United States and Panama and the Hay–Pauncefote Treaty of 1901 between the United States and Great Britain in the matter of exemption of Panama from tolls levied on ships passing the Canal – the dispute never came for judicial determination.

2. The effect of Article 16 is that an international tribunal requested to enforce a treaty the performance of which involves a breach of a treaty obligation previously undertaken by one or more of the parties to the new treaty must decline to enforce the subsequent treaty. It must do so on the ground that the latter is void. The Article does not adopt alternative solutions such as that the obligations of the former treaty take priority over those of the latter treaty which otherwise remains valid. It proceeds on the assumption that if parties to a treaty bind themselves to act in a manner which is a violation of the rights of a party under a pre-existing treaty, they commit a legal wrong which taints the subsequent treaty with illegality. This result follows cogently from general principles of law governing the subject, from requirements of international public policy and the principle of good faith which must be presumed to govern international relations. These considerations are summarized in an extract reproduced below in note 1 to this comment.

3. The knowledge, at least on the part of one contracting State, of such incompatibility must – unless in exceptional circumstances of which it is not easy to conceive – be assumed. This is so, in particular, having regard to the fact that since the Covenant of the League of Nations the obligation of registration, followed as it is by publication, rests upon most States. In those exceptional cases in which one of the

parties to the new treaty had, for no fault of its own, no knowledge of the pre-existing treaty, principle requires that the other party should compensate it for the damage caused by the fact that the subsequent treaty is declared void. This is the effect of the second paragraph of the Article. The possibility that the incompatibility was unknown to both parties to the new treaty must be regarded as remote – except in so far as it is due to the mistaken belief that no legally relevant inconsistency with the former treaty existed.

4. As in the case of invalidity on other grounds, so also the invalidity of the subsequent treaty on account of its inconsistency with a previous treaty, must, if it is to excuse a party from performance, be declared by an international tribunal, when called upon to enforce that subsequent treaty, on the application of one of the parties. Moreover, international tribunals must also be deemed competent to declare the nullity of the subsequent treaty at the request of a party to the prior treaty even if no attempt has yet been made to put the subsequent treaty into effect. For the very existence of the subsequent offending treaty, in so far as it is a source of challenge and uncertainty for the parties to the previous treaty, provides a legitimate occasion for protest by the parties to the prior treaty and for a request on their part that the subsequent treaty should be formally declared void. This in fact has been the attitude of Governments in most of the cases in which they considered their interest to be affected by the conclusion of the subsequent treaty.

5. The principle that the subsequent treaty, violative of a prior conventional obligation, is invalid requires a substantial modification in cases in which that subsequent treaty partakes of the nature of a general rule of international law of a legislative character. Within the municipal sphere a statute may effectively interfere with pre-existing contracts. Some such principle must also apply in international relations in cases in which the subsequent treaty is – in effect (though not in strict law seeing that there is as yet no legislation proper in the relations of States) – of a legislative character. Thus Article 103 of the Charter of the United Nations provides that 'in the event of a conflict between the obligations of the Members of the United Nations under the present Charter and their obligations under any other international agreements, their obligations under the present Charter shall prevail'. In referring, in the matter of the obligations of the Members of the United Nations, to 'their obligations under any other international agreement' the Charter refers to agreements concluded both prior and subsequent to the acceptance

of the Charter. In so far as it is directed to the latter the Charter merely upholds the principle that the obligations of a prior treaty have precedence over those of a treaty concluded subsequent to it. Under the present Article 16, which is intended to be declaratory of existing law, treaties inconsistent with the Charter and concluded subsequent to its acceptance are void whether concluded with Members of the United Nations or with States which are not members. However, in so far as Article 103 of the Charter in referring to 'obligations under any other international agreement' aims at treaties entered into prior to the acceptance of the Charter, that Article, being inconsistent with treaties previously concluded, would itself be void unless we apply to it the principle adopted in paragraph 4. That principle provides an exception with regard to 'subsequent multilateral treaties, such as the Charter of the United Nations, partaking of a degree of generality which imparts to them the character of legislative enactments properly affecting all members of the international community'. The same principle has been sanctioned in a different sphere by the International Court of Justice in the advisory opinion concerning *Reparation for Injuries Suffered in the Service of the United Nations*. To that extent this part of paragraph 4 of Article 16 must be regarded as being *de lege lata*. (Article 20 of the Covenant of the League of Nations merely provided, with respect to obligations undertaken by a State prior to its becoming a member of the League and inconsistent with the Covenant, that it is its duty to take immediate steps to procure release from such obligations. With regard to other obligations the Covenant adopted the rule that 'the Covenant is accepted as abrogating all obligations and undertakings *inter se* which are inconsistent with the terms thereof' which meant in effect that they were void. This result – with regard to future treaties – would have followed, it is believed, even without the express provision of Article 20 with regard to treaties concluded by Members of the League both *inter se* and with non-member States.)

6. Similar considerations, although in a more limited sphere, may apply to paragraph 4 in so far as it refers to treaties, inconsistent with previous treaty obligations, 'which must be deemed to have been concluded in the international interest'. At present, the possibility of quasi-legislative international enactments, such as the Charter of the United Nations, being accepted by a vast majority of States is distinctly limited. But situations may arise in which a treaty concluded by a considerable number of States, though not so numerous as to approach universality, coincides so patently with general

international interest that it may properly be entitled to claim to override previous treaty obligations – especially if in cases of this description an attempt is made to compensate the beneficiary of the prior treaty. In exceptional cases this might be held to apply even to a bilateral treaty. Thus there is room for the view that the Treaty of 1903 between the United States and Panama which promised the latter exemption for Panamanian ships passing the Canal and which was considered inconsistent with the treaty concluded in 1901 with Great Britain was concluded in the international interest inasmuch as its purpose was to make possible the opening of a great international highway of paramount importance and inasmuch as the special concessions granted to Panama were an essential condition of the conclusion of the treaty. It is not suggested that the above example necessarily falls within the provision of the exception formulated in paragraph 4. However, that example lends emphasis to the view that some such exception may properly find a place in any general rules as laid down in that paragraph. While this specific provision of paragraph 4 is essentially *de lege ferenda*, it is believed to merit full consideration in connection with the codification of the law of treaties. The safeguarding of the authority of treaties must be reconciled with the equally important international interest involved in preventing the development of international law from being hampered by the obligations of existing treaties. In some cases parties have expressly provided against the contingency of a treaty becoming a stumbling block in the way of general international regulation. Thus the Air Navigation Agreement between the United Kingdom and Canada of 19 August 1949 provided, in Article 11 (2), that 'in the event of the conclusion of any general multilateral convention concerning air transport by which both contracting parties become bound, the present agreement shall be amended so as to conform with the provisions of such convention' (*U.N.T.S.* 44, 240).[1]

7. Considerations of similar nature apply also to the qualification of the general rule as expressed in paragraph 3. That qualification is specially relevant to the case of multilateral conventions. The

---

[1] With this there may be contrasted the way in which the Hague Convention of 1930 on Certain Questions Relating to the Conflict of Nationality Laws attempted to resolve the problem of inconsistency by providing, in Article 19, that nothing in the convention 'shall affect the provisions of any treaty, convention or agreement in force between any of the high contracting parties relating to nationality or matters connected with it'. A provision of this character substantially reduces the legal effect of the multilateral treaty – although it cannot be interpreted as leaving the parties freedom of action with regard to treaties concluded subsequent to the acceptance of the multilateral treaty.

latter are often in need of revision. It is clearly undesirable that such revision should be possible only through unanimous agreement of the original contracting parties. If such unanimity is impossible, the parties to the original convention must, in proper cases, be in a position to alter, *inter se*, its provisions by means of a new treaty concluded by them. This, for instance, has been the case in the matter of the various Hague Conventions of 1899 and 1907 and the successive Geneva Conventions for the amelioration of the condition of the sick and wounded in the armies in the field. These new treaties did not adversely affect the interest of the original contracting parties or impair the purpose of the original treaties. A different situation was said to have arisen in connection with the case, mentioned above in paragraph 1 of this comment, of the Treaties of Berlin of 1885 and of St Germain in 1919. Two of the dissenting judges in the *Oscar Chinn* case, which was concerned with the relation between these two treaties, were of the opinion that the latter treaty had, to a substantial extent, the effect of frustrating the object of the Treaty of 1885, which was still in force, and for that reason the Treaty of 1919 was null and void. (The opinions of Judges Nyholm and Negulesco in the case concerning the *Competence of the European Commission of the Danube* (*P.C.I.J.* Series B, no. 14 pp. 73, 129) were substantially to the same effect.) If that were so – the present comment expresses no opinion on the question – the view of the dissenting judges must be regarded as unobjectionable. The fact that the parties directly concerned in the case did not challenge the validity of the Treaty of 1919 was probably not relevant. It is believed that if the Court had examined the allegation that the Treaty of 1919 frustrated the purpose, to which some of the original signatories legitimately attached importance, of the Treaty of 1885, and if the Court had come to the conclusion that it was so, then it would have been consistent with and required by correct legal principle to hold that the Treaty of 1919 was void. An international court cannot properly enforce a treaty whose purpose or effect amounts to a legal wrong, in matters of substance, against some of the signatories of the original treaty. The proper course for States wishing to conclude a new treaty inconsistent with their obligations under the prior multilateral treaty is to denounce it, if they can do so consistently with its provisions, and to conclude a new treaty. On the other hand – in particular if such termination of the original treaty is not legally possible – the continued existence of the original multilateral treaty cannot legitimately provide a reason for preventing developments which are desirable and generally beneficial and which, although departing from or amplifying, however considerably, the terms of the original treaty, cannot be regarded as unduly interfering with the rights of the original parties or the true purpose of that treaty. Moreover, it is clear that, *de lege ferenda*, consideration ought to be given to the adoption of a rule permitting changes in the original treaty by a decision which, if necessary, falls short of an unanimous decision of the original parties.

Note

1. The importance of the subject matter of this article from the point of view both of the law of treaties and of international law in general justifies, it is believed, a detailed treatment of the matter in the Article itself and in the comment. The special rapporteur ventures to refer in this connection to the following passage in an article, of which he is the author:

In the international sphere the reasons for regarding later inconsistent treaties as void and unenforceable are even more cogent than in private law. It is, as a general rule, incompatible with the unity of the law for the courts to enforce mutually exclusive rules of conduct laid down in a treaty, a statute, or a contract. But among individuals contracts are infinite in variety and number; among States they are relatively few and a matter of general knowledge. The shock, therefore, resulting from any recognition of the later contract to the sentiment of the unity of the law is greater in the latter than in the former case. Moreover, in so far as there is any disposition by municipal courts to treat the later contract as subsisting, the logical exclusiveness of the subject matter of the two contracts is mitigated by substituting the right to damages for the second inconsistent obligation. In the international sphere damages, by the very nature of things, are in most cases not likely to offer adequate compensation for the wrong. For these reasons it is difficult to accept the view that the treaties in question are valid and that the only effect of the inconsistency is that the obligations of the former treaty take priority over the conflicting provisions of the later agreement. This would be the position in any case. For, obviously, a state cannot lawfully terminate a treaty by the simple device of concluding another treaty inconsistent with the first. The flaw in the later treaty has an effect reaching beyond the mere reproduction of an obvious rule of international law. It makes that later treaty unlawful and incapable of enforcement.

This insistence on the nullity of the later treaty is not, it is submitted, mere pedantry. Treaties, woven into the structure of customary international law, are the substance of the growing and changing law of nations.

International law cannot recognize and it must actively discourage a state of affairs in which the law-creating faculty of States is abused for violating existing law as laid down in valid agreements. Governments cannot be permitted to discredit international law and to render it unreal by filling it with mutually exclusive obligations and by reducing treaties to conflicting makeshifts of political expediency. (*B.Y.* 17 (1936), 63–4.)

2. The principle that contracts entered into by the parties in violation of previous contractual obligations binding upon them are void must be regarded as a general principle of law. As to English law, Sir Frederic Pollock (*Principles of Contracts* (9th ed., 1921), p. 475) lays down, without apparent qualification, the rule that if A concludes a contract with B and then another contract with C which, to the knowledge of both B and C, is inconsistent with the first contract, then the second contract is void. For an elaboration of this rule in private law see Lauterpacht, 'Contracts to create a contract' in *L.Q.R.* (1936), pp. 434–54. (See also *ibid.* pp. 524–7, for an examination of French and German law.) The principal French decision on the subject is that of the French Court of Cassation of 13 October 1912 in *Deutsche Celluloid Fabrik* v. *Schwerber* (Sirey (1913), 1, 259) where it was held that a contract of service between the plaintiff and the defendant made in disregard of a contract which, to the knowledge of both parties, was binding on the defendant, was void.

3. Some treaties, including Article 20 of the Covenant of the League of Nations referred to above, include express provisions in which the parties undertake not to conclude treaties inconsistent with the obligations already undertaken. As already suggested, such provisions, in which the parties undertake not to violate an existing obligation, are redundant and of doubtful legal elegance.[1] They do not provide an argument either in support or in refutation of the principle formulated in Article 16.

4. The importance of that principle assumes particular importance in relation to conventions codifying international law. If the parties were to be in a position to conclude, *inter se*, treaties inconsistent with the general purpose of the convention, the resulting situation would indeed be confusing. Reference may be made in this connection to an article by Professor M. Hudson in *A.J.* 24 (1930), 461, in which he

[1] The same probably applies to such provisions as Article 6 of the Brussels Treaty of 17 March 1948 of Economic, Social and Cultural Collaboration and Collective Self-defence in which the parties declared 'each so far as he is concerned, that none of the international engagements now in force between him and any other of the high contracting parties is in conflict with the provisions of the treaty'.

discusses the possibility of States concluding treaties modifying *inter se* the conventions resulting from The Hague Codification Conference of 1930. He suggested that 'such action would, in a sense, be contrary to the spirit of codification'. He recalled that in the report of the drafting committee such conventions were not considered improper provided that they affected 'only the relations between the States parties thereto'. However, the purport of these conventions would not thus be limited if their effect were to frustrate or seriously impair the purpose of codification.

5. For the reasons stated the present Article 16 does not adopt the solution proposed in Article 22 (*c*) of the Harvard Draft Convention which, while leaving on one side the question of the nullity of the offending subsequent treaty, merely lays down that 'the obligation assumed by the earlier treaty takes priority over the obligation assumed by the latter treaty'. That formulation of the legal position is, it is believed, contrary to principle (see note 1) and to the views of practically all writers who have considered the question. Neither does it take into account the nature of the situation confronting a court adjudicating on a claim to enforce the subsequent treaty. The question of priority of obligations is not before the court. It is not called upon to pronounce whether the prior obligation is to be enforced or not.

6. In this connection it may be noted that the question of the nullity of the subsequent inconsistent treaty does not arise if the party to the prior treaty which is adversely affected by the subsequent treaty expressly or by implication waives its rights thereunder. This happens on occasions as, for instance, in the case of the British protest against the Hay–Varilla Treaty in 1903. Once waiver has taken place, there is no longer any inconsistency and therefore no question of the nullity of the subsequent treaty.

1954 REPORT

ARTICLE 16

CONSISTENCY WITH PRIOR TREATY OBLIGATIONS

1. *A bilateral or multilateral treaty, or any provision of* a treaty, is void if its performance involves a breach of a treaty obligation, previously undertaken by one or more of the contracting parties.

2. A party to a treaty which has been declared void by an

international tribunal on account of its inconsistency with a previous treaty may be entitled to damages for the resulting loss if it was unaware of the existence of that treaty.

3. The above provisions apply only if the departure from the terms of the prior treaty is such as to interfere seriously with the interests of the other parties to that treaty or substantially to impair an *essential aspect of its original purpose*.

4. The rule formulated above does not apply to subsequent multilateral treaties, partaking of a degree of generality which imparts to them the character of legislative enactments properly affecting all members of the international community or which must be deemed to have been concluded in the international interest. *Neither does it apply to treaties revising multilateral conventions in accordance with their provisions or, in the absence of some provisions, by a substantial majority of the parties to the revised convention.*

1. The following changes, which have been italicized and which are the subject of this comment, have been introduced in Article 16 of the original report:

(a) The contention of the principal provision of paragraph 1 has been clarified so as to make it cover both unilateral and multilateral subsequent treaties;

(b) A further clarification has now been introduced in this paragraph in the sense that the invalidity of the subsequent treaty may extend to some of its provisions only as distinguished from the treaty as a whole – a recognition of the principle of severability which is of special importance in connection with the subject matter of this Article;

(c) The present version of paragraph 3 of Article 16 now qualifies the rule of the invalidity of the inconsistent subsequent treaty, namely that the serious impairment of the original purpose of the prior treaty must extend to an essential aspect of that original purpose;

(d) In paragraph 4 the reference to the Charter of the United Nations has been omitted in order to avoid too narrow a reference to multilateral treaties which permit of an exception to the general principle enunciated in the Article;

(e) In the same paragraph, in relation to subsequent multilateral treaties generally, the principle has been introduced that such multilateral treaties are valid if they constitute a revision of the prior treaty accomplished either in accordance with its original terms or by a substantial majority of the parties thereto.

2. While the changes now introduced into Article 16 represent some alterations of substance, they are intended mainly to clarify and to supplement the original object of that Article. Their object is also to draw attention to the fact that the question of the co-existence and the conflict of multilateral treaties raises problems other – and in some respects more important – than that of the validity or otherwise of the subsequent treaty inconsistent with treaty obligations previously undertaken. These problems include those of interpretation of the prior and subsequent treaties and of termination[1] – or degree of termination – of the prior treaty in the light of the subsequent instrument. Above all, there arise in this connection complicated problems of legislative technique as the result of the co-existence of multilateral treaties unavoidably covering the same subject matter, of regional agreements, and of constitutions of international institutions – based on treaty – with overlapping spheres of activity. With regard to these questions, the issue of invalidity of the subsequent treaty or of its individual provisions is not of primary significance. Although this aspect of the problem falls more conveniently within the part of the report concerned with the operation and implementation of treaties, it is of importance that the codification of the law of treaties should, at every stage, draw attention to the wide ramifications of this aspect. In particular, it has a direct bearing upon the question of the revision of multilateral conventions. Any revision of a multilateral convention amounts to the conclusion of a

---

[1] *As between the same parties* the question of inconsistency of the prior and subsequent treaties is not relevant to the question of the validity of the latter. Here – but only here – the maxim *lex posterior derogat priori* fully applies. To the extent of inconsistency the subsequent treaty abrogates the former treaty. The degree of the inconsistency is a question of interpretation. See, for example, Hackworth, v, 306–507, on the controversy between the United States and Turkey concerning the implied abrogation of the Treaty of Commerce and Navigation of 1930 between the United States and the Ottoman Empire by the Treaty of 28 October 1931. It will be noted that in the case of the *Free Zones of Upper Savoy and the District of Gex* the Permanent Court of International Justice was called upon to decide whether Article 435, paragraph 2, of the Treaty of Versailles 'has abrogated or is intended to lead to the abrogation' of the provisions of the Treaty of Paris of 1815 regarding the régime of the Free Zones of Upper Savoy and the District of Gex (*P.C.I.J.* Series A/B, no. 46). While in the *Mavrommatis* case the Court considered that a Protocol annexed to the Peace Treaty of Lausanne overruled the provisions of the Mandate for Palestine (Series A, no. 2, p. 30), it held in the case of *Minority Schools in Upper Silesia* that the contracting parties could not validly abrogate or modify in one part of the convention, the protection afforded by a decision of the Conference of Ambassadors and embodied in a preceding part of the same convention (Series A, no. 15). There may be circumstances in which two parties may properly cancel a treaty to which a third State is a party. Thus Article 8 of the Treaty of Peace and Friendship of 31 July 1950 between the Governments of India and Nepal (*U.N.T.S.* 94 (1951), 8) provides as follows: 'So far as matters dealt with herein are concerned, this treaty cancels all previous treaties, agreements, and engagements entered into on behalf of India between the British Government and the Government of Nepal.'

new treaty which, even if it merely adds to the obligations of the revised treaty, creates a new set of obligations potentially inconsistent with the latter. The question arises whether, in the absence of express provisions regulating the process of revision, the second treaty – however otherwise justified, reasonable and beneficent – is void on account of inconsistency with the prior treaty. This and similar questions affect the whole process of so-called international legislation – including that covered by the codification of international law – and a further detailed examination of the problem seems to be indicated.

3. In the first instance, it has seemed desirable to clarify the first paragraph of Article 16 by stating expressly that the main principle there formulated applies both to subsequent bilateral and multilateral treaties. The contrary principle is adopted in the Havana Convention on Treaties of 1928 which provides in Article 18 that 'two or more States may agree that their relations are to be governed by rules other than those established in general conventions celebrated by them with other States'.[1] The Governments participating in The Hague Codification Conference of 1930 were conscious of the implications of the question. However, the final recommendation of the conference on the subject was inconclusive. It stated that 'in the future, States should be guided as far as possible by the provisions of the Acts of the First Conference for the Codification of International Law in any special conventions which they may conclude among themselves'.[2] The Report of the Drafting Committee added a further element of uncertainty by contriving, in one passage, to give expression to – and, apparently, approve of – two contradictory considerations. It referred to the concern felt in the Committee on Nationality 'as to how far it would be possible for two States to conclude between themselves special agreements which were not entirely in accordance with the principles contained in the instruments adopted by the Conference'.[3] It proceeded to express the view that 'doubtless nothing prevents the conclusion of such agreements, provided they affect only the relations between the States parties thereto'.[4] The committee then added to the inconclusiveness of its statement by putting on record its opinion that it would not be desirable to adopt a rule expressly permitting States to avoid the obligations of the convention by allowing them to conclude

[1] Printed in Hudson, *Legislation*, iv, 2378 *et seq.* at p. 2383.
[2] *Acts of the Conference for the Codification of International Law*, vol. i, *Plenary Meetings*, Publications of the League of Nations, *V. Legal, 1932.V.14.*, p. 171.
[3] *Ibid.*, p. 68.　　　　[4] *Ibid.*

agreements of this nature and that this was the reason for the recommendations referred to above.

4. It would thus appear that the solution adopted by The Hague Conference was essentially in the nature of a diplomatic formula, contradictory in itself, which left on one side the principal issue. No such course is open to the International Law Commission in its codification of the law of treaties. The problem is admittedly of pronounced complexity. Can it be said that any *inter se* agreement affects only the relations of the parties thereto? If a number of States are parties to a general convention whose provisions are designed to eliminate statelessness, can those States validly conclude *inter se* an agreement departing from these provisions? If a number of States are parties to a general treaty providing for full freedom of air navigation in respect of all the 'freedoms of the air', can they subsequently validly conclude *inter se* an agreement limiting the operation of that principle? If some States are parties to general conventions which prohibit forced labour, or traffic in slaves, or white slave traffic, or the right to have recourse to force, or absolute freedom to produce and import narcotic drugs, can these States validly conclude *inter se* a convention which limits the operation of the principal convention? Can a number of States parties to the Geneva Conventions on Prisoners of War or on the Treatment of Civilians subsequently agree *inter se* that, contrary to the provisions of these conventions, in any war in which they may be engaged, reprisals shall be admissible against prisoners of war or that all or some of the safeguards provided for the civilian population shall not apply? The same question can be asked in respect of a convention which codifies the law of treaties. In this case, however, a negative answer does not suggest itself as readily as with regard to other questions. It might not seem improper, when a general convention on treaties provides for the requirements of ratification as a condition of the validity of a treaty, that some of the parties should in a subsequent treaty *inter se* dispense with that requirement. The same applies to the requirement of written form as a condition of the validity of a treaty. But are the parties to a general convention on treaties equally at liberty to provide *inter se* that, unlike the general treaty, treaties imposed by force or treaties inconsistent with general international law shall be valid?

5. Possible questions of this character are probably as many as there are multilateral conventions. The fundamental difficulty arises out of the consideration that it is of the essence of multilateral

conventions that, as a rule, they do not, in respect of the subjects covered by them, regulate matters which affect only the relations between the States parties thereto. If five States parties to any of the conventions referred to above adopt as between themselves provisions and principles contrary to – or perhaps only differing from – those of the general conventions they may fairly be said to affect by their action all parties to the general convention. It is in the general and particular interest of all parties to these conventions that all other parties to the convention adhere *among themselves* to the provisions and principles of that convention. The latter may otherwise have no meaning or purpose – even if that general interest has no other object than that of securing uniformity for the sake of certainty and smoothness of international intercourse. For this reason it would appear that once States have become parties to a multilateral treaty of a legislative character, none of the questions covered by it affects only a limited number of the contracting parties; all contracting parties are affected. In fact, in conventions of this type the main interest of some parties, whose participation in the convention is no more than declaratory of a practice which they have followed as a matter of course, may be that *other* parties should individually or *inter se* abide by the purpose and the rules of the convention. For their purpose is not the regulation of a contractual *quid pro quo*. In such a convention the object is not to give or receive a specific tangible consideration for benefits received: the decisive consideration is the general observance of the convention. This is the position with regard to most – or perhaps all – multilateral conventions.[1] This being so, the prohibition of *inter se* arrangements inconsistent with the previous treaty obligations applies to all multilateral treaties unless, in accordance with paragraph 4 of Article 16, the *subsequent* inconsistent treaty belongs to the exceptional category of enactments of a fundamental character or unless it is concluded in the general international interest and is of such a nature as properly to override previous undertakings. In view both of the actual increase of the practice of multilateral treaties and its possible extension as the result of the growing integration of international society, the time seems to be ripe for the authoritative affirmation of the principle that parties to a multilateral treaty cannot legitimately claim the right to avoid

---

[1] In this respect the special rapporteur has felt compelled to adopt a view differing from that expressed in the Harvard Research Draft on treaties which limits the multilateral conventions in question to conventions of a fundamental character such as the Covenant of the League of Nations or the Statute of the Permanent Court of International Justice. See *A.J.* 29 (1935), Supplement, 1016 *et seq.* especially at 1018.

its obligations through the device of concluding a bilateral or multilateral arrangement *inter se*.

6. While, for these reasons, the special rapporteur has deemed it necessary to clarify paragraph 1 of Article 16 by extending its principal provision to both bilateral and multilateral treaties, the fact must be taken into consideration that international practice shows numerous instances of subsequent *inter se* agreements and that such agreements are necessary and desirable. The Covenant of the League of Nations provided for – and encouraged – regional agreements. So does the Charter of the United Nations. The Universal Postal Convention of 1952 authorizes, in Article 9 (*U.N.T.S.* 169 (1953), 25), the establishment of limited unions – subject to the restriction that they do not introduce conditions less favourable to the public than those laid down by the Convention and Regulations of the Universal Postal Union. Similar latitude is provided for in Article 42 of the International Telecommunication Union. The Convention of 1934 for the Protection of Industrial Property and the Convention of 1928 for the Protection of Literary and Artistic Works permit, in Articles 15[1] and 20[2] respectively, *inter se* arrangements provided that they are not inconsistent with the provisions of those conventions. In some cases the authorization extends specifically to conventions already concluded. Thus the Safety of Life at Sea Convention of 1948 lays down that matters falling within the provisions of that Convention but governed by the International Telecommunications Convention shall be governed by the latter as supplemented by the Safety of Life at Sea Convention. The same principle has been made applicable in the relations between the International Telecommunications Convention and the International Civil Aviation Convention as well as between the International Sanitary Regulations and the International Civil Aviation Convention. Above all, upon analysis, those treaties which terminate an existing multilateral treaty and provide for the continuation of such prior treaty between and in relation to those States who do not become parties to the new treaty, amount to what is called an *inter se* arrangement. Such treaties, which may or may not be inconsistent with a previous treaty in *pari materia* between the same parties, constitute a prominent and constant feature of international practice. This takes place through provisions such as that of Article 27 (1) of the Convention for the Protection of Literary and Artistic Works of

---

[1] *L.N.T.S.* 192, 17 *et seq.* 43.
[2] Printed in Hudson, *Legislation*, IV, 2463 *et seq.*, at 2475–6.

2 June 1948 which reads as follows: 'The present convention shall replace in the relations between the countries of the Union the Convention of Berne of 9 September 1886, and the Acts by which it has been successfully revised. The Acts previously in effect shall remain applicable in the relations with the countries which shall not have ratified the present convention.'[1] The Hague Convention for the Pacific Settlement of International Disputes provided that it shall replace as between the Contracting Parties the corresponding convention of 1897. Similar provisions were incorporated in the Sanitary Convention of 21 June 1926. The Geneva Conventions of 1949 include analogous provisions in relations to the Geneva Convention of 1929 which, in turn, made similar reference to the provisions of the Hague Convention no. 4 in so far as they bore on the treatment of prisoners of war.

7. Two factors would thus seem to emerge from the preceding observations. The first is that successive treaties which are concluded between some of the parties to the previous treaty and which cover the same subject and, to that extent, are potentially mutually inconsistent, are a frequent and necessary occurrence. The second is that any such subsequent treaty, although concluded only as between some States, as a rule affects, in some way, the former treaty and all the parties thereto. The question is whether it affects them so vitally and so adversely as to bring into play the general principle of the invalidity of the subsequent inconsistent treaty. This problem, in turn, resolves itself into two questions: the first is whether the subsequent multilateral treaty is in fact inconsistent with the prior multilateral treaty. This is a question of considerable difficulty which can be decided only by reference to the character and the purpose of the two treaties. In the nature of things, although the decision must somehow be made, it cannot be made, with any assurance, in advance and by reference to any abstract standard. Very often, an inconsistency – a conflict – will, upon closer scrutiny, prove to be no more than a divergence or variation with regard to the scope of the treaty and the method of its application. Often the departure, though apparent, is not such as to affect the true purpose of the prior treaty – especially in the light of an actual assessment of the relative importance of the interests involved. Thus, from this point of view, there is no conflict – even if the resulting situation amounts to more than mere overlapping – as the result of the fact that the various

---

[1] *Ibid.* p. 2479.

Trusteeship agreements cover such subjects, regulated in other conventions, as traffic in arms, slavery and forced labour; or that the Convention of 1951 relating to the Legal Status of Refugees or the Conventions of 1949 on Prisoners of War and the Treatment of Civilians regulate questions which form the subject matter of various international labour conventions with regard to such matters as labour legislation and social security; or that, while some conventions between the same contracting parties aim at the relaxation of restrictions of the freedom of movement of goods or persons, others introduce specific limitations by reference to public health (as in the case, referred to above, of the International Sanitary Regulations and the International Civil Aviation Convention).

8. In all these matters the ensuing problem – and the correct method of approach – ought not to be conceived so much in terms of any invalidity of the subsequent treaty or its particular provisions as of deciding which, in all the circumstances, must prevail. For there is little substance in the suggestion that, in pure logic, if a provision is made to yield to a provision of another treaty it is, *pro tanto*, invalid. For that provision may be otherwise – i.e. in relation to other treaties and generally – fully valid and operative. This being so, unless the inconsistency is so gross, irremediable and raising the issue of good faith as to call urgently for the application of the principle and of the sanction of invalidity, the problem is one of resolving the conflict by application of principles appropriate to the case. Such principles may be found in the application of the maxim *lex specialis derogat generali* or in an inquiry into the degree of generality or hierarchical order of the treaties in question. It cannot be found in the application of a rule of thumb.[1] It must, more properly, be sought in the provision of some organs of international advice and assistance equipped with an up-to-date knowledge of existing treaties in the same way as parliamentary draftsmen in national legislatures among whose principal qualifications is a thorough and ready familiarity with the large mass of statutory law of their country. It must further be sought in a consistent practice of consultation between and with the various specialized agencies within whose province any particular multilateral convention may fall. The Administrative Committee on Co-ordination of the United Nations and the Specialized Agencies has made far-reaching

---

[1] An illuminating survey of these possible principles is contained in an article by Jenks entitled 'The conflict of law-making treaties' in *B.Y.* 30 (1953), pp. 401 *et seq*. See also the valuable contribution by Aufricht in *Cornell Law Quarterly*, 37 (1952), 655–700.

recommendations to that effect.[1] In many cases the problem may be solved by the conclusion of more general – consolidatory – treaties aiming at the removal of inconsistencies between treaties as in the case of the United Nations Convention on Road Traffic of 19 September 1949[2] (which attempted to remove the inconsistencies between the Washington Convention of 6 October 1930 on the Regulation of Automotive Traffic[3] and the Paris Convention of 24 April 1926 on Motor Traffic[4]) or in the case of the Universal Copyright Convention of 1952[5] (which, partially, attempted to achieve the same object as between the Berne and Inter-American Conventions for the Protection of Literary and Artistic Works).[6] Last – but not least – there remains recourse to judicial settlement for determining, in relation to any particular conflict, either the priority or, in extreme cases, the voidance of any particular inconsistent obligation. It is clear that in such cases the task confronting a judicial body is of an exacting nature. Inasmuch as on occasion it may amount to assigning the same treaties and provisions a hierarchical priority of importance by reference to the character and objects of the treaties in question, it may tend to assume the complexion of legislative activity. However, the performance of such tasks may be unavoidable in some cases. It may be aided by a codification, on the lines suggested, of this aspect of the law of treaties.

9. At the same time it is of importance not to exaggerate the importance of conflict. On occasion, the apparent conflict resolves itself, upon analysis, into no more than an assumption of additional obligations. Thus, for instance, it was widely maintained for a time that there existed a conflict between the obligations of the Pact of Paris, which prohibited war as an instrument of national policy, and the provisions of the Covenant of the League of Nations which allowed war in certain contingencies (such as the failure of the Council to make a valid recommendation or a valid finding that a dispute fell within the domestic jurisdiction of a State). There was in fact no such conflict. There merely existed an additional obligation under the Pact of Paris – an obligation clearly not inconsistent with the Covenant. Neither was there a conflict when, in addition to the

[1] See Jenks, 'Co-ordination in international organization: an introductory survey' in *B.T.* 28 (1951), 75 and 84; *ibid.* 30 (1953), 401 *et seq.* and in *Hague Recueil* 77 (1950), 189–293.
[2] *U.N.T.S.* 125 (1952), 22 *et seq.*
[3] Hudson, *Legislation*, v, 786 *et seq.*
[4] *Ibid.* III, 1859 *et seq.*
[5] Cmd. 8912 (1952).
[6] The special rapporteur is indebted to Dr Jenks for these examples: *B.T.* 30 (1953), 401 *et seq.*

obligation to submit disputes to the Council of the League of Nations, the parties became bound by special treaties of conciliation and other means of pacific settlement – a contingency which in any case does not arise under chapter VI of the Charter of the United Nations owing to the elastic nature of its provisions. The same applies to the multiplicity of obligations of judicial settlement – as when parties to the optional clause of Article 36 of the Statute of the International Court of Justice are also bound by other obligations of judicial settlement. In such cases it is probably for the body first seized with the dispute to determine which obligation enjoys precedence. The co-existence of multilateral conventions in cognate fields must unavoidably cause a great deal of overlapping and divergence. When the International Law Commission approaches in due course the question of the operation and implementation of treaties it will be necessary, in the light of recent authoritative research on the subject, to consider constructive proposals in the field of legislative technique in this matter. However, as a rule the problem is in many cases of a less drastic nature than that arising from obvious or deliberate inconsistency which renders relevant the principle of the invalidity of the subsequent treaty. This applies even to such widely acknow-ledged instances of inconsistency of treaties as occurred in the case of the Convention of 1919 for the Regulation of Aerial Navigation and the Havana Commercial Aviation Convention of 1928.[1]

10. In this connection there arises the question of what weight must be given to the provision of treaties affirming that they are not intended to conflict with other – specified or unspecified – treaties. Thus Article 7 of the North Atlantic Treaty of 4 April 1949 (*U.N.T.S.* 34 (1949), 248) provides as follows: 'This treaty does not affect, and shall not be interpreted as affecting, in any way the rights and obligations under the Charter of the parties which are Members of the United Nations.' Article 10 of the Inter-American Treaty of Reciprocal Assistance of 2 September 1947 (*U.N.T.S.* 21 (1948), 101) provides that 'none of the provisions of this treaty shall be construed as impairing the rights and obligations of the high con-tracting parties under the Charter of the United Nations'.[2] The

[1] See Warner in *Air Law Review* (1932), p. 225.

[2] Provisions of this character are to be found in a variety of recent treaties. Thus the Mutual Defence Assistance Agreements between the United States of America and other States (see above, Article 1, para. 7) provide that the financing of any assistance under these agreements shall be consistent with the obligations of the contracting Governments under the Charter of the United Nations and of the North Atlantic Treaty. The Treaty of Friendship between Thailand and the Philippines of 14 June 1949 lays down, in Article 2 (*U.N.T.S.* 81 (1951), 54), that the undertaking to settle disputes between the parties by

Agreement between the United Nations and the Universal Postal Union of 15 November 1948 provides in Article 6 (*U.N.T.S.* 19 (1948), 224) that 'as regards the Members of the United Nations, the Union agrees that in accordance with Article 103 of the Charter no provision in the Universal Postal Convention or related agreements shall be construed as preventing or limiting any State in complying with its obligations to the United Nations.' Similar provisions were inserted in the various and numerous treaties of friendship and pacific settlement between Members of the League of Nations providing for neutrality of the parties in case of any – usually defensive – war in which they may become engaged. These treaties provided, having regard to the obligations of Article 16 of the Covenant, that they were not intended to conflict with the obligations of the Covenant.[1] These treaties included the Locarno Treaty of Mutual Guarantee of 16 October 1925 (Article 7). Provisions of this nature were also found in treaties of a technical character such as the Barcelona Statute of 1921 concerning navigable waterways of international interest, the Geneva Statute of 1921 concerning railways, and the convention of the same year relating to transit of electric power. What effect is to be attributed to such declarations of compatibility? It may be said that they are no more than declaratory of the general presumption – which is a principle of interpretation – that the parties to a convention do not intend to undertake obligations conflicting with their duties under previous treaties. It may be argued, on the other hand, that such declarations of compatibility are no more than a form of words which cannot do away with the fact that the subsequent treaty cannot be performed without violating the provisions of the prior treaty. An inconsistent treaty cannot, it may be said, be made consistent with the prior treaty by the simple device of the parties affirming that it is so. However, the better view is probably that such declaration of compatibility is not devoid of effect and that it serves a useful purpose. It amounts to a clear expression of intention that the subsequent treaty should not be operative in case it should

various pacific means, including reference to the International Court of Justice, 'shall not affect the application of the Charter of the United Nations'. The Convention between the United States of America and Costa Rica for the establishment of an Inter-American Tropical Tuna Commission of 31 May 1949 (*U.N.T.S.* 80 (1951), 4) provides in Article 4 (*ibid.* p. 10) that 'nothing in this convention shall be construed to modify any existing treaty or convention with regard to the fisheries of the eastern Pacific Ocean previously concluded by a high contracting Party, nor to preclude a high contracting party from entering into treaties or conventions with other States regarding these fisheries, the terms of which are not incompatible with the present convention'.

[1] For an enumeration and discussion of some of these treaties, from this point of view, see Rousseau, pp. 774–6, 789–92.

in fact, in any particular instance, conflict with the prior treaty. To that extent the presumption that the parties do not intend the subsequent treaty to be inconsistent with the first receives a considerable accession of strength as the result of an express provision to the effect that no conflict is intended.[1]

11. Having regard to the general tendency of international practice, as expressed in Article 16, to treat the subsequent inconsistent treaty as void only if no other solution can reasonably be adopted, the special rapporteur has deemed it desirable to clarify the first paragraph of that Article by adding the words '*or any provision of a treaty*'. The object of that addition is to incorporate expressly in the Article the principle of severability, that is to say, the principle that, as a rule, the voidance resulting from the absence of any of the conditions of the validity of a treaty need not affect the treaty as a whole; it may, and as a rule does, affect only the relevant provision. The principle of severability applies generally to the whole subject of treaties and will be examined in the appropriate parts of this report, in particular in connection with the application and the termination of treaties. However, it has been considered convenient to give to it express formulation in the present Article which is concerned largely with multilateral treaties. In relation to these the principle of severability is of special importance.

12. The reasons for the change introduced in paragraph 3 – namely, the substitution of the words 'essential aspect of its original purpose' for the words 'original purpose' – appear from the preceding sections of this comment. The fact that the subsequent treaty alters *some* aspect of the original purpose of the prior treaty need not be decisive. The decisive question must be whether it contravenes an essential aspect of that treaty.

13. In paragraph 4 the words 'such as the Charter of the United Nations' have been omitted as suggesting too narrow a scope of multilateral treaties which, although inconsistent with previous obligations, are nevertheless valid (i.e. which in effect may override previous treaties). There may be other multilateral treaties of such generality and importance that they may properly be attributed that effect. Thus, for instance, if a general air navigation convention effectively securing 'the freedoms of the air' were to come

---

[1] This same principle is occasionally expressed in connection with the provisions of the same instrument. Thus the Agreement of 27 February 1953 on German External Debts (Cmd. 8781 (1953)) lays down, in Article 27, that 'in the event of any inconsistency between the provisions of the present agreement and the provisions of any of the annexes thereto, the provisions of the agreement shall prevail' (*ibid.* p. 19).

into existence that convention might properly claim validity even if inconsistent with the previous treaty obligations of the parties; it might do so to the point of releasing the parties thereto from previous treaty obligations. This is to some extent recognized in various bilateral treaties in which the parties agree that in the event of their becoming parties to a general air convention the bilateral treaty should be amended accordingly. Thus Article 14 of the Agreement of 29 October 1948 between the Netherlands and the Argentine concerning regular air services provides as follows: 'If the two contracting parties should ratify or accede to a multilateral air transport convention, then this agreement and its annex shall be amended so as to conform with the provisions of the said convention as from the date on which it enters into force between them' (*U.N.T.S.* 95 (1951), 57). Article 14 of the Agreement of 8 December 1949 between the Netherlands and Egypt concerning the establishment of scheduled air services is to the same effect (*ibid.* p. 141). So is Article 14 of the Agreement of 11 March 1950 between Norway and Egypt for the establishment of scheduled air services (*ibid.* p. 184). So are many other treaties in this sphere.[1] The adoption of some such principle may also assist in solving the difficulties raised by treaties incorporating the most-favoured-nation clause and the subsequent desire of the parties to participate in general treaties providing for a comprehensive economic régime in the direction of liberalizing international commercial relations. It is clear that, in view of the general practice of giving an unconditional interpretation to the most-favoured-nation clause, the participation in such general treaties would become illusory or impossible if the benefits of such treaties had to be extended to States refusing to take part in the general treaty. For this reason there may be room for extending the principle now introduced in paragraph 4 to economic multilateral treaties of general character concluded in what may fairly be regarded as the overriding international interest. In fact some such solution has been suggested by writers who have devoted close study to the subject.[2]

---

[1] Thus Article 13 of the Agreement concerning air communications between Poland and Bulgaria of 16 May 1949 (*U.N.T.S.* 84 (1951), 338) provides as follows: '1. The present agreement shall be ratified by the two contracting parties and shall come into force on the date of the exchange of the instruments of ratification. . . It annuls and replaces all previous Polish-Bulgarian agreements and arrangements concerning air communications. 2. Should the two contracting parties ratify or adhere to a multilateral aviation convention, the present agreement and its annex shall be amended so as to conform to the provisions of that convention as soon as it has entered into force, as between the two parties.'

[2] See, for example, Ito, *La clause de la nation la plus favorisée* (1930).

14. The special rapporteur deems it necessary to draw attention to the wide implications of the principle as now proposed in paragraph 4 of Article 16. In so far as that principle sanctions and treats as valid departure from the terms of a binding treaty as the result of the conclusion of a multilateral treaty of a sufficient degree of significance and generality, it amounts to an interference with the legal rights of States without their consent. To that extent it amounts to a pronounced measure of international legislation in the literal sense. That consequence is probably unavoidable in a progressive and developing international society. However, it is of importance to realize the implications of that aspect of the codification of the law of treaties.

15. The same considerations apply to the addition now introduced at the end of paragraph 4 of Article 16. The rule as now formulated provides that the general principle of the voidance of the subsequent incompatible treaty does not apply to treaties revising multilateral conventions in accordance with the provisions of these conventions or, in the absence of such provisions, by a substantial majority of the parties to the original convention. To some extent this rule overlaps with that expressed in the first sentence of paragraph 4 which refers, in the same sense, to 'subsequent multilateral treaties, partaking of a degree of generality which imparts to them the character of legislative enactments properly affecting all members of the international community or which must be deemed to have been concluded in the international interest'. However, the multilateral treaties referred to in the paragraph now added cover also multilateral treaties falling short of the stringent requirements of the first sentence. As stated above, any revision of a treaty, unless extending to matters of minor importance, is more or less inconsistent with the original treaty. If the revision of the prior treaty does not impair, in the words of paragraph 3, 'an essential aspect of its original purpose' then, under the principle there stated, there is no question of the subsequent treaty being void. However, this will not always be the case. It is for this reason that the provision now added seems to be necessary. There is a substantial body of practice which is based on that principle. Thus Article 14 of the Postal Convention of 1930 (and, substantially, Article 15 of the Universal Postal Convention of 1947) provide for the possibility of a repeal, by a majority vote, of Acts of the preceding Congress of that Union. The revised convention was, as from the date fixed by the Congress, binding on all members except those withdrawing from the Union. Under Article 17 of the Articles of Agree-

ment of the International Monetary Fund (*U.N.T.S.* 2 (1947), 98) amendments to most[1] Articles of the agreement require the concurrence of three-fifths of the members having four-fifths of the total voting power and are binding for all members within the time prescribed in the agreement. Article 8 of the Articles of Agreement of the International Bank for Reconstruction and Development (*U.N.T.S.* 2 (1947), 184–6) is to similar effect. The provisions of the Convention on the Privileges and Immunities of the Specialized Agencies of 21 November 1947 (*U.N.T.S.* 33 (1949), 262 *et seq.*) go in the same direction.

16. The amendment as proposed refrains from specifying in detail the kind of majority required for revision. While a detailed regulation of that aspect of the matter is possible – and indicated – in particular conventions, such as the Postal Union or the Monetary Fund, an Article in the codification of the law of treaties must leave room for elasticity in this respect. A purely numerical majority – even if qualified by a requirement of two-thirds – may on occasion provide no more than a nominal solution.[2] Possibly a definition of what constitutes a 'substantial majority' might include, as one of the relevant factors, a system of weighting votes such as that expressed in the Universal Postal Convention or in similar instruments. However that may be, the revision of multilateral treaties constitutes one of the most important aspects of the international legislative process and attention must be given to it either in connection with the present Article 16 or in some other part of the codification of the law of treaties.

---

[1] This does not apply to some Articles, namely, those requiring unanimous consent for amendments modifying the right to withdraw from the Fund and the provisions relating to the quota of a member and the par value of its currency.

[2] Thus the United States, Great Britain and France consider as invalid the Belgrade Convention of 1948 relating to the Danube and revising the Convention of 1921 although that convention was agreed upon by seven out of the ten States participating in the Conference of 1948. However, as Italy, Belgium and Greece, who were parties to the Convention of 1921, were not – contrary to Article 42 of that convention – invited to participate in the Conference of 1948, it appears that the revision was not accomplished by a majority of the original signatories.

THE COVENANT AS THE 'HIGHER LAW'

Editor's note A much earlier work by Lauterpacht on the legality and object of treaties, with special reference to their compatibility with the Covenant of the League of Nations, is to be found in an article which he published under the above title in *B.Y.* 17 (1936), 54.

Treaties, including the Covenant of the League, are, in principle, of equal status. Although fulfilling a variety of objects,[1] they are all contractual transactions based on agreement. The principal rules relating to the conditions of validity and the canons of construction are the same in various categories of treaties. They are not governed by any hierarchical order of importance or precedence attaching to any of them an overriding power by virtue of either their subject matter or the number of their signatories. Some of them are frequently, for reasons of convenience, referred to as law-making or legislative, as distinguished from ordinary, treaties. These terms are adequate so long as it is borne in mind that they are used in a specific and metaphorical sense. There is no legislature in the international society; all treaties, whether bilateral or comprehensively multi-lateral, are law-making. That law-creating effect is, in terms of political importance, proportionate to the number of signatories and the scope of the treaty. But it is in principle present in every treaty. All treaties constitute binding law. It follows that so long as they are in force they govern not only the conduct but also the contractual capacity of the parties; they prevent, in law, the effective rise of obligations inconsistent with their provisions. This, it will be submitted here, is a general principle of law to which international law forms no exception and which, for cogent reasons, obtains with special force in the international society.

However, in cases in which the contracting parties attach particular significance to a treaty there is nothing to prevent them from placing that general principle of law beyond doubt by endowing the treaty with express attributes of superiority, for so long as it is in force, over any other contractual obligation, present or future. An explicit provision of this nature hardly adds to the juridical effects of the treaty. But it lends emphasis and certainty to a rule which, while unimpeachable in legal logic and fully entitled to recognition in the

[1] See McNair in *B.Y.* 11 (1930), 100 *et seq.*

relations of States, has not so far received sufficient clarification either in the practice of States or in the literature of international law. It appears that Article 20 of the Covenant of the League constitutes an enactment of this character. In the course of the application of sanctions against Italy during the war with Abyssinia that Article grew considerably in stature. Events revealed some of its hitherto unexplored implications. This article is an attempt to assess their bearing on the more general question indicated in the title. For the sake of convenience Article 20 may be here reproduced *in toto*:

ARTICLE 20

1. The Members of the League severally agree that this Covenant is accepted as abrogating all obligations or undertakings *inter se* which are inconsistent with the terms thereof, and solemnly undertake that they will not hereafter enter into any engagements inconsistent with the terms thereof.

2. In case any Member of the League shall, before becoming a Member of the League, have undertaken any obligations inconsistent with the terms of this Covenant, it shall be the duty of such Member to take immediate steps to procure its release from such obligations.

Prior to September 1935, that Article was seldom mentioned. It received little attention during the drafting of the Covenant; the principal question which weighed on the minds of the draftsmen seems to have been who will decide as to the alleged inconsistency.[1] Unlike most Articles of the Covenant it has never been made the subject of a proposal for an amendment. Commentators, if they did not dismiss it either as a truism or as a statement of political views, have concentrated on technical questions of phrasing and divergencies between the English and French texts,[2] or on specific questions like the compatibility of treaties of alliance with the Covenant of the League.[3] But a number of questions arising out of the application of sanctions against Italy have helped to draw attention to the interpretation of that Article as establishing the absolute primacy of the Covenant over any other treaty engagements of Members of the League *inter se* whether concluded prior or subsequent to the membership of the League, and, in some contingencies, over treaties concluded with non-member States.

Some of these questions came before a legal sub-committee set

---

[1] Hunter-Miller, *Drafting of the Covenant* (1928), ii, 279–81, 370–4, 380–4.

[2] See e.g., Ray, *Commentaire du Pacte de la Société des Nations* (1930), pp. 569, 570.

[3] Schücking und Wehberg, pp. 667–9.

up by the Co-ordinating Committee of the Assembly. The answers given by the sub-committee cover a wide range and are highly significant.[1] Thus they expressed the opinion that the application of sanctions suspended, as against nationals of the Covenant-breaking State, the operation of such treaties as those for the reciprocal enforcement of judgments 'for the treaties could not override the effect of Article 16 of the Covenant, which constitutes the law by which the two States concerned are bound'. They were, secondly, of the opinion that although the application of sanctions against Italy may prevent the execution of a commercial treaty with that State, Italy would 'have no legal right to complain, since the situation so created would be the result of the provisions of the Covenant, which is legally binding on both Italy and the other State and prevails over the treaty in question'; neither, they thought, would Italy, bound as she was by the Covenant, be entitled to retaliate by refraining on her part from carrying out the treaty. Thirdly, they held that a treaty between two Members of the League obliging the parties not to participate in any international *entente* to prevent the purchase or sale of goods or provision of credits must be interpreted subject to Articles 16 and 20 of the Covenant with the effect that 'application of sanctions by one of the contracting parties against the other is entirely legitimate, even if the treaty contains no reservation regarding the provisions of the Covenant or if one of the contracting parties was not a Member of the League of Nations at the moment when it concluded the treaty'. Fourthly, they expressed the view that as the result of the obligation of mutual support as laid down in paragraph 3 of Article 16, it is in accordance with the spirit of that provision that Members of the League applying sanctions shall continue to benefit from the advantages of the most-favoured-nation clause in cases in which the application of sanctions against Italy has resulted in the suspension of advantages which were granted to Italy and which constituted the basis of the most-favoured-nation treatment accorded to other States. Fifthly, they were of the opinion that a State (which, apparently, is a Member of the League but does not participate in sanctions) is not entitled to invoke the benefits of a most-favoured-nation treaty in respect of special advantages accorded to a State applying sanctions. Finally, with regard to conventions concluded with States non-members of the League, which contain provisions for freedom of communications,

[1] Doc. General 1935. 6. Co-ordination Committee 40. Also in *L.N.O.J.* Special Supplement, no. 145, pp. 21, 26.

the sub-committee held that the latter cannot absolve a Member of the League from giving effect to its obligations under the Covenant. The committee declined to say how far the obligations under the Covenant affected the rights of non-member States. It seems that they envisaged the possibility of distinguishing in this respect between treaties concluded prior to the Covenant and those subsequent to it. It is clear, from the answer to this and other questions, that, in the view of the committee, the obligations of Article 16 were in any case of overriding effect as between Members of the League.

The views of the legal sub-committee are, in their cumulative effect, striking and unusually definite. This ought not to give cause for surprise. The answers were conceived not as a product of academic deliberation concerned with putting both sides of the difficulty, but as an aid to urgent international action of unprecedented significance. Nevertheless, these answers, it is submitted, constitute a sound interpretation of the letter and spirit of Article 20. The Co-ordinating Committee acted upon them. They were in effect invoked, in a number of cases, by States Members of the League confronted with complaints of Governments adversely affected by the interpretation. Thus, for instance, the British Government seems to have relied upon the interpretation suggested in the replies of the sub-committee when, in January 1936, Hungary, a Member of the League who did not apply sanctions, demanded that Hungarian poultry should, having regard to a most-favoured-nation treaty with Great Britain, be granted customs concessions accorded to Yugoslav imports. Great Britain rejected that demand on the ground that the special concessions allowed to Yugoslavia were conceded in pursuance of an action under the Covenant.[1] When, in January 1936, Turkey, in reply to an inquiry by Great Britain, declared her readiness to comply with the obligations of mutual support under paragraph 3 of Article 16, Italy complained that the Turkish assurance was contrary to the Turco-Italian Treaty of Friendship of 1928. The Turkish answer to this complaint was based on the view that the admission of Turkey to membership of the League subsequent to the signature of the treaty *ipso facto* subordinated to the Covenant all previous agreements.[2]

The principal obligation of Article 20 is in fact much more comprehensive than the abrogation of such treaties inconsistent with

[1] *The Times* newspaper (9 January 1936). And see The Treaty of Peace (Covenant of the League of Nations) (no. 4) Order, 1935 (S.R. & O., no. 1248), reducing duty on certain Yugoslav goods by making an exception to the Import Duties Act, 1932.
[2] *The Times* newspaper (4 February 1936).

the Covenant as are in existence when the State concerned ratifies its adhesion to the League. It applies to all treaties between Members of the League regardless of whether they were concluded before or after they became Members of the League. The express undertaking, in the concluding sentence of paragraph 1, not to conclude in the future treaties inconsistent with the Covenant is not a substantial addition to the principal provision of Article 20, except in so far as the conclusion of such treaties is made to constitute in itself a breach of the Covenant and a wrong involving the international responsibility of the State in question. But their invalidity or unenforceability results from the first, not the second, sentence of Article 20. Treaties concluded in breach of that undertaking are inoperative because 'the Covenant is accepted as abrogating all obligations or undertakings *inter se* which are inconsistent with the terms thereof'. The Covenant, like any other treaty, is the 'higher law'; or, as the purist would have it, it is *the* law. The expression 'abrogates' means in effect 'is superior to' – now and for the future.

The answers of the legal sub-committee throw further light on what is meant by the term 'inconsistent' as used in Article 20. It seems that inconsistency means not only patent inconsistency appearing on the face of the treaty – e.g. an offensive alliance or a treaty providing for the cession, without the consent of the Council, of Mandated territory held by the contracting party, or an absolute promise of strict neutrality notwithstanding Article 16 – but also what may be called potential or latent inconsistency. Such potential or latent inconsistency in relation to the Covenant may be concealed in an otherwise innocuous treaty of commerce or extradition or for the enforcement of judgments or for the exchange of postal parcels. There is, on the face of it, nothing in such treaties which runs counter to the Covenant. But they may become inconsistent, and therefore abrogated, as soon as it becomes clear that their continued validity or operation is incompatible with the negative or positive obligations of the Covenant. These positive obligations, in particular those under paragraphs 1 and 3 of Article 16, are such that their fulfilment cannot be reconciled with the continued operation of most treaties concluded with the State against which the action of the League is directed. These treaties are abrogated *pro tanto*, that is to say, for such time and to such an extent as may be required by the obligations of the Covenant. Article 20 is not a knife blunted by the cutting of the dead wood of inconsistent treaties in force when States enter the League. It is a perpetual source of legal energy possessed of a dynamic force of its own and calculated to ensure the effectiveness of the Covenant unhampered by any treaties between Members, whenever concluded. It is this latent inconsistency which is successfully attacked by the emphatic terms of Article 20, for treaties patently inconsistent with the Covenant would, without special provision, be caught by the more general rule of international law, discussed below, relating to treaties which are in terms contrary to former treaty obligations. So, of course, would even latent inconsistency. For, in strict logic, there is no difference in kind between the two. Latent inconsistency can be easily avoided by a safeguarding clause in some such terms as 'Nothing in the present treaty shall be deemed to be inconsistent with or render illegal the fulfilment of the obligations laid down in or resulting from the Covenant'. In fact, a number of treaties concluded after 1919 provide that they apply only subject to the obligations of the Covenant.[1] Reservations of this nature hardly modify the legal position. With or without express proviso such treaties are subject to the obligations of the Covenant. However, Article 20 removes from the orbit of doubt a point of some nicety and difficulty.

The consequences of the construction here put forward may appear, so far as the Covenant is concerned, to be alarmingly wide. But they follow not because there is any hierarchical superiority about the Covenant as a legislative instrument – for there is none. Neither do they ensue for the mere reason that the Members of the League, not content to rely on general international law in the matter of inconsistency of treaties, have expressly endowed the Covenant with comprehensive overriding powers – for such caution is merely declaratory of existing principle. The grave consequences in the shape of possible incompatibility are the direct result of the comprehensiveness of the Covenant, which not only limits the right of resort to war but also imposes most far-reaching obligations for the enforcement of the Covenant.

Finally, the answers of the jurists are suggestive as to the meaning of the last paragraph of Article 20. A distinction must here be drawn between treaties concluded with third States by a Member of the League prior to the fact of membership and those concluded subsequently to that event. With regard to the first, non-members are not legally affected. Politically, their position is not as impregnable as might appear at first sight. For, as suggested by the legal

---

[1] For an enumeration of some of these treaties see Rousseau in *R.G.* 39 (1932), 140–2, 156–62, and Ray, *Commentaire du Pacte de la Société des Nations*.

sub-committee, dilatory Members of the League, who have failed to secure release, may find themselves confronted with two conflicting obligations the choice between which must remain a matter of conjecture and uncertainty.

As to treaties which a Member concludes with third States subsequent to his entry into the League, the position is more complicated. The difficulty for the third States is no longer merely a political one. Undoubtedly, the Covenant does not bind non-members, and they cannot therefore be directly affected by any abrogation of treaties inconsistent with its terms. But they *are* affected by international law inasmuch as it generally invalidates treaties so inconsistent with previous treaties as to prejudice the interests of other co-signatories. When third States conclude a treaty with a Member State they know or ought to know that the latter has, by ratifying the Covenant, limited its contractual capacity to the extent both of not concluding treaties inconsistent with the Covenant and of not being bound by treaties in so far as they prove to be incompatible with the obligations of the Covenant in any given situation. For the obligation of Article 20 not to conclude treaties inconsistent with the Covenant applies to treaties both with Members and with non-members. The third State has concluded a treaty with a State whose contractual capacity is limited. To the extent of that incapacity the treaty is inoperative. The third State may ignore the Covenant; it is not at liberty to ignore international law.

The interpretation of Article 20 here put forward proceeds on the view that treaties, other than those between the same contracting parties, which conflict with the provisions of previous treaties so as to cause injury to the interests of some of their signatories[1] are, to the extent of such incompatibility, invalid and unenforceable before international courts. This principle, it is submitted, forms part of international law. It is regarded as such, in terms even wider than those suggested here, by positivist writers like Oppenheim,[2] Hall,[3] De Louter,[4] and others.[5] It is recognized, notwithstanding occasional

---

[1] For the reasons for this qualification see the writer's note in *B.Y.* 16 (1935), 166, commenting on the dissenting opinions of Judges Van Eysinga and Schücking in the *Oscar Chinn* case.

[2] *International Law*, 1, 4th ed. by McNair (1928), 713.

[3] *International Law*, 6th ed. (1909), p. 334.

[4] *Droit international public positif*, 1 (1920), 480.

[5] See, e.g. Vattel, Book 11, ch. 12, § 165. See, on the other hand, Wright in *A.J.*, 11 (1917), 576–9; Salvioli in *Rivista*, 12 (1918), 229–41; Rousseau in *R.G.* 39; and, in particular, *Harvard Research* (1935), 111, 1016–29.

departures, in the practice of States.[1] Great Britain has frequently appealed to it.[2] The so-called doctrine of non-recognition, recently revived[3] by the United States and the Assembly of the League in connection with the Manchurian dispute, constitutes, upon analysis, a different formulation of the same principle. For non-recognition is not a purely political act; it is, in the absence of a court competent to adjudicate on the matter, an attitude expressive of a legal judgment to the effect that the new treaty is incompatible with the law as laid down in binding treaties and, therefore, legally non-existent. This absence of legal force in the inconsistent later undertakings, such inconsistency being known to both parties to the new agreement, is not a rule confined to international law. It is a general principle

[1] For a survey of cases and incidents see Tobin, *The Termination of Multilateral Treaties* (1933), pp. 206–49, who summarizes that practice as showing that 'there is nowhere in the discussion a denial of its validity, and frequent affirmations of its existence' (at p. 217). In the case between Costa Rica and Nicaragua the Central American Court of Justice, while finding that the Bryan–Chamorro Treaty between the United States and Nicaragua violated the provisions of former treaties between Nicaragua and Costa Rica, refused to pronounce that treaty null and void for the merely jurisdictional reason that one of the parties, namely, the United States, was not a party to the dispute (*A.J.* 11 (1917), 228). See also, to the same effect, the decision of the same Court in the action brought *in pari materia* by Salvador against Nicaragua (*ibid.* p. 729). But the Court found that Nicaragua 'is under the obligation – availing itself of all possible means provided by international law – to re-establish and maintain the legal status that existed prior to the Bryan–Chamorro Treaty . . . in so far as it relates to the matters considered in this section'.

[2] See, in particular, the British protest, in 1846, against the Treaty between Russia, Prussia, and Austria providing for the annexation of Cracow. The protest was based on the ground that the treaty was contrary to the provisions of the General Act of Vienna of 1815 (see Lord Palmerston's dispatch to Viscount Ponsonby of 23 November 1846, *Br. and For. St. Papers*, 35, 1085; and see *ibid.* pp. 1042–107, for the correspondence on the matter). See also the protest against the Preliminary Treaty of St Stephano on account of its incompatibility with the Treaty of Paris of 1856 (Oppenheim, *International Law*, I, 713); and the British refusal, which was subsequently withdrawn, to recognize the validity of the Hay–Varilla Treaty between the United States and Panama inasmuch as it conflicted with the Hay–Pauncefote Treaty between the United States and Great Britain (*Diplomatic History of the Panama Canal*, U.S. Sen. Doc. no. 474, 63rd Congress, 2nd Session, pp. 81, 91). For a recent example of a painstaking effort to avoid what must be regarded as merely formal inconsistency between two international instruments, see the observations of the Swiss delegate to the Co-ordinating Committee questioning the propriety of including in the recommendation concerning the arms embargo against Italy the category of articles useful for chemical and incendiary warfare on the ground that such weapons were in any case forbidden 'by the *jus gentium*, by the conscience of mankind, and by certain declarations to which all states had subscribed their names'. In deference to these objections the Committee appended the following footnote to the relevant passage of the recommendation in question: 'It should be observed that the utilization of these articles has been, and still is, prohibited under the Convention of June 17 1925. These articles are only mentioned above because their manufacture being free (the more so, as in many instances they serve various purposes), the Committee desires to emphasize that the export of such products could in no circumstances be tolerated' (*L.N.O.J.* Special Supplement, no. 145, p. 20).

[3] A practically identical formula was used by the United States in 1915 in its communication to the Chinese and Japanese Governments concerning the Japanese demands presented to China: see McMurray, *Treaties and Agreements concerning China*, II (1921), 1236.

of law. The exact degree of its adoption in private law may be controversial, but the principle itself is not open to doubt.[1]

[1] As to English law, Sir Frederick Pollock (*Principles of Contract*, 9th ed. (1921), p. 475) lays down, without any qualification, the rule that if A makes a contract with B and then another contract with C which, *to the knowledge of both A and C*, is inconsistent with the first contract, then the second is void. (In the matter of international treaties such knowledge must be presumed, especially under a binding regime of registration as adopted in Article 18 of the Covenant.) Sir Frederick Pollock quotes no direct authority in support of this view and it seems difficult to find one, but its soundness, it is submitted, ought not lightly to be questioned. The illegality and voidance of the contract concluded in these circumstances may be asserted on various grounds. For C knowingly to conclude such a contract with A is in effect to induce him to break the contract with B. Such a contract, involving as it does interference with an existing contractual relation, is in itself a tortious act (*Quinn* v. *Leathem* [1901] A.C. 495; *South Wales Miners' Federation* v. *Glamorgan Coal Co.* [1905] A.C. 239). For the very making of the new contract may be an inducement to break the old one. A contract brought about in this manner falls under the rule avoiding contracts to commit a tort; the tort *in casu* is unlawful interference with an existing contract. Apart from this it is a clear rule that a contract cannot be valid if in order to prove it it is necessary to prove an immoral or illegal fact: Lord Mansfield in *Holman* v. *Johnson* (1775), 1 Cowp. 341, 348. Deliberate interference with an existing contractual relation is such a fact. Possibly such contracts might also fall under the rules avoiding contracts because of legal impossibility (*nemo dat quod non habet; nemo ad alium plus juris transferre potest quam ipse habet* – a reason which underlies the unenforceability of such contracts in Continental systems of law) or for reasons of public policy. There is a suggestive passage in the judgment of Buckley L.J. in *Smithies* v. *National Association of Operative Plasterers* [1909] 1 K.B. 310, at 357: 'No doubt there are circumstances in which A is entitled to induce B to break a contract entered into by B with C. Thus, for instance, if the contract between B and C is one which B could not make consistently with his preceding contractual obligations towards A, A may not only induce him to break it, but may invoke the assistance of a Court of Justice to make him break it.' It seems to follow that, if there was no lawful justification for inducing the breach of the first contract, then the assistance of the Court cannot be invoked to enforce the second. However, the writer has found no direct judicial authority supporting Sir Frederick Pollock's view, and the reasoning here adduced as an explanation of that view is therefore put forward with no little hesitation.

The fact that the Court, because of the circumstances of the case (as in contracts of personal service: *Whitwood Chemical Co.* v. *Hardman* [1891] 2 Ch. 428), may refuse to grant an injunction restraining A, who is already bound by the same contract with B, from fulfilling the contract with C, does not necessarily mean that the Court will enforce that contract. It is one thing to say we cannot, in some cases, compel A not to fulfil a contract which he has unlawfully concluded; it is another thing to help A or C to enforce the contract which they made unlawfully in disregard of the pre-existing contract with B. With regard to the frequently quoted cases of *Lumley* v. *Gye* (1853), 2 E.Bl. 216, and *Lumley* v. *Wagner* (1 D.M. & G. 604), it may be asked whether Miss Wagner's contract with Gye, in addition to constituting a tort, at least on the part of the latter, was not in itself void and unenforceable. Could the court by injunction restrain Miss Wagner from singing elsewhere than at Lumley's theatre (*Lumley* v. *Wagner*) and then proceed in an action on the contract to compel Miss Wagner to sing at Gye's theatre or to pay him damages for breach of a contract which she had been restrained from performing for reasons of which Gye knew at the time when he made his contract?

Apart from the *dicta*, which are not quite clear, of Lord Holt in *Harrison* v. *Cage* (1698), 1 Ld. Raym. 386, and Hill J. in *Beachey* v. *Brown* (1800), E.B. & E. 796, there is no authority in support of the view that the inconsistent subsequent contract, when the inconsistency was known to the third party, is enforceable. See also the observations of Sir John Fischer Williams in *Grotius Society*, 18 (1933), 122, and Smith, *Leading Cases*, 13th ed. (1929), 1, 432, whose authorities, however, do not in fact support the view that a contract is not illegal or void simply because private rights are interfered with e.g. where the consideration is a breach of contract.

In German law the case here discussed seems to be covered by the provisions of Articles

In the international sphere the reasons for regarding later inconsistent treaties as void and unenforceable are even more cogent than in private law. It is, as a general rule, incompatible with the unity of the law for the courts to enforce mutually exclusive rules of conduct laid down in a treaty, a statute, or a contract. But among individuals contracts are infinite in variety and number; among States they are relatively few and a matter of general knowledge. The shock, therefore, resulting from any recognition of the later contract to the sentiment of the unity of the law is greater in the latter than in the former case. Moreover, in so far as there is any disposition by municipal courts to treat the later contract as subsisting, the logical exclusiveness of the subject matter of the two contracts is mitigated by substituting the right to damages for the second inconsistent obligation. In the international sphere damages, by the very nature of things, are in most cases not likely to offer adequate compensation for the wrong. For these reasons it is difficult to accept the view that the treaties in question are valid and that the only effect of the inconsistency is that the obligations of the former treaty take priority over the conflicting provisions of the later agreement. This would be the position in any case. For, obviously, a state cannot lawfully terminate a treaty by the simple device of concluding another treaty inconsistent with the first. The flaw in the later treaty has an effect reaching beyond the mere reproduction of an obvious rule of international law. It makes that later treaty unlawful and incapable of enforcement.

This insistence on the nullity of the later treaty is not, it is submitted, mere pedantry. Treaties, woven into the structure of customary international law, are the substance of the growing and changing law of nations. International law cannot recognize and it must actively discourage a state of affairs in which the law-creating faculty of States is abused for violating existing law as laid down in valid agreements. Governments cannot be permitted to discredit international law and to render it unreal by filling it with mutually exclusive obligations and by reducing treaties to conflicting makeshifts of political expediency. The necessity of discouraging such a state of affairs is so compelling that it is imperative to disregard the theoretical possibility of maintaining both treaties, for instance, when the injured contracting party fails to protest or when

138 (voidance of juristic acts which are *contra bonas nores*) and 826 (compensation for such acts) of the Civil Codes. For a survey of judicial decisions see Staudinger, *Kommentar zum Bürgerlichen Gesetzbuch*, 9th ed. by Loewenfeld and Riezler (1925), I, 576, and II, Part III (1929), 1825.

the offending State obtains release from the former treaty. States which deliberately choose to bind themselves to act in a manner contrary to obligations which they have undertaken, as well as States which induce such conduct, must know that the new treaty does not create a legal bond and that courts will refuse to enforce it. Jurists, it is believed, will be fulfilling a useful function by disclosing to the full these consequences of the law-making effects of treaties – of all treaties. They cannot by their own incantations conjure into existence a higher, legislative, type of international agreement. But they may help to reveal the far-reaching legal consequences common to all treaties.

The following summary of conclusions is submitted:

(a) The principal provision of Article 20 of the Covenant is essentially declaratory having regard to the rule of international law avoiding treaties, other than those between the same parties, conflicting with former treaty obligations of either of the parties.

(b) The same rule probably invalidates treaties of Members of the League with third States if such treaties are inconsistent with the obligations of the Covenant and are concluded after the State in question has become a Member of the League.

(c) The provisions of Article 20, although declaratory, are valuable inasmuch as they tend to remove doubts surrounding the application of a somewhat neglected principle of international law and to draw attention to the wide range of possible inconsistency with the comprehensive obligations of the Covenant.

(d) In particular, Article 20 brings into relief the fact that while the Covenant of the League is no more 'law-making' than any other treaty, the substance of its law differs so radically from other international conventions in its scope and significance as a purposeful instrument in the process of political integration of mankind as to deserve the designation of a 'higher law'.

(e) The rule postulating the invalidity of treaties conflicting with previous treaty obligations is a necessary deduction from the law-making effect of treaties in general and must be regarded as a beneficent principle calculated to enhance the authority of the Law of Nations and to safeguard its unity as a system of law.

THE OSCAR CHINN CASE

Editor's note   This note appeared in *B.Y.* 16 (1935), 164–6.

This note refers to the same question as is discussed in the preceding note in connection with the dissenting opinions of Judges Van Eysinga and Schücking in the *Oscar Chinn* case.[1] It is therefore convenient to omit a statement of the facts which gave rise to the observations of these two judges. The question is, whether two or more parties to a multilateral treaty are legally in a position to modify *inter se* or in treaties concluded with third states the position established by the terms of the original treaty in a manner which does not directly and on the face of it conflict with the rights acquired by the other signatories of the multilateral treaty. (It is, of course, clear that if the new treaty infringes directly and patently the rights of the other signatories[2] it is contrary to law.)[3] The Covenant of the League apparently refers to situations of this nature by laying down, in Article 20, that Members of the League 'solemnly undertake that they will not hereafter enter into any engagements inconsistent with the terms thereof'. The consequences of a failure to comply with this obligation are not clear; they are not beyond doubt even in the case of Article 18, which provides expressly that treaties not registered in conformity with that article shall not 'be binding until so registered'.[4] What would, for instance, be the effect of an agreement between two members of the League waiving the right to invoke the consequences of non-registration of any particular treaty?

The position is even more difficult in multilateral treaties containing no provisions analogous to Article 20 – provisions, that is to say, calculated to safeguard the general purpose of the treaty as

---

[1] *P.C.I.J.* Series A/B, no. 63.

[2] The judgments of the Central American Court of Justice in 1916 and 1917 in connection with the Bryan–Chamorro Treaty (*A.J.* 11 (1917), 181–229 and 674–730) and the advisory opinion of the Permanent Court of International Justice in the *Austro-German Customs Union* case (Series A/B, no. 41) afford illustrating examples of judicial treatment of questions of this nature. See on this aspect of the question an admirable article by Rousseau in *R.G.* 39 (1932), 133–92, entitled 'De la compatibilité des normes juridiques contradictoires dans l'ordre international'.

[3] The effect of such illegality of the new treaty may be a matter of dispute. See a discussion of this point by Sir John Fischer Williams in *Grotius Society*, 18 (1933), 119–21, in connection with the new doctrine of non-recognition.

[4] The matter is discussed in Anzilotti, pp. 374–92, and by McNair in Oppenheim, *International Law*, vol. I, § 518a.

distinguished from the particular interests of the parties. Some hypothetical cases may be mentioned by way of example: Can two or
more signatories of the General Treaty for the Renunciation of War,
faced with a final failure of all means of pacific settlement, lawfully
agree to settle a particular dispute by resort to war? – 'lawfully'
meaning 'without disregarding the rights of the other contracting
parties'.[1] Can two or more signatories of the Barcelona Convention
and Statute of 1921 on the Régime of Navigable Waterways of
International Concern agree, for reasons which they find compelling,
that they will mutually subject the nationals of the states parties to
the new treaty to dues and charges other or higher than those levied
upon the subjects of the other contracting parties of the Barcelona
Convention? Can two or more parties to a multilateral convention
exempting aliens from the duty to deposit security for costs when
appearing as plaintiffs agree to abrogate that provision, *inter se*,
wholly or in part? Can two states, parties to a multilateral treaty
providing for equality for national and foreign workers as regards
workmen's compensation for accidents, subsequently agree to adopt
a different method in their reciprocal relations?

It would be easy to multiply these questions by reference to most
of the multilateral conventions. They have been framed so as to show
the diversity of possible situations and the difficulty of suggesting a
solution equally applicable to all of them. Their common feature is
that, on the face of it, no interests are directly involved except those
of the signatories of the new treaty. Nevertheless it is clear that in
some of these cases the rights of other signatories of the original
multilateral treaty may be deeply, although indirectly, affected. The
signatories of the original convention may have a general legal
interest in the abolition of war as an instrument of national policy, or
in the maintenance of the principles of the freedom of navigation on
international rivers, or of easy access to courts, or of certain standards
for the international protection of workers. States conclude multilateral treaties not only in order to secure for themselves concrete
mutual advantages in the form of a tangible give and take, but also in
order to protect general interests of an economic, political or
humanitarian nature, by means of obligations the uniformity and
general observance of which are of the essence of the agreement. The
interdependence of international relations frequently results in
states having a vital interest in the maintenance of certain rules and

[1] It is common ground that such rights are violated if one signatory attacks the other by
resorting to war.

principles, although a modification or breach of these principles in any particular single case is not likely to affect adversely some of them at all or at least not in the same degree. The Aaland Islands controversy illustrated the fact of the existence of treaties which contain provisions transcending the interests of the parties directly concerned. Judge Anzilotti, in his opinion in the case of the *Austro-German Customs Union*, apparently had in view a similar contingency when he questioned whether the states parties to the Geneva Protocol of 1922 were in a position to modify in that protocol the provisions of Article 88 of the Treaty of St Germain, which 'form an essential part of the peace settlement, and were adopted not in the interest of any given state but in the higher interest of the European political system and with a view to the maintenance of peace'.[1]

It is submitted that it is possible to approach this subject without placing too much reliance upon the distinction between law-making and other treaties – a distinction the scientific value of which is highly controversial. Neither is it necessary, for this purpose, to establish a hierarchy of treaties and to regard some of them as being of a higher, legislative value. No such distinction has so far been established by positive international law. Although there has been an increased tendency to use the term 'international legislation', such terminology, when used with reference to existing multilateral treaties of a general character, is purely metaphorical and likely to conceal the fact that an international legislature, however desirable it may be, does not as yet exist. The problem is simply how far international law recognizes a general interest of the signatories in the maintenance of a treaty regardless of the question whether any particular or individual interest is directly and immediately involved. That it does and ought to recognize such interests there is no doubt. The immediate interests of a state are not necessarily the most important or enduring. On the other hand, an attitude of rigid adherence to a purely formal immutability of the law is hardly entitled to respect. It is clearly impossible to accept the view that the provisions of a multilateral treaty can never be modified and its obligations limited by particular agreements unless with the consent of all other contracting parties. It is equally difficult to acquiesce in the opinion that the stipulations of a multilateral treaty can always be modified at will by particular agreements provided that in their terms they are limited to the new contracting parties. In the absence of express treaty provisions bearing on the matter, the approach

[1] *P.C.I.J.* Series A/B, no. 41, p. 64.

must, it is submitted, be a pragmatic one. We ought to proceed from the assumption that the interest of the original signatories in the maintenance of the régime established by the treaty may be either direct or indirect, and that both are entitled to legal protection. But such indirect interest must be real; it must not be a cloak for petty legalism or mere obstruction. If this test is adopted, then it would be in each case for an international tribunal to determine, either on its own initiative or on the complaint of the signatory of the original instrument, whether the new treaty has interfered to such an extent with the true legal interests protected by the general instrument that it must be regarded as an inadmissible attempt at a substantive change of the law without the consent of the joint authors of the original treaty. As the law cannot legally be changed in this way, the new treaty would have to be held in certain cases to be invalid and therefore unenforceable. In some cases a less drastic sanction might be appropriate, for instance, the right of the original signatories to withdraw from the treaty. But where unenforceability and invalidity are the only possible solution, then that result would follow quite independently of any doctrine of non-recognition in all cases in which treaties are concluded in violation of or in consequence of violation of the principles established by previous treaties to which at least one of the signatories of the new treaty is a party. The suggested solution is in the nature of a tentative suggestion which cannot be elaborated within the limits of a short note. But it is submitted that the matter deserves careful study. It is not merely a question of the scientific unity of a system of law impatient of inconsistencies; it is a question of the reality of international law as established by treaties.

CONTRACTS TO BREAK A CONTRACT

Editor's note This section consists of the only article which Lauterpacht ever wrote exclusively on a question of English law. Even here, however, his interest in comparative legal method and in international law led him to append a note on the treatment of the problem in French, German and international law.

In view of the commitment of the present work to the systematic presentation of Lauterpacht's papers in terms of international law, it seems appropriate to include the present paper at this point as an appendix to Lauterpacht's consideration of the validity of treaties which are incompatible with prior treaty obligations of the parties.

Lauterpacht wrote this article at the time when he was preparing for his Bar examinations. He was delighted to be able to say in later years that he was probably the only candidate for that examination who could, in one of his answers, refer to an article of his own authorship. The article appeared in *L.Q.R.* 52 (1936), 494.

I

It is not an altogether unusual event that a court of law is confronted with a case *primae impressionis* arising out of a situation which no person would regard as exceptional. In this category there must be included the question, raised in a recent case, of the validity of a contract which, to the knowledge of both parties, cannot be performed without a breach of a prior contract binding upon one of them. In that case – *British Homophone Co., Ltd.* v. *Kunz and Crystallate Gramophone Record Manufacturing Co., Ltd.*[1] – one of the grounds on which the defendant resisted the claim for damages for the breach of a contract of service with the plaintiffs was that the latter, in concluding the contract, wrongfully induced him to break his pre-existing contract with the co-defendant company and were therefore *in pari delicto* with him.[2] Du Parcq J., in dealing with this contention of the defendant, recalled that his counsel was unable to produce any authority for the proposition that 'a service agreement made between two parties, both of whom know that it cannot be performed without the breach by one of them of another pre-existing service agreement, and one of whom is inducing the other to break the pre-existing contract, is itself [? not[3]] capable of being enforced'. In spite of such absence of authority the learned judge was not inclined to rule that the contention could be lightly dismissed. He said generally, without confining his remarks to contracts of service: 'It is an unlawful act or, in other words, a legal wrong, to break a contract, as it is to induce another person to break a contract without lawful excuse. . . It seems to be consistent with principle that an agreement to do a legal wrong to a third party should be

[1] (1935), 152 L.T. 589.
[2] The facts of the case are somewhat complicated: the defendant entered in 1934 into a contract with the plaintiffs in which they acquired the exclusive right to his services for twelve months. The contract contained an option (which the Court held not to be binding), in favour of either party, to extend its duration for a further period of twelve months on terms to be agreed. The co-defendants, who knew of the contract but not of the option, then concluded with the defendant a contract in which he promised them his services after the expiry of the existing contract with the plaintiffs. The plaintiffs thereupon persuaded the defendant to conclude a new contract with them.
[3] This word, which is essential for the understanding of the passage, has been omitted from the report by mistake.

unenforceable by reason of its illegality.' However, he did not find it necessary to come to a clear decision on this question on the ground that the evidence had not satisfied him that the plaintiff company had knowingly induced the defendant to break his contract with the co-defendant company.

The absence, alluded to in the judgment, of express judicial authority on this point was not, it seems, due to any lack of diligence on the part of counsel for the defendant. For, so far as the common law and its remedies are concerned,[1] there is, it is believed, no direct authority bearing on this subject. Neither, with two not very pronounced exceptions, is it possible to find a clear exposition of this question in the works of text-book writers in this country. They do not, as a rule, discuss the validity of the second inconsistent agreement under the conditions described above, namely, when the promisee of the second contract knows that the consideration on the part of the promisor is a breach of another contract by which he is still bound.[2] The exceptions referred to are Sir Frederick Pollock's and Sir John Salmond's treatises on Contracts. Their contributions to the subject are not as emphatic as may be desired for the reason that the first discusses the matter only incidentally and the second does not make it sufficiently clear whether the answer suggested covers the case in which the inconsistency is known to the promisee of the second contract.

Sir Frederick Pollock gives an answer which, although parenthetic, may seem to some embarrassingly comprehensive. He lays down, without any qualifications, the rule that if 'A makes an agreement with B the execution of which would involve an unlawful act on B's part (e.g. a breach of B's contract with C)', then 'if A does know the facts, the agreement is void'.[3] He adduces no judicial authority in support of his view.

Sir John Salmond was, it seems, inclined to adopt a different solution:

A contract is not illegal and void merely because its performance would amount to the breach by one of the parties of a prior and inconsistent contract made by him with some third person. If any man chooses to make two inconsistent contracts with different persons he is bound by both of

---

[1] As to equitable jurisdiction see below, p. 361.

[2] It is with that particular situation that we are here concerned. When the promisee of the second contract has no knowledge of the first contract the law is, in general clear. The contract is valid and enforceable.

[3] *Principles of Contract*, 10th ed. (1936), p. 441. See below, p. 364, n. 2, for a possible qualification of this view.

them, even though it is impossible for him to perform them both. He must perform one of them and pay damages for the breach of the other.[1]

This statement is compatible with Sir Frederick Pollock's view so long as it is limited to cases in which the promisee of the second contract does not know of the existence of the prior and inconsistent contract.[2] However, it appears that Sir John Salmond was prepared to go much further. He refers to the case of a person agreeing to sell his goods first to A and then to B, and goes on to say that 'he who enters into a contract *is not concerned with the question* whether the other contracting party has or has not already entered into a rival contract of such a nature that the performance of both of them is impossible'.[3] The language used is perhaps not quite clear. Do the italicized words mean that knowledge of the promisee in the second contract is legally irrelevant or merely that he is under no duty to make inquiries? It would seem from the context that Sir John Salmond has in mind the first alternative. The only substantive argument[4] which he adduces in support of his view is one *ab inconvenienti*. The second inconsistent contract, he says, is valid, for 'otherwise he who had promised to marry one woman could never afterwards effectively promise to marry another, and he who had agreed to sell his property to one man could never afterwards effectively agree to sell it to another'. Contracts of marriage and, to a lesser extent, promises to marry, are, as will be shown later,[5] in an exceptional category. As to agreements to sell, the result foreshadowed is far from being absurd. It is in many cases good law.[6] There is authority for the proposition that at least some agreements to sell or lease property in breach of a former contract are ineffective not only as against the promisee of the first contract but also as between the parties to the second.[7]

On the other hand, the answer given by Sir Frederick Pollock

---

[1] Salmond and Winfield, *Principles of the Law of Contract* (1927), pp. 145, 146.

[2] The same applies to the statement in Smith, *Leading Cases*, 13th ed. (1929), I, 432, that 'a contract is not illegal or void, simply because private rights are interfered with by the act stipulated for; e.g. where the consideration is a breach of contract or of private trust, the contract may be enforced, and the persons injured by its performance are left to the ordinary means of redress'. The usefulness of this statement is, again, limited so long as it is not made clear whether the promisee of the second contract knows that the promise of the other party implies a breach of the previous contract.

[3] Salmond and Winfield, *Principles of the Law of Contract*, p. 146. The italics are the writer's.

[4] The two cases to which he refers in this connection – *Ford* v. *Tiley* (1827), 6 B. & C. 325 and *Bowdell* v. *Parsons* (1808), 10 East 359 – are, it appears, irrelevant to the issue. In neither of them was the question raised whether the second promisee had knowledge of the former contract; nor did the question of the validity of the second contract constitute an issue in either of these cases. In both cases the defendants were the promisors of the first contract and in both cases they were held liable in damages.

[5] See below, p. 365. [6] See below, p. 357. [7] See below, p. 358.

is undoubtedly startling when all its implications are realized. If it is good law then we must hold that in situations covered by such cases as *Lumley* v. *Wagner*[1] the second contract (i.e. the contract between Miss Wagner and the producer Gye) is void as between the parties to the second contract and cannot be enforced at the suit of either of them; that, generally, a contract made in breach of a former and valid contract in restraint of trade, is void and unenforceable; that, more generally, every contract the conclusion of which would be actionable at the instance of the first promisee as falling under the doctrine of *Lumley* v. *Gye*[2] is void as between the parties to the second contract; that the range of these contracts, far from being limited to contracts of service, extends to all contracts; that, in particular, it reaches contracts for the sale of goods with the result that if A agrees to sell real property or a chattel to B (whom we may call the first promisee) and then agrees to sell the same land or chattel to C (the second promisee) who has knowledge of the former contract, then the second contract is void as between the parties thereto; that it covers those situations in which the terms of the second agreement of sale or contract to sell are inconsistent with the covenants and terms of a prior contract by which the vendor is bound; that it embraces agreements containing restrictions on user and prohibitions of underselling with the result that in cases like *Dunlop Pneumatic Tyre Co., Ltd.* v. *Selfridge & Co., Ltd.*[3] in which the courts, in reliance upon the doctrine of privity of contract, have declined to go the length of the full recognition of restrictions of user on chattels[4] and have refused to admit that the plaintiffs had enforceable rights as against the defendants, the contract between the latter and the purchasers from the Dunlop Company is nevertheless void; and that – we must not shrink from extreme examples – if A promises to marry B and then promises to marry C, who knows of the promise to B, the second promise is void. These instances, *all of which are based on the assumption that the second promisee knows of the first inconsistent contract,*[5] show some of the practical consequences following from the adoption of the view accepted by Sir Frederick Pollock and apparently approved in principle by Mr Justice du Parcq. They open up a formidable vista of possibilities.

---

[1] (1852), 1 De G.M. & G. 604. [2] (1853), 2 E. & B. 216. [3] [1915] A.C. 847.
[4] As recognized in *De Mattos* v. *Gibson*, 4 De G. & J. 276, and *Lord Strathcona Steamship Co., Ltd.* v. *Dominion Coal Co., Ltd.* [1926] A.C. 108.
[5] An apology is due to the reader for this unseemly use of italics, but it is useful to indicate to the point of repetition that the proviso embodied in the italicized sentence is of the essence of the problem here discussed.

There are other considerations which may well make us pause before we fully subscribe to the view that the second contract is, in the circumstances here described, void. There is the fact that inconsistent contracts of this nature are a relatively frequent occurrence and that if the principle laid down by Sir Frederick Pollock and approved by Mr Justice du Parcq were law, it seems improbable that a long series of cases would not be available to substantiate it. There is a multitude of cases in which injunctions have been issued to prevent a breach of contract threatened by a subsequent contract or in which damages have been granted for a breach, in that way, of a prior contract – and yet, with inconspicuous exceptions,[1] there is nothing in judicial pronouncements to point to the invalidity of the second contract as between the parties thereto. There is a long string of cases on record in which courts have expressly refused to interfere, at the suit of the original promisee, in order to prevent the promisor from fulfilling his second promise inconsistent with the first.[2] Moreover, it would appear that there are some contracts as to which there is no doubt that the court will uphold them although the promise is, to the knowledge of the promisee, contrary to a previous contract binding upon the promisor.[3] All these considerations are a summons to caution. And yet it will be submitted here that the rule as laid down by Sir Frederick Pollock is, subject to suitable exceptions, sound and, in fact, inescapable; that the absence of direct judicial authority on the subject is due largely to the fact that, as will be shown here, the law has found other means than formal invalidity for taking the teeth out of the inconsistent contract and for protecting the original promisee; that the isolated instances of express recognition of the validity of the inconsistent contract are capable of an explanation leaving intact the principal rule; and that instead of questioning that rule in its entirety attention may usefully be devoted to an elucidation of the limits of its operation.

It is of interest to find that Sir Frederick Pollock's view is adopted in the recent attempt of the American Law Institute to restate the law of contract. It is laid down there, in § 576, that 'a bargain, the making or performance of which involves breach of a contract with a third person, is illegal'.[4] The reason given, in the comment, is that

---

[1] See above, p. 341.   [2] See below, p. 363.   [3] See below, p. 364.

[4] *Restatement of the Law of Contracts*, as adopted and promulgated by the American Law Institute (1932), II, 1081. Of the illustrations of the rule given in support of that section the following is of interest: 'A bargains with B, a member of a stock exchange, to give B stock brokerage business in consideration of B's charging reduced commissions in violation of the rules of the Stock Exchange, by which B had agreed to be bound when he became a member. The agreement is illegal.'

345

'since breach of contract is a legal wrong, a bargain that requires for its performance breach of a contract with another, is opposed to public policy'.[1] This also seems to be the view of some American writers. Thus Professor Gardner, in a recent article, says: 'No remedy . . . will be allowed for breach of any promise which the promisee relied upon knowing that performance would involve a violation of the promisor's duty to third parties. . . . A promisee may not recover compensation for services which necessarily involved a violation of the law or of his own duty to the third parties.'[2] Professor Williston is more hesitating. He admits that a contract of service which, to the knowledge of the parties, can be fulfilled only by violating an existing contract of service with another, has been held invalid. But, he says, it is not clear 'whether an agreement to sell goods which to the buyer's knowledge the seller was under contract to sell to another would be illegal and unenforceable'.[3] There are cases decided by courts in the United States which go to the full length of invalidating the second inconsistent contract.[4] But that practice is not uniform.[5]

II

When A promises to do for C something which he has exclusively promised to B, and if C knows of the existence of the first contract and its inconsistency with the second, the following two questions immediately arise: (a) Can B sue C in tort for damages for inducing

[1] There is a proviso added to this rule to the effect that a completed sale 'though made in pursuance of such a bargain is effective to transfer ownership' (*ibid.*). This statement lends itself to misunderstanding unless it is explained: (a) that, at least in certain cases, the passing of the property is subject to the rights of the promisee of the first contract (see below, p. 359); and (b) that although property in goods acquired under an illegal contract may pass, this does not necessarily mean that that contract is otherwise enforceable as between the parties. No action will lie, in general, to recover money paid or property transferred under such contract.

[2] *H.L.R.* 46 (1932–3), 36, 37. See also, to the same effect, the editorial note *ibid.* 27 (1913–14), 273–5.

[3] *The Law of Contracts* (1922), III, §§ 1138, 3036.

[4] Thus in *Rhoades* v. *Malta Vita Pure Food Co.*, 112 N. W. 940, the plaintiff was under a contract for one year with a competitor of the defendant. The latter then made a secret agreement with the plaintiff to employ him for two years. It was held that the plaintiff could not recover his salary, or for materials furnished. For comment thereon see *H.L.R.* 21 (1907–8), 290. See also *ibid.* 28 (1913–14), 274, and 31 (1917–18), 1017. In a Dominion case – *Wanderers Hockey Club* v. *Johnson*, 25 West. L. R. 434 (Brit. Col.) – it was held that if A induced B to enter into a contract the performance of which would necessarily involve the breach of a pre-existing contract between B and C, A could not recover for non-performance.

[5] See the note in *H.L.R.* 21 (1907–8), 290, and some of the cases referred to in Williston, *The Law of Contracts*, III. See also the conflicting cases cited in *Yale Law Journal*, 34 (1924–5), 213; and those referred to by Carpenter in *H.L.R.* 41 (1927–8), 747, n. 77, and 764–8.

A to break his contract with B? (b) Can A sue C or can C sue A in respect of the new contract, or, in other words, is the contract between A and C a valid and enforceable contract? The present article is, as stated, concerned only with the second of these questions, but in answering it it will be necessary to touch on the first.[1]

The invalidity, in the circumstances here assumed, of the second inconsistent contract may, in addition to reasons based on morality and public policy,[2] be postulated on one or both of the following two grounds: it may be asserted by reference to and as a development of the law laid down in *Lumley* v. *Gye*; or it may be based on the wider ground of invalidity of contracts whose object is the commission of an unlawful act. The first of these two aspects will now be considered.

The connection between the doctrine laid down in *Lumley* v. *Gye* and the invalidity, as a general rule, of the second inconsistent contract is not as obvious as may appear at first sight. Even if we accept without qualification the principle that it is a tort to induce a breach of contract, it is still a long way from that principle to the rule that the second contract, brought about by the tortious act, is illegal and unenforceable. In order to establish generally a direct connection between the doctrine of *Lumley* v. *Gye* and the invalidity of the second contract it is necessary to demonstrate all of the following propositions: (a) that the doctrine of *Lumley* v. *Gye* applies to all contracts, and not only to what have been termed 'contractual relations'; (b) that the tortious character of 'inducing' is not conditioned either by the state of mind or the initiative of the 'inducing' party, but that mere knowledge on his (i.e. the second promisee's) part of the first inconsistent contract must be regarded as the decisive factor in the situation; (c) that, accordingly, the tort *in casu* consists in the conclusion of and persevering in the new contract with the result that that contract is in itself both a tort and a contract to commit a tort; (d) that a tort of this nature is one falling under the general principle avoiding contracts to commit a tort.

(a) There is, in the matter of the breadth of the rule in *Lumley* v. *Gye*, a curious discrepancy between the authoritative and unqualified

---

[1] When the contract in question is one concerned with the sale of a chattel and a restriction upon its use, a further question arises: Can B compel C to fulfil the terms of the contract in accordance with the still binding agreement between A and B? For a discussion of this aspect of the matter see Winfield, *The Province of the Law of Tort* (1931), p. 106; Hanbury, *Modern Equity* (1935), p. 40; Wade in *L.Q.R.* 42 (1926), 139–41, and 44 (1928), 51–65; Chafee in *H.L.R.* 41 (1927–8), 945–1013. And see the principal cases referred to below, p. 359.

[2] See below, pp. 367–9.

acceptance of a comprehensive principle and the willingness to apply it to all situations apparently covered by it. There is abundant authority in favour of the view that the principle of *Lumley* v. *Gye* covers all contracts and is not confined to contracts of service or those analogous to contracts of service. *Bowen* v. *Hall*[1] and *Temperton* v. *Russell*[2] are generally regarded as putting that proposition beyond doubt. Actually the judgment of Erle J. in *Lumley* v. *Gye* is most explicit on the matter. It expressly includes within the orbit of the rule not only inducement leading to breaches of contracts of service, but also to non-delivery of goods and non-payment of debts. And yet how many would be prepared to subscribe, without reservations, to the view that the rule of *Lumley* v. *Gye* applies, for example, to all the categories of contracts which we have enumerated as instances of inconsistent contracts? How general will be the assent to the proposition that 'a sub-buyer may . . . be liable in tort to the original seller if he have procured a violation by the buyer of his contract with the seller'?[3] The fact is that judges did not easily shake off the reluctance to face fully the consequences following from the application of the doctrine in *Lumley* v. *Gye* to all contracts. In *Bowen* v. *Hall* the majority of the Court (Brett L.J. and Selborne L.C.) were inclined at the hearing to base their decision on the view that the contract in question was one of personal service though not necessarily one which established strictly for all purposes the relation of master and servant between the original parties. It was only in their considered judgment that they abandoned this narrower ground and relied on considerations applicable to all contracts. Even after *Temperton* v. *Russell* the view that *Lumley* v. *Gye* is limited to contracts of service and those of a similar nature died hard. In *Quinn* v. *Leathem*[4] Lord Macnaghten used in this connection the expression 'contractual relations', and judicial conservatism subsequently fastened on that expression and distinguished it from 'contract' proper. In *Exchange Telegraph Co., Ltd.* v. *Gregory*[5] Rigby L.J. was not prepared to accept the view that every procuring of a breach of contract will give a right of action. 'The nature of the contract broken', he said, 'must be considered.'[6] In *National Phonograph Co.,*

---

[1] (1881), 6 Q.B.D. 333.   [2] [1893] 1 Q.B. 715.

[3] Benjamin, *Sale of Personal Property*, 7th ed. by Kennedy (1931), p. 545.

[4] [1901] A.C. 495, 510.

[5] [1896] 1 Q.B. 147, at p. 157. This was an action for maliciously inducing a breach of contract in order to obtain information which the committee of the London Stock Exchange reserved to certain subscribers. See also for a similar case *Hamlyn* v. *Houston Co., Ltd.* [1903] 1 K.B. 81.

[6] [1896] 1 K.B. at p. 157.

Ltd. v. *Edison–Bell Consolidated Phonograph Co., Ltd.*[1] Joyce J. fully associated himself with this view and pointed to the difficulties which might arise if the doctrine of *Lumley* v. *Gye* were extended to all contracts. He referred to the hypothetical case of a lady who having promised to marry A is induced by B to change her mind and to accept his own offer to marry her. He asked whether in that case A, instead of bringing an action for breach of promise against the lady, could recover damages against B in an action of tort, or, what is more, if, had he commenced the action soon enough, he could obtain against B an injunction restraining him from marrying the lady. And he applied the same question to other embarrassing situations like contracts in breach of valid contracts or in restraint of trade or of contracts containing a prohibition of reselling at less than the fixed price. The Court of Appeal reversed the judgment of the Court below and expressly disapproved of the view in this matter of both Joyce J., and Rigby L.J., on which he relied.[2] The law is thus well established. Yet the doubts voiced in both these cases are not without significance. They show the startling implications of a thorough-going extension to all cases of the doctrine laid down in *Lumley* v. *Gye*. The judges of the Court of Appeal have discounted these implications. The present comprehensiveness of the rule is neither an accident nor a rash generalization. It is in keeping with the modern tendency of the law to afford increased protection to contractual rights. This being so we are not entitled to attach importance to the fact that somehow most of the relevant cases in the law reports are confined to contracts of service and those analogous thereto.

(b) The second link between the doctrine of *Lumley* v. *Gye* and the invalidity of the second inconsistent contract is the elimination of 'malice' in its ordinary meaning as a condition of the application of that doctrine. Here again we encounter a phenomenon similar to that which confronts us with regard to the scope of the doctrine. There is, on the one hand, a clear determination[3] to rule out 'malice' proper conceived as a mental attitude responsible for and leading to the tortious act; there is, on the other hand, some lack of appreciation of the true meaning of that simplification. As appears clearly from the judgment of Crompton J. in *Lumley* v. *Gye*,[4] malice on the

---

[1] [1908] 1 Ch. 335, at p. 350.

[2] See in particular the observations of Kennedy L.J. at p. 367.

[3] See, e.g., the observation of Lindley L.J. in *South Wales Miners' Federation* v. *Glamorgan Coal Co., Ltd.* [1905] A.C. 239, at p. 255, explaining why he had 'purposely abstained from using the word "malice" ' in this connection.

[4] (1853) 2 E. & B. 216, at p. 224.

part of the inducer means merely that he has notice of the pre-existing contract. In *Bowen* v. *Hall*[1] the Court was of the opinion that malice in this connection did not necessarily mean the intention to injure the plaintiff; it is enough if there is the intention to benefit the defendant at the expense of the plaintiff. Subsequent decisions exhibited the same tendency to eliminate malice as a condition of tortious 'inducing'.[2] The significance of that development has been somewhat obscured by the fact that some of the leading cases of interference with contractual relations by inducing a breach of contract have been cases of 'malice' accompanied by fraud[3] or coercion.[4] But, as said, no such qualified malice is necessary. The declarations and counts usually refer in this connection to 'maliciously and wrongfully inducing'. So do judges from time to time. There may be historical reasons explaining the language used.[5] But it is now generally agreed that that form of words need not be taken literally. This is one of the branches of the law where 'maliciously' means 'knowingly'. However, although this is now generally recognized, it is essential to push analysis a bit further. If the element of malice is eliminated, are we not justified in maintaining that the inducement consists in nothing else than the conclusion of the second inconsistent contract, i.e. in a promise to do or to forbear from doing something in consideration of the promisee breaking his prior contract? If, in the example just quoted, C concludes the (second) contract with A, is it relevant – and, in many cases, possible – to inquire into the history of that contract and to ascertain whether the overtures were made by A or C? Would the result in *Lumley* v. *Gye* have been different if Gye could have proved that his contract with

---

[1] (1881), 6 Q.B.D. 333.

[2] In *South Wales Miners' Federation* v. *Glamorgan Coal Co., Ltd.* [1905] A.C. 239, James L.J. went to the length of saying that the defendants would have had no excuse even if they had sincerely believed that their employers would benefit by their collieries being interrupted (at p. 251). And see the observations of Buckley L.J. in the *National Phonograph Co.* case (at p. 360).

[3] See, e.g., *National Phonograph Co. Ltd.* v. *Edison–Bell Consolidated Phonograph Co., Ltd.* [1908] 1 Ch. 335.

[4] *Read* v. *The Friendly Society of Operative Stonemasons of England, Ireland and Wales* [1902] 2 K.B. 732.

[5] There is in the judgment of Collins M.R. in *Read* v. *Friendly Society of Operative Stonemasons of England, Ireland and Wales* [1902] 2 K.B. 732 an interesting passage suggesting that the requirement of malice was a necessary concession to the doctrine of privity of contract indirectly challenged by the rule in *Lumley* v. *Gye*. He said that at common law it was not a case of 'a *prima facie* cause of action based on the fact that a breach of contract had been brought about to the detriment of the plaintiff, party thereto, by a stranger to the contract. The common law did not lightly extend rights arising out of contracts to and against persons not parties thereto, owing to the absence of privity. Some nexus had to be established between the plaintiff and the stranger, and this was found in malice' (at p. 739).

Miss Wagner was due solely to the initiative and insistence of the latter?[1] The test, which is an unavoidably simple one, is: Has C concluded the contract with knowledge of the previous conflicting contract? If he has, he has 'induced' A to break his contract with B. The tort established in *Lumley* v. *Gye* does not, as is widely assumed,[2] consist in persuasion, solicitation and other acts aiming at inducing the person already bound by one contract to make the second inconsistent contract. It consists in the making of the second contract with full knowledge of the first. The majority of the relevant cases illustrate and confirm this proposition. Thus, for instance, in *Long* v. *Smithson*[3] a number of discharged sailors entered into a partnership with a view to performing together at certain music-halls. The plaintiffs, who were members of the company, maintained that the defendant induced some of the partners to break the contract by promising to get them other engagements. In the pleadings and the judgments of the County Court and the Divisional Court the terms 'wrongfully and maliciously induced' were freely used. Both Courts found for the defendant on the ground that there was no evidence at all that she had induced, in 'the ordinary sense', or 'maliciously or at all', these persons to break their contract. In what did the evidence consist? It consisted in the proof that, to the knowledge of the defendant, the first contract was no longer existent; she was told, and had good reason to believe, that the first contract was at an end. The question is simply this: Did the defendant, or did she not, have knowledge of the continued existence of the first contract?

(c) We are thus led to the third proposition, which is vital for establishing the link between *Lumley* v. *Gye* and the invalidity of the

---

[1] In *Lumley* v. *Gye* Lord Coleridge pointed, in an impressive passage, to the difficulty of drawing a line between advice, persuasion, enticement, and procurement. 'Who', he asked, 'shall say how much of a free agent's resolution flows from the interference of other minds, or the independent resolution of his own?' The answer is that no such fine psychological investigation is necessary. It certainly did not trouble the majority of the judges in *Lumley* v. *Gye*.

[2] See, for instance, Iyer, *The Law of Torts* (1932), p. 356: 'The breach of contract must be the direct consequence of the defendant's words or acts.' That conception of 'inducing' seems to have inspired Professor Chafee's view that the doctrine of *Lumley* v. *Gye* cannot be resorted to as an instrument for enforcing against third parties contractual restrictions upon the user of chattels (*H.L.R.* 41 (1927–8), 971). Thus, he says, although it might be possible to bring within the rule of *Lumley* v. *Gye* the sub-purchaser who purchased an article in violation of the original contract containing a price restriction if that sub-purchaser had *induced* the second contract, the remedy would not be available if he merely knew of the first contract. There is, in law, no difference between the two situations. The reason why the doctrine of *Lumley* v. *Gye* is of no avail for upholding restrictions on the use of chattels is that it is impossible to introduce by a back door an innovation which courts have, in cases like *Taddy & Co.* v. *Sterious & Co.* [1944] 1 Ch. 354 and *McGruther* v. *Pitcher* [1904] 2 ch. 306, so far expressly refused to accept.

[3] (1918), 118 L.T. 678.

351

second contract. It follows from what has been said that the 'inducement' and the second contract are largely co-terminous. This being so, there is, apart from that contract, no 'inducement' of which the law will take notice for the purposes of the doctrine of *Lumley* v. *Gye*. As Collins M.R. said in *Read* v. *Friendly Society of Operative Stonemasons of England, Ireland and Wales*: 'Persuasion by an individual for the purpose of depriving another person of the benefit of a contract, *if it is effectual in bringing about a breach*[1] of the contract to the damage of that person, gives a cause of action.'[2] An inducement not consummated by a breach of the old contract is not a tort. An *attempt* to commit a tort is unknown to the law. The tort of inducing is constituted by the very fact of the new contract inasmuch as the latter involves in its performance a breach of the prior contract. The second contract is illegal not only in its making but also in its performance. With regard to the latter it may be said, by analogy with the doctrine of continuing trespass, that the second contract is a continuing tort on the part of C, the inducer, and the promisee of the new contract.[3]

(d) Finally, there remains, as the last link, the question of the scope of the rule that a contract to commit a tort upon a third party is illegal and void. Does that principle apply to all torts or only to some of them? The answer given by the authorities is, generally and without qualification, in favour of the first alternative, and, but for the doubts recently raised by Professor Winfield,[4] there ought to be little hesitation in accepting it. Just as there is no rigid limit to the range of possible torts, so there is no finality about the number of possible torts which when constituting the subject matter of a contract render it illegal and void. Undue importance need not be attached to the fact than any particular tort has not yet received judicial recognition as a cause of the illegality of the contract.

The attempt here made to establish a direct nexus between the doctrine of *Lumley* v. *Gye* and the invalidity of the contract to break a contract may seem to some unduly elaborate. The justification, if any, for this is that it is still necessary to bring into relief some of the consequences inherent in the doctrine of *Lumley* v. *Gye* but recognized only with reluctance, like its applicability to all contracts

---

[1] Italics are the writer's.   [2] [1902] 2 K.B. 732, at p. 737.

[3] If, on the other hand, stress is laid on the act of inducing prior to the conclusion of the second contract, it might possibly be argued that the contract is illegal as being the direct result or the consummation of the tort or the means of giving effect thereto. But see, for a possible corrective, *Holman* v. *Johnson* (1775), Cowper 341.

[4] *The Province of the Law of Tort* (1931), p. 84.

and the absence of active 'inducement' as separate from the conclusion of the new contract. It is difficult to deny that this interpretation of *Lumley* v. *Gye* may lead in the domain both of contract and tort to results which take one's breath away. But, subject to definite exceptions, that interpretation has been judicially recognized as inherent in that doctrine. It is too late to challenge it. The truth is that with the passage of years the doctrine of *Lumley* v. *Gye* has grown in stature. It continues, in a sense, the development begun with the extension of assumpsit to contracts – the development, that is to say, in which the instruments of the law of tort are used for the protection of contract. It signifies – parallel to the principles laid down in *De Mattos* v. *Gibson*,[1] *Tulk* v. *Moxhay*,[2] and the *Strathcona*[3] case – an addition, at the expense of the doctrine of privity of contract, to the legal protection of rights acquired by contract. It marks another step in the recognition of the property character of the contractual right. And, inasmuch as it expressly recognizes a right of the promisee not only against the promisor but also, in a specific sphere, against the whole world, it is not without some effect on the traditional distinction between rights *ad rem* and rights *in personam*. In view of this, the importance of its consequences for the question of the validity of contracts in breach of contract is almost trifling.

III

The first reason for the invalidity of the second inconsistent contract is, as we have seen, the fact that, so far as the 'inducing' party is concerned, the contract is a tortious act defined by *Lumley* v. *Gye* and on that account invalid under the general rule avoiding contracts constituting a tort. The second reason for invalidity has its source in the legal position and the acts of the 'induced' party, i.e. the author of the two inconsistent promises. His part in the new contract is the agreement to commit a breach of a prior contract; it is an agreement to commit an unlawful act, a civil injury. That civil injury is, from this point of view, committed principally and in the first instance by the party who has made the two inconsistent promises; the rôle of the 'inducing' third party is here a secondary one. It is generally admitted that a contract to inflict a civil injury upon a third party is illegal. Most authorities expressly refer to breach of contract as an example of such illegality.[4] It is a wrongful act to agree to break a

---

[1] See below, p. 365.   [2] See below, p. 359.   [3] See below, p. 359.
[4] See Pollock, *Principles of Contract*, 9th ed. (1921), p. 343: 'An agreement . . . to carry

contract. This is so, in the first instance, because to break a contract is in itself an unlawful act. In legal theory there is no warrant for the view that the obligation of the promisor is an alternative one, namely, either the promised performance or the duty to pay damages. Quite apart from the equitable and statutory remedies of specific performance and injunction, that view seems to be incorrect also so far as the common law is concerned. The point was put lucidly and emphatically by Lord Lindley in *South Wales Miners' Federation* v. *Glamorgan Coal Co., Ltd.*[1] He said:

> To break a contract is an unlawful act, or, in the language of Lord Watson in *Allen* v. *Flood*, 'a breach of contract is in itself a legal wrong'. The form of action for such a wrong is quite immaterial in considering the general question of the legality or illegality of a breach of contract. Any party to a contract can break it if he chooses; but in point of law he is not entitled to break it even on offering to pay damages. If he wants to entitle himself to do that he must stipulate for an option to that effect. Non-lawyers are apt to think that everything is lawful which is not criminally punishable; but this is an entire misconception. A breach of contract would not be actionable if nothing legally wrong was involved in the breach.

Other authority is not lacking in support of the same view.[2] The payment of damages is not fulfilment of the object of the contract; it is compensation for the unlawful act of its breach.[3] There is no

---

out some object in itself not unlawful by means of an apparent trespass, breach of contract, or breach of trust is unlawful and void'; Snell, *Principles of Equity*, 21st ed. by Rivington (1934), p. 547.

[1] [1905] A.C. 239, at p. 253.

[2] Pollock, *Jurisprudence*, 6th ed. p. 93, has pointed out that it is not impossible to regard a breach of contract 'as a wrong in the strictest sense, a trespass or deceit'. And he observes that the history of the common law substantiates that view. Mr Justice Holmes in a vivid passage suggests that to consider a breach of contract as an illegal act is to confuse legal and moral ideas. He says, relying on Lord Coke (*Bromage* v. *Genning*, I. Roll. Rep. 368): 'The duty to keep a contract at common law means a prediction that you must pay damages if you do not keep it – and nothing else' (*H.L.R.* 10 (1896–7), 462; also in *Collected Legal Papers*, edited by Laski (1920), p. 175). As mentioned, it is doubtful whether this view is in fact in keeping with the common law. It seems more accurate to assume that specific relief is as old as the action of damages (see Pollock and Maitland, *History of English Law*, 2nd ed., II, 595 *et seq.*). There is impressive evidence for holding that the refusal of common law courts to grant specific performance is a comparatively late development: see Barbour, 'The "right" to break a contract' in *Michigan Law Review*, 16 (1917), 106. See also Corbin in *Yale Law Journal*, 27 (1917–18), 363. And see a series of cases in which it was held that when the contract provides that the promisor shall pay a sum of money if he fails to perform the contract, he cannot escape performance by offering to pay the sum, but may be compelled by injunction to perform the contract specifically: *per* Lord St Leonards in *French* v. *Macale* (1842), 2 Dr. & War. 274; *Hardy* v. *Martin* (1783), 1 Cox 26; *Weston* v. *Managers of the Metropolitan Asylum District* (1882), 9 Q.B.D. 404; *Aliter*, if it is clear that, in the intention of the parties, the obligation is an alternative one: *Jones* v. *Green* (1829), Y. & J. 298.

[3] In fact it is mainly on the assumption that the breach of contract is an unlawful act that decisions like that in *Allen* v. *Flood*, [1898] A.C. 1, can be distinguished from those in

such thing in law as a conspiracy to break a contract but if it is unlawful to break a contract it cannot be less unlawful to agree to break a contract.

There is a second, and more concrete, reason for the unlawfulness of the second agreement arising out of the fact that the contemplated breach involves actual damage and, consequently, a civil injury to a third party. That damage may be infinitesimal, but even in that case the illegality of the breach will be penalized to the extent of awarding nominal damages.[1] The injury may, on the other hand, be a substantial one, and it may be of such a nature as to be entirely incapable of adequate redress by way of damages. The existing law relating to damages[2] (and, until recently,[3] interest) is not invariably such as to make it a matter of indifference to the creditor whether the contract will be fulfilled or whether he will receive damages. This inadequacy of damages is particularly conspicuous in cases, like those of contracts of personal service, in which the remedies of injunction or specific performance are not available. Moreover, the very fact of the conclusion of the second inconsistent contract is, independently of an accomplished breach of the prior contract, injurious to and, in principle, actionable at the suit of the first promisee on grounds which led to the adoption of the doctrine of anticipatory repudiation of contracts.[4] It is for these reasons that some will prefer to base the invalidity of the second contract on the fact that it contemplates an unlawful act aiming at the commission of a civil injury upon a third party rather than on its connection with the specific tort constituted by *Lumley* v. *Gye*. Actually, the difference between illegality arising out of the application in the doctrine of *Lumley* v. *Gye* and that grounded in the principle avoiding contracts to commit an unlawful act by inflicting a civil injury is probably that between the operation of a specific and a general rule.

IV

The main factor which renders it difficult to adopt the view that the second contract is invalid is the absence, with the partial exception of equitable jurisdiction,[5] of any judicial authority supporting that

which the inducement to break a contract was held to be tortious. The explanation is that in *Allen* v. *Flood* the action of the defendant was aimed at inducing conduct which was not unlawful.

[1] *Marzetti* v. *Williams* (1830), 1 B. & Ad. 415.
[2] See the rule in *Hadley* v. *Baxendale* (1854), 9 Ex. 341, at 354.
[3] See 24 & 25 Geo. 5, c. 41.   [4] See below, p. 360.   [5] See below, p. 361.

proposition. However, there is an explanation of the dearth of direct authority on the subject. The law, in avoiding certain categories of contracts to the point of rendering them unenforceable, pursues two objects: the first is to protect those injuriously affected by the contract; the second is the vindication of the law in general inasmuch as the courts find it repugnant to enforce contracts which are contrary to a legal prohibition, to morals, or to public policy. Contracts in breach of contract, although naturally obnoxious, are not tainted by a sufficient degree of turpitude to render the vindication of the law by means of emphatic unenforceability of the new contract a conspicuous and decisive feature of the situation. It has been submitted here that such contracts are in principle unenforceable. But if this be the law, it does not loom large in practice. This is so for the simple reason that the law has found manifold means of discouraging such contracts by giving adequate protection to the promisee of the first contract.

(a) In the first instance, there is, in appropriate cases, the remedy of injunction. The injunction to restrain a breach of contract is a recognized and well-developed branch of equitable jurisdiction. It includes cases in which the contemplated or accomplished breach is due to a subsequent inconsistent contract. That remedy renders the second contract nugatory and affords, at least for the time being, full protection to the original promisee. If A agrees to sell an estate to B, and subsequently agrees to sell it to C, B may restrain A by injunction from carrying out his (A's) contract with C. If A grants an option to B to purchase two jars of unusual rarity and beauty and subsequently agrees to sell the same jars to C who has knowledge of B's option, the court will, in principle, restrain A from completing the second agreement.[1] If A, an author, grants to publisher B an option for his next three books and then in disregard of the contract agrees with publisher C, who has notice of the option, to publish his next novel with him, the Court will restrain him from proceeding with the agreement.[2] The same applies generally to contracts concluded in breach of a valid prior contract if the relevant stipulation

---

[1] *Falcke* v. *Gray*, 4 Drew. 651. In *Heathcote* v. *North Staffordshire Ry.* (1850), 2 Mac. & G. 100, Cottenham L.C. doubted whether if A contracts with B to deliver goods at a certain time, equity will restrain A from doing anything which may prevent him from delivering the goods. He had no doubt that if A had agreed to sell an estate to B and then proposed to deal with it in a manner inconsistent with the contract, equity would interfere on the ground that, unlike the case of goods, B would by contract have obtained an interest in the estate itself. It is difficult to follow this reasoning. It is refuted by cases like *Falcke* v. *Gray* (4 Drew. 651) and *Donnell* v. *Bennett*, referred to below.
[2] *MacDonald* v. *Eyles* [1921] 1 Ch. D. 631.

of the first contract is negative in substance or in form[1] – with the exception of (not necessarily all[2]) contracts of personal service, which are governed by special considerations inherent in the nature and effectiveness of equitable remedies.[3] Moreover, the protection granted to the first promisee has gone to the length of disregarding the strictness of privity of contract and of granting injunctions not only upon the author of the two inconsistent promises but also on the person who induced the second promise so as to restrain him from taking advantage of the promisor's unlawful conduct. *Manchester Ship Canal Co.* v. *Manchester Racecourse Co.*[4] is an interesting example of this development and as this case is one of the rare instances of a general treatment of the question under discussion a detailed reference to it seems to be justified. A series of disputes between the two companies had been settled by an agreement including a clause that should the latter at any time in the future propose to use land or cause it to be used for other than racing purposes it should give the former the 'first refusal' thereof. Subsequently the defendants, without, as the Court found, effectively giving the plaintiffs the promised option, agreed to sell the racecourse for use for dock purposes to another company, the Trafford Park Company, who knew of the prior agreement. The Court not only granted an injunction restraining the defendant company from completing or carrying out the proposed sale but, relying on *Willmott* v. *Barber*,[5] in which Fry J. refused to enforce as between the parties an agreement in breach of a former contract, the Court held that, by an inverse application of the principle of *Willmott* v. *Barber*, it could restrain the intending purchaser from accepting a conveyance of the legal estate in breach of his vendor's prior contract. Farwell J. said:

If, as in *Willmott* v. *Barber*,[6] the Court refuses to grant specific performance of an agreement involving a breach of a prior contract with a third person,

---

[1] *Metropolitan Electric Supply Co., Ltd.* v. *Ginder* [1901] 2 Ch. 799.

[2] *Lumley* v. *Wagner* (1852), 1 De G. M. & G. 615.

[3] See, e.g. *Rely-A-Bell Burglar and Fire Alarm Co.* v. *Eisler* [1926] Ch. 609. The only reason why the Court declared itself unable to grant an injunction to restrain the new employer from continuing the employment of the defendant was that the ultimate result of a series of injunctions granted against each successive new employer would mean in effect decreeing specific performance of the contract of personal service. See also the interesting case *Gladstone* v. *Ottoman Bank* (1863), 1 H. & M. 505, in which, however, the Court refused to issue an injunction on the ground that the defendants were the agents of a foreign independent sovereign over whom the Court had no jurisdiction. The plaintiff asked the Court to restrain the execution of a contract made between the defendants and the Sultan of Turkey on the ground that the concession granted by him to the defendants was in contravention of a former contract granted by the Sultan to the plaintiff.

[4] [1900] 2 Ch. 352; [1901] 2 Ch. 37.   [5] See below.   [6] (1880), 15 Ch. D. 96.

why should it not by parity of reasoning say to a purchaser, 'You shall not aid or abet a breach of your vendor's prior contract with a third person so as to deprive that person of the estate for which he contracted'? I do not see any reason against interfering before conveyance to prevent such a breach of contract as that. The Trafford Park Company cannot complain, because they entered into the agreement with their eyes open . . . If they find that the Canal Company intervene and prevent the completion of their contract before they can get the legal estate, they have only themselves to thank for entering into a contract the completion of which would compel the Racecourse Company to commit a breach of a prior contract.[1]

The judgment of the Court of Appeal is equally instructive:

It seems to us to follow that one ought to treat this case on the basis of an action to restrain a breach of a contract threatened to be carried out in pursuance of a subsequent contract by the defendant with a third person having full knowledge of the first contract. . . If the action had been brought against the Racecourse Company, the party to the contract, alone, the injunction asked for could not have been granted without affecting the rights and interests of the Trafford Park Company. They are necessary parties to the action, just as Mr Gye was a necessary party to the action of *Lumley* v. *Wagner*.[2]

A further step in the same direction is the application of the same rule to executory contracts for the sale of chattels. Thus, for instance, in *Donnell* v. *Bennett*,[3] the Court granted an injunction not only against the defendant, named in the title of the case, to restrain him from selling fish except to the plaintiff in pursuance of an existing agreement; the injunction was sought for and granted against one Cormack to whom the defendant, in violation of the contract with the plaintiff, bound himself by a similar contract. The Court restrained Cormack from buying fish from the defendant.[4]

(b) There is, secondly, the remedy of specific performance which, again, in appropriate cases, will render the actual subject matter of the new contract impossible of execution and thus afford sufficient protection to the original promisee. Here again, there has asserted itself, not without some hesitation, the same tendency to protect the original promisee not only against the first promisor, but also against the new party to the second contract. If the latter acquires

[1] [1900] 2 Ch., at p. 367.
[2] *Per* Vaughan Williams L.J. delivering the judgment of the Court of Appeal [1901] 2 Ch. 37, at p. 51. The injunction was in fact granted also against Gye.
[3] (1883) 22 Ch. D. 835. For American cases see Vold in *H.L.R.* 41 (1927–8), 359, n. 73.
[4] *Ibid.*

the subject matter of the prior contract, with notice of it, his conscience is deemed to be affected by it and he can be made, jointly with the other defendant, a party to a suit for specific performance. Thus in *Potter* v. *Sanders*[1] the defendant contracted with the plaintiff for the sale to him of an estate which he afterwards conveyed to C who, at the time of the conveyance, had notice of the former contract. In an action for specific performance brought against Sanders and C both defendants were ordered to convey the estate to Potter and to pay the cost of the action. In a previous case – *Cutts* v. *Thodey*[2] – the Court refused in similar circumstances to grant a specific injunction against a stranger to the first contract. This summarily reported decision is generalized in Snell's *Principles of Equity*[3] as establishing the rule that the third party cannot properly be made a co-defendant in such cases. But *Cutts* v. *Thodey* was not only contrary to previous decisions; it was overruled in *Potter* v. *Sanders* and *Holmes* v. *Powell*.[4] It may now be regarded as established that, in suitable cases, a party to the second inconsistent contract, although a stranger to the first contract, may be made co-defendant in an action for specific performance of a contract for the sale of land.

(c) There is, thirdly, the operation of the doctrine of constructive trusteeship as laid down in *Lord Strathcona Steamship Co.* v. *Dominion Coal Co.*[5] In this and similar cases the second transaction is an out and out sale, but the position is not radically different from that of agreements to sell. The purchaser who acquires property under a contract with notice of a pre-existing contract restricting the use of the object acquired will, in some cases, be treated as a constructive trustee bound to give effect to the previous contract. The second contract is thus rendered inoperative – and the inconsistency removed, in fact, *ab initio* – in so far as it conflicts with the first, and the interests of the original promisee are fully protected. The doctrine of *Tulk* v. *Moxhay* gives effect, by means of an injunction, to the same principle in a different, and somewhat artificially restricted, sphere. The merits of the refusal of courts to extend the operation of these doctrines to chattels generally by way of what has been termed 'equitable servitudes on chattels' have been a matter of controversy.[6] However, this is not the place to inquire whether the dividing line between the cases recognizing in this connection the principle of

---

[1] (1846), 6 Hare 1.   [2] (1844), 1 Coll. 212, 223.
[3] 21st ed. by Rivington (1934), p. 536.   [4] (1856), 8 De G. M. & G. 572.
[5] [1926] A.C. 108.
[6] *Taddy & Co.* v. *Sterious & Co.* [1904] 1 Ch. 354; *McGruther* v. *Pitcher* [1904] 2 Ch. 306; *Dunlop Pneumatic Tyre Co., Ltd.* v. *Selfridge & Co., Ltd.* [1915] A.C. 847.

constructive trusteeship and those adhering with strictness to privity of contract is justified by considerations of convenience and caution rather than by logic.[1] For the purpose of the present inquiry it is sufficient to note that the principle of constructive trusteeship, as laid down in the *Strathcona* case and cognate cases, goes a long way in the direction of rendering inoperative the second transaction to the extent of its inconsistency with the first contract.

(d) There is, fourthly, the remedy available to the original promisee as the result of the operation of the doctrine of anticipatory repudiation of the contract. If A after having made a contract with B enters into a second and inconsistent contract with C, B may probably rely on *Hochster* v. *De La Tour* and sue A as soon as he is apprised, from whatever source, of the existence of the second contract. There are, it appears, no cases in the Law Reports in which the doctrine of anticipatory breach of contract was invoked *eo nomine* in connection with a second inconsistent contract, but there is no good reason why it should not apply to a contingency like this. Judges, it is true, have not been inclined to impute rashly to the party concerned a disposition to break the contract, but no violence is done to the doctrine of *Hochster* v. *De La Tour* by spelling out the noxious intention to break a contract from the clear fact of concluding a formal contract promising, in effect, to break the prior obligation. A cannot be allowed to plead that he may, after all, break his contract with C or obtain release. In the analogous cases in which a person by a subsequent sale or executed lease has put it out of his power to perform a former agreement, the courts have uniformly held that the chance of release from the second contract or of re-acquisition of the thing sold is too remote and hypothetical to upset the assumption of the repudiation of the first contract. This is shown by the various cases of impossibility created by a party before performance like *Ford* v. *Tiley*,[2] *Bowdell* v. *Parsons*,[3] *Lovelock* v. *Franklyn*,[4] *Omnium d'Entreprises* v. *Sutherland*.[5] Closely related as these cases are to the doctrine of anticipatory repudiation of a contract, they permit the inference that the immediate remedy of *Hochster* v. *De La Tour* might be available to the promisee of the first contract.

(e) There is, finally, the action for damages in contract against the promisor of the first contract and, at least in some cases, an action

---

[1] 'When the courts wish to enable the beneficiary to sue they make the promisor a trustee, and when they wish to prevent him from doing so they fall back on the shibboleth of privity of contract' (Winfield, *The Province of the Law of Tort* (1931), p. 107).
[2] B. & C. 325.   [3] 10 East 359.   [4] (1847), 8 Q.B. 371.
[5] [1919] 1 K.B. 618.

in tort, based on *Lumley* v. *Gye*, against the new party to the second contract who has induced a breach of the first.[1]

All these instances of the interference of courts with the effective operation of the second contract do not supply a direct answer to the question of the validity of the second contract. But they show in what ways the law fulfils the object of protecting the original promisee and of discouraging the inconsistent contract. Their cumulative effect is such as to explain why the question of the validity of the second contract as between the parties thereto is to some extent an academic one and why it has not produced a rich crop of cases in the law reports.

V

The only direct authority pointing to the, at least partial, unenforceability of the second inconsistent contract as between the parties to it will, not unnaturally, be found in equity. Courts of equity have refused to countenance the impropriety involved in the fact of a contract knowingly made by both parties with the view to interfering with the contractual rights acquired by a third party. In the first instance, it is well established that no specific performance will be granted to compel the defendant to perform a contract which it would be a breach of trust on his part to perform[2]; similarly, specific performance will be refused to the plaintiff if the contract was a breach of trust on his part. Thus in *Dunn* v. *Flood*[3] the purchasers of trust property were held to be entitled to rely on the fact

---

[1] It would thus appear that the second inconsistent contract creates yet another example of breaches of contract which constitute at the same time a tort. But the combination is here a peculiar one. While the fact of the second contract can, on the strength of *Hochster* v. *De La Tour*, be treated as a breach of contract on the part of A, the promisor in the first contract, the author of the *tort* is C, the new party to the contract, who by inducing it has brought himself within the rule of *Lumley* v. *Gye*. And see Vold, 'Tort aspect of repudiation of contracts' in *H.L.R.* 41 (1927–8), 340–76, who puts the question whether the repudiation of the contract by A is not a tort and gives reasons why it ought to be treated like one. The courts have not, of course, regarded it in that light, but if any anticipatory repudiation of contract is to be treated as a tort, this ought to apply in the first instance to anticipatory repudiation expressed in the conclusion of a second inconsistent contract. There is all the difference between anticipatory repudiation in cases where the promisor is unable to fulfil the contract and those in which, induced by a better offer, he deliberately incapacitates himself from fulfilling his obligation.

[2] *Ord* v. *Noel* (1820), 5 Madd. 438; *Wood* v. *Richardson* (1840), 4 Beav. 174; *Sneesby* v. *Thorne* (1855), 7 De G. M. & G. 399. And see as to contracts in fraud of a power, *Harnett* v. *Yielding* (1805), 2 Sch. & L. 549.

[3] (1885), 28 Ch. D. 586. See also *Rede* v. *Oakes* (1864), De G. J. & S. 505; *Dance* v. *Goldingham* (1873), L.R. 8 Ch. 902. But see now for certain modifications Trustee Act, 1925, 13. Also, agreements to indemnify trustees against purely nominal breaches of trust are treated as valid both in law and equity. Conveyance of property or the creation of a trust to defraud creditors are voidable (s. 172 (1) of the Law of Property Act) – and not void as before (13 Eliz. c. 5) – at the option of the person who is prejudiced thereby.

that the inclusion, by the trustees, of certain conditions of sale was contrary to their duty as trustees. 'How', asked Bowen L.J., 'can an unconscientious trustee be entitled to the assistance of the Court in carrying out out a contract which is a breach of trust?'

The refusal to enforce specifically the second inconsistent contract extends also to cases in which the first transaction is an agreement to sell. Thus in *Willmott* v. *Barber*[1] the Court refused to grant specific performance to compel the defendant to commit a breach of his prior covenant not to assign without licence. *Manchester Ship Canal Co.* v. *Manchester Racecourse Co.*[2] shows that *Willmott* v. *Barber* was not only regarded as good law but was also used as a starting point for further developments.

The fact that the second contract cannot be enforced by means of specific performance or injunction does not necessarily mean that it is altogether unenforceable. There may be no remedy in equity, but there may still be a remedy at law – a remedy which can now be given by a court normally exercising equitable jurisdiction. The Court may refuse specific performance of an option to purchase void for remoteness but will nevertheless, in the same action, grant damages for breach of contract.[3] It may refuse specific performance of a contract of personal service but it may, in the same judgment, fix the amount of damages or order an inquiry to ascertain them.[4] In fact, in *Willmott* v. *Barber*, Fry J., after refusing specific performance, said: 'As no case for substantial damages has been opened to me, I must dismiss the action altogether.' However, the general rule governing the matter is probably that laid down by Jessel M.R. in *Sykes* v. *Beadon*[5]: 'I think the principle is clear that you cannot directly enforce an illegal contract, and you cannot ask the Court to assist you in carrying it out. You cannot enforce it indirectly; that is, by claiming damages or compensation for the breach of it.' Undoubtedly in many cases a party who is unsuccessful in a suit for specific performance may sue at law for damages. But this is not invariably so; in particular it is not so where a party coming into equity submits the whole case to the jurisdiction of the Court.[6] Thus in the leading case, *Lord Tredegar* v. *Windus*,[7] Sir

---

[1] (1880), 15 Ch. D. 96.   [2] 2 Ch. 352; 2 Ch. 37.
[3] *Worthing Corporation* v. *Heather* [1906] 2 Ch. 532.
[4] See, for instance, *Rely-A-Bell Burglar and Fire Alarm Co.* v. *Eisler* [1926] Ch. 609.
[5] 11 Ch. D. 170.
[6] For a clear statement of the law, see *Phelps* v. *Prothero*, 7 D. M. & G. 722. See also *Brandlyn* v. *Ord*, 1 Atk. 571; *Peterborough* v. *Germaine*, 6 Bro. P.C. 1; *Moss* v. *Anglo-Egyptian Navigation Co.*, 2 Russ. & My. 1; *Reynolds* v. *Nelson*, 6 Madd. 290; *M'Namara* v. *Arthur*, 2 B. & B. 349, 353.   [7] L.R. 19 Eq. 607.

Charles Hall V.-C., after reviewing the authorities, laid down the rule that although 'in certain cases' the party who has failed to obtain specific performance may proceed at law, this is so 'only when the Plaintiff's so doing is not inconsistent with, and does not raise the same question as has been already dealt with by the Court of Equity'. It would appear, therefore, that when the Court refuses to grant the equitable remedy the position is in general as follows: in some cases the Court may expressly reserve the right of the plaintiff to pursue his remedy at law.[1] In others, even without such express authorization, the remedy at law is open when specific performance has been refused either for reasons, discretionary but not arbitrary, governing the granting of equitable remedies, or on account of a defence, like unfair dealing, which affords no answer in a court of law. But in the vast residuum of cases where the action is dismissed, without an award of damages, for reasons which would not be disregarded in a court of law the refusal of the equitable remedy must, unless the Court expressly reserves the right of redress at law, be regarded as finally disposing of the action.

VI

It is now necessary to consider the evidence pointing to the validity of the second inconsistent contract. Some of it may be disposed of without difficulty. This applies, for instance, to the numerous cases in which the Court, for reasons peculiar to the granting of the remedy, refuses to interfere by injunction or specific performance with the second inconsistent contract. Such refusal does not mean that the Court recognizes as valid the contract between the defendant and the party who has induced the new contract. The Court might say: 'We cannot compel you to perform your first contract; but we are certainly not going to assist you in breaking the prior contract by enforcing the new inconsistent agreement.' The fact that in cases of underselling the Court will not enforce against the sub-purchaser the covenants between the original vendor and the purchaser, does not necessarily mean that the sub-purchaser may not be liable for

---

[1] *Langmead* v. *Maple*, 18 C.B. (N.S.) 255; *Ord.* v. *Noel*, 5 Madd. 438; *Mortlock* v. *Buller*, 10 Ves. 292, 312. As according to the Judicature Act, 1873, § 124 (7), re-enacting in part the provisions of Lord Cairns' Act, 1858, referring to the award of damages in the Chancery Court, the High Court and Court of Appeal are authorized to grant in the same action all the remedies, legal or equitable, to which the parties appear to be entitled so that all matters in controversy between the parties may be finally decided, it would seem that the cases in question, in so far as they include no decision as to damages, show that the matter is at an end.

inducing a breach of contract or that the contract between the purchaser and the sub-purchaser is enforceable.

But there exist instances of inconsistent contracts which apparently will be enforced even if the new party knows of the prior conflicting contract. Thus when a tenant who is bound by a restrictive covenant not to sub-let or not to assign without the consent of the landlord assigns or sub-lets without having asked for the required consent, the assignment is nevertheless valid as between the tenant and the assignee even if the latter knew of the former contract – although, of course, the sub-demise or assignment is invalid as against the landlord. It is of no consequence whether the assignee or sub-tenant knew of the restrictive covenant. Similarly, prior to the Conveyancing Act, 1881, the mortgagor could not make a lease of his property. If he did the lease was valid as between himself and the lessee, but invalid against the mortgagee. However, cases like these may be explained in a number of ways. The most obvious of them is that, in the first example, in view of the landlord's inexorable right of forfeiture, the second contract cannot be regarded as conflicting with the covenants of the lease.[1] It must, if the assignee or sub-tenant knew of the covenant, be considered as having been made subject to the implied condition that the consent of the landlord will first be forthcoming.[2] The law removes any inconsistency *ab initio* by subjecting the rights acquired by the second transaction to the restrictions of pre-existing covenants. It does exactly the same, in a different sphere,

---

[1] In view of this the position would probably not be different if instead of an executed assignment or sub-lease we were confronted with an agreement to sub-let or to assign in violation of the covenants of the lease.

[2] It is by dint of some such explanation that it is possible to understand the manner in which an American court dealt with the following case: The defendant was a contractor under a contract for railway construction which provided that the constructors shall not be allowed to sub-contract without the permission of the railway company. He sub-let part of the work to the plaintiff without the consent of the railway company. Both parties to the second contract were aware of the clause in the principal agreement. The plaintiff performed part of the work, but was prevented by the railway company from completing it. He now sued to recover on the sub-contract. The defendant resisted the claim and asked for damages on the ground that the plaintiff failed to complete the performance of the contract. Neither party pleaded the invalidity of the second contract; nor was the question raised by the Court. The judgment was for the plaintiff on the ground that the failure to perform was excusable. 'As both parties had in view the contingency that performance might not be permitted by the railroad company, it was an implied part of their contract that if such were the result, both were to be released as to the future, but bound as to the past' (*Dolan* v. *Rogers*, 149 N.Y. 489). See also the observations of Sir Frederick Pollock added in the tenth edition (1936) of his *Principles of Contract*: 'An agreement conditional on M's consent to something for which that consent is required is of course good enough. Likewise A may well promise Z that he will do such a thing and for that purpose will procure M's consent. Whether a condition or undertaking of this kind can ever, in special circumstances, be implied, may be a question of some nicety' (p. 441).

through the operation of the doctrines of notice and constructive trusteeship as laid down in *Tulk* v. *Moxhay, De Mattos* v. *Gibson*,[1] and the *Strathcona* case.[2] In fact if the law had not shrunk, as it has done,[3] from following the same principles in regard to chattels generally and the subject matter of contracts of service, there would, in the great majority of cases, be no room for the inconsistency of the second contract. Both contracts would be perfectly consistent.

The same considerations apply, in inverse order, to the case of unregistered estate contracts and restrictive covenants entered into, after 1925, which are not binding upon the purchaser even if he has notice of them.[4] In this case there is no inconsistency for the reason that the unregistered estate contract does not confer enforceable rights against third persons to whom the land has been conveyed.[5]

Finally, there is the question of contracts of marriage and of promises to marry in breach of a previous promise to marry known to both parties. It is convenient to discuss these two separately while bearing in mind at the same time the fact that contracts of marriage and, to some small extent, promises to marry are creatures of both public and private law and that their importance for the law of contract in general is accordingly limited. The first question is whether the Court will enforce a promise to marry given in such circumstances. Curiously enough, there seems to be no decision bearing directly upon this particular matter. Sir John Salmond refers to two cases as substantiating the view that such promises are valid: *Caines* v. *Smith*[6] and *Short* v. *Stone*.[7] But neither of these is an authority for the proposition contended for. In both cases the second transaction was an actual marriage and not a promise to marry. In neither case was the Court concerned with the validity of the marriage; and in neither case was the question discussed, nor was it relevant to know, whether the person actually married had knowledge of the pre-existing engagement. Text-book writers freely state the rule that a pre-existing promise to marry will not invalidate a subsequent promise, and the reason given is that a person ought not to be

---

[1] 4 De G. & J. 276. [2] A.C. 108. [3] See above, p. 359.

[4] Prior to the Law of Property Act, 1925, such contracts were in equity binding upon the purchaser with notice.

[5] The situation might possibly be different if the second transaction is itself an agreement which, to the knowledge of both parties, is contrary to a previous and still subsisting unregistered estate contract relating to the same property. A question of this kind may arise as follows: A makes with B an agreement for a lease. That agreement is an estate contract within the meaning of the Law of Property Act, 1925. Neither party registers the agreement. B then agrees to sub-demise the property to C under conditions inconsistent with the covenants laid down in the agreement for the lease.

[6] (1846), 15 M. & W. 189. [7] (1846), 8 Q.B. (N.S.) 358.

allowed to avail himself of his own wrong.[1] But that statement does not cover, and is not intended to cover, cases in which not only the promisor but also the promisee of the second promise knew of the prior engagement.

The writer has found only one judicial pronouncement, clearly in the nature of an *obiter dictum*, to the effect that the second promise is valid in these circumstances: *Beachey* v. *Brown*.[2] This was an action for breach of promise to marry. The defendant pleaded that the promise was void on the ground that at the time when it was given the plaintiff was, to her knowledge *although not to the knowledge of the defendant*, bound by an agreement to marry another person. It was held, in accordance with the rule stated above, that the defendant was liable. But in the course of the short judgment of Hill J. there occurs the following passage: 'The defendant might be the very person who induced the plaintiff to break that contract, by winning her from her first love; it would be hard that he should be allowed to set that up as a reason for not performing his contract or paying damages for the breach of it.'[3] This *obiter dictum*, contemplating as it does a situation in which both parties know of the former promise, is the only authority for holding that the second promise is valid even if both parties know of the former promise. Possibly, or even probably, it is. But more convincing arguments than those given by Sir John Salmond are required in order to make that proposition plausible. The objection that otherwise 'he who had promised to marry one woman could never afterwards effectively promise to

---

[1] See e.g., Chitty on *Contracts*, 18th ed. (1930), p. 627.

[2] El. Bl. & El. 796; L.J.Q.B. 105.

[3] There is a passage in the judgment of Shearman J. in *Long* v. *Smithson*, 118 L.T. 678, which seems to support the same view, but that passage refers in fact only to the case of *continuing* a second inconsistent contract concluded without knowledge of the first. The learned judge said: 'If that [knowingly harbouring a servant] is to be extended to every kind of contract it produces remarkable results, and, as has been pointed out to us, it would enable a man who has been engaged to a lady who had jilted him to sue another person who married her. He would be guilty of an actionable wrong, because if he had promised to marry her, he would have prevented her performing the contract she had already made with the plaintiff.' And he expressed the opinion that the wrong of knowingly continuing an inconsistent contract must be confined to the relations between master and servant on which the relevant cases are based. This last conclusion is, perhaps, a *non sequitur*. Between master and servant cases and marriage contracts there is a vast territory of situations to which the law expressly adopted in *De Francesco* v. *Barnum* (1890), 45 Ch. D. 730, and *Smithies* v. *National Association of Operative Plasterers* [1909] 1 K.B. 310, can be applied. The difficulty alluded to by Mr Justice Shearman does not raise nor answer the question whether the disappointed suitor could bring an action against his successor if the latter knew of the pre-existing promise when he caused the lady to promise to marry him. This is obviously a case in which a court of law would refuse to apply the doctrine of *Lumley* v. *Gye*. This does not necessarily mean that the second promise is enforceable as between the new parties. Its invalidity may, as pointed out, have its source in the more general rule avoiding contracts to commit a wrong upon a third party.

marry another' is not too alarming. The second promise can be validly given if the promisee does not know of the pre-existing promise. The difficulty begins only when both parties know of the prior promise. Even in that case there is probably nothing to prevent them from marrying forthwith. But, it might be argued, with regard to a mere promise to marry, it is not altogether unreasonable to withhold from them the benefit of enforceability of the second promise which, to the knowledge of both of them, is a wrong upon a third party. Moreover, apart from the precariousness of the legal situation, the second promisee will be wise to insist on an immediate marriage. For, in the light of the experience of the less fortunate predecessor, what assurance is there that the second promise will be more sacrosanct than the first?

There still remains the question of a contract of marriage concluded in disregard of a promise to marry known to both parties. The law is, of course, that such a contract is valid. It has apparently been so treated in decided cases, and there are obvious grounds of public policy why it should be so. The contract of marriage constitutes a relation which is primarily one of public law. In so far as it is a transaction of a private character, it furnishes a good occasion for asserting the truism that there are limits to legal logic. There are contingencies to which the doctrine of constructive trusteeship cannot possibly apply. The contract of marriage is one of them.[1]

VII

It has been shown that the practical importance of the question of the validity of the contract to break a contract is distinctly limited. In some cases the law removes *ab initio* the very possibility of inconsistency as the result of the operation of the equitable doctrines of notice and constructive trusteeship. In others it blunts the edge of the second contract by dint of the remedies available to the first promisee against both parties to the new contract. But in the residuum of cases as well as in legal theory[2] the problem here raised,

---

[1] In the converse case of promise to marry made by a person already married the knowledge, on the part of the promisee, of the existing marriage is not without importance. If he (or she) knows of the marriage, the promise is not actionable; if he does not know, an action will lie (*Wild* v. *Harris* (1849), 7 C.B. 999; *Wilson* v. *Carnley* [1908] 1 K.B. 729; *Spiers* v. *Hunt* [1908] 1 K.B. 720).

[2] Sir William Holdsworth says with reference to the change incorporated by the recognition in *Lumley* v. *Gye* of the tortious character of interference with contractual relations: 'A new chapter of the greatest importance has been added to that branch of legal doctrine which is on the border line between contract and tort' (*History of English Law*, IV, 385). And see above, p. 367.

bearing as it does on mixed questions of contract and tort, is not without interest. In that residuum of cases the law, it has been submitted, is probably that the second contract is invalid and unenforceable between the parties thereto as the result of the operation of the doctrine of *Lumley* v. *Gye* and/or of the principle avoiding contracts whose object is the infliction of a civil wrong upon a third party. There are broader reasons of public policy urging the same solution. It is against public policy to permit the use of the instrument of contract for interfering with the rights of others: and it has been shown that such rights may be seriously and irreparably interfered with by the second contract notwithstanding the available remedies. At first sight, there is no suggestion of impropriety or immorality about the conduct of C who, knowing of the prior agreement, offers A a higher price for an article which A has already agreed to sell to B.[1] But this, surely, must be only the first impression.[2] Apart from the moral aspect, it is only the lack of appreciation of the property character of the contractual right which renders possible such indifference. Wealth and property consist not only in tangible things, but also in legitimate expectations in the fulfilment of legally binding promises. The law has in the last fifty years shown a marked tendency to implement the development from status to contract and to afford to contractual rights the same measure of recognition and protection as to other proprietary rights.[3] This process of implementing that tendency has been slow but persistent. Its slowness may well be measured by contrast with the jealous protection afforded to ownership and possession of things, of tangible property rights. An infringement, however innocent, of

---

[1] See, e.g., the observations of Sir John Fischer Williams in *Grotius Society*, 18 (1932), 122n. On the other hand, it may be argued that there is no fundamental difference between a contract to break a contract and a contract to defraud a creditor. As to the illegality and unenforceability of the latter there is, of course, no dispute.

[2] It may be possible to remove the stigma of impropriety from the second contract by construing it as being made under the implied condition that the consent of the first promisee would be forthcoming, but there are obvious limits to that charitable construction. See above, p. 364, n. 2.

[3] For an interesting example see *G. W. K., Ltd.* v. *Dunlop Rubber Co.*, 42 T.L.R. 376. In this case the plaintiffs successfully sued the defendant company which substituted their own tyres for those with which certain cars sent to an exhibition were fitted out in pursuance of a contract made between the first and second plaintiffs. The Court found that the defendants caused damage to the plaintiffs by interfering with existing contractual relations to which they were a party. This case shows the consequences which would follow from the acceptance of the view that the tort of interference with contractual relations does not extend to contracts other than those of personal service. It would mean that, in the present case, the Dunlop Company would have escaped liability if, knowing of the prior contract, they had removed the tyres in pursuance of an express contract with the first plaintiff.

ownership or possession will give rise to an action of damages in tort.[1] In the domain of the law of property the rule is paramount *nemo plus iuris ad alium transferre potest, quam ipse habet.* The two major exceptions to that rule, namely, those resulting from the separation of the legal from equitable ownership and of ownership from possession, are subject to the absence of notice in the acquiring party.[2] Even in market overt a person cannot acquire property over a thing which he knows belongs to someone other than the vendor. A person knowingly acquiring converted goods may be sued without a demand as a joint tortfeasor. In all these cases the contracts are illegal and although property may pass as between vendor and purchaser the law will do nothing to enforce such contracts as between them. With this strictness of the law there must be contrasted the tardiness in the recognition of the rule that a person cannot validly by contract acquire enforceable contractual rights[3] which by virtue of a prior agreement, of which he has notice, belong to someone else. The property character of such rights is being increasingly recognized[4] in the teeth of the still powerful hold of the dogma of privity of contract, and there seems to be good reason for revealing all the implications of that development.

One of these implications is the unenforceability, as a broad rule, of contracts to break a contract. It is only by the application of that principle that the law can avoid the unedifying spectacle of enforcing, be it only by way of damages, agreements which it treats as torts and which it prevents the parties from fulfilling, at the suit of the injured party, either by injunction or in consequence of a decree of specific performance of the first contract. Law is not a system of logic, but

---

[1] *Hollins* v. *Fowler* (1875), L.R. 7 H.L. 757.

[2] But while a person cannot as a rule convey to another ownership of property which he does not own, he may validly agree to convey such property in the future. The rule *nemo dat qui non habet* does not apply here. It does not matter that the promisor in the second contract has promised something which he does not possess and which he is not in a position to acquire at will. It is axiomatic that impossibility due not to the nature of the performance but to the substantive inability of the promisor to fulfil the promise is irrelevant for the validity of the contract. There is no difference in this respect between the legal and equitable remedies. See Fry, *On Specific Performance*, 6th ed. by Northcote (1921), p. 464. However, the position is different if an agreement to convey a thing which the promisor does not own is in breach of an agreement by which he is still bound and of which the purchaser has notice.

[3] See e.g., the dissenting judgment of Romer L.J. in *Corbett* v. *South Eastern and Chatham Railways Managing Committee* [1906] 2 Ch. (C.A.) 12, where the *dicta* seem to suggest that, even if the plaintiff had known of the clause in a prior contract binding upon the defendant and inconsistent with the new contract concluded between the plaintiff and the defendant, that would not render the plaintiff's contract void.

[4] The judgments in *National Phonograph Co.* v. *Edison–Bell Consolidated Phonograph Co.* ([1908] 1 Ch. 335) are a significant expression of that tendency. See also Markby, *Elements of Law*, 6th ed. (1905), p. 320.

there is more than a question of *symmetria iuris* involved in the (hypothetical) situation in which the Court helps Mr Gye to recover damages from Miss Wagner for breach of an agreement which the same or another Court restrained her from fulfilling for reasons of which both Gye and Miss Wagner had notice when they made the agreement in question. There is nothing pedantic in the insistence that the law shall not assist a person in enforcing what is in effect a conspiracy to commit a legal wrong upon a third person. It would be unsatisfactory if it were otherwise.

Undoubtedly if that is the law the consequences may frequently be startling and embarrassing. The idea that, if A agrees to sell to B the entire output of his factory for the next two years and then, tempted by a better offer from C, who knows of the former agreement, agrees to sell to him the same output for the same two years – the idea that neither C nor B can enforce the second contract and that C is in addition liable in tort strikes one as unduly far-reaching. It is no less far-reaching in the domain of contracts of service, or those relating to underselling, or generally restricting the user of chattels. But it still remains to be proved that it is bad law. The proper approach, it is believed, is to accept the view that the second inconsistent contract is illegal and unenforceable and to inquire what exceptions courts[1] or statute[2] have already engrafted upon that rule, what further exceptions courts ought or are likely to admit with regard to various categories of contracts, and what is the best way of disposing of the difficulties arising out of its application.[3]

[1] As, e.g., in cases in which the vendor had obtained the legal estate without notice of the restrictive covenant (*Wilkes* v. *Spooner* [1911] 2 K.B. 473; *Harrison* v. *Forth* (1695), Prec. Ch. 51); or where a servant acting *bona fide* within the scope of his authority procures the breach of a contract between his employer and a third person (*Said* v. *Butt* [1920] 3 K.B. 497); or where the prior contract was itself in breach of a former contract (*Smithies* v. *National Association of Operative Plasterers* [1909] 1 K.B. 310, at p. 337); or where the matter is subject to section 3 of the Trade Disputes Act, 1906; or where the first contract is, for reasons of morality and public policy, unworthy of protection (*Brimelow* v. *Casson* [1924] 1 Ch. 302).

[2] As, for instance, in the case of purchases by a public body under the Land Clauses Consolidation Act, 1845.

[3] Some of them may be mentioned here: If the second contract is void *ab initio*, is the vice fundamental so that it cannot be purged by a subsequent discharge of the first contract with the concurrence of the first promisee? Can A, the promisor of the first contract, be sued for damages not only in contract, but also in tort as joint tortfeasor, the principal tortfeasor being C who induced the breach of contract (just as in the case of conversion if the transferee is aware of the defect of the transferor's title he is a joint wrongdoer and is liable without a demise)? What is the position if the second contract conflicts only in part with the first? Do the ordinary rules as to severability apply? What is the position if only C, the inducing party, but not A, the promisor, knows of the inconsistency? How far does the rule as to knowingly harbouring the servant of another apply to executory contracts entered into without knowledge of the prior contract but continued with knowledge of such contract (see p. 366, n. 3 above)?

NOTE ON FRENCH, GERMAN, AND INTERNATIONAL LAW

In view of the general jurisprudential interest of the question discussed in this article the following comparative note may perhaps prove helpful:

The invalidity of the second inconsistent contract[1] seems, in French Law, to follow from the provisions of the *Code Civil* governing the conditions of the validity of contracts. Article 1131 lays down that a promise in return for an unlawful consideration has no legal effect; according to Article 1133 the consideration is unlawful if it is prohibited by law, or contrary to morality or public order. The principal decision on the matter is that of the Court of Cassation of 23 October 1912 in *Deutsche Celluloid Fabrik* v. *Schmerber* (Sirey (1913), I, 259). It was held there that a contract of service between the plaintiff and the defendant, an employee of a factory, made in disregard of a contract which, to the knowledge of both parties, was binding on the defendant, was void. A contrary decision of the Court of Cassation given in 1890 (*Belaval* v. *Saint-Pé*) must therefore be regarded as overruled (Sirey (1890), I, 193, with a note by Labbé which will well repay reading). It is by reference to Articles 1131 and 1133 that Planiol and Ripert (cited below, VI, 331) summarize, without qualifications, the legal position to the effect that a contract is void 'as between the contracting parties if its object is to commit a fraud on a third party or if it implies, to the knowledge of both parties, a breach of an obligation of one of them in regard to a third party'. In addition, French law, like English and German law, discourages the second inconsistent contract by imposing a liability in tort upon the third party inducing a breach of the first contract.[2] The liability is grounded in that living fountain of what may be called the French law of tort – Article 1382 of the *Code Civil*: 'Any act whatsoever done by any person and causing damage to another obliges him by whose fault the damage was caused to repair it.' It is by reference to that Article that a doctrine similar to that of *Lumley* v. *Gye* has been adopted in French law. The jurisprudence of the Court of Cassation in this matter is well established (see, e.g. *Doeuillet* v. *Randnitz*,

---

[1] The question seems only recently to have attracted the attention of French writers. Aubry and Rau, in a note inserted in the 1920 edition of their work (cited below), refer to it as 'cette question curieuse, qui donne un intérêt nouveau à la distinction célèbre de la faute délictuelle et de la faute contractuelle' (VI, 338). See also Ripert, *La règle morale dans les obligations civiles*, 3rd ed. (1935), § 170.

[2] On this aspect of the question see Hugueney, *De la responsabilité du tiers complice de la violation d'une obligation contractuelle* (1910) – a monograph which may be fittingly used as a starting point for a comparative study of the doctrine of *Lumley* v. *Gye*.

Sirey (1910), I, 118). Moreover, it is of interest in view of what has been submitted above (see p. 351) that French courts expressly rule out the element of active inducement as a condition of tortious action: 'It is not necessary that the defendant should have personally induced the breach of the contract; it is enough if he dealt with him [the servant] knowing that he was bound by a previous contract' (judgment of the Court of Besançon of 13 November 1911, Sirey (1912), II, 166). A representative selection of cases will be found in Planiol and Ripert, *Traité pratique de droit civil français* (1930), VI, 809, 810, and Aubry and Rau, *Cours de droit civil français* (1920), VI, 338, 339. It is also established that the liability under Article 1382 covers not only inducement to break contracts of service,[1] but contracts generally (Planiol and Ripert, VI, 809, 810). Thus, for instance, a sub-purchaser from a vendor bound by a price-fixing agreement is in such case liable under Article 1382: see *Dalloz* (1905), II, 394, and Sirey (1921), I, 158 (*Beaujoint* v. *Lagrillière*). But the law goes beyond securing redress from the inducing party. It will in proper cases declare the invalidity of the second contract at the instance of the injured party. This is accomplished by means of the remedy of the Paulian action derived directly from the *actio Pauliana* (Dig. 42. 8) and grounded in Article 1167 of the Code. That Article lays down that creditors 'may, in their own names, impeach acts done by their debtor in fraud of their rights'. Thus, in what may be regarded as the leading case in the matter (*Josserand* v. *Leclère*, Sirey (1906), II, 242, with an exhaustive note by Bourcart), the Court found that an agreement of sale involving, to the knowledge of both parties, a breach of a former contract with a third party who had an option in respect of the property bargained to be sold, not only gave that party a right of damages, but could itself be pronounced to be invalid as the result of the combined effect of Articles 1167 and 1382. The decision of the Court of Cassation of 15 April 1902 in the case *Grand Bazars* v. *Teyssèdre* is to the same effect (Sirey (1902), I, 316).

In German law the *sedes materiae* is in Articles 138, which avoids juristic acts which are *contra bonos mores*, and 826, which lays down that one who wilfully causes damage to another in a manner *contra*

---

[1] In regard to contracts of service these decisions have now been given statutory form in Article 23 of chapter I of the *Code de Travail* as amended in February 1932. That Article provides: 'If a servant, after having wrongfully broken his contract, makes a new contract with another employer, the latter is jointly responsible for the damage caused to the former employer: (1) if it is proved that he took part in the enticement; (2) if he enticed a servant who, to his knowledge, was already bound by another contract; (3) if he continued to employ the servant after learning that he was still under a contract with another employer.

bonos mores is bound to compensate him for the damage. By reference to the latter Article German courts have given numerous decisions the total effect of which seems to justify the conclusion reached in the leading commentary of Staudinger that the inducing of a breach of contract falls 'without doubt' within the terms of Article 826 (Staudinger, *Kommnentar zum bürgerlichen Gesetzbuch*, 9th ed. by Loewenfeld and Riezler (1925), *Recht der Schuldverhältnisse*, II, Part III, 1825).[1] And as inducing a breach of contract is thus, as a rule, stigmatized as being *contra bonos mores*, it is not surprising that the Reichsgericht has in a number of cases treated the second contract as invalid under Article 138. The leading decision is that given in 1912 in the case of *S. R.* v. *Bayerische Bierbrauerei zum Karlsberg* (*Decisions of the Reichsgericht in Civil Matters*, 79, 279). In this case the plaintiff, in return for a money consideration, agreed to join a combine of brewers formed with the view of raising the price of beer. The agreement provided, *inter alia*, that the parties shall not, 'regardless of any prior contract by which they may be bound', supply beer to any publican who refuses to recognize the higher prices as fixed by the brewers. It was also provided that should any of the parties find himself compelled to pay damages on account of the failure to fulfil the prior contracts, such damages shall be paid out of a joint fund of the combine. In an action on the agreement brought by the plaintiff, the Reichsgericht, upholding the judgment of the Court below, found that the agreement was unenforceable as being void within the meaning of Article 138. The Court said: 'A general undertaking to break a former contract is immoral even if the promisor recognizes his duty to pay damages and makes provision for that contingency.' For, the Court said, no one can be compelled to forgo his contractual rights and accept damages. In another decision, given in 1924, the Reichsgericht held that if in similar circumstances C acquires from A goods which A, to C's knowledge, had already agreed to sell to B, the latter is entitled to demand that C hand over the goods to him (*S. L.* v. *B. & R.*; *Decisions of the Reichsgericht in Civil Matters*, 108, 58). The Court refused to follow a former decision of the Reichsgericht which laid down that the only remedy available to C in such circumstances was a claim for damages.

---

[1] See also Hein, 'Die Verleitung zum Vertragsbruch nach B.G.B.' in Leonhard's *Studien zur Erläuterung des Bürgerlichen Rechts*, Part 18 (1906), and Kiss, 'Die Verleitung zum Vertragsbruch', in *Deutsche Juristen Zeitung* (1906), pp. 684 *et seq.* But see, for a qualification of the view expressed in Staudinger, the important commentary entitled *Das Bürgerliche Gesetzbuch* (1923) and edited, *inter alios*, by a number of the judges of the Reichsgericht (1, 1118).

Staudinger's commentary lays down without hesitation the rule that a promise to break a contract is in principle void in the meaning of Article 138 (1, 576).

In international law the question of the validity of treaties inconsistent with former treaties binding on either or both parties is of special significance inasmuch as treaties constitute the bulk of the growing and changing Law of Nations. They fulfil the function not only of contracts in private law, but, in a sense, of statutes laying down general rules of conduct. The opportunities for authoritative judicial determination of the question of the validity of the second inconsistent treaty are naturally rare in the international sphere. The results reached in this matter by a comparative study of the principal systems of law are therefore not without importance for international law seeing that the Permanent Court of International Justice is by Article 38 of its Statute empowered to rely on 'general principles of law recognized by civilized nations'. In a recent case before that Court (the *Oscar Chinn* case, *P.C.I.J.* Series A/B, no. 63), Judges Van Eysinga and Schücking expressed the view, in a dissenting opinion, that the Convention of St Germain of 1919 relating to the Congo was void between its signatories as it modified the General (Berlin) Act of 1855 without the assent of all the signatories thereto. (The judgment of the majority of the Court did not deal with this aspect of the case.) In 1917 Costa Rica and Salvador brought an action before the Central American Court of Justice on account of the violation by Nicaragua of her treaties with these two States by a treaty concluded with the United States. The Court, for purely jurisdictional reasons, declared itself unable to pronounce on the validity of the treaty in question (*A.J.* 11 (1917) 228). Writers of authority (see, e.g., Oppenheim, *International Law*, 4th ed. by McNair, 1 (1928), 713) have expressed the view that the second inconsistent treaty is invalid. But this view is not unchallenged. See, for example, Sir John Fischer Williams in *Grotius Society*, 18 (1932), 122; *Harvard Research* (1935), III, 1016–29. The author of the present article has elsewhere expressed the view that there are cogent reasons against the exclusion from the international sphere of a principle generally recognized in the law of contract; that the shock to the unity of law resulting from the recognition of the validity of the second inconsistent transaction would be specially serious in the international sphere where treaties are relatively few and a matter of general knowledge; that the remedy of damages for the breach of the prior treaty must as a rule be inadequate among States; and that the recognition of the validity of the subsequent inconsistent treaty must tend to discredit international law by reducing treaties to conflicting makeshifts of political expediency (see pp. 337 and 326 above). In view, however, of the requirement of unanimity in the international sphere the rule postulating the invalidity of the second inconsistent treaty must be subject to suitable modifications so as to prevent a beneficent legal principle from becoming a source of absurdity and of obstruction of the peaceful process of international change.

SECTION 4

FORM AND PUBLICITY

.

CHAPTER 17

WRITTEN FORM

Editor's note   This material is taken from the 1953 Report. In the Vienna Convention the requirement that a treaty be in writing is contained in the definition of 'treaty' in Article 2(1) as an international agreement concluded 'in written form'. Moreover, in the Vienna Convention Article 4 expressly provides that the fact that the convention does not apply to agreements not in written form shall not affect the legal force of such agreements.

ARTICLE 17

WRITTEN FORM

An agreement is void as a treaty unless reduced to writing.

Comment

1. There is slight – and occasionally exotic[1] – authority in support of the view that a treaty may be the result of an oral agreement. It is not certain to what extent certain passages in the judgment of the Permanent Court of International Justice in the case of *Eastern Greenland* (*P.C.I.J.* Series A/B, no. 53, pp. 69, 70) can be regarded as supporting that view. It is probable that, as the fact and the contents of the oral declaration made, in that case, by the Norwegian Minister for Foreign Affairs were not disputed, the Court did not address itself to that question at all. It appears also that the declaration was recorded simultaneously with its oral transmission. In view of this no decisive importance need be attached to the observation of Judge Anzilotti in his dissenting opinion that 'there does not seem to be any rule of international law requiring that agreements of this kind must necessarily be in writing, in order to be valid' (*ibid.* pp. 91, 92). In the *Kulin* case decided in 1927 by the Roumanian–Hungarian Mixed Arbitral Tribunal the latter refused to recognize the binding force of alleged verbal engagements, as recorded in the minutes of a

---

[1] See for example, the agreement referred to by Grotius between Mithridates and Sulla in 84 BC (Grotius, Book II, Ch. xvi, § xxx); between King Ludwig and King Charles the Bald in 870, referred to in Bittner, *Die Lehre von den völkerrechtlichen Urkunden* (1924), p. 4; and an arrangement for an alliance between Peter the Great and Frederick III in 1697, Elector of Brandenburg (von Martens, *Traité de droit international*, translated Leo (1883), p. 541).

conversation, made by Hungary (*Recueil des décisions des tribunaux arbitraux mixtes*, VII, 38). In the arbitral award given in 1889 in the dispute between Germany and Great Britain concerning a concession on the Island of Lama the Arbitrator, in declining to attach importance to an alleged oral statement of the Sultan of Zanzibar declaring his immediate readiness to grant a concession, expressed the view that 'although there is no law which prescribes a written form for agreements between States, it is nevertheless contrary to international usage to contract orally engagements of this nature and character'. In the course of the Manchurian dispute between Japan and China, the former relied on a 'protocol' consisting of the minutes of conversations between the Chinese and Japanese representatives in Peking in 1905 in which China agreed not to construct railways in certain districts of Manchuria. China contended that the 'protocol', which was never incorporated in a formal treaty, consisted of an 'arbitrary selection' of various Articles of provisional understandings embodied in the daily records of the conference. The Lytton Commission of Inquiry in its Report of 4 September 1932 treated the 'protocol' as a binding agreement having the force of a 'formal commitment' although the results of the conversations were not subsequently embodied in the treaty.

2. Whatever may be the interpretation of the above inconclusive incidents and pronouncements, it is submitted that a code of the law of treaties must expressly lay down the requirement of written form as a condition of their validity. In view of the conflicting conclusions which can be drawn by reference to such rare authority as there exists on the subject, it is of little importance whether the requirement of writing as a condition of validity of treaties is regarded as being *de lege lata* or *de lege ferenda*. The decisive consideration in favour of the solution adopted in the present article is: (i) that international precedents suggesting that oral agreements are binding as treaties are but few, insignificant and controversial; and (ii) that it is desirable, having regard to the security and certainty of international transactions and to the significance of their subject matter, that treaties be recorded in writing. Treaties to which States and international organizations are parties are concerned with matters of importance. Within the State the law provides uniformly that certain types of important contracts should be in writing or an even more solemn and recorded form. It is an obvious requirement of the certainty and the convenience of international intercourse that this should be so invariably in the case of treaties. At a time when the

additional requirement of registration is in most treaties regarded as a condition of their enforceability before the organs of international society (see Article 18), the mere requirement of writing is a self-evident minimum.[1] This statement is not inconsistent with the occasional and still surviving practice of so-called 'verbal notes' which are, in point of fact, neither *verbal* nor instruments constituting agreements. They are communications transmitted and recorded in writing.[2] It is significant that practically all unofficial and official drafts or Codes of the Law of Treaties postulate written form as a condition of the validity of treaties. Article 2 of the Havana Convention of Treaties of 20 February 1928 lays down that 'the written form is an essential condition of treaties'.[3]

3. The rule that an oral undertaking does not constitute a treaty does not necessarily signify that, on occasions, it may not result in the creation of an international obligation. For international obligations may be created by acts other than treaties such as, for instance, the declarations of or conduct by agents in the course of oral proceedings before international tribunals.[4] Such declarations made by authorized agents have frequently been regarded by the Permanent Court of International Justice and its successor as binding upon the parties. But this does not mean that such acts are treaties.

4. The principle formulated in Article 17 according to which writing is a condition of the validity of the treaty does not signify that any special requirement of form or formality attaches to the requirement of writing. What matters is the existence of a record of the agreement – provided that such record does not emanate exclusively from one of the parties. Thus the minutes of a conference or of a meeting recording the agreement of the parties or a recorded

---

[1] J. W. Garner, who generally favoured the view that oral agreements are binding, stated that 'it is not easy to see how parties to an oral treaty can comply with this requirement [of registration]' (*A.J.* 27 (1933), 494).

[2] See for example, the verbal note of 1 March 1948 by which the Czechoslovak Government in pursuance of Article 10 of the Peace Treaty with Roumania notified the Roumanian Government of those pre-war bilateral treaties between the two countries which Czechoslovakia desired to keep in force. The communication, registered in the *U.N.T.S.* (26, 112), ends with the request to the Roumanian Minister of Foreign Affairs 'to acknowledge the receipt of the present verbal note'.

[3] See also Field's draft, Article 188; Bluntschli's draft, Article 422; Fiore's draft, Article 744; Pessoa's draft, Article 200; the draft of the International Commission of American Jurists, Article 2.

[4] See for example, *Mavrommatis* case (*P.C.I.J.* Series A, no. 5, p. 37); *Upper Silesian* case (*ibid.* Series A, no. 7, p. 13); *Free Zones* case (*ibid.* Series A/B, no. 46, pp. 170, 172); case of *Société commerciale de Belgique* (*ibid.* Series A/B, no. 78, p. 178); *Corfu Channel* case (*I.C.J. Reports* 1949, pp. 24, 25).

unilateral declaration accepted by the other party may be sufficient for the purpose. The fact that such unilateral declaration, duly recorded, took originally the form of an oral declaration is irrelevant.[1] The same applies essentially to cases in which the written agreement is stated to constitute the acceptance of proposals made verbally[2] or in confirmation of an oral agreement.[3]

[1] See the oral declaration made at the signing of the Anglo-Egyptian Treaty of Alliance of 1936 (*Parliamentary Papers: Egypt*, no. 1 (1936)) It is probable that the Oral Declaration of the Norwegian Foreign Minister and the 'protocol' relating to the Manchurian railway, both referred to above in paragraph 1 of this comment, belong to this category. And see note 5 following upon the comment to Article 2 above on *memoranda of understandings constituting an agreement, agreed combined statements*, and the like.

[2] As in the Exchange of Notes of 18 and 19 December 1922 between the Netherlands and Roumania (*L.N.T.S.* 14, 191).

[3] As in the Exchange of Notes of 23 March 1944 between the United Kingdom and Turkey (*U.N.T.S.* 2, 227).

CHAPTER 18

REGISTRATION

Editor's note This material is taken from the 1953 Report. Although Lauterpacht's draft Article reflects directly the terms of Article 102(2) of the Charter of the United Nations, the Vienna Convention contains no corresponding provision on the effect of a failure to register. The matter is dealt with only in Article 80:

Registration and publication of treaties

1. Treaties shall, after their entry into force, be transmitted to the Secretariat of the United Nations for registration or filing and recording, as the case may be, and for publication.

2. The designation of a depositary shall constitute authorization for it to perform the acts specified in the preceding paragraph.

ARTICLE 18

REGISTRATION

Treaties entered into by Members of the United Nations subsequent to their acceptance of the Charter of the United Nations cannot be invoked by the parties before any organ of the United Nations unless registered, as soon as possible, with the Secretariat of the United Nations.

Comment

1. This Article does no more than reproduce the substance of Article 102 of the Charter of the United Nations. It is not certain to what extent, in its present formulation, it has a direct bearing on the question of validity of treaties. For Article 102 does not lay down that treaties which have not been registered are invalid. It merely provides that they cannot be invoked before any organ of the United Nations. This means substantially – though not inevitably – that they cannot be enforced before any organ of the United Nations. As enforceability is the hallmark of validity, the effect is that such treaties are, to that extent, invalid.

2. It may be said, in reliance upon the wording of Article 102, that there is nothing to prevent an organ of the United Nations from

applying a non-registered treaty if the latter is not invoked by the parties. Any such argument is believed to be a refinement. If a non-registered treaty is likely to be of advantage to one party, it will be 'invoked' by the other in order to prevent its application. Moreover, it is believed that an accurate – as distinguished from a literal – interpretation of this provision of the Charter is that a non-registered treaty cannot be *applied* by an organ of the United Nations (and not merely that it cannot be invoked before an organ of the United Nations).[1]

3. The Article as drafted does not prevent non-member States from registering treaties concluded either between themselves or with Members of the United Nations. No such limitation follows from the terms of the Charter. In fact, as the consequences of non-registration of a treaty to which a Member of the United Nations is a party may adversely affect contracting parties who are not members, it is proper that they should be permitted to register treaties concluded by them and it is in their interest that they should avail themselves of that facility. The practice of the United Nations has been in accordance with that view.[2]

4. The term 'treaties' used in Article 18 is here intended to be identical with the expression 'every treaty and every international agreement' used in Article 102 of the Charter and to cover the entire field of treaties in the meaning of Article 2 of the present draft.[3]

Note

1. The present Article, in so far as it reproduces substantially an Article of the Charter of the United Nations, seems to be out of place in a general codification of the law of treaties applicable, in principle, to all States. However, it has been deemed proper to include it in the present draft for the reason that, as stated elsewhere (comment to Articles 1 and 12), the Charter must be regarded in some ways as an expression of general international law; that, in the matter of

---

[1] For an expression of a somewhat different view on the subject see Brandon in *B.T.* vol. 29 (1952).

[2] See the following comment in the Report of the Rapporteur of Committee IV/2 of the San Francisco Conference in the matter of paragraph 2 of Article 102: 'This provision also covers treaties and agreements to which both Members and non-members are parties. It is open to the latter to have such treaties or agreements registered. Moreover, it is necessary that they should be able to do so, seeing that their right to invoke the treaty or agreement before an organ of the organization is made subject to registration' (*United Nations Conference on International Organization*, 13, 706).

[3] The subject is discussed by Brandon in an article entitled 'Analysis of the Terms "Treaty" and "International Agreement" for Purposes of Registration under Article 102 of the United Nations Charter' and published in *A.J.* 47 (1953), 49–69.

registration of treaties the effects of the Charter extend – not improperly – to States which are not members of the United Nations (see below, note 2); and that the reasons which have led to the adoption of Article 102 as well as of the corresponding Article 18 of the Covenant of the League of Nations are of general validity (see below, note 3).

2. No legal impropriety attaches to a rule which affects with unenforceability – so far as organs of the United Nations are concerned – non-registered treaties the parties to which are non-member States. No obligation of registration is imposed upon such States. The Charter – and the present Article – merely provide that if a non-member State desires to be in the position to invoke a treaty before the organs of the United Nations it must avail itself of the opportunity offered to it to register the treaty. Moreover, a non-member State, when concluding a treaty with a Member of the United Nations, must be deemed to be affected with the knowledge of the provision of the Charter which requires registration as a condition of enforceability before the organs of the United Nations. To that extent the contractual capacity of Members of the United Nations is limited. Non-members enter into treaty relations with Member States with the full knowledge of that limitation. They are in the position, by availing themselves of their right to register the treaty, to safeguard themselves against its consequences.[1]

3. The reason for viewing the principle of registration as an incipient rule of general international law is particularly cogent if it is considered that the principle of registration – and subsequent publication – is a principle adopted in the general interest of the international community, of certainty of international intercourse, and of the authority and effectiveness of treaties within such spheres, for instance, as that covered by Article 16 of the present draft relating to consistency of treaties with prior treaties. The importance of that principle was stressed in a memorandum approved in 1920 by the Council of the League of Nations, in a passage which merits quotation:

Publicity has for a long time been considered as a source of moral strength in the administration of national law. It should equally strengthen the

---

[1] The somewhat restrictive interpretation, in this respect, of the corresponding provision of the Covenant of the League of Nations by the President of the French–Mexican Claims Commission in the *Pablo Nájera* case (*Annual Digest* (1927–8), case no. 271) can partly – but only partly – be explained by the manner in which the fact of non-registration of the French–Mexican Claims Convention of 1924, which established the Commission, was relied upon by Mexico.

laws and engagements which exist *between nations*. It will promote public control. It will awaken public interest. It will remove causes for distrust and conflict. Publicity alone will enable the League of Nations to extend a moral sanction to the contractual obligations of its Members. It will, moreover, contribute to the formation of a clear and indisputable system of International Law. (*L.N.O.J.* (1920), p. 154.)

It was by reference to these considerations that Judge Hudson, when commenting upon the registration of treaties by the United States with the League of Nations, spoke of 'the general benefit to be derived from the provision of Article 18 of the Covenant' (*A.J.* 28 (1934), 345).

4. While the present Article, following Article 102 of the Charter, makes it possible for Members of the United Nations to invoke a non-registered treaty before a tribunal or body other than an organ of the United Nations, the practical importance of the remedy thus left open is insignificant. As a rule, apart from any treaty conferring obligatory jurisdiction upon a tribunal other than the International Court of Justice, proceedings before any such outside body or tribunal would require the consent of both parties to the treaty. In the circumstances, it is not likely that any such consent would be forthcoming. However, there ought to be little doubt as to the unsatisfactory nature of a provision which makes the enforceability of a treaty dependent upon the organ called upon to apply it. In some cases that organ may be designated by the United Nations as, for instance, in the case of the Security Council acting under chapter VI of the Charter and recommending, as a proper method of settlement, recourse to an arbitral tribunal. These considerations appear to militate in favour of the adoption, *de lege ferenda*, of some such rule as proposed in note 5 below.

5. It may be a matter for consideration whether in its codification of the law of treaties the International Law Commission ought not, in the exercise of its function to develop international law, formulate a rule both more comprehensive and more explicit than that formulated in the present Article on the basis of Article 102 of the Charter. In the sphere of municipal law the requirement of registration is a condition of the validity of many instruments of an importance smaller than that usually attaching to treaties. There is no apparent reason why such requirement should not be adopted without qualification in the matter of treaties. That rule might be formulated as follows: 'A treaty concluded by a Member of the United Nations

shall be void if not registered with the United Nations within six months of its entry into force.' A formulation of this nature would avoid many of the existing obscurities of Article 102 of the Charter. In particular, it would have the merit of providing a time limit for registration; of rendering unnecessary the determination, both by the organs concerned and by the parties, of the period within which a treaty is to be deemed to have been registered 'as soon as possible'; and of discouraging a practice of delaying registration until the necessity arises for invoking the treaty. Some such time limit would not necessarily have the effect of permanently nullifying a treaty which has not been registered as the result of oversight or for similar reasons. It would always be open to the parties to conclude a new treaty, in terms identical with those of the non-registered treaty, and to register it within the period prescribed. Moreover, the provision of a time limit might be accompanied by the conferment, upon some international organ, of the power to grant relief, in appropriate cases and for cogent reasons, by sanctioning an extension of the time limit as prescribed. Such power of relief may extend, in particular, to cases in which the treaty has actually been published by the parties. For in such case the main reason of the requirement of registration has, in fact, been complied with. The latter circumstance explains, in part, why the Permanent Court of International Justice on two occasions admitted as relevant instruments which had not been registered with the League of Nations.[1] Similarly, some such element of reasonable interpretation in accordance with the spirit of the principle of registration may justify the assumption of jurisdiction by the Court by reference to a special agreement which has not been registered and is immediately acted upon by the parties. In a different sphere, provision might be made for permitting the disregard of the absence of registration, *by the parties*, of multilateral treaties or such instruments as the trusteeship agreements or declarations of the acceptance of the jurisdiction of the International Court of Justice under Article 36 of the Statute. In all or most of these cases registration may be effected *ex officio* by the depositary authority or the Secretary-General of the United Nations. It may be possible

---

[1] In the *Mavrommatis Palestine Concession* cases the Court assumed jurisdiction, in its judgment of 30 August 1924 (*P.C.I.J.* Series A, no. 2, p. 33) by reference to a protocol concerning concessions signed at Lausanne on 30 August 1924. In the advisory opinion concerning the *Polish Postal Service in Danzig* (*ibid.* Series B, no. 11) the Court took note of the so-called Warsaw Agreement between Danzig and Poland which had not been registered but the text of which had been communicated to the Council of the League of Nations.

to make some general provision for such latitude of interpretation in cases involving a departure from the letter – though not the spirit – of an otherwise mandatory rule adopted in pursuance of what has become recognized as an important principle of international public policy.

V INTERPRETATION OF TREATIES

SECTION I

THE DOCTRINE OF PLAIN MEANING

CHAPTER 19

THE DOCTRINE OF PLAIN MEANING

Editor's note   In 1950 Lauterpacht acted as rapporteur for the Institute of International Law on the subject of interpretation of treaties. Both his principal and supplementary reports are printed in French in *Annuaire*, 43 (1950) (i), 366–460 and 44 (1952)(i), 197–223. In *B.T.* 26 (1949), p. 48, which actually appeared in 1951(?), Lauterpacht published an article entitled 'Restrictive Interpretation and the Principle of Effectiveness in the Interpretation of Treaties'. This article appears as chapter 20. In the first footnote to that article, Lauterpacht indicated that it was based 'to some extent' on his reports for the Institute. In fact the article absorbs virtually the whole of his reports to the Institute with the exception of two sections – one on 'the doctrine of plain meaning' and the other on preparatory work in the interpretation of treaties.

In the course of the report, Lauterpacht referred to the doctrine of plain meaning as 'the pivot of the traditional doctrine of interpretation'. As no useful purpose would be served by printing both the *B.T.* article and the reports to the Institute, it seems appropriate to introduce the present section on Interpretation of Treaties with the material on the doctrine of plain meaning, taken from the original English text of the report to the Institute; to follow it, as the next chapter, with the *B.T.* article, and to bring in the section on preparatory work taken from the report under an appropriate later heading.

The following are the relevant provisions of the Vienna Convention:

Section 3. Interpretation of Treaties

ARTICLE 31

General rule of interpretation

1.   A treaty shall be interpreted in good faith in accordance with the ordinary meaning to be given to the terms of the treaty in their context and in the light of its object and purpose.

2.   The context for the purpose of the interpretation of a treaty shall comprise, in addition to the text, including its preamble and annexes:

(a)   any agreement relating to the treaty which was made between all the parties in connection with the conclusion of the treaty;

(b)   any instrument which was made by one or more parties in connection with the conclusion of the treaty and accepted by the other parties as an instrument related to the treaty.

393

3. There shall be taken into account together with the context:

(*a*) any subsequent agreement between the parties regarding the interpretation of the treaty or the application of its provisions;

(*b*) any subsequent practice in the application of the treaty which establishes the agreement of the parties regarding its interpretation;

(*c*) any relevant rules of international law applicable in the relations between the parties.

4. A special meaning shall be given to a term if it is established that the parties so intended.

ARTICLE 32

Supplementary means of interpretation

Recourse may be had to supplementary means of interpretation, including the preparatory work of the treaty and the circumstances of its conclusion, in order to confirm the meaning resulting from the application of Article 31, or to determine the meaning when the interpretation according to Article 31:

(*a*) leaves the meaning ambiguous or obscure; or

(*b*) leads to a result which is manifestly absurd or unreasonable.

In addition, Article 33 deals with the interpretation of plurilingual texts – a matter with which Lauterpacht did not deal.

The doctrine of 'plain meaning' or 'clear meaning' is the rule – or the principle – of interpretation which is relied upon most frequently in diplomatic correspondence and in arbitral and judicial proceedings – both by the parties to the dispute and the tribunal. That principle was expounded nearly two hundred years ago by Vattel with a characteristically deceptive lucidity. He said:

La première maxime générale sur l'interprétation est qu'il n'est pas permis d'interpréter à qui n'a pas besoin d'interprétation. Quand un acte est conçu en termes clairs et précis, quand le sens en est manifeste et ne conduit à rien d'absurde, on n'a aucun raison de se refuser en sens que cet acte présente naturellement. Aller chercher ailleurs des conjectures, pour le restraindre ou pour l'étendre, c'est vouloir l'éluder.[1]

The rule thus formulated seems to be pre-eminently reasonable. Its obviousness explains the frequency with which it is invoked. Its only – but, upon analysis, decisive – drawback is that it assumes as a fact what has still to be proved and that it proceeds not from the starting point of the inquiry but from what is normally the result of it. As in argument generally the disputants attempt to obtain a tactical advantage over their opponents by describing themselves – or their contentions – as sound and realistic while labelling their adversaries

[1] Book II, ch. xvii, para. 263.

as utopian, so in the matter of interpretation parties incline to characterize the construction which they favour as following from the 'clear' terms of the treaty. If, therefore, the law on the subject had to be deduced from the pronouncements of Governments in the past, the search could hardly lead to results which are wholly reliable or sound. For Governments are seldom in the position to lay down principles of interpretation independently of disputes in which they are engaged. A welcome and much needed opportunity of that nature for an impartial statement of views of Governments on the question of interpretation would arise in connection with the codification of the law of treaties as proposed in 1949 by the International Law Commission. It is likely that when free to speak their minds independently of any particular controversy, Governments would give their support to the view which, as Sir Arnold McNair suggests, the British Government would probably adopt in the matter, namely, that if they

were called upon to face squarely the question of 'plain terms' they would take the view that this so-called rule of interpretations like others is merely a *prima facie* guide and cannot be allowed to obstruct the essential quest in the interpretation of treaties, namely, to search for the real intention of the contracting parties in using the language employed by them.[1]

This, essentially, is the opinion of other writers of authority who have devoted special study to the practice of international tribunals. In particular Professor Hyde's weighty chapters on interpretation of treaties, with special reference to the International Court of Justice and the Supreme Court of the United States, have emphasized this crucial aspect of the problem of interpretation. 'One must reject', he says, 'as an unhelpful and unscientific procedure the endeavour to test the significance of the words employed in a treaty by reference to their so-called "natural meaning" or any other linguistic standard, and then to attempt to reconcile therewith the thought or conduct of the contracting parties'.[2] Professor Hudson, who speaks with particular authority on the subject, in referring to the 'earlier jurisprudence' of the International Court in making the 'natural' meaning the starting point of the inquiry, has pointed to some danger inherent in allowing the 'natural' meaning to overcome the results of other investigations[3] – though his warning is tempered by the suggestion that to treat the 'natural meaning' as a starting point 'may be a wise tendency' and that 'no objection is to be made to a

---

[1] McNair, p. 175.   [2] Hyde, II, 1470. And see generally, *ibid.* pp. 1468–502.
[3] *The Permanent Court of International Justice, 1920–1942* (1943), p. 645.

term which has a soothing effect and which tends to avoid arousals because of its indefinite content'.[1] Yet the fact is that, in the view of many, the reliance upon the 'natural meaning' may have a soothing effect, in an adverse sense, upon the energy and vitality of the interpretative effort of international tribunals – one of the principal, if not *the* principal, tasks which confront them – and that, far from 'avoiding arousals' it has justifiably given rise to general criticism. Neither, as may be seen from the advisory opinion of the International Court of Justice in the matter of the *Admission of Members of the United Nations,* is that tendency confined to the earlier jurisprudence of the Court.

The present attitude, largely critical of the doctrine of 'plain meaning', of the science of international law has been determined not so much by individual pronouncements of international tribunals – for these often tend in the opposite direction – as by the accumulated experience and the lessons of international judicial activity in that sphere. Individual judgments, opinions and awards incline to favour the doctrine of plain meaning – although more often than not the affirmation of that doctrine, far from being the decisive consideration, is due to the desire to make the decision appear more convincing and to give the embellishment of plausibility and apparent soundness to a result reached in other ways. But cases have occurred in which an international tribunal in invoking the 'clarity' of a provision has contented itself with what must be regarded as a partial and essentially incomplete investigation of the intention of the parties. When a court describes a contested clause as clear and in consequence refuses to have recourse to a source of interpretation other than the assumed textual and grammatical meaning, the only factor which is obvious is, often, that the provision is not clear at all. The very fact that the clause is so controversial that the parties are willing to go to the expense and the trouble of a litigation or that the request for an advisory opinion is preceded by a hotly debated controversy as to the legal merits of the issue is evidence that the provision or term in question is not 'clear'. When, in addition, the Court itself is almost equally divided on the subject, for the majority or the minority to assert the 'clarity' of the controversial clause is a highly subjective proceeding which begs the question the answer to which is being sought. It may be useful to give some illustrations of the problem involved.

In the advisory opinion given in 1948 on the *Conditions for Admission*

[1] *Ibid.*

of a State to Membership in the United Nations (Article 4 of the Charter) the majority of the Court relied almost exclusively on the 'natural meaning of the words used'[1] as clearly demonstrating the intention of the authors of the Charter. It did not altogether exclude the possibility of an 'interpretation other than that which ensues from the natural meaning of the words'. But to do that, it said, 'a decisive reason would be required which has not been established'. Yet the majority of the Court in effect ruled out the main possibility of finding such a decisive reason which could be found, in particular, in an examination of the relevant preparatory work. It said:

> The Court considers that the text is sufficiently clear; consequently, it does not feel that it should deviate from the consistent practice of the Permanent Court of International Justice, according to which there is no occasion to resort to preparatory work if the text of a convention is sufficiently clear in itself.[2]

As is pointed out below the consistency of the practice of the Court in this matter is more apparent than real. However that may be, a method of interpretation which, with reference to an essential aspect of a basic international instrument, confines itself to a rigid deduction from the 'natural meaning' of words runs the danger of simplifying the difficult process of interpretation to a point at which it carries little conviction. This is so in particular with a regard to a clause the formulation of which, according to common knowledge, has been the product of a prolonged controversy on a fundamental issue. It is by no means certain that if, as did some of the minority of the judges, the majority had considered the clause in question in the light of the circumstances, recorded and otherwise, of its adoption, they would have arrived at a conclusion different from the one which they in fact reached.[3] But it would have been a conclusion the authority of which would have been enhanced by the fact of its having taken into account evidence of the intention of the parties more tangible and more convincing than exclusive reliance on the assumed natural meaning of the clause in question.

When in the *Lotus* case the Court applied, not for the first time,

---

[1] *I.C.J. Reports*, 1948, p. 63.   [2] *Ibid.*

[3] For it is arguable that although the preparatory work of the San Francisco Conference revealed the disinclination of the majority of the original signatories of the Charter to deprive the Members of the United Nations of a substantial measure of freedom of action in admitting new members, such freedom of action was quite consistent with the reply given by the majority of the Court to the question put to it: see p. 63 of the opinion where the Court pointed to 'the very wide and very elastic nature of the prescribed conditions' and to the fact that 'no relevant political factor – that is to say, none connected with the conditions of admission – is excluded'.

the doctrine of 'plain meaning' by stating that 'there is no occasion to have recourse to preparatory work when the text of a convention is sufficiently clear in itself',[1] it was apparent that the relevant provision of the treaty was not in fact clear either when standing by itself or even when viewed in the context of the Preamble and other Articles of the Treaty of Lausanne. In laying down that questions of jurisdiction shall, as between Turkey and other contracting parties, be decided in accordance with the principles of international law, the treaty did not register a clear agreement of the parties on the subject. The study of the records of the conference pointed conclusively to the different views held by Turkey and France in the matter. The expression 'principles of international law' is not one which explains itself with automatic clarity. Neither, as the equal division of the Court showed, was it quite clear what are the principles of international law with regard to the particular problem before the Court. To say, therefore, that in this – and similar – cases the treaty is clear and that therefore no reference to other sources of evidence is required is to use a formula the artificiality of which is only partly reduced by the circumstance that in fact the Court did proceed to examine other evidence of the intention of the parties. When, on the other hand, the formula of 'plain meaning' is applied rigidly to the point of excluding evidence extraneous to the text it is calculated to give rise to legitimate criticism.

It is too much to expect that in their legal argument, whether conducted in diplomatic correspondence or before arbitral or judicial tribunals, Governments will abandon recourse to a doctrine so plausible – unless it receives at the hands of international tribunals a degree of discouragement which will make resort to it a source of weakness rather than of strength to the party relying upon it. However, unlike parties to a controversy, international tribunals are in the position to discard a doctrine which is not conducive either to the effectiveness or, in the long run, the economy of the task of interpretation. In fact, it would be inaccurate to assume that the practice of international tribunals, taken in its entirety, supports the doctrine of plain meaning. That doctrine, when fully acted upon, tends to attach decisive importance to the literal meaning of words. As such it may often be contrary to the principle of good faith – which is perhaps the only non-controversial principle of interpretation and which, lucidly expressed by Cicero, was fully approved by Grotius: 'In fide quid senseris non quid dixeris cogitandum'.[2]

---

[1] *P.C.I.J.* Series A, no. 10, p. 16.   [2] Book II, chapter xvi.

International tribunals have often declined to act upon the plain or literal meaning of terms. It is sufficient to refer in this connection to the award in the case of the *Island of Timor* given in 1913, between the Netherlands and Portugal[1] and other boundary disputes where tribunals refused to attach literal importance to terms and names used in treaties; in the *Chevreau* case, decided in 1930 between Great Britain and France, where the Arbitrator assumed jurisdiction as to one aspect of the dispute notwithstanding the fact that the plain terms of the *compromis* seemed to exclude it;[2] in the *Sarropoulos* case, where the Greco-Bulgarian Mixed Arbitral Tribunal held in 1927 that notwithstanding the clear wording of the Treaty of Neuilly it had no jurisdiction except with regard to claims directly connected with the war;[3] in the case of *Polyxène Plessa* v. *Turkish Government* in which, although Article 58 of the Treaty of Lausanne provided for the renunciation by all contracting powers, except Greece, of pecuniary claims for loss and damage, the Tribunal held that notwithstanding the very plain wording of the treaty, the study of the circumstances accompanying the conclusion of the treaty and the *travaux préparatoires* led to the conclusion that that renunciation applied to Greece also;[4] in the *Ottoman Debt* arbitration where, with regard to an important aspect of the dispute, the Arbitrator preferred what he believed to be the common intention of the parties to a literal interpetation of the Treaty of Lausanne;[5] or in the significant case of *Lederer* v. *German State* in which the Anglo-German Mixed Arbitral Tribunal held in 1923, in disregard of the literal and 'clear' provision of Article 297(h) of the Treaty of Versailles, that the proceeds of liquidation were not to be credited to the State of which the owner of the claim was a national.[6]

Undoubtedly, there exist arbitral decisions which not only adopt with emphasis the doctrine of plain meaning but also combine it with the enunciation of one or more of the current rules of construction. Thus in the opinion of Parker, Umpire, in the *Lusitania* case, Vattel's 'first principle' – 'it is not allowable to interpret that which has no need of interpretation' – was given decisive weight. The Umpire held that the 'clear and unambiguous' language of the treaty did not authorize the imposition of penalties. Moreover he

---

[1] Scott, *Hague Reports*, pp. 355, 382.
[2] See award as printed in *A.J.* 27 (1933), 176.
[3] *Annual Digest* (1927–8), case no. 291.
[4] 'The exception in favour of Greece was intended not so much to regulate legal interests as to take into account certain sentimental considerations' (*Annual Digest* (1927–8), case no. 299).
[5] *Ibid.* (1925–6), case no. 270.   [6] *Recueil T.A.M.* 3 (1928), 762, 769.

insisted, after quoting Vattel, that 'if it were competent for us to look to them' all of the other rules of interpretation would lead to the same result. Of these rules he instanced two: The first was that as the treaty was framed for the benefit of the party, namely, the United States, it must be 'strictly construed against it'. The other was that treaty provisions must be construed as to best conform to the accepted principles of international law rather than to be in derogation of them and that as 'penal clauses in treaties are odious' they must be construed most strongly against those asserting them.[1] In the *Georges Pinson* case, decided by the American–Mexican Mixed Claims Commission, a distinguished arbitrator not only committed himself in unequivocal terms to the doctrine of 'plain meaning'. He said: 'Inasmuch as the text of the convention is clear in itself, there is no reason to appeal to alleged contrary intentions of its authors unless both parties agree that the text does not cover their common intention.'[2] He amplified that statement by adding that 'in so far as the text is not sufficiently clear, it is allowable to have recourse to the intention of the parties concerned'. He then proceeded to enumerate a number of rules of interpretation. It would appear that the Arbitrator assumed the possibility – or the duty – of international tribunals acting upon an assumed clear meaning irrespective of the intention of the parties. In general, however, reliance on plain meaning has been less conspicuous in international arbitration than in the jurisprudence of the Permanent Court of International Justice and its successor – although even there 'plain meaning' has often been more in the nature of a formula than a decisive factor in reaching the decision.

On the other hand, any criticism of the tendency to attribute decisive authority to 'plain meaning' must be tempered by the following two considerations: In the first instance, it would be inaccurate to assume that the doctrine of 'plain meaning' has been invariably resorted to as an artificial device for avoiding the more substantial task of eliciting the intention of the parties by means other than a speculative exercise in logical or grammatical interpretation. For the 'plain meaning' of the treaty has often been relied upon as a method of defeating appeals to technical and other rules of interpretation which are of questionable usefulness and validity. Thus on a number of occasions when confronted with the argument that clauses imposing obligations must be interpreted restrictively the Permanent Court of International Justice, while broadly conceding

[1] *Decisions and Opinions* (1925), p. 31.   [2] *Annual Digest* (1927–8), case no. 292.

that principle, denied its applicability to cases in which the treaty is clear or in which its meaning cannot be ascertained by other means of interpretation. Secondly, in so far as the process of interpretation must start from *somewhere*, it is not unreasonable – it is essential – that it should begin with what appears to be the natural, the common, the 'plain' meaning of the terms used. It is also legitimate to insist, in the interest of good faith and of a requisite minimum of certainty in legal transactions, that the burden of proof should rest upon the party asserting that the term in question is used not in its common but in its technical or in an unusual connotation or that the 'clear meaning' is not what on the face of it it appears to be. At the same time the burden of proof must not be so exacting or rendered so onerous by technical rules of construction as to give the effect of finality to what ought to be no more than a starting point or so as to relieve the Court of its own duty of investigating the true intention of the parties. Occasionally the Permanent Court of International Justice showed an appreciation of the relativity of natural meaning. Thus while in the case concerning the *Legal Status of Greenland* the Court started from the proposition that the expression 'Greenland' used by the contracting parties referred to the geographical meaning of the term as shown in the maps, it added that that fact did not exclude the possibility that that expression was used in some special sense. But, the Court said, the burden of proof that this was so rested upon Norway to show that in the treaties in question the term 'Greenland' meant only the colonized area.[1] In its advisory opinion on the *Employment of Women during the Night* it found the provisions of the relevant Article of the convention in as much as it applied to 'women without distinction of age' to be 'general in its terms and free from ambiguity'. But it did not on that account exclude the possibility that notwithstanding the generality of the terms used the convention did not apply to some categories of women. In that case, however, 'it is necessary to find some valid ground for interpreting the provision otherwise than in accordance with the natural sense of words'.[2] In the award of the British–American Claims Arbitral Tribunal in the case of *The David J. Adams* the Tribunal found, not unnaturally, that the provision admitting American fishermen for certain enumerated purposes and 'for no other purposes whatever' was 'perfectly clear'. But it did not rule out on that account the possibility of 'sufficient evidence of contrary intention of the high contracting parties . . . to contradict

[1] Series A/B, no. 53, p. 52.   [2] Series A/B, no. 50, p. 373.

such a clear meaning'.[1] It examined the evidence produced, including that of preparatory work, and found that it did not substantiate a derogation from the literal meaning of the treaty.

While the apparent degree of clarity must be a measure of the degree of exactness of the proof required for displacing the initial presumptions of plain meaning, no apparent amount of clarity is a sufficient justification for ruling out an independent investigation of intention. Plain meaning may, at the highest, be treated as rebuttable *presumptio juris*. It ought not to be regarded as an irrefutable *presumptio juris et de jure*. An ounce of external evidence or of consideration based on historical inquiry of the purpose of the treaty may be more decisively illuminating than a ton of logic operating by interpretation through analogy, by textual comparison with other parts of the treaty or with other treaties, or even by means of such apparently unassailable rules as *expressio unius est exclusio alterius*.

Finally, the doctrine of 'plain meaning' suffers from the disadvantage that it does not answer – in fact it often delays the answer to – the question of interpretation of technical terms. There is a natural tendency to consider the popular meaning to be the 'plain', the natural, meaning. But treaties are legal documents which as a rule are drawn up by legal experts or by persons availing themselves of legal advice. In view of this it must be assumed that whenever parties have recourse to terms which in legal terminology have an accepted connotation, they intend to use them in their technical – not in their popular – meaning. This is a presumption which can be rebutted by cogent consideration as was the case in the advisory opinion of the Permanent Court of International Justice in the matter of the interpretation of the Greco-Turkish Agreement where the Court held that the term 'arbitration' applied in the Final Protocol was not used in its ordinary technical meaning.[2] But in the absence of such proof to the contrary technical terms must be deemed to have been resorted to as such. Thus, for instance, the term 'intervention' in Article 2(7) of the Charter of the United Nations must be considered to refer to intervention in its technical

---

[1] *A.J.* 16 (1922), 315. In *The Francisca* Dr Lushington expressed himself in the following way: 'I apprehend that I must first look to the Articles themselves, and if the meaning intended to be expressed is clear, I am not at liberty to go further' ((1855) Spinks *Prize Cases*, 111, 151). In *The Ionian Ships* the same judge said: 'terms, however strong and clear in themselves, whatever meaning may be attributed – necessarily attributed – to them standing alone, may be modified by other parts of the same instrument' (*ibid.* 193, 198). Both cases are referred to in McNair, pp. 184, 198, respectively.

[2] Series B. no. 16, p. 22.

sense as distinguished from the popular notion of interference or demonstration of interest not accompanied by compulsion or a threat of compulsion or a claim to compliance conceived as a legal duty. Similarly the term 'lease' when used in a treaty is a lease and not a vague expression intended to conceal an outright annexation of territory. The terms 'mandate' or 'trust' are technical terms expressive of the idea of tutelage and delegation of powers incompatible, among others, with the full sovereignty of the mandatory or trustee over the territory concerned. On occasions, as in the latter case, the technical meaning coincides to a large extent with its popular understanding. Failing that it is the technical connotation which supplies the accurate standard of the interpretation notwithstanding any 'plain meaning' to the contrary.

CHAPTER 20

RESTRICTIVE INTERPRETATION AND THE PRINCIPLE OF EFFECTIVENESS IN THE INTERPRETATION OF TREATIES

Editor's note The first footnote in the present chapter states that it is based 'to some extent' upon two sections of a report on the 'Interpretation of Treaties' which Lauterpacht prepared for the Institute of International Law in 1950. Comparison of the texts shows great similarities between them and even extended passages with identical wording. But the later character of the present chapter is established by a number of additions – mainly by way of further illustration of points – and the statement of some important conclusions with greater emphasis or less qualification.

Thus, in describing the jurisprudence of the International Court of Justice in the report, Lauterpacht said: 'The Court has given its sanction, with qualification, to the principle of restrictive interpretation. It has approved, on occasions, the opposite rule of effectiveness.' In the present chapter, however, these sentences were altered to read: 'The Court has given its sanction, however nominal, hesitating and inconclusive, to the principle of restrictive interpretation. It has approved, more frequently and decisively, the opposite rule of effectiveness'.

The other important difference between the present chapter and the report to the Institute lies in the omission of a substantial section of the report dealing with the doctrine of 'plain meaning' (now printed as chapter 19 above) and of another section dealing with the use of preparatory work (printed as chapter 22 below).

The present chapter appeared in *B.Y.* 26 (1949), at pp. 48–85.

I. RULES OF CONSTRUCTION AND THE TASK
OF INTERPRETATION

The formulation of rules of interpretation of treaties has proved the object of strong temptation to writers, to arbitrators, and, occasionally, even to Governments assembled at a conference.[1] Grotius

---

The present article is based to some extent upon two sections of a report on the Interpretation of Treaties submitted in 1950 by the writer to the Institute of International Law.

[1] See the Resolution of the Seventh International Conference of American States in 1933 submitting to study by the International Commission of American Jurists a list of rules of interpretation (printed in *Harvard Research* (1935), III, 1225, 1226).

devoted to it an entire chapter[1] which, when compared with some modern treatises, does not create the impression of being out of date. In various respects Grotius' treatment of the subject constitutes an advance upon some modern pronouncements by international tribunals and writers. Thus with regard to the doctrine of plain meaning he qualifies the statement that 'words are to be understood in their ordinary sense' by adding: 'if other implications are lacking'.[2] Vattel's chapter on 'The Interpretation of Treaties'[3] probably represents the most detailed discussion of the subject by any author of a general treatise. The chapter seems to concentrate on the frequently cited rule that 'it is not permissible to interpret what has no need of interpretation' and that 'when a deed is worded in clear and precise terms, when its meaning is evident and leads to no absurdity, there is no ground for refusing to accept the meaning which the deed naturally presents'.[4] Yet it is most improbable that Vattel regarded this 'first general principle' as being of decisive practical importance. For it was followed by other general principles, by presumptions, and by elaborate distinctions between things favourable and things odious. It is doubtful whether any party to a dispute involving the interpretation of a treaty can fail to derive some advantage from the rich choice of weapons in Vattel's armoury of rules of interpretation. To a large extent Vattel followed the rules of the *Digest*. That fact, and not any conscious borrowing, was responsible for the circumstance that when three years later Pothier published his treatise on Obligations, his rules of interpretation – subsequently taken over almost textually by the *Code Civil* and the Italian Code[5] – showed a striking resemblance to those formulated by Vattel.

The majority of text-book writers have followed in this respect in the footsteps of Grotius and Vattel.[6] They have not all been writers given to mere speculation and generalization. Thus Hall, while admitting that there are rules of interpretation which are unsafe in their application and of doubtful applicability, believed that there can be found some to which no objection can be raised and which 'are probably sufficient for all purposes'. He proceeded to elaborate them in detail.[7] Others, while expressing scepticism as to the

---

[1] 'On Interpretation': Book II, ch. xvi. [2] *Ibid.* § ii.
[3] Vol. I, ch. xvii. [4] Para. 263.
[5] For an illuminating analysis see Fairman in *Grotius Society*, 20 (1934), 129, 130.
[6] For an enumeration of some of them see *Harvard Research* (1935), III, 939–40. See also ss. 797–821 of Fiore, *Code*.
[7] *A Treatise on International Law* (3rd ed., 1890), para. 111.

usefulness of rules of interpretation in general, nevertheless give a detailed catalogue of them. Thus Oppenheim – in a section which the present editor has left without substantial changes more out of piety than conviction – states expressly that there exist neither customary nor conventional rules of interpretation concerning the interpretation of treaties. He then adds that 'it is of importance to enumerate some rules of interpretation which commend themselves on account of their suitability'.[1] He enumerates fifteen of these rules. More recently, notwithstanding the growing criticism of the method of laying down fixed rules of interpretation, most writers find it difficult to dispense with them. Professor Guggenheim speaks of 'the supremacy, recognized in international practice, of restrictive as distinguished from extensive interpretation'.[2] He admits that that interpretation applies only in case of doubt, but is of the opinion that the rule is of great importance (it will be noted – although this is often forgotten – that, necessarily, all rules of interpretation apply only in case of doubt; where there is no doubt, there is no necessity for interpretation). Professor Podestá Costa, while admitting the justification of recent opinion critical of the formulation of rules of interpretation, nevertheless adopts as fundamental two principles of construction which are, in fact, most controversial, namely, that clear terms do not require interpretation and that in case of doubt restrictive interpretation must be the rule.[3] These two principles are also adopted – among others – by Professor Rousseau in his exhaustive treatment of the subject.[4] Only very few text-book writers attach importance to consistency by declining resolutely to formulate rules of construction, by way of illustration or otherwise, other than that of the fundamental requirement of *uberrima fides*. Professor Hyde – a no mean authority on the subject – has made a powerful contribution to the elucidation of this branch of international law without suggesting any specific rules of interpretation.[5] He has expressly discouraged recourse to them. More recently, Professor Balladore Pallieri has been equally consistent in exercising the same kind of restraint.[6] However, while the great majority of writers who, in monographs, have devoted special attention to the subject,[7]

---

[1] *International Law*, I (7th ed., 1948), §§ 553, 554.
[2] Guggenheim, Part I, p. 128.
[3] *Manual de derecho internacional público* (2nd ed., 1947), pp. 197, 198.
[4] Rousseau, I, 678, 686–94.
[5] Hyde, II, 1468–1502.
[6] *Diritto internazionale pubblico* (4th ed., 1948), pp. 235–40.
[7] See, in particular, Yü, *The Interpretation of Treaties* (1927); Chang, *The Interpretation of Treaties by Judicial Tribunals* (1933); *Harvard Research* (1935), III, 937–77.

show little respect for rules of interpretation, others have stressed their general usefulness.[1]

Whatever may be the results which the science of international law is reaching gradually but emphatically in the matter of rules of interpretation, the latter have constituted a prominent feature of the activity of international tribunals – although it is only by way of exception that, as in the *Georges Pinson* case, the Arbitrators have gone to the length of enunciating a system of rules of interpretation.[2] The International Court of Justice and its predecessor have constantly applied rules of interpretation.[3] The Court has given its sanction,

[1] Professor Ehrlich, in a valuable course of lectures, undertook a spirited defence of rules of interpretation (*Hague Recueil*, 24 (1928), pp. 13–79). The author of a doctoral dissertation – Prieur, *Die Auslegung völkerrechtlicher Verträge* (1930) – has suggested twenty-two rules of interpretation of treaties and has urged that only a steady increase in the number of these rules will make possible a further development of that branch of international law. Sir Eric Beckett in his observations, submitted in 1950, on the present writer's Provisional Report on Interpretation of Treaties, said: 'It must be presumed (although, in fact, it is by no means always the case) that treaties have been drafted by experts who have full knowledge of the rules of interpretation which international tribunals apply. International tribunals above all have good reasons to endeavour to base their conclusions on the application of legal principles and precedents and to avoid the suspicion of favouritism and arbitrariness.'

[2] France and Mexico, Mixed Claims Commission (Verzijl, President). The rules are reproduced verbatim in *Annual Digest*, 4 (1927–8), case no. 292. But see below, p. 408, for the view of Professor Verzijl, who as Arbitrator formulated these rules, on the value of rules of interpretation.

[3] This aspect of the work of the Court is surveyed lucidly and exhaustively by Professor Hudson in *The Permanent Court of International Justice, 1920–1942* (1943), pp. 631–61. It may be difficult to assent to the view of the learned writer that the Court 'has formulated no rigid rules'. The Court is free to decline to apply them, not, perhaps, because they are in a form which is guarded and qualified, but because it is not bound to follow its own decisions. Thus there is a measure of rigidity in the frequent statement that there is no room for recourse to preparatory work when the treaty is clear. Though it is a rigidity mitigated by the fact that in actual practice the Court has often had recourse to that method of interpretation either on account of the fact that the treaty was not clear or by way of 'confirming' a result reached independently of 'preparatory work', the Court has occasionally acted in that way. Thus in the advisory opinion of May 1948 on *Conditions for Admission of a State to Membership in the United Nations* the Court considered that 'the text is sufficiently clear' and that 'consequently, it does not feel that it should deviate from the consistent practice of the Permanent Court of International Justice, according to which there is no occasion to resort to preparatory work if the text of a convention is sufficiently clear in itself' (*I.C.J. Reports* 1948, p. 57, at p. 63; *Annual Digest*, 15 (1948), at p. 335). In the advisory opinion of March 1950 on *Competence of the General Assembly for the Admission of a State to the United Nations* the Court in relying on the 'natural and ordinary meaning' of the words of the treaty held that 'it is not permissible, in this case, to resort to *travaux préparatoires*' (*I.C.J. Reports* 1950, p. 4, at p. 8; *International Law Reports*, 17 (1950), at p. 329). Yet although the Court found 'no difficulty in ascertaining the natural and ordinary meaning of the words in question and no difficulty in giving effect to them' (*ibid.*), it proceeded to consider 'the structure of the Charter, and particularly the relations established by it between the General Assembly and the Security Council' – a fact suggesting that the 'natural and ordinary meaning' of the words in question was not fully obvious. However, the examination of the question of preparatory work falls outside the purview of the present article.

however nominal, hesitating, and inconclusive, to the principle of restrictive interpretation. It has approved, more frequently and decisively, the opposite rule of effectiveness. In a variety of ways it has given its adherence to the doctrine of 'plain terms' or 'clear meaning'. It has made a distinct, though controversial, contribution to the question of the use of preparatory work. It has applied rules of interpretation by reference to the immediate and general context. It has relied on such technical rules of interpretation as *expressio unius est exclusio alterius* or that doubtful clauses must be construed *contra proferentem*.[1] It has qualified some of these rules by the overriding principle that they can be legitimately resorted to only when the treaty is not clear or when all other means of interpretation have failed. Yet notwithstanding the accompanying qualifications, some of the rules enunciated by the Court, especially those in the matter of restrictive interpretation and of preparatory work, seem to have acquired what would have been a substantial degree of rigidity but for the fact that the Court is not bound by its previous pronouncements and that often it has not acted upon them in the very cases in which it gave utterance to them. As such they must continue to be a source of uncertainty. This is so although – or perhaps because – they have been put forward subject to qualifications. For these qualifications are themselves not free from doubt. To say that the rule as to restrictive interpretation or preparatory work may be relied upon only when the treaty is not clear is to lay down a condition the actual application of which is the result of the process of interpretation, and not its starting point. To say that the principle of restrictive interpretation may be invoked only when other means of interpretation have failed is to suggest that it serves a distinctly limited purpose – for it is seldom, if ever, that some result, however deceptive, cannot be achieved by resort to one or more of the multifarious rules of interpretation.

However, notwithstanding the frequency of the resort by international tribunals to rules of interpretation, the general trend in the literature of international law seems to deprecate them and to stress their essential unhelpfulness. This is not a case of writers being wiser than the practice of courts. It is merely a case of writers being more easily in a position to assess the cumulative result of experience. Thus Professor Verzijl, who in 1928 in his capacity as President of the French–Mexican Mixed Claims Commission formulated a detailed list of rules of interpretation, said ten years later, in referring to the

[1] See below, p. 422.

rules of interpretation adopted by the Permanent Court of International Justice: 'In principle they are all correct, but on concrete application they often abrogate each other and frequently appear worthless. . .'[1] The view which is gaining increasing acceptance seems to be that some of the current rules of construction of treaties are in themselves of controversial validity; that many of them are mutually exclusive and contradictory – such as the rule of restrictive interpretation when related to the rule that treaties must be interpreted so as to be effective rather than ineffective; and that instead of aiding what has been regarded as the principal aim of interpretation, namely, the discovery of the intention of the parties, they end by impeding that purpose. It may be added that in so far as 'revealing the intention of the parties' has in itself assumed the complexion of a somewhat stereotyped formula, it may, on occasions, conceal the true difficulties of interpretation. For the question frequently arises whether the intention of the parties can be the decisive factor in cases where, as often happens in international instruments, the treaty – far from giving expression to any common intention of the parties – actually registers the absence of any common intention (either in general or in relation to the subject matter of the dispute) or contains provisions which are mutually inconsistent and which the creative work of interpretation must reduce to some coherent meaning.[2] That absence of relevant common intention is not confined to treaties. In relation to the interpretation of contracts situations frequently arise in which the decision must be given by reference to the implied intention of the parties for the reason that the actual subject matter of the dispute was not present to the minds of the parties at the time of the conclusion of the agreement or for other reasons. In the international sphere the occasions for such necessity of acting on implied intention are more frequent.[3]

It is not the object of the present article to examine in detail the various rules of interpretation or to survey the entire field of construction of treaties. On the other hand, the experience of arbitral and judicial settlement seems to justify – and to call for – a re-examination of the main principles governing the subject. Such re-examination may help to clarify the legal position, to discourage appeal to time-honoured but essentially unhelpful formulas, and, as a result, to contribute to the economy of the judicial process and to

---

[1] Before the Royal Netherlands Academy of Science – as quoted by Fockema Andreae, *An Important Chapter from the History of Legal Interpretation* (1948), p. 75.
[2] See below, p. 442.   [3] See below, p. 443.

the scientific character of the process of interpretation. Parties to controversies, before international tribunals and elsewhere, will probably continue to rely on arguments drawn from rules of interpretation of long standing. But there may be merit in an effort calculated to discourage resort to facile formulas.

In a sense the controversy as to the justification of rules of interpretation partakes of some degree of artificiality inasmuch as it tends to exaggerate their importance. For as a rule they are not the determining cause of judicial decision, but the form in which the judge cloaks a result arrived at by other means. It is elegant – and it inspires confidence – to give the garb of an established rule of interpretation to a conclusion reached as to the meaning of a statute, of a contract, or of a treaty. But it is a fallacy to assume that the existence of these rules is a secure safeguard against arbitrariness or partiality. The very choice of any single rule or of a combination or cumulation of them is the result of a judgment arrived at, independently of any rules of construction, by reference to considerations of good faith, of justice, and of public policy within the orbit of the express or implied intention of the parties or of the legislature. What fixed canons of law are there which can uniformly impose upon the judge the choice of one of the three classical rules of interpretation: the doctrine of 'literal' or 'plain meaning' according to which if the words are plain and unambiguous they must be construed in their ordinary sense, even if such an interpretation leads to an absurdity or a manifest injustice; the 'golden rule' according to which 'the grammatical and ordinary sense of words is to be adhered to, unless that would lead to some absurdity, or some repugnance or inconsistency with the rest of the instrument, in which case the grammatical and ordinary sense of the words may be modified, so as to avoid that absurdity and inconsistency but no farther';[1] or the 'mischief rule' which, although formulated as far back as 1584,[2] must for ever continue to be the inspiration, avowed or actual, of all work of interpretation? What rigid rules of law or construction can prevent the judge from assuming an ambiguity or absurdity, as he sees it, in order to make the interpretation conform with his understanding of the purpose of the treaty or the object of the statute?[3]

---

[1] *Gray* v. *Pearson*, 10 E.R. at p. 1234.   [2] In *Heydon*'s case, 3 Co. 7 b.

[3] 'A word is not a crystal, transparent and unchangeable, it is the skin of a living thought and may vary greatly in colour and content according to the circumstances and the time it is used' (Mr Justice Holmes in *Towne* v. *Eisner* (1918), 245 U.S. at p. 425). In *Ellerman Lines* v. *Murray* [1931] A.C. 126, all the judges were agreed that the meaning was 'plain', but there were at least three different views as to what that 'plain meaning' was. For a

Conversely, there is nothing easier than to purport to give the appearance of legal respectability and plausibility – by the simple operation of selecting one or more rules of interpretation – to a judicial decision which is lacking in soundness, in impartiality, or in intellectual vigour.

There are three other factors which severely limit the part of rules of interpretation as an absolute check upon the free use of judicial discretion. In the first instance, the selection of any particular rule, out of a number of competing and occasionally mutually inconsistent rules, is necessarily a matter of discretion. The discretion is proportionate to the number and the elasticity of the rules available. Secondly, there is no assurance that a judge, bent upon achieving a desired result, will not purport to base his decision upon a rule which nominally covers the issue but in fact has little to do with it. Thirdly, it is not necessary for the judge formally to use any rules of interpretation at all – even as a mere device for achieving a desired result which he considers to be consistent with the common intention of the parties or, in its absence, with justice and good faith. This is shown, for example, by the way in which, in the *Corfu Channel* case, the International Court of Justice interpreted the special agreement conferring upon it jurisdiction to determine whether 'there is any duty to pay compensation' with respect to the liability of Albania for the explosion in the Channel and the resulting damage and loss of life. It referred specifically to the 'generally accepted principles of interpretation' and held that it would be incompatible with these rules 'to admit that a provision of this sort occurring in a special agreement should be devoid of purport or effect'.[1] But this was not the only reason underlying the decision. The Court inquired in detail into the history of the Special Agreement, beginning with the Resolution of the Security Council of April 1947 which recommended that the two Governments should refer the dispute to the Court. The Court could have appended to that aspect of its interpretation one of the appellations current with regard to historical interpretation. It then construed the special agreement by reference to the 'subsequent attitude of the parties'.[2] It could have invoked here the rule of *contemporanea expositio* on which it relied on previous occasions. Instead, after recalling the subsequent conduct of the parties

survey of the origin and limitations of the doctrine of 'plain meaning' in the interpretation of statutes see Willis in *Canadian Bar Review*, 16 (1938), 11 *et seq.*, and Corry in *University of Toronto Law Journal*, 1 (1936), 286–312.

[1] *I.C.J. Reports* 1949, p. 24.   [2] *Ibid.* at p. 25.

as an element of interpretation of the intention of the parties, it preferred to construe that subsequent conduct as 'an implied acceptance of the Court's jurisdiction'. It then proceeded, without invoking any particular designation, to apply the rules of what is often described as logical interpretation or interpretation by reference to the context. It referred to the second part of the special agreement, in which the Court, with respect to any liability of the United Kingdom in the matter of the alleged violation of Albanian sovereignty, was asked to decide whether there was 'any duty to give satisfaction'. The Court pointed out that that particular part of the special agreement had been signed by both parties on the basis that this question should be decided by the Court. The Court said:

If, however, the Court is competent to decide what kind of *satisfaction* is due to Albania under the second part of the special agreement, it is difficult to see why it should lack competence to decide the amount of *compensation* which is due to the United Kingdom under the first part. The clauses used in the special agreements are parallel. It cannot be supposed that the parties, while drafting these clauses in the same form, intended to give them opposite meanings – the one as giving the Court jurisdiction, the other as denying such jurisdiction.[1]

Finally, the Court interpreted the special agreement in the light of the various declarations of the parties which preceded it and in which they manifested their intention to accept the recommendation of the Security Council to the effect that the dispute in its entirety – i.e. including the question of the amount of compensation – should be settled by the Court. That method of applying principles of interpretation without appending to them any technical description is a constant feature of the activity of the Court.

It thus appears that the importance of rules of interpretation is limited in the sense that, when used by the Court, they are not necessarily the decisive factor in reaching the decision and that a decision reached by reference to what is generally described as a rule of interpretation is often arrived at without any specific mention of the rule in question. That fact does not mean that we are at liberty to ignore the problems, outlined above, resulting from actual or potential recourse to them. It means that the examination must be directed not so much to a criticism of rules of interpretation in general, or of their number, as to the accuracy of particular rules, the manner of their application, and their hierarchical importance

[1] At p. 26.

when viewed in their totality. Thus the relevant questions are: Is the doctrine of plain meaning an accurate or workable rule? What is the value, as a matter of principle and practice, of the rule of restrictive interpretation? What is the justification for the limitation of the part of preparatory work? What are the limits of the doctrine of effectiveness? What are the problems arising out of the application of the fundamental principle of interpretation by reference to the intention of the parties? It is not the purpose of this article to answer all these questions. In particular, no attempt will be made to discuss here the problem of recourse to preparatory work which, although apparently of a technical nature, constitutes, when related to the doctrine of 'plain meaning', one of the main problems of interpretation of treaties. In the present article it is proposed to examine, in the first instance, to what extent the doctrine of restrictive interpretation has actually found a place in the practice of international tribunals and in particular of the International Court of Justice. Secondly, it is intended to inquire into the degree of the adoption of the rival principle of effectiveness and its implications in relation to the rule of restrictive interpretation. Finally, it is proposed to consider, in relation to the principles both of restrictive interpretation and of effectiveness, the problems and limitations of what must remain the main task of interpretation, namely, the discovery of the intention of the parties.

II. THE PRINCIPLE OF RESTRICTIVE INTERPRETATION OF OBLIGATIONS AS A GENERAL PRINCIPLE OF LAW

Most of the current rules of interpretation, whether in relation to contracts or treaties, are unobjectionable. They are no more than the elaboration of the fundamental theme that contracts must be interpreted in good faith. This, in fact, is the only provision of the German Civil Code on the subject. It lays down, in a single Article,[1] that contracts must be interpreted in good faith having regard to general usage. That overriding rule must indeed be regarded as one of the general principles of law recognized by civilized States in the matter of interpretation. Yet it is surprising to find that the application of that principle produces divergent results with regard to one of the main aspects of the question, namely, whether in case of doubt the contract must be interpreted in favour of or against the party bound by the obligation. The French *Code Civil* accepts the first of

[1] Article 157.

these solutions: 'Dans le doute, la convention s'interprète contre celui qui a stipulé et en faveur de celui qui a contracté l'obligation.'[1] Up to 1942 the Italian Civil Code followed, in identical terms, the same rule.[2] On the other hand, the rule of interpreting the contract in favour of the party bound by the obligation is not a principle adopted by the common law countries, in particular in England and the United States. It is an established rule in English law that a deed or other instrument must be interpreted 'most strongly' against the grantor or contractor.[3] In a different sphere the principle – which is not confined to English law – that the grantor must not derogate from his grant belongs to the same category.[4]

It is of interest to note that in these two groups of countries the varying principles adopted are explained in the same way, i.e. by reference to the same logical and equitable consideration as expressed in the maxim – of which there are a number of variants – *verba ambigua accipiuntur contra proferentem*. The terse formulation of the French Code clearly expresses that connection. The contract is interpreted against the party which has *stipulated* and in favour of the one which has contracted the obligation. *Obscuritas pacti nocet ei qui apertius loqui potuit*. The party which stipulates – i.e. which formulates the contract – is the party which is the creditor, the obligee. This was the position in Roman law. Savigny gives an explanation of the historic origin of the rule: The essence of the contractual relation consists in the mutually conforming declaration of will as to the contents of the obligation. Accordingly, the party which undertakes the drafting of the contract undertakes the responsibility for such conformity. It follows that in case of an ambiguity the drafting party is responsible for any mistake of the other party. For the party responsible for the drafting either deliberately introduced the

---

[1] Article 1162.
[2] Article 1137. The new Italian Code of that year introduced a significant change. It laid down that restrictive interpretation in favour of the debtor is to be applied only when all other rules of interpretation have failed – 'quod nullo modo potest intellegi', as Ruggiero and Maroi put it in *Istituzioni di diritto privato* (6th ed., 1947), p. 203 – and only if there was no consideration for the benefit of the obligee. Otherwise the contract is to be interpreted by reference to an equitable apportionment of the interests of the parties ('nel senso que realizzi l'equo contemperamento degli interessi delle parti').
[3] *Chitty on Contracts* (20th ed., 1947), p. 170. But this is so only in case of ambiguity and only when other means of construction have failed. See Lord Sumner in *London & Lancashire Fire Insurance Co.* v. *Bolands* [1924] A.C. 836, at p. 848.
[4] See, for example, *Harmer* v. *Jumbil (Nigeria) Tin Areas Ltd.* [1921] 2 Ch. 201; *Grosvenor Hotel Co.* v. *Hamilton* [1894] 2 Q.B. 836; *Browne* v. *Flower* [1911] 1 Ch. 219. See also the decision of the French Court of Cassation, Chambre des Requêtes, of 25 April 1893 (*Dalloz Périodique*, 93, 1, 287), and that of the German Reichsgericht of 19 January 1906 (372/05).

ambiguity in order to mislead the other party or he was negligent. In either case the interpretation must be against him. This reasoning was adduced in particular with regard to the *stipulatio*, where the questioner was responsible for the form of the question which determined the reply of the opposing party.[1] Williston, the leading American authority on the subject, gives a similar explanation:

Since one who speaks or writes, can by exactness of expression more easily prevent mistakes in meaning, than one with whom he is dealing, doubts arising from ambiguity of language are resolved in favour of the latter; and as he will ordinarily be the promisee of the promise in question, it is sometimes stated that the contract, if ambiguous, will be interpreted in favour of the promisee. This rule finds frequent application to policies of insurance which are ordinarily prepared solely by the insurance company and the words therefore are construed most strongly against it.[2]

Thus as the result of an interesting legal development the same principle of interpretation *contra proferentem* which in English and American law has led to the acceptance of the rule that the contract is to be construed against the giver of the promise was responsible in the Roman law system for the appropriate principle of restrictive interpretation in favour of the debtor. Accordingly, while the interpretation *contra proferentem* may fairly be regarded as a general principle of law – though, as will be shown,[3] the field of its application in the sphere of international law is limited – the rule of restrictive interpretation in favour of the debtor can hardly claim the character of a principle of law of unchallenged generality.

However, the main reason why the rule of restrictive interpretation has acquired prominence in international law is not that it has been considered by many to represent a general principle of law. The main explanation of the prominence of the rule of restrictive interpretation in the international sphere is that it has been resorted to by reference to and on account of the sovereignty of independent States. It is not

---

[1] Savigny, *Das Obligationenrecht*, II (1853), 193. See also L. 99 pr. de V.O. (45.1): 'ac fere secundum promissorem interpretamur, quia stipulatori liberum fuit verba late concipere'; *Dig.* xlv. i. 38. 18: 'In stipulationibus quam quaeritur, quid actum sit, verba contra stipulatorem interpretanda sunt'; *ibid.* ii. 14. 39: 'Veteribus placet pactionem obscuram vel ambiguam venditori et qui locavit nocere, in quorum fuit potestate legem apertius conscribere'; and see *ibid.* xviii. 1, 21; L. 17. 172; xviii. 1. 33. Attention to this aspect of the matter is drawn in a suggestive footnote in Phillimore, p. 109, n. x.

[2] *A Treatise on the Law of Contract* (revised ed., 1936), vol. III, § 621. The same view is expressed in the American Law Institute's *Restatement of the Law, Contracts*, I (1932), 328 (§ 236), where the rule is laid down that terms must be interpreted against the party from whom they proceed, *unless their use by him is prescribed by law*.

[3] See below, p. 422.

only that in case of doubt the contractual obligation must be inter-preted in favour of the debtor; it is because States are sovereign that a restrictive interpretation must be put upon their obligations. In the first contentious case which came before the Permanent Court of International Justice,[1] Judges Anzilotti and Huber in a dissenting opinion urged a restrictive interpretation of the obligation under-taken by Germany because, in their words: 'The right of a State to adopt the course which it considers best suited to the exigencies of its security and to the maintenance of its integrity, is so essential a right that, in case of doubt, treaty stipulations cannot be interpreted as limiting it, even though these stipulations do not conflict with such an interpretation.' In the proceedings arising out of the first important advisory opinion rendered by the Permanent Court of Inter-national Justice – the opinion relating to the *Competence of the Inter-national Labour Organization in the Matter of the Regulation of Conditions of Work of Persons Employed in Agriculture* – it was urged on behalf of the Governments which denied that the organization had com-petence that, as the very establishment of the International Labour Organization implied a relinquishment of rights of national sover-eignty, it was not permissible to extend the jurisdiction of the organization by way of interpretation. Counsel appearing on behalf of the French Government admitted that the restriction of sover-eignty involved in membership of the organization was inconsider-able, but he was insistent that as some restriction was placed on the sovereignty of the States concerned, the text must be construed strictly and in a narrow sense.[2] In fact, a substantial part of the pleadings before international tribunals has been conducted in terms of the argument of restrictive interpretation. 'International law governs relations between independent States. The rules of law binding upon States therefore emanate from their own free will. . .

---

[1] The *Wimbledon*: Series A, no. 1, at p. 37.

[2] He said, 'It is a fundamental principle that States, justly jealous of their sovereign prerogatives, do not abandon them willingly and that all limitations of their sovereignty must be formally embodied in the text. One of the great principles of civil law is that in case of doubt, liberty cannot be presumed to have been restricted; *a fortiori*, when im-portant legal personalities such as States are concerned, it is a principle that, in case of doubt, their special attributes, which include not merely liberty, but sovereignty, cannot be considered as having been in any way restricted' (Professor de Lapradelle: *P.C.I.J.* Series C, no. 1, p. 174). It will be noted that learned Counsel limited himself, rightly, to civil law – by which is probably meant the system of Roman law. See also Series C, no. 12, p. 63, for a somewhat similar argument by Professor Borel (who, it will be noted, ex-pressed similar views in the arbitration between the United States and Sweden: see below, p. 421). And see to the same effect the argument on behalf of Bulgaria summarized in the award of 23 March 1933, in the arbitration between Bulgaria and Greece concerning the *Interpretation of the Treaty of Neuilly: U.N.R.I.A.A.* III (1949), 1400.

Restrictions upon the sovereignty of States cannot therefore be presumed.' That principle, which in *The Lotus* case[1] the Permanent Court of International Justice enunciated – perhaps without compelling necessity – with regard to customary international law, lends itself even more easily to application in the field of treaties. It has been so used.

It has been shown that the principle *in dubio mitius*, in so far as it implies an interpretation unfavourable to the recipient of benefits under the contract and one which is less onerous to the party burdened with an obligation, is not a general principle of law. Moreover, quite independently of that fact its merits do not seem to be as apparent as is generally assumed. It is a principle which is open to the objection that it does not take into account the benefits which the party bound by the commitment has reaped in consideration of its undertaking. It considers the contractual obligation as implying, *prima facie*, an impairment of freedom. The very reverse may often be the case. Contract, in the relations of parties of unequal economic power, may be a legalization of subjection and servitude. But that is not its typical characteristic. Neither is it easy to assert without qualifications the proposition, occasionally put forward, that the principle of *favor debitoris* represents a precept of good faith inasmuch as it must be presumed in case of doubt that the obligor intended to be bound to the least possible extent. For can it not be contended that the obligee, who has given valuable consideration, is entitled in case of doubt to interpretation in his favour? There are only two factors which may, in moderation, legitimately be taken into account in support of the principle *in dubio mitius*. The first is that the burden of proof must rest, as a rule, on the party alleging the restriction on the obligation.[2] It is reasonable to assert that, in the

---

[1] Series A, no. 10, p. 18.

[2] See, for example, the award of the Special Arbitrators of 13 April 1935, in the case of *Radio Corporation of America* v. *National Government of China* (*Annual Digest*, 8 (1935–7), case no. 12): 'The Chinese Government can certainly sign away a part of its liberty of action, and this also in the field of establishment of international radio-communications, and of co-operation therein ... But as a sovereign Government, on principle free in its action for the public interest as it sees it, it cannot be presumed to have accepted such restriction of its freedom of action, unless the acceptance of such restriction can be ascertained distinctly and beyond reasonable doubt ... It is a correct rule, known and recognized in common law as well as in international law, that any restriction of a contracting Government's right must be effected in a clear and distinct manner' (*U.N.R.I.A.A.* III, 1627). See also the advisory opinion of the Permanent Court of International Justice in the case of *Access to, or Anchorage in, the Port of Danzig, of Polish War Ships* (Series A/B, no. 43, at p. 142; *Annual Digest*, 6 (1931–2), case no. 208), where the Court held that exceptional derogations from the rights of the Free City must be established on a clear basis.

absence of proof to the contrary, a party cannot be presumed to have undertaken an obligation or agreed to a restriction. The second is grounded in the principle of good faith and convenience expressed in the rule, discussed below,[1] as to the interpretation *contra proferentem*. Unlike the principle of restrictive interpretation of obligations, that rule must be regarded as a general principle of law. However, even in those systems of law in which the principle of restrictive interpretation in favour of the debtor is recognized, its practical significance is reduced to the minimum by the fact that it applies only when all other means of interpretation have failed – a rare and improbable contingency.[2] That limitation of its application goes back to Ulpian, who accepted only as the *ultima ratio* the principle *ad id, quod minimum est, redigenda summa est.*[3]

In the international sphere there seems to be no justification for it unless we make the notions of sovereignty and of presumptive freedom of action the decisive considerations and the starting point of the task of interpretation. There is no warrant for doing that. The purpose of treaties – and of international law in general – is to limit the sovereignty of States in the particular sphere with which they are concerned. Their purpose is to lay down rules regulating conduct by restricting, in that particular sphere, the freedom of action of States. To a large extent treaties have no meaning except when conceived as fulfilling that function. For the same reason there is less substance than is generally assumed[4] in the suggestion that, in particular with

[1] See p. 422.
[2] See Grassetti, *L'interpretazione del negozio giuridico con particolare riguardo ai contratti* (1938), p. 219.
[3] Fr. 34, *in fine*, Dig. de div. reg. Jur. 50. And see the French and Italian Codes, referred to at pp. 413–14 above.
[4] Thus in the *Wanderer* the British–American Claims Arbitral Tribunal held in 1921 that as the United States in seizing a British vessel in alleged enforcement of the Behring Sea Regulations acted under a special agreement and that as 'any such agreement, being an exception to the general principle, must be construed *stricto jure*', the mere possession of firearms and munitions was not a contravention of the Regulations, which prohibited only the *use* of such firearms and munitions (*Annual Digest*, 1 (1919–22), case no. 120). The question of interpretation of exceptional treaty provisions was highly relevant in the case of the *I'm Alone*, decided in 1933 and 1935 between Canada and the United States (see *ibid.* 7 (1933–4), case no. 86). However, as no reason accompanied the award it is not certain to what extent the Commissioners accepted the Canadian contention as to the necessity for a restrictive interpretation of such provisions. See, for a discussion of this aspect of the question, Fitzmaurice in *B.Y.* 17 (1936), 97–100. See also the separate opinion of Judge Anzilotti in the *Lighthouses* case between France and Greece (*P.C.I.J.* Series A/B, no. 62, p. 39; *Annual Digest*, 7 (1933–4), case no. 36), and the dissenting opinion of Judge Loder in the *Lotus* (Series A, no. 10, p. 95). And see the following passage in the award of Borel, Arbitrator, in the case of the *Kronprins Gustaf Adolf*, decided in 1932, between the United States and Sweden: 'The general rule that limitations imposed by a treaty on the natural liberty of a State are to be strictly interpreted applies with special emphasis to provisions of so exceptional a nature as those of Separate Article 5.

regard to treaties, there is a presumption against derogations from a general principle and that restrictive interpretation must be the rule in such cases. For the very object of a treaty may be to derogate from an accepted general principle. There is no compelling reason to assume that treaties are merely of a declaratory nature or confined to regulating matters of detail. If the parties, in a freely accepted treaty, go to the length of inserting a provision of an exceptional nature, it must be presumed that they intended that provision to be fully effective and its operation unhampered by restrictive rules.

In the light of these considerations we may now examine the application of the doctrine of restrictive interpretation by international tribunals and, in particular, by the International Court of Justice and its predecessor.

III. THE RULE OF RESTRICTIVE INTERPRETATION AND THE PRACTICE OF INTERNATIONAL TRIBUNALS

There were indications in the very first judgment which the Permanent Court of International Justice was called upon to give – in the *Wimbledon* case[1] – that it might make a decisive contribution towards putting this aspect of interpretation on an adequate basis when, in a frequently quoted passage, it said:

The Court declines to see in the conclusion of any treaty by which a State undertakes to perform or refrain from performing a particular act an abandonment of its sovereignty. No doubt any convention creating an obligation of this kind places a restriction upon the exercise of the sovereign rights of the State, in the sense that it requires them to be exercised in a certain way. But the right of entering into international engagements is an attribute of State sovereignty.[2]

Yet in the same judgment the Court laid the foundations for a series of pronouncements,[3] almost identical in wording, in which it committed itself to the doctrine – however nominal – of restrictive interpretation of provisions implying a limitation of State sovereignty. The latter circumstance, the Court said, 'constitutes a sufficient reason for the restrictive interpretation, in case of doubt, of the

This Article stipulates that, once on board, merchandise, the export of which is forbidden, can no longer be stopped; . . . It does not go further and does not allow any inference beyond its strict terms' (*U.N.R.I.A.A.* II (1949), 1239, at p. 1287; *Annual Digest*, 6 (1931–2), at p. 377).

[1] Series A, no. 1, p. 18.

[2] *Ibid*, at p. 25. See also to the same effect, and in almost identical terms, the case of *Jurisdiction of the European Commission of the Danube* (Series B, no. 14, p. 36), and the case of *Exchange of Greek and Turkish Populations* (Series B, no. 10, p. 21).

[3] See below, p. 420, n. 3.

clause which produces such a limitation'.[1] It then proceeded to qualify the principle of restrictive interpretation: 'But the Court feels obliged to stop at the point where the so-called restrictive interpretation would be contrary to the plain terms of the Article and would destroy what has been clearly granted.'[2]

The combination of recognition of the principle of restrictive interpretation with the refusal to apply it in individual cases on the ground that the treaty is clear or that restrictive interpretation can be resorted to only if all other methods of interpretation have failed is a frequent feature of the jurisprudence of the Court.[3] Yet there seems to be no case on record in which the Court decided the issue exclusively on the basis of the principle of restrictive interpretation. In fact, the way in which it has formulated that principle has reduced to the minimum the likelihood of its application. No other result could be expected from such statements as that there is no room for restrictive interpretation unless all other means of interpretation have failed.[4] That latter contingency is hardly likely to arise – especially if recourse to preparatory work is acknowledged to be a legitimate means for ascertaining the intention of the parties. For, presumably, in laying down that recourse to preparatory work is permissible only when the treaty is not clear, the Court has not intended to proceed on the view that the rule of restrictive interpretation has sufficient potency to render clear what is otherwise a doubtful provision and thus make recourse to preparatory work unnecessary or illegitimate. As the principle of restrictive interpretation is applicable only when the treaty is not clear, it cannot be a factor which makes recourse to other means of interpretation unnecessary. This means, in particular, that prior to assuming that 'all other means of interpretation have failed' and that therefore the

---

[1] Series A, no. 1, at p. 24.   [2] *Ibid.*

[3] The case of the *Polish Postal Service in Danzig* (Series B, no. 8, at p. 40); case of the *Territorial Jurisdiction of the International Commission of the River Oder* (Series A, no. 23, at p. 26; *Annual Digest*, 5 (1929–30), at p. 382); case concerning the *Competence of the International Labour Organization to Regulate, Incidentally, the Personal Work of the Employer* (Series B, no. 13); case of the *Free Zones of Upper Savoy and the District of Gex* (Series A/B, no. 46, at p. 167).

[4] See, in particular, the manner in which the Court dealt with the argument of restrictive interpretation in the case of the *Territorial Jurisdiction of the International Commission of the River Oder*: 'This argument, though sound in itself, must be employed only with the greatest caution. To rely upon it, it is not sufficient that the purely grammatical analysis of a text should not lead to definite results; there are many other methods of interpretation, in particular, reference is properly had to the principles underlying the matter to which the text refers; it will be only when, in spite of all pertinent considerations, the intention of the parties still remains doubtful, that the interpretation should be adopted which is most favourable to the freedom of States' (Series A, no. 23, at p. 26; *Annual Digest*, 5 (1929–30), at p. 382).

rule *in dubio mitius* has to be applied, the Court would have to exhaust the sources of information available in the preparatory work and the vast reservoir of judicial inspiration available in the principle of effectiveness of treaty provisions. Thus, for instance, in interpreting the provisions of the Convention of Paris of 1920 between Poland and Danzig – a treaty which, *inter alia*, imposed upon Danzig substantial obligations in the sphere of protection of minorities – the Court admitted that the provision in question was not 'absolutely clear'.[1] That circumstance did not lead it to interpret the convention restrictively in favour of the 'natural liberty' and sovereignty of Danzig. Instead, it proceeded 'to recall here somewhat in detail the various drafts which existed prior to the adoption of the text now in force'.[2]

The International Court of Justice has not only refrained, apart from one doubtful exception,[3] from applying in actual practice the rule of restrictive interpretation. As will be shown presently, it has often relied, in a conspicuous manner, on the opposite of that rule by acting on the principle of effectiveness of treaty obligations and of the general purpose of the treaty as a whole. Yet the frequency with which it has conceded the theoretical relevance of the rule of restrictive interpretation has helped to keep it alive in some arbitral awards,[4] in the pleadings of parties, and in the literature of international law. In view of the fate which the doctrine has suffered in

---

[1] Series A/B, no. 44, at p. 33; *Annual Digest*, 6 (1931–2), p. 384.   [2] *Ibid.*
[3] In the *Free Zones* case (Second Phase) (Series A, no. 24, at p. 12) – but it is doubtful whether the question of interpretation of a specific treaty provision was at issue in that case.
[4] See, for instance, the following passage in the award given in 1930 by Professor Borel, Sole Arbitrator, in the case of the *Kronprins Gustaf Adolf* between Sweden and the United States: 'considering the natural state of liberty and independence which is inherent in sovereign States, they are not to be presumed to have abandoned any part thereof, the consequence being that the high contracting parties to a treaty are to be considered as bound only within the limits of what can be clearly and unequivocally found in the provisions agreed to and that those provisions, in case of doubt, are to be interpreted in favour of the natural liberty and independence of the party concerned' (*U.N.R.I.A.A.* II, at p. 1254; *Annual Digest*, 6 (1931–2), at p. 375). And see the award of the Special Arbitral Tribunal of 3 September 1924, in the case of *Reparation Commission* v. *German Government* (*Annual Digest*, 2 (1923–4), case no. 194), where the Tribunal held with regard to bilingual treaties that 'if there were two texts equally clear but not agreeing with one another, it would be arguable that the text involving the smaller obligation for the party obliged ought to be preferred. But if one text is clear and the other is not, the necessary solution is to interpret the less clear text in the light of the other text...'. See also the dissenting judgment of Judge Moore in the *Mavrommatis Palestine Concessions* case to the effect that in case of a difference of opinion as to the sense to be given to a term differently understood in the languages of the contracting parties, preference is to be given to the language of the country which is bound (*P.C.I.J.* Series A, no. 2, pp. 69–70). See also the case of *Radio Corporation* etc., above, p. 417. But see the award of the Arbitrator in *French High Commission to the States of the Levant* v. *Egyptian Government* (*Annual Digest*, 10 (1941–2), at p. 423).

practice at the Court's own hands, the question may properly be asked whether, quite apart from the absence of any inherent merits in the doctrine of restrictive interpretation, the continued reference, however nominal, to its potential usefulness is not a source of confusion which deserves greater discouragement than it has as yet received. What value – except a negative value as an element of confusion – can be attached to a rule of interpretation which, in the language of a carefully worded arbitral award, is to be resorted to only 'in the case of absolute impossibility of ascertaining the exact meaning' of a treaty?[1] Other arbitral decisions, while accepting it nominally, in effect refuse to follow it: 'Le fait que cet article consacre une limitation de l'exercice du droit de souveraineté impose le droit de l'interpréter strictement, mais ce devoir ne pourra jamais faire refuser à l'article le sens qui est commandé par des termes formels.'[2]

With the rule that treaties must be interpreted restrictively on account of State sovereignty there is connected a cognate rule of construction to the effect that they must be interpreted, in case of doubt, against the party which was responsible for the drafting of the disputed clause – that they must be interpreted *contra proferentem*. The rule has not been prominent in international practice,[3] but, like many other rules of construction, has been conspicuous in textbooks where it has been used occasionally as a reason, the cogency of which is not apparent, for substantiating the distinction between law-making and other treaties.[4] It has not been prominent in practice because, although – unlike the principle of restrictive interpretation in favour of the debtor – it constitutes a general principle of law,[5] in relation to treaties the rule can hardly be

[1] *Georges Pinson* case, referred to above, p. 407.

[2] Award of Count van Sandenburg of 26 April 1926 in the arbitration between *Germany and the Commissioner for Pledged Revenues* (*U.N.R.I.A.A.* III, 773).

[3] The Permanent Court of International Justice relied upon it on one occasion – in the *Brazilian Loans* case – in connection with an instrument which was not an international treaty (Series A, no. 21, p. 114). See also the opinion of Parker, Umpire, in the *Lusitania* case (*Annual Digest*, 2 (1923–4), case no. 198); the decision of the Roumano-German Mixed Arbitral Tribunal, given in 1926, in *Weitzenhoffer* v. *Germany* (*Annual Digest*, 3 (1925–6), case no. 278); and the decision of the Arbitrator in *Goldenberg* v. *Roumania*, decided in 1928 (*U.N.R.I.A.A.* II, 907). And see *Annual Digest*, 6 (1931–2), case no. 206 (*Sch.* v. *Germany*), decided by the German Supreme Court in respect of the Treaty of Versailles.

[4] See Rousseau, I, 745, 762. And see, to the same effect, the submission of French Counsel in the *Wimbledon* case (*P.C.I.J.* Series C, I, no. 3, 172–4).

[5] See above, p. 415. See also Article 1137 of the old and Article 1730 of the new Italian Code. For comment on the former see Polignani, *Di un antica regola di diritto* ('*interpretatio contra stipulatorem*') in *Filangieri* (1881), pp. 1 *et seq.* See also Article 1162 of the French *Code Civil*; and see Williston, *Treatise on the Law of Contract*, § 621, who lays down in em-

regarded either as persuasive or as being of considerable practical application. Treaties, except those imposed by force, are the result of common effort and the product of prolonged negotiations. They do not originate from drafts imposed by one party. Accordingly, in so far as a particular provision is based on a draft proposed by one negotiator, there is no imperative reason to credit that party with a degree of ingenuity and foresight which cannot be matched by the other party and which permits the implication that the *proferens* has provided fully for his own interests and that therefore the task of interpretation is to safeguard, by way of compensation, the interests of the other party. The following passage from the decision of the Arbitrator, given in 1934, in the dispute between Germany and the Governing Commission of the Saar in the matter of the *Interpretation of the Baden-Baden Agreement* concerning officials, illustrates this aspect of the rule *contra proferentem*:

The rule that, in case of doubt, the text of a treaty is to be interpreted against the party which drafted it can only be applied when, as in the case of the Treaty of Versailles, one of the parties handed a prepared text to the other for signature. The Baden-Baden Agreement was the object of lengthy negotiations, precisely in regard to the question of officials' pensions, and the parties came to mutual agreement on their proposals step by step. In such a case, which party it was that drafted the final text is, from the standpoint of this rule of interpretation, irrelevant. . .[1]

The doctrine of restrictive interpretation is not only of questionable value in itself. Once it has been adopted there is a tendency to generalize it and to apply it with special emphasis to selected categories of treaties. Thus it has been maintained that clauses conferring jurisdiction upon international tribunals must be interpreted restrictively seeing that they are in derogation of sovereignty.[2]

phatic terms the rule that 'language will be interpreted most strongly against the party using it'. The rule is expressed in identical terms in Anson's *Principles of the Law of Contract*, ch. xi, § 1, the reason for the rule being that 'a man is responsible for ambiguities in his own expression, and has no right to induce another to contract with him on the supposition that his words mean one thing, while he hopes the Court will adopt a construction by which they would mean another thing, more to his advantage'. For the suggestion that the clause is to be interpreted in favour of the party in whose interest it was inserted regardless of who inserted it, see Oertman, 'Interests and Concepts' in *The Jurisprudence of Interests* (ed. by Magdalena Schoch, 1948), p. 63. (See the judgment of the Germano–Polish Mixed Arbitral Tribunal in *Kunkel et Al.* v. *Polish State*, which seems to have acted on that principle: *Annual Digest*, 3 (1925–6), case no. 279). But the author admits that this is not the case when standardized forms of contract contain inconspicuous and apparently harmless clauses with the aid of which large business concerns, assisted by ingenious counsel, attempt to secure an advantage over their less adroit customers.

[1] *U.N.R.I.A.A.* iii, 1564.
[2] See Rousseau, I, 688; Guggenheim, p. 128.

The Permanent Court of International Justice has said so occasionally – as in the case of the *Free Zones*[1] and of the *Phosphates in Morocco*.[2] Actually, the practice of the Permanent Court showed a clear tendency in the opposite direction. With the exceptions of the *Phosphates* case, in which the wording of the declaration of signature of the optional clause left little room for doubt, and of one aspect of the *Mavrommatis Palestine Concessions* case,[3] the Court interpreted jurisdictional clauses so as to assume jurisdiction rather than to deny it. On occasions it did so in a way significantly approaching judicial legislation. In the *Mavrommatis* case it assumed jurisdiction grounded in a treaty which had not yet entered into force at the time when the application submitting the case to the Court was filed; it did so for the reason that 'the Court, whose jurisdiction is international, is not bound to attach to matters of form the same degree of importance which they might possess in municipal law'.[4] In the same case it gave a very wide – not a restrictive – interpretation to the provision which conferred upon it jurisdiction only if negotiations had failed. It considered that abortive negotiations between the private party concerned and the defendant Government could be assimilated to negotiations between the two Governments in question. It expressed the view that it would be incompatible with the flexibility which should characterize international relations to require the two Governments to reopen a discussion which had in fact already taken place and on which they relied.[5] In the first phase of the case concerning *Certain German Interests in Polish Upper Silesia* the Court refused to be hampered 'by a mere defect of form' – that defect of form being such that it could be remedied at any time by the plaintiff Government.[6] In the second phase of that case the Court went much further in interpreting extensively the clause conferring jurisdiction upon it. It held that jurisdiction given to it in the matter of the interpretation and application of the convention gave it jurisdiction to decree and assess reparation in respect of the disregard of the obligations of the convention. As reparation, it considered, was an indispensable complement of a failure to apply a treaty, it was not necessary that jurisdiction in respect of such reparation should be specifically provided for. Only 'an express provision to the contrary' could have excluded that implied jurisdiction of the Court.[7] In a less drastic manner, but equally by way

[1] Series A/B, no. 46, at p. 138; *Annual Digest*, 6 (1931–2), at p. 431.
[2] Series A/B, no. 74, p. 23; *Annual Digest*, 9 (1938–40), at p. 505.
[3] Series A, no. 2.　　　　[4] *Ibid.* at p. 34.　　　　[5] *Ibid.* at p. 15.
[6] Series A, no. 6, p. 14.　　　　　　　　[7] Series A, no. 9, p. 23.

of implication, the International Court of Justice held in the *Corfu Channel* case that the jurisdiction to determine the question whether there is any duty to pay compensation implied the competence to assess the amount of compensation. The Court held that the jurisdiction to decide what kind of *satisfaction* was due to *Albania* included the jurisdiction to decide the *amount of compensation* due to the *United Kingdom*.[1] In giving that interpretation of the special agreement the Court referred to the ruling of the Permanent Court of International Justice in the *Free Zones* case[2] in which it expressed the opinion that 'in case of doubt, the clauses of a special agreement by which a dispute is referred to the Court must, if it does not involve doing violence to their terms, be construed in a manner enabling the clauses themselves to have appropriate effects'.

There is no trace in all these pronouncements or, what is more important, in the unambiguous instances of assumption of jurisdiction, of any restrictive interpretation of jurisdictional clauses. The opposite is the case – not to mention the numerous cases in which the Court assumed jurisdiction by virtue of the conduct of the parties such as submissions made in a counter-case.[3] It is not surprising that in a period during which the Court was in a general way expressing approval of restrictive interpretation of jurisdictional clauses while in effect acting in an opposite manner, an international Arbitrator should have followed the practice of the Court rather than its general and qualified language and that he should have preferred expressly to dissociate himself from the view that such clauses must be interpreted restrictively. He said:

The defendant Government maintains that, in case of doubt as to the meaning of an arbitral clause, the incompetence of the Arbitrator must be presumed, according to the general rule by which a State is not obliged to have recourse to arbitration except when a formal agreement to that effect exists. The Arbitrator cannot agree with this principle of interpretation of arbitral clauses. Such a clause should be interpreted in the same way as other contractual obligations. If analysis of the text and examination of its purpose show that the reasons in favour of the competence of

[1] *I.C.J. Reports* 1949, p. 26; *Annual Digest*, 16 (1949), at p. 170. And see above, p. 411.
[2] Series A, no. 22, p. 13; *Annual Digest*, 5 (1929–30), at p. 463.
[3] See the case of *Rights of Minorities in Upper Silesia* (Series A, no. 15, p. 24). And see the *Mavrommatis Jerusalem Concessions* case, where the Court considered that a declaration made by Great Britain in the course of the proceedings was sufficient to invest the Court with jurisdiction on one aspect of the dispute on which it could not otherwise have had jurisdiction to pronounce (Series A, no. 5, pp. 27–8).

the Arbitrator are more plausible than those which can be shown to the contrary, the former must be adopted.[1]

It would thus appear that the time is ripe for drawing the necessary consequences both from the inherent shortcomings of the doctrine of restrictive interpretation of treaties and from the circumstance that it has been more honoured in the breach than in the observance – in particular from the fact of the wide adoption of the principle of effectiveness of treaty obligations as an element of interpretation. These two principles – that of restrictive interpretation and that of effectiveness – are mutually incompatible. The more there is of one, the less there is of the other. The greater effectiveness of a provision can be secured, by dint of liberal interpretation, only at the expense of the freedom of action of the State bound by it – unless, of course, we limit severely, to the point of practical obliteration, the rule of restrictive interpretation by saying that it is applicable only when all other considerations, including that of effectiveness, have failed to produce a result. This, in fact, has been the practice of international tribunals.

IV. THE PRINCIPLE OF EFFECTIVENESS

While, in the decisions of international tribunals, the doctrine of restrictive interpretation of treaties limiting the sovereignty of States has been no more than a form of words, the principle of effectiveness has played a prominent and ever-growing part in the administration of international law.[2] The principle of effectiveness in the interpretation of treaties appears in national and international jurisprudence in various forms. In the United States it has been repeatedly invoked and acted upon by the Supreme Court in the form of 'liberal interpretation'. In *Nielsen* v. *Johnson*, a case concerning a treaty limiting the right to levy discriminating taxes upon

---

[1] Undén, Arbitrator, in the case between Greece and Bulgaria concerning the *Interpretation of Article 181 of the Treaty of Neuilly of 1920* (4 November 1931); *A.J.* 28 (1934), 773; *Annual Digest*, 7 (1933–4), at p. 392.

[2] For this reason it is not perhaps necessary to view with alarm the fact that there is an obvious inconsistency between the rule that treaty obligations ought to be interpreted so as to impose the minimum of obligation upon the party bound by the treaty and the principle that provisions of a treaty ought to be construed so as to display a proper – if not the maximum – degree of effectiveness. For the same reason there is less harm than may appear at first sight in the fact that these two rules are often not only enumerated together in the same catalogue of rules, but that they follow one upon the other without any attempt at explaining what is on the face of it a contradiction. For the nominal character and ineffectiveness of the rule of restrictive interpretation tends to remove the inconvenience resulting from the inconsistency of the two sets of rules.

the property of aliens, the Court, citing a long line of precedents, said: 'When a treaty provision fairly admits of two constructions, one restricting, the other enlarging rights which may be claimed under it, the more liberal interpretation is to be preferred.'[1] In *Factor* v. *Laubenheimer*,[2] a case concerning extradition in relation to the requirement of double criminality, the Court used identical language – thus raising, incidentally, the question whether 'liberal interpretation' of the rights granted by a treaty refers to the rights of the State requesting extradition or to the rights of the person whose extradition is requested. In English jurisprudence and practice the term 'liberal interpretation' seems to have been used in a somewhat wider sense as connoting a generous rather than a pedantic interpretation, in accordance with principles of good faith – though the dividing line between liberal interpretation thus conceived and the principle *ut res magis valeat quam pereat* is somewhat elastic. In fact, in the sphere of municipal law the rule of effectiveness in the interpretation of contracts is so widely accepted that it may fairly be described as a general principle of law.[3]

International jurisprudence – and particularly that of the Permanent Court of International Justice and its successor – has constantly acted upon the principle of effectiveness as the governing canon of interpretation. This the Court has done in practically every sphere of its activity: in giving, notwithstanding occasional disclaimers to the contrary, a 'liberal' interpretation to clauses conferring jurisdiction upon it; in pronouncing, almost invariably, in favour of an interpretation extending the competence of international institutions such as the International Labour Organization or the

---

[1] (1929), 279 U.S. 41, 51–2; *Annual Digest*, 5 (1929–30), at p. 377. For a long list of decisions of American courts based on the principle of liberal interpretation see Hackworth, v, 256, and Hyde, II, 1478–80. On the question of liberal interpretation in favour of American Indians see *North-Western Shoshom Indians* v. *United States* (1945), 324 U.S. 335; *Annual Digest*, 13 (1946), at p. 195.

[2] (1933), 290 U.S. 276, 293–6, 300; *Annual Digest*, 6 (1931–2), at p. 301 (*sub nom. Laubenheimer et Al.* v. *Factor*).

[3] 'An agreement ought to receive that construction which will best effectuate the intention of the parties to be collected from the whole of the agreement' (*Ford* v. *Beech*, 11 Q.B. 866). For an emphatic example see *Simpson* v. *Vaughan* (1739), 2 Atk. 32, in which case it was held that where a man, for good consideration, gave a note expressed to be 'for money borrowed, which I promise never to pay', the word 'never' was rejected. And see generally in that sense on the principle of effectiveness *Chitty on Contracts*, pp. 147–9; Williston, *Treatise on the Law of Contract*, vol. III; American Law Institute, *Restatement*, § 236. As to French law see vol. I Article 1157 of the *Code Civil*, where the principle of effectiveness occupies the first place in the enumeration of rules of interpretation. See also Grassetti, *L'interpretazione del negozio giuridico*, pp. 217–23, who discusses what he considers the apparent inconsistency between Article 1132 which lays down the principle of effectiveness and Article 1137 which sanctions *il principio del favor debitoris*.

international river commissions; and in construing, without exception, minorities treaties and similar obligations in a manner calculated to enhance their effectiveness and to limit, *pro tanto*, the freedom of States bound by the clauses in question. In the advisory opinion concerning *German Settlers in Poland* the Court declined to adopt a literal interpretation of the Minorities Treaty and to hold that the jurisdiction of the Council of the League ceased whenever it involved the interpretation of an international engagement other than the Minorities Treaty itself. If that were so 'the Minorities Treaty would to a great extent be deprived of value... In order that the pledged protection may be certain and effective, it is essential that the Council, when acting under the Minorities Treaty, should be competent, incidentally, to consider and interpret the laws or treaties on which the rights claimed to be infringed are dependent.'[1] Similarly, when in the case of the *Acquisition of Polish Nationality*[2] the Court extended the protection of the Minorities Treaty to persons who were not Polish nationals – for the reason that 'if this were not the case, the value and sphere of application of the treaty would be greatly diminished' – it did not act in accordance either with the plain meaning of the terms or with the principle of restrictive interpretation. In the advisory opinion concerning the *Minority Schools in Albania* it refused to give a literal interpretation to the clause providing for equality of treatment – an interpretation the result of which would have been that the clause 'would become a weapon by which the State could deprive the minority régime of a great part of its practical value'.[3] Neither did it rely on the doctrines of plain meaning or restrictive interpretation when in the advisory opinion on the *Competence of the International Labour Organization* it held that the treaty which conferred upon the latter jurisdiction concerning the regulation of conditions of work of persons employed in industry bestowed upon it jurisdiction with regard to persons employed in agriculture;[4] or when it held that a treaty which gave it competence to regulate the conditions of work of employees entrusted it also with the jurisdiction to regulate the conditions of work of the employer when such jurisdiction was incidental to or necessary for the regulation of the work of employees.[5] The same applies to most of the cases in which the Court acted on the principle that it must give effect to the ostensible object of the treaty as it (the Court) saw

---

[1] Series B, no. 6, p. 26.   [2] Series B, no. 7, p. 17.
[3] Series A/B, no. 64, p. 182; *Annual Digest*, 8 (1935–7), at p. 390.
[4] Series B, no. 20.   [5] Series B, no. 13.

it. As it said in the last-mentioned case: 'The Court, in determining the nature and the scope of a measure, must look to its practical effect rather than to the predominant motive that may be conjectured to have inspired it.'[1]

The issue thus raised brings into the forefront one of the cardinal questions of interpretation – that of the relation of the principle of effectiveness to the intention of the parties. If the intention of the parties was that the treaty should not be fully effective – if they intended that its clauses should be limited in their scope and operation – to what extent does it lie with an international tribunal to add to the efficacy of the treaty because of its own conception of international interest or of the purpose of the agreement? Undoubtedly, when confronted with an attempt at interpretation which, if accepted, would reduce the treaty to an absurdity or an empty form, the tribunal would have to do its utmost to prevent any such result from eventuating – although, as we shall see presently, contingencies may arise in which that negative result may constitute the nearest approximation to the intention of the parties bent upon producing a non-committal political declaration rather than a statement of legal rights and obligations. However, it is seldom that the unavoidable choice is between requiring a total frustration of the apparent purpose of the treaty and endowing it with a full measure of effectiveness in disregard of the intention of the parties. In the same way as, in another sphere, the choice is usually not between the simple alternatives of a literal interpretation or an interpretation leading to an absurdity, but between two opposing contentions neither of which is absurd, so also in this matter the choice is not between full effectiveness and utter frustration of the purpose of the treaty. The decision, as we have seen, is usually between a higher and a lower degree of effectiveness. If the parties have decided for the latter, is it within the province of a court – acting by reference to maxims of 'liberal' interpretation or of *ut res magis valeat quam pereat* – to bring about the former? There is really in such cases no question of choosing between *valeat* and *pereat* – the question is one of less or more *valeat*. The following four examples will illustrate the issue.

1. *The principle of effectiveness and finality of adjudication.* In laying down in the Covenant of the League of Nations the general principle of unanimity, the authors of the Covenant must have envisaged the possibility that because of that limitation the action of its organs, such as the Council or the Assembly, was bound on occasions to lack

[1] *Ibid.*

full effectiveness. This applied, for instance, to its action under Article 11 – assuming that absolute unanimity, including the votes of the parties to the dispute, was required for the validity of resolutions of the Council. In the advisory opinion on the *Interpretation of the Treaty of Lausanne* the Permanent Court found that, notwithstanding the comprehensive language of the Covenant to the contrary, the principle *nemo judex in re sua* applied generally to the interpretation of the Covenant[1] – in particular to cases where the Council was asked to decide a dispute submitted to it not under Article 15 but by virtue of a treaty concluded between the parties. Otherwise, the Court held, the action of the Council in solving the dispute could not be fully effective. However, the requirement of unanimity under the Covenant did not deprive the action of the Council of all effectiveness. It left room for the display of the wide possibilities of conciliation and of the moral and political effect of recommendations and decisions reached by a consensus of opinion falling short of unanimity. Such result could not be as effective as a binding legal decision, but it was not altogether lacking in effectiveness. To what extent was it within the province of an international tribunal to add, by way of interpretation, to the efficacy of the action of the Council? If the principle *nemo judex in re sua* and the consequent requirement of qualified, as distinguished from absolute, unanimity of the Council applied to action of the Council in its capacity as an arbitrator, was there any compelling reason why it should not apply to Article 11 generally? The interpretation of arbitration agreements in a way calculated to ensure the finality of adjudication has not been limited to the International Court.[2]

2. *The principle of effectiveness and the binding force of recommendations.* The powers of the Security Council under chapter VI of the Charter of the United Nations are exercised almost exclusively by way of recommendations. The fact that these recommendations are not binding is undoubtedly calculated to diminish the effectiveness of the action of the Security Council. But it does not deprive them of all effectiveness. For they are of considerable moral and political value. They may have a legal effect in relation to the organs of the United Nations; if disregarded, they may become a powerful factor in the

[1] Series B, no. 12.

[2] See, for example, the decision of the Swiss Federal Council of March 1922 in the *Boundary Dispute between Colombia and Venezuela*; *Annual Digest*, 1 (1919–22), case no. 262. And see *ibid.* 5 (1929–30), case no. 243, at p. 390, for the award of Asser, Arbitrator, in the dispute between the *Compagnie d'Electricité de Varsovie* and the *Municipality of Warsaw*, in which he declined to sanction an interpretation of the convention which would result in a duality of jurisdiction.

decision of the Security Council to proceed to enforcement action under chapter VII of the Charter. But as the law now stands they are not legally binding and therefore far from being fully effective. In the course of the proceedings in the *Corfu Channel* case before the International Court of Justice it was urged by Great Britain that certain recommendations of the Security Council under chapter VI were binding. It was asserted, *inter alia*, that such an interpretation was required by reference to the principle of effectiveness. The Court did not consider that submission. A considerable number of the judges found it necessary to refute it expressly.[1]

3. *The effectiveness of jurisdictional clauses.* As pointed out above,[2] the Court has held that jurisdiction to find whether the conduct of a State has amounted to a breach of an obligation of customary or conventional law implies also the competence to pronounce judgment on the reparation due by the offending State, and that the jurisdiction to pronounce on the question whether reparation is due implies also the competence to assess the amount of compensation. Otherwise, the Court held, the jurisdictional clause would lack effectiveness. Perhaps it would be more accurate to say that otherwise it would lack *full* effectiveness. For the finding that there was a breach of an international obligation would create the duty – the legal duty, to be fulfilled in good faith – to make reparation. As such it would not be without legal, not to mention moral and political, effect. The Court found – and it is not easy to challenge its finding with any confidence – that the principle of effectiveness required that one kind of jurisdiction implied the other. Similarly, it is conceivable, though perhaps not lightly to be assumed, that the parties – or one of the parties – in giving the Court jurisdiction to find whether it has violated an international obligation and whether therefore reparation is due, did not wish to endow it with the further jurisdiction to determine, because of the principle of effectiveness, the amount of reparation due to the other party. Effectiveness is a matter of degree. For, in the existing state of international organization and having regard to the terms of Article 94 (2) of the Charter, there is no assurance that a binding judgment of the Court will be given full effect. However, it will be noted that in the case in question the decision of the Court was not based solely on the requirement of effectiveness.[3]

4. *The effectiveness of international organization.* The advisory opinion

---

[1] *I.C.J. Reports* 1948, at pp. 31–2; *Annual Digest*, 15 (1948), at p. 355.
[2] See p. 425.   [3] See above, p. 411.

of the International Court of Justice given in 1949 in the matter of *Reparation for Injuries Suffered in the Service of the United Nations*, in particular in so far as it referred to the right of the United Nations to bring an international claim in respect of injury done to its agents, relied largely on the principle of effectiveness.[1] The opinion of the Court was based to a considerable extent on the view that it was necessary to render fully effective the purpose of Article 100 of the Charter in so far as it is intended to safeguard the international and independent character of the functions and status of officials of the United Nations.[2] Yet it cannot plausibly be maintained that the right of the United Nations to bring claims in respect of damage suffered by its officials is essential to the fulfilment of the purpose of Article 100 of the Charter – although there ought to be no doubt that a right of that nature is beneficial to the fulfilment of that purpose. If the opinion of the majority of the Court on the subject had run counter to a principle more firmly grounded in international law and deserving of greater respect than the rule of nationality of claims, it would have raised in a more conspicuous manner than it did the issue whether the function of interpretation can legitimately aim at extracting every possible element of effectiveness from international instruments.[3] It is arguable that once the Court had come to an affirmative decision in the matter of the international personality of the United Nations, its right to bring an international claim on behalf of its officials followed from the fact of its international personality without it being necessary to rely on the desire to make the Charter effective. International juridical personality implies the right to prosecute claims in the international sphere – an indirect reminder of the necessity of revising Article 34 of the Statute of the International Court of Justice which, in its present formulation, makes it impossible for the United Nations to bring before the Court a claim against a State even with the consent of that State.

The examples referred to above may help to draw attention to the complications of the principle of effectiveness as an element in the interpretation of treaties and its relation to what is properly assumed to be the primary object of interpretation, namely, the revealing of

[1] The Court invoked specifically in support of its ruling the advisory opinion of the Permanent Court of International Justice, referred to above, in the matter of the right of the International Labour Organization to regulate, incidentally, the conditions of work of employers – an opinion based, in turn, upon the same principle.

[2] See, in particular for emphasis on this aspect of the question, the statement made before the Court by Mr [now Sir Gerald] Fitzmaurice (United Kingdom) on 9 March 1949: I.C.J. *Pleadings, Oral Arguments, Documents* (1949), pp. 123-6.

[3] See above, pp. 411, 412.

the intention of the parties. The intention of the parties – express or implied – is the law. Any considerations – of effectiveness or other-wise – which tend to transform the ascertainable intention of the parties into a factor of secondary importance are inimical to the true purpose of interpretation. The answer, though perhaps not the complete answer, to that call for caution is that in applying the principle of effectiveness the Court does not supplant the intention of the parties and substitute for it a factor extraneous to it – especially if it is borne in mind that this is a principle applicable only when the intention of the parties is doubtful. That explanation may not be wholly satisfactory. For it leaves unanswered the question as to the degree of doubt which is required in order to render legitimate recourse to the principle of effectiveness. In particular, it leaves open the question whether the latter enjoys priority over other principles of interpretation. Moreover, it is idle to pretend that that particular presumption – that of effectiveness – follows invariably from the attitude usually adopted by States engaged in concluding treaties. Parties to treaties often wish their obligation to go so far and no farther. They – or some of them – desire the treaty to be only partly effective. They use language which, in their view, adequately expresses their determination not to concede to the treaty a full measure of realization of all its inherent and potential purposes.

On the other hand, in interpreting treaties it seems legitimate to act on the view that in availing themselves of the faculty of entering into treaties Governments intend to pursue a purpose which, in accordance with the requirement of good faith, treaties must be considered to fulfil. If parties – or a party – abuse that faculty by reducing it to the level of a device calculated to deceive one another, or to mislead others, they cannot rule out the contingency that the judge will attach to words the meaning usually associated with them. Nothing save explicit language will reduce the incidence of that risk. Once an instrument has assumed the form of a treaty, signed and ratified, good faith requires that, in the absence of compelling reasons to the contrary, it should not be treated as a non-committal enunciation of principle. That consideration is the reason for such superiority as the principle of effectiveness as an element of inter-pretation enjoys over the doctrine of restrictive interpretation and other rules of construction. But it is a superiority which must be invoked sparingly if international tribunals are not to incur the reproach of acting as legislators in a manner which is outside their legitimate province and which, in the long run, must react unfavourably upon their power and authority. Some inarticulate legislative element there must be in their activity, as there must be in the judgments of national courts. This applies to the application of both conventional and customary law. The judicial function is not that of an automaton which registers a gap, an obscurity, an absurdity, a frustrated purpose, without an attempt to fill the lacunae by reference to the intentions of the parties in the wider context of the agreement as a whole and the circumstances accompanying its adoption, to the needs of the community, and to the requirement of good faith. In particular, in cases of doubt it may not be improper to rely on the rule of effectiveness so as to promote the operation of general principles of law and of the rule of law in international society. But, as within the State, that quasi-legislative function ought not to be so deliberate or so drastic as to give justifiable ground for the reproach that the tribunal has substituted its own intention for that of the parties. Moreover, on occasions there may be a certain deceptiveness in the suggestion that the provisions of a treaty ought to be interpreted so as to achieve the object intended rather than to leave that object unfulfilled. For the question is: what is the object intended? Is it the aim contemplated by the parties, or what the judge or arbitrator assumes ought to have been the purpose of the treaty? Views as to the object of certain categories of treaties undergo substantial changes in proportion as international relations are in a state of progress or retrogression. When the Permanent Court of International Justice in its advisory opinion on the *Minority Schools in Albania* considered the object of the Minority Treaties and Declarations to be the securing of a 'true equality' between the majority and the minority – an equality which, in its view, would not exist 'if the latter were deprived of its own institutions, and were consequently compelled to renounce that which constitutes the very essence of its being as a minority'[1] – it adopted a view of the purpose of protection of minorities which was not likely to secure support in the period following the Second World War, when no room could be found for the recognition of the rights of minorities either in the non-committal Universal Declaration of Human Rights or in the drafts of more stringent instruments.

Undoubtedly, in so far as the rule of effectiveness is identical with the principle of good faith it has a full justification of its own and cannot be regarded as a technical or artificial rule of construction.

[1] Series A/B, no. 64, at p. 17; *Annual Digest*, 8 (1935–7), at p. 388.

But it is for that very reason that it must not deliberately be allowed to assume an existence independent of the intention, express or legitimately implied, of the parties. No rule or principle of interpretation is acceptable unless it proceeds from or acts upon that paramount consideration. In particular, no principle of effectiveness can properly endeavour to give legal efficacy to clauses or instruments which were not intended to produce such results. Thus, for instance, judicial activity could not legitimately aim at giving the force of a binding rule of conduct to Articles 16 and 38, respectively, of the Hague Conventions of 1899 and 1907 for the Pacific Settlement of International Disputes, which laid down that 'in questions of a legal nature, especially in the interpretation or application of international conventions, arbitration is recognized by the signatory Powers as the most effective, and at the same time the most equitable, means of settling disputes which diplomacy has failed to settle'. These provisions did not contemplate the assumption of the legal obligation to submit disputes to compulsory judicial settlement. They repudiated, in effect, any such obligation. This was also the position with regard to Article 12 of the Covenant of the League of Nations, which described as generally suitable for arbitration certain enumerated categories of disputes and which the Committee of Jurists who in 1920 drafted the Statute of the Permanent Court of International Justice interpreted as an implied obligation to submit such disputes to the Court. The same applies to the Universal Declaration of Human Rights which was approved in 1948 by the General Assembly of the United Nations. While professing to attribute to it a moral and political significance of the first order, practically all the Members of the United Nations declined to consider it as imposing upon them a legally binding rule of conduct. There would be no warrant for endowing it with legal effectiveness either directly or by the back-door of an assertion that it constitutes a legally binding interpretation of existing obligations of the Charter. Similarly, no considerations of effectiveness would provide a legitimate reason for reading a judicially ascertainable element of legal obligation into the declaration of the United States, made in 1946, accepting the compulsory jurisdiction of the International Court of Justice in certain categories of so-called legal disputes enumerated in Article 36 of the Statute of the Court. That declaration was made subject to the reservation, *inter alia*, of matters essentially within the domestic jurisdiction of the United States *as determined by the United States*. It cannot be made effective by judicial interpretation in cases in which the United States elect to deny the jurisdiction of the Court on account of that particular reservation.

V. INTERPRETATION IN THE ABSENCE OF A COMMON INTENTION OF THE PARTIES

An attempt has been made in the preceding section to show that the intention of the parties must be the paramount factor in the interpretation of treaties and that studied caution must be exercised in acting upon rules of interpretation, including those of such apparent attractiveness as the principle of effectiveness, which may play havoc with the intention of the parties. Such rules may, upon analysis, prove to be little more than presumptions. To presume – to imply – intention is to predicate that intention does not matter. To do that without circumspection would be to introduce into the work of interpretation an element of wide and uncontrolled discretion inconsistent with the legitimate exercise of the judicial function. At the same time there must be envisaged situations in which an international tribunal, faced with the duty of interpreting a disputed provision of a treaty, is not in a position to do so by reference to the common intention of the parties for the reason that, in relation to the particular provision, there is no such common intention. This does not mean that the treaty falls to the ground and that no question of interpretation arises at all. While common intention, if it can be ascertained, is the governing factor which must not be sacrificed to presumptions and technical rules of construction, it does not necessarily follow that the existence and the express manifestation of a common intention in relation to any specific provision of a treaty are an essential condition of its operation. It is the treaty as a whole which is law. The treaty as a whole transcends any of its individual provisions or even the sum total of its provisions. For the treaty, once signed and ratified, is more than the expression of the intention of the parties. It is part of international law and must be interpreted against the general background of its rules and principles. It is part of the legal system and, as such in the absence of a clear intention of the parties to the contrary, it allows of no gaps resulting in the impossibility of an adequate judicial decision. That absence of an effective common intention of the parties may occur, primarily, in the following five ways.

In the first instance, there may be no common intention for the reason that the parties, although using identical language, did not intend the same result. Such cases may be due to the fact that the parties, acting in good faith, attached differing meanings to the language of the treaty. Thus, for instance, a party may have attached to a term a meaning dictated by the peculiarity of its own language or of its own law or practice; the other party may have done the same. Or, when a map is attached to a treaty, one of the parties may have considered the map to be in the nature of a general identification of the territory in question while the other may have viewed it as exhaustively describing the boundaries, the islands, the creeks, and so forth. In such cases it would be idle to speak of the common intention of the parties, and the judge may legitimately have recourse to what may be considered the common intention of the treaty taken in its entirety, by reference to the historical circumstances of its creation, to its object as ascertained by the general tendency of its clauses, and, in cases of discrepancy of versions in different languages, to an analysis of the history of the adoption and of the meaning of all relevant versions.[1] Such wider considerations may be more useful than controversial technical rules such as that each party is bound only by the text in its own language.

Secondly, it is possible that the different meanings attached to the same expression by the parties to a dispute are due not to an accident but to the deliberate design of one or more of the parties bent upon benefiting from an ambiguity surrounding the expression or provision which it succeeded in having inserted – or which it allowed to be inserted – in the treaty without the other party being aware of the pitfall thus prepared for it or waiting for it.[2] The chapters on Interpretation in Grotius and Vattel abound in examples of this character. It is not unavoidable in such cases to have recourse to the principle that mistake induced by the active fraud or deceitful acquiescence or misrepresentation of one party is, at the option of the injured party, a cause of nullity. For there is hardly a question of mistake in cases of such absence of common intention as can be reduced to an instance of ambiguity. In such cases the principle of good faith and consideration of the general purpose of the treaty may legitimately

---

[1] See the method adopted by the Permanent Court of International Justice in the case relating to the *Competence of the International Labour Organization* (Series B, no. 2, pp. 35 *et seq.*) and in the *Mavrommatis Palestine Concessions* case (Series A, no. 2, pp. 19, 20).

[2] It is this aspect of the situation which brings to mind the drawbacks of any rigid reliance upon the rule *contra proferentem*. See above, p. 423. There is, consistently with good faith, no room for its application if it can be shown that the party which produced the draft containing the ambiguous expression acted in all innocence whereas the other party, hoping and intending to reap an advantage from the ambiguity, allowed or encouraged its incorporation in the treaty.

provide a substitute for any lack of common intention. The principle of good faith impels the assumption of a common purpose. Thus in the case, referred to above, of the *Interpretation of the Special Agreement between Great Britain and Albania of March 1948*, it was possible that at the time of the signature of the agreement the Albanian representatives, while being under no illusion as to the comprehensive interpretation – which, in the circumstances, was the natural interpretation – given to the agreement by the British representatives, envisaged the possibility of and eventually relied upon a restrictive construction of the terms used.[1] To that extent there did not exist a common intention of the parties on the particular subject. Yet, independently of the other reasons given by the Court,[2] such common intention could legitimately be assumed from the provisions of the special agreement as a whole.

Thirdly, and this is one of the most typical aspects of the subject here discussed, the absence of an effective common intention may be due to the circumstance that, being unable to reach an agreed solution, the parties are content to use an ambiguous or non-committal expression and to leave the divergence of views to be solved in the future by agreement or in some other way. Some examples will illustrate the issue. In the negotiations preceding the Treaty of Lausanne of 1924 the parties were unable to agree on the question of the exercise of jurisdiction over aliens for offences committed abroad. They accordingly postponed the settlement of the controversy on that point by inserting a non-committal phrase to the effect that such jurisdiction shall be exercised in accordance with international law. It fell to the Permanent Court of International Justice, in *The Lotus* case,[3] to resolve the difficulty. Similarly, in the same treaty the parties, unable to agree either on the delimitation of the boundary with Iraq or on entrusting the decision on the subject to a final award of an impartial body, adopted a formula which left the latter question in abeyance. That question came before the Permanent Court of International Justice when it was requested to give its Twelfth Advisory Opinion.[4] When the Definitive Statute of the Danube was being drafted, Roumania declined to concede to the Danube Commission the right to exercise jurisdictional powers. The Statute as adopted did not resolve the difficulty. It reflected the

[1] See above, pp. 411, 412. [2] *Ibid.*
[3] Series A, no. 10.
[4] Concerning the *Interpretation of Article 3, para. 2, of the Treaty of Lausanne*; Series B, no. 12.

divergence of views on the subject. When the Permanent Court was asked to give an advisory opinion on the *Jurisdiction of the European Commission of the Danube*,[1] it was maintained by Roumania that the intention of the parties was to perpetuate their disagreement on the question – a contention which, in view of its practical consequences, the Court declined to accept. The Charter of the United Nations abounds in examples of deliberate ambiguities concealing the absence of an effective common intention of the original signatories of the Charter on the questions at issue. It is sufficient to mention the terms of Article 79 of the Charter, which provided that 'the terms of trusteeship' for each territory to be placed under the Trusteeship system '. . . shall be agreed upon by the States directly concerned'. It was clear at the time of the adoption of that Article that there was no agreement as to the meaning of the term 'States directly concerned'.

In all these, and similar, cases, although the common intention of the parties may have been to avoid giving a definite meaning to the clauses in question – that is to say, although there was no common intention of the parties to adopt a positive and clear-cut solution on the particular subject – it is the right and duty of international judicial and arbitral agencies to impart an effect to these clauses by reference to the purpose of the treaty as a whole and to other relevant considerations, including the finality of adjudication. *Interest rei publicae ut sit finis litium.* Undoubtedly the treaty is the law of the adjudicating agencies. But, at the same time, the treaty is law; it is part of international law. As such it knows no gaps. The completeness of the law when administered by legal tribunals is a fundamental – the most fundamental – rule not only of customary but also of conventional international law. It is possible for the parties to adopt no regulation at all. They may expressly disclaim any intention of regulating the particular subject matter. But, in the absence of such explicit precaution, once they have clothed it in the form of a legal rule and once they have found themselves in a position in which that subject matter is legitimately within the competence of a legal tribunal, the latter is bound and entitled to assume an effective common intention of the parties and to decide the issue. That common intention is no mere fiction.

The same fundamental consideration of the completeness of the law applies to the fourth aspect of the question here discussed – an aspect which is not unfamiliar in the interpretation of contracts

[1] Series B, no. 14.

generally.[1] While the common intention of the parties provides an effective basis for the interpretation of the treaty as a whole, it is possible that it affords no clue to the solution of any particular problem or difficulty which, demonstrably, did not occur to them when they concluded the treaty but which falls within the purview of its general provisions. The Permanent Court of International Justice was confronted with that question in its advisory opinion on the *Interpretation of the Convention of 1919 concerning the Employment of Women during the Night*.[2] The question before the Court was whether the provisions of the convention applied to women holding positions of supervision or management in industrial undertakings. The Court pointed to the contention that the application of the convention to women holding such posts had not been considered at the time when the convention was adopted. The Court refused to admit the relevance of that argument:

Even if this were so . . . it does not by itself afford sufficient reason for ignoring the terms of the convention. The mere fact that, at the time when the Convention on Night Work of Women was concluded, certain facts or situations, which the terms of the Convention in their ordinary meaning are wide enough to cover, were not thought of, does not justify interpreting those of its provisions which are general in scope otherwise than in accordance with their terms.[3]

The same considerations clearly applied to the advisory opinion on the *Competence of the International Labour Organization to Regulate, Incidentally, the Personal Work of the Employer*.[4] The Court admitted that the treaty in question did not contain a provision expressly conferring upon the organization jurisdiction 'in such a very special case as the present'. But it gave an affirmative answer to the question put to it for the reason that such competence of the International Labour Organization was essential to the accomplishment of the purpose of the organization as revealed in its constitution.

In these and similar cases the common intention in relation to the particular case must be derived from the common intention of the treaty as a whole – from its policy, its object, and its spirit. It is a matter of legitimate controversy, bordering on dialectics, whether in

---

[1] On the other hand, the frequent artificiality and the nominal character of provisions of treaties constitute a peculiar feature of international relations, where the demonstration of a semblance of agreement is often considered preferable to an acknowledgement of unresolved differences.

[2] Series A/B, no. 50; *Annual Digest*, 6 (1931–2), case no. 217.

[3] *Ibid.* p. 377; *Annual Digest*, 6, at p. 413.

[4] Series B, no. 13.

these cases we do not in fact treat intention as irrelevant – just as it may be a matter of dispute to what extent the function of courts in such cases assumes the complexion of an activity which is essentially legislative. However that may be, it is a function which no legal tribunal in a community under the rule of law can hope – or is entitled – to escape. It must not usurp it when it can be avoided; it must not stretch it beyond what is reasonably necessary. But, when confronted with it, the judge must face it – in effect, though not, perhaps, in form – with the same freedom which is enjoyed by the legislature or by the contracting parties. It is a freedom which may often be exercised with a foresight, responsibility, and detachment not given to law-making agencies proper. Gaps in the law – and resulting cases *primae impressionis* – are an unavoidable phenomenon. But that law, in its larger outlines and against its wider background, has its source in the will and in the interests of the parties to the dispute as interpreted by the judge by reference to their intention manifested by the treaty as a whole. That particular problem of interpretation is not confined to treaties. It is a general problem of interpretation. In a sense it is one of the main problems of construction. There is no difficulty in interpreting a provision relating to a situation which the parties had in mind when making the contract. The difficulty – the solution of which is within the true province of the judge – arises in relation to matters falling within the general terms of the agreement but not at all present to the minds of the parties when they negotiated it or put their signatures to it. It is in such cases for the judge to act on the implied intention of the parties, i.e. on his understanding, having regard to the contract as a whole and to surrounding circumstances, as to what would have been the attitude of the parties if confronted with the issue.[1]

Fifthly, there is an absence of effective common intention when two or more provisions of the same treaty are mutually inconsistent. This may occur in bilateral and, in particular, in multilateral conventions covering a great variety of subjects. The taking, in the

[1] The treatment of the subject by Planiol and Ripert (*Traité pratique de Droit Civil français*, p. 514) with regard to French law clearly shows the general jurisprudential character of the problem involved – though it is possible that these writers tend to over-emphasize the legislative character of the function of the judge in such cases. The judge, in their view, acts in cases of that nature as if he were a legislator who supplements the law. He weighs the respective interests of the parties in the balance of justice and general interest as well as in the light of usage and the conduct of the parties. This is so even if he professes to follow strictly the intention of the parties. Similarly, they add, in the sphere of private international law the courts deduce the proper law of the contract from the intention of the parties although it is clear that there was no intention bearing on the matter. See also Salmond, *Jurisprudence* (8th ed., 1930), p. 185, n.

midst of and after protracted negotiations, of rapid decisions which are often the result of a compromise or of appearance of compromise, is not conducive to consistency. But the judge, confronted with the task of interpreting a provision the apparent meaning of which is contradicted by another provision of the same treaty, cannot confine his efforts to construing the isolated clause directly before him. He must view the treaty as a whole. He must, if only possible, assume an intention of the parties – an intention which is not self-contradictory. This may not always be feasible. Thus if the constitution, in the form of a treaty, of an international organization were to lay down in a number of Articles the duty of the organization and of its members to adopt a certain line of conduct and if the same constitution, in another Article or set of Articles, were to remove the matter in question from the sphere of action of the organization, both sets of rules would, taken in isolation, convey a definite meaning. Taken together, they would amount to a contradiction which could only be resolved by a judicial decision giving preference to one or the other set of provisions – assuming that the court had not previously arrived at the conclusion that, upon examination, there was no inconsistency or that any apparent inconsistency could not be resolved by reference to other provisions of the treaty. In deciding which object of the treaty is to be preferred the court will take into consideration the purpose of the treaty as a whole and what, in its view, is the relative importance of the provisions in question. In so doing the court – although deciding on legal, as distinguished from political, grounds – will be imputing rather than discovering a common intention underlying the treaty as a whole. A problem of this nature would arise, for instance, with regard to Article 2 (7) of the Charter – the clause of domestic jurisdiction – and its numerous provisions relating to human rights and fundamental freedoms. If, which is controversial, the latter constitute a legal obligation, to what extent is its effectiveness limited or rendered nugatory by the prohibition of intervention in Article 2 (7) – assuming, which is once more controversial, that the question of observance of human rights and fundamental freedoms is a matter essentially within the domestic jurisdiction of States? What is the position with regard to inconsistent versions in different languages – all being authentic – of the same provision? It is idle, in relation to a clearly ascertained contradiction, to speak of an effective common intention directly covering the matter at issue. The determination, in such cases, of the overriding – the higher – common intention of the parties, not less real because it is necessarily implied, may constitute an important aspect of the judicial function of interpretation – a timely and accurate reminder that that function, far from being limited to discovering the meaning of a text, may legitimately impart to it a meaning by reference to the paramount principle of the completeness and the rational development of the law and of the requirements of justice in the light of the purpose of the treaty viewed as a whole. This does not mean that the judgment thus given is based on 'political' considerations and that when confronted with a variety of possible interpretations the judicial decision is in the last resort a political act. For although there are many possible interpretations of a disputed provision there is in theory – in what is believed to be the accurate legal theory – only one correct interpretation of the law. The balance in favour of that correct interpretation may be indeed slight and the merits of alternative interpretations may be considerable, but to say that in every case there are a number of *equally* correct legal interpretations and that the choice between them is – legitimately, avowedly, and consciously – the result of a political decision and of political predilections of the judge[1] is to put forward an assertion which denies the very essence of the judicial function in a society under the rule of law. Undoubtedly, the judicial choice of the standard of interpretation may be influenced by a variety of factors seemingly extraneous to the text. But these factors – such as considerations of justice, canons of fairness and good faith, and, in proper cases, an equitable reconciliation of the interests at stake – are of legitimate legal relevance. They do not obliterate the borderline between the function of the judge and the powers of the legislator.

VI. CONCLUSIONS

The discussion, in the last two sections of this article, of the principle of effectiveness and of the relevance of the common intention of the parties appears, on the face of it, to be inconclusive. It is hoped that that inconclusiveness will not be attributed solely to the indecision of the writer. For the matter there discussed neither permits nor calls for excess of assurance. It touches upon one of the most controversial

---

[1] See Kelsen, *The Law of the United Nations* (1950), Preface, p. xvi. The very notion of interpretation conceived as a scientific and critical task is based on the assumption that, although there are a number of possible interpretations of the law, some of them are, in terms of legal relevance, more accurate than others and that it is the business of the judge to choose the most accurate of all. This implies the possibility – and the necessity – of one interpretation being the most accurate having regard to all pertinent legal considerations.

and elusive problems of jurisprudence – the nature and the limits of the judicial function. That function consists largely in the interpretation of the law, whether laid down in statutes or in agreements. In the international sphere the problem is complicated by a number of factors sucn as the frequent absence, for a variety of reasons, of a common intention of the parties bearing directly upon the subject of the dispute and the similarly frequent fact of the positive intention of the parties to the treaty to deny to it what would appear to be a natural degree of effectiveness. The chief of these reasons is that, unlike contracts in the sphere of municipal law, treaties, or some of their provisions, are often a political substitute for rather than a legal expression of the agreement of the parties. In the circumstances it will perhaps be more useful to draw attention to the salient features of the problem here discussed rather than to attempt a rigid summary of conclusions.

Unlike the rule of restrictive interpretation of international obligations, the principle of effectiveness constitutes a general principle of law and a cogent requirement of good faith. It finds abundant support in the practice of international tribunals. On the other hand, the principle of effectiveness is in the last resort no more than an indication of intention, to be interpreted in good faith, of the parties. It is the intention of the authors of the legal rule in question – whether it be a contract, a treaty, or a statute – which is the starting point and the goal of all interpretation. It is the duty of the judge to resort to all available means – including rules of construction – to discover the intention of the parties; to avoid using rules of interpretation as a ready substitute for active and independent search for intention; and to refrain from neglecting any possible clues, however troublesome may be their examination and however liable they may be to abuse, which may reveal or render clear the intention of the authors of the rule to be interpreted.

Accordingly, with regard both to the question of effectiveness and to other matters, there would seem to be no merit in an attitude or doctrine which, in view of the difficulties attendant upon the discovery of the authors or of the fact of intention, discards it altogether and concentrates exclusively upon what is considered the plain text of the rule. Undoubtedly, when confronted with a statute the judge may find it difficult to determine whose intention it is that must be interpreted. Is it that of the members of the Government who brought forward the measure; or of the amorphous, docile, and often self-contradictory mass of the supporters of the measure; or of the officials who drafted it; or of the particular interests and organizations which prompted it? Similar difficulties arise in the case of multilateral treaties. But to assert, on that account, that intention is irrelevant and that what matters are the 'plain words' of the text, is, in the long run, to divest the task of interpretation of its scientific character and its true purpose. Words have no absolute meaning in themselves. They are an expression of will. That will is not the will of the judge. There is latent in any consistent doctrine of 'plain meaning' the danger of the substitution of the will of the judge for that of the parties. Undoubtedly, the judge's notions of the purpose of the law, of right and wrong, of convenience, of the social consequences of any particular construction, and of an equitable apportionment of the interests of the parties may often be the decisive factor in the situation, but they may legitimately be so only as an element in the interpretation of the meaning of the statute or treaty. The law-creating autonomy and independence of judicial activity may be an unavoidable and beneficent necessity. But they are so only on condition that the judge does not consciously and deliberately usurp the function of legislation. That fact sets a natural limit even to a principle as cogent as that of effectiveness. It is a principle which can give life and vigour to an intention which is controversial, hesitant, or obscure. It cannot be a substitute for intention; it certainly cannot claim to replace it.

These considerations are of particular importance in relation to international judicial and arbitral settlement. The jurisdiction of the International Court of Justice – and of other bodies and persons administering international law in the international sphere – is still, in principle, of a voluntary character. Any justifiable impression that it either relegates the intention of the parties to a factor of secondary importance or that it simplifies unduly the task of discovering the intention of the parties must, in the long run, impair the scope and usefulness of their activity and the authority of their pronouncements. Thus, for instance, no international tribunal could properly attempt the task of amending the Charter of the United Nations – by reference to considerations of effectiveness or otherwise – for the reason that, as framed by its authors, some of its provisions are unworkable, or are liable to be abused, or are in fact abused.

In comparison, the rules concerning the restrictive interpretation of treaty obligations do lend themselves to summary by way of conclusions. The principle of restrictive interpretation of contractual obligations is not a general principle of jurisprudence. It is due to a large extent to the historical peculiarities of *stipulatio* in Roman law. It is of doubtful – if any – application in other systems of law. In the matter of treaties it has received no substantial support either from international tribunals in general or from the International Court in particular. It has been discouraged as a matter of both practice and principle. Such occasional endorsement as it has received has been purely nominal. For its application has been made dependent upon the double condition of doubt and of the complete absence of any other means of interpretation. The same applies to treaty obligations conferring jurisdiction upon international tribunals. These obligations the Court has interpreted in accordance with the principle of effectiveness and with conspicuously scant respect for the rule *in dubio mitius*. Such element of justification as the doctrine of restrictive interpretation possesses lies in the domain of burden of proof and of the emanations, which are of little relevance in the sphere of international law, of the rule *contra proferentem*. In so far as there is a case – and there is some case – for eliminating unnecessary and cumbersome rules of interpretation, that relating to restrictive interpretation of treaty obligations ought to be considered as first on the list of priorities. The aggregate result of rules of interpretation is probably to hinder rather than to promote the proper fulfilment of the task of the judge. It is not only that occasionally they tend to obscure the intention of the parties instead of clarifying it. The more frequent occurrence is that they help to cloak with an appearance of orthodoxy and soundness an unwillingness or inability to inquire, in all requisite detail and with all requisite vigour, into all the material factors pointing to the intention, express or implied, of the parties or the legislator. However, the remedy is not to assail rules of interpretation in general. The more helpful approach is to examine individual rules in the light of principle and of their application in practice.

SECTION 2

PREPARATORY WORK

CHAPTER 21

PREPARATORY WORK IN THE INTERPRETATION OF TREATIES (1934)

Editor's note Lauterpacht examined in detail the rôle of preparatory work in the interpretation of treaties on at least five occasions: in 1934 in his lectures at the Hague Academy of International Law (*Hague Recueil*, 48 (1934)(ii)); in chapter 2 of *The Development of International Law by the Permanent Court of International Justice* (1934), pp. 35–41; in an article entitled 'Some observations on preparatory work in the interpretation of treaties', published in *H.L.R.* 48 (1935), 549; in his report on the 'Interpretation of Treaties' prepared for the Institute of International Law in 1949–50; and, finally, in chapter 7 of *The Development of International Law by the International Court*, published in 1958. Notwithstanding the period of nearly a quarter of a century which separates the first from the last of these contributions, there is a common strand which runs through them – a concern not so much to justify uncontrolled recourse to preparatory work as to repudiate the absolute and arbitrary exclusion of this aid to interpretation. This basic theme involves, however, some repetition of argument and material; and in consequence no useful purpose would be served by reprinting every item here.

It has not been easy to choose between these contributions. But of the earlier ones, it seemed sensible to select the fullest presentation of the material, namely the Hague lectures of 1934, and to omit the article in the *H.L.R.* The latter followed soon after, and is essentially a truncated version of the former. An additional factor justifying the choice of the Hague lectures is that hitherto they have been published only in French. The chapter which follows contains the original English version.

No question arises, of course, of reprinting here the contributions on the subject which have appeared in the two books mentioned above. But as a later reflection of Lauterpacht's thought – showing, for example, his adherence to the ideas which he presented originally in 1934, even though some of the instruments upon the interpretation of which he was commenting were quite different, being constitutional rather than merely contractual – it appears appropriate to print as chapter 22 the section on *travaux préparatoires* of his 1950 report to the Institute of International Law on the 'Interpretation of Treaties'. This provides in a conveniently condensed form the essentials of his thought on the subject.

It would, of course, have been interesting to see how, if Lauterpacht had reached this topic in his approach to the codification of the law of treaties, he would have dealt with it. In the concluding paragraphs of the section of *The Development of International Law by the International Court* (1958) Lauterpacht observed that 'the time is ripe for putting beyond doubt the full justification of the use of preparatory work in its own right and within proper limits, as a legitimate element in the interpretation of treaties'. A few lines earlier he had suggested that 'the nature of the treaty-making process necessitates in the matter of preparatory work, a solution which lies half-way between the finality of the text and the indiscriminate use of preparatory work' (p. 140).

A pragmatic approach of this kind marks the treatment of the problem in Article 32 of the Vienna Convention on the Law of Treaties, under the heading 'Supplementary means of interpretation':

> Recourse may be had to supplementary means of interpretation, including the preparatory work of the treaty and the circumstances of its conclusion, in order to confirm the meaning resulting from the application of Article 31, or to determine the meaning when the interpretation according to Article 31:
> (*a*) leaves the meaning ambiguous or obscure; or
> (*b*) leads to a result which is manifestly absurd or unreasonable.

While these words may lead to a solution which in practice would have been acceptable to Lauterpacht, it will be clear upon a study of the chapters which follow that he would have been critical of the assumption that it is possible first to identify a 'meaning' and then to seek to confirm it by recourse to preparatory work. In his judgment – and as practical experience in the process of interpretation confirms – unless an effort so deliberate as to be to some extent forced and artificial is made to exclude consideration of preparatory work before a 'meaning' is found, consideration of preparatory work cannot, in either temporal or intellectual terms, be clearly distinguished from the rest of the process of interpretation.

I. Introductory

The study of the cases of interpretation of treaties by international and municipal tribunals is a good practical test of the usefulness of the various and elaborate rules of interpretation which are found in treatises of international law. This test shows them to be of small practical significance. They are a cherished instrument in forensic argument; they are a tool of questionable efficiency in the administration of justice. No writer has been more frequently quoted before or by international tribunals than Vattel, and of Vattel's treatise no part has been more frequently referred to than his exhaustive list of canons of interpretation in the seventeenth chapter of the second Book. In practice, however, this long list of rules of construction has been conspicuous not for its usefulness but for its irrelevancy and artificiality. It is difficult to imagine a situation in which a State putting forward a contention could not rely upon some rule of interpretation in Vattel's list. Upon analysis most of them cancel themselves out.

Municipal courts have increasingly insisted on the serious limitations of the traditional rules of construction, many of which are regarded as hampering rather than facilitating the task of interpretation. As Cockburn C.J. said: They were framed with a view to general results, but are sometimes productive of injustice by leading to results contrary to the intention of the parties.[1] The position is the same in the interpretation of treaties. Thus the rule – the first rule in Vattel's list – that it is not admissible to interpret what is in no need of interpretation[2] is impressive at first sight, but, although international tribunals have relied upon it on a number of occasions,[3] its hollowness reveals itself clearly upon analysis. It is an assertion of literal construction which, if acted upon, would render other rules, and, indeed, the task of interpretation itself, superfluous. It is a useful rule so long as there is no dispute between the parties. But when the parties disagree as to the meaning of a term then, obviously, there is need of interpretation at least to the extent of finding that the term must be assumed to have been used in the ordinary meaning and that there is no evidence to show that another meaning was intended. Or, to give another example, the rule that treaties have to be interpreted so as to be effective rather than ineffective may be reduced to a shadow of its own self if we apply at the same time the various rules, based on Vattel's subtle distinction between things favourable and things objectionable, authorizing restrictive interpretation.

In so far as international arbitrators have invoked Vattel's – and other – rules of interpretation their real function has been to give the authority of a legal maxim to the result at which the arbitrator has arrived at the conclusion of his task of ascertaining the intention of the parties. Grotius' treatment of rules of construction is almost equally elaborate and equally lacking in practical usefulness;[4] they are calculated to obstruct rather than to promote the achievement of the principal task of interpretation as defined by Grotius himself:

---

[1] 2 C.P. Div. at p. 93.   [2] § 263.

[3] See, for instance, the *Lusitania*, United States–Germany Mixed Claims Commission, *A.J.* 18 (1924), 373, where the confident view was expressed that 'all the rules governing the interpretation of treaties would lead to the same result'.

[4] Book II, ch. xvi.

'Rectae interpretationis mensura est collectio mentis ex signis maximae probabilibus.'[1] But the example of these two most distinguished classics of international law has been widely followed. The usual method of presenting the question of interpretation of treaties has been to set up a long list of technical rules of construction.[2] There have indeed been, in the last fifty years, a minority of writers who have uttered a warning against the traditional method. Thus Westlake insisted that the principal object of interpretation is to get at the real intention of the parties and that 'the inquiry is not to be shackled by any rule of interpretation which may exist in a particular national jurisprudence but is not generally accepted in the civilized world'.[3] It was in connection with the interpretation of treaties that Hall – who, it ought to be said, put before the reader his own list of rules of construction – coined the frequently quoted phrase that 'there is no place for the refinements of the courts in the rough jurisprudence of nations'.[4] Lawrence, without otherwise contributing substantially to the subject, deplored the 'vast amount of misplaced ingenuity'[5] expended by writers on this matter. More recently Professor Hyde has emphasized the inconvenience of purely technical rules by insisting on the necessity of not limiting the freedom of the judge in ascertaining the true intention of the parties from all available sources.[6] But, with the exception of the last mentioned author, there has been no attempt on the part of text-book writers to translate this criticism into action by a consideration of the practical problems of interpretation.

It may be an interesting theme for speculation to explain this predilection of early writers for detailed rules covering all contingencies. Probably at a time when the interpretation of treaties by the impartial agency of an international judge was unknown or exceptional there was a desire to limit by a number of clear-cut rules the freedom in interpretation enjoyed by States acting as judges in their own cause. However that may be, the result of the preponderance of technical and abstract rules of interpretation has been to neglect almost entirely a question of interpretation with which tribunals are constantly confronted when construing treaties, namely, the question of the relevance of so-called preparatory work.

---

[1] Book II, ch. xvi, § i.
[2] See, for instance, Phillimore, II, ch. VIII; Fiore, §§ 1117–31: Rivier, II, 122–5; Fauchille, vol. I, no. 840; Oppenheim, *International Law*, vol. I (5th ed., 1935), § 553; Hershey, *International Law* (1927 ed.), § 290.
[3] Westlake, I, 282.   [4] § 112.
[5] *The Principles of International Law* (3rd ed., 1905), p. 287.
[6] See below, p. 491.

It is, as we shall see, a problem which has been confronting international tribunals from the very inception of modern international arbitration. It has occupied them in the majority of cases in which these tribunals have been called upon to interpret treaties. It has constituted a constant feature of the work of the Permanent Court of International Justice which has been called upon to deal with it in almost all cases of treaty interpretation. It is not only before tribunals that the question of preparatory work has assumed importance. It has, for instance, loomed large in the discussion concerning the meaning of the General Treaty for the Renunciation of War, in particular of the various declarations made in the course of the negotiations which preceded the signature of the treaty and which had reference to resort to war in self-defence. The relative infrequency of international adjudication prior to the establishment of the Permanent Court of International Justice partly accounts for this neglect of a question of pre-eminently practical importance. There are indications that as the result of the increased judicial activity in the post-war period more attention is now being devoted to this subject.[1]

At the same time, however, the study of the question of preparatory work as an element of interpretation of treaties has been seriously hampered by a view which experience has shown to be effective out of all proportion to the accuracy of its premises. It is believed by many that this subject is yet another example of the difference between the so-called Continental and Anglo-American schools of thought. It is maintained that while the Continental school favours resort to preparatory work in the interpretation of contracts, statutes and treaties, the Anglo-American practice tends in the opposite direction. Prior to the establishment of the Permanent Court of International Justice little was heard of this particular aspect of the divergence between the two schools of thought. The establishment of the Permanent Court assumed to represent various systems of jurisprudence has made it feasible to emphasize the real or apparent divergencies between the various systems and to couple such emphasis with an expectation that the majority of the Court

---

[1] See, in particular, Hyde, *International Law* (1922), II, 63–72; and the same in *A.J.* 23 (1929), 824–8 and 27 (1933), 502–6; Fachiri in *ibid.* 23 (1929), 745–52; Marshall Brown in *ibid.* pp. 819–24; Wright in *ibid.* pp. 97–104; and the same, *Mandates under the League of Nations* (1930), pp. 353–64; Yü, *The Interpretation of Treaties* (1927), *passim*; Ehrlich in *Hague Recueil* (1928) (iv), pp. 117–31; Miller in *Iowa Law Review*, 17 (1931–3), 206–22, 366–73; Chang, *The Interpretation of Treaties by Judicial Tribunals* (1933), pp. 95–140; Crandall, *Treaties: Their Making and Enforcement* (2nd ed., 1916), pp. 384–6; Bittner, *Die Lehre von den Völkerrechtlichen Vertragsurkunden* (1924), §§ 28, 53.

would carefully refrain from deciding international disputes by reference to their own system of law. General phrases of this nature are impressive. In fact, the Permanent Court of International Justice has shown in this matter a degree of caution which is due not so much to the inherent difficulties of the question as to the desire not to make the Court appear to have committed itself to one particular 'school of thought'. As a result the Court, whose activity is conspicuous for constant recourse to preparatory work, has taken a very long time to make that contribution to the matter which ought to be expected from a tribunal of its authority and permanence.

The insistence on the fundamental divergence in this matter between two schools of thought has further resulted in concealing the fact that the question of preparatory work is only one aspect of the general problem of admissibility of extrinsic evidence for the inter-pretation of written instruments and that this question again constitutes a problem of general jurisprudence. It constitutes one aspect of the ever-topical question in the matter of interpretation – a question which formed one of the subjects of the controversy between the Proculeians and the Sabinians. It is the problem of the choice between literal and liberal interpretation, between the word and the intention. The immutable meaning of the word, given by the general as distinguished from the individual standard, represents the requirement of convenience and certainty, the realization of the intention of the author of the expression, disregarding if necessary the common standard, represents the element of equity and justice. The early stage of legal development is characterized by formalism and rigidity, which in turn are due to the desire to maintain certainty and security. For this reason undeveloped law exhibits a tendency to rigid textual interpretation excluding extrinsic evidence. Legal development tends to make of interpretation an equitable process of adjusting, by all legitimate means, the written expression to the intention of its author if inquiry reveals that there is a discrepancy between the two. Historical reasons may have retarded this develop-ment in some countries and accelerated it in others, but the process is essentially the same in all systems. The problem is much wider and more general than one may be inclined to assume from vague references to fundamental differences between the Anglo-American and Continental schools of thought. This is one of the reasons why it is deemed necessary here to begin the inquiry by an examination of some systems of municipal law in the matter of interpretation of contracts and statutes.

Before proceeding it may be useful to mention that 'preparatory work' in relation to treaties may be understood in two meanings: (a) It may refer to the various written instruments emanating from or recording the declarations of the views of the negotiators of the treaty from the commencement of negotiations to the ratification and bearing upon the treaty in question. Such 'preparatory work' includes diplomatic correspondence through which the treaty is negotiated in cases in which the treaty is not negotiated at a special conference. It includes, in other cases, the negotiations preceding the conference; the original and successive drafts of the treaty; the negotiations at the conference and its committees as recorded in the minutes or otherwise; instructions issued to the delegates. (b) It may refer to the expression of opinion of Governments or authoritative members or committees of legislative bodies during the deliberations of these bodies. In these lectures we shall be primarily concerned with the first type of preparatory work, i.e. with the negotiations leading to the conclusion of the treaty.

II. *Preparatory Work in the Interpretation of Contracts*

It may be a matter for discussion whether treaties are analogous to contracts or statutes, or whether some of them – the so-called 'law-making' treaties – are comparable to statutes and the other treaties to contracts. The accurate view probably is that while all treaties are of a contractual nature inasmuch as they are the result of the common agreement of the signatories, some of them fulfil the function which statutes perform within the State, namely, the function of laying down rules of conduct of universal or general application among a considerable number of members of the community. In any case contracts, statutes, and treaties are juridical acts which have to be interpreted by reference to the common intention of their authors. It is therefore convenient to study the question of preparatory work from the point of view of the rules applicable to these various categories of documents in various systems of law.

In the matter of interpretation of contracts, the private law of the various countries is the result of the working of a number of factors. There is, in the first instance, the doctrine of merger embodying the principle that the written contract is the final expression of the intention of the parties, that is to say, that all contemporaneous and preceding oral expressions are merged in the writing and displaced by it. There are, secondly, historical factors which, at various stages of

455

legal development, have worked for the exclusive rigidity of rules of evidence. There are, finally, the requirements of substantive justice demanding that no artificial hindrances shall be placed in the way of elucidating the common intention of the parties. English and French law – which on this matter are very much alike – offer good examples of this development.

The student who first approaches the study of English law is struck by the apparent rigidity of the law of evidence in the matter of interpretation of contracts; by the mass of subtle and elaborate exceptions; and, generally, by the conspicuous place which the question of extrinsic evidence occupies in the law. The rigid rule is expressed in two propositions which are in fact different expressions of the same idea. The first is that when a transaction has been reduced to writing the latter becomes the exclusive record thereof and no evidence, other than the document itself, can be given to prove the terms of the transaction. The written contract is the best evidence; it is superior testimony and no inferior, i.e. extrinsic, evidence can be admitted to prove its terms. In the words of Chief Justice Baron Gilbert, whose book on *Evidence*, published in 1756, was most instrumental in giving expression to the 'best evidence' principle, 'a man must have the utmost evidence that the nature of the fact is capable of'. The second rule, connected with the first, is that when the transaction has been reduced to writing, parole evidence in general and in particular drafts, deleted clauses or informal agreements preceding the contract will not be admitted to contradict, vary, add to or subtract from a contract.[1] There were historical reasons which influenced this rigid exclusion of evidence in substitution and variation of documents.[2] Much was probably due to the Roman law doctrine that a form of evidence can be dissolved only by matter of equal or higher, but not of inferior, degree. The same analogy of Roman law stimulated the indisputability of mercantile instruments. The exclusion of parole evidence was also influenced by 'special reasons, which are partly historical and partly precautionary, but wholly arbitrary'. There was the tendency of judges to keep the construction of writings out of the jury's hands by applying strict rules in matters of evidence. To this there was added the professional interests of conveyancers bent upon preserving

---

[1] *Inglis* v. *Buttery*, 3 App. Cas. 352; *Legott* v. *Barrett*, 15 Ch.D. 306; *National Bank* v. *Falkingham* [1902] A.C. 585, 591; *Roden* v. *London Small Arms Co.*, 46 L.J.Q.B. 213; *Smith* v. *Thompson*, 8 C.B. 44.

[2] Phipson, on *Evidence* (7th ed., 1930), pp. 544–6, 582–8; and the same in *L.Q.R.* 20 (1904), 245–71; Wigmore, on *Evidence*, §§ 2426 and 2461.

the rigidly professional standards of interpretation, and the presumption in favour of the legal heir with the result that there was no inducement to use all available means of liberal interpretation in order to save a will from failing.

Upon these rigid rules of interpretation practice has engrafted a number of exceptions like the one that evidence is admissible to contradict or to vary documents intended as an informal memorandum of a transaction (like a receipt), and not as a binding legal instrument; or when it is clear that the writing was not intended to contain the full agreement; or in order to show the true nature of the transaction, or the legal relationship of the parties; or in order to prove allegations affecting the legal validity of the document, e.g. incapacity, duress, forgery, etc.; or to explain the meaning of a particular term having regard to the customary use of language in the neighbourhood or in the branch of business. Alongside the rule excluding evidence in substitution for or alteration of a written instrument there has established itself a clear rule that, where the language is peculiar or its application to the facts is ambiguous or inaccurate, extrinsic evidence is as a rule admissible. This rule has not established itself without difficulty and without the resistance of the factors militating in favour of literal interpretation. But it may now be regarded as firmly established in the law. The principles governing this rule were expressed, with such clarity as the difficult subject permits, in the famous propositions of Sir John Wigram, the author of a book on *Extrinsic Evidence* published in 1831.

Although Wigram's propositions signify a landmark in the development towards less rigid rules of interpretation, he has in turn become responsible for a classification which has in many respects been regarded as hampering. While he admitted extrinsic evidence 'explanatory of words themselves', he barred it rigidly in regard to evidence of intention. Practice has shown this classification to be artificial.[1] The only limitation which is generally recognized as still valid is that direct evidence of intention is not admissible except in such cases as equivocation, i.e. when the language of a document though intended to apply to one person or thing only is equally applicable in all its parts to two or more and it is impossible from the document itself to decide to whom it applies.

It is not surprising that among this maze of rigid rules and no less rigid exceptions there has been a tendency to forget that – at least in the interpretation of contracts with which alone we are

---

[1] Wigram, on *Extrinsic Evidence*, p. 587.

concerned here – the inadmissibility of extrinsic evidence in the shape of preceding negotiations and otherwise refers only to cases in which it is sought to 'contradict, vary, add to or subtract from' a written document. Extrinsic evidence in the form of preceding negotiation is admissible to *interpret* a doubtful provision. It may be used as an instrument of interpretation when the words of the contract are not clear and whenever it is necessary to ascertain whether it was intended to give them a narrower or wider meaning.[1] It is here after all that the crux of the matter lies. For once extrinsic evidence is admitted as an element of interpretation it will as a rule be admitted in all cases except when the party putting forward the evidence admits that it is meant 'to contradict, vary, add to or subtract from' the document. For the question whether the evidence put forward interprets or varies the instrument is one which cannot be decided on the face of the document. It is true that these relaxations of the rule are qualified by the ever-present limitation that in no case is direct evidence of intention admissible, but it is permissible to doubt whether there is a clear line of demarcation between direct evidence of intention and evidence, which is admissible, as to what was in the mind of the parties in regard to the circumstances and subject matter of the contract or the meaning of an ambiguous term – so long as evidence is not admittedly put forward in order 'to contradict, vary, add to or subtract from' the agreement.

There are a number of instructive cases which show to what extent extrinsic evidence and preceding negotiations may be resorted to. In *Bank of New Zealand* v. *Simpson* the Privy Council had to decide whether the Court below properly admitted extrinsic evidence in order to interpret certain words as used by the parties in the contract. The respondent was allowed to give evidence as to what took place at the interview in which the appellant confirmed the contract, and as to the intention of the parties. There were also tendered a circular prepared by the respondent and certain correspondence between the parties said to support the view of the appellants. Their Lordships dismissed the appeal: 'Extrinsic evidence is always admissible, not to contradict or vary the contract, but to apply it to the facts which the parties had in their minds and were negotiating about.'[2] But their Lordships affirmed the rule that

[1] *Bank of New Zealand* v. *Simpson* [1900] A.C. 182; *Charrington* v. *Wooder* [1914] A.C. 71, 77; the *Curfew* [1891] P. 131; *Heffield* v. *Meadows*, L.R. 4 C.P. 595; *Henniker* v. *Wigg*, 4 Q.B.D. 792.

[2] [1900] A.C. 182, at p. 187. Reference was made to *Grant* v. *Grant*, L.R. 5 C.P. 727; *Ogilvie* v. *Foljambe* (1817), 3 Mer. 53; *Macdonald* v. *Longbottom*, 1 E.E. 977; *Smith* v. *Thompson*, 8 C.B. 44.

parole evidence is not admissible to show that the parties meant something different from what they have said. In the *Curfew* the Court below considered the language of the charterparty ambiguous, and admitted evidence of the previous correspondence between the parties to show what was their intention in entering the charterparty.[1] It was held, on appeal, that there was sufficient ambiguity in the language of the charterparty to warrant the admission of this evidence. It would appear therefore that there is in English law in the matter of contracts no such rigidity as that which, as we shall see, obtains in the matter of interpretation of statutes. Preparatory work in the form of written records emanating from the parties may or may not be inadmissible. Analogous material is, as will be seen, always excluded in the interpretation of statutes.

The position with regard to the interpretation of contracts is not altogether different in French law. At the outset the student is confronted with a rule of apparent rigidity resembling that of exclusion of parole evidence in English law. Article 1341 of the *Code Civil* provides expressly that 'no verbal evidence can be given against or beyond the contents of the instrument, nor as to what may be alleged to have been said before, at the time of, or after the drawing up of the instrument'. This Article has its origin in the well-known Ordinance of Moulins of 1556, which was re-enacted with some substantial changes[2] in 1667, and is now reproduced in the Code. Its main purpose was to shorten procedure and to prevent perjury. However, the apparent rigidity of Article 1341 disappears when it is considered that according to the most authoritative interpretation of courts and commentators, parole evidence is *not* excluded when the evidence put forward aims not at contradicting the document or varying it, but at interpreting obscure or ambiguous clauses or at determining the scope of the declaration.[3] For Article 1341 must be read and has been read in the light of the overriding Article 1156 which lays down that 'in construing agreements, one must seek to ascertain what was the common intention of the parties, rather than to be tied down by the literal meaning of the terms used'. It is in connection with this Article that *jurisprudence* and commentators have allowed full use of extrinsic evidence.[4]

---

[1] See also *Lewis* v. *Great Western Railway*, 3 Q.B.D. 195.

[2] The Ordinance of Moulins prohibited parole evidence to add to the writing; the Ordinance of 1667 prohibited parole evidence to vary the writing.

[3] See the decision of the Chambre des Requêtes, 9 March 1909, Sirey (1910), I, 28; Planiol and Ripert, *Traité pratique de droit civil français*, VII (1931), 866, 867; Aubry and Rau, *Cours de droit civil français* (5th ed., 1902), IV, 570 and n. 3.

[4] Planiol and Ripert, *Traité pratique de droit civil*, VI, 513.

Moreover, the effect of Article 1341 has been seriously limited by a number of important exceptions. In the first instance, it has no application to commercial matters. Secondly, parole evidence, even when intended to vary or contradict the written instrument, is admissible when there exists a so-called commencement of proof in writing, i.e. a written document emanating from the person against whom the claim is made, or from the person whom he represents.[1] The *Code Civil* explains this exception by adding that the commencement of proof makes the fact alleged probable. And Article 1348 contains further detailed exceptions of a less comprehensive nature. On the other hand, in regard to documents of a solemn and formal character, like wills, the tendency has been to restrict recourse to extrinsic evidence so far as possible[2] – yet another reminder that in these matters much depends upon the nature of the document to be interpreted. This applies to most systems of law.

The German Civil Code has avoided these difficulties by dispensing with all restrictive rules of evidence. The *sedes materiae* is generally held to lie in Article 133 of the Code which provides that in the interpretation of a declaration of intention the true intention is to be sought without regard to the literal meaning of the expression. This Article has been interpreted as meaning, *inter alia*, that the intention of the parties may be elucidated from all accompanying circumstances including the preceding negotiations and the drafts.[3] This liberality in the matter of interpretation has by no means resulted in uncertainty and confusion. Thus it is a clear rule with German courts that in the case of a written contract the first and direct evidence of the contents of the contract is the writing itself, and not the records of preceding negotiations. The presumption is that the written instrument is accurate and complete.[4] But the law does not exclude parole evidence to exclude that presumption. It merely shifts the burden of proof upon the party alleging *aliud scriptum atque actum*.[5]

It has been deemed necessary here to consider in some detail the question of preparatory work in the interpretation of contracts in

[1] Article 1347.

[2] See Geny, *Méthode d'interprétation et sources en droit privé positif*, vol. 1 (2nd ed., 1919), § 104 (*in fine*); Sirey (1896), 1, 308; Sirey (1888), 1, 479.

[3] Staudinger, *Kommentar zum bürgerlichen Gesetzbuch* (9th ed. by Loewenfeld and Riezler, 1925), 1, 551; Siméon-David, *Lehrbuch des bürgerlichen Rechtes* (12th ed., 1923), 1, 205; *Decisions of the Reichsgericht*, 59, p. 218; 62, pp. 50, 382. See also Article 18 of the Swiss Code of Obligations.

[4] *Decisions of the Reichsgericht*, 52, p. 23.

[5] Siméon-David, *Lehrbuch des bürgerlichen Rechtes*, p. 230. And see *Decisions of the Reichsgericht*, 62, p. 49; 88, p. 370.

private law. An examination of this question shows that it would be superficial to reduce it to a clear cut divergence between the common law and Roman law systems; that the position in English and French law is in essential aspects the same; and that from the network of rigid rules and the exceptions there emerges the tendency to leave the field free for the ascertainment of the real intention of the parties. This result is not without importance for the solution of similar problems confronting the interpretation of treaties.

III. Preparatory Work in the Interpretation of Statutes

The interpretation of statutes is of interest for the subject of this course, not only because of the tendency to regard some (including the most important) treaties as statutes, but also because of the influence which the rigid rule of English law on this matter seems to have exercised on the treatment of this question in international law. The apparent rigidity of the English rule excluding parole evidence in the interpretation of private documents shows itself even more conspicuously in the matter of statutes. It is a well-established rule of law that in order to construe a statute it is not permissible to have recourse to the parliamentary history of the enactment – like the original draft of the bill, the changes which it underwent, and the speeches in Parliament.[1] The reasons and the origin of this rule have never, so far as I know, been thoroughly investigated. Some of them may be tentatively mentioned here. In the first instance, as Dicey points out, there is the principle that the will of the sovereign legislature can be expressed only through an Act of Parliament, i.e. through the combined action of its three constituent parts. This principle, which has its origin in historical causes, is in turn due to the fact that an Act of Parliament was once in reality – and not, as it is today, only in form – a law 'enacted by the King by and with the advice and consent of the Lords and Commons in Parliament assembled'.[2] This reason is also given in a judicial decision as early as 1769.[3] In this connection it is useful to

---

[1] *R. v. Capel* (1840), 12 Ad. & El. 382; 113 E.R. 857; *R. v. Whittaker* (1848), 2 Car. & Kir. 636; *A.G.* v. *Sillem* (1864), 2 H. &. C. 431; *Richard* v. *McBride* (1881), 8 Q.B.D. 119; *Herron* v. *Rathmines and Rathger Improvement Commissioners* [1892] A.C. 498; *Millar* v. *Taylor* (1769), 4 Burr. 2303; *R.* v. *Board of Education* [1909] 2 K.B. 1045; *Administrator-General of Bengal* v. *Prem Lal Mullick* (1895), L.R. 22 Ind. App. 107; *R.* v. *West Riding of Yorkshire County Council* [1906] 2 K.B. 676; *Hollinshead* v. *Hazleton* [1916] 1 A.C. 428; *Viscountess Rhondda's claim* [1922] 2 A.C. 339

[2] *Law of the Constitution* (8th ed., 1920), p. 403 and n. 1 on p. 404.

[3] See Willes J. in *Millar* v. *Taylor* (1769), 4 Burr. 2303, 2332: 'The sense and meaning of an Act of Parliament must be collected from what it says when passed into law, and

note the frequent decisions which refuse to recognize that there is any force of law in the resolutions of a part of the legislature.[1] If the resolutions of one House are legally irrelevant for the purpose of determining private rights, then it is not surprising that isolated expressions of opinion during debate are not admissible. Thirdly, it may be possible to trace here the influence of the English constitutional usage which, in the seventeenth and eighteenth centuries, prohibited the publication of parliamentary debates and proceedings. If parliamentary debates could not be published it would be inappropriate and might become a source of abuse if they could be referred to in courts as an interpretation of the will of the legislature. Finally, in this connection it is not impossible that the rigidity of the rule as to the exclusion of parole evidence may to some extent have influenced the law in the matter of statutes. The student of constitutional history may see also in the tenacity of this rule yet another manifestation of the strong position of the judiciary as compared with that of other countries. The rejection of the parliamentary history of statutes as an element of interpretation is yet another assertion of judicial freedom of interpretation.[2] There are many important reasons – some of which will be considered later – which necessitate caution in the use of the parliamentary history of statutes, but, as has been suggested, the reasons which in England became responsible for this rule have been not so much reasons of convenience as historical peculiarities. This explains partly its tenacity and imperviousness to criticism which has recently been levelled against it.[3] On the other hand there must be noted the relaxations of the rule on account of the admissibility: (a) of reports of commissions appointed to investigate the subject matter of the bill prior to its introduction before Parliament;[4] (b) of extrinsic evidence showing the state of the law prior to the passing of the statute and the cause

not from the history of changes it underwent in the House where it took rise. That history is not known to the other House or to the Sovereign.'

[1] *Stockdale* v. *Hansard* (1839), 9 A. & E. 1; *Bowles* v. *The Bank of England* [1913] 1 Ch. 57.

[2] Such freedom, it may be added, is not necessarily opposed to a progressive and creative interpretation of the statute. An interpretation based on the intention of the legislature, as revealed in the parliamentary history of the bill, may be less progressive and less in accordance with social change than that which is the result of the unhampered freedom of judicial interpretation. This aspect is not always, it appears, sufficiently realized by the critics of the established rule.

[3] See Smith in *J.C.L.* 3rd ser., 9 (1927), 155–8; Amos in *Cambridge Law Journal*, 5 (1934), 171–3.

[4] *Eastman Photographic Materials Co.* v. *Comptroller-General of Patents* [1898] A.C. 571; *Curran* v. *Treleaven* [1891] 2 Q.B. 545, 557; *Powell* v. *Kempton Park Co.* [1899] A.C. 143, 157; *Taff Vale Railway Co.* v. *Amalgamated Society* [1901] A.C. 426.

and necessity of the statute.[1] In Coke's words, in *Heydon*'s case, extrinsic evidence is admissible to ascertain, *inter alia*, what was the common law before the Act and what was the mischief for which the common law did not provide.[2] Also, the occasional departures, by judges of distinction, from the established rule are not without interest. These departures have not imperilled the rule and in some cases they have been criticized in subsequent decisions, but they testify to the inconvenience of the present position.[3]

In the United States the original attitude of courts in the matter of the interpretation of statutes was the same as in English law. The decisions of the Supreme Court during the nineteenth century are quite uncompromising on this matter.[4] But there were even then instances of the Supreme Court referring to the reports and the journals of the Constitutional Convention.[5] Recently, there has been a more marked departure from the original practice, although the departure is a gradual one. Thus while the Supreme Court in interpreting an Act of Congress relating to naturalization of aliens supported its decision by reference to Congressional debates,[6] it still safeguarded itself by saying that the Congressional debates 'furnished no basis for judicial construction of the statute'. But it attached importance to them 'as an important historic incident, which may not be altogether ignored in the search for the true meaning of the words which are in themselves historic'. This

---

[1] *Wallis* v. *Russell* [1902] 2 Ir. Rep. 585; *per* Bramwell B. in *A. G.* v. *Sillem* (1863), 2 H.C. 431, at p. 531; *per* Coleridge J. in *R.* v. *Rlane*, 13 Q.B. 773; *Viscountess Rhondda's Claim* [1922] 2 A.C. 339. And see Maxwell, *On the Interpretation of Statutes* (6th ed., 1920), pp. 39–48; Craies, *A Treatise on the Interpretation of Statutes* (3rd ed., 1923), pp. 116 *et seq.*; Phipson, *The Law of Evidence*, p. 595.

[2] *Heydon*'s case (1584), 3 Co. Rep. 8. And see Lindley M.R. in *In re Mayfair Property Co.* [1898] 2 Ch. 28, at p. 35.

[3] See Maxwell, *On the Interpretation of Statutes*, pp. 49 *et seq.* on Lord Nottingham's interpretation of the Statute of Frauds by reference to the fact that he had brought it into the House of Lords; on the Privy Council referring, in an ecclesiastical case (*Ridsdale* v. *Clifton*, 46 L.T.P.C. 27) to the parliamentary history of a proviso; on Lord Westbury referring to the speech made by himself as Attorney-General in introducing the Bankruptcy Bill in 1860; and others. See also Cockburn C.J. in *South Eastern Railway Co.* v. *The Railway Commissioners* (1880), 5 Q.B.D. 217, 236. And see the frequently quoted case of Chief Justice Hengham who is reported to have said that he knew better than counsel the meaning of the 2nd Statute of Westminster as he was instrumental in drawing it up; *Y.B.* 33 Ed. I, 82. When Brabazon C.J. was in doubt as to the nature of *Scire Facias* in that Statute, c. 45, he said: 'We will advise with our companions who were at the making of the statute': *Bygot* v. *Ferrers*, *Y.B.* 33–5 Ed. I, 385 (as quoted in Plucknett, *Statutes: Their Interpretation in the First Half of the Fourteenth Century* (1922), p. 50).

[4] See, e.g., *Alridge* v. *Williams*, 3 How. 9, 24, where the reasoning closely approaches that in *Millar* v. *Taylor*. See also *United States* v. *Trans-Missouri Freight Association*, 166 U.S. 290, 316.

[5] *Blake* v. *National Banks*, 23 Wall. 307, 317.

[6] *United States* v. *Bhagat Singh Thind*, 261 U.S. 204, 214.

obeisance to a traditional doctrine seems almost antiquated when we consider that of late the reference to parliamentary history as an element of interpretation has become a constant feature of the work of the Supreme Court and of Federal courts.[1] This is so in particular in reference to reports of committees.[2] Undoubtedly the Supreme Court has proceeded with caution. It has differentiated between the various elements of parliamentary history. It has attached importance to statements of chairmen of committees and to reports of the latter; but it has refused to be guided by individual expressions of opinion in the general debate.[3] In any case the general position may be summarized to the effect that the old rule is no longer the sole authority. 'The statute, as punctuated, reads as its legislative history shows Congress intended it to read' – say three justices of the Supreme Court in their concurring opinion in a recent case.[4]

In the courts of the British Dominions, like Canada[5] and Australia, the English rule still prevails. In the High Court of Australia O'Connor J. while objecting to the quotation of debates in the Federal Convention of the United States, insisted that reference to the *Federalist* in American courts was no more than reference to a text-book or an expert opinion.[6] However, it is of interest to note that in the same case Griffith J., while equally questioning the propriety of the reference to debates in the Convention, said: 'They are no higher than parliamentary debates, and are not to be referred to except for the purpose of seeing what was the subject-matter of discussion, what was the evil to be remedied, and so forth.'[7] This is not the English rule which excludes the parliamentary history of the bill altogether. Griffith J. would admit them for certain purposes.

While it would be a mistake to exaggerate the rigidity of the exclusion of the parliamentary history in English-speaking countries

[1] See *Omaechevarria* v. *Idaho* (1917), 246 U.S. 343. See in particular the monumental opinion of Taft C.J. in *Myers* v. *United States*, 272 U.S. 52 *passim*; *Okanogan and other Indian Tribes* v. *United States*, 279 U.S. 672, in particular at p. 684; *Oceanic Navigation Co.* v. *Stranahan*, 214 U.S. 320. As to Federal courts see *Buttfield* v. *Bidwell*, 96 Fed. 328 (reference to the report of the Senate Committee and the successive amendments); *In re Marshall Paper Co.*, 102 Fed. 872 (reference to early drafts of the bill); *Frank Cook* v. *United States*, 288 U.S. 102.
[2] For a valuable collection of cases bearing on this matter see Chamberlain in *University of Chicago Law Review* (May 1933), pp. 81–8. See in particular *Duplex Printing Press* v. *Deering*, 254 U.S. 443, 477.
[3] *United States* v. *Trans-Missouri Freight Association*, 166 U.S. 290, 310.
[4] *United States* v. *Shreveport Grain and Elevator Co.*, 287 U.S. 77.
[5] *Gosselin* v. *R.*, 33 Canada S.C. 255, 264.
[6] *Sydney Municipal Council* v. *Commonwealth* (1904), 1 C.L.R. 208, 213.
[7] *Ibid.*

it is a mistake to overrate their importance on the Continent. They are not a source of law; they serve to interpret the law. The German theory and practice in the matter have been stated by a writer of the authority of Binding in a manner meriting quotation:

With the promulgation of the statute there disappears with one stroke the whole structure of the intentions and the wishes of the spiritual authors of the statute and of the legislature itself; henceforth the statute rests on itself, supported by its own force and weight, filled by its own meaning; it may be wiser or less wise than its author; it may be more fortunate in expression; and in places which the legislator regarded as clear beyond doubt it may become hopelessly controversial by juxtaposition with other parts of the statute.[1]

German writers distinguish between the will of the legislator and the meaning of the law. In order to ascertain the latter preparatory work – the so-called *Materialien* – may be resorted to so long as no attempt is made to use them as a vehicle of authentic interpretation.[2] German courts have as a rule carefully examined this preparatory work. They have been alive to the possible dangers of this instrument of interpretation and have relied not on isolated expressions of opinion in the legislature but on the official drafts and commentaries thereon. Even these have never been regarded as in any way binding, and there are decisions in which the Court found that the final text of the law was in direct opposition to the official commentary on the draft, and acted accordingly.[3] But this caution in approach has not had the result of seriously questioning the right and duty of courts to have recourse to the legislative history of enactments. It is in particular in the complicated sphere of labour law that German courts have in post-war years had recourse to the legislative history of various enactments.[4]

The position is on the whole the same in France, although for a time French courts exhibited, for similar reasons of caution, the

---

[1] Binding, *Handbuch des Strafrechts*, 1 (1885), 454. And see the judgment of the *Reichswirtschaftsgericht* of 4 December 1920 (*Juristische Wochenschrift* (1921), p. 693) in which this passage is quoted with approval.

[2] See Staudinger's *Kommentar zum Bürgerlichen Gesetzbuch* (9th ed. by Riezler, 1925), p. 19. See also Siméon-David, *Lehrbuch des bürgerlichen Rechtes*, pp. 37, 38; Dernburg, *Pandekten*, § 35, n. 6; Windscheid, *Pandekten*, 1, 100, n. 6; Schuster, *The Principles of German Civil Law* (1907), p. 11. And see Bekker, *Ernst und Scherz über unsere Wissenschaft* (1892), pp. 145, 146.

[3] *Decisions of the Reichsgericht in Civil Cases*, 74, p. 81.

[4] See *Decisions of the Federal Labour Court*, 11, p. 268 (decision of 25 June 1932); *ibid.* 10, p. 253 (decision of 27 February 1932); *ibid.* p. 343 (decision of 19 March 1932). See also decision of the Federal Labour Court of 29 April 1931, *International Series of Decisions in Labour Law* (1931), p. 213.

tendency to limit recourse to *travaux préparatoires*.[1] But the principle itself has never been seriously questioned, and may be regarded as being fully in force today.

A survey of the municipal law of some of the principal States has thus shown that the existing differences in the matter of interpretation of contracts and statutes cannot be understood with the help of the short-cut of an alleged difference between the Anglo-American and Continental systems of law; that in some cases these differences cut across the various systems of law; that in others they are due to historical circumstances; and that they do not apply uniformly to all types of written expressions of will which are subject to interpretation. Different principles may apply to the interpretation of contracts, and different ones to statutes. And, it will be shown, the principles applicable to both do not necessarily apply to treaties. This does not mean that the examination of municipal law on the subject has proved fruitless. It has shown that there is on this subject no uniform and sufficiently 'general principle of law recognized by civilized nations' which can be adopted as a ready made rule for the interpretation of treaties. But although there is no generally recognized uniform rule there is a visible tendency operating in most systems of law towards eliminating hampering and technical rules. This in itself is a significant lesson.

IV. *Resort to Preparatory Work in the Interpretation of Treaties by Municipal Tribunals*

The resort to preparatory work in the interpretation of contracts and to parliamentary history in the interpretation of statutes has been considered here not, indeed, because the rules applicable in these matters apply also to treaties, but because they throw light on the general problem of extrinsic evidence in the interpretation of legal instruments and because they save us from the mistake of considering the matter from the point of view of alleged fundamental differences between various systems of law. There is always a temptation to assume such difference as it provides a simple and ready solution of the legal problem involved. There is equally a temptation to regard the rules of law applicable to the interpretation of any particular class of instruments as applicable to others. Thus some English lawyers have assumed that English courts do and will apply to the interpretation of treaties the same principle of exclusion of

---

[1] See on this question Gény, *Méthode d'interprétation et sources en droit privé positif*, § 104; Vander Eycken, *Méthode positive de l'interprétation juridique* (1907), nos. 80–85.

preparatory work which they apply to the admissibility of parliamentary history of statutes. This view was expressed in 1932 by a representative committee of English lawyers appointed by the Lord Chancellor to report on the reciprocal enforcement of foreign judgments.[1] It has been given support by Professor Gutteridge, one of the most distinguished comparative lawyers in the English-speaking countries.[2] It has been given expression by British representatives before the Permanent Court of International Justice.[3] However, with great respect, it must be doubted whether this is the law. The practice of British courts seems to point to the contrary. This may be seen not only from the course adopted in individual cases but also from general pronouncements to the effect that the principles applicable to the interpretation of contracts and statutes are not necessarily applicable to treaties and, generally, to interpretation of acts of an international character.

In *Maltass* v. *Maltass* Dr Lushington, a distinguished judge who had frequent occasion to interpret treaties and, generally, to apply international law, had to decide what law, having regard to the treaties between Great Britain and the Ottoman Empire, was to govern testacy and intestacy in the case of a British subject long resident as a merchant in Smyrna. It is not necessary to give an account of this case here except to the extent of stating that it depended largely on the interpretation of a number of treaties of commerce and establishment between Great Britain and Turkey. But the following extract from the judgment may fittingly be quoted, as showing the true attitude of English courts in the matter of interpretation of treaties as distinguished from the interpretation of statutes.

In the construction of treaties of this description, we cannot expect to find the same nicety of strict definition as in modern documents, such as deeds, or Acts of Parliament; it has never been the habit of those engaged in diplomacy to use legal accuracy, but rather to adopt more liberal terms. I think, in construing these treaties, we ought to look at all the historical circumstances attending them, in order to ascertain what was the true intention of the contracting parties, and to give the widest scope to the language of treaties in order to embrace within it all the objects intended to be included.[4]

In the *Leonora*, the *locus classicus* on retaliation in naval warfare,

[1] Committee Report (1932), Cmd. 4213, para. 18, p. 19.
[2] 'A Comparative View of Interpretation of Statute Law', in *Tulane Law Review*, 8 (1933) 1–20, especially p. 9.
[3] See below, pp. 498–9.   [4] 1 Robb. Ecc. 76; 163 E.R. 970.

Sir Samuel Evans devoted no less than twelve pages of the report to quotations from parliamentary utterances of Sir William Grant, Sir William Scott, and Lord Erskine on the British retaliatory Orders in Council of 1807. He did so, apparently, not without having before his mind the general rule as to the inadmissibility of parliamentary records. For we find him prefacing the lengthy exposition of the parliamentary debate by the following significant passage: 'There is no legal impropriety, I think, in referring to views of statesmen and lawyers – outside the courts – upon questions touching the law of nations, particularly in the special instances which I shall give.'[1] Apart from these pronouncements of a general character pointing to the necessity of using a different standard for instruments of an international character, there is a great number of cases of specific application of this view.

In *Webster*'s case the King's Advocate (Sir Herbert Jenner) again argued by reference to the intention of the framers of the Treaty of 1814 with France.[2] In support of this argument the King's Advocate, without, it seems, any opposition on the part of the court, produced a letter from Lord Castlereagh to the effect that it was not 'the intention of those who were entrusted with the negotiation of that treaty to bind the French Government to the restitution of any other property than such as had, prior to its seizure or confiscation, been placed under the implied protection and *bona fide* guarantee of that Government'.[3] In *Drummond*'s case (an appeal from the award of the Commissioners for liquidating the claims of British subjects on France) the representatives of the Crown, the King's Advocate (Sir Herbert Jenner) and the Attorney-General (Sir John Campbell) did not hesitate to invoke the intention of the framers of the treaty. They asked: 'How could, indeed, a French negotiator be acquainted with the technical rule of English law, by which a man, whose father and himself were born in France, is to be considered a British subject?'[4] In *Daniel* v. *Commissioners for Claims on France*,[5] relating to the inter-

---

[1] 3 B.C.P.C. at p. 212.   [2] ii Knapp 386; 12 E.R. 532.
[3] Lord Castlereagh's letter, *ibid*.
[4] ii Knapp 305; 12 E.R. 496. And see *Wall*'s case, ii Knapp 19; 12 E.R. 553. That British lawyers do not always show reluctance to invoke the parliamentary history of the laws of other States may be seen from the fact that in this case both counsel (Dr Lushington) and the Court (Sir Lancelot Shadwell) had no hesitation in referring to the history of the relevant article of the *Code Civil*.
[5] ii Knapp 48; 12 E.R. 397. See also *Marryat* v. *Wilson* (1 Bos. & Pul. 436; 126 E.R. 996) for an instance of the interpretation of the Treaty of 19 November 1794 between Great Britain and the United States by Eyre C.J. who rejected a restrictive construction of the treaty on the ground that it would be 'a chicanery unworthy of the British Government and contrary to the character of its negociations'. And see Lord Sumner's reference

pretation of the Treaty of Paris of 1814 with France concerning compensation for confiscation of British property, Lord Gifford interpreted the treaty looking 'at the occasion and the object' of the convention. In the case of the *Ships Taken at Genoa*[1] Lord Stowell had to interpret the Articles of a capitulation entered into by the British and Austrian commanders and the Government of Genoa. Lord Stowell admitted as evidence on the part of the Crown an affidavit of Lord Keith, the British commanding admiral, on the question whether the Article of the capitulations providing for the immunity from seizure of 'money, merchandise, moveables, or other effects either by land or sea' included ships. In particular, he admitted the declaration of Lord Keith to the effect that the proposal to exempt shipping '*was* made, but that it was rejected, and expunged with his own hand'.[2]

There was no departure from this practice during the First World War. In *Porter* v. *Freudenberg*[3] the Court of Appeal was called upon to interpret Article 23(h) of the Hague Convention of 1907 upon the Laws and Customs of War on Land. Lord Reading C.J., in giving the judgment of the Court, examined in detail the 'legislative history' of that Article. He referred at some length to the original form of the Article as introduced by the German delegates and to the interpretation which they put on it. He then discussed the changes in the language of the Article in the course of the drafting and referred to the fact that they were adopted by the Conference without discussion or debate. This departure from the practice followed in the matter of statutes was not seriously weakened by the observation that the paragraph in question must be interpreted as it stood in the ratified convention and that the intention of the proposer was immaterial.[4]

In the *Paklat* the Supreme Court of Hong Kong, sitting in Prize, had to decide whether an enemy ship carrying women and child fugitives from a naval base of the enemy, a blockade of which was expected, was 'employed on a philanthropic mission' within the meaning of Article 4 of the Eleventh Hague Convention and was

in the *Blonde* to an interpretation of the Sixth Hague Convention described as not consistent 'with the dignity of negotiations' (3 B.C.P.C. 1042) and to the impossibility 'whatever the imperfection of their phrasing, that the framers of such instruments should have intended any Power to escape its obligations by a quibbling interpretation' (*ibid.* at p. 1041).

[1] 4 Ch. R. 388.

[2] *Ibid.* at p. 399. I am indebted to Dr McNair (*Hague Recueil* (1933)), for the reference to this case.

[3] [1915] 1 K.B. 857.   [4] *Ibid.* at p. 876.

therefore exempt from capture. Rees-Davies C.J. applied to the Foreign Office for the official report of the Committee of the Second Hague Conference[1] which, he thought, 'leaves no reasonable doubt as to the construction to be placed on the Article in question'.[2]

In the *Tubantia* the Attorney-General, Sir Frederick Smith (as he then was), cited in argument the speech of the German delegate at the Hague Conference who, while proposing the regulation in question, explained that Article 1 of the Eleventh Hague Convention did not include parcels.[3]

In the *Marie Leonhardt*, Sir Henry Duke, when dealing with the question whether the concessions occasionally granted to enemy merchantmen in ports of the belligerents at the outbreak of war were recognitions of a right or acts of grace, said: 'I am guided to the true answer to this inquiry by the proceedings at the Hague Conference of 1907 which led to the formulation of Convention VI.'[4]

These cases ought to be distinguished from the numerous cases in which British courts during the First World War interpreted the provisions of the Declaration of London by reference to the General Report (the so-called Renault Report) of the Drafting Committee of the Conference which was presented to and adopted by the Conference.[5] In the Declaration of London Order in Council (no. 1) of 20 August 1914[6] the British Government, while putting into force, with some modifications, the Declaration of London, directed British courts to treat the General Report of the Drafting Committee as an authoritative interpretation of the declaration. This act was in itself significant seeing that prior to the War the question of the authority of the report was widely discussed and that writers like Holland questioned its authoritative character.[7] But British courts went beyond the Governmental declaration and frequently had recourse to the proceedings of the London Conference and the preparatory work which preceded it.

---

[1] *Deuxième Conférence Internationale de la Paix* (1907), *Actes et Documents.*
[2] 1 B.C.P.C. 515.   [3] 5 L.R.P.C. 286.   [4] 3 B.C.P.C. 769.
[5] *London Gazette* (21 August 1914).
[6] Thus in the *Kim* (1 B.C.P.C. 405, at p. 491) Sir Samuel Evans referred to the Renault Report of the Declaration of London in the matter of Article 42 of the declaration (penalty for carriage of contraband). In the *Sorfareren* he had no hesitation in referring to the same report in the matter of Article 43 (*ibid.* p. 589, at p. 603). He followed the same course in the *Axel Johnson* where he referred at length to the Renault Report relating to absolute contraband (Article 30) (*ibid.* p. 532, at p. 536). See also the *Leda* (1 B.C.P.C. 239) and the *Thor* (*ibid.* p. 232), both quoted by Garner, *Prize Law during the World War* (1927), s. 115.
[7] Holland in *R.I.* 2nd ser., 13 (1911), 342–6. But see Westlake, *Papers*, pp. 652–4, 667–70.

In the *Lorenzo* the Chief Justice of St Lucia, sitting in Prize, in interpreting the provision of Article 40 of the Declaration of London had recourse to the Proceedings of the Conference upon the reading of which the meaning of the convention became 'reasonably clear' to him. He pointed out that 'for the interpretation of a code, recourse may be had to the deliberations of the codifiers, who, unlike members of Parliament, are presumed to have expert knowledge of the matters which they discuss'.[1] In the *Hakan* Sir Samuel Evans reviewed at length the memoranda exchanged by the various Governments and showing their attitude on the matter of the penalty for the carriage of contraband.[2]

Finally, in the post-war period, there must be mentioned the case of *Amodu Tijani* v. *The Secretary, Southern Rhodesia*[3] in which the Judicial Committee of the Privy Council was called upon to interpret a treaty of cession in which the King of the Island of Lagos (near Southern Nigeria) ceded to the British Crown the port and island of Lagos. In giving judgment, Lord Haldane referred to the debate which took place in the House of Commons in 1862 and which showed the interpretation put upon the treaty by the British Government. It was mainly by reference to this interpretation that Lord Haldane construed the general terms of the cession as referring primarily to sovereign rights and as leaving intact private property rights.[4] This case is of particular interest when we consider that it was Lord Haldane who in another judgment strongly deprecated recourse to the parliamentary history of a statute.[5]

This, it is submitted, is an impressive array of authority which ought to act as a check upon the notion that English courts are under a necessity to apply to the interpretation of treaties the rule applied by them in the matter of interpretation of statutes. While thus the contention as to the peculiarity of the Anglo-American practice in the matter of treaties appears to be open to serious doubt in regard to England, it has no foundation whatever so far as the United States is concerned. The Supreme Court of that country has not only as a matter of constant practice had recourse to preparatory work for the interpetation of treaties: it has expressly affirmed its right and duty to do so. This was the early practice of the Supreme Court, at a time when the exclusion of parliamentary history for the interpretation of

---

[1] 1 B.C.P.C. 226, at p. 228.
[2] 2 B.C.P.C. 210, at p. 220. See also the *Jeanne, ibid.* p. 302.
[3] [1921] 2 A.C. 399.
[4] *Ibid.* pp. 406, 407.
[5] *Vacher and Sons, Limited* v. *London Society of Compositors* [1913] A.C. 113.

statutes was more rigid than it is nowadays.[1] But recently recourse to preparatory work has become an approved tool of interpretation. In the recent case of *Factor* v. *Laubenheimer*[2] the Supreme Court in interpreting the provisions of the Extradition Treaty with Great Britain of 1842 laid down that 'in ascertaining the meaning of a treaty we may look beyond its written words to the negotiations and diplomatic correspondence of the contracting parties relating to the subject matter'.[3] In this particular case the diplomatic negotiations in question followed upon the Treaty of 1842. In *Cook* v. *United States*[4] the Supreme Court reviewed at length the diplomatic negotiations and successive proposals preceding the conclusion of the 'Liquor Treaty' between the United States and Great Britain in 1924: 'In construing the treaty its history should be consulted.'[5] In *Nielsen* v. *Johnson*,[6] which was an appeal from a judgment imposing an inheritance tax on the estate of a decedent, a Danish subject, the Supreme Court was called upon to interpret the Treaty of Commerce with Denmark of 1826. The Court found that the history of the crucial Article 7 of the treaty and the references to its provisions in the diplomatic exchanges between the United States and Denmark left no doubt that the purpose of the treaty was to relieve the citizens of the contracting parties of onerous taxes and to compel them to pay only such duties on disposal of their property as were exacted from the inhabitants of the place. The Court, quoting a long list of precedents,[7] said that when the meaning of the treaty is uncertain 'recourse may be had to the negotiations and diplomatic correspondence of the contracting parties relating to the subject matter'.[8]

German courts have no hesitation in regarding preceding negotiations as a valid element of interpretation. They have gone to the length of laying down that, in the silence of a treaty, preparatory work, construed in accordance with principles of good faith, may show that the treaty intended a departure from generally recognized principles.[9] In a more recent decision[10] the Reichsgericht, while

---

[1] *M'Culloch* v. *Maryland* (1819), 4 Wheaton 434; *Prigg* v. *Pennsylvania* (1842), 16 Peters, 561, 587, 593, 616, 620; *United States* v. *Yorba*, 1 Wall. 421; *Kinkead* v. *United States*, 150 U.S. 483; *More* v. *Steinbach*, 127 U.S. 70; *John Doe* v. *Joseph Addison Bradden* (1853), 16 How. Rep. 635. And see for other examples Crandall, *Treaties, their Making and Enforcement* (2nd ed., 1916), § 166.

[2] *A.J.* 28 (1934), 149.   [3] *Ibid.* p. 155.   [4] (1933), 288 U.S. 102.
[5] *Ibid.*   [6] 279 U.S. 607.
[7] *Re Ross*, 140 U.S. 467; *United States* v. *Texas*, 162 U.S. 1, 23, 40; *Terrace* v. *Thompson*, 263 U.S. 197, 223.
[8] At p. 610. For comment on this case see Hyde in *A.J.* 23 (1929), 824.
[9] *Decisions of the Reichsgericht*, 104, p. 352 (decision of 20 May 1922).
[10] 4 February 1931, *Juristische Wochenschrift* (1932), p. 243; *Clunet*, 60 (1932), 1009. See also the decision of the Reichsgericht of 14 April 1932, *Entscheidungen in Zivilsachen*, 137, 6.

affirming in principle the usefulness of preparatory work, actually reversed a decision of the Court below on the ground that it decided the case without inquiring sufficiently into the extrinsic evidence adduced by one of the parties. It is in this connection of interest to note that the German Reichsgericht in interpreting Article 307 of the Treaty of Versailles relating to industrial property resorted to the proceedings of the United States, namely, to a declaration of the Chairman of the Committee on Foreign Affairs, in order to ascertain the intention of the parties. The Court did this in view of the fact that 'the negotiations preceding the Treaty [of Berlin] with the United States did not offer any clue for the interpretation of the provision in question.'[1]

The attitude of French courts is on the whole the same notwith-standing the solitary exception of the *Federico* in which the Conseil d'État refused to accept the report of the drafting committee as an authoritative interpretation of the Declaration of London.[2] But in the *Dacia* the French Prize Council interpreted Article 56 of the Declaration of London relating to the validity of transfer of merchant vessels by reference to the original proposals made at the Conference, to the interpretation put on these proposals by the various delega-tions, and to the text offered for adoption by the Conference.[3]

The conclusions which may be derived from the above survey of the attitude of municipal courts in the matter of interpretation of treaties do not require much elaboration. This survey shows that whatever may be the law, under various systems, in regard to the interpretation of contracts and statutes, there is general recognition evidenced by practice that preparatory work may be used for the purpose of interpreting treaties. This result is not only instructive in itself. It shows that there may be reasons inherent in the nature of treaties and of inter-State relations which permit and necessitate recourse to preparatory work even if recourse to this kind of evidence may be excluded or limited so far as other instruments are concerned.

V. The Practice of International Arbitration

To give an account of recourse to preparatory work by international tribunals would mean to survey a large part of the history of

---

[1] *Annual Digest* (1923–4), case no. 195. As to frequent recourse by German courts to the preparatory work of the Declaration of London, see Garner, *Prize Law during the World War*, s. 115.

[2] Fauchille, *Jurisprudence française des prises*, p. 19, and Garner, *Prize Law during the World War*, ss. 115, 449.

[3] *A.J.* 9 (1925), 1024.

international arbitration – in the case of the Permanent Court of International Justice of a larger part of its activity. This task cannot be attempted in these lectures. What is intended in the survey which follows is, in the first instant, to show how far recourse to preparatory work has characterized arbitral and judicial settlement to which Great Britain and the United States were a party either as between themselves or with other States. There is no better means of reducing to its true proportions the belief in a peculiar Anglo-American practice in this matter than by showing how frequent has been resort to preparatory work on the part of these two States.[1] Secondly, it is intended to draw attention to those cases which are specially instructive for the study of the problem under discussion either because of the nature of the question decided or the extent to which recourse was had to preparatory work.

Modern arbitration begins with the adjudications under the Jay Treaty of 19 November 1794, between Great Britain and the United States, and it is of interest to see how the question of preparatory work became of importance in the very first case dealt with under the Treaty by the Mixed Commission under Article v of the Treaty, namely, in the *St Croix River* arbitration. According to that Article the Mixed Commission was to decide what was the river truly intended under the name of St Croix River under the Treaty of Peace of 1783. The United States claimed that the St Croix River was the River Magaguadavic falling into the Passamaquoddy Bay, whereas according to Great Britain the river intended by the treaty was the Schoodiac. The mouths of the two rivers lie about nine miles apart, and the territory involved in the dispute was from seven to eight thousand square miles. Early in the proceedings the United States requested that the Commissioners who negotiated the Treaty of 1783 should be called to prove what river was intended by them at the time when they negotiated and signed the treaty. This request was opposed by the British agent. The recent publication by Professor Moore of the records of the proceedings of this Commission[2] sheds

[1] It is proposed in these lectures to consider only judicial practice as distinguished from cases in which Governments in the course of diplomatic correspondence invoked preparatory work as a factor in the interpretation of treaties. See, for instance, the correspondence concerning the *Panama Canal Toll* controversy between Great Britain and the United States (*U.S. For. Rel.* (1912), p. 785), and in particular Sir Edward Grey's reliance on statements made by Secretary Hay as negotiator of the Hay–Pauncefote Treaty. And see Hyde, II, 69, on the controversy between the United States and Switzerland concerning the interpretation of the most-favoured-nation clause in connection with the Treaty of 1850.

[2] Moore, *International Adjudications*, vol. I (1929); vol. II (1930).

interesting light on the controversy, and it may therefore be useful to reproduce some of the reasoning of the parties.

The British agent maintained emphatically that the intention of the treaty can 'never consistently with the rules and principles of that law [of nations], with reason or with common sense, be proved by the Commissioners themselves who made the treaty'.[1] He insisted that the moment the law is made and duly ratified, the Commissioners who made it can have no further concern with it, and that the interpretation must be governed by established rules which he proceeded to quote copiously from Vattel and Pufendorf. He pointed to the complications inherent in admission of evidence of this nature, e.g., in the case of the Commissioners on both sides giving contradictory evidence.[2] He adduced the analogy of statutes and said that it would indeed be a novelty if members of the legislative body were permitted, in case of doubt as to the construction of a statute, to give evidence as to what they intended; he remarked that if in the case of the treaty in question such evidence were admissible, the arbitral proceedings would be unnecessary; and he concluded by reiterating that 'the contracting parties only agreed on what was mutually *signed* and *sealed,* and the admission of such testimony as competent would be to all intents making a supplemental and *verbal* treaty, instead of a just interpretation of the former one, which is the sole and exclusive object of the present Commission'.[3]

Undoubtedly the British agent weakened the force of his argument by suggesting that the evidence which the United States sought to put forward was contrary to the clear intention of the treaty – a suggestion which anticipated the results of the inquiry. The American agent, in an elaborate discussion of the subject, did not fail to point to this weak link in the British argument.[4] He readily admitted that evidence is not admissible as to what an individual member of a legislature meant, but – and here lies the crux of the question – he pointed out that the testimony of the Commissioners was intended to refer not to their direct intention but to certain circumstances throwing light on the intention of the treaty, and that their evidence in this matter was only one link in the chain of evidence. The Commissioners were called upon to testify as to the maps used by them; they were not asked to say which river they intended.

But if the map was before the Commissioners when they framed the

---

[1] *Ibid.* I, 260.
[2] The British Commissioner was not alive at the time of the arbitration.
[3] Moore, *International Adjudications,* I, 267.   [4] *Ibid.* p. 371.

Second Article of the Treaty of Peace, and those lines were then marked by them all, is it not a fact which in justice ought to be proved? and would not any clerk, or bystander, who happened to be present at that time, be a good witness as to the fact? Can the witness having been a Commissioner, disqualify him from giving evidence?[1]

The Commission decided that the negotiators of the Treaty of 1783 – i.e. the surviving American negotiators: John Adams, John Jay, and Benjamin Franklin – ought to be heard in evidence. The principal object of their evidence was to elucidate how far and in what way a certain map (Mitchell's map) was used by the negotiators.[2] It is stated that the result of their evidence was disappointing to the American agent.[3] This pathetic outcome of a protracted controversy was not due to the circumstance that the questions which the witnesses were asked were strictly speaking questions of fact. They were questions as to intention although they were framed as if they referred to mere facts only. Thus, for instance, questions 3 and 6 put to John Adams were, respectively, as follows: What rivers were claimed, or talked of, by the Commissioners on either side, as a proposed boundary, and for what reason; what were the lines claimed on each side and how was the matter ultimately settled? But – it will be recalled – the problem confronting the Commission was one very much approaching equivocation, and on such occasions even the strict English law of evidence does not exclude direct statements of intention. However that may be, the case is of great importance for a number of reasons. It introduces at the very threshold of modern international arbitration one of the persistent themes of discussion; and it introduces it in a prominent manner in the form of direct evidence by the negotiators themselves not only as to surrounding circumstances but also, in fact, as to their intention.

The subsequent history of arbitral settlement between Great Britain and the United States is a continuous example of reliance, by one or both of the parties, on preparatory work in the interpretation of treaties. This occurred in the proceedings before various Mixed Commissions, e.g., before that constituted under Article IV of the Treaty of Ghent of 24 December 1824, between Great Britain and the United States and relating to the title over some islands in Passamaquoddy Bay, where the United States again relied to a large extent on this evidence of the negotiators of the Treaty of 1783.[4]

---

[1] *Ibid.* p. 362.   [2] For the text of the depositions see *ibid.* pp. 62–7.   [3] *Ibid.* p. 67.
[4] Moore, *International Adjudications*, v, 163, 231, 240. And see also the account of the proceedings of the Commission under the Treaty of 30 April 1803 between the United

Similarly in the proceedings under Article VI of the same treaty concerning compensation for losses and damages resulting from unlawful impediments to the recovery of pre-war debts, the American Commissioners relied on the history of the peace negotiations as showing that the British suggestions in favour of the loyalists and refugees had been uniformly rejected by the American negotiators: 'It is impossible, with such evidence of the intent of the Parties, to yield to mere constructions and by such constructions to extend the extent of the treaty to cases which we know to have been the subject of long and earnest demands on the one side and inflexible and final denial on the other.'[1]

Recourse to this means of interpretation has also characterized most of the later well-known arbitrations in which the two countries were engaged. In the course of the *Alabama* arbitration there arose the disturbing question, which threatened to frustrate the arbitral settlement, whether the Tribunal had jurisdiction to adjudicate on the very comprehensive claims for indirect damages put forward by the United States. Great Britain made extensive use of the negotiations preceding the Treaty of Washington in order to show that claims of this nature were not contemplated by the negotiators of the treaty as coming within the jurisdiction of the Tribunal.[2] In the *Behring Sea* arbitration, Great Britain referred throughout to the negotiations leading to the Treaties of 1824 and 1825 with Russia which recognized the rights of the United States and Great Britain to fish and navigate in the area of the Behring Sea. It was pointed out by Great Britain that the contention of the United States that a narrow interpretation should be given to the expression 'north-west coast' used in the Treaty of 1825 was inaccurate on the ground, *inter alia*, that throughout the negotiations which preceded the treaty these words were used to include not less than the whole of the North American coast in dispute.[3]

In the *Alaskan Boundary* arbitration much use was made on the part of the United States of the negotiations leading to the Treaty of 28 February 1825 between Great Britain and Russia which the

States and France where Livingstone, the American negotiator of the treaty, insisted on the authoritative character of his own interpretation (*ibid.* pp. 231–4).

[1] Moore, *International Adjudications*, III, 301. See also the award of Bates, Umpire, in the case of the *Washington*, under the Convention of 1853 between Great Britain and the United States (Moore, p. 4342).

[2] *Ibid.* I, 625, 627 *et seq.*

[3] See Argument of Great Britain, U.S. no. 4 (1893), Cmd. 6921, p. 19; Counter-Case of Great Britain, U.S. no. 3 (1893), Cmd. 6920, p. 27. And see the Case of the United States, U.S. no. 6 (1893), Cmd. 6949, p. 53.

Tribunal was in the arbitration agreement requested to consider. The right to have recourse to preliminary negotiations appeared to have been conceded by Article III of the arbitration agreement which provided that 'the Tribunal shall also take into consideration any action of the several Governments or of their respective representatives, preliminary or subsequent to the conclusion of the said treaties as far as the same tends to show the original and effective understanding of the parties . . .'. Counsel for Great Britain, while not excluding altogether the propriety of resort to previous negotiations, questioned, by reference to the common law rule of evidence, any extensive use of this instrument of interpretation. He referred to the rule of common law that when a bargain is made, the previous negotiations are superseded altogether.[1] He admitted that it might be difficult to apply the rigid common law rules to the interpretation of a treaty, for instance, between France and Great Britain, but he urged that in the case before the Tribunal the common law rules of evidence could properly be applied as the dispute was between 'two nations both governed by the common law of England' and that 'it would be more reasonable to say that rules of that law of England should apply here than it would be in a contest between two nations where the rules as to admissibility of evidence are different'.[2] This contention was vigorously opposed by the United States. Their counsel went to the length of asserting that 'the substructure of the whole international system is the Roman law as developed and embodied in the codes of continental nations'; that 'we have absolutely nothing in the world to do with the common law rules of evidence in any shape or form'; and that 'this being a Tribunal governed by the rules of procedure and the rules of evidence which prevail in Roman law tribunals, every fact is admissible which is pertinent to the issue, and its pertinence is a question to be determined by judges themselves'.[3] However, it may be doubted whether the parties were really so wide apart. The British attitude was mainly one of warning against an exaggerated recourse to previous negotiations. It was acknowledged on behalf of Great Britain that there 'was no use in urging' the strict common law rule on the Tribunal 'because we know that negotiations on the question of the construction of the treaty have been referred to in other cases, and always are referred to'.[4] And British counsel volunteered to give reasons for

---

[1] Argument of Mr Christopher Robinson, *Proceedings of the Alaskan Boundary Tribunal*, U.S. Senate Doc. no. 162, 58th Congress, 2nd Session, p. 502.
[2] *Ibid.* pp. 503, 507.   [3] *Ibid.* p. 557.   [4] *Ibid.* p. 502.

this departure from the common law rule of evidence. The first was that negotiations between nations, evidenced by their protocols and despatches, are more formal and precise than negotiations between individuals. The second was that rules of evidence are not uniform in all countries, and that it would be difficult to expect France, for instance to be bound by common law rules of procedure. This point of view was also adopted in the Argument of Sir Robert Finlay (as he then was).[1] What is even more significant is that Lord Alverstone, a distinguished judge with wide experience in cases of an international character, in his opinions supplementing the award of the Tribunal on individual questions referred to the negotiations preceding the Treaty of 1825. This he did in particular with regard to Question 5 of the Arbitration Agreement, namely, whether the eastern boundary was to run round the bays, ports, and waters of the ocean or not. He found that the language of the treaty was not clear enough of itself to enable this question to be answered distinctly, and proceeded to inquire in detail into the negotiations preceding the Treaty of 1825; in particular the various drafts leading up to the treaty.[2] The other members of the Tribunal, American and Canadian, adopted the same course in much greater detail.[3]

The voluminous records of the oral and written proceedings in the *North Atlantic Fisheries* arbitration show the clear absence of hesitation on the part of both States to rely on diplomatic negotiations. There was a particular inducement in this case to rely on the negotiations preceding the Treaty of 1818 in which fishery rights were granted to and renounced by the United States, for this treaty was preceded by a lengthy diplomatic correspondence arising from the fact that the Peace Treaty terminating the war of 1812 left open the question whether, as contended by the British negotiators, the war abrogated the fishery rights conferred upon the United States in the Treaty of 1783. The award of the Tribunal was in its vital parts based on the negotiations preceding the treaty. The Tribunal relied largely on 'preparatory work' in answering the general question as to the nature of the rights conferred in the Treaty of 1818 (Question 1). Thus, contrary to the contention of the United States, it found that no peculiar character need be claimed for the rights in question in order to secure their enjoyment in perpetuity 'as is evidenced by the American negotiators in 1818 asking for the insertion of the

---

[1] *Ibid.* p. 185.
[2] *Ibid.* pp. 37–41. See also pp. 33–5 for the opinion of Lord Alverstone on Question 2 (What Channel is the Portland Channel?).
[3] *Ibid.* pp. 53–8, 73–8, 90–6.

words 'for ever';[1] it attached importance to the question of the use
by the negotiators of the term 'servitude';[2] it rejected the American
theory of the exclusive right of fisheries for American citizens on
the ground, *inter alia*, that the American negotiators themselves
advanced the theory of partition;[3] it found that the British negotiators refused to place the right of British subjects on the same footing
with those of American inhabitants and that they refused to insert
certain words proposed to this effect by the American negotiators;[4]
it examined Lord Bathurst's letters alleged by the United States to
have contained an acknowledgement of the exclusion of British
interference.[5] The Tribunal adopted the same method in answering
the question whether the renunciation by the United States of the
fishery rights applied to all bays in general or only to certain bays.
In interpreting the term 'bay' the Tribunal proceeded on the basis of
what 'might be reasonably supposed to have been considered as a
bay by the negotiators of the treaty'; it pointed out that it 'has not
been shown by the documents and the correspondence that the
application of the three mile limit to bays was present to the minds
of the negotiators in 1818'.[6]

Of special interest, in view of the parties to the dispute, is the
Manica arbitration between Great Britain and Portugal concerning
the delimitation of their spheres of influence, in particular in regard
to the Zambezi boundary. It was provided in the *compromis* of 7
January 1895 that the Arbitrator be asked 'to take into consideration',
inter alia, 'the reports of the negotiations'.[7] The parties, in particular
Great Britain, made full use of this provision. The Arbitrator followed
the same line. He investigated the history of the negotiations, both
at the conference and in the course of the diplomatic correspondence
preceding it, leading to the Treaty of 1891 which laid down the
boundary, and found that the line agreed to was the result of compromise and that therefore Portugal was not at liberty to reject, as
she in fact claimed to do, that part of the bargain which she now
deemed disadvantageous.[8]

An instructive and frequently quoted decision in this connection
is the one given in the *Aroa Mines* case by the British–Venezuelan
Claims Commission created by the Protocol of 13 February 1903.[9]
In this case Plumley, Umpire, reviewed at great length the history of
the negotiations which led to the conclusion of the Protocol of 1903

[1] Scott, *Hague Reports*, p. 159.   [2] *Ibid.*   [3] *Ibid.* p. 163.
[4] *Ibid.* p. 164.   [5] *Ibid.* p. 166. See also p. 191.   [6] *Ibid.* p. 184.
[7] Moore, *International Arbitrations*, v, 4987.   [8] *Ibid.* pp. 5008, 5009.
[9] Ralston, *Venezuelan Arbitrations, 1903*, pp. 344 *et seq.*

in which Venezuela admitted liability 'in cases where the claim is for injury to, or wrongful seizure of property'. The question was how far this phrase covered damage caused by revolutionary troops. In these negotiations, the Umpire found, there was constant reference to claims based on justice and recognized by international law, but there was no allusion to claims occasioned by losses due to acts of insurgents. It is also of interest, in view of a different pronouncement of the Permanent Court of International Justice,[1] that the Umpire relied not only on the correspondence exchanged in this matter between the two parties but also on that exchanged *in pari materia* between Venezuela and Germany.[2]

Of other arbitral decisions given in this period and illustrating recourse to preparatory work space permits merely a mention of decisions like those given in the *Capitulation Tax* case between the United States and Colombia where the Umpire, Sir Frederick Bruce, refused to accept an interpretation which, he said, the United States 'has not formally adopted and urged in its correspondence' and which the executive authority of the other party expressly rejected;[3] the arbitral award given in 1900 by the Swiss Federal Council in the boundary dispute between France and Brazil;[4] or the decision given on 14 October 1902 by the King of Norway and Sweden in the dispute between Germany and the United States and Great Britain concerning the justification of the military action taken by the two latter States in Samoa, where the Arbitrator attached importance to the fact that the Protocols of the Berlin Conference of 1898 clearly showed that the plenipotentiaries who framed the General Act relating to Samoa wished to establish the principle that, in their dealings with Samoa the Powers would only proceed by common accord.[5]

Before the Permanent Court of Arbitration recourse to previous negotiation seems to have become a rule which no one sought to question. With the doubtful exception of one case,[6] whenever a Hague Tribunal of the Permanent Court of Arbitration has been confronted with the interpretation of a treaty it has approached this task to a large extent through the medium of the preparatory work leading to the treaty. In the *Venezuelan Preferential Claims* case

---

[1] See below, p. 494.   [2] See also the *Kummerow, Betancourt,* and *Sambiaggio* cases.

[3] Award of 9 May 1866 (Moore, *International Arbitrations,* p. 1415).

[4] See Lafontaine, *Pasicrisie internationale* (1902), p. 160.

[5] *Br. and For. St. Papers,* 105 (1901–2), 167.

[6] *The Muscat Dhows* case, Scott, *Hague Reports,* p. 93. But see the reference to the 'elevated aims' of the Brussels Conference.

decided on 22 February 1904 the Tribunal in deciding that the blockading Powers were entitled to preferential treatment adduced as a ground of its decision the facts that during the diplomatic negotiations Venezuela always made a formal distinction between the 'allied Powers' and the 'neutral Powers'; and that during the negotiations the German and British Governments insisted on guarantees being given for a 'sufficient and punctual discharge of the obligations' of Venezuela.[1] In the *Japanese House Tax* case, decided on 22 May 1925 the Tribunal in holding that the buildings erected on land held by virtue of perpetual leases were exempted from taxation attached importance to the fact that in the course of the drafting of the crucial Article of the treaty in question a proposal was made to place aliens on the same footing as Japanese subjects, but that the project was subsequently abandoned.[2] The *North Atlantic Fisheries* arbitration has already been noted.

But it was in the *Island of Timor* case that preparatory work became the principal and most conspicuous ground of the decision of the Tribunal. This was an arbitration arising out of a dispute between Holland and Portugal over the boundaries of their possessions in the Island of Timor. After prolonged negotiations the two countries concluded a treaty in 1904 which contained a settlement of the disputed boundary with the exception of one sector the delimitation of which was entrusted to a mixed commission. The inability of the Commission to reach agreement on this question gave rise to a new arbitration agreement in which the Tribunal was called upon to interpret the Convention of 1904. The voluminous award[3] is almost entirely based on the record of the negotiations – reviewed by the Tribunal in their progress day by day – which led to the treaty. These negotiations the Tribunal found it necessary to reproduce in detail 'since it throws positive light on the real and mutual intention of the parties'.[4] The 'preparatory work' as examined by the Tribunal showed a clear renunciation, by way of concession prompted by mutual compensations, on the part of Portugal of the line which she claimed before the Tribunal. Moreover, the examination of preparatory work helped the Tribunal to overcome a difficulty resulting from a *falsa demonstratio*, i.e. from the fact that the negotiators of the previous treaties gave a false name to a crucial river by confusing it with that of another river.[5] In doing this the Tribunal referred to Article 18 of the Swiss Code of Obligations which lays down that

---

[1] *Ibid.* p. 60. [2] *Ibid.* p. 83. [3] *Ibid.* pp. 355–86.
[4] *Ibid.* p. 369. See also pp. 376–8. [5] *Ibid.* pp. 374 *et seq.*

'to appreciate the character and clauses of a contract there is occasion to look for the actual common intention of the parties, without dwelling on inexact names or expressions of which use might have been made, either erroneously, or to disguise the true nature of the convention'.

The jurisprudence of the various arbitral tribunals after the First World War is particularly instructive in view of the shadow which the apparently hesitating practice of the Permanent Court of International Justice has cast over the question in discussion. There has been no inclination to abandon or to modify the firmly established rule admitting preceding negotiations as a legitimate instrument of interpretation. This can especially be seen in the work of the mixed arbitral tribunals established by the Peace Treaties. Their work offers instructive instances of the varying application and the various degrees of boldness and caution exhibited by international tribunals when dealing with preparatory work.

There are, first, cases in which tribunals have sounded a note of caution in the use of preparatory work. Thus in the case of *Heim and Chamant* v. *The German State*,[1] the defendant asked for a revision of some previous decisions of the Tribunal on the ground of discovery of new facts. These facts, it was alleged, consisted of the minutes, hitherto inaccessible, of the so-called Alsace–Lorraine Conference, a meeting of politicians and jurists which took place before the Peace Conference at Paris. It was contended that the minutes of the Alsace–Lorraine Conference, which could fittingly be described as part of the preparatory work of the conference, influenced to a considerable extent the Alsace–Lorraine Committee of the Peace Conference on the matter at issue before the Tribunal. The Tribunal rejected the application on the ground that even in municipal law the discovery of new facts in the shape of preparatory work did not constitute a good ground for revision. In any case, the Tribunal expressed disagreement with the German view that the preparatory work of a treaty and the 'motives' of a statute within the State were on the same level. The assimilation, it said, of a treaty to a legislative enactment is not accurate; a treaty is a contractual act; although like a statute it has the force of law, this does not mean that the same rules of interpretation apply to treaties and statutes. In addition, the Tribunal pointed to some special reasons which diminished the weight of preparatory work. It said:

[1] *Recueil T.A.M.* 3 (1924), 50; *Annual Digest*, 1 (1919–22), case no. 268.

Att., en effet, qu'en droit interne il est pour le moins douteux que les travaux préparatoires d'une loi constituent une source décisive d'interprétation; que la découverte de tels travaux après qu'un jugement aurait été rendu ne pourrait être considérée comme un fait de nature à ouvrir une procédure de revision; qu'aux motifs qui, en droit interne, s'opposent à ce qu'on attache une telle signification à des travaux préparatoires, viennent s'ajouter d'autres considérations encore lorsqu'on se trouve sur le terrain international; qu'ici, en effet, la source des travaux cesse d'être unique pour devenir multiple et multiforme; qu'émanant de divers États, ces travaux peuvent procéder de conceptions et d'intérêts divergents, voire opposés; qu'en outre les documents de ces travaux préparatoires, en tant qu'ils appartiennent aux archives des États, ne peuvent pas toujours être connus du juge ou peuvent ne lui être révélés que fragmentairement, ce qui diminue encore la sureté, très relative déjà, d'un tel mode d'interprétation; qu'il convient d'être d'autant plus prudent et réservé, à cet égard, qu'en droit international, un État, signataire d'une convention, n'a pas la faculté – qu'il a en droit interne, vis-à-vis de sa propre loi – de la modifier souverainement et de réduire ainsi à néant, pour l'avenir, la valeur que le juge aurait attachée à tort à des travaux préparatoires. . .

Even more explicit is the summons to caution in the case of *Roumanian Minister of War* v. *Turkish Government*[1] where Turkey contended that although the text of Article 65 of the Treaty of Lausanne made no distinction between various categories of property subjected to the duty of restitution, some such distinction followed from the preparatory work of the Lausanne Conference. The Tribunal examined this preparatory work at length and found that it did not warrant the Turkish contention. But it prefaced its inquiry by some general considerations which may fittingly be quoted. It said:

Il est vrai que parmi les moyens dont le juge dispose pour ces recherches figure sans doute le recours aux travaux préparatoires qui peuvent et doivent, en cas de besoin, servir à l'interprétation de la loi qui en est dérivée. Mais il est aussi reconnu que la valuer des arguments tirés de ces travaux est très limitée et qu'il ne faut les utiliser qu'avec une extrême prudence pour ne pas tomber dans l'erreur de modifier, par des raisons qui y sont empruntées, un texte clair et précis par lui-même. Si cela est vrai en ce qui concerne les lois internes, lesquelles sont en règle générale le résultat d'un travail laborieux se prolongeant le plus souvent – au moins lorsqu'il s'agit d'une loi de quelque importance – pendant de longues années, il est encore plus exact quant à un traité dont, par la force des choses, l'élaboration a dû être faite plus ou moins hâtivement et souvent

[1] *Recueil T.A.M.* 7 (1927–8), 993; *Annual Digest*, 4 (1927–8), case no. 299.

sans que les intentions des hautes parties contractantes n'aient pris corps que par les clauses mêmes de l'acte qu'elles ont signé. En outre, il ne faut pas perdre de vue que le traité ne constitue pas une loi proprement dite, mais une convention synallagmatique et que par conséquent les travaux préparatoires, pour être utilement mis à profit pour l'interprétation du texte, doivent établir l'intention *commune* des parties contractantes de donner à une certaine clause du traité une signification et une portée qui ne découlent pas directement de ses termes. Pour que l'on puisse s'en écarter, il faut qu'il soit nettement et incontestablement prouvé que les parties contractantes ont voulu dire autre chose que ce qu'elles ont dit. Mais dans la règle il est à présumer qu'elles aient su fidèlement traduire leur pensée par les termes employés.

Secondly, there are cases in which the Tribunal, while admitting that recourse to preparatory work may be had to interpret provisions which were not clear and where doubts existed as to the intention of the parties, regarded as unnecessary recourse to previous correspondence in cases where the meaning of the treaty was clear. This occurred in the case of *Ascherberg Hopwood and Crew, Ltd.* v. *H. Quaritch*[1] in connection with the interpretation of Article 310 of the Treaty of Versailles which provided that licences in respect of industrial, literary, or artistic property shall be considered as cancelled as from the declaration of war. Germany maintained that having regard to the preparatory work of the Peace Conference (Reply of the Allied and Associated Powers to the German Observations), that Article ought not to be read literally and that the licences in question should be treated like contracts in conformity with Articles 299 to 305 of the treaty. Similarly, in *Hartrodt* v. *Olsen*,[2] Germany contended that an Australian vesting order, made in June 1919, was invalid as being contrary to the Treaty of Versailles. It was urged on behalf of Germany that the order was in violation of an undertaking given in the course of the Reply of the Allied and Associated Powers to Germany. The Tribunal contented itself with stating that the treaty contained no express provisions forbidding the making of vesting orders after the armistice.

With this there must be contrasted the third category of cases in which the result reached through the use of preparatory work seems directly to contradict the text of the treaty. Thus in the case of *Polyxène Plessa* v. *Turkish Government*[3] the Tribunal found that although

---

[1] *Recueil T.A.M.* 5 (1925–6), 332; *Annual Digest*, 3 (1925–6), case no. 286.
[2] Anglo-German Mixed Arbitral Tribunal, 18 June 1928; *Recueil T.A.M.* 8 (1929–30), 26.
[3] *Recueil T.A.M.* 8 (1929–30), 224; *Annual Digest*, 4 (1927–8), case no. 299.

Article 58 of the Treaty of Lausanne provided that the contracting parties *except Greece* renounce claims for compensation as the result of acts of war, Greece was not entitled to put forward claims for reparation in respect of Turkish war measures undertaken in conformity with the laws of war. The Tribunal was of the opinion that in this case the text of the treaty did not reproduce with sufficient precision the intention of the parties, and that it must be read as containing also in regard to Greece a mutual waiver of claims for compensation. The exception in favour of Greece, the Tribunal said, was not intended to regulate legal interests, but merely to take into account certain sentimental considerations. The Tribunal reached this result simply on the basis of an analysis of the preparatory work of the treaty.[1] It is of interest to note that the majority of the Tribunal were identical with that of the Tribunal in the case of *Roumanian Minister of War* v. *Turkish Government*,[2] which was conspicuous for its attitude of caution. It is true that even in the case under discussion the Tribunal reiterated the view that preparatory work should be used only with the utmost caution for the purpose of interpreting and supplementing a treaty; it is also true that, in its opinion, it merely filled a gap in the treaty without modifying it in any way. But the decision does in fact depart from the literal and clear expression of the treaty. The decision in *Eastern Bank Ltd.* v. *Turkish Government*[3] was based on a similar interpretation of Article 58 of the Treaty of Lausanne. The Tribunal referred here to the preparatory work of the Convention of Lausanne in which the mutual renunciation of claims for damages for war measures was described as a *conditio sine qua non* of reopening negotiations between the parties at Lausanne.

There are, fourthly, cases in which preparatory work without actually contradicting the treaty, appears to add to it considerations which do not appear on the face of it. Thus in *Antippa* v. *Germany*[4] the Tribunal in interpreting the expression 'acts committed' as used in section 4 of the Annex to Article 297 of the Treaty of Versailles based its decision on the fact that the history and origin of section 4 showed that it was the intention of the parties to establish the responsibility of Germany for *all* acts of destruction of neutral vessels regardless of whether they were allowed or prohibited by international law. The Tribunal adopted this interpretation in face

---

[1] See below, p. 518.   [2] See above, p. 484.
[3] *Recueil T.A.M.* 8 (1929–30), 188; *Annual Digest*, 4 (1927–8), case no. 298.
[4] German–Greek Mixed Arbitral Tribunal, 3 November 1926, *Recueil T.A.M.* 7 (1927–8), 23; *Annual Digest*, 3 (1925–6), case no. 285.

of overwhelming authority in the shape of judicial decisions to the effect that the Treaty of Versailles referred only to acts committed in violation of international law.

Fifthly, in some cases preparatory work, without on the face of it varying or adding to the treaty, constitutes the sole basis of interpretation. Thus in *Katz and Klump* v. *Yugoslavia*[1] the Tribunal, basing itself on the preparatory work leading up to Article 297(h) of the Treaty of Versailles decided that the Kingdom of the Serbs, Croats and Slovenes was not a 'new State' within the meaning of that Article. The Tribunal drew certain conclusions from the fact that that Article was a concession granted to Germany at the last moment.

Sixthly, in a great number of cases the purpose of reference to and examination of preparatory work is to corroborate conclusions reached otherwise. Thus in the case of *Schmid* v. *Chemische Werke Fürstenwalde*[2] the Tribunal, in addition to the indications drawn from the text of Article 299(b) of the Treaty of Versailles, adduced the correspondence between the Allied and Associated Powers and Germany as showing that the decision as to construction of pre-war contracts was to rest with the Allied and Associated Powers to the exclusion of the jurisdiction of the mixed arbitral tribunals.[3]

Finally, in other cases the Tribunal deals with the argument based on preceding negotiations as put forward by the parties in order to point out that they do not in fact support the argument advanced.[4]

The practice of the various other mixed commissions after the First World War has provided further instances of reliance on preparatory work. The Umpire in the German–American Mixed Claims Commission relied on it on a number of occasions. It was by reference to the negotiations preceding the Treaty of Berlin between the United States and Germany that he ruled out claims for punitive damages and interpreted the provisions of the treaty relating to loss of earnings and damages in respect of intangible property[5] and to the insurance premium claims.[6] And he even went to the length of examining in detail the history of the negotiations leading up to the Treaty of

---

[1] German–Yugoslav Mixed Arbitral Tribunal, 30 September 1925, *Recueil T.A.M.* 5 (1925–6), 963; *Annual Digest*, 3 (1925–6), case no. 24.

[2] Franco-German Mixed Arbitral Tribunal, 30 July 1921, *Recueil T.A.M.* 1, 345; *Annual Digest*, 1 (1919–22), case no. 248.

[3] See also *Karl Toth* v. *Yugoslav State*, *Recueil T.A.M.* 6, 850; *Kauroklis* v. *Turkey*, *ibid.* 8, 398; *Megalidis* v. *Turkey*, *ibid.* p. 390; *Kulin* v. *Roumanian State*, *ibid.* 7 (1927–8), 138.

[4] See *Roumanian Minister of War* v. *Turkish Government*, *ibid.* 7 (1927–8), p. 993; *Abbas Holmi Pasha* v. *Great Britain*, *ibid.* p. 909; *Ekrem Bey* v. *Italy*, *ibid.* p. 965.

[5] *A.J.* 18 (1924), 361; *Maud Thompson de Gennes* v. *Germany*, *ibid.* 19 (1925), 803 (see below, p. 503). See also *Administrative Decision no. 2*, *ibid.* 18 (1924), 177.

[6] *Ibid.* p. 593.

Washington relating to the *Alabama* claims in order to throw light on the use of the term 'indirect damages'.[1] He followed the same method in the Tripartite Claims Commission between the United States, Austria and Hungary.[2] The British–American Mixed Claims Commission was on a number of occasions confronted with the same problem.[3] So were some tribunals connected with the question of reparations.[4]

The award of 18 April 1925 in the *Ottoman Debt* arbitration constitutes another signal contribution to the subject. In this case the Arbitrator (Professor Borel) had to interpret Article 51 of the Treaty of Lausanne which provided for the distribution of the Ottoman Public Debt among the States comprising territories formerly belonging to the Ottoman Empire. The Arbitrator prefaced his award by a general exposition of the task of the arbitrator in the matter of interpretation.[5] He emphasized that his central task was to ascertain the common intention of the parties 'avec la liberté d'appréciation nécéssaire et à l'aide de ce que l'historique du traité peut révéler en fait d'indication véritablement sûres, pertinentes et de caractère suffisamment probant'.[6] Some of the most important parts of the award are based on the evidence supplied by the 'Actes de la Conférence de Lausanne sur l'affaire du Proche-Orient'. Thus the Arbitrator found that 'it follows from the evidence' drawn from this source that the negotiators of the treaty were agreed that it was not within their province to determine the currency of the payments;[7] that the documentary evidence of the conference 'démontrent effectivement' the adoption by the conference of the system of proportionality in the distribution of the debt and the reasons therefor;[8] that the pronouncements made at the Lausanne Conference showed clearly that at least some of the contracting parties refused to admit the general principle of succession in regard to the public debt;[9] that an analysis of the work of the relevant committee and sub-committee of the conference and of the successive changes in the wording of the treaty showed that the principle of proportional distribution of the debt applied also to Turkey;[10] that the preparatory works showed clearly that Cyprus and Turkey were not included

---

[1] *Ibid.* pp. 595 *et seq.*   [2] *Ibid.* 21 (1927), 609.
[3] See the *Cayuga Indians Claims*, below, p. 505, and see *The David J. Adams, A.J.* 16 (1922), 315.
[4] See below, p. 522.   [5] *Sentence Arbitrale* (printed at Geneva, 1925), pp. 31–3.
[6] *Ibid.* p. 33.   [7] *Ibid.* p. 34.
[8] *Ibid.* p. 39. See also p. 47 as to the changes in the course of the conference in the various drafts relating to Article 54.
[9] *Ibid.* p. 62.   [10] *Ibid.* pp. 63, 64.

among the territories charged with the debt;[1] that the various declarations made at the conference showed that the revenue derived from the Hedjaz Railway was to be included in the revenue serving as the basis of the distribution of the debt.[2]

The question of preparatory work assumes particular importance in cases in which it is necessary to interpret that part of the arbitration agreement which is concerned with the source of the powers conferred upon the arbitrator. The recent arbitration between the United States and Egypt in the *Salem* case affords a striking example of decisive importance being attached to preparatory work.[3] Paragraph 3 of the Arbitration Agreement of 20 January 1931 between the two States laid down that the Tribunal shall decide the following question: 'Is the Royal Government of Egypt, under the principles of law and equity, liable in damages to the Government of the United States of America on account of treatment accorded to the American citizen, George J. Salem?' At an early stage of the proceedings the Egyptian Government raised the question of the right of the United States to espouse Salem's claim. It maintained that Salem acquired American nationality by fraud and that as the result the United States Government was not entitled to act on his behalf. The Tribunal admitted that on the obvious grammatical construction of the arbitration agreement Salem was indicated to be an American citizen and ought to be acknowledged as such by both parties. However, the Tribunal refused to admit that this grammatical construction was the only possible one. It pointed to the possibility of an interpretation according to which the term 'American citizen' indicated the juridical basis of the claim and that 'as the claim is disputed between the high parties in its entirety the investigation of the validity of this basis would also fall under the jurisdiction given by them to the Arbitral Tribunal'.[4] As on the face of it the arbitration agreement allowed of several meanings the Tribunal proceeded to investigate which meaning best accorded with the joint will of the parties. It expressed the opinion that in order to ascertain the joint will of the parties an arbitral tribunal is entitled, 'according to the predominating international practice', to refer to the discussions and negotiations preceding the *compromis*. A detailed examination of this correspondence showed that the question of Salem's nationality was a subject of contention in the course of the negotiations; that there had never taken place an

---

[1] *Ibid.* pp. 64–6.　　　　　　[2] *Ibid.* p. 78. See also p. 87.
[3] Award of 8 June 1932 (1932), p. 25.　　　[4] *Ibid.* at p. 190.

unequivocal admission on the part of the Egyptian Government that it regarded the question of his nationality as closed; that one of the Egyptian communications placed on record its view that the *compromis* was purposely drafted in broad terms in order to enable the Egyptian Government 'to raise all points at the arbitration with reference to the general question of their responsibility to the United States'; and that the United States took notice of that communication. For these reasons the Tribunal deemed itself at liberty to examine whether Salem in fact possessed American nationality. The American member of the Tribunal, while doubting the usefulness and the relevancy of the correspondence relied upon by the Tribunal, agreed generally with the view of the majority that a tribunal may properly examine negotiations leading up to the conclusion of the *compromis*.[1]

This ascertainment by reference to preceding negotiations of the scope of the powers conferred upon arbitrators is a frequent occurrence. In determining the 'arbitrability' of the claims submitted by Great Britain against Spain in connection with the operations in Morocco, M. Huber, Arbitrator, had recourse to the 'genèse' of the arbitration agreement and the negotiations preceding it.[2] The French–Mexican Mixed Claims Commission when confronted with opposing contentions of the parties as to the scope of the provisions of the Claims Convention formulated a number of rules of interpretation, one of which may be conveniently quoted:

In order to determine the true sense of the text, or the intention of the parties, the diplomatic negotiations which led up to the conclusion of the convention may be taken into account, unless the parties have finally adopted a text which is incompatible with the original scope of the negotiations or have consciously waived their right to invoke the elements of interpretation which those negotiations might furnish.[3]

In the case of *Illinois Central Railroad Company* v. *United Mexican States* the Mexican–American General Claims Commission in interpreting the arbitration convention on the question whether the Commission was competent to adjudicate upon contractual claims, referred to the fact that it was 'well known to have been the purpose of the negotiators to have by this convention removed a source of irritation between the two nations and a constant menace to their friendly relations'.[4] The Commission also pointed out that if the negotiators

---

[1] *Ibid.* p. 64.   [2] Spanish Zone of Morocco Claims: *Sentence Arbitrale*, pp. 41, 42.
[3] *Per* Verzijl, President: *Annual Digest*, 4 (1927–8), case no. 292.
[4] *A.J.* 20 (1926), 796.

had been in doubt as to the attitude of the American Government relative to contract claims they could have obtained reliable information from Professor C. C. Hyde's treatise.[1]

THE PRACTICE OF THE PERMANENT COURT OF INTERNATIONAL JUSTICE

The survey of international arbitral practice before and even during the existence of the Permanent Court of International Justice has shown such a wide recognition of the admissibility of preparatory work for the purpose of interpreting treaties that what is usually regarded as the attitude of the Court on this matter strikes one almost as an innovation. The general impression which is conveyed by the reading of the pronouncements of the Court is that its attitude towards preparatory work is not only one of the utmost caution, but also one of refusal to recognize its importance as an independent factor in the process of interpretation. As late as the year 1933 Professor Hyde, who has devoted special attention to this subject, wrote that in regard to this matter the battle of interpretation in the Permanent Court of International Justice still remains to be fought.[2] It will be submitted here that this battle has now in fact been closed; that the initial attitude of the Court on this question has undergone a substantial change; and that the cumulative result of its activity is not only a distinctive contribution to the question of recourse to preparatory work but also an affirmation of the great value of this means of ascertaining the intention of the parties. This result is the outcome of an interesting development in which we may distinguish some distinctive stages.

The first phase is that of an attitude which may generally be described as a negative one. The Court either ignored altogether the argument based on preparatory work or was satisfied with a bare negative reference to it. Thus, in the course of the proceedings in connection with the Second Advisory Opinion on the question of the *Competence of the International Labour Organization*, part of the oral and written argument was devoted to the preparatory work of the Commission on the International Labour Organization which formulated and submitted to the Peace Conference Part xiii of the Treaty of Versailles. France – not an Anglo-American country – questioned the admissibility of evidence of this nature on the ground that the treaty was clear and also that preparatory work could not be

[1] *Ibid.* p. 798.   [2] *A.J.* 27 (1933), 506.

invoked against States which acceded to the treaty after its signature. The Court's answer was a laconic one:

La Cour estime qu'il n'est pas nécessaire pour elle de discuter ces arguments: elle est, en effet, déjà en interprétant le texte même du traité, arrivée à la conclusion que le travail agricole se trouve compris dans la compétence de l'Organisation internationale du Travail; et il n'y a certainement rien dans les travaux préparatoires qui puisse l'amener à modifier cette conclusion.[1]

We are not told why the Court arrived at this negative conclusion. In the Fourth Advisory Opinion on the *Tunis and Morocco Nationality Decrees* the Court ignored the question altogether although the matter loomed large in the oral argument.[2] Similarly, in the *Wimbledon* case the Court's interpretation of Article 380 of the Treaty of Versailles on the status of the Kiel Canal was based on considerations limited to the text of the Treaty without any reference to preparatory work. But it is clear both from the oral proceedings[3] and from the dissenting opinion of two judges that the matter was before it.[4]

In the second phase, the somewhat dogmatic indifference yields to detailed consideration of preparatory work. This change of practice is obscured by the constant repetition of the formula that there is no need to have recourse to preparatory work when the meaning of the treaty is clear. The Court still does not, at least in the form of its pronouncements, regard preparatory work as an independent means of interpretation which it is entitled and bound to consider, alongside other means of interpretation, on its own initiative. The Court seems to reach its conclusion by way of interpreting the text, and the text only. Preparatory work, to which it refers only in order to refute a contention put forward by the parties, merely seems to corroborate conclusions reached in another way. It is, as will be seen, difficult to say whether this sequence of events is an exact description of what happens in the course of the elaborate process of shaping the judgment.[5] But whatever may be the garb which the examination of preparatory work assumes in the pronouncement of the Court, the fact is that at this second stage it looms prominently in the Court's pronouncements.

This period is inaugurated by two pronouncements. One is the advisory opinion on the *Exchange of Greek and Turkish Populations*, where the Court, without any qualifications, examined the Turkish

---

[1] Series B, no. 2, at p. 41.   [2] See below, pp. 498-9, 520.
[3] Series C, no. 2 (vol. 3), p. 325.   [4] Series A, no. 1, p. 40.   [5] See below, p. 509.

contention said to be based on some observations made by the French delegate at the Lausanne Conference.[1] The other is the judgment relating to the *Mavrommatis Palestine Concessions*, where the Court in interpreting Article 11 of the Palestine Mandate referred to the draft of that Article prepared at a time when it was thought that the Treaty of Sèvres would shortly be ratified.[2] These cases were not in themselves significant except inasmuch as they showed the abandonment of an attitude of mere negation. In the first mentioned case the point at issue proved to be of small compass; in the second the reference was not so much to the intention of the negotiators as to accompanying historical circumstances. But it is in the three cases referred to below that the changed attitude reveals itself quite clearly. In the case of the *Jurisdiction of the European Commission of the Danube* Roumania requested that the disputed Article should be interpreted in the light of the elaboration of the treaty. She contended that that Article was only a new form of a draft adopted by the Conference at the first reading and substantially harmonizing with the attitude adopted by Roumania. The Court recalled that preparatory work should not be used for the purpose of changing the plain meaning of a text but proceeded to inquire whether the records of the preparation of the Definitive Statute of the Danube furnished anything calculated to overrule the construction adopted by the Court.[3] Previously, in the *Lotus* case, the Court sounded the same note of caution, but proceeded to inquire in detail into the preparatory work of the Treaty of Lausanne.[4] This was also the case in the advisory opinion on the *Interpretation of the Treaty of Lausanne*.[5] In all these cases the examination of preparatory work resulted in a corroboration of the result reached by the interpretation of the text itself.

This changed attitude shows itself indirectly also in the way in which the Court definitely declared inadmissible certain categories of preparatory work. Thus in the matter of the *Jurisdiction of the European Commission of the Danube* it refused to consider certain aspects of the preparatory work of the Treaty of Versailles invoked by Roumania on the ground that the record in question was confidential and was not placed before the Court by or with the consent of the competent authority.[6] In the case of the *Territorial Jurisdiction of the*

---

[1] Series B, no. 10, p. 22. [2] Series A, no. 2, p. 24.
[3] Series B, no. 14, p. 31. See also below, p. 521. [4] See below, pp. 515–16.
[5] *Interpretation of the Treaty of Lausanne, Article 2(3)*, Series B, no. 12.
[6] Series B, no. 14, p. 32.

International Commission of the River Oder the Court declared as in-admissible records of the preparatory work of the Treaty of Versailles on the ground that three of the parties to the dispute did not participate in this work,[1] and it also refused, although not quite consistently,[2] to consider the preparatory work of treaties other than that directly before it.[3] The same changed approach is shown by the fact that the Court while refusing to admit the authoritative character of certain instruments invoked by a party declared itself willing to consider it as part of the preparatory work.[4] Thus, while refusing to recognize the authoritative character of the so-called Interpretative Protocol of Article 6 of the Definitive Statute of the Danube, it was ready to consider it as part of the preparatory work. The Court, at this stage, unhesitatingly relaxed its practice when it was confronted with preparatory work of a specially authorized character, like the Replies of the Allied and Associated Powers at the Peace Conference – even in cases when for a particular reason it declared preparatory work inadmissible.[5]

In the third stage consideration of preparatory work becomes a normal, independent, feature of the process of interpretation. The Court engages in it *ex officio*, as a matter of course. Its purpose is more dignified than to prove the inaccuracy of a contention of one party. The transition is almost imperceptible. It assumes the form of reciting the successive stages of the *travaux préparatoires* as part of the exposition of the facts preceding the exposition of the law. This was the course followed by the Court in the final judgment in the *Free Zones* case.[6] It gave a detailed account of the informal and the official negotiations and of the various drafts leading to Article 435 of the Treaty of Versailles and, then, to the arbitration agreement instituting proceedings before the Court.[7] How far this consideration of preparatory work influenced every detail of the Court's interpretation of these two instruments it is difficult to say. It is possible that it did furnish the inarticulate background by reference to which the Court performed its task of interpretation. But there are indications that it went beyond that. Notice, for instance, the emphasis on

---

[1] Series A, no. 23, p. 42. But see below, pp. 520–1.
[2] See Series A, no. 15, p. 40, where the Court considered the attitude adopted by Poland in her negotiation of a previous treaty with Danzig, which was a party to the dispute.
[3] *Ibid.* p. 30.   [4] Series B, no. 14, p. 34.
[5] Series A, no. 23, at p. 30. See also p. 29. In the case of *Serbian Loans* it appears that the Court examined 'preliminary documents' of instruments of a private law character, namely, of agreements relating to bonds and their gold clause (Series A, no. 20, p. 31).
[6] Series A/B, no. 46.   [7] At pp. 125–31, 132–5.

the fact that 'Article 435, both by reason of its position in the Treaty of Versailles and of its origin, forms a complete whole';[1] or, in regard to the arbitration agreement, the passage referring to 'the information given about the negotiations which took place between the Parties prior to the conclusion of the special agreement'.[2] In the advisory opinion on the *Access of Polish War Vessels to the Port of Danzig* the exposition of the relevant preparatory work occupied almost one half of the opinion.[3]

This course was followed, even more prominently, in the advisory opinion on the *Treatment of Polish Nationals in Danzig*,[4] where the Court reviewed in minute detail the preliminary and final drafts, the unofficial conversations and the correspondence between the interested States and the Conference of Ambassadors. This was also the course adopted in the advisory opinion on the *Interpretation of the Convention of 1919 concerning the Employment of Women during the Night.*[5] The transition, as mentioned, is slow, and in another part of the same advisory opinion we find the Court reiterating that it 'n'entend en rien déroger à la règle précédemment posée par elle à diverses reprises, à savoir qu'il n'y a pas lieu de recourir aux travaux préparatoires lorsque le texte d'une convention est suffisamment clair en lui-même'.[6] But – and the phenomenon is again significant – this was a passage prefacing an examination by the Court of an apparent difficulty raised largely by the Court itself. In the previous periods of its activity the Court examined preparatory work in order to dispel doubts raised by the parties. Here the question is raised by the Court itself:

Au cours des débats auxquels a donné lieu, en 1930 et 1931, à Genève, la proposition de reviser la Convention de Washington sur le travail de nuit des femmes, plusieurs délégués, expert en la matière ont exprimé catégoriquement l'opinion que la convention ne s'appliquait qu'aux ouvrières. Ces opinions ont tellement frappé la Cour que celle-ci a été amenée à examiner les travaux préparatoires de la convention afin de rechercher s'ils confirmaient ou non les opinions exprimées à Genève.[7]

In his dissenting opinion Judge Anzilotti made some very outspoken remarks on the very relative value of a statement to the effect that 'an Article of the convention is clear' and on the necessity of finding a sufficiently broad basis for the view that the natural meaning of a

---

[1] At p. 140.   [2] At p. 152.   [3] Series A/B, no. 43, pp. 132 *et seq.*
[4] Series A/B, no. 44, pp. 13–17.   [5] Series A/B, no. 50, pp. 369 *et seq.*
[6] At p. 378. See also to the same effect Series A/B, no. 47, p. 249 (*Interpretation of the Statute of the Memel Territory: Preliminary Objection*).
[7] Series A/B, no. 50, at p. 378.

disputed term is clear. These remarks are referred to and commented on elsewhere.[1] But it is submitted here that so far as the present case was concerned they were directed not so much against the substance of the Court's efforts to discover the intention of the parties as against some of the expressions used by it. *In fact* the Court resorted in this case in a conspicuous manner to an investigation of preparatory work.

What remained was to put the formal impress of legal respectability upon this practice and to announce *ex cathedra* that recourse to preparatory work has always formed part of the work of the Court. This is the fourth stage in the development. The transition is again almost imperceptible, for instance, when in the case on the *Legal Status of Eastern Greenland* the Court, without any precautionary expressions, examined the various drafts of the Treaty of Kiel of 1819 in order to ascertain how far it contained a recognition by Norway of Danish sovereignty over the whole of Greenland.[2] But the change becomes conspicuous and significant when the Court used preparatory work not merely in order to refute an argument or in order to corroborate a view reached otherwise, but in order to solve what it regarded as a real difficulty, i.e. as to expressions which the Court itself declared to be doubtful. This took place in the advisory opinion on the *Treatment of Polish Nationals in Danzig*.[3] There the Court was called upon to interpret Article 33 of the Convention of Paris between Poland and Danzig. That Article provided as follows:

La Ville libre de Dantzig s'engage à appliquer aux minorités de race, de religion ou de langue, des dispositions semblables à celles qui sont appliquées par la Pologne sur le territoire polonais, en exécution du chapitre I du Traité conclu à Versailles, le 28 Juin 1919, entre la Pologne et les Principales Puissances alliées et associées, notamment à pourvoir à ce que, dans la législation et la conduite de l'administration, aucune discrimination en soit faite au préjudice des nationaux polonais et autres personnes d'origine ou de la langue polonaise . . .

The parties differed as to the interpretation of the expression 'notamment à pourvoir'. Danzig maintained that the word 'notamment' referred logically to the first paragraph of the principal clause of the Article with the effect that the second paragraph, being a subsidiary one, must be read in the light of the first and that everything said in the second paragraph must necessarily be included in

---

[1] See below, pp. 507–8.   [2] Series A/B, no. 53, p. 67.   [3] Series A/B, no. 44.

the first. The Polish Government contended that while the first paragraph referred to the protection of minorities in general, the second had reference to the treatment of Polish subjects, which, according to the Polish interpretation, must be national treatment. Confronted with this divergent interpretation the Court found – for the first time, it appears – that the text 'not being absolutely clear, it may be useful, in order to ascertain its precise meaning, to recall here somewhat in detail the various drafts which existed prior to the adoption of the text now in force'.[1] This task the Court then proceeded to perform in great detail.

Of no less interest is the separate opinion delivered in that case by Judge Hurst. He was prepared to regard as decisive the fact that the Article was so divided as to distinguish the two undertakings. This being so, he said, 'le texte devient si clair qu'un renvoi aux travaux préparatoires de la convention ne semble guère se justifier'.[2] But he did not stop here. He expressed the opinion that the history of that Article was 'interesting', and that there was one fact, not mentioned in the passage of the opinion dealing with the drafting of the Article, which appeared to him 'of considerable importance'. This was the fact that at one stage of the negotiations Poland refused for a number of reasons to accept the draft submitted to her. One of these reasons was her objection to the words 'à l'effet de' connecting the two sentences of the paragraph. These words were then suppressed. 'L'effet de cette suppression', said Sir Cecil Hurst, 'fut de transformer la partie par laquelle se terminait le paragraphe en un engagement positif, au lieu d'un simple explication de la première partie.'[3] He explained that 'il est concevable que dans la hâte et la presse des négociations à Paris, on se soit insuffisamment rendu compte de l'importance de la modification', but he was emphatic in his view that the effect of the change, as shown by the preparatory work, was such as fully to support the Polish contention.[4] This separate opinion, coming as it does from an English international lawyer, is of considerable interest. It shows how an originally deprecatory attitude towards preparatory work changes in the very course of judicial reasoning with the result of transforming it into an important or even decisive element of interpretation.

The last case decided by the Court, at the time of writing these lectures, is, by the generality of its language, of particular significance. This is the judgment in the *Lighthouses* case between France and

[1] *Ibid.* p. 33.   [2] *Ibid.* p. 56.   [3] *Ibid.* p. 58.
[4] *Ibid.* p. 59.

Greece, given on 17 March 1934.[1] The Court was asked, in the arbitration agreement, to decide whether a contract made between a French firm and the Turkish Government in 1913 in respect, *inter alia*, of certain lighthouses situated at that time in Turkish territory occupied by Greek forces and subsequently ceded to Greece 'est dûment intervenue et partout est opérant vis-à-vis du Gouvernement héllènique en ce qui concerne les phares situés sur les territoires qui lui furent attribués à la suite des guerres balkaniques ou postérieurement'. Before the Court the parties disagreed as to the meaning of the words 'contrat . . . dûment intervenu'. In particular, Greece maintained that the effect of these words was to give the Court jurisdiction on the question whether the contract had binding force also in regard to Greece in respect of the lighthouses situated in the territory ceded to her. The French view was that these words had reference only to the validity of the contract under Ottoman law. The Court, after examining the arbitration agreement, put solemnly on record the fact that it 'has reached the conclusion that the precise import of the question in Article 1 of the special agreement, when read in conjunction with its context, is not clear'.[2] It expressed the view that the term 'duly entered into' was not a technical term which possesses invariably the same meaning, and then proceeded to say: 'Where the context does not suffice to show the precise sense in which the parties to the dispute have employed these words in their special agreement, the Court, in accordance with its practice, has to consult the documents preparatory to the special agreement, in order to satisfy itself as to the true intention of the parties.'[3] This reference to the 'jurisprudence' of the Court is undoubtedly somewhat startling; it is not entirely in keeping with the cautious expressions to which the Court has accustomed us in this matter. But, as has been shown, it is certainly not out of accord with its practice. It definitely frees our appreciation of this aspect of the Court's work of an excessively cautious formula of little helpfulness.

Twelve years of experience have proved necessary in order to effect this change. The reasons for the original negative attitude have been clearly indicated. The majority of the Court probably deemed it unseemly to follow a method which some held to be contrary to the traditions of a great system of law. Thus in the oral argument in the case concerning the *Tunis and Morocco Nationality Decrees* Sir Ernest Pollock, speaking on behalf of Great Britain, objected to references to the history of paragraph 8 of Article 15 of

---

[1] Series A/B, no. 62.   [2] Series A/B, no. 62, at p. 14.   [3] At p. 13.

the covenant on the ground that 'to those who are accustomed to what I may call the Anglo-Saxon procedure, a reference to the history or debates concerning the origin of a clause is inadmissible'.[1] But this objection, in itself of doubtful accuracy, was soon abandoned in deference to the obvious requirements of the process of interpretation of treaties. Representatives of the British Government began to raise their objections on grounds not peculiar to English law. In the case concerning the *Iraq Boundary*, Sir Douglas Hogg (as he then was) insisted that 'it is a fundamental rule of English law that a written document must be interpreted according to the intention of the parties as expressed in or to be gathered from its actual terms'.[2] But he did not regard his view as based on a legal principle peculiar to English law; he submitted that it was based on reasoning and good sense and he quoted copiously from French authorities. Similarly, in the advisory opinion concerning the *Employment of Women during the Night* the British counsel, while objecting at length to the use of preparatory work, deprecated the suggestion that his objection was based on a peculiarity of English law.[3] In the case concerning the *Territorial Jurisdiction of the International Commission of the River Oder* Sir Cecil Hurst, speaking on behalf of the six Governments (including the British Government), based his argument not only on the wording of Article 344 of the Treaty of Versailles but also on that of the Allied Reply to Germany, and he drew 'almost irresistible' conclusions from both documents.[4] And it is not without interest that in the *Iraq Boundary* case the British Government while objecting to recourse to previous negotiations devoted eight pages of the written argument to a consideration of this work.[5]

Thus in the second period of its activity the Court was in a position to deal with the question of preparatory work on its merits unhampered by the argument of the divergence of two systems of law. The result has been a final affirmation of the usefulness of this source of evidence. The question of admissibility of preparatory work before the Court has now ceased to be a problem. What remains is to avail ourselves in this matter to the full of the experience of the cases decided by the Court for the purpose of accurately assessing the possibilities and the limits of preparatory work as an element of interpretation.

[1] Series C, no. 2, p. 197. [2] Series C, no. 10, p. 20.
[3] Series C, no. 60, p. 232. See also p. 219. [4] Series C, no. 17, p. 59.
[5] Series C, no. 10, pp. 207–15.

THE PLACE OF PREPARATORY WORK IN THE PROCESS OF INTERPRETATION OF TREATIES

I. Relevance of the Distinction between Various Categories of Treaties

The examination of municipal jurisprudence in the matter of contracts, statutes and treaties and the survey of the practice of international tribunals afford a sufficient basis for the consideration of the place of preparatory work in the interpretation of treaties. The term 'preparatory work' is here used as referring to expressions of opinion, statements of fact, and declarations of intention[1] on the part of the representatives and organs of the contracting parties relating to the treaty in question from the commencement of the negotiations to the signature – and, in some minor respects, to the ratification – of the treaty.

In studying this question the international lawyer must steer clear of two notions which may prove a trap for the unwary. The first of these has already been dealt with, and it is sufficient merely to mention it here. It is necessary to disabuse one's mind of the fascinating misconception that the subject is governed by or germane to any difference between the English (or Anglo-American) and the Continental practice. This view has – at least in the matter of interpretation of treaties – been shown to be a preconception which can be dispelled, without undue difficulty, by a study of the judicial decisions on the subject.[2] The second possible source of confusion is the attempt to divide treaties into categories and to favour recourse to preparatory work in regard to some of them and exclude it in regard to others. Thus, it has been suggested that preparatory work is admissible in the interpretation of bilateral treaties, which, it is said, approach contract: whereas it must be excluded from multilateral treaties of a law-making character, to which there ought to apply the rules governing the construction of statutes, namely, the exclusion of preparatory work.[3] This view is based on two assumptions both of which are inaccurate.

In the first instance the distinction between law-making treaties and other, purely contractual, treaties is – if not actually non-

---

[1] Preparatory work, it will be noted, is not only evidence of intention. It is also a record of circumstances surrounding the conclusion of the treaty. In the English law of evidence the distinction between direct evidence of intention and other parole evidence is sharply drawn. See above, p. 457.

[2] See above, p. 473.

[3] See, e.g. Wright in *A.J.* 23 (1929), 97–104, and *Mandates under the League of Nations* (1930), pp. 353–64.

existent – of a highly relative and controversial value.[1] Even if such a distinction is assumed for the sake of convenience, it does not follow from such an assumption that 'law-making' treaties are identical or even analogous with statutes and the others with contracts in private law. International legislation is a very useful term so long as it is remembered that it is a legislation *sui generis*, not comparable either in the matter of its creation or its functions with legislation within the State. But such identity or analogy, even if admitted, does not carry us very far. There is, it has been shown, no general principle of private law admitting preparatory work for the interpretation of contracts; neither is there a general rule of municipal law excluding preparatory work in the matter of statutes. In this matter international law must stand on its own feet.[2] But although there are in the domain of contracts and statutes no specific rules, enjoying general recognition, which can be made directly applicable to the interpretation of treaties in the matter of preparatory work, all these types of instruments contain certain common features of importance.

II. *The Doctrine of Merger*

The most important of these common features is that treaties – like contracts and statutes – are juridical acts which represent the final expression of the will of the authors of the juridical act in question. The presumption of law – and of common sense – is that it is this final expression of will, and not anything which may have preceded it, that reveals the legally relevant intention of the parties. It is of little importance whether we clothe this principle in the garb of a substantive or procedural doctrine; whether we call it the principle of merger, or of interpretation of the legal act, or of 'best evidence', or of exclusion of parole evidence. The result is the same. The principle that the final instrument supersedes the former expressions of intention is not a rigid principle of legal formalism but a necessary requirement of legal certainty, justice and convenience. In this sense the principle of merger must be constantly kept in mind as a summons to caution whenever preparatory work is resorted to for the purpose of interpretation.

On occasions this element of merger is such as to leave no doubt. This is so particularly in cases in which the treaty contains a clear renunciation of rights and pretensions. In such cases, to quote the

[1] See Lauterpacht, *Analogies*, § 70.
[2] But see below, p. 523, as to the special problems raised by multilateral, as distinguished from bilateral, treaties.

language of Dr Lushington in *The Ionian Ships*, 'it is obvious that this clause entirely removes . . . the necessity of looking into any part of the antecedent history, because, whatever might have been the claims of any of the contracting Powers, they have so completely ceded and merged them by this treaty, that it were perfectly vain to look back to them to obtain any information which can by possibility be of use on the present occasion'.[1] Similarly the problem is simplified when it appears from the pleadings themselves that a party attaches to undertakings given prior to the signature of the treaty the importance of an independent factor going beyond that of mere interpretation. Thus in the case concerning *Access to, or Anchorage in, the Port of Danzig of Polish War Ships*, Poland relied to a considerable extent on the promise given to her by some of the Allied and Associated Powers that she was to enjoy free and secure access to the sea. She maintained that it was the principle underlying this promise, and not the specific terms of the treaty, which ought to govern the opinion of the Court on the issue placed before it.[2] The Court declared itself prepared to take notice 'as a matter of history' of the promise given to Poland, but, it said, no materials and no reasons had been submitted to it for assuming that the treaty did not constitute a complete fulfilment of the promise given. 'The Court is not prepared to adopt the view that the text of the Treaty of Versailles can be enlarged by reading into it stipulations which are said to result from the proclaimed intentions of the authors of the treaty, but for which no provision is made in the text itself.'[3] A treaty may violate an undertaking given in the course of negotiations, but this does not necessarily mean that it is to be interpreted in the light of the broken promise. The undertaking is merged in the treaty; the part of the tribunal is limited to the finding that it does not appear in the treaty.[4] For the same reason the promises said to have been given to Germany by the Allied and Associated Powers prior to the Armistice of November 1918 have seldom, if ever, been adduced by German writers as a factor in the interpretation of the Treaty of Versailles; although the alleged disregard of these promises, construed as a preliminary treaty, has been given by some of them as a reason vitiating the legal validity of the treaty.[5]

But it is only by way of exception that parties admittedly oppose

---

[1] 2 Spinks 212, at p. 219; 164 E.R. 398.　　　[2] Series A/B, no. 43, p. 143.
[3] *Ibid.* at p. 144.
[4] *Hartrodt* v. *Henry Olsen & Co.*, Anglo-German Mixed Arbitral Tribunal, 18 June 1928, *Recueil T.A.M.* 8, 26; *Annual Digest*, 4 (1927–8), case no. 301.
[5] See, for instance, Hold-Ferneck, *Lehrbuch des Völkerrechts*, II (1932), 152–7.

preparatory work to the clear wording of the treaty; as a rule they invoke it to confirm their own interpretation of the treaty. For this reason although international tribunals have had occasion to act on the somewhat obvious principle embodied in the requirement of merger, the term itself does not appear frequently in their pronouncements. The case of the *Chilean–Peruvian Accounts*[1] which is frequently cited as the only judicial affirmation of the doctrine of merger,[2] is, in fact, a denial of it. The Arbitrator seems to have misunderstood the true meaning of the doctrine. He was of the opinion that the doctrine of merger means not that the treaty supersedes the previous communications, but that they form part of the treaty.[3] But the doctrine does appear *eo nomine* in more recent pronouncements. Before the Mixed Claims Commission between the United States and Germany it was contended that during the negotiations following upon the sinking of the *Lusitania* Germany made an offer to pay a suitable indemnity for the loss of life of the United States citizens. This offer was never accepted and the Tribunal refused to act on it: 'All offers therefore made by Germany, as well as all her obligations to the United States or its nationals, whatever their nature, arising during the war period, were merged in and fixed by the Treaty of Berlin.'[4] A State may, at some stage of diplomatic negotiations relating to the treaty in question or otherwise, make an offer designed to meet the wishes of the other party. But such offer need not be regarded as necessarily indicative of that State's view of the legal position. When the offer is not accepted its force is spent. This principle was reaffirmed, in another connection, by the Permanent Court of International Justice when it held 'que la Cour ne saurait faire état de déclarations, admissions ou propositions qu'on put faire les parties au cours des négociations directs qui ont lieu entre elles, lorsque ces négociations n'ont pas abouti à un accord complet'.[5] While fully admitting the importance of preparatory work as expressed in the negotiations, care must be taken not to attach to the latter the importance of a binding obligation. Negotiations are a process of bargaining. They cannot be

---

[1] Award of C. A. Logan, 7 April 1875; Moore, II, 2086.

[2] Ralston, p. 8.   [3] Moore, II, 2092.

[4] *Maude Thompson de Gennes* v. *Germany*, *A.J.* 19 (1925), 805. See also, to the same effect, *Administrative Decision No. 5, ibid.* p. 622. In the arbitral award of 16 February 1933, under the Final Act of the Hague Reparations Agreement of 1930, the Tribunal found that the conclusion by Germany and Portugal of a further agreement in 1931 rendered irrelevant certain declarations and statements made by the Portuguese Government at the Hague Conference in 1930 (*A.J.* 27 (1933), 543).

[5] Series A, no. 17, p. 51. And see below, p. 516, as to the Twelfth Advisory Opinion on the *Interpretation of the Treaty of Lausanne.*

regarded as solemn and binding declarations. Any appreciable tendency to attach to them an importance of this nature would result in diminishing their usefulness which is now being increasingly recognized, especially in treaties of obligatory judicial settlement. International tribunals have on occasions drawn attention to this aspect of the matter. Thus in the *North Atlantic Fisheries* arbitration, one of the grounds advanced by the United States was that in the course of diplomatic negotiations following upon the conclusion of the Treaty of 1818, Great Britain made use of expressions inconsistent with a claim to exclusive regulation of the fisheries. The Arbitrators said: 'The Tribunal, unwilling to invest such expressions with an importance entitling them to affect the general question, considers that such conflicting or inconsistent expressions as have been exposed on either side are sufficiently explained by their relation to ephemeral phases of a controversy of almost secular duration, and should be held to be without direct effect on the principal and present issues.'[1] The Arbitrator in the *Chamizal Boundary* dispute between the United States and Mexico adopted the same view.[2]

There is all the difference between using declarations made in the course of negotiations for the purpose of interpreting a final agreement and regarding them as the agreement itself.[3] The intentions, possibly of an uncompromising nature, revealed prior to the signature of the treaty may have undergone a change in the course of the process of arriving at a mutual *quid pro quo*. For, ultimately, what matters in the process of interpretation is the common intention of the parties, not the intention of one of them as expressed in his drafts or declarations – except when there is evidence to show that the point of view there expressed has been accepted by the other

[1] Scott, *Hague Reports*, p. 166.
[2] Award of 5 June 1911, *A.J.* 5 (1911), 797, 802, 803.
[3] And see below, pp. 515–16, on the necessity for caution in the appreciation of fragments of preparatory work torn out of their context.

Cases may, of course, occur in which the arbitrator may, having regard to the circumstances, regard as binding notes, public or secret, exchanged in the course of negotiations but not included in the final document. This was the case in regard to certain formal notes signed and exchanged in connection with the signature of the Treaty of 20 October 1904 between Bolivia and Chile. The Arbitrator (acting, it may be recalled, as an amiable compositeur) was not to ignore these notes altogether. He said: 'It would be very dangerous if States were at liberty to repudiate notes exchanged by their respective plenipotentiaries appointed to negotiate a treaty when those notes had an intimate relation with the subject matter of the treaty and when the action of the plenipotentiaries had not been disavowed by their Governments as soon as it was known.' However, this is not really a case of treaty interpretation. (Award of the King of England of 5 July 1911, *A.J.* 5 (1911), 1103.)

party. But even that may not be enough. For what is ultimately decisive is not only the common intention of the parties, but their common intention at the time of signature, i.e. their intention as expressed in the treaty. The common intention may have changed in the course of the preparation of the treaty; so also may have changed the intention of the parties who had a decisive influence on the framing of the treaty. Thus in *Weitzenhoffer* v. *Germany* the plaintiff referred to the drafts presented to the Peace Conference by the British and French plenipotentiaries in regard to Article 297(e) of the Treaty of Versailles. The Tribunal simply pointed out that the treaty adopted a different point of view.[1]

The treaty – and nothing else – is the final expression of the will of the parties. It must be recognized as a clear rule that wherever there is an admitted contradiction between the treaty and preparatory work, it is the former that prevails. Preparatory work must not vary, add to or subtract from the treaty. But it may interpret it. Whether such interpretation in fact amounts to varying, adding to or subtracting from the treaty must in each case be determined by the Tribunal. In practice, the party adducing preparatory work will only seldom admit that it is in flat contradiction to the apparent meaning of the treaty. In the *Cayuga Indians Claims* case it was urged on behalf of the United States, by reference to the history of the negotiations of the Treaty of 1812, that a provision of the treaty granting certain privileges to the Indian tribes was merely a 'nominal' provision intended to save the face of the negotiators. The Tribunal refused to accede to this proposition: 'We are not asked to choose between possible meanings. We are asked to reject the apparent meaning and to hold that the provision has no meaning. This we cannot do.'[2] But, as mentioned, an outspoken admission on the part of the State invoking it that preparatory work materially changes the content of the treaty is in the nature of an exception. As a rule the State in question maintains that the treaty reveals the true intention of the parties in an imperfect manner, and that the preparatory work invoked by it puts a proper interpretation on an expression which is doubtful, obscure or even apparently contradictory of the true intention of the treaty. Whether this is really so must be decided by the Court. But the Court can properly give its decision only after it has examined the preparatory work in question.

[1] Roumanian–German Mixed Arbitral Tribunal, 18 January 1926, *Recueil T.A.M.* 5, 935; *Annual Digest*, 3 (1925–6), case no. 284.
[2] American and British Claims Arbitral Tribunal (award of 22 January 1926), *A.J.* 20 (1926), 574.

III. Preparatory Work and 'Clear Meaning'

While these considerations based on the principle of merger set the limits of recourse to preparatory work, they do not substantially affect the right and duty of international tribunals to make full use of preparatory work, as, indeed, of all other means of extrinsic evidence. In international law as elsewhere, the object is to arrive at the intention of the parties *ex signis maxime probabilibus*. The battle of interpretation has been fought elsewhere and the tendency is an obvious one. We have shown that the actual practice of international tribunals has been not to repeat formulas and rules based on the historical peculiarities of one country or group of countries, but to explore the intention of the parties by reference to all available sources of evidence. The first and principal lesson that can be deduced from their practice is that in no circumstances ought preparatory work to be excluded on the ground that the treaty is clear in itself. Nothing is absolutely clear in itself. Most words and expressions have many meanings – complementary, parallel, and even directly contradictory. They have a general meaning; or a local one; or a meaning confined to a trade or profession; or an arbitrary individual meaning. Most of the cases of treaty interpretation before the Permanent Court of International Justice had reference to expressions which are in themselves 'clear'. Its pronouncements turn on the interpretation of such otherwise 'clear' terms as 'indus-try',[1] 'workers'[2] (a category of which Judge Anzilotti said that it is 'far from being clear and definite'[3]), 'established',[4] 'contract duly entered into'[5] (an expression which a practically unanimous Court held not to be clear[6]), and so on. The preference for what may be called the natural meaning is helpful, but inquiry frequently reveals that a term may possess many natural meanings. Most of the various meanings of a word in a dictionary are natural meanings. The choice of any one of these meanings may yield a result which is logical and far from being absurd.

Just as in strict law there are no gaps in a legal provision from the point of view of its logical completeness, so also it is only in exceptional cases that a term is itself obscure. As a rule both parties, while putting forward diametrically opposed contentions, claim

---

[1] Series B, no. 2 (*Competence of the International Labour Organization*).
[2] Series A/B, no. 50 (*Interpretation of the Convention of 1919 concerning the Employment of Women during the Night*).
[3] *Ibid.* p. 389. [4] Series B, no. 10 (*Exchange of Greek and Turkish Populations*).
[5] Series A/B, no. 60 (*Lighthouses* case between France and Greece). [6] *Ibid.*

that the disputed provision is clear. This, for instance, was the contention of France in connection with the Advisory Opinion (No. 2) on the *Competence of the International Labour Organization*. She advanced the view that the term 'industry' in the Treaty of Versailles was clear as referring to industry in the limited meaning of the term. The Court held it to be clear in the opposite meaning. This very fact is in itself an indication of the relative value of the phrase that 'the treaty is clear'. A term is not 'clear' when taken in isolation – even by reference to its 'natural meaning'. The natural meaning of the passage that the régime of certain rivers as laid down in the Treaty of Versailles shall be superseded by a convention *drawn up* by the Allied and Associated Powers is clear enough. But the Permanent Court of International Justice held the expression 'to draw up a convention' to be 'some whatill-chosen'[1] and one which it was not permissible to take literally; it held that 'drawn up' means also 'duly ratified'. The controversial expression becomes scientifically clear only after we have caused to pass through it the 'galvanic stream' – to use Mr Justice Holmes' phrase[2] – not only of the whole document, but of all evidence available. An overwhelmingly 'clear' decision may be plunged into the depths of uncertainty by a ray of evidence; a doubtful and controversial term may by the same process achieve a decisive accession of strength and clarity. It is useful to quote in this connection the remarkable passage in Judge Anzilotti's dissenting opinion in the case of the *Interpretation of the Convention of 1919 concerning the Employment of Women during the Night*. He said:

Mais je ne vois pas comment il est possible de dire qu'un article d'une convention est clair avant d'avoir déterminé l'objet et le but de la convention, car c'est seulement dans cette convention et par rapport à cette convention que l'Article assume sa véritable signification. Ce n'est que lorsqu'on connaît ce que les parties contractantes se sont proposées de faire, le but qu'elles ont voulu atteindre, que l'on peut constater, soit que le sens naturel des termes employés dans tel ou tel Article cadre avec la véritable intention des parties, soit que le sens naturel des termes employés reste en deçà ou va au delà de la dite intention. Dans le premier cas, on dit avec raison que le texte est clair et qu'on ne saurait, sous couleur d'interprétation, lui donner une signification différente de celle qui répond au sens naturel des mots. Dans les autres cas, puisque les mots n'ont de valeur qu'en tant qu'expression de la volonté des parties, on

[1] Series A, no. 23 (*Territorial Jurisdiction of the International Commission of the River Oder*), p. 20.
[2] In *Harvard Law Review*, 12 (1898–9), 417.

constatera, soit que les termes ont été employés dans un sens plus large que celui qui leur revient normalement (interprétation dite extensive), soit que les termes ont été employés dans un sens plus étroit que celui qui leur revient normalement (interprétation restrictive).[1]

The importance of this pronouncement, it may be said with respect, is not impaired by the fact that on several former expressions Judge Anzilotti had joined the Court's positive affirmation that the text was clear. No clarity is so absolute as not to admit of proof to the contrary. There are many pronouncements of international tribunals which while refusing in a given case to depart from the meaning of the treaty as accepted by the tribunal safeguard themselves by adding the phrase 'in the absence of evidence to the contrary'. In the *North Atlantic Fisheries* arbitration we find a statement to the effect that 'words in a document ought not to be considered as being without any meaning, *if there is no specific evidence to the contrary*'.[2] The same safeguarding clause has been noted in the passage, quoted above, of the advisory opinion of the Permanent Court of International Justice in the dispute between Poland and Danzig.[3]

Undoubtedly as the process of interpretation cannot be suspended *in vacuo* the tribunal must base its investigation on what according to the circumstances appears to it to be the most natural meaning of a term or of a clause. Equally, the tribunal must attach importance to the degree of discrepancy between the natural meaning thus provisionally adopted and that suggested by preparatory work. But this fixation of meaning is, as mentioned, only a provisional assumption. This presumption may not be altogether without importance; it shifts the burden of proof upon the party who, basing himself on preparatory work, alleges a discrepancy between the natural meaning and the true one as it appears to him. But it is a presumption which can be rebutted. It is not a *presumptio juris et de jure*. While it is inadmissible to depart from the absolutely clear meaning of the treaty there ought to be the greatest reluctance to assume, without exhaustively examining the available sources, that the meaning is absolutely clear. It follows from what has been said that the statement that an expression is clear is – or ought to be – the result of the process of interpretation, not the starting point. Some

---

[1] Series A/B, no. 50, p. 383.   [2] Scott, *Hague Reports*, p. 146.
[3] See above, p. 497. See also the award of the British–American Claims Arbitral Tribunal of 9 December 1921, in the *David J. Adams* (*Annual Digest*, 1 (1919–22), case no. 243) in reply to the contention of the United States, based on preparatory work, that 'the literal meaning of an isolated clause is often shown not to be the meaning really understood or intended'.

of the decisions of the Permanent Court make it appear to be the beginning, but the form of these pronouncements is not necessarily indicative of the sequence of events in the actual framing of the judgments and advisory opinions.[1]

IV. The Special Position of Preparatory Work in International Adjudication

There are special reasons which tend to increase the importance of preparatory work as an element of interpretation of treaties as compared with the interpretation of statutes or contracts. These reasons are grounded both in the substance of controversies involved in the interpretation of treaties and in the particular problems of the international judicial function. In the first instance, a method of interpretation which relies on the text to the exclusion of extrinsic evidence in the form of preparatory work is less suitable for international adjudication than for the normal activity of municipal courts. A purely grammatical or logical interpretation is one which leaves larger scope to unfettered judicial reasoning and to freedom of judicial construction than one which takes into account the objective factors as given by extrinsic evidence. There is something almost arbitrary in purely grammatical or logical interpretation. On the face of it, it is an objective process – as objective as logic or grammar. But it is the logic of the judge. It is his individual logic, and nothing but logic. It is clear therefore that reliance on this method of interpretation is feasible in a political society where the position of the judiciary is traditionally a strong one. There is in the judgment of Farwell L.J. in the case of *Rex* v. *West Riding of Yorkshire County Council*[2] an interesting passage upholding the inadmissibility of reference to parliamentary proceedings as an instrument of interpretation. The learned judge, while pointing to the deliberate ambiguity of many an Act of Parliament where each side hopes to have expressed its own point of view, added: 'The generality of public understanding is quite incapable of proof, and is beside the mark unless as an appeal to timidity. "*Securus judicat orbis terrarum.*"' Such austere serenity cannot always be assumed by an international judge. In international relations the position of the judiciary is not yet so exalted as to be able to rely entirely on the impersonal authority of the bench. It is imperative that the international decision shall be based on as many factors independent of the subjective reasoning

---

[1] See on this point Lauterpacht, *The Development of International Law by the Permanent Court of International Justice* (1934), p. 38.
[2] [1906] 2 K.B. 676, at p. 716.

of the judge as circumstances allow. When, therefore, matters affecting States are concerned, it would be utterly undesirable to derive the judicial decision from what is in fact only a mental operation. Undoubtedly, extrinsic evidence also – including preparatory work – becomes part of the decision through a mental operation performed by the judge, but nevertheless the nature, the method, and the ingredients constituting this process are of the utmost importance. A decision of a municipal tribunal based on a technical rule of interpretation or on a merely textual analysis may on occasions seem inappropriate; for the reasons stated, a similar decision by an international tribunal is open to much stronger objections. The question of preparatory work is yet another illustration of the view that in international relations it is as important that justice should appear to be done as that it should be done in fact. Such appearance is seriously diminished if the tribunal excludes from consideration or from sufficiently careful consideration any kind of evidence likely to throw light on the intention of the parties. As a matter of practice international, as, indeed, other tribunals do not confine themselves to ascertaining the intention of the parties from the document alone. They endeavour to elucidate their intention by various indirect means like the assumption that the parties intended a result in conformity with international law. This being so, it is, to mention one example, almost strange to see the Permanent Court in the *Wimbledon* case[1] considering in detail the international position of various international waterways as evidence of existing rules of international law assumed to underlie the intention of the parties, and failing to have recourse to the available extrinsic sources of information.

The impropriety of relying upon mere textual interpretation becomes even more striking when one considers the importance of the subject matter of international adjudications. They frequently involve national interests of significance. The responsibility placed in such cases upon the international judge is correspondingly great. The availability of extrinsic evidence, including preparatory work, diminishes the burden placed upon him. It makes the result dependent upon something more tangible than mere analysis of the text. No legal theory and no political safeguards can or ought to do away with creative judicial activity and freedom of judicial appreciation. But the voluntary nature of international jurisdiction requires that whatever may, with judicial activity, appear purely personal and

[1] Series A, no. 1.

subjective, should be counterbalanced and strengthened by enlarging the basis of judicial reasoning. This consists in taking into consideration objective facts in the form of recorded statements and declarations. An international tribunal which, in deciding the question whether the Hay–Pauncefote Treaty between the United States and Great Britain conferred rights upon third parties, would rely merely on the text without reference to the recorded and detailed history of the treaty as shown in its original form, its rejection by the Senate, and its subsequent amendment, would be guilty of a dogmatism approaching levity. An international judge who would interpret the provisions of an important arbitration treaty without reference to the prolonged correspondence which preceded it and which throws abundant light upon every expression and nuance of expression, upon what is included and what is omitted, would run the risk of reducing his work to the point of devastating barrenness.[1] For there exists in treaties a further element of considerable importance, which increases the evidential value of the negotiations preceding the treaty as compared with the preparatory work of statutes or contracts. In the case of treaties the preparatory work is as a rule recorded, formal, authoritative, explicit and continuous. If thoroughly studied it permits to trace, in an illuminating chain of continuity, the development of a clause from the first instruction to the delegate or from the first note initiating the correspondence to the final provision as adopted in the treaty. A party aiming at securing a forensic advantage may deliberately disturb this continuity, but a thorough investigation by the judge will without undue difficulty restore the missing link.[2]

There are other weighty reasons which make reliance on preparatory work particularly important in the international sphere. The judge within the State interprets documents whose language is his language and whose incidents take place against a social and historical background with which he is intimately acquainted. This undoubtedly is both an inducement to and a partial justification of textual and logical interpretation. The position is different in the case of treaties. Terms which in national jurisprudence have acquired a distinct meaning become the prey of controversy when applied to situations between States. They acquire a connotation said to be dictated by the specific requirements of international law. A 'lease' is said to connote annexation; a 'mandate' is said to be only in name connected with its prototype in private law. Apparent

---

[1] See, for instance, British Diplomatic Documents.   [2] See below, p. 515.

termini technici like 'war' become the subject of controversy – witness the prolonged discussion on the meaning of the term 'resort to war' as used in the Covenant of the League of Nations.[1] The very term 'principles of international law' was hotly debated in the *Lotus* case.[2] There is little, if any, authoritative definition of terms in international law; there is only a limited amount of traditional usage in terminology; there is no sufficiently powerful ray of illuminations flowing from a community of language, history, and experience. This is an additional reason for assisting the process of interpretation by available extrinsic evidence.

V. The Objections against the Use of Preparatory Work

It is convenient to answer here some of the objections against the use of preparatory work. These objections do not affect the by now clear rule of international law admitting evidence of preparatory work, but they ought to be considered.

In the first instance, it is maintained that what matters in the interpretation of treaties is not the intention of the negotiators but of the ratifying authority. The ratifying authority, it is said, does not know what happened at the conference in the course of the negotiations leading up to the treaty; it has before it only the text of the treaty.[3] It ratifies the treaty as it stands, and it ought not to be bound by anything else. Upon examination it will be found that there is little substance in this objection. It raises the difficult question as to who is the ratifying authority. Is it the legislative body which in most countries takes part directly or indirectly in the process of ratification? Or is it that section of the legislative body which deals specifically with foreign relations? Or is it the executive department which in fact examines the treaty, frequently in consultation with other departments, and submits the treaty to Parliament? Or is it the Head of the State who performs the formal act of ratification? In a sense all these persons or bodies take part in the process of ratification. Any attempt to interpret the treaty by reference to *their* intention must render the work of interpretation almost impossible; but reference to *someone's* intention there must be. This is of the essence of the process of interpretation. The invariable practice of international tribunals has been to investigate the intention of those who negotiate and sign the treaty. It is they who make

[1] See Lauterpacht in *A.J.* 27 (1934), 43–60. And see above, pp. 506–9, where the 'clear meaning' of treaties is discussed.
[2] See below, pp. 515–16.   [3] See Fachiri in *A.J.* 23 (1929), 745 *et seq.*

the treaty. The act of ratification is of decisive importance for the validity of the treaty, but it is formal in its nature and must not be confused with the substantive act of making the treaty. There is no question of the ratifying authority being *bound* by preparatory work; the latter is in no case binding. It merely serves to interpret the treaty. At the same time while it cannot be expected that the several hundred members of the legislative body have made themselves acquainted with the records of the negotiations it is not unreasonable to assume that the competent executive department has made itself acquainted with them and also that it has drawn the attention of the legislature to points of importance.

Secondly, it has been asserted that recourse to preparatory work may, particularly in the case of multilateral treaties, result in divergent interpretations of the same treaty by various tribunals.[1] This objection can apply to cases in which a municipal tribunal in interpreting a treaty relies exclusively upon that part of the preparatory work which shows the intention of its own State, the assumption being that the tribunals of other countries will adopt the same course and limit their investigations to the preparatory work favourable to their State. But this is an assumption, not supported by evidence, which questions the impartiality and thoroughness of municipal tribunals. It does not apply to international adjudication. Far from resulting in divergent interpretations, recourse to preparatory work connecting the process of interpretation with tangible and extrinsic sources of proof must, assuming a thorough fulfilment of their task by international tribunals, result in a uniformity greater than that achieved by textual and logical elucidation of the meaning of the text.

A more weighty objection is contained in the view that adherence to preparatory work may result in an unprogressive and rigid interpretation which, by fastening on the expressions and declarations of the negotiators, debars the judge from taking into consideration the development and changes subsequent to the signature. There may be a certain amount of truth in this objection; undoubtedly there may occur cases in which reliance on preparatory work diminishes the element of judicial freedom in developing the law beyond the intention of the parties as expressed in the treaty. But, on the other hand, there may be cases in which preparatory work will reveal possibilities of creative development of the law which might seem to be unwarranted if reference is made to the text alone.

---

[1] See Wright in *A.J.* 23 (1929), 101.

In fact, while the duty to rely on preparatory work may impose limits upon judicial freedom to develop the law, the question is not highly relevant to the problem of progressive interpretation or otherwise. It does not apply in any case to so-called executed treaties or to treaties in which the purely contractual element predominates over the legislative aspect, if any.[1] However, as suggested, even in multilateral treaties of a general character the danger of a rigid and unprogressive interpretation on account of reliance on preparatory work is largely imaginary.

VI. Examination of the Whole of Preparatory Work by Judicial Tribunals

The most weighty, and not altogether groundless, objection to admissibility of preparatory work is that recourse to it may be abused for the purpose of disintegrating the work of interpretation by diverting the attention of the judge from the consideration of the final text of the treaty and by compelling him to study and disentangle a bulky mass of evidence. There is no doubt that a consideration of preparatory work, although it may on occasions reduce the burden of responsibility, imposes a considerable strain upon judicial activity. It may be abused in a variety of ways. It may add to the artificiality, evasiveness and uncertainty, already considerable, of international obligations. However, if it is admitted that recourse to preparatory work is necessary on the grounds both of legal principle and for reasons peculiar to international adjudication, then the objection based on the possible abuse of this source of evidence and on the addition to the work of tribunals is not decisive. The dangers resulting from the admission of preparatory work are real only so long as there is no court to probe the relevance and the accuracy of the argument based on preparatory work. But the whole discussion of the relevance of preparatory work as an element of interpretation presupposes the existence of tribunals which are able and which regard themselves as under an imperative duty to exhaust to the full the possibilities of available sources of interpretation. In this matter there do not obtain in international adjudications the reasons which

[1] This is clearly brought out in a passage of the award in the *Ottoman Debt* arbitration: 'La tâche des négociateurs n'était pas, comme celle du législateur, de poser des règles générales auxquelles des tribunaux eussent altérieurement à donner, par leur jurisprudence, les développements nécessaires en face de la diversité des situations concrètes régies par elles. Leur besogne était bien plutôt de résoudre des questions et des difficultés concrètes, de stipuler des droits et des obligations, de fixer des prestations et des charges, en un mot de mettre fin à des conflits de volontés et d'intérêts par un accord obtenu et consacré sur une séries de points déterminés. L'Arbitre n'a d'autre tâche que d'assurer l'effet de cet accord à l'égard des questions donnant lieu aux différends portés devant lui' (*Sentence Arbitrale*, p. 32).

historically prompted the introduction of restrictive rules in municipal law like the desire to minimize the dangers arising from the possibility of juries being unduly influenced by inferior evidence.

That recourse to evidence of preparatory work may on occasions introduce ambiguity where none appears on the face of the treaty, there is no doubt. But that ambiguity can as a rule be removed by a conscientious analysis of the whole of the preparatory work. The problem raised by a piece of extrinsic evidence can be examined and solved by the same type of evidence. In Bacon's much quoted and much abused phrase, *ambiguitas verborum latens verificatione suppletur, nam quod ex facto oritur ambiguum verificatione facti tollitur.* Such conscientious analysis renders the work of interpretation immune against incomplete or misleading appeal to preparatory work. It is the incompleteness of the approach which is a prominent feature. Thus, for instance, it happens frequently that a party refers only to one stage of the negotiations or of the elaboration of the treaty. The fact invoked supports its contention – but it supports it only so long as only part of the preparatory work is examined. The examination of the whole preparatory work may show that the statement appealed to was made at a very early stage of the proceedings; that it was rejected by the other party; or that there was no occasion to answer it; or that it does not in fact support the argument; or that it was subsequently abandoned by its author. It may be necessary to reconstitute all the links of the long chain of preparatory work in order to gain a full and reliable picture. A number of examples will illustrate this aspect of the matter.

In the *Lotus* case the Permanent Court had to interpret Article 15 of the Convention of Lausanne which provided that 'les questions de compétence judiciaire seront ... réglées conformément aux principes du droit international'. The French Government contended that the meaning of the expression 'principles of international law' must be sought in the light of the preparatory work. It pointed out that in the course of the drafting of this Article Turkey submitted an amendment asserting her right to exercise in certain cases jurisdiction over foreigners for crimes committed abroad. This amendment, which was met by reservations on the part of Great Britain and Italy, was rejected by France, and the Drafting Committee thereupon adopted the wording as it appeared in the convention. From this France inferred that it was the intention of the convention to exclude jurisdiction over foreigners for crimes committed abroad.

However, the Court found that this was only one half of the story. In the first instance, it found that the preparatory work did not show for what reasons France and Italy objected to the Turkish draft; these reasons, the Court said, 'sont inconnus et auraient pu n'avoir aucun rapport avec les raisons que la France invoque maintenant'. Secondly, the examination of the whole of the preparatory work showed that the original draft of the Article which limited Turkish jurisdiction to crimes committed in Turkey was also discarded. 'Ce fait', dit la Cour, 'pourrait, au même titre, porter à croire que la pensée des rédacteurs de la Convention a été de ne restreindre aucunement cette juridiction.'[1]

In the Advisory Opinion No. 12, concerning the *Interpretation of the Treaty of Lausanne*, the Court dealt in detail with the Turkish attempt to interpret the crucial provision by reference to the preparatory work of the convention. Turkey relied on a speech of the chief British representative in the course of the first stage of the Lausanne Conference in which he explained that the proposed Article conferring upon the Council the power to lay down the frontier must be interpreted in the light of the fact that the decisions of the Council, on which Turkey would have to be represented, must be unanimous and that no decision could be arrived at without her consent. The Court went into the details of this aspect of the preparatory work of the conference. It found that the passage in question formed part of a proposal which was rejected by Turkey – a fact which it would be difficult to understand unless one assumed that at that time Turkey did not understand the proposal in the sense which she sought to give to it subsequently. Secondly, the Court pointed out that at the time of the speech referred to it the relevant provision of the Treaty of Lausanne did not exist, and that when five months later the conference adopted the Article in question the legal position was fundamentally modified and 'il n'est donc pas possible d'interpréter cet Article au moyen de déclarations qui se rapportent à l'état antérieur des choses'.[2]

How strong is the temptation to rely on part only of the preparatory work may be seen from the fact that occasionally not only parties but also judges have rendered themselves guilty of this omission. The student searching for such examples of judicial sins of omission will find a conspicuous one in Judge Kellogg's Observations, in the *Free Zones* case, with regard to the history of the last

---

[1] Series A, no. 10, p. 17.
[2] Series B, no. 12, p. 23.

paragraph of Article 38 of the Statute of the Permanent Court of International Justice.[1]

In the advisory opinion on the *Interpretation of the Convention of 1919 concerning Employment of Women during the Night,* the Court was

[1] Series A, no. 24. This argument was put forward by Judge Kellogg in support of the view that the last paragraph of Article 38 of the statute did not empower the Court to disregard existing law even at the wish of both parties to the dispute. In Judge Kellogg's submission the paragraph in question was submitted by M. Fromageot who desired to add to Article 38 a provision that the Court might decide in accordance with principles of 'law and justice'. 'C'est pour exprimer cet avis', said M. Kellogg, 'que fut adoptée la clause autorisant la Cour a statuer *ex aequo et bono.* Mais M. Fromageot déclara que cette clause n'impliquerait aucunement que le Cour pût ne pas tenir compte des règles existantes; or, les règles existantes étaient celles qui sont énoncées à l'Article 38, aux termes duquel la Cour doit fonder ses décisions sur des conventions et traités internationaux et sur des principes de droit' (Series A, no. 24, at p. 41). A more detailed examination of the preparatory work in question would have resulted in an entirely different picture.

The present last paragraph of Article 38 did not appear in the draft of the Committee of Jurists. It grew out of a proposal submitted to the Third Committee of the First Assembly by M. Fromageot (*Meetings of Committees*, First Assembly, pp. 385, 386) with a view to enabling the Court to give judgments by consent. With this object in view he proposed that to the clause instructing the Court to decide in accordance 'with general principles of law' there should be added the words 'and justice'. The proposal was made with a view to enabling the Court 'to state as the sole reason for its judgments that the award had seemed to it to be just', a 'just' award being a decision rendered in accordance with the wish of both parties. In amplifying his proposal M. Fromageot then said: 'Ceci n'impliquerait aucunement, d'ailleurs, [this adverb does not appear in the English translation] que la Cour puisse ne pas tenir compte des règles existants', the intention being obviously to convey that the words 'and justice' did not empower the Court to disregard the existing law 'd'ailleurs', i.e. apart from the special agreement of the parties. It is in this light that we must read Judge Kellogg's remark that 'M. Fromageot stated that this "clause" did not imply that the Court might disregard existing rules'.

Judge Kellogg's researches into the origin of the present last paragraph do not appear to go beyond the first meeting at which the question was discussed. However, the further history of the Article throws more light on the matter. At one of the subsequent meetings of the Committee M. Politis raised the question whether the formula 'in accordance with generally recognized principles of law and justice' reflected the true wishes of the committee. He pointed out that the clause thus adopted would enable the Court to apply not only existing law, but also general principles of justice as distinguished from the existing law. He insisted that the Court should not be allowed to exercise such wide powers except with the consent of the parties. He therefore proposed the following formula: 'The general principles of justice recognized by civilized nations'. The report of the meeting tells us that after some discussion M. Fromageot suggested that M. Politis' view should be met by adding to the end of the Article the clause: 'This provision shall not prejudice the power of the Court to decide a case *ex aequo et bono* if the parties agree thereto' (*ibid.* p. 403). The intentions of the committee on that point were embodied in the report of the chairman, M. Hagerup, who referred to the decision of the committee in regard to the original wording of M. Fromageot's amendment as intended 'permettre, le cas échéant, à la Cour de rendre avec l'agrément des parties, une décision fondée en bonne justice sans avoir à se référer expressement à tels ou tels textes de droit' (*ibid.* p. 608). In his report to the full committee, M. Hagerup again referred to the amendment, as finally adopted, as permitting the Court 'if necessary and with the consent of the parties, to make an award *ex aequo et bono*' (*ibid.* p. 534; see also *Minutes of the Plenary Session*, p. 463).

If, as suggested by Judge Kellogg, the term '*ex aequo et bono*' means legal justice not inconsistent with the existing law, then, in fact, it is difficult to see why an express authorization of the parties should be necessary in order to enable the Court to do what is plainly its duty.

prepared to attach importance to the fact that, as shown by the preparatory work, at first the intention of the framers of the convention was that there should be no departure from the stipulations of the Berne Convention, but it found that in the course of the preparatory work 'this intention had receded into the background by the time that the draft convention was adopted'.[1] In the *Lighthouses* case between France and Greece, the Court was prepared to accept the contention, based on deductions from preparatory work, that a controversial term in the arbitration agreement was derived from Protocol XII of the Treaty of Lausanne, but it found that from the very beginning the parties attached a different meaning to this term of the protocol.[2] At times the consideration of all relevant facts will reveal that the argument based on preparatory work is simply due to a misunderstanding.[3]

An important consideration which courts have constantly to bear in mind in sifting evidence of this character is that the object of interpretation is to elicit the common intention of both parties, and not of one party only. Unless the declaration of intention of a party is instrumental in disclosing the common intention of all signatories, its value is limited. What one party understood by the treaty is of little importance if the other party disagreed with that interpretation or if circumstances show that it could not be expected or that there was no opportunity to repudiate it expressly. For in the atmosphere of international conferences it is not always that an unpalatable proposal or interpretation is expressly rejected.[4] At times it is merely ignored by others; frequently the delegates are not sufficiently acquainted with the intricacies of the ordination in order to grasp and to reply to the implications of a subtle declaration.[5] In such cases it would be unreasonable to attach to the unilateral proposal much evidential value. Now such thorough investigation undoubtedly

---

[1] Series A/B, no. 50. See also for similar examples Series A/B, no. 47 (*Interpretation of the Statute of the Memel Territory: Jurisdiction*), p. 25, and Series A/B, no. 53 (*Legal Status of Eastern Greenland*), p. 67. See also the award of W. D. Hines on certain cessions by Germany to the Allied and Associated Powers by virtue of Article 339 of the Treaty of Versailles, *A.J.* 18, 187.

[2] Series A/B, no. 62, p. 17.

[3] Series B, no. 10 (*Exchange of Greek and Turkish Populations*), p. 22.

[4] As was the case, for instance, in *Abbas Holmi Pasha* v. *Great Britain* (award of 29 June 1927 by the Anglo–Turkish Mixed Arbitral Tribunal, *Recueil T.A.M.* 7 (1927–8), 909). Here the Tribunal pointed out that the Turkish declaration, refusing to accept a British declaration, was followed by a British statement reiterating the British position. On the other hand, in the case of *Polyxène Plessa* v. *Turkish Government* (quoted above, at p. 486) the Tribunal attached importance to the fact that the Greek delegate failed to make a certain statement.

[5] See Series B, no. 14 (*Jurisdiction of the European Commission of the Danube*), p. 3.

imposes a strain upon the work of the tribunal. It is much easier to give a decision on the basis of a logical deduction or by the short-cut of a technical rule of interpretation. But, with slight exceptions, international and national tribunals have refused to ease their burden in this way.

Neither is it feasible to lighten the task by developing a set of rules as to the method of examining preparatory work adduced by the parties. For the process of examining preparatory work is a pragmatic one. There are no ready made rules – and there ought not to be – for dealing with the various problems raised by an appeal to preparatory work. This may be seen, for instance, in regard to the perennial problem as to whether in case of an apparent discrepancy between preparatory work and the final text of the treaty the text ought to be qualified by what has been revealed by the preparatory work or whether the final wording signifies that the point of view as revealed in the preparatory work has been abandoned. Thus, for instance, in interpreting the term 'resort to war' as used in the Covenant of the League the question has arisen of the importance to be attached to the fact that at a late stage of the work of the Peace Conference these words were substituted for the term 'resort to force' which appeared in the original drafts of the relevant articles of the Covenant. What is the meaning of this change? Does it mean that the draftsmen did not attach any particular importance to the change except as one of form and manner – a view for which some support may be found in the records of the conference?[1] Or does it mean that the existing text must be qualified by or interpreted in the light of the original one? Or, finally, are we justified in assuming that the change was deliberately one of substance and that it amounted to an alteration of one of the vital aspects of the Covenant? To these questions there is no answer by a reference to any ready made rules. The right solution must be sought by inquiring into the whole and nothing less than the whole of the preparatory work. This may be a protracted task beset with perplexing difficulties like deciding on the authority and reliability of the various sources of the *travaux préparatoires*. Thus in regard to the minutes of a conference the question may arise as to the significance to be attached to the fact that the records at times constitute an amended version of what was actually said at the conference. The question may arise as to the authority of private records, memoirs and diaries. In view of this one might regard as

---

[1] See Hunter Miller, *My Diary at the Conference of Paris*, v, Doc. 396, p. 277, where this alteration is mentioned in a reference to a 'change in verbiage'.

natural the inclination to avoid the complexities of this additional task either by eliminating it altogether through the short cut of an interpretation restricted to the text or by simplifying it through some cut and dried rules relating to the use of preparatory work. Such a procedure cannot be regarded as commendable. The more significant the subject of the controversy the less satisfactory will appear attempts to shorten and to simplify radically the task of interpretation.

VII. *Particular Categories of Preparatory Work*

The necessity for caution in framing fixed rules relating to the consideration of preparatory work shows itself in a subject on which the activity of the Permanent Court of International Justice reveals a tendency to fix rules of a certain rigidity. Thus the Court has declared as inadmissible preparatory work based on confidential negotiations or on negotiations between States other than the parties to the dispute. In the Preliminary Order concerning the *Territorial Jurisdiction of the International Commission of the River Oder* the Court laid down that the records of the Peace Conference which prepared the Treaty of Versailles could not be used for the purpose of interpreting the treaty in relation to those parties to the dispute, like Sweden and Denmark, who did not take part in the work of the conference. And the Court then proceeded to say: 'In any particular case, no account can be taken of evidence which is not admissible in respect of certain of the parties'[1]. This is a rule whose reasonableness is not, on the face of it, open to doubt, but it may be useful to point to some of the consequences of its rigid application. The Court, by limiting the application of the rule to the parties to the dispute, apparently refused to go to the length suggested by Great Britain in the *Tunis and Morocco Nationality Decrees* case. There it was argued that as the Covenant of the League was binding also upon States other than those which took part in its elaboration, it was not permissible to rely on the preparatory work of the Covenant; such third States, it was said, might otherwise be bound by an interpretation based on statements and declarations of which they had no knowledge when adhering to the treaty.[2] The Court did not in that case pronounce on the matter. In its decision in the *Oder* case the Court went only to the length of excluding preparatory work of this nature in cases in which one or more parties did not participate in its elaboration. The situation would, it appears, have been different if

---

[1] Series A, no. 23, p. 42.
[2] Statement of Sir Ernest Pollock, Series C, no. 2, p. 197.

the States which did not participate in the preparatory work of the convention in question were not directly involved in the actual dispute. If it were otherwise, important multilateral conventions might be deprived of a valuable instrument of interpretation as the result of the accession of new States – a situation vividly reminiscent of the notorious effects of the so-called general participation clause in the various Hague Conventions. A somewhat similar result would follow if, in accordance with the decision in the *Oder* case, this rule were to be uniformly adopted in all cases in which one of the disputants which *is* a party to the dispute did not take part in the preparatory work. A rigid rule is not here necessarily a wise rule. Due weight ought to be attached to such questions as whether the adhering State could have knowledge of the nature of the preparatory work; the relative importance of the adhering State; the number of other signatories; and so on.[1] As a matter of broad principle it must be urged that the adhering States accede to a concrete and definite product of the will of others, and that their own part in its interpretation is necessarily of a somewhat secondary character. It is the original convention and the intention of its makers which must be clarified and interpreted, and if this task cannot be performed satisfactorily and scientifically without recourse to preparatory work then there is no room for hampering rules excluding that preparatory work because some States took no part in it.

Neither, it is respectfully submitted, is it possible as a matter of principle to exclude preparatory work for the simple reason – to use the words of the Court in the case on the *Jurisdiction of the European Commission of the Danube* – of its record 'étant confidentiel et n'ayant pas été communiqué à la Cour par l'autorité compétente ou avec son consentement'.[2] If the preparatory work in question in fact sheds light on the intention of the parties then it is difficult to see how this effect can be destroyed by its being confidential. It can be rejected because its authority is doubtful, or creditably denied, or difficult of ascertainment, or directed against an adhering State which could have no knowledge of it; these, and not other, factors ought to constitute the ground for its exclusion. The fact that it has not been placed before the Court by or with the consent of the competent authority – which may mean the opposing party – is hardly relevant. Such submission against the will of the other party may

[1] In the *Oder* case the situation was particularly interesting inasmuch as Denmark and Sweden, who were parties to the dispute by virtue of a special agreement, never adhered to the Treaty of Versailles.

[2] Series B, no. 14, p. 32.

constitute a breach of diplomatic decorum or of a definite undertaking, but this cannot legally affect the evidential value of the
record[1] – unless the matter can, in appropriate circumstances, be
brought within the orbit of Article 18 of the Covenant of the League
which destroys (or, perhaps, merely diminishes) the effectiveness of
secret engagements.

While circumstances may in some cases impair the evidential value
of preparatory work, e.g. in case of confidential records of negotiations,
in other cases preparatory work may possess a particularly authoritative character. This is so, for instance, in declarations which amount
to an authentic and decisive interpretation of the document in
question. When a victorious State drafts a treaty which it imposes
upon the vanquished without giving him the opportunity of discussion, then the statements by which it accompanies such imposed
conditions are of obvious usefulness for the purpose of interpreting
the treaty. To a large extent only the intention of one of the parties is
here relevant. For this reason there has been a disposition to attach
great weight to the communications of the Allied and Asssociated
Powers addressed during the Peace Conference to Germany and the
other Central Powers.[2] In one case the parties, while agreeing that
preparatory work shall not be taken into account, exempted from
this provision the notes exchanged at the Peace Conference between
the German delegates and the Allied and Associated Powers.[3]

VIII. Authentic Interpretation and Preparatory Work Subsequent to the Signature of the Treaty

With the question discussed in the last section there is connected
the question of authentic interpretation of a treaty, prior to its
signature, by the contracting parties. The matter can be treated here
only in large outline. When Governments in answer to a proposed
text of a treaty issue declarations and statements, addressed to some
or all of the co-signatories and giving their view of its terms, then
such statements constitute preparatory work which must be taken
into consideration. In the first instance there ought not to be any
doubt that when there is a series of concurrent interpretations,
prior to the signature of the treaty, as to the meaning of the treaty,
such interpretations must be taken into account and decisive effect

[1] See also the *Alsop* case, *U.N.R.I.A.A.* ix, 349.

[2] See Series B, no. 14 (*Jurisdiction of the European Commission of the Danube*), p. 32; Series A, no. 23 (*Territorial Jurisdiction of the International Commission of the River Oder*).

[3] *Reparation Commission* v. *German Government*, Award of Special Arbitral Tribunal (Beichmann ‚Arbitrator) of 3 September 1924: *Annual Digest*, 2 (1923–4), case no. 194.

must be attributed to them. Thus with regard to the much-discussed question of the relevance of the various communications preceding the signature of the General Treaty for the Renunciation of War and relating to wars of self-defence, it would be unwarranted and pedantic to disregard them. This is so particularly in cases in which the interpretation contained in the preparatory work thus expressed can be adopted without depriving the treaty of its effect. In regard to the Treaty for the Renunciation of War the difficulty is diminished inasmuch as the interpretation in question merely gives expression to a self-evident legal principle recognized in all systems of law. It is true that in some of these interpretations the parties reserved to themselves the right to remain judges as to the exercise of the right to resort to war in self-defence, but, as has been pointed out elsewhere, even this safeguard is entirely compatible with a reasonable interpretation of the treaty which leaves intact its principal object.[1]

In the case of a multilateral treaty such concurrent constructions, by the bulk of the signatories, have the effect of impressing the treaty with an interpretation of considerable authority even against those isolated States which did not concur in this interpretation. Their remedy is not to sign the treaty and to refuse to be party to it. The situation is different in the case of a divergency of interpretation represented on each side by a considerable number of signatories. In such cases it is not unreasonable to assume that the divergent interpretations cancel themselves out, and that by finally agreeing to sign and ratify the treaty the contracting parties have tacitly agreed that the treaty should be construed without reference to the divergent interpretations. Preparatory work is useful and legally relevant only if it helps to reveal the *common* interpretation of the parties. By the same token, an interpretation of the treaty by a relatively small number of signatories – even if not expressly rejected by others – cannot, it would seem, be of legal effect if it is held by the Court to be contrary to the natural meaning and the common intention of the other parties. A State cannot be permitted by the device of a unilateral interpretation to append what is in fact a reservation requiring the express assent of the other parties.[2]

The position might perhaps be different in the case of a bilateral treaty. An official interpretation by one party prior to the signature if not contradicted by the other party cannot well be disregarded.

---

[1] Lauterpacht, *The Function of Law*, pp. 159–60.
[2] See, on declarations not amounting to reservations, Shatzky in *R.I.* 14 (1933), 231, and Baldoni in *Rivista*, 8 (1929), 356–70.

But, as in the case of a multilateral treaty, clearly divergent interpretations on both sides cannot well be invoked as such; they are merged in the treaty. On the other hand, concurrent interpretation must be regarded as an authoritative expression of the common intention of the parties.

It is not necessary to consider here in any detail the question of the relevance of communications and declarations subsequent to the signature but prior to ratification. They cannot be properly regarded as preparatory work preceding the formation of the treaty. They usually assume the form of statements made in connection with the submission of the treaty for approval by the legislative assembly. It would appear that, as in the matter of statutes, the expressions of opinion of the private members of the legislature are hardly relevant for the purpose of interpretation. On the other hand, the declarations of the members of Governments and the official reports of committees and of their chairmen cannot be altogether disregarded. They certainly throw light on the interpretation put upon the treaty by the State in question. It would be difficult for a State to maintain an interpretation at variance with such pronouncements. But it is doubtful whether their effect goes further than that. It is obvious that any expressions of opinion calculated to limit or qualify the treaty cannot be given that effect as regards the other contracting party. Only formal reservations can produce a legal effect. Even declarations and resolutions of parliamentary assemblies as such, however official and solemn, when not forming part of the act of ratification are in no way binding.[1] They are not addressed to the other party. It frequently has no knowledge of them; or it may be informed of them after it has itself ratified the treaty.[2] On the other hand, there is nothing to prevent it from regarding such interpretation at variance with its own and emanating from the other contracting party as a reason for refusing to proceed with ratification. This may

[1] The courts of the United States have repeatedly refused to attach importance to resolutions of the Senate not formally embodied in the act of ratification. See *New York Indians* v. *United States*, 170 U.S. 1; the case of *Fourteen Diamond Rings*, 183 U.S. 176. See also Kellogg in *A.J.* 13 (1919), 767–73. And see Foster, *The Practice of Diplomacy* (1906), p. 286, on the incident connected with the ratification of the Naturalization Treaty of 1874 between Turkey and the United States. In the course of the exchange of ratifications Turkey put her own construction on the resolution of the Senate amending the treaty. The American Government then held the exchange of ratifications to be invalid.

[2] See Mandelstam in *R.G.* 40 (1933), 537 *et seq.* and 41 (1934), 179 *et seq.* See in particular the repeated statements of the rapporteur of the French Chamber who distinguished between preparatory work proper, to which he attributed a definite place in the process of interpretation, and declarations and commentaries in foreign legislative bodies which, in his view, could not be used for this purpose.

be a wise act of precaution. There is little merit in a treaty which, even prior to its formally entering into force, shows lack of an agreement *ad idem*. An international tribunal may, of course, reject the interpretation thus put forward, but it is a bad augury for a treaty if it begins with a certain prospect of future litigation. And in the case of a multilateral treaty, what is otherwise an act of precaution may become a positive duty if an interpretation with which a State feels itself at variance emanates from a considerable number of other signatories. A court would not be justified in ignoring such interpretation communicated to or obviously known to the State in question.

IX. *Preparatory Work and the Doctrine* rebus sic stantibus

This doctrine of *rebus sic stantibus*, in so far as it is not a disintegrating political catchword but a principle capable of judicial application, is essentially a question of the interpretation of the intention of the parties. It is not every change of conditions which will in law give rise to the application of the doctrine, but only such change of circumstances as amounts to the frustration of the object of the treaty as contemplated, expressly or impliedly, by the parties at the time of its completion. For this reason in the matter of the doctrine *rebus sic stantibus* it is not only the interpretation of a particular term which is of importance: it is the view of the negotiating parties as to the object of the treaty and, to some extent, the reasons which led to its conclusion. Naturally, preparatory work is of great if not decisive importance for ascertaining these factors. In the French–Swiss *Free Zones* case France invoked the doctrine of *rebus sic stantibus* on the ground that the conditions which underlay the Treaty of 1815 creating the régime of free zones had undergone a substantial change. It was contended that the régime of free zones was embodied in the Treaty of 1815 in view of the fact that at that time the Canton of Geneva was in effect an area of free trade; that the withdrawal of the French customs line made the area of Geneva and of the free zones one economic unit; and that the establishment of the French Customs Union in 1849, by destroying this economic unit, 'mis fin aux conditions en considération desquelles les zones avaient été crées'.[1] The Court examined these contentions in detail. It agreed that there had taken place changes in the food supply of Geneva, with the development of communications and so on. But it was of the opinion that these changes must be relevant to the object of the

[1] Series A/B, no. 46, p. 156.

treaty as conceived by the parties when they entered into the treaty. 'Il est nécessaire, au premier lieu, de prouver que c'est en considération de l'absence de droits de douane à Genève que les Puissances se prononcèrent en 1815 en faveur de la création des zones.' It then found that these changes 'ne portent pas sur l'ensemble des circonstances ... que les hautes parties contractantes avaient en vue lors de la création des zones franches.'[1] And it is clear that the Court in order to find out what were the motives of the parties was prepared to look not only at the text of the treaty, but also at its preparatory work.[2]

The same approach to the problem will be found in another recent pronouncement on the doctrine of *rebus sic stantibus*, namely, in the decision of the German *Staatsgerichtshof* in the dispute between Bremen and Prussia, decided in June 1925.[3] Before the First World War there had taken place an exchange of small pieces of territory between these two States. The treaty stipulated for certain conditions to be observed by the parties in regard to the territories ceded, one of the conditions being the obligation of Bremen to refrain from constructing works connected with the fishing industry in the territory received by her. Bremen now asked to be relieved of this condition on the ground that her expectations to use the territory for developing her shipping did not materialize on account of the outbreak and the outcome of the War. The Court inquired in great detail into the motives which led the parties to enter into the treaty. It went so far as to examine the project of the law introduced by the Prussian legislature in this matter and part of the parliamentary history of the law. It found that those very clauses for the abrogation of which Bremen now asked were the principal consideration which induced Prussia to enter into the treaty. It therefore refused to apply the doctrine. These examples suggest that if resort to preparatory work helps to assert the juridical element in what may be the otherwise anarchic comprehensiveness of the doctrine of *rebus sic stantibus*, then this function alone would go a long way towards vindicating its usefulness in the process of interpretation.

This course of lectures is, for reasons of space, not intended as an exhaustive treatment of the subject of preparatory work in the

---

[1] *Ibid.* p. 158.

[2] See *ibid.* p. 156 for a reference to the declaration of the Swiss representative at the Allied gatherings in 1815.

[3] *Entscheidungen des Reichsgerichts in Zivilsachen*, 112, Appendix, 21; *Annual Digest*, 3 (1925–6), case no. 266.

interpretation of treaties. Its purpose is rather to bring together the available judicial decisions on the matter and to discuss, from this aspect, the problems raised by the use of preparatory work. There is little doubt that international law admits this particular source of evidence. But both the extent and the desirability of its acceptence have been obscured by certain notions which are here subjected to some criticism. In this matter, as in many others, the practice of international law and of international tribunals can be regarded as a distinct contribution to general jurisprudence by helping to reveal the common element and the uniformity of tendency on a question obscured by historical peculiarities of various systems of law. The treatment of preparatory work in the practice of international tribunals shows also that in the matter of interpretation of treaties it is not so much the elaboration of detailed rules that is to be aimed at as the elimination of artificial restrictions upon the elucidation of the common intention of the parties. This is the general and uniform tendency of the principal systems of law. For reasons peculiar to the international judicial function, it is particularly true to say that in the matter of interpretation of treaties the absence of definite and elaborate rules means not arbitrariness and anarchy but the fulfilment of the purpose of the law.

CHAPTER 22

PREPARATORY WORK IN THE
INTERPRETATION OF TREATIES (1950)

Editor's note A general introductory note to this section on preparatory work appears at p. 449 above. The present chapter consists of section III, entitled 'Travaux Préparatoires', of the original English text of Lauterpacht's report on the Interpretation of Treaties prepared for the Institute of International Law. In the French translation, which is printed in *Annuaire*, 43(1) (1950), it appears at pp. 390–402.

Probably the main factor which has tended to reduce the authority of the doctrine of 'plain meaning' has been the growing realization of the importance of preparatory work as an element of interpretation and the circumstance that recourse to it has become a prominent feature of the work of international tribunals. It is seldom that resort to it is challenged without qualification.

Undoubtedly the Permanent Court of International Justice – and its successor – have occasionally used language in the contrary sense. Thus the Permanent Court of International Justice has often expressed the view that it is not bound – or entitled – to have recourse to preparatory work when the meaning of the treaty is 'clear'. However, in most cases in which the Court has declared the admissibility of recourse to preparatory work to be dependent upon the absence of clarity of meaning it has actually inquired into the preparatory work either because the treaty was not deemed to be clear[1] or, more often, by way of confirmation of a result reached by other means. In the latter case, as has been rightly suggested, it is by no means certain that the actual sequence of events has been as it has appeared in the judgment or the opinion of the Court – it is not certain that the clarity of meaning said to have been confirmed by the preparatory work was not in fact due to the illumination obtained

---

[1] As in the *Lighthouses* case between France and Greece where the Court said: 'The Court cannot regard the expression "duly entered into" as a technical term, invariably possessing the same signification. Where the context does not suffice to show the precise sense in which the parties to the dispute have employed these words in their special agreement, the Court, in accordance with its practice, has to consult the documents preparatory to the special agreement, in order to satisfy itself as to the true intention of the parties' (Series A/B, no. 62, p. 13). See also to the same effect the advisory opinion on the *Treatment of Polish Nationals in Danzig* (Series A/B, no. 44, p. 33).

by the study of the latter. It is only by way of exception, as in the Advisory Opinion, referred to above, on admission of Members of the United Nations, that the Court declined altogether to consider the *travaux préparatoires* on the ground that the relevant clause was clear. As will be suggested below, such attitude is open to serious question.

The paramount fact is that the recourse to preparatory work is a constant feature of interpretation of treaties by international tribunals.[1] It is not surprising that it should be so. If the task of interpretation is to discover the intention of the parties what better method can there be, in case of dispute, for achieving that object than the examination of the written record of the negotiations leading to the treaty, of the instructions sent to the representatives and of the discussions, of successive drafts, of agreed declarations, and of authorized reports which preceded the adoption of the treaty? This is not the easy method. It is much easier and seemingly more economical to let the sharp knife of logical or grammatical interpretation cut the knot of controversy. Preparatory work is frequently lengthy, repetitive, contradictory, and, with regard to multilateral treaties, revealing the views of the more articulate rather than the more important, better instructed and influential participants. The record of preparatory work is often incomplete, faulty or misleading. Much depends in this connection on the adequacy of the secretarial arrangements of the conference. It often happens that in the heat or enthusiasm of the debate views are advanced or expressions used which it is subsequently deemed wiser to modify or to qualify in the written record[2] – and yet it is the spoken work which provokes the answers and supplies the substance of the debate. Moreover, in the course of negotiations the participating States change their views as expressed on previous occasions, and the examination of any particular stage of the preparatory work, to the exclusion of others, is therefore liable to be incomplete and

[1] This is the general result of the examination of this question by the author of the present report in *Hague Recueil* 48 (1934) (ii), 713–815 [chapter 21 above] and in *Harvard Law Review*, 48 (1935), 549–91 [not reprinted – see Editor's note, p. 449 above]. This is also the view of practically all writers, including the authors of *Harvard Research* (1935), III (Article 19, pp. 956–66), who have devoted detailed study to the matter. For a list of these writers see Oppenheim's *International Law* (7th ed., 1948), I, 862.

[2] The Universal Declaration of Human Rights adopted by the General Assembly in December 1948 is not a legal instrument subject to ordinary legal rules of interpretation. For that reason it is not germane to the issue here discussed. But it is of interest to compare the record of the speeches made at the final meetings of the Assembly and embodied in the Summary Record with the more sombre version reproduced in the Records of the General Assembly.

misleading.[1] There are other reasons why, unless care is taken to examine preparatory work in its entirety, it may lead to conclusions which are inaccurate and one-sided. Thus in the *Lotus* case the French Government supported its principal contention by reference to the fact that a Turkish draft which claimed for Turkey jurisdiction over offences committed, in certain cases, outside Turkish territory was rejected by the conference. The Court found that, with one exception, no reasons were given for the rejection of the Turkish draft and that, therefore, from the mere circumstance of its rejection no conclusion could be drawn that such jurisdiction was contrary to international law. Moreover, an examination of the preparatory work as undertaken by the Court showed that another draft expressly limiting the jurisdiction of the parties to offences committed in their territory was equally rejected.[2] Similarly, it is only the examination of the preparatory work as a whole which can reveal whether there is room for the application of the doctrine of 'merger' according to which the conflicting manifestations of intention are merged in and absorbed by the treaty as finally concluded or whether the divergent expressions of intention can legitimately be permitted to play an independent part in the process of interpretation.

Such thorough examination of the bulky record of preparatory work imposes a considerable strain upon international tribunals. Yet it is improbable that there is an effective alternative to the laborious unravelling of the sequence and inconsistencies of preparatory work whenever such is available. It is not suggested that preparatory work is the only method of discovering the intention of the parties. Logic, context, grammar, 'natural meaning', presumptions, the principle of effectiveness, the historical circumstances and presumed object of the treaty (in the discovery of which preparatory work is not an unimportant element), action taken subsequent to its adoption – they all have an important and legitimate place in the task of disclosing the intention of the parties. But if an international judge confronted with a controversial provision of an important multilateral treaty were to confine himself to the text before him and to disregard the written record showing what the parties actually said or solemnly declared – his decision would leave a disturbing

[1] Professor Guggenheim in *Lehrbuch des Völkerrechts*, 1 (1947), 126, in questioning the applicability of preparatory work to multilateral treaties, attaches importance to the fact that it passes through various stages. Yet it is the business of the interpreting agency to survey and mutually to relate the various phases of the preparatory work.

[2] See Series A, no. 18, pp. 16, 17.

impression of incompleteness. There is all the difference – in so far as the authority and the persuasive force of the judgment are concerned – between disregarding preparatory work altogether and examining it and finding that either because of its incompleteness or contradictions it offers no clue to the intention of the parties or that it does not in fact support the contention of the party which invokes it as against what appears *prima facie* to be the natural meaning of the terms of the treaty.[1]

There is certainly no justification for ignoring preparatory work in cases in which it is unambiguous and to the point. It may be unprofitable to speculate whether an uncontradicted report of the rapporteur of a commission approximates in authority to a provision of a treaty. But it is equally idle to deny its probative value for the elucidation of the intention of the parties. The same applies, even more cogently, to express and solemn declarations made by a commission as a whole or by individual members of it. As in the case of the question of withdrawal from the membership of the United Nations, there may be reasons which prompt the parties to refrain from inserting a formal Article in the treaty and to be satisfied with what appears to them to be a less formal but adequate expression of their will. The procedure adopted may be open to criticism, but such criticism is irrelevant to the question of discovering and of

---

[1] Thus it would appear that the considerable authority of the unanimous advisory opinion of the International Court of Justice in the matter of *Reparation for Injuries Suffered in the Service of the United Nations* is somewhat impaired – perhaps unnecessarily impaired – by the failure of the Court to consider or to refer to the relevant preparatory work of the San Francisco Conference. Part of that work – but only part of it – seems to point to the view that the authors of the Charter deliberately refrained from attributing international personality to the United Nations. In fact they rejected the Belgian proposal to recognize expressly that it possesses international status and the corresponding rights (Doc. 524. iv/2/26). This was also the understanding of the Secretary of State of the United States in his report to the President (*The Charter of the United Nations, Hearings before the Senate Committee on Foreign Relations* (1945), p. 135). He explained the omission of an express attribution of international personality to the United Nations on the ground that the committee which discussed the matter 'was anxious to avoid any implication that the United Nations will be in any sense a "super-State" ' (*ibid.*). If no other part of the preparatory work were available the opinion of the Court would be less acceptable than it is. However, it appears from the report of the rapporteur of the relevant committee (iv/2) that the fact of the non-acceptance of the Belgian proposal could not properly be regarded as a rejection of the view which prompted it. The report described such express attribution of international personality as 'superfluous' and added that such personality 'will, in effect, be determined by implication by reference to the entirety of the provisions of the Charter' (Report of the Committee iv, 2, A., Doc. 803). That is what the Court did in effect. It acted upon the intention of the parties, as shown in the preparatory work, to leave to future developments the exact determination of the juridical status of the United Nations. The persuasive force and the authority of the opinion would have been enhanced by evidence, such as here outlined, that, notwithstanding some appearance to the contrary, it did not disregard the proclaimed intention of the authors of the Charter.

acting upon a clearly revealed intention of the parties. There is no escape from the fact that, unlike in the matter of most private contracts, the preparatory work leading to the conclusion of treaties – especially those of a multilateral character – partakes of a deliberation and a degree of authentication commensurate with the importance of their subject matter. This is one of the main explanations of the ease and alacrity with which the parties appeal to it – including, frequently, the party which at the opening stage of the pleadings denies the probative value of preparatory work. This is also the reason why such appeal has become prominent in modern times when the negotiations and the conferences preceding the conclusion of treaties, general or particular, are as a rule public and recorded – often with an almost embarrassing abundance of documentation. The question of preparatory work may be, in a sense, a technical problem of evidence. In essence it is a fundamental and perhaps the most important aspect of interpretation of treaties. This applies, in particular, to the interpretation of general international instruments such as the Charter of the United Nations. To attempt an interpretation of the Charter without references to the vast resources of preparatory work which preceded its adoption is to adopt the method of 'jurisprudence of concepts' in its most questionable connotation. The author of the present report knows of no commentary of the Charter, either in its entirety or with regard to any of its comprehensive aspects, which has appeared so far[1] and which is not based predominantly or exclusively on what may be described generally as *travaux préparatoires*.

In this connection reference must be made to the specific limitation put by the Permanent Court of International Justice on the use of preparatory work in cases in which some of the parties to the dispute did not take part in the preparatory work of the clause forming the subject matter of the controversy. In connection with the case concerning the *Territorial Jurisdiction of the International Commission of the River Oder* the Court issued in 1929 an Order laying down that as three of the parties concerned in the case before it did not take part in the conference which preceded the Treaty of Versailles, 'the record of this work cannot be used to determine, in

---

[1] Reference may be made in particular to Goodrich and Hambro, *Charter of the United Nations* (2nd ed., revised, 1949); Kopelmanas, *L'Organisation des Nations Unies*, I (1947) (a work of exceptional merit); Dr Kaeckenbeeck's Commentary of the Charter in *Hague Receuil*, 70 (1947) (i), and the comprehensive work of Professor Kelsen, *The Law of the United Nations* (1950).

so far as they are concerned, the import of the treaty'.[1] The Court then proceeded to make its ruling more specific – and more controversial – by laying down that it applied with equal force to passages of the record which had been previously published and to those which were produced for the first time in the written proceedings before the Court. It is not believed that the ruling when thus explained – i.e. when referring to preparatory work previously published – can stand the test either of principle or convenience. When applied, for instance, to the Charter of the United Nations, the effect of the ruling would be that, assuming that resort to preparatory work is admissible in relation to States which participated in the Conference of San Francisco, the interpretation of any particular provision of the Charter might be subject to different methods and sources of interpretation with resulting differing or contradictory consequences – the answer in each case being dependent on whether any of the parties to the dispute had an opportunity to participate in the preparatory work. In proportion as the number of States adhering to the Charter increases, the effect of the ruling might be that recourse to preparatory work – a vital source of interpretation – would be ruled out for most practical purposes. It would be sufficient if one of the parties to the disputes was absent from the Conference at San Francisco, to exclude resort to *travaux préparatoires*. Moreover, quite independently of any dispute, any provision of the Charter would be subject to a double standard of interpretation – that in relation to the participants at the Conference of San Francisco *inter se* and that among the Members of the United Nations at large.

But there are reasons even more compelling than the inconvenience of the consequences of the adoption of the principle of the case of the *Territorial Jurisdiction of the International Commission of the River Oder* which render it difficult to accept it as a sound legal proposition. The very basis of that principle is open to serious question inasmuch as it assumes the existence of an objective meaning of a term or clause – of a natural 'plain' meaning – divorced from the intention of the parties responsible for it. Apparently, on that view, the States which adhere to a treaty after it has been formulated are bound by an abstraction expressed in words independent of the intent of those who shaped the treaty. However, to assert that once the treaty has

---

[1] Series A, no. 23, p. 42. The same view was propounded by Great Britain in the case of the *Tunis and Morocco Nationality Decrees* in relation to the Covenant of the League of Nations (Series C, no. 2, p. 197).

been concluded it has an existence independent of the negotiations which preceded it is to maintain that it has a meaning independent of the intention of the parties who evolved it. There is no more reason why the adhering States should not be bound by the *travaux préparatoires* than that they should not be bound by the final expression of intention as recorded in the treaty. For they have no part in either. The only adequate solution seems to be that the adhering States should accept the treaty as, *to their knowledge*, it was agreed upon – as it was intended – by the original parties. This means that the preparatory work in question must be recorded, public, and accessible. To that extent the Order of the Court in the case of the *Oder Commission* commends itself as a sound and working rule.

The hesitation which has surrounded the use of preparatory work, the cautious and essentially unhelpful formula used occasionally by the International Court to the effect that there is no room for recourse to preparatory work when the meaning of the treaty is clear, and the appeal to that formula by parties to the dispute whenever that has suited their purpose, have been fostered to a considerable extent by the suggestion that there is in this respect a cleavage between the so-called Anglo-American and the Continental schools of thought. With isolated exceptions that view has not been advanced by American writers, and it is contrary to the American judicial practice in interpreting constitutional and other statutes. Neither does it find support in British practice. Sir Arnold McNair, in an exhaustive examination of the subject, has come to the conclusion that although British courts in general exclude preliminary negotiations, successive stages of drafting, and parliamentary debates in connection with the interpretation of statutes 'there is ample evidence that in the interpretation of treaties a different practice is sanctioned both by governmental opinion and judicial decisions'.[1] Although before international tribunals British representatives at times have objected to the use of *travaux préparatoires*, on other occasions they have relied on them. There are cases on record in which after objecting as a matter of principle to the use of preparatory work they found it useful to invoke it in support of some aspects of their thesis. Judges of British nationality on the International Court have often relied on preparatory work either in individual opinions or in joint pronouncements to which they

[1] *The Law of Treaties* (1938), p. 262. The author of the present report advanced the same view in an article on 'The So-called Anglo-American and Continental Schools of Thought in International Law' in *B.Y.* 12 (1931), 43, 44 [reprinted as chapter 17 of volume 2 of these *Collected Papers*], and in the works referred to above, at p. 529, n. 1.

subscribed. The alleged divergence between the Anglo-American and Continental principles and approach in the field of international law has been exaggerated out of all proportion to its true significance. Probably, it is non-existent. This applies in particular to the question of *travaux préparatoires*. But 'the divergence of two schools of thought' is an argument of a high degree of attractiveness, and this fact explains to a large extent the pronouncements of international tribunals, in particular of the Permanent Court of International Justice, on the matter. An international tribunal which considers itself bound to apply principles of international law as generally accepted and general principles of law, is reluctant to give its imprimatur to a practice said to be contrary to an important system of law. As has been pointed out, it is doubtful whether the Court has in fact acted literally upon the rule, frequently formulated, that there is no room for recourse to preparatory work when the treaty is clear. It has relied upon it, with conspicuous regularity, for confirming its interpretation of a provision held to be clear. But the border-line between confirming a view already reached by other methods and finding support for it before its final crystallization is elastic and indefinite. However that may be, both the cumulative experience of international arbitral and judicial settlement and a critical examination of the problems involved suggest that the time is ripe for putting beyond doubt the full justification of the use of preparatory work, in its own right, as an essential element in the interpretation of treaties. Such clarification of the position would, by discouraging some redundant forensic argument, conduce to economy in the written and oral argument. It would also diminish the danger that international tribunals, when confronted with the difficult task of unravelling the complexities of preparatory work, might feel inclined to solve the difficulty in a manner which is hardly calculated to assist the cause of international justice, namely, by disregarding preparatory work altogether.

535

VI OPERATION OF TREATIES

CHAPTER 23

GUARDIANSHIP CASE — SEPARATE OPINION

Editor's note An explanation is given in the Preface to volume III of these *Papers* of the considerations underlying the decision to distribute through the work Lauterpacht's various judicial opinions. His separate opinion in the *Guardianship* case is printed at this point because it is primarily concerned with the extent to which various factors such as *ordre public* might affect the operation of a treaty – the Convention of 1902 between the Netherlands and Sweden governing the Guardianship of Infants. The case is reported in *I.C.J. Reports* 1958, p. 55. Lauterpacht's opinion appears at pp. 79–101.

While, for reasons which I deem it incumbent upon me to state, I am unable to accept some of the contentions advanced by the defendant Government and upheld by the Court, I arrive on other grounds at the same results as does the judgment. I do so by reference to considerations of public policy, or *ordre public* – a question which occupied the main part of the written and oral pleadings, which figures exclusively in the formulation of the legal issue in the final conclusions of both parties, and which I feel therefore bound to examine in the present opinion.

The facts underlying the controversy between the parties are stated in detail in the judgment of the Court. For the purpose of this opinion it is sufficient to recapitulate briefly the crucial aspect of the dispute: The Hague Convention of 12 June 1902 on Guardianship of Infants, to which both Sweden and the Netherlands are parties, provides in Article 1 that the guardianship of an infant shall be governed by the national law of the infant. It is clear from the various Articles of the Convention, and it is not disputed by the parties, that such guardianship extends normally to the custody of the person of the minor. In accordance with the provisions of the convention, a Dutch guardian was appointed in 1954 by a Dutch Court over Elisabeth Boll who, although born in Sweden and permanently resident there since her birth, is of Dutch nationality. In the same year, various Swedish authorities, in a series of

539

decisions and in circumstances which appear from the judgment, applied to Elisabeth Boll the Swedish Law of 1924 concerning the Protection of Children and Young Persons (Child Welfare Act) – which will be referred to in this opinion as the Law on Protective Upbringing. By one of these decisions the custody of the person of Elisabeth Boll was taken over in 1954 by the Child Welfare Board at Norrköping, the place of residence of Elisabeth Boll. The Board, in turn, entrusted the custody of Elisabeth to her maternal grandfather – such custody to be exercised on behalf of the Board. That measure was finally confirmed by the Supreme Administrative Court of Sweden. It must be noted that in a series of decisions the Swedish courts and authorities otherwise recognized the guardian appointed by the Dutch Court.

The principal justification which the Swedish Government adduced for the action taken by the Swedish authorities was that the Law on Protective Upbringing is a measure of *ordre public* and that the reliance on it, far from being in violation of the convention, is implied in it. In the course of the written and oral pleadings subsidiary arguments were relied upon by the Swedish Government. One of them was the contention that the Convention of 1902, being a convention on guardianship, does not cover the Swedish Law on Protective Upbringing said to pursue a different object and to lie in a different field. It is that line of argument which has acquired prominence in the present case and which must be examined in the first instance.

That manner of approach, as expressed in or as underlying the Swedish argument, may be summarized as follows: There is no incompatibility between the Guardianship Convention and the Law on Protective Upbringing. The convention, which is concerned with guardianship, does not cover protective upbringing. The latter is outside the convention. This is so although the effect of the Law on Protective Upbringing is such as to render impossible, for the time being, the exercise by the Dutch guardian of the right of custody of the person of Elisabeth Boll. The object and purpose of the Law on Protective Upbringing is wholly different from that of the Guardianship Convention. The Court is not concerned with the incidental effects of the Law on Protective Upbringing but with its nature and purpose. Guardianship and protective upbringing are wholly different institutions. The former is concerned with the interests of the minor, the latter with the interests of society. Guardianship is in the sphere of private law. Protective upbringing is in the sphere of public law. The convention, which is one on *private* international law, can be violated only by legislation in the sphere of private international law. From the point of view of their nature and purposes, the convention and the Law on Protective Upbringing operate on wholly different planes and there is, therefore, no question of the law and the measures taken thereunder being incompatible with the convention.

The reasoning underlying these contentions raises important questions, transcending the issue immediately before the Court, of interpretation and observance of treaties. If a State enacts and applies legislation, which in effect, renders the treaty wholly or partly inoperative, can such legislation be deemed not to constitute a violation of the treaty for the reason that the legislation in question covers a subject matter different from that covered by the treaty, that it is concerned with a different institution, and that it pursues a different purpose? I have considerable difficulty in answering that question in the affirmative. The difficulty is increased by the fact that the conflict between the treaty and the legislation in question may be concealed, or made to be concealed, by what is no more than a doctrinal or legislative difference of classification. An identical provision which in the law of one country forms part of a law for the protection of children may, in another State, be included within the provisions relating to guardianship. That, as will be shown, is no mere theoretical possibility. It is in fact a conspicuous feature of the present case.

What is the meaning of the expression: 'The Convention of 1902 does not cover a system such as that set up in the Swedish Law on Protective Upbringing'? It is admitted that guardianship under the convention covers the right to decide on the residence and education of the minor – a right claimed and exercised by a Swedish authority and, on its behalf, by the Swedish maternal grandfather acting in pursuance of the Law on Protective Upbringing. If that is so, then the convention does cover, in one of its essential aspects, the same powers and functions which are now exercised by Swedish authorities in pursuance of the Law on Protective Upbringing. The substance is the same although the purpose of the convention and of the law may be different. It may be said that what matters is not the substance of these functions but their object. It is not easy to follow that distinction. When a State concludes a treaty it is entitled to expect that that treaty will not be mutilated or destroyed by legislative or other measures which pursue a different object but which, in effect, render impossible the operation of the treaty or of part thereof.

The treaty covers every law and every provision of a law which impairs, which interferes with, the operation of the treaty. It has been said that the law in question may have an adverse effect upon subject matter of the treaty without being covered by the treaty. However, what the Court must be concerned with is exactly the effect of the law inasmuch as it impairs the operation of the treaty, and not the notional identity or otherwise of the objects pursued by the law and the treaty. The treaty prohibits interference with its operation unless there is a justification for it, express or implied, in the treaty; that justification cannot be found in the mere fact that the law pursues an object different from the object pursued by the treaty. It can be found only in the fact that that particular object is expressly permitted by the treaty or implicitly authorized by it by virtue of some principle of public or private international law – a principle such as stems from public policy or from a cognate, although more limited, principle, which is often no more than another formulation of public policy, namely, that certain categories of laws, such as criminal laws, police laws, fiscal laws, administrative laws, and so on, are binding upon all the inhabitants of the territory notwithstanding any general applicability of foreign law.

The following example will illustrate the problem and the consequences involved: States often conclude treaties of commerce and establishment providing for a measure of protection from restrictions with regard to importation or export of goods, admission and residence of aliens, their right to inherit property, functions of consuls, and the like. What is the position of a State which has concluded a treaty of that type and then finds that the other party whittles down, or renders inoperative, one after another, the provisions of that treaty by enacting laws 'having a different subject matter' such as reducing unemployment, social welfare, promotion of native craft and industry, protection of public morals, in relation to admission of aliens, racial segregation, reform of civil procedure involving the abolition of customary rights of consular representation, reform of the civil code involving a change of inheritance laws in a way affecting the right of inheritance by aliens, a general law codifying the law relating to the jurisdiction of courts, and involving the abolition of immunities, granted by the treaty, of public vessels engaged in commerce, or any other laws 'pursuing different objects'? It makes little or no difference to the other party that the treaty has become a dead letter as the result of laws which have so obviously affected its substance, but which pursue a different object. As stated, some of these laws may be justified as being within the domain of public policy or for some cognate reason. However, the argument here summarized does not proceed on these lines. It is based on the allegation of a difference between the treaty and the law which impedes its operation.

Another example, directly relating to the Convention of 1902, will illustrate the problem from a different point of view. Article 2 of the convention lays down that in some cases the diplomatic or consular agents authorized by the law of the State of which the infant is a national may make provision for guardianship in accordance with the law of that State. What is the position if a contracting party enacts a general law – a law of public character on a quite different plane – relating to the immunities and functions of foreign diplomatic and consular representatives providing that in the future foreign diplomatic and consular representatives shall not perform any act affecting private rights in the territory of that State? Can that State plead that, as the convention and the law pursue a quite different purpose, it does not matter that the effect of the law is to frustrate one of the provisions of the convention?

The conspicuous fact in the present case is that the Dutch guardian acceptable to the father of the infant and appointed under Dutch law in accordance with the convention was replaced, in respect of the exercise of the right of custody, by the Swedish maternal grandfather of Elisabeth Boll acting on behalf of the Children's Bureau. The Dutch authorities and the Dutch guardian may not unnaturally hold the view that the custody exercised by the Swedish grandfather is, in fact and in the circumstances of the case which reveal some dissension between the Dutch and the Swedish branches of the family, to a large extent a rival guardianship. They may find it difficult to appreciate the suggestion that there is no conflict between the convention and the measures taken seeing that they lie on a different plane and pursue different objects. The situation is not affected by the continuing right of the Dutch guardian to administer the property of the child or to institute proceedings for the restoration of her functions of custody. So long as the exercise of the right of custody is vested in the hands of the Swedish authority and the Swedish maternal grandfather of Elisabeth Boll acting on its behalf, there is a nullification of the essential attributes of the guardianship as instituted by the convention.

543

There may be – and as will be suggested later on, there is – a full justification for that measure in considerations of a different character. That justification cannot be found in the allegation, which is controversial, that the Dutch guardianship and the Swedish protective upbringing are wholly different institutions.

A State is not entitled to cut down its treaty obligations in relation to one institution by enacting in the sphere of another institution provisions whose effect is such as to frustrate the operation of a crucial aspect of the treaty. There is a disadvantage in accepting a principle of interpretation, coined for the purpose of a particular case, which, if acted upon generally, is bound to have serious repercussions on the authority of treaties. As stated, the convention and the particular provision of the Law on Protective Upbringing cover, in relation to the present dispute, the same ground, and the same subject matter. It has been said that there is a technical difference, inasmuch as they lie on different planes, between the convention and the Law on Protective Upbringing. Assuming that there is a technical difference, it may still be considered undesirable that a dispute between two Governments shall be decided by reference to a controversial technicality in a case relating to significant issues of substance – a technicality which, if acted upon generally, would introduce confusion, or worse, in the law of the operation of treaties. Once we begin to base the interpretation of treaties on conceptual distinctions between actually conflicting legal rules lying on different planes and for that reason not being, somehow, inconsistent, it may be difficult to set a limit to the effects of these operations in the sphere of logic and classification.

The view has been put forward that there can be no conflict between a Convention on Guardianship and the Law on Protective Upbringing for the reason that the Convention of 1902 is a convention of private international law and that guardianship with which it is exclusively concerned is an institution of private law, in particular of family law, while the Law on Protective Upbringing and the various measures authorized therein are in the sphere of public law seeing that they are concerned with safeguarding the interests of society. Even if these reasons were otherwise acceptable, an essentially doctrinal classification and distinction provides a doubtful basis for judging the question of the proper observance of treaties. However, there is in the present case a particular difficulty in acknowledging the force of that distinction.

An examination of the main systems of municipal law in the

matter of guardianship does not corroborate the view that it is a mere family institution of a purely private law nature. The principal justification for that view is that, by way of traditional classification, guardianship finds a place in codes of private law and that it creates numerous rights and duties in the sphere of private law. However, at the same time guardianship can rightly be described as an institution in which the guardian acts as an organ of the State, as it were, and therefore partakes of the nature of an institution of public law. He acts under the active supervision of the State which may step in at any time – in the interest both of the child and society – and supplant the guardian, wholly or in part. There are very few countries the law of which is based exclusively upon a private law and family conception of guardianship. The law of the majority of States, including Holland and Sweden, on this matter is characterized by an active intervention of the State as an organ of control and supervision at every stage. In some countries, such as Germany, the protection of minors is entrusted mainly to the State which acts through a special tribunal – the Guardianship Court – and it is only by way of exception that these functions are delegated to the family council. It is of interest to note that prior to the Hague Conventions which examined the various drafts of the Convention on Guardianship, the difference between the two systems – 'tutelle de famille' (family guardianship) and 'tutelle d'autorité' (authority guardianship) – was clearly recognized. That distinction was, for instance, elaborated in 1902 by M. Lehr, Secretary of the Institute of International Law, which had a substantial share in the preparation of the first drafts of the Convention.[1] He classified both the Dutch and Swedish systems of guardianship as belonging to the group of 'tutelle d'autorité'.[2]

In view of this, it does not seem to me possible to accept the argument based on the notion of a purely private law and family character of guardianship. How artificial are the distinctions between the supposed private law character of guardianship and the assumed public law character of systems of protective supervision or upbringing of children, apart from the normal operation of guardianship, may be gauged from the fact that the matter is entirely a question of legislative technique and drafting. That may be seen, for instance, from the provisions of the Dutch Civil Code relating

[1] Lehr, 'De la tutelle des mineurs d'après les principales législations de l'Europe' in *R.I.* 2nd ser., 4 (1902), 315 *et seq.*
[2] *Ibid.* pp. 320, 326, 329.

to guardianship and contained in Part xv of Book 1 of the Code. Section A 1 of Part xv covers Paternal Power; section B 2 covers Paternal Guardianship; while section B 3, which according to section B 9 is applicable to guardianship, embodies largely the same provisions as are embodied in that part of the Swedish Law on Protective Upbringing which was applied in the case of Elisabeth Boll. That section, in language almost identical with that of the above-mentioned Swedish law, provides, in paragraph 365, for the taking of certain steps 'if a child grows up in any such a way as to be threatened with moral or physical harm'. These steps may be taken at the instance of Guardianship Councils, for which provision is made in the same part of the law and which, under the authority of courts of law, fulfil functions similar to those of the Children's Bureau under the Swedish Law of 1924 (sections 461 *et seq.*). The same section A 3 makes provisions for children in that situation being placed by the judge of the Children's Court in an observation centre for mental or physical examination, or, if the child needs special observation, in an institution selected for that purpose (paragraph 372*a* and *b*). The German Civil Code, in the section on Guardianship, provides in a single Article – Article 1838 – that the Guardianship Court can order the placing of the minor with an appropriate family or in an educational or reformatory institution – a kind of provision which is found in the Swedish Law of 1924. It is a matter of legislative technique and drafting whether the provisions for the protection of children in relation to whom normal guardianship has proved insufficient are, as in Holland, made part of the legislation relating to guardianship or whether, as in the case of Sweden, they are embodied in a separate enactment. In both instances they are intended to protect both the child and the society.

For it is clear that the distinction between the protection of the child and the protection of society is artificial. Both the laws relating to guardianship and those relating to protective upbringing are laws intended primarily for the protection of children and their interests. At the same time, the protection of children – through guardianship or protective upbringing – is pre-eminently in the interests of society. They are part of it – the most vulnerable and most in need of protection. All social laws are, in the last resort, laws for the protection of individuals; all laws for the protection of individuals are, in a true sense, social laws. There is an element of unreality in making these two aspects of the purpose of the State the starting point for drawing legal consequences of practical import. It is wholly unreal to insist that the measures taken under the Law on Protective Upbringing for the safety, health and happiness of Elisabeth Boll were not measures taken primarily in the interest of that child – and therefore not measures of guardianship of her person – but primarily in the interest of society at large and therefore falling within a quite different category. It is in the light of these considerations that it is necessary to judge the view that as the Guardianship Convention of 1902 is concerned only with a private law institution of family relationship devoid of any public element, there can be no conflict between it and an enactment of an exclusively public law character such as the Swedish Law on Protective Upbringing. Even if every link of that proposition could be substantiated by reference to national law as operating in most countries – and that does not appear to be the case – there would still remain the difficulty of assessing the content of the statement that there can be no conflict between a treaty regulating a sphere of private law and national enactment in the realm of public law.

Undoubtedly, the Convention of 1902 was intended to regulate conflicts of law in the sphere of guardianship. But there is no persuasive reason for accepting the suggestion that the relevant provisions of the Swedish Law on Protective Upbringing, under which the custody of Elisabeth Boll was entrusted to the care of her maternal grandfather in his home under the authority of the Children's Board, has nothing to do with guardianship, seeing that they are of a public law nature. Similarly, it is difficult to accept the suggestion that guardianship, instituted in the private interest of the child, is devoid of a substantial public element of social purpose. The rights of the parties, especially in an international dispute, ought not to be determined by reference to the controversial mysteries of the distinction between private and public law. The fact that the purpose of the Convention of 1902 is to establish rules for avoiding conflicts of laws in the sphere of guardianship does not mean that that sphere is confined to laws *described* as guardianship; it covers all laws, however described or classified, which fulfil an essential function of guardianship. It is part of the firmly established jurisprudence of this Court that with regard to national laws bearing upon treaty obligations what matters is not the letter of the law but its actual effect.

However, it is not necessary to labour this point. The preceding considerations are, in my view, sufficient to show the decisive difficulties inherent in the proposition that a State can properly claim to depart from the obligations of a treaty by enacting laws which, although they impair the operation of the treaty, are said not to conflict with it on the ground that they lie on different planes or are concerned with a different subject matter.

Clearly, the guardian does not enjoy immunity from the operation of local law, such as criminal law, which may deprive him of the custody of the minor placed in a penal or reformatory institution. The guardian is subject to laws relating to education, health, revenue and so on. However, although, in the absence of a more substantial justification than differences of classification, the guardian enjoys no immunity from local law, he is entitled, in principle, to immunity from being deprived permanently or semi-permanently of some of the main attributes of guardianship such as custody of the child – especially if such custody is made the subject of what, in the circumstances of the case, is apt to give the impression of a rival guardianship. There may be a justification for such deprivation but that justification cannot properly be based upon factors which are essentially of a technical character. In my view, the more accurate approach to the question is not that the system of protective upbringing is outside the convention or that it pursues a different object but, rather, that it is not inconsistent with the convention. In other words, that it is both covered and permitted by the convention by virtue of public policy – *ordre public* – or some similar reason based on the right, conceded by international law, of a State to apply a particular law impairing or preventing the operation of the convention.

In fact, it is in that sense that I understand – and concur in – that part of the Court's judgment which stresses the beneficent social objects, of an urgent character, of the Swedish law in question. That is a consideration closely related to those underlying the notion of *ordre public*. It is this aspect of the question which I deem it incumbent upon me to examine in some detail in the present opinion.

Prior to that, reference must be made to an ancillary submission of Swedish Counsel bearing upon the possible effects of a ruling that the Swedish Law on Protective Upbringing does not apply to children of Dutch nationality. It was pointed out on behalf of the Swedish Government that any such interpretation of the convention would result in a dangerous legal vacuum. It was urged that as Dutch administrative authorities are responsible for giving effect to the provisions of the Dutch law in the sphere of the protection of children and that as, according to international law, no State can perform administrative acts in the territory of another State, the result would be that Dutch children in Sweden who are in need of care outside guardianship would remain altogether without protection.

It must be conceded that, if only possible having regard to the intention of the parties, a treaty ought to be interpreted so as to permit rather than to impede desirable measures of social protection. However, it appears to me that the spectre of a legal vacuum, as pictured on behalf of the Swedish Government in this connection, is illusory. Normally, the Dutch guardian would, in such cases, take the necessary steps to remove the child to Holland. In cases when that is not possible, the Dutch guardian would place the child in an appropriate home (as was, in fact, contemplated for a time by the Dutch guardian of Elisabeth Boll) or take other steps required by the physical or mental condition of the child, such as placing it in an institution for observation or treatment. In exceptional cases in which, for one reason or another, the guardian fails to act or to act satisfactorily, necessary measures would be decreed by the Dutch authorities. However, according to Dutch law these are not administrative authorities. They are judicial authorities applying Dutch law which Sweden, by virtue of the convention, is bound to recognize and the respect for which she is bound to ensure in good faith without requiring any additional treaty arrangements for that purpose. Thus the above-mentioned Article 365 of the Dutch Civil Code provides that if the child grows up in such a way as to be threatened with moral or physical harm the judge of the Children's Court may place it under supervision. It is also upon the judge of the Children's Court that Articles 372a and 372b of the Code confer the power to place the child in an observation centre or, if it needs special discipline, in an appropriate institution. Under Article 461c it is for the judge, on the initiative of the Guardianship Council, to order the necessary steps when the infant is not under required legal authority or in other cases of urgency. It must be added that such exceptional measures of protection with regard to a child remaining in Sweden would, in practice, be the same as would be taken by Swedish authorities in similar circumstances and that therefore no considerations of Swedish *ordre public* would stand in the way of their execution.

Undoubtedly, the task of Dutch judicial authorities in taking the measures in question might be rendered somewhat more difficult than would otherwise be the case seeing that they might have to obtain the necessary information with regard to a situation in a foreign country. But these difficulties – which lie wholly outside any legal problem of the applicability of foreign administrative law – are inherent in a convention which sanctions and prescribes the operation of the national law of the infant. In days of rapid travel, which makes possible visits by the interested parties or representatives of Guardianship Councils or other institutions, and facilities of postal communication, these difficulties are considerably reduced. In any case, as stated, they refer to a wholly exceptional situation; as such they appear somewhat unreal when adduced as a decisive factor with regard to the interpretation of the convention. They seem to me an unsubstantial ground for permitting a departure from its language and purpose. For these reasons, I cannot accept that particular argument advanced on behalf of the Government of Sweden.

As already stated, reliance upon *ordre public* – public policy – constitutes the main feature in the written and oral pleadings of the parties. This is the only submission, in the nature of legal principle, in the final conclusions of the parties. The Court is not rigidly bound to give judgment by exclusive reference to the legal propositions as formulated by the parties in their conclusions. However, I consider that I ought not to disregard the conclusions of the parties formulating exhaustively the legal issue between them. The position is analogous to that in which the parties have concluded a special agreement defining the legal issue between them and asking the Court to pronounce upon it as part of its operative decision. It is only when it is abundantly clear that the formulation, adopted by the parties, of the legal issue cannot provide a basis for the decision and that there is another legal solution at hand of unimpeachable cogency, that I would feel myself free to disregard the conclusions of the parties. Neither of these conditions seems to me to obtain in the present case. (It may be pointed out in this connection that the position is here different from that in the *Fisheries* case in which the Court declined to render judgment by reference to general 'definitions, principles and rules' formulated by *one* Party.[1]) Admittedly, the legal issue as thus expressed by the parties in their pleadings and conclusions in the present case touches directly upon a difficult and controversial question which has constituted one of the crucial

[1] *I.C.J. Reports* 1951, p. 126.

problems in the sphere of private international law and which brings into prominence the relation between private and public international law.

Does the Guardianship Convention of 1902, which contains no express exception of *ordre public*, permit reliance upon it? This seems to be the crucial question. However, before an attempt is made to answer it, there are two preliminary observations which must be made in this connection.

The first is that caution must be exercised with regard to the manner in which the question is put in the present context. It seems incorrect to put the problem in some such form as: 'Shall the Court apply the convention or shall it apply *ordre public*? Which comes first?' For there is no question here of choosing between the convention and *ordre public*. If that were the alternative, clearly the Court would have no option but to apply the convention. The question is whether the convention, viewed in its entirety and in the light of relevant principles of interpretation – and not merely by reference to its bare letter – permits the exception of *ordre public*. For these reasons no assistance can be derived from the various pronouncements of the Permanent Court of International Justice to the effect that national legislation cannot be validly invoked as a reason for non-compliance with an international obligation. The problem now for the Court is, exactly, what is the international obligation at issue.

The second preliminary question is whether legislation relating to protective upbringing of children is properly comprised within the sphere of *ordre public*, that is to say, whether, notwithstanding any apparent treaty provision to the contrary, *ordre public* covers exceptional measures for the protection of minors in addition to and to the exclusion of guardianship operating in normal circumstances. That question must clearly be answered in the affirmative. Apart from criminal law, it is difficult to conceive of a more appropriate and more natural object of *ordre public*, as generally understood, than the protection by the State of infants, especially when they are helpless, ill, an actual or potential danger to themselves or to society, a legitimate object of its compassion and assistance, and an occasion for public resentment whenever the State fails to measure up to its responsibilities in this respect. There are, in that wide and highly controversial province of *ordre public*, matters which are the object of uncertainty and occasional exaggerations of national prejudice reluctant to apply foreign law. But there is a hard core within that field which is not open to reasonable challenge. The protection of children, in the sense indicated above, is an obvious particle of that hard core. Mention may be made in this connection, as emphasizing this aspect of guardianship (which is exemplified, in its wider sense, in the system of protective upbringing), of the fact that in English law the Crown as the *parens patriae* – the parent of the country as a whole – is the supreme guardian of infants and, through its courts, exercises its authority in this respect, at every stage, with total disregard of any artificial formalities of the law. The Guardianship Act of 1925 provides in section 1 that, when in proceedings before any court custody or upbringing of an infant are in question, the court in dealing with the matter 'shall regard the welfare of the infant as the first and paramount consideration' and shall not decisively take into account any claim, based on any particular rule of law, of the father or the mother to a superior right of custody and control.

The notion of *ordre public* is generally used in two meanings: It is either applied as referring to specific spheres of the law, such as territorial laws, criminal laws, police laws, laws relating to national welfare, health and security, and the like; from this point of view, protective upbringing clearly comes within the notion of *ordre public*. Secondly, it is resorted to as embracing, more generally, fundamental national conceptions of law, decency and morality. From this point of view, too, the protection of the interests of the minor through measures such as protective upbringing falls naturally within the notion of *ordre public*. (It may be stated in the present context that although in this opinion the French term *ordre public* is mainly used, it is not used as implying a substantial difference between it and the notion of public policy in common law countries such as the United Kingdom or the United States of America – although probably the conception of *ordre public* is somewhat wider. It is used here for the reason that it is current in the law of two States which are parties to the dispute.)

Admittedly, in answering the question as here put we are confronted with the following dilemma: Is it the Swedish *ordre public* by reference to which that question must be answered? If that is so, is the Court competent and in the position to examine a matter of Swedish *ordre public*, of Swedish municipal law? It is clear that that question must be answered in the affirmative. The examination of municipal law, wherever that is necessary, is a proper function of the Court; it has undertaken it on repeated occasions. Neither do the intricacies of *ordre public* set a limit to that legitimate function of the Court. In the *Serbian Loans* case the Court examined the French law and the French judicial practice in the sphere of *ordre public* in relation to currency legislation.[1] However, the question that must be answered in this connection is not only whether protective upbringing of children falls, according to Swedish law, within the Swedish *ordre public* but also whether it can properly be included as falling within that sphere. That question cannot be answered by reference to Swedish law only. It can be answered in reliance on a notion of *ordre public* conceived as a general principle of law – an aspect of the question referred to below.

If protective education of children falls legitimately within the sphere of public order, then – and only then – there must be considered the main question, namely, whether public order, if not expressly permitted by the convention, can be invoked at all; whether it has been properly invoked in the present case; and, if so, whether the Law on Protective Upbringing has been applied by the Swedish authorities in a manner which is reasonable and not manifestly contrary to the object and the principles of the convention.

Does the conception of *ordre public* operate at all in the present case? This is the central issue before the Court. It can be examined here only in brief outline:

In the first instance, the convention now before the Court is a convention of public international law in the sphere of what is generally described as private international law. This means: (i) that it must be interpreted, like any other treaty, in the light of the principles governing the interpretation of treaties in the field of public international law; (ii) that the interpretation must take into account the special conditions and circumstances of the subject matter of the treaty, which in the present case is a treaty in the sphere of private international law.

Secondly, in the sphere of private international law the exception of *ordre public*, of public policy, as a reason for the exclusion of foreign law in a particular case is generally – or, rather, universally – recognized. It is recognized in various forms, with various degrees of emphasis, and, occasionally, with substantial differences in the manner of its application. Thus, in some matters, such as recognition of title to property acquired abroad, the courts of some countries are more reluctant than others to permit their conception of *ordre*

[1] *P.C.I.J.* Series A, nos. 20 and 21, pp. 46, 47.

public – their public policy – to interfere with title thus created. However, restraint in some some directions is often offset by procedural or substantive rules in other spheres. On the whole, the result is the same in most countries – so much so that the recognition of the part of *ordre public* must be regarded as a general principle of law in the field of private international law. If that is so, then it may not improperly be considered to be a general principle of law in the sense of Article 38 of the Statute of the Court. That circumstance also provides an answer to the question as to the nature and the content of the conception of public policy by reference to which there must be judged the propriety of the Swedish legislation in the matter. Clearly, it is not the Swedish notion of *ordre public* which can provide the exclusive standard in this connection. The answer is that, the notion of *ordre public* – of public policy – being a general legal conception, its content must be determined in the same way as that of any other general principle of law in the sense of Article 38 of the Statute, namely, by reference to the practice and experience of the municipal law of civilized nations in that field. It is by reference to some such considerations that I have, in an earlier part of this opinion, attempted to answer the question whether the Swedish Law on Protective Upbringing can properly be regarded as falling within the domain of *ordre public*.

For these reasons the correct interpretation of a convention on private international law must take that general recognition of public order fully into account. The same result is reached by way of another, no less cogent, principle of interpretation: In a case concerned with the interpretation of a treaty relating to a particular matter with regard to which the law and practice of both parties recognize the applicability of certain principles, due weight must be given to those principles. To give an example: If the law and practice of Sweden and Holland were to recognize that the distance of twenty miles is the proper limit of territorial waters, and if these two States were to conclude a treaty laying down that their vessels shall be bound to submit to certain restrictions within their respective territorial waters, then the expression 'territorial waters' would have to be interpreted in the sense attached to it by the law and practice of those two States, namely, as extending to twenty miles. By the same token, if the law of Sweden or Holland recognizes the exception of public order in the sphere of private international law, then that factor must be considered as relevant to the interpretation, as between them, of the treaty in question. It is well known, and it is admitted by both parties, that both in Sweden and Holland *ordre public* constitutes a valid reason for the exclusion of foreign law. Accordingly, the fact that a particular subject of private international law is covered by a convention does not, in the absence of an express prohibition to the contrary, in itself exclude the operation of *ordre public*, even if the convention is otherwise silent in the matter – provided always that the State invoking *ordre public* is, if its decision to invoke it is challenged, willing to submit to an impartial judicial or arbitral determination of the issue. The latter condition follows inevitably from the principle that a State which invokes an exception not expressly recognized by the treaty cannot claim the right to determine unilaterally whether that exception applies.

At the same time, and this is the third main consideration in the present context, the circumstance that the parties are bound by treaty in relation to a particular subject of private international law sets a limit to the application of *ordre public*. It does so in three respects.

In the first instance, the existence of the treaty imposes upon municipal courts an obligation of restraint in invoking *ordre public* – a restraint additional to that which they impose upon themselves in matters of private international law generally. This is admitted by both parties. In fact, it is one of the objects of a treaty bearing upon private international law to set some further limit to reliance upon *ordre public*.

Secondly, the existence of a treaty limits the discretion of national courts in determining whether a particular subject is within the domain of *ordre public*; it limits it in the sense that in case of a dispute, and provided that an international tribunal is endowed with the requisite jurisdiction, it is for that tribunal to determine the matter. This, too, is in substance admitted by both parties.

Thirdly – a view contended for by Holland but denied by Sweden – in the case of a dispute as to the manner in which the national authority has applied the exception of *ordre public*, that question is subject to review and determination by an international tribunal, if otherwise competent in the matter. That aspect of the question is examined later in this opinion.

Applied to the present case, these principles mean, in general, that the exception of public order is admissible within proper limits and that, there being a dispute as to whether these limits have been observed, it is for the Court to decide whether the notion of public order has been properly invoked and applied. As stated, I have come to the conclusion that reliance on *ordre public* in relation to a Law on Protective Upbringing is fully justified and that, therefore, *ordre public* has been properly invoked. I will revert presently to the question whether the proper *application* of *ordre public* has been satisfactorily proved in this case.

Reference must be made in this connection to certain views expressed during the written and oral proceedings with regard to *ordre public*, in particular the opinion that reliance upon it is inconsistent with the purpose of treaties on private international law and that *ordre public* ought to be interpreted restrictively in that sphere or refused recognition altogether. In particular, it was argued that because of its comprehensiveness and elasticity it has been the cause of uncertainty and confusion, that it has been a disturbing element in that field, and, more emphatically, that it has been destructive of private international law. There is some substance in these considerations. However, they cannot in any way be decisive.

Admittedly, the notion of *ordre public* – like that of public policy – is variable, indefinite and occasionally productive of arbitrariness and abuse. It has been compared in this respect, not without some justification, with the vagueness of the law of nature. Admittedly also, it has often been the instrument or the expression of national exclusiveness and prejudice impatient of the application of foreign law. Yet these objections, justified as they are, do not alter the fact that the principle permitting reliance on *ordre public* in the sphere of private international law has become – and that it is – a general principle of law of most, if not all, civilized States. More than that: It is, on its own merits, part and parcel of the entire doctrine and practice of private international law almost from its very inception; the two are inseparable, not only as a matter of history but also of necessity; they have grown together in a mutual interaction and compromise. The purpose of private international law is to make possible the application, within the territory of the State, of the law of foreign States. This is an object dictated by considerations of justice, convenience, the necessities of international intercourse between individuals and indeed, as has occasionally been said, by an elightened conception of public policy itself. But there is an obvious element of simplification in the view that the law of a State should be deemed to have consented or that it should reasonably be expected to consent in advance to the application of foreign law without any limitations, in any circumstances whatsoever, without a safety valve, without a residuum of contingencies in which, because of the very nature of its structure and the fundamental legal, moral and political conceptions which underlie it, it should be able to decline to apply foreign law.

Within the State, the judicial use of public policy – of *ordre public* – has often been exposed to criticism. But it is seldom, if ever, suggested that it is not an indispensable instrument of the interpretation, application and development of the law. If that is so in relation to the national law of the State which may be changed by ordinary legislative processes, it is particularly so in relation to foreign law over which the State has no control and which, in certain circumstances, its courts may find it inconceivable to apply. History – modern history – has occasionally produced examples of legislation manifesting eruptions of malevolent injustice, or worse, to which courts of foreign countries may find it utterly impossible to give effect and with regard to which the right to denounce the treaty may not provide a timely or practicable remedy.

It is that residuum of discretion, it is that safety valve, which has made private international law possible at all, and which, if kept within proper limits, is one of the principal guarantees of its continued existence and development. It is significant that an important part of the contribution of the most illustrious exponents of private international law – such as Story, Savigny and Pillet – lay in their effort to formulate the notion of *ordre public* and the limits, often wide and general, of its application. *Ordre public* is, and ought increasingly to be, subject to reasonable limitations in accordance with the main purpose of private international law. But the problem cannot be solved by the device of shelving it. It can be alleviated by the existence of international remedies of judicial control and review whenever there exists the requisite jurisdiction of an international tribunal. The present case afforded an opportunity for acting in that way.

The preceding considerations may also offer assistance in answering the question whether the existence of a treaty sets a limit to reliance on public policy in the sense that the latter cannot be properly invoked unless the treaty contains an express exception to that effect. That question must be answered in the negative. Obviously, the treaty may expressly, or by implication, prohibit recourse to *ordre public*. Thus it is occasionally maintained that the Hague Convention of 1902 on the Conclusion of Marriage contained such prohibitive implication by enumerating exhaustively the reasons for which the *lex fori* could disregard the impediments to marriage established by foreign law. (Yet it is significant that, in spite of the convention, practically all parties to it refused to recognize, prior to the Second World War, the impediments established by the German Nuremberg Laws. Although Dutch courts applied the convention in this respect, they often found circuitous means of defeating the Nuremberg Laws in question.)

However, apart from an express or clearly implied prohibition, the correct principle seems to be that a convention in the sphere of private international law does not exclude reliance on *ordre public*. Nothing short of an express prohibition can rule out reliance on a firmly established principle of private international law. This seems to me to be the fairly unanimous view of writers. They include authorities of the calibre of Professors Batiffol and Niboyet. This is also the emphatic view of an author who has devoted special attention to questions of private international law in relation to treaties.[1] Professor Lewald, a balanced and authoritative writer to whose views I attach importance, provides no clear exception to that virtual unanimity. In 1928, writing in the *Revue de droit international privé*, he stated, though with very considerable hesitation, that, *a priori*, if the treaty is silent on the question of *ordre public*, the latter cannot be invoked.[2] In 1930, when writing in the *Répertoire de droit international*, he expressed a different view, namely, that in such cases the answer to the question depends on the interpretation of a particular treaty and that it is impossible to give an answer *a priori*.[3] There is little judicial practice directly applicable to this matter.

In this connection reference may also be made to the preparatory work of the Convention of 1902. The study of that preparatory work shows that there was opposition – effective opposition – to incorporating in the Hague Conventions any general clause permitting reliance on *ordre public* (though no discussion on the subject took place with regard to the Convention on Guardianship). Does that mean that there was an intention to exclude altogether recourse to *ordre public* unless in cases expressly authorized? It may be doubted whether that was so. The authors of the conventions wished to avoid the complications of a general and express authorization, of a general

---

[1] Plaisant, *Les règles de conflit de lois dans les traités* (1946), pp. 91–4.
[2] At pp. 164 *et seq*.   [3] Vol. 7, p. 308.

blank cheque, with regard to a notion so elastic and so comprehensive as *ordre public*. It is natural that they did not wish to inject into the conventions, in express terms, a potential source of controversy or abuse. But does that mean that, by mere silence, the authors of the conventions excluded indirectly from the operation of the convention a firmly-established principle of private international law? That is not probable. It is doubtful whether Governments would have signed and ratified these conventions if they had expressly denied the right to invoke, in any circumstances, their *ordre public* as a reason for excluding foreign law.

There is one factor of importance which is directly relevant to the question whether *ordre public* can be invoked by the parties in the present case in relation to the Convention of 1902. That factor is that in this respect the Court is confronted with a substantial measure of agreement between the parties. The Dutch Government has repeatedly, although in a highly qualified manner, given an affirmative answer to that question – subject to the obligation of the parties to the convention to proceed with particular caution, with special restraint and with exacting meticulousness in limiting the operation of the treaty by reference to *ordre public*. That attitude was maintained in Conclusion II of the Netherlands, in which the denial of the right to invoke *ordre public* is qualified by the word 'generally' and, even more so, in Conclusion III, A and B, which asserts the power of the Court to determine whether the conditions of *ordre public* have been complied with, having regard to the character of the case and the provisions of the Swedish Law on Protective Upbringing – a conclusion which can be understood only on the assumption that there was no intention to deny, in principle, the right to invoke *ordre public*. This – the agreement of the parties on a matter of basic principle – is a significant legal aspect of the situation; it makes it difficult to maintain that public order cannot be invoked unless specifically provided for in the Convention.

Admittedly, the Dutch Government denies that in the *present case* there is room for resort to *ordre public*. It does so for two reasons: The first is that the obligation of caution and restraint binds the parties not to invoke it unless there is a requisite element of close territorial connection, and that there is no such connection in the present case. It is difficult to follow that contention. It is not easy to imagine a closer connection between the minor in question and the country which relies on *ordre public*. Elisabeth Boll was born in

Sweden; so far as is known, she speaks Swedish only; she has resided permanently in Sweden since her birth. I do not find convincing the argument that, according to Dutch law, Elisabeth Boll shares the legal Dutch domicile of her Dutch guardian or that, if she is not domiciled in Holland, it is only because the Swedish measure of protective upbringing, said to be in violation of the convention, prevents her from being being brought to Holland. The question of domicile, which is a question of fact and intention, is not properly answered by arguments of this nature.

Neither is it easy to follow the second reason advanced by the Dutch Government in the sense that the necessary territorial connection is lacking, seeing that this is a 'transfer case', namely, that if only the transfer of the child to Holland were made possible, in accordance with the convention, then there would be no question of anything happening on Swedish territory which is contrary to Swedish *ordre public*. There is no more force in this argument than in the suggestion that a State has no reason to refuse to hand over a political refugee to prosecution and persecution in a foreign country considering that such prosecution and persecution will take place in foreign territory. Yet it is apparent that in cases such as these the very fact of intended transfer is decisive for the purpose of relying upon *ordre public* seeing that the transfer is deemed contrary to the fundamental notions of public law of that State and that it may be productive of a revulsion of public opinion as being flagrantly offensive to national conceptions of decency. Public opinion is not easily reconciled to the view that the moral and social responsibility of the State has been discharged by the simple device of removing to a foreign country the object of possible persecution and suffering. This would be too easy a means of salving the conscience. When, therefore, it is argued that a 'removal case' is not sufficiently connected with the country of the forum to warrant the application of *ordre public*, the correct answer is probably that there are very few occasions in which the connection is more obvious.

These, then, are the two main grounds – the two only grounds – which the Netherlands have adduced against the application of *ordre public* in this case: the absence of connection and the character of a 'removal case'. Neither of these grounds seems to be acceptable. If they are not acceptable, then there are no grounds which, on the Dutch submission, prevent reliance upon *ordre public*.

There must now be considered the question of the extent to which the Court is called upon to examine the issue of the propriety of the appeal to and of the manner of application of *ordre public* in the present case. It is upon the answer to a question of this kind that there must, to a substantial degree, depend the position of *ordre public* in the development of this branch of the law.

Both parties are in agreement that the Court is competent to decide whether the Swedish Law on Protective Upbringing comes within the sphere of *ordre public* and whether it has been properly invoked for that purpose. In particular, the Government of Sweden does not deny that the Court is competent to determine whether in principle the Swedish Law on Protective Upbringing belongs to the category of *ordre public*. In its conclusions it asked the Court to hold that the Convention of 1902 does not affect the right of the parties to impose upon foreign guardians the restrictions called for by their public order. The agreement of the parties on this question removes to a large extent the ground from the criticism directed at reliance on public order by reference to its disintegrating effect as opening wide the floodgates of wholesale nullification of this and similar conventions by the simple means of asserting unilaterally that a particular law under which the measure was taken is in the domain of *ordre public*. For both parties agree that it is for the Court, and not for them, to decide that issue.

At the same time, the parties are not in agreement on the question whether the Court is entitled to examine the grounds on which, by reference to the Law on Protective Upbringing, the Swedish authorities decided to decree and to maintain the measure which they had taken. Sweden denied such competence in her conclusions and in the course of the written and oral proceedings. On the other hand, the Government of the Netherlands repeatedly asserted the competence of the Court in that respect. This it did both in the conclusions and by way of a formal intervention in the course of the oral proceedings. The agent for the Netherlands insisted that the Court was competent to examine 'every fact, every circumstance, every motive' pertaining to the application of the Swedish law and that this being a case of a treaty obligation no reliance on a charge of denial of justice was necessary for that purpose.

I accept the Dutch Conclusion III A, according to which the Court is competent to appreciate, in the light of the relevant facts and circumstances, whether the conditions of *ordre public* have been complied with. The Court is competent to decide not only whether the Law on Protective Upbringing falls within the notion of *ordre public*, but also whether it has been applied reasonably and so as not to defeat the true objects of the convention. I am unable to accept the Swedish view that the Court, not being a court of appeal, is not entitled to examine that aspect of the question. Suppose the Swedish authorities had decided to apply the Law of Protective Upbringing to a child of Dutch nationality, born in Holland and speaking Dutch only, and who had been resident in Sweden only for one month. Would this Court be precluded from taking these facts into consideration? Recourse to *ordre public*, especially if not expressly authorized by the convention, is in the nature of an exception. It is a permissible exception. But it is an exception which must be justified with some particularity. If a State takes action which, on the face of it, departs from the language of the convention, then it cannot confine itself to proving generally that the law under which it acted falls within the permissible exception; it must show that the exception was applied reasonably and in good faith.

When there is no treaty binding upon a State, it has very considerable – although not unlimited – discretion in applying its system of private international law in relation to *ordre public*. But when that State is bound by a treaty in relation to a particular subject matter, it can invoke public order only if, in case its action is challenged, it is prepared to submit the legality of its action to impartial decision. It is that jurisdiction which removes the notion of and recourse to *ordre public* from the orbit of uncertainty, pure discretion and arbitrariness and which endows the treaty with the character of an effective legal obligation. It is that subjection to judicial or arbitral determination, as the very condition of legitimate reliance on *ordre public* in cases not expressly provided by the treaty, which saves *ordre public* in such cases from the reproach of being a cover for a unilateral repudiation of the treaty and which gives it the character of an attempt to secure a just and reasonable interpretation of treaty obligations. The present case provided an opportunity for asserting and giving effect to that principle. The task of such factual examination may be difficult, and, occasionally, invidious. Nevertheless, it constitutes a proper exercise of the judicial function in relation to a dispute which is one both as to the law and fact in the meaning of Article 36 of the Statute of the Court.

In the present case the parties have not laid before the Court the facts which would enable it to decide with any assurance on this aspect of the question. The Government of Sweden did not act upon the offer, formally made by it in the final Submissions in the Counter-

Memorial and repeated during the oral proceedings, to lay before the Court the relevant documents. It is true that it was open to the Court, at any stage of the proceedings, to ask for their production. In particular, Article 49 of the Statute provides that 'the Court may, even before the hearing begins, call upon the agents to produce any document or to supply any explanation'. However, it is not necessary in this connection to consider the problem of the function of the Court, under that and other Articles of the Statute and the Rules, as an agency called upon to clarify and substantiate the basis of its decisions by active initiative in the elucidation of the relevant factors before and during the oral proceedings. For there was no reason why the Government of Sweden should not have supplied the necessary information of its own accord, in the event that the Court should find that it could properly examine it. A State invoking an exception cannot be too forthcoming in producing evidence in justification of it. It ought not to limit itself to vague – and, from the point of view of ordinary rules of evidence, probably inadmissible – allusions as the possible contents of the evidence which, by its own decision, it has failed to produce. At the same time, in the exercise of its jurisdiction of review, a legal tribunal must attach importance to the appreciation of the facts, by local authorities – of the authorities of the State where the child was born and is domiciled. Their decision must not be lightly disturbed. This is so in particular if the applicant Government, while inviting the Court to decide upon the factual aspects of the issue and the motives underlying the decision of the local authorities, has failed to bring to its notice any facts suggesting that the discretion of the Swedish authorities has not been exercised properly and in good faith. In all the circumstances, on such evidence as there is, I am bound to assume that the action of the Swedish authorities was not such as to constitute a misapplication of the Law on Protective Upbringing on which they were clearly entitled to rely as part of their *ordre public*.

The above considerations explain why, subject to differences of approach and reasoning, I concur in the operative part of the judgment rejecting the demand of the Government of the Netherlands.

INDEX